Actors
YEARBOOK
2010

Actors' YEARB OOK 2010

Edited by Simon Dunmore and Hilary Lissenden

methuen | drama

Sixth edition 2009
A & C Black Publishers Limited
36 Soho Square, London W1D 3QY
www.acblack.com

ISBN 978–1–408–11562–6
A CIP catalogue record for this book is available from the British Library.

The publishers make no representation, express or implied, with regard to the accuracy of the information contained in this book and cannot accept any legal responsibility for any errors or omissions that may take place.

This book is produced using paper that is made from wood grown in managed, sustainable forests. It is natural, renewable and recyclable. The logging and manufacturing processes conform to the environmental regulations of the country of origin.

Typeset by QPM from David Lewis XML Associates Ltd
Printed in the UK by CPI William Clowes Beccles NR34 7TL

Contents

Foreword

Equity (see page 392) is a relatively small union covering a wide variety of issues – not just contracts – of importance to those working in the performing arts. Despite our size we are expert in all the issues we cover, thanks to a dedicated staff with a wide variety of specialist knowledge to support our members.

However, you, as lone actor, also have a range of other concerns that are outside Equity's remit. For instance, how do you go about finding a specialist photographer capable of capturing the essential 'you'? What unforeseen pitfalls can you expect to encounter on a small-scale tour? Which agents and casting directors are happy to receive unsolicited showreels?

The joy of this wonderfully comprehensive book is that it gives you not only detailed listings for every aspect of work-related issues, but also great insights into the experiences of seasoned practitioners. The really helpful introductions and articles are written with warmth and humour. It is a valuable companion and an essential tool for all actors at whatever stage in their careers.

Christine Payne
General Secretary of Equity

Introduction

It is well known that an actor's life is not an easy one. Those who aspire to the 'bright lights' face a seemingly bewildering array of courses, audition processes and funding methods. Drama school graduates confront a bedazzling array of agents, casting directors and production companies (in all media) to whom they could send their precious CVs and photographs. Experienced actors try to become philosophical about how secure-seeming 'contacts' they once had have been superseded by a new generation. ('There's a new bunch of schoolboys running the networks each week.' Joan Collins) The art and crafts of acting are difficult enough – the prospect of navigating through 'bald' lists of services and potential employers can overwhelm all but the most determined. Those with time and money can simply blitz every agent (for instance) that they can find, in the hope that some may respond with offers of representation – this will cost several hundred pounds, let alone the time spent stuffing envelopes. And the chances of success, with this kind of unfocused approach, will be extremely limited. Judicious targeting, using the information in this book and your own research (especially on the Internet), can save a considerable amount of money and will give you a greater chance of satisfaction and success.

The aim of this book is also to make some more detailed sense of the ever-diversifying world of professional acting – from training to the wide range of companies offering work in all media, via the 'brokers' (agents and casting directors) of much of that work. In addition, you will find more details of the available services (photographers, showreel companies, and so on) so that you can make detailed comparisons before committing your precious funds. In order to help you cut your way through the 'jungle' of performing arts information, the listings are restricted to those directly relevant to aspiring and work-seeking actors. (For instance, agents who only represent directors, designers, and so forth, are not included.) Careful study of the section(s) appropriate to you at a particular moment could save you time and money through more accurate 'targeting' of your intentions – whether looking for appropriate training, whom to send your CV and photograph to, where to get your showreel made, and so forth.

This book contains details of those organisations and individuals from whom we were able to glean more full information, beyond the basic contact details. Some were prepared to provide helpful information but requested that their telephone numbers, for instance, should not be included. You'll find more organisations listed in *Contacts* (published annually by The Spotlight). Some individuals and organisations declined to contribute to this book, apparently fearful of attracting even more actor-submissions. Some simply did not respond. Some information will go out of date – new companies will start up and others go out of business – and personnel will change; this profession has a highly mobile population. However, the listings will help focus your research and enable you to 'target' more accurately and efficiently.

Actors' Yearbook is designed to work in harmony with my *An Actor's Guide to Getting Work* (4th edition, A&C Black, 2004), in which you will find much more detailed advice on how to market yourself and enhance your chances as a professional actor.

Simon Dunmore, Consultant Editor
www.simon.dunmore.btinternet.co.uk

Important note – the new postage rates

As of 2nd April 2007, postage rates started to vary according to size as well as weight. There are three basic formats (more details available from **www.royalmail.com**):

'Letter': A thin (less than 5mm – i.e. probably not padded in any way), just over A5-sized package, which could contain:
• a letter
• a folded CV
• a postcard-sized photograph
• a CD/DVD (in a paper or plastic sleeve)
• an sae (stamped with sufficient postage) for return of your photo and CV/DVD

'Large letter': A just over A4-sized package, which can be up to 25mm (nearly an inch) thick; this could contain:
• a letter
• an unfolded CV
• a 10x8in photograph
• a CD/DVD (in a paper or plastic sleeve)
• a board-backed envelope (stamped with sufficient postage) for return of your photograph and CD/DVD

'Packet': Any package that exceeds the dimensions of the above – or where the weight exceeds 750g. If you are sending a video cassette (these are wider than the 'Large letter' maximum thickness) your package will fall into this charge zone.

Your submission

As most submissions will contain a 10x8in (unfolded) photograph, they will be classified as 'Large letters'. These have charge bands by weight. A board-backed envelope with a 10x8in photo, A4 CV and A4 or A5 letter weighs in at just under 100g and should therefore be fine with a standard 'Large letter' 1st or 2nd Class stamp (61p and 50p respectively, at the time of writing). If you're adding a stamped addressed envelope for return of your photo, however, this will probably push you over the 100g limit and you will need a stamp for the next band up. (At the time of writing this is 90p for 1st Class and 72p for 2nd Class.) You'll also go into the higher band if you add a CV or DVD in a paper or plastic sleeve.

If you're sending a light, A5 padded envelope with a CD or DVD then your choice of case will affect the postage: the chunky old-style CD cases, the full-size DVD cases, and the heavier-style padded envelopes will need the higher postal rate, whereas a paper or plastic sleeve, or some of the modern, lighter-style cases, will probably still come in at under 100g. If you use a padded envelope you will probably need a 'Large letter' stamp; without a padded envelope a standard 'Letter' stamp will probably suffice.

The video cassette in a padded envelope will fall into the 101-250g 'Packet' charge band, which will cost £1.62 (1st Class) and £1.49 (2nd Class). Even if the video cassette weighed less, then it would still be charged at the 'Packet' rate because they are thicker than the 25mm maximum allowable in the 'Large letter' charge band.

It is very important to get the postage right on a submission, as it's the recipient who has to pay an excess charge. Many companies – fed up with people getting this wrong – will simply not accept delivery and it will be returned to you unopened ... with all your hard work and postage costs wasted.

It is also important to consider the cost of the postage on your sae, especially if you want your photograph returned intact.

Note: The larger style of envelope, unless board-backed, does not survive the postal system very well, and your photo and CV will probably arrive looking rather dog-eared. If you're sending a 10x8in photograph, then always use a board-backed envelope; if you're not sending a 10x8 then consider folding your letter/CV and using a C5 envelope (takes A5 or A4 folded once).

Postage costs usually go up each April, so if you're reading this after April 2010 then check the Royal Mail website for the latest rates.

Training
Introduction

This section is largely devoted to those who are 18 and older. This is not to dismiss the fact that there is training (of varying kinds) for those under that age. However, the field is so wide that the confines of this book limit listings to the major organisations only.

In spite of the fact that a minority of well-known actors did not formally train, it is very important for today's aspirant to do so. An ever-increasing number of people want to become actors, so those with 'casting clout' (agents, casting directors and directors) have more and more people to choose from. Doesn't it make more sense to select from those who've undergone the rigours of a respected training process? It is an essential fact that the acting industry works on very tight time-scales and budgets – trained actors should be quicker, more reliable and, usually, more inventive than their untrained counterparts. For instance, an untrained voice that cracks up after a few days of live performance is time-consuming and costly for a management – only the larger productions can afford under-studies. An untrained actor, who may look good on camera, will take time to learn how to work on a television set, where time spent keeping technicians waiting is very, very expensive. A fight (in a theatre or on camera) has to be staged so that it (a) looks real, (b) is safe for the participants and (c) can be seen properly by camera and/or audience – actors who've been trained in the essentials of combat will make this staging process much, much quicker. Moving correctly in period costumes, performing all kinds of formal dance and using microphones properly are just a few of the other time-saving skills that the trained actor can bring to a production. It is only an exceptional few who, nowadays, have the opportunity to 'learn on the job'.

For today's aspiring actor, it is important to train on a professionally recognised course. The established drama schools are the focus of such training. There are acting-related university degree courses which have a reasonable proportion of vocational training (as well as academic work) and there are numerous part-time, short-term and 'foundation' courses which will give you basic insights into the many crafts involved in acting. However, because of the intense competition, a full-time drama school course of at least a year is essential for most people.

For those who have already trained, there are opportunities to learn new skills and refine those already acquired, or simply to keep them in trim when the acting work is not coming in. The latter is very important, as you can be asked to demonstrate your skills at very short notice. Being an actor is a bit like being a fireman – without the regular salary. Also, the more you can legitimately add to the 'Skills' section of your CV, the more you can enhance your chances of finding work.

Editor's Note: It is especially important to **check for the latest information on all fees listed** under all headings in this section. *Actors' Yearbook* makes every effort to ensure that such information is correct and up-to-date, but prices especially are liable to ongoing amendment.

Training for the under-18s

It is a fact that many child stars do not succeed as adult actors. There are notable exceptions – Nicholas Lyndhurst, Dennis Waterman and Jenny Agutter, for instance – but they are the exceptions that prove the rule. I also wonder whether a childhood largely devoted to performing is entirely healthy: what about learning about life? And what about learning other essential skills in order to earn one's living when the acting work is not coming in? Generally speaking, the best thing for the stage-struck child is to send him or her to one of the numerous youth theatre groups and drama workshops that exist in almost every town and city. These are often listed in *Yellow Pages*, and many are members of the National Association of Youth Theatres – see below. Public productions are often the last priority of such groups – especially for the younger ages – but a terrific amount can be learnt by the young from what seem like simple make-believe games. Children in such groups won't learn many of the technical skills necessary to acting, but they will learn a lot of important social skills and the fundamental business of 'interacting' that is so important to an acting ensemble: that it's not just what you can create that matters, it's what you can create with other people. Some youth theatres are allied to agencies who will promote their members for professional work, but it is important to note that employment of the under-16s is very strictly regulated.

National Association for Youth Drama (NAYD)

34 Upper Gardiner Street, Dublin 1, Ireland
tel 353-1 878 1301 *fax* 353-1 878 1302
email info@nayd.ie
website www.youthdrama.ie

NAYD (National Association for Youth Drama) is the development organisation for youth theatre and youth drama in Ireland. It supports youth drama in practice and policy, and supports the sustained development of youth theatres in Ireland.

NAYD advocates the inherent value and the unique relationship between young people and theatre as an artform, and is committed to extending and enhancing young people's understanding of theatre and raising the artistic standards of youth theatre across the country. The organisation supports youth drama in practice through an annual programme that includes the National Youth Theatre, National and Regional festivals of youth theatres, commissioning new writing, publications, resources, training and other services, as well as research and policy development.

With a membership of more than 50 youth theatres throughout the country, NAYD supports the sustained development of youth theatres in partnership with local authorities, youth services, theatres and arts centres. Its productions are produced to a professional standard and cast from youth theatres around Ireland. Previous productions

include: *Our Town*, by Thornton Wilder and directed by Ben Barnes; *A Midsummer Night's Dream*, directed by Andy Hinds; *Young Europeans*, written and directed by Gerard Stembridge; and *The Crucible* by Arthur Miller, directed by Ben Barnes. For further details about NAYD's work, please refer to the website.

National Association of Youth Theatres (NAYT)

Arts Centre, Vane Terrace, Darlington DL3 7AX
tel (01325) 363330 *fax* (01325) 363313
email nayt@btconnect.com
website www.nayt.org.uk

Founded in 1982, the National Association of Youth Theatres (NAYT) is the development agency for youth theatre practice in England. The organisation supports the development of youth theatre activity through training, advocacy, participation programmes and information services. Registration is open to any group or individual using theatre techniques in their work with young people, outside formal education. NAYT is an educational charity (No. 1046042) and a company limited by guarantee (No. 2989999).

NAYT responds to more than 800 enquiries a year from young people, teachers, parents, carers, youth workers and social services looking for information and advice about youth theatre provision or career and educational opportunities. This free service puts young people in direct contact with youth theatres.

National Youth Arts Wales (NYAW)

245 Western Avenue, Cardiff CF5 2YX
tel 029-2026 5060 *fax* 029-2026 5014
email nyaw@nyaw.co.uk
website www.nyaw.co.uk/nytw.html
NYTW Artistic Director Tim Baker (there are other
Artistic Directors with the other disciplines)

NYAW represents the National Youth Brass Band of
Wales, National Youth Choir of Wales, National
Youth Chamber Ensemble of Wales, National Youth
Dance Wales, National Youth Orchestra of Wales,
and National Youth Theatre of Wales (NYTW).

The National Youth Theatre of Wales was founded in
1976 and has since provided opportunities for
hundreds of young people, many of whom are now
actively involved with the theatre as professional
actors, directors, writers, designers and stage
managers. The NYTW is aimed at young people aged
16-21 who are drawn from all over Wales. With
guidance from its Artistic Director, the youth theatre
prepares and rehearses during the summer of each
year for a series of high-profile public performances.

In addition, the NYTW spearheads a development
programme of workshops and education activities,
designed to increase interest and participation in
youth theatre.

National Youth Music Theatre (NYMT)

2–4 Great Eastern Street, London EC2A 3NW
email enquiries@nymt.org.uk,
auditions@nymt.org.uk (Auditions),
sheena.clark@nymt.org.uk (Sponsorship & Support)
website www.nymt.org.uk

The National Youth Music Theatre exists to produce
challenging music theatre work (both major
productions and workshops) for young people of all
backgrounds as participants; and, in helping them to
explore new and existing works, to inspire themselves
and each other – giving them the opportunity to
achieve their highest aspirations and realise their
talent, imagination and creativity.

In 2006 they produced 7 exciting new music theatre
projects around the UK; 2 of these were adaptations
of novels and 5 were completely new projects or
developments of new musicals created in 2005.

National Youth Theatre of Great Britain (NYT)

443-45 Holloway Road, London N7 6LW
tel 020-7281 3863
website www.nyt.org.uk
Artistic Director Paul Roseby *Executive Director* Sid
Higgins *General Manager* Alexa Cruickshank

Founded in 1956, the NYT is the UK's premier youth
arts organisation, providing young people aged 13-21
with the opportunity for creative participation and
learning through theatre arts. Courses are offered in
Acting, Stage Management, Lighting & Sound,

Scenery & Prop Building and Costume Making at a
professional standard, which culminate in a season of
productions and community projects around the UK
and abroad, in professional theatres and site-specific
locations.

Many leading names in the creative industries started
out at the NYT, including Sir Ben Kingsley, Sir Derek
Jacobi, Dame Helen Mirren, Daniel Craig, Daniel
Day Lewis, Chiwetel Ejiofor, Timothy Spall, Liza
Tarbuck and Matt Smith.

The NYT auditions approximately 3000 applicants
each year at one of 20 audition centres across the UK.
Approximately 650 new members are recruited
annually. Successful applicants are offered a place on
one of the courses, and, having completed a course,
members are eligible to audition for the NYT's
production season or to become Peer Mentors within
the Creative Learning programme. Major
productions are mounted each year.

The NYT also has a robust Creative Learning
programme which embeds learning throughout all
projects, and also runs accredited courses for NEETs
groups, as well as many open access projects and
community productions.

Scottish Youth Theatre

The Old Sheriff Court, 105 Brunswick Street,
Glasgow G1 1TF
tel 0141-221 5127 *fax* 0141-221 9123
email info@scottishyouththeatre.org
website www.scottishyouththeatre.org
Artistic Director Mary McCluskey

Founded in 1977, Scottish Youth Theatre is
Scotland's national theatre for and by young people.
Runs weekly drama classes for young people aged 3-
25, in addition to a variety of training courses,
festivals, educational workshops, youth theatre
projects and productions throughout the year. There
is no audition process to attend the drama classes,
but participants in the annual summer festival are
asked to prepare a 2-minute speech and a song. In
2003 almost 2000 applications were received and
1000 places offered. Stages at least 5 productions each
year, which in recent years have included: *Mary
Queen of Scots* and *Dying for It.* Staff are happy to
help applicants with any enquiries.

Youth Music Theatre UK

London Office 40 Parkgate Road, London SW11 4JH
tel 0844-415 4858
Edinburgh Office c/o FST, Theatre Workshop,
Hamilton Place, Edinburgh EH3 5AX
website www.youthmusictheatreuk.org

Youth Music Theatre UK, also known as YMT, is a
national charity whose principal aim is the personal
and creative development of young people through
the medium of musical theatre. Set up in 2003, the
organisation is the UK's biggest and most active
music theatre provider for young people aged 11-21.

The company provides a wide range of residential workshops around the country, in the form of summer productions and Studios. Each year, YMT presents work in all corners of the UK and works with hundreds of young people from a wide range of backgrounds.

The charity also provides a wide range of Outreach opportunities with schools, youth services and cross-cultural groups, and is dedicated to giving every young person who participates a unique and memorable experience.

Auditions for young performers take place around the UK from January to March, and successful applicants join the company of around 8 fully staged productions at venues and festivals around the country in the summer holidays.

YMT also runs The Studio, a non-auditioned residential summer course which allows young performers and musicians the chance to work with professional artistic teams to create a unique new musical. In 2008, YMT also introduced the Young Writers' and Composers' Course, led by professional musical theatre creators working with 15 young writers and composers to create new work with the intention of possible future development.

YMT also offers training opportunities for graduate directors, assistant directors, assistant MDs, designers and choreographers alongside our professional summer teams – check the website for details early each year.

For further information on YMT's work, visit www.youthmusictheatreuk.org.

Drama schools

Currently there is a core of established drama schools which belong to an organisation called the Conference of Drama Schools (CDS – **www.drama.ac.uk**). Most of these run courses that are 'accredited' by the National Council for Drama Training (NCDT – **www.ncdt.co.uk**); for more details, see the article on the NCDT and accreditation. At present, all courses that have 'accreditation' are provided by schools who are members of the CDS. However, there are also courses within these schools which don't have 'accreditation', and there are a few well-respected courses that are neither 'accredited' nor part of CDS schools. The reasons for these variations are too complex to explain here. However, if you get a place on a three-year accredited course, you stand a higher than 'evens' chance of getting funding in the same way as those accepted on conventional university courses.

It is important to check the current funding arrangements for each course you intend applying for. Don't simply rely on what arrangements were in place last year, as things have a habit of changing. Many three-year accredited courses have 'degree' status – in spite of the fact that there is little or no written component to the courses, let alone formal, written exams. (Historically, the schools took the 'degree' route to help students get funding on the same basis as those following conventional academic courses.) Degree status actually means very little in the acting profession, and courses with degree status are not necessarily better than those without it. Some schools have been quite vociferous about not wishing to become embroiled in the whole philosophy and bureaucracy that is fundamental to degree education – believing that joining with a university would compromise the purely vocational character of their courses. One such adds: 'Universities are academic institutions, and the intelligence required of an academic is different from that required of an actor. While some are blessed with both kinds, many talented and intelligent actors are of indifferent academic ability. We would not wish to exclude them.' Degree status will enable you to go on to a higher degree and enhance your employment prospects outside the profession – but not within it.

Funding for some accredited one- and two-year courses is available, but not with the same frequency as for three-year courses. However, there is advice on finding funds from private sources on both the NCDT and the CDS websites, and some schools have scholarships and/or are good at helping students with this task.

It is worth spending time checking through all the courses listed below – also, read through the CDS's *Guide to Professional Training in Drama and Technical Theatre* which is available from their website. (Additionally, if possible seek the opinion of those with recent knowledge of drama schools.) Then get prospectuses for any school that you feel could be viable for you – and read each one thoroughly. Important considerations include whether you could be eligible for funding for your fees (and a maintenance loan), and potential living costs – central London is significantly more expensive to live in than Manchester, for example. (Bear in mind, too, whether a degree qualification at the end of the course is important to you.) Above all, it's important to try to assess which courses you feel would suit you best, and to apply – some require application via UCAS **www.ucas.ac.uk** – to as many as you can afford the audition fees and travel costs for. Don't forget to factor in the cost of overnight accommodation, if necessary. The plain truth is

Training

that competition for places is so intense (especially for women) that you need to audition for as many places as possible. Every time you do another audition you will learn more about the techniques of auditioning than any book or class can teach you – particularly if it's your first time. It is important to take on board the fact that many people take two or three years of auditioning, and sometimes more, before they get places. If you are determined to become a professional actor, you have to take rejection in your stride – learn from it and keep on trying until you succeed.

Finally, carefully check the application deadlines, funding details and audition specifications of each school you intend applying to – there are some considerable variations. You may find it useful to read *An Applicant's Guide to Auditioning and Interviewing at Dance and Drama Schools*, which is available from the NCDT's website. Andrew Piper's website **www.andrew-piper.com** contains useful advice on auditioning and fundraising for drama school, as well as an account of his own first year. Simon Dunmore's website **www.simon.dunmore.btinternet.co.uk** also contains auditioning advice, suggests playwrights suitable for audition material and lists over-used Shakespeare characters.
Notes
• For general information on funding for fees and maintenance loans, see **www.directgov.uk/en/EducationAndLearning/index.htm** and click on Student Finance.
• Places on some accredited courses are currently funded through Dance and Drama Awards (DaDAs). These were introduced in the late 1990s and provide funding for about two-thirds of successful applicants. For more details check each relevant school's prospectus and website – also look at **www.direct.gov.uk/danceanddrama**.
• It is especially important to **check for the latest information on all fees listed** in this section. *Actors' Yearbook* makes every effort to ensure that such information is correct and up-to-date, but prices especially are liable to ongoing amendment.

* denotes membership of the Conference of Drama Schools

Academy Drama School
www.the-academy.info
Following the tragic death of the Principal, Tim Reynolds, the Academy closed in January 2007.

The Academy of Live and Recorded Arts (ALRA)*
Studio One, The Royal Victoria Patriotic Building, John Archer Way, London SW18 3SX
tel 020-8870 6475
email info@alra.co.uk
website www.alra.co.uk
Co-directors Clive Duncan, Adrian Hall

Accredited acting courses
• BA (Hons) Acting. A full-time, 3-year course to prepare students for a varied career as a professional actor.
• MA Acting. A full-time, intense, 1-year course to prepare students for a career in the stage and screen industries.
• Stage Management and Technical Theatre Foundation Degree. A full-time, 2-year course to

equip students with the necessary skills to gain employment in the theatre industry.
• Acting Foundation Course. A part-time, 3-term course to prepare students for full-time vocational training.
• Acting for Deaf BSL Users. A part-time, 3-term introduction to acting for TV and the theatre.

Consult the website for more details.

The Academy of the Science of Acting & Directing
9-15 Elthorne Road, Archway, London N19 4AJ
tel 020-7272 0027 *fax* 020-7272 0026
email info@asad.org.uk
website www.asad.org.uk
Principal Helen Kogan *Administrator* Philip Pritchard

Full-time acting courses
No public funding is available for the courses listed below, but students may apply for a limited number of scholarships. There are daytime and evening courses.

• Three Year Acting Course. Applicants must be aged 18 or over. Course fee is £11,120 p.a. Offers 14 places each year. *Audition requirements*: 1 modern, 1 classical and 1 other speech, and 1 song for solo audition. *Audition fee*: £30
• Two Year Acting Course. Applicants must be aged 18 or over. Course fee is £11,120 p.a. Offers 14 places each year. *Audition requirements/fee*: as above
• One Year Acting Course. Applicants must be aged 18 or over. Course fee is £11,120 . Offers 14 places each year. *Audition requirements/fee*: as above.

The Actor Works

1 Knighten Street, Wapping, London E1W 1PH
tel 020-7702 0909
email info@theactorworks.co.uk
website www.theactorworks.co.uk
Director Daniel Brennan

Full-time evening and weekend courses

This course is designed for those who may:

• need to work during the day to pay for their training
• have family commitments that prevent them from studying in the day
• be considering changing their career and need to keep 'the day job' until the acting bug finally bites for good

It is an intensive, two-year vocational training, which covers all aspects of an actor's work. Subjects covered include: acting for stage, screen acting, actors' movement, speech, voice, reading, audition technique, stage combat, dance, singing and theatre history. During the course students will take part in up to five different productions, normally at the end of every term.

The course culminates in an agents showcase at a major theatre and a season of graduation plays on the London fringe.

Students on this course must be aged 20 +. There is no upper age limit.

The fee for this course is £1500 per term. There are six terms.

Postgraduate course

This course is designed for those who:
• studied drama at university and would like some more 'hands on' experience
• have had actor training and would like to hone their skills

This is a one-year daytime course, which offers full actor training. Subjects covered include: acting for stage, screen acting, actors' movement, speech, voice, reading, audition technique, stage combat, dance, singing and theatre history. During the course students will take part in up to four different productions, normally at the end of every term.

The course culminates in an agents showcase at a major theatre and a season of graduation plays on the London fringe.

Students on this course must be aged 21 +. There is no upper age limit.

The fee for this course is £2200 per term. There are three terms in all.

Foundation course

This course is designed for younger students who:
• need guidance and support through the gruelling process of auditioning for major drama schools
• have not yet decided whether acting is for them
• want to do something productive with their gap year

This one-year daytime course is not full actor training as such, but it prepares students for what they will experience should they choose to take up acting as a career. Emphasis is placed on preparation, application and discipline. We encourage confidence and a feeling of self-worth which helps students through the audition process. Subjects covered include: voice, speech, actors' movement, audition preparation, stage combat, theatre history and reading. Students can expect to take roles in three different productions over the year.

Students on this course must be between the ages of 17 and 20 inclusive.

The fee for this course is £1300 per term and includes the cost of LAMDA examinations. There are three terms in all.

Other courses offered

Also now runs a part-time course designed for those who wish to pursue acting as a leisure interest. "You may wish to 'test the water' before considering full-time training; to improve your self-confidence in group situations; to improve your public-speaking skills; or perhaps simply enjoy a new activity one night a week." These qualifications are currently NVQ Level 3 equivalent and from 2008 count for between 20 and 65 points towards UCAS tariffs. The cost for 10 Tuesday evenings is £350. For LAMDA tuition on Thursdays, an extra £100 (plus the cost of exam – £40-£50).There is no need to audition, though "please phone us in the first instance to reserve a place, before sending payment".

The Arden Theatre School

1 Universal Square, North Devonshire Street, Manchester M12 6JH
tel 0161-279 7257 *fax* 0161-279 7218
email AMurray@ccm.co.uk
website www.thearden.ac.uk (School) or www.ccm.ac.uk (College)
Head of School David O'Shea *Administrator* Angela Murray

The Arden was established over 15 years ago, in a unique collaboration between Manchester University, City College and The Royal Exchange Theatre. The School now offers 3 BA (Hons) programmes and a postgraduate Diploma in Writing for the Stage.

Full-time acting courses

• BA (Hons) Acting Studies (3 years full-time). Applicants must be aged 18 or over at the start of the course with a minimum of 12 UCAS tariff points. Entry to the School is by audition only, applications from mature students with relevant experience in place of qualifications will be considered. Applications must be made through UCAS and auditions run from December to June.
• BA (Hons) Musical Theatre Studies (3 years full-time). Application procedures as above. This course accepted its first intake of students in September 2006.

Arts Ed London*

Cone Ripman House, 14 Bath Road, London W4 1LY
tel 020-8987 6666 fax 020-8987 6699
email drama@artsed.co.uk
website www.artsed.co.uk
Director of the School of Acting Jane Harrison Director of the School of Musical Theatre Chris Hocking Key contacts Nicola Ramsbottom (Acting), Vivienne Hobbs (Musical Theatre)

Part of the Dance and Drama Awards scheme. Applications for courses and awards should be made direct to the school. All courses are accredited by the National Council for Drama Training or the Council for Dance Education and Training, and validated by City University.

Accredited acting courses

• BA (Hons) Acting (3 years). Applicants must be aged 18 or over. Course fee is £8790 p.a.; public funding is available for some students. In 2004 the school received 500 applications for 35 places. Audition requirements: 1 modern and 1 Shakespeare speech for solo audition. Audition fee: £30
• BA (Hons) Musical Theatre Programme (3 years). Applicants must be aged 18 or over. Course fee is £9294 p.a.; public funding is available for some students. In addition, the school has a limited number of bursaries. Applications will be accepted until the end of February but the academy recommends early applications. Audition requirements: first round consists of a movement audition and a song from a musical; second round involves an acting audition, a further singing audition, an interview and an Orthopaedic Assessment. Course is accredited by the Council for Dance Education and Training (CDET – www.cdet.org.uk). Audition fee: £30
• MA Acting (1 year postgraduate). Applicants must be aged 21 or over. Course fee is £9297; public funding is available for some students. In 2004 the school received 300 applications for 30 places. Audition requirements/fee: as for 3-year course

Birmingham School of Acting* (formerly Birmingham School of Speech and Drama)

Millennium Point, Curzon Street,
Birmingham B4 7XG

tel 0121-331 7200 fax 0121-331 7221
email info@bsa.uce.ac.uk
website www.bsa.uce.ac.uk
Principal Stephen Simms Admissions Manager Roger Franke

Accredited acting courses

• BA (Hons) Acting (3 years). Applicants must be aged 18 or over with 2 A levels (grade E or above) or equivalent. Course fee is £3000 p.a. Applications should be made direct to the school by 31st March. In 2003 the school received 450 applications for 42 places. Audition requirements: 1 modern and 1 other speech for solo audition; 2nd audition requires 1 modern and 1 classical speech and 1 song. Audition fee: £20 for first round, £10 for second
• Graduate Diploma in Acting (1 year). Applicants must be aged 21 or over with a university degree or relevant professional experience. Course fee is £3000. In 2003 the school received 110 applications for 16 places. Applications should be made directly to the school by 31st March. Audition requirements/fee: as above

The Birmingham Theatre School

The Old Rep Theatre, Station Street,
Birmingham B5 4DY
tel 0121-643 3300 fax 0121-643 3300
email info@birminghamtheatreschool.co.uk
website www.birminghamtheatreschool.co.uk
Principal Chris Rozanski Key contact Andrea Cobham (Arts Admin Manager)

Full-time acting courses

• HND Performing Arts/Theatre Acting (2 years). Applicants must be aged 18 or over with 12 points at A level or BTEC. 300 applications were received in 2006 and 60 places offered. Audition requirements: 1 modern and 1 classical speech for solo audition. Audition fee: no charge
• BTEC National Diploma in Performing Arts. Applicants must be aged 16 or over
• Advanced Acting Diploma (1 year). Applicants must be aged 17 or over. Course fee is £6900 for which no public funding is available. More than 35 applications were received in 2003 and 25 places offered. Audition requirements/fee: as above
• Open Access Foundation in Acting (1 year). Applicants must be aged 16 or over

The Bridge Theatre Training Company

Cecil Sharp House, 2 Regent's Park Road,
London NW1 7AY
tel 020-7424 0860 fax 020-7424 9118
email admin@thebridge-ttc.org
website www.thebridge-ttc.org
Joint Artistic Directors Mark Akrill, Judith Pollard Company Administrator Alex Abbott

The Bridge is a non-profit organisation which provides intensive training for a career in professional acting. Courses include comprehensive career guidance, and a graduating season of public productions in London theatres with a West End showcase at the Criterion Theatre in front of agents, directors and casting directors.

Full-time acting courses

• Professional Acting Course (2 years). Applicants must be aged 18 or over. Course fee is £4650 p.a.
• Professional Acting Course (1 year postgraduate/post-experience). Applicants must be aged 21 or over with a university degree or significant relevant experience. Course fee is £5250 p.a.

Audition fee: £30

Bristol Old Vic Theatre School*

2 Downside Road, Clifton, Bristol BS8 2XF
tel 0117-973 3535 *fax* 0117-923 9371
email enquiries@oldvic.ac.uk
website www.oldvic.ac.uk
Principal Paul Rummer *Artistic Director* Sue Wilson

An affiliate of the Conservatoire for Dance and Drama. All courses are entirely vocational and are validated by the University of West England.

Accredited acting courses

Fees for the courses listed below were £3000 p.a. for 2006/7. The official age for entry is 18-30 but the school frequently makes exceptions in the case of older applicants. Applications should be made direct to the school.

• BA Professional Acting (3 years). *Audition requirements*: 1 classical verse speech (preferably Shakespeare), 1 modern prose piece – each lasting no longer than 2 minutes for solo audition. Candidates should also prepare a short song. Recalls take the form of a weekend school in Bristol. *Audition fee*: £30 for first audition; no charge for the weekend-school recall
• Diploma of Professional Acting (2 years). *Audition requirements/fee*: as above

Other full-time acting courses

• Certificate of Higher Education in Professional Acting (1 year). *Audition requirements/fee*: as above
• Professional Acting Course for Overseas Students (1 year). *Course fee*: £12,370. See the website for audition procedures.

Central School of Speech and Drama*

64 Eton Avenue, London NW3 3HY
tel 020-7722 8183 *fax* 020-7722 4132
email enquiries@cssd.ac.uk
website www.cssd.ac.uk
Principal Gavin Henderson

Scholarships/Bursaries Diana Wade Memorial Award, Gary Bond Memorial Award, Robert Tunstall Memorial Award

Accredited acting courses

• BA (Hons) Acting (Acting for Stage) – 3 years. Applicants must be aged 18 or over. For 2007 start, normal entry requirements are a minimum of 2 Cs at A level, a minimum of 3 Cs at GCSE, and selection by audition. Exceptionally, applicants who do not meet this requirement but demonstrate appropriate academic potential may be accepted. Applications should be made through UCAS by January. For 2006 start, course fees were: £3000 p.a. for home/EU students, for which some public funding is available; £9000 p.a. for overseas students. In 2005 the school received 3058 applications for a maximum of 66 places for its BA (Hons) Acting course. *Audition fee*: £30
• BA (Hons) Acting (Music Theatre) – 3 years. Applicants must be aged 18 or over. For 2007 start, normal entry requirements are a minimum of 2 Cs at A level, a minimum of 3 Cs at GCSE, and selection by audition. Exceptionally, applicants who do not meet this requirement but demonstrate appropriate academic potential may be accepted.
• BA (Hons) Acting (Physical and Visual Theatre) – 3 years. Applicants must be aged 18 or over. For 2007 start, normal entry requirements are a minimum of 2 Cs at A level, a minimum of 3 Cs at GCSE, and selection by audition. Exceptionally, applicants who do not meet this requirement but demonstrate appropriate academic potential may be accepted. Applications should be made through UCAS by January 2007. For 2006 start, course fees were: £3000 p.a. for home/EU students, for which some public funding is available; £9000 p.a. for overseas students. *Audition fee*: £30

Other full-time acting courses

• Alternative Theatre and New Performance Practices (qualification, BA (Hons) Theatre Practice). For 2007 start, normal entry requirements are a minimum of 2 passes at A level plus 3 GCSEs at grade C or above. Applications should be made through UCAS by January or March 2007. For 2006 start, course fees were: £3000 p.a. for home/EU students, for which some public funding is available; £9000 p.a. for overseas students. In 2005 the school received 587 applications for a maximum of 131 places for its BA (Hons) Theatre Practice course.

All the 1-year courses listed below are for postgraduates or actors (aged 21 or over) with significant professional experience. Applications for all postgraduate courses should be made direct to the school. For 2006 start, course fees were £5200 or £5500 (dependent on course) for home/EU students, and £10,200 or £10,500 (dependent on course) for overseas students.
• Acting Musical Theatre. In 2005 the school received 116 applications for a maximum of 31 places.
• Classical Acting. In 2005 the school received 195 applications for a maximum of 33 places.

• Advanced Theatre Practice – Performing. In 2005 the school received 211 applications for a maximum of 57 places.
• Movement Studies. In 2005 the school received 17 applications for a maximum of 6 places.
• Actor Training & Coaching. In 2005 the school received 11 applications for a maximum of 6 places.
• Acting for Screen. In 2005 the school received 76 applications for a maximum of 20 places.

The Cygnet Training Theatre*

New Theatre, Friars Gate, Exeter EX2 4AZ
tel (01392) 277189 *fax* (01392) 277189
email CygnetArts@btconnect.com
website www.cygnetnewtheatre.com
Principal Rosalind Williams *Key contact* Mary G Evans

A member of the Conference of Drama Schools, Cygnet offers a 3-year, full-time training course based in its own studio theatre. Functions as a small touring company, drawing its members from all over the UK and abroad. The small number of applicants selected each year (6-8) are chosen for their flexibility, maturity, awareness and self-discipline. They are expected to work with professional commitment from the first day in this ensemble training. Financial assistance is occasionally available to third-year students.

Full-time acting courses

• Professional Acting Certificate (3 years). Applicants must be aged 18 or over. Course fee is £7500 p.a. for which no public funding is available. More than 200 applications were received in 2003 and 8 places were offered. *Audition requirements*: 1 modern and 1 classical speech lasting 1-3 minutes each, and 1 unaccompanied song. Applicants are auditioned on their own and in a group. *Audition fee*: £35

Other options include: Acting with Music, and Acting with Directing. People may come to train straight from school, after a university degree, or as a career change. All need stamina, commitment and an ability to put the work of the ensemble before their personal feelings. This training, regardless of the option, requires serious commitment.

Drama Centre London*

Central Saint Martins College of Art and Design, 10 Back Hill, London EC1R 5EN
tel 020-7514 7022 *fax* 020-7514 8777
email drama@arts.ac.uk
website www.csm.arts.ac.uk/drama
Principal Dr Vladimir Mirodan *Key contact* Maggie Wilkinson

Trains students to become professional actors, directors and screen writers. Established 47 years ago, it is now part of the University of the Arts London, and is a member of the Conference of Drama Schools. The school awards 3 Foundation

Scholarships; 1 Malmgren Scholarship; 1 Reeves Scholarship; 5 UK/EU Leverhulme Scholarships; and 2 International Leverhulme Scholarships.

Accredited acting course

• BA (Hons) Acting (3 years). Applicants must have 2 A levels. Course fee for 2009 is £3225 p.a.; public funding is available for all UK/EU students doing their first degree. Applications should be made through UCAS. In 2009 the school received 1948 applications for 16 places. *Audition requirements*: 1 modern speech (post-1830) and 1 classical verse speech (Shakespeare or other Renaissance playwright) for solo audition. Ear test will be required at recalls. *Audition fee*: £40

Other full-time acting courses

• MA in European Classical Acting (45 weeks). 20 places are available
• MA in Screen: Acting, Directing, Writing (60 weeks over 18 months). 20 places are available

Applicants for both MA courses must have a related degree, a diploma in dance or drama, an honours degree in another discipline supported by performance-related experience (professional, amateur or student), or significant professional experience. Applications are made direct to the school. *Audition fee*: £40
• Diploma in Foundation Studies – Performance (30 weeks). Applicants must have 1 A level and a BTEC National Diploma in Performing Arts or equivalent. 20 places are available. Applications are made direct to the school. *Audition fee*: £40

Drama Studio London (DSL)*

1 Grange Road, London W5 5QN
tel 020-8579 3897 *fax* 020-8566 2035
email registrar@dramastudiolondon.co.uk
website www.dramastudiolondon.co.uk
Director Peter Craze *Registrar* Sue Quelch-Woolls

Drama Studio London (DSL) provides training for mature and postgraduate students in acting and directing, and both courses are full-time and intensive. A maximum of 60 acting and 2 directing places are offered each year. Acting auditions are held throughout the year: applicants will be contacted by the course director to arrange auditions. Contact the registrar (**registrar@dramastudiolondon.co.uk**) for a prospectus, an application form or information about Open Days and course fees. This information is also available on the website.

Some scholarship funding is available according to need. All successful candidates will be offered the chance to apply.

Accredited acting courses

• DSL Diploma in Acting (1 year postgraduate). Applicants are usually aged 21 or over. *Audition requirements*: 1 speech of any genre of a maximum of

2 minutes, and a group-based workshop. *Audition fee*: £30

Other full-time acting courses

• DSL Diploma in Acting (2 year postgraduate). "Includes all the same subjects as the 1-year course, but allows us to offer a greater variety of teaching styles and devote more time to developing techniques." Applicants are usually aged 21 or over. *Audition requirements*: 1 speech of any genre of a maximum of 2 minutes, and a group-based workshop. *Audition fee*: £30

East 15 Acting School*

Hatfields, Rectory Lane, Loughton IG10 3RY
tel 020-8508 5983 *fax* 020-8508 7521
email east15@essex.ac.uk
website www.east15.ac.uk
Director Professor Leon Rubin *Key contact* Linda Humphreys

Accredited acting courses

• BA Acting (3 years). 40 places were offered in 2004. Deadline for applications is June. Applicants must be aged 18 or over with A level grades EE, AVCE grades EE or BTEC National overall pass or equivalent. (If an applicant does not meet the specific criteria, he or she may discuss the application with East 15 admissions.) Students over the age of 21 are not required to fullfil the same A-level grade criteria. There is no upper age limit, although it is unusual to admit students over 40 years. Deadline for applications is June. Course fee is £3000 p.a. for qualifying UK and EU students (£8500 for overseas students). *Audition requirements*: In the first instance, all students must apply using the application forms available through the school or on the school's website. Students must also register through the UCAS system. Auditions are required of all acting students. Students are offered 2 alternative dates for UK auditions, which are held on Saturdays from October to June. These sessions start at 11am and are usually completed by 6pm. In the UK, all auditions are held at East 15's campus. The audition consists of a series of workshops (movement and singing), as well as the presentation of audition speeches and a prepared song, during which helpful suggestions and feedback are often given. East 15 Acting School's audition procedures have been praised for being a thorough experience, through which students are encouraged to do their best. While many drama schools give students 3 minutes, East 15 Acting School gives its auditionees up to 6 hours – including the opportunity to ask questions. Overseas students may apply via video or through personal interview in certain countries. For audition purposes each candidate must perform 3 contrasting, short speeches as follows: 1 speech from a Shakespeare or Jacobean play of 10 lines only; 1 'serious' speech from a 20th-century play; 1 contrasting speech from a contemporary play (post-1950). Speeches should not exceed 2 minutes each. Each applicant should also prepare a short song, and bring sheet music (in the correct key) for use by the accompanist. *Audition fee*: £35 (non-refundable) for UK auditions and for video applicants; £50 for overseas auditions (held in the spring – contact the school for details)

• MA/PG Acting (1 year). Selection for this course is based upon experience and potential. All applicants must be over the age of 21; there is no upper age limit. Applicants must hold a BA degree (normally at least a 2:1) or have suitable previous life professional or academic experience. Course fee is £8700 for UK/EU students (£10,200 for overseas); public funding is available for some students. 28 places were offered in 2004. Deadline for applications is June. *Audition requirements/fee*: as above

• MA/PG Acting for TV, Film and Radio (1 year). Selection for this course is based upon experience and potential. All applicants must be over the age of 21; there is no upper age limit. Applicants must hold a BA degree (normally at least a 2:1) or have suitable previous life professional or academic experience. Course fee is £8900 for UK/EU students (£10,700 for overseas); public funding is available for some students. 16 places were offered in 2004. *Audition requirements/fee*: as above

Other full-time acting courses

• BA in Contemporary Theatre (3 years). All applicants must be aged 18 or over at time of enrolment. There is no upper age limit, although it is unusual to admit students over 40 years. Applicants must hold A-level grades EE, AVCE grades EE or BTEC National overall pass or equivalent. (If an applicant does not meet the specific criteria, he or she may discuss the application with East 15 admissions.) Students over the age of 21 have no minimum educational requirements. Deadline for applications is June. Course fee is £3000 p.a. for UK/EU students (£8500 p.a. for overseas). 14 places were offered in 2004. *Audition requirements/fee*: as above. This course is pending NCDT Accreditation.

• Foundation in Acting (1 year). Applicants must be aged 18 or over with 2 A levels or equivalent. Course fee is £3000 for UK/EU students (£8500 for overseas). 50 places were offered in 2004. *Audition requirements/fee*: as above

• MA in Professional Theatre (see website for details)

• Certificate of Higher Education in Theatre Arts (see website for details)

• Foundation Degree/BA Degree in Community Theatre (see website for details)

• Foundation Degree/BA Degree in Specialist Performance Skills (Stage Combat) (see website for details).

GSA Conservatoire* (formerly Guildford School of Acting)

Millmead Terrace, Guildford GU2 4YT
tel (01483) 560701 *fax* (01483) 535431

Training

email enquiries@conservatoire.org
website www.conservatoire.org
Director Peter Barlow

GSA was founded in 1935 and from 1964 onwards has concentrated on the vocational training of actors and stage managers. Since 1987 the Musical Theatre Course has held a leading position in the world of actor training.

Accredited full-time acting courses

Applications for the courses listed below should be made direct to the Conservatoire by the end of January.

• BA (Hons) Acting (3 years). Applicants must be aged 18 or over with 2 A levels. Course fee is £10,167 p.a. for which some public funding is available. 18 places were offered in 2006/07. *Audition requirements*: 2 modern and 2 classical speeches, each lasting 2 minutes for solo audition. *Audition fee*: £35
• BA (Hons) Theatre, Musical Theatre (3 years). Applicants must be aged 18 or over with 2 A levels. Course fee is £11,130 p.a. for which some public funding is available. 52 places were offered in 2006/7. *Audition requirements*: 2 modern speeches, each lasting 2 minutes and 2 x 3 minutes musical theatre repertoire for solo audition. *Audition fee*: £35
• MA in Acting (4 term postgraduate) [subject to validation]. Applicants must be aged 21 or over. Course fee is £10,167 p.a. 10 places were offered in 2006/7
• MA in Musical Theatre (4 term postgraduate). Applicants must be aged 21 or over. Course fee £14,270. p.a. 14 places were offered in 2006/7

Guildhall School of Music & Drama*

Silk Street, Barbican, London EC2Y 8DT
tel 020-7628 2571 *fax* 020-7256 9438
email registry@gsmd.ac.uk
website www.gsmd.ac.uk
Director of Drama Wyn Jones

Accredited acting courses

• BA (Hons) Acting (3 years). Applicants are normally at least 18 years old with a minimum of 2 A-level passes or equivalent. Applications should be made direct to the school as early as possible, and by mid-January at the latest. Student Support from the UK Government is available for most EU students. Audition requirements: 1 piece in verse from Shakespeare or other Jacobean playwright, 1 modern (after 1956), and 1 other contrasting piece – each lasting no longer than 2 minutes. A short unaccompanied song is also required. Recall auditions include voice, movement and improvisation work (some of this in small groups), more detailed work on audition pieces, and a short interview. *Audition fee*: £44

In the final year of training, clear guidance is given on starting in the acting profession. There are regular talks and visits by regional theatre directors, agents, casting directors, income tax advisers and representatives from Equity.

Hertfordshire Theatre School

c/o The Market Theatre, 6A Sun Street, Hitchin SG5 1AE
email info@htstheatreschool.co.uk
website www.htstheatreschool.co.uk
Principals Kirk Foster, John Gardiner *Bursar & key contact* Annie Wilkinson

Has been providing training for actors for 17 years. Current total of 50 students. Graduation showcase takes place at a West End theatre.

Full-time acting courses

• Acting and Musical Theatre Course (3 years). Applicants must be aged 18 or over with a good level of education, either at A level or at BTEC. Course fee is £6500 p.a.; no public funding is available, but the school has a charitable trust offering reduced fees to students paying privately. A maximum of 20 places are available. *Audition requirements*: 1 modern, 1 classical and 1 comedy speech and 1 song. *Audition fee*: £25
• Advanced Acting and Musical Theatre (1 year postgraduate). Applicants must be aged 21 or over with a university degree or relevant professional experience. Course fee is £6500 for which no public funding or bursaries are available. A maximum of 6 places are available. *Audition requirements/fee*: as above

InterACT Training Scheme

c/o NTC Touring Theatre, The Playhouse, Bondgate Without, Alnwick, Northumberland NE66 1PQ
tel (01665) 602586 *fax* (01665) 605837
email interact@northumberlandtheatre.co.uk
website www.northumberlandtheatre.co.uk
Artistic Mentor Gillian Hambleton *Managed by* Northumberland Theatre Company

Not a formal drama-school training, but a 44-week scheme to provide a bridge between education or training and the profession, with the aim of encouraging and retaining talent within the North of England. The training consists of a series of workshops, masterclasses and placements within professional companies. There are no fees. Trainees are awarded a modest weekly bursary, based on Equity's average annual wage for a professional actor. Accommodation, travel and theatre tickets are also provided. *Audition requirements*: 1 modern speech and 1 classical speech (2 minutes each), and an unaccompanied song. At least 1 of the speeches should demonstrate an awareness of physical theatre. In 2005 there were 67 applications for 7 places. Minimum age is 18, although most applicants will have a degree. "All applicants *must* either originate from Northumberland, Tyne & Wear, Cumbria, Durham or Cleveland, or have trained or studied in those regions within the past 5 years. We endeavour to provide facilities and access to accommodate all disabilities."

International School of Screen Acting

3 Mills Studios, Unit 3, 24 Sugar House Lane, London E15 2QS
tel 020-8555 5775
email office@screenacting.co.uk
website www.screenacting.co.uk
Key contact David Craik

Founded in 2001 to specialise in offering full-time training specifically in television and film acting, taking a holistic approach to creativity in relation to students' personal development. No public funding or scholarships are available for these courses. Both courses are currently seeking NCDT accreditation. The school also offers a number of short courses - see their entry under *Short-term and part-time courses*. While the school is happy to receive applications from disabled students, there are currently significant access issues with the school's premises.

Full-time acting courses

• One Year Postgraduate Screen Acting. Students should be between 21 and 35 on entry to the course. In 2005 there were 110 applicants for the 14 places offered. No formal qualifications are required for entry. Course fee is £8812 (inc VAT). *Audition requirements*: No pre-rehearsed speeches are required; after an interview applicants are asked to read from a film script into camera. *Audition fee*: £25
• Two Year Screen Acting. Students should be over 18 on entry to the course. In 2005 there were 130 applicants for the 14 places offered. *Course fee*: £7637 (inc VAT) p.a. *Audition requirements/fee*: as above

Italia Conti Academy of Theatre Arts*

'Avondale', 72 Landor Road, London SW9 9PH
tel 020-7733 3210 *fax* 020-7737 2728
email acting@lsbu.ac.uk
website www.italiaconti-acting.co.uk
Course Director (Acting) Chris White

A member of the Conference of Drama Schools, the Academy offers a 3-year BA (Hons) Acting Degree, validated by London South Bank University and accredited by the National Council for Drama Training. This course takes a unique approach to actor training. Based loosely on the teachings of Sanford Meisner, whose work now dominates in the United States, it trains actors to be open, responsive and spontaneous.

Accredited acting courses

• BA (Hons) Acting (3 years). Applicants must be aged 18 or over with 5 GCSEs (grade C or above), including English, and 2 A levels (grade E or above)

or equivalent. Course fee for 2004 for UK/EU students was £3000 p.a. with public funding available for some students. *Audition fee*: £30

The Liverpool Institute for Performing Arts (LIPA)*

Mount Street, Liverpool L1 9HF
tel 0151-330 3232/3116/3084/3022 *fax* 0151-330 3131
email admissions@lipa.ac.uk
website www.lipa.ac.uk

LIPA is dedicated to providing the best teaching for people who want to pursue a lasting career in the arts and entertainment industry, and offers a variety of styles of courses aimed at different age groups. It looks for more than acting talent in its students, and applicants should show evidence of versatility and trainable ability in other performance-related skills.

Full-time acting courses

• BA (Hons) Performing Arts – Acting (3 years). Applicants must be aged 18 or over; there is no upper age limit. Educational attainment, relevant experience and interdisciplinary interest and ability will be taken into account when applying. Applications should be made through UCAS initially. If invited to audition, further information will be required. Course fee is £3000 p.a. with some public funding available.
• Postgraduate Diploma in Acting (1 year). Applicants are usually aged 21 or over, and educated to degree-level standard with some acting experience. Mature students without degree qualifications but with considerable related professional experience are welcome to apply. Course fee is £8250. This is an intensive year-long programme enabling students to become flexible, multi-skilled practitioners.

London Academy of Music and Dramatic Art (LAMDA)*

155 Talgarth Road, London W14 9DA
tel 020-8834 0500 *fax* 020-8834 0501
email enquiries@lamda.org.uk
website www.lamda.org.uk
Principal Peter James *Admission Assistants* Amy Richardson, Elissa Perrau, Philip McDonnell

LAMDA is one of the oldest and most celebrated drama schools in the English-speaking world. The Academy is dedicated to helping actors, directors, stage managers and theatre technicians acquire the necessary skills and levels of creativity to meet the highest demands in theatre, film and television. LAMDA's continuing success derives from its ability to adopt its traditional teaching to match modern advances. "At the Academy, we offer classical training for the modern acting profession. Through our affiliation with the Conservatoire for Dance and Drama, the Academy strives to ensure that the most talented students can continue to benefit from the outstanding vocational training we offer, regardless of their background or financial circumstances."

Training

Training

LAMDA also conducts an eminent set of Speech and Drama examinations through LAMDA Examinations, and has gained acclaim in the corporate sector through LAMDA Business Performance (LBP).

There are a limited number of scholarships available for the Three and Two Year Acting Courses and the Two Year Stage Management & Technical Theatre Course. Scholarships are allocated at the Academy's discretion – there is no application procedure prior to being offered a place.

LAMDA operates an equal opportunities policy for all students, and welcomes applications from disabled students. Disabled students are encouraged to disclose their needs to ensure that they are supported in the training. For more information, please see the website, or contact LAMDA Admissions (**admissions@lamda.org.uk**).

Accredited acting courses

• BA (Hons) in Professional Acting (3 years). Applicants must be aged 18 or over. Applications should be made directly to the school; please see the website for application deadline and course fee. 24-30 places are offered. *Audition requirements*: 1 Modern and 1 Classical speech, plus interview. Song required at recall stage; refer to the website for full details
• Foundation Degree in Acting (2 years). Applicants must be aged 18 or over. Applications should be made directly to the school; please see the website for application deadline and course fee. 24-30 places are offered. *Audition requirements*: 1 Modern and 1 Classical speech, plus interview. Song required at recall stage; refer to the website for full details
• Foundaton Degree in Stage Management & Technical Theatre (2 years). Applicants must be aged 18 or over. Applications should be made directly to the school; please see the website for application deadline and course fee. 22 places are offered. *Audition requirements*: interview; for fee, see website

Other full-time acting courses

• Postgraduate Diploma in Classical Acting (1 year). Applicants must be aged 18 or over; please see the website for fees and further details. 20 places are offered
• Single Semester Acting Course (14 weeks). Applicants must be age 18 or over; please see the website for fees and further details. 20-25 places are offered
• One Year Diploma Course for Postgraduates (1 year) – Directors, Designers, Musical Director & Repetiteur, Movement Instructor. Applicants must be aged 18 or over; please refer to the website for further details

London Academy of Radio, Film & TV

1 Lancing Street, London NW1 1NA
tel 0870-850 4994
website www.media-courses.com
Director of Courses Andy Parkin *Key contact* Estelle Burton

The academy has more than 30 teaching staff; around 1200 students take one or more of its 100+ courses. It is situated opposite Euston Station.

Full-time acting courses

• Diploma in Screen Acting. In 2005 there were 24 applicants for 24 places. Application deadline is June. Age range: 16+. Entry is by audition: 1 modern and 1 classical speech. There is no audition fee. Course fee: £6000

London Drama School

30 Brondesbury Park, London NW6 7DN
tel 020-8830 0074 *fax* 020-8830 4992
email enquiries@startek-uk.com
website www.startek-uk.com
Key contact Sarah Mann

Established 1996. All teachers are actors, directors, writers or producers currently working in the industry. 2 bursaries are available to talented students with financial difficulties; these bursaries cover half the tuition fees.

Full-time acting courses

• One Year Advanced Acting Course. Course fee is £7860 for which some public funding is available. More than 80 applications were received in 2006 and 15 places were offered. *Audition requirements*: 1 modern speech (from a play or film) lasting 3-5 minutes for solo audition. An unaccompanied song is optional. Advises applicants to choose a character close to own age and experience. *Audition fee*: £30
• One Year Foundation Acting Course. Prepares students to audition for either the course above or for other Drama Schools. Course fee is £6950. *Audition requirements*: 1 speech or poem lasting 1 minute. *Audition fee*: £30

London School of Musical Theatre

83 Borough Road, London SE1 1DN
tel 020-7407 4455 *fax* 020-7407 4455
email info@lsmt.co.uk
website www.lsmt.co.uk
Principal/Course Producer Adrian Jeckells
Administrator Laura Blundell

Full-time acting courses

• Musical Theatre Diploma Course (1 year). Age range for entry is 18-35. Course fee is £13,000 with public funding available for some students. 450 applications were received in 2008 and 40 places were offered. *Audition requirements*: 1 speech of applicant's choice lasting 2-3 minutes, and 2 contrasting musical theatre songs (i.e. 1 ballad and 1 up-tempo) for solo audition. *Audition fee*: £35

London Studio Centre (LSC)

42-50 York Way, London N1 9AB
tel 020-7837 7741 *fax* 020-7758 0222

Training

email sarah.tudor@london-studio-centre.co.uk
website www.london-studio-centre.co.uk
Director Nic Espinosa *Audition Enquiries* Sarah Tudor
Head of Studies Robert Penman

Primarily a dance college offering a BA Hons in
Theatre Dance, accredited by the Council for Dance
Education and Training and validated by the
University of the Arts, London. The LSC also offers a
1-year full-time diploma in Musical Theatre, for
those students who have completed a performing arts
course elsewhere and who wish to further their
training in this specialist area. Public funding is not
available for this 1-year course. More details are
available from the website.

Manchester Metropolitan University School of Theatre*

School of Theatre, Mabel Tylecote Building,
All Saints, Manchester M15 6BH
tel 0161-247 1305 *fax* 0161-247 6875
email k.daly@mmu.ac.uk
website www.theatre.mmu.ac.uk
Course Director Niamh Dowling *Key contact* Kath
Daly

See entry under *University acting-oriented courses* on
page 30 for further details.

Accredited acting courses

BA (Hons) Theatre Arts/Acting (3 years). Applicants
must be aged 18 or over with 2 A levels or equivalent.
Course fee is £3000 p.a. for which some public
funding is available. Applications should be made
through UCAS by January. Receives more than 1000
applications for around 28 places each year. *Audition
requirements*: 1 modern, 1 classical and 1 other speech
for both group and solo auditions. *Audition fee*: £30

Mountview Academy of Theatre Arts*

Ralph Richardson Memorial Studios,
Clarendon Road, London N22 6XF
tel 020-8881 2201 *fax* 020-8829 0034
email enquiries@mountview.org.uk
website www.mountview.org.uk
Principal Sue Robertson

Scholarships/Bursaries Sir John Mills Scholarship,
Dame Judi Dench Scholarship, Margaret Rutherford
Scholarship, Peter Coxhead Scholarship (all for
postgraduate performance courses)

Accredited acting courses

Applications for the courses listed below should be
made direct to the school, by March for the BA
(Hons) and by July for the postgraduate diploma.

• BA (Hons) Acting (3 years). Applicants must be
aged 18 or over, usually with A levels but these are
not essential. Course fee is £9402 p.a.; Dance and
Drama Awards are available for a significant number
of students. The school received more than 700

applications in 2004 and offered 32 places. *Audition
requirements*: 1 modern speech (post-1945) and 1
Shakespeare for both group and solo auditions.
Audition fee: £30
• BA (Hons) Musical Theatre (3 years). Applicants
must be aged 18 or over, usually with A levels but
these are not essential. Course fee is £10,077 p.a.;
Dance and Drama Awards are available for a
significant number of students. The school received
more than 700 applications in 2004 for 32 places.
Audition requirements: 1 modern speech (post-1945),
1 contrasting speech and 2 contrasting songs for both
group and solo auditions. *Audition fee*: £30
• PG Dip in Acting/MA in Performance (1 year).
Applicants must be aged 21 or over, usually with a
university degree. Course fee is £12,368. The school
received 300 applications in 2004 for 30 places.
Audition requirements/fee: as above
• PG Dip in Musical Theatre/MA in Performance (1
year). Applicants must be aged 21 or over, usually
with a university degree. Course fee is £12,220. The
school received 300 applications in 2004 for 30 places.
Audition requirements/fee: as above

Other full-time acting courses

• PG Dip in Acting – Screen and Radio (1 year).
Applicants must be aged 21 or over, usually with a
university degree. Course fee is £12,368. *Audition
requirements/fee*: as above

Oxford School of Drama*

Sansomes Farm Studios, Woodstock,
Oxford OX20 1ER
tel (01993) 812883 *fax* (01993) 811220
email info@oxforddrama.ac.uk
website www.oxforddrama.ac.uk
Principal George Peck *Executive Director* Kate
Ashcroft

The smallest of all the drama schools with accredited
status. Awarded Beacon Status by the Minister for
Education in 2006. Provides a significant number of
Dance and Drama Awards for its 1- and 3-year
courses. Also offers its own Hardship fund which is
distributed each year to students on full-time courses
at the school. Students not in receipt of a DaDA are
prioritised for funding. The Lionel Bart Foundation
and the Sir John Gielgud Charitable Trust currently
support the school; in addition, students have also
won the Lawrence Olivier Bursary, the Henry Cotton
Memorial Fund Award, the *Evening Standard*/Patricia
Rothermere Award, the Alan Bates Award, and the
BBC Carleton Hobbs bursary award.

Accredited acting courses

Applications for the courses listed below should be
made direct to the school by May. The fees for both
courses were set at £12,480 p.a for 2009/10.

• Diploma in Acting (3 years). Applicants must be
aged 18 or over. 18 places were offered in 2008.

Audition requirements: 1 modern and 1 classical speech, each lasting no longer than 90 seconds for solo audition, and 1 group movement/improvisation session. *Audition fee*: £35
• One Year Acting Course. Applicants must be aged 21 or over. 18 places were offered in 2008. *Audition requirements/fee*: as above

Poor School

242 Pentonville Road, London N1 9JY
tel 020-7837 6030 *fax* 020-7837 5330
email acting@thepoorschool.com
website www.thepoorschool.com
Principal Paul Caister

The school was created in 1986 with the aim of providing high-quality acting training that is financially within the reach of all, or almost all. Training lasts 2 years and operates in the evenings and at weekends until the final 2 terms, when daytime work is involved. Since March 1993 the Poor School has owned its own theatre, the Workhouse. This is a flexible studio theatre seating 50-80.

Full-time acting courses

• Two Year Acting Course (6 terms). Most students are in their early 20s but the school offers many places to older and younger people. Course fees are £1350 per term. Accepts 39 students each October. *Audition requirements*: 2 dramatic speeches (1 from Shakespeare) each lasting between 90 seconds and 2 minutes. *Audition fee*: £20

Queen Margaret University College*

Drama and Theatre Arts Programme Queen Margaret University, Edinburgh EH21 6UU
tel 0131-317 3900 *fax* 0131-317 3902
email cowen@qmuc.ac.uk
website www.qmuc.ac.uk
Key contact Catherine Owen

Full-time acting courses

• BA (Hons) Acting and Performance (3-4 years). Applicants must be aged 18 or over with Scottish Higher CCC, A level at grade E, BTEC or HNC/NC. Applications should be made through UCAS by March. Course fee is £1700 p.a. with public funding available to some students. In 2004 the college received 900 applications for this course and offered 22 places. *Audition requirements*: 1 modern and 1 classical speech for first audition; may also be asked to sing. Recall involves improvisation and movement workshops, sight-reading, singing, 2 additional pieces and an interview. *Audition fee*: £30 for first audition and £10 for recall. Initially the core subjects of acting, voice, text and movement are taught separately; as the course progresses, they combine and focus on performance through a wide variety of productions and projects. In the past few years, highly successful collaborations with students on other courses (stage

managers, directors, playwrights, etc.) have become a feature of the course. Close collaborations with professional theatre companies provide another dimension to the training.
• BA (Hons) Drama and Theatre Arts (4 years). This course is designed to develop understanding and practical experience in the broad canvas of drama. In years 1 and 2, students have classes in drama and performance and study the texts and contexts of theatre crossing between theory and practice. In years 3 and 4, students complement their studies with intensive work in a specialist area of study, including playwriting, directing, contemporary performance, producing, dramaturgy, community theatre and arts journalism.

The REP College

17 St Mary's Avenue, Purley on Thames, Berks RG8 8BJ
email tudor@repcollege.co.uk
website www.repcollege.co.uk
Key contact David Tudor

Provides acting students with 1 year of practical education, including 14 public performances. Course includes classes on audition techniques and planning. 4-8 scholarships of £1187-2375 are awarded annually.

Full-time acting courses

• Acting Course (1 year). Applicants must be aged 18 or over. Course fee is £8400 with public funding available for some students. Receives on average 300 applications per year, with 20 places offered. *Audition requirements*: group full-day workshop. *Audition fee*: £25

Rose Bruford College*

Lamorbey Park, Burnt Oak Lane, Sidcup DA15 9DF
tel 020-8308 2600 *fax* 020-8308 0542
email enquiries@bruford.ac.uk
website www.bruford.ac.uk
Principal Professor Michael Earley

Accredited acting courses

Applicants for the BA degree courses listed below must be over the age of 18 with the equivalent of a minimum of 2 A Levels at grade C or above. Course fees for 2009/10 were £3225 p.a. with some public funding and loans available. Applications should be made through UCAS.

• BA (Hons) Acting (3 years). *Audition requirements*: 1 modern and 1 classical speech each lasting no longer than 90 seconds. 1 song from musical theatre repertoire for recall audition. *Audition fee*: £30
• BA (Hons) Actor Musicianship (3 years). *Audition requirements/fee*: as above but with an additional instrument audition at recall stage

Other full-time acting courses

• BA (Hons) American Theatre Arts (3 years). *Audition requirements*: 1 modern speech (post-1945) lasting no longer than 2 minutes

• BA (Hons) European Theatre Arts (3 years). *Audition requirements*: 1 speech from a European (including a UK) play, lasting no longer than 3 minutes

Royal Academy of Dramatic Art (RADA)*

62-64 Gower Street, London WC1E 6ED
tel 020-7636 7076 *fax* 020-7323 3865
email enquiries@rada.ac.uk
website www.rada.org
Key contact Sally Power

Founded in 1904 by Sir Herbert Beerbohm Tree at His Majesty's Theatre, the Academy moved to its present premises a year later. In 1996 the Academy received a Lottery Grant from the Arts Council and embarked on a £32 million rebuilding programme, opening its new premises in 2000. The final stage of the estate's strategy was completed at the end of 2004. Some maintenance bursaries are available for students to supplement their own fundraising efforts. Applications should be made direct to the school by March.

Accredited acting courses

• BA (Hons) Acting (3 years). Normal age-range for entry is 18-30. Course fee is £3000 p.a. for which some public funding is available. Receives approximately 2000 applications each year for a maximum of 32 places. *Audition requirements*: 1 Shakespeare or Jacobean speech and 1 contrasting speech, each lasting no longer than 3 minutes for solo audition. Recalls may take the form of second audition, group workshop or individual working session; an unaccompanied song is also required. The auditions are 'lengthy and rigorous' and the process may span several months. *Audition fee*: £40

The course is for students who wish to earn a living working not only in the more traditional outlets, but also in the many alternative areas of theatre, film, television and radio. It is intensive, with a minimum working day of 10.00am – 6.00pm and individual classes in the evening. When public performances take place, the working day can be from 10.00am – 11.00pm.

Royal Academy of Music

Musical Theatre Department, Marylebone Road, London NW1 5HT
tel 020-7873 7483 *fax* 020-7873 7484
email mth@ram.ac.uk
website www.ram.ac.uk/mth
Head of Music Theatre Mary Hammond F.R.A.M, L.R.A.M *Course Leader* Karen Rabinowitz

Students are enrolled at the Royal Academy of Music, one of Europe's leading conservatories and a full member of the University of London. Fellow students include instrumentalists, pianists, concert and opera singers, composers, jazz and commercial musicians.

Full-time acting courses

• One Year Music Theatre Course. Aimed at graduates, mature students and professionals wishing to refocus their careers. The aim of the course is to give a thorough professional musical and dramatic training to students of postgraduate (or equivalent) level to equip them for performance in contemporary musical theatre, through the integration of singing, acting and movement. It aims to bridge the gap between the acting singer and the singing actor. Course fee for 2006/07 was set at £9800. Audition requirements, along with a full prospectus, can be found on the website. No public funding is available for this course. *Audition fee*: £60

Royal Scottish Academy of Music and Drama*

100 Renfrew Street, Glasgow G2 3DB
tel 0141-332 4101 *fax* 0141-332 8901
email registry@rsamd.ac.uk
website www.rsamd.ac.uk
Principal John Wallace

Accredited acting courses

Applications for the courses listed below should be made direct to the school by March. Public funding is available for some students.

• BA (Hons) Acting (3 years). Applicants are normally aged 18-21 but this is flexible. Course fee is £1700 p.a. Received 584 applications for 20 places in 2004. *Audition requirements*: 1 Shakespeare speech and 1 other for solo audition. *Audition fee*: £35

Other full-time acting courses

• Master of Performance in Musical Theatre (1 year). Course fee is £7500. 12 places are available. *Audition requirements*: contact the Academy. *Audition fee*: £35

Royal Welsh College of Music and Drama*

Castle Grounds, Cathays Park, Cardiff CF10 3ER
tel 029-2039 1327
website www.rwcmd.ac.uk
Principal Hilary Boulding *Drama Admissions Officer* Luise Moggridge

Accredited acting courses

• BA (Hons) Acting (3 years). Applicants should normally be at least 18 years old by the time of enrolment. The tuition fees for UK and other EU students is currently £3225 p.a. and is subject to inflation. There is a range of support in place to help cover the cost of tuition, the details of which will depend on where the student normally lives. Applications should be made through UCAS. Normally offers 20 places per year.
• MA in Acting for Stage, Screen and Radio (4 terms – September 2010 until January 2012). Applicants

should normally be at least 21 years old by the time of enrolment. The tuition fees are currently £8000. Applications should be made directly to the college. Normally offers 10 places.

• Postgraduate Diploma in Acting for Stage, Screen and Radio (1 year). Applicants should normally be at least 21 years old by the time of enrolment. The tuition fees are currently £7000. Applications should be made directly to the college. Normally offers 10 places.

• MA in Musical Theatre (Subject to validation; 3 terms – January 2011 until December 2011). Applicants should normally be at least 21 years old by the time of enrolment. The tuition fees are currently £11,000. Applications should be made directly to the college. Normally offers 10 places.

The School of the Science of Acting – now The Academy of the Science of Acting & Directing

Checklist of Drama School deadlines and audition requirements

Only schools with 'accredited' courses are included, and postgraduate courses often have later application deadlines.

School	Definition of 'Classical'	Definition of 'Modern/ Contemporary'	Application deadline
ALRA	Shakespeare	After 1950 – to camera	Mid-January – via UCAS
Arts Ed	Classical	Modern	31st March
Birmingham	Shakespearean/ Jacobean (they provide you with a list that you *may* choose from)	'Last 20 years'	1st March
Bristol	Classical (preferably Shakespeare) – verse	Modern Prose	1st March
Central	2 from supplied list	After 1960	Mid-January – via UCAS
Drama Centre	Shakespeare/ Contemporaries – verse	After 1830	Mid-January – via UCAS
Drama Studio	Classical	Modern	No specific deadline
East 15	Shakespearean/ Jacobean – '10-15 lines only'	20th/21st century – 'Serious'	Mid-January – via UCAS
Guildford	2 Classical – ideally Shakespeare and in verse	2 Modern	31st January
Guildhall	Shakespeare/ Jacobean – verse	Modern	Mid-January
Italia Conti	1 from supplied list	After 1870	31st May
LAMDA	Elizabethan/ Jacobean	20th/21st century	1st March
Manchester Met.	Shakespeare – blank verse	After 1970	Mid-January – via UCAS

Training

School	Definition of 'Classical'	Definition of 'Modern/ Contemporary'	Application deadline
Mountview	Elizabethan/ Jacobean	After 1945	Mid-March
Oxford	Shakespeare	Modern	31st May
Rose Bruford	16th/17th/18th century or Ancient Greek	After 1960 – 'Not verse'	Mid-January – via UCAS
RADA	Elizabethan/ Jacobean	Modern	1st March
Royal Scottish	Shakespeare – 'Preferably in verse'	A contrasting speech of your choice	Mid-January
Royal Welsh	Elizabethan/ Jacobean	Modern	Mid-January – via UCAS

Notes:

• **All schools have additional audition parameters (a third speech and/or a song, for example); it is important to check with each for full details.**

• When only 'Classical' is specified, this can mean anything written before about 1800.

• When only 'Modern' or 'Contemporary' is specified, you should be fine with anything written after 1945 – and speeches written between 1900 and 1945 have often proved acceptable in this category.

• 'Verse' is sometimes specified – this doesn't mean that it necessarily needs to rhyme.

• You'll find various definitions in the 'Classical' column: 'Shakespearean/Jacobean', 'Elizabethan/Jacobean', 'Shakespeare/Contemporaries'. Strictly, these all imply slightly different (but overlapping) periods in history. In practice, anything written between about 1560 and 1640 should be fine.

• See individual schools' websites for more detailed audition requirements and advice.

• Also see *Effective Audition Speeches* on page 154.

Warning:

Some of these details may change for entry in future years. Please inform the Editor of any such changes at **Simon.Dunmore@btinternet.com**.

Conference of Drama Schools (CDS)

Saul Hyman

What is the CDS?

The Conference of Drama Schools (CDS) is an organisation made up of Britain's leading drama schools. Its role is to help guide prospective students through the training options and to define what is required to achieve the highest standards of training within the vocational drama sector. For the past 40 years it has also lobbied the Government for the necessary funding, and spoken in funding debates on behalf of the member schools.

Contact details

Conference of Drama Schools (CDS)
The Executive Secretary, CDS Ltd,
PO Box 34252, London NW5 1XJ
email info@cds.drama.ac.uk
website www.drama.ac.uk

Training

Founded in 1969, the CDS defines a drama school as 'an organisation or recognisable part of an organisation for students over the age of 18, offering a vocational course in acting, plus in some cases musical theatre, stage management and technical theatre skills'. There are currently 22 member schools of CDS (listed at the end of this article), offering a wide range of courses from diplomas and degrees through to short courses and summer schools. They are all committed to developing creativity, originality and skills. Their aim is to ensure that all students have the necessary training and the best opportunity to enter their chosen profession. Although the different schools have a variety of approaches to teaching, they share a proven track record of success and excellence.

The three qualities that are common to all CDS schools are:

1. **Extensive input from the industry**. Students are taught by staff with professional experience, as well as by visiting professionals. They also have the opportunity to work in professional theatres and studios.
2. **Full-time training**. As a student, you can expect to be in classes for at least 30 hours a week, plus research and preparation time.
3. **Vocational courses**. This is work-orientated, vocational training – you are being trained to do a job. Although courses lead to an academic qualification, including Bachelors' and Masters' degrees, these courses are practical training for work.

Acting and musical theatre courses

Actors who have attended CDS schools include: Daniel Day-Lewis, Tom Baker, Michael Ball, Helen Baxendale, Samantha Bond, Kenneth Branagh, Pierce Brosnan, Christopher Eccleston, Rupert Everett, Colin Firth, Tara Fitzgerald, Rhys Ifans, Jeremy Irons, Lennie James, Sarah Lancashire, James McAvoy, Ewan McGregor, Jimmy Mistri, Gary Oldman, Pete Postlethwaite, Miranda Richardson, Simon Russell Beale and Claire Skinner.

Who applies?

In 2005, CDS did some research into those applying to its schools, and found that it was harder to get into an acting course at a CDS school than to get into Oxford and Cambridge! Most applicants were aged between 18 and 21 with an average of seven applicants for each place. There were more female applicants than male; in fact, women made up two-thirds of the applications. Despite these odds, nearly half of all applicants applied to only one school and only a quarter of applicants applied to more than three schools. (See also the introduction to the drama schools listings, starting on page 5.)

Auditions

Auditions and interviews can be nerve-wracking. For all CDS acting courses you will be expected to prepare at least two short (2-3 minutes) audition speeches, which you will have to perform from memory without a text. You will have to pay a fee for the audition. Technical theatre applicants may be asked to bring along examples of their work to an interview. CDS contributed to the useful free *Applicants Guide to Auditioning and Interviewing*, which is available from the National Council for Drama Training (NCDT – see below, and page 469).

Accreditation

Many of the acting and musical theatre courses available at CDS schools are accredited by NCDT. Applicants to drama school often get the CDS and NCDT confused: NCDT accredits courses, whereas CDS is a membership organisation whose members are drama schools. Today most courses are also degree courses validated by different universities. CDS cannot give

The CDS schools

ALRA – Academy of Live and Recorded Arts

Arts Educational Schools London: The School of Acting

Birmingham School of Acting

The Bristol Old Vic Theatre School

The Central School of Speech and Drama

Cygnet Training Theatre

Drama Centre London

Drama Studio London

East 15 Acting School

Guildford School of Acting

Guildhall School of Music and Drama

Italia Conti Academy of Theatre Arts

LIPA – Liverpool Institute for Performing Arts

LAMDA – The London Academy of Music and Dramatic Art

Manchester Metropolitan University School of Theatre

Mountview Academy of Theatre Arts

The Oxford School of Drama

Queen Margaret University College: Department of Drama

Rose Bruford College

RADA – The Royal Academy of Dramatic Art

The Royal Scottish Academy of Music and Drama

Royal Welsh College of Music and Drama

financial assistance to help students attend drama schools, but most courses are eligible for Government assistance – either student loans or the Drama and Dance Awards (DaDAs). Students graduating from courses accredited by the NCDT can get student membership whilst at drama school and automatically qualify for Equity membership when they graduate.

Multiple offers

Those applicants who are best able to show their talent and potential at audition may be offered places on a number of courses. Deciding factors might include the location of the school, the atmosphere in the building, the style and content of the course and the destinations of the graduates. Applicants may want to attend a student show to help with their decision and schools are generally happy to provide auditioning applicants with information about forthcoming productions. CDS only allows applicants to accept a place at one school. All schools make decisions regarding offers of places by 1 July each year and exchange offer lists.

Employment

If your training is in stage management or technical theatre (see below), then provided you are competent you should be able to get jobs relatively easily: there is virtually 100%

visualeyes
photorepro services

Attention All Drama Students!
You may be entitled to benefits provided by our

STUDENT HEADSHOT REPRO SERVICE*

Service includes:

- ☑ **FREE scan of your image**
  if you only have a print and no access to a digital file

- ☑ **10% off all photographic print runs**
  on orders over £12.00

- ☑ **20% off name caption creation and application**
  with a choice of typefaces

- ☑ **Label creation for stickering to back of prints**
  - Sheet of 21 x 3 line labels @ £1.15 per sheet
  - Sheet of 10 x 5 line labels @ £1.15 per sheet
  choose your own text & font per sheet

- ☑ **Save on carriage charges**
  by ordering as a group and arranging delivery dates to the college

- ☑ **Upload image(s) & order online 24/7**
  go to www.visphoto.co.uk/order
  you only pay when we call to confirm order

PRICES QUOTED INCLUDE VAT @ 15% AND MAY BE SUBJECT TO CHANGE WITHOUT NOTICE

*STUDENT HEADSHOT REPRO SERVICE IS ONLY AVAILABLE TO PARTICIPATING COLLEGES - TERMS & CONDITIONS APPLY
FOR MORE INFORMATION VISIT THE 'WHAT WE DO' PAGE OF OUR WEBSITE www.visphoto.co.uk

95 mortimer street, london w1w 7st | t: 020 7323 7430 | www.visphoto.co.uk

ROSIE STILL (PHOTOGRAPHER)

Zoe Heyes

Christopher Parker

Bella Emberg

Michael Barber

Debra Stephenson

Charlie Clements

Gabrielle Bradshaw

Mia McKenna-Bruce

Liz Fraser

John Judd

Maureen Sweeney

Chris Jarvis

*Special SPOTLIGHT prices*Student rates*Free prints*Free airbrushing*
Very relaxed atmosphere in my own South London studio
*View work instantly*Whole shoot put onto CD*

020 8857 6920 ** www.rosiestillphotography.com

Why is it so hard to find quality acting work?

Being a trained professional doesn't count for much when the number of actors looking for work is so much greater than the amount of work available. Most actors have a very limited choice when it comes to hearing about quality acting opportunities:

Your Agent

Most agents will submit only one or two clients for each role. Employers who may have preferred to cast you for a role will often never get the opportunity to see your CV and headshot. As a result, many actors find that they receive fewer than 6 casting invitations a year via their agent.

Casting Reports and Casting Websites

Many employers find that publishing a casting breakdown in a casting report or on a casting website will result in them being swamped with hundreds of completely unsuitable CVs and headshots. Many of those suggestions will be from untrained, inexperienced actors who do not meet the requirements of the role. As a result, many employers refuse to publish breakdowns for paid acting work. This is the reason why casting reports are often filled with details of unpaid work or only seeking actors with very unusual physical characteristics or skills.

CastNet is a casting service with a difference. We are very selective about the actors we allow to join this service. You must have trained at an accredited drama school and have a minimum of three professional acting credits before we will even consider your application.

We do not simply distribute casting information. We carefully check that you only receive details of projects that you want to do containing roles that precisely match your skills, physicality and playing age. We then send your CV and headshot directly to the employer or casting director on your behalf. We take no commission from any work found so this service does not conflict with your agent if you are represented.

Because we are so selective about the actors allowed to join CastNet and only send employers suggestions of actors that precisely meet their requirements, many actors find that they gain more work from CastNet than from any other source.

A subscription to CastNet is only £6.50 per week and is fully tax-deductible. This includes the cost of all submissions, headshots and all of the benefits listed opposite. There is no minimum commitment. You may stop, start or suspend your subscription at any time.

To read more information about this service and to request an application form, please contact us or visit the website at www.castingnetwork.co.uk

The Benefits

• Have submissions made on your behalf for personally selected film, TV, commercials, corporate and theatre work. The cost of all headshots is included in the subscription fee.

• Receive a free text message when new casting information is available and new casting invitations are received.

• Get a FREE professional actor's website including photo-gallery, showreel and video demos pages.

• Receive a weekly report detailing every production for which you have been submitted.

• Receive free independent assessments of your headshot for character type and playing age.

• Have the chance to be considered for productions exclusively available to CastNet actors.

Plus many other benefits – See website for details

Exclusive Offer to the readers of Actor's Yearbook. Get a FREE 4-week subscription to CastNet!

web: www.castingnetwork.co.uk - tel: 0800 542 4459 - email: admin@castingnetwork.co.uk

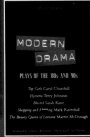

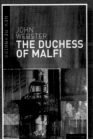

Tel:
0208
438
0303

Picture Credits Sinitta actresss and singer, Martina Miss Slovakia, Sir Richard Branson Virgin, Andy Hamilton Whitbread, Jana Hyncociva, Miss Pinto with Rat, Kate Melton actress, Elizabeth actress

Will C specialises in actors, actresses and personalities in advertising, editorial, film and television. He has been principal photographer on over 30 major films and has directed and shot 40 commercials. Actors and actresses portraits can be taken in our fully equipped film and digital studio in NW2 - just 15 minutes from Marble Arch or Baker Street.

WillC

Tel: 0208 438 0303 Mobile: 07712 669 953
e-mail: billy_snapper@hotmail.com
www.london-photographer.com
www.theukphotographerexhibition.co.uk - www.billysnapper.com

Will C - Photographer to the Stars

employment among graduates in this area and there will be increasing demand for these skills in the run-up to the Olympics. Actors who get taken on by a good agent early in their careers may quickly get into television, but only a few are cast in lead roles immediately. Television work may be lucrative and good for the CV, but a long run in regional theatre may be a better way of developing skills. It can take 10-15 years before you get your 'break', but most actors who stick with it eventually find their niche: a recent survey showed that 86% of British actors working in the profession had relevant professional training.

Stage management and technical theatre courses
As well as training actors, many CDS schools also offer courses in stage management and technical theatre.

Stage Management
It is the Stage Management team who co-ordinate and manage both the rehearsal process and the performance itself, working closely with the director, actors and the creative team. To work in stage management you will need skills in diplomacy, organisation and time management, and be an excellent communicator. You should have a flair for research and attention to detail.

Lighting
In any performance the lighting creates mood and atmosphere. There is a big demand for good lighting technicians in theatre, dance, trade shows, rock concerts and other related industries. However, opportunities for those interested in becoming a lighting designer are fewer. The work is creative but also requires a substantial amount of technical knowledge.

Sound
Sound also has a substantial role to play in creating mood and atmosphere by the application and creation of sound effects. Musical theatre relies heavily on skilful and sensitive amplification. Sound technology is constantly developing. As well as having a good ear, good people skills are needed in this area as sound brings you into close contact with performers.

Design
Design offers a range of careers which include scenic design, artist, prop maker, wardrobe, costume design and set design. In all these areas you will have to acquire the relevant craft,

Note:
- Students on acting courses will generally receive training in singing and movement. However, those wishing to specialise in singing or dance should either take a course in musical theatre, or look beyond the drama schools to dance or music colleges.
- CDS cannot recommend a particular drama school – each school produces its own prospectus and has its own website, where you can find out more information and the dates of their open days. There are links from the CDS website.
- CDS cannot give information about drama schools that are not members of CDS and cannot advise British students about studying overseas.
- CDS cannot give information about classes for school children (except for short courses run by our members).
- CDS cannot give financial assistance to help students attend drama schools.
- CDS cannot recommend drama teachers to individuals.
- CDS cannot receive applications or give information about closing dates or auditions – applicants need to contact the individual school directly.
- Some CDS schools require applications via UCAS.

as well as skills in budgeting, research, problem-solving and versatility. Skilled professionals are always in demand and the work is usually varied and creative, although there are fewer opportunities for set designers.

Construction

The construction team is responsible for realising the creative vision of the set designer. To do this they use a variety of materials and techniques and often need to apply their skills in unusual and innovative ways. To work in construction you need to be practical, and good at budgeting and problem-solving. A good understanding of maths and a flexible approach helps, too. There is a skills shortage in this area and good construction professionals are much in demand.

The CDS publishes the free *Guide to Professional Training in Drama and Technical Theatre*, which is updated each year and contains information on the training opportunities at each member school. As well as the information in the *Guide*, each school produces its own prospectus and there are links to all members from the CDS website **www.drama.ac.uk**. The CDS also publishes the free *Guide to Careers Backstage*. For copies of both documents, contact: French's Theatre Bookshop, 52 Fitzroy Street, London W1T 5JR; 020-7255 4300; **theatre@samuelfrench-london.co.uk**; **www.samuelfrench-london.co.uk**.

Saul Hyman has been Executive Secretary of the CDS since 2002. Prior to that he worked for the Arvon Foundation, the Arts Council, the British Council and BBC Worldwide. He has also worked as an actor and assistant stage manager and taught screenwriting at the London College of Communication and Royal Holloway College.

The NCDT and accreditation

Ian Kellgren

If you were going to buy electrical goods and wanted some reassurance about the quality of a particular product – making it fit for purpose, and safe – you might well look to see if it had an industrial kitemark. If you wanted reassurance about a particular vocational drama course, you would be wise to look and see if it was accredited by the National Council for Drama Training (NCDT).

This accreditation aims to give students confidence that the courses they choose are recognised by the drama profession as being relevant to the purposes of their employment. In its turn, the profession can have confidence that any people they employ who have completed these courses will possess the skills and attributes required for the continued well-being of the industry.

NCDT was formed in 1976, after a Gulbenkian Foundation report, 'Going on the Stage', recommended its establishment. There were fears then that a recent severe increase in unemployment in the profession, coupled with a multiplication of training establishments, was leading to a critical situation for vocational drama training. NCDT was created to provide some way of judging which courses were truly vocational – realistically leading to a career. Local authorities were the major funders of drama students, and they wanted some way of distinguishing those courses that the profession would recognise as being of value.

At that time, there were only seven universities offering drama degrees: there are now more than 2000 degrees with 'drama' in the title. The need for potential students and the current funders to have some way of knowing which are vocational is stronger than ever – not least because of the changes that have taken place since 1976.

• Equity is no longer a closed shop (although there are 37,000 members, and extensive use of Equity contracts is made by employers); the profession has undergone massive change.

• Few, if any, reps exist in the way that they did in the early 70s.

• Musical theatre is a much more dominant force, demanding a supply of 'triple threat' performers – that is, those who can act, sing and dance, all to a high standard.

• Technological advances have revolutionised the ways in which the recorded media operate, and this area provides many more first-employment opportunities.

• Local Education Authority student grants have given way to the Dance and Drama Awards and core funding from the three national funding councils, in England, Scotland and Wales, at various rates.

• In Further and Higher Education, the Conference of Drama Schools (CDS) schools are now subject to the relevant Quality Assurance requirements.

NCDT accredits courses, not drama schools. Currently, there are about 50 courses in 20 drama schools that are accredited by NCDT: in acting, stage management and technical and musical theatre. Some courses that are not currently accredited may well apply to be so in the near future, and these would have to pass stringent tests as to their 'vocationality'. If they became accredited, they would have to apply for re-accreditation after six years.

The accreditation process

The application process for both accreditation and re-accreditation is similar. This involves the school submitting documentation about the course, which is examined in detail by specialists. The course is then visited by a panel, which talks to the staff who deliver the course and to the students who are on it, as well as attending classes. Panel members are looking all the time at the professional relevance of the programme of training.

For this, they really need to have their finger on the pulse – so that everyone contributing to the accreditation process has to have at least five years' professional experience; a good general knowledge of current practice relevant to the course, with some being subject specialists as well; and a keen interest in the development of drama training in this country. Panel members are all well trained for their tasks.

At the end of a re-accreditation visit, the panel decides if the course should be re-accredited or not. They may decide to re-accredit but with recommendations or conditions. The Chair of the panel submits a recommendation in a report to the Review Committee; this is a group of 14 people who are current practitioners with demonstrable knowledge in at least one of the following skill areas: acting, casting, dance & movement, directing, knowledge of funding and statutory inspectorate regimes, film, musical theatre, production management, radio, representation, stage management, technical, television, vocational drama school training, and voice. The Review Committee decides on this recommendation and passes its judgement to the Council of NCDT for formal approval.

In addition to the accreditation visits, schools are required to submit annual reports, and there is a system of show reporting. This is where professionals visit the shows or showcases of a course and complete a report for NCDT. Each year, NCDT is therefore able to decide if a particular course is still fulfilling the aim of accreditation.

Embracing change

Recently, NCDT recognised that it needed to check its operation in the light of the host of changes since its inception. A period of intense research produced a programme of reform that has now been implemented.

NCDT is a unique partnership of employers in the theatre, broadcast and media industry, employee representatives and training providers. When it began, it had three 'wings': the industry, Equity and CDS. Now, under its new Chair, Sir Brian Fender, it has a more widely composed membership which, as well as Equity and CDS, includes the BBC, Channel 4, ITV, the Theatre Managers Association, the Film Council and up to five independent members.

Their brief is to not only to work to safeguard the highest standards, and to provide a credible process of quality assurance through accreditation for vocational drama courses in the UK; it is also to ensure that NCDT exists to act as a champion for the industry, by working to optimise support for professional drama training and education, and embracing change and development.

The discerning shopper will want the electrical goods they buy to be not only fit for purpose and safe, but also to have benefited from development and innovation. NCDT offers such 'shoppers' a means of identifying those vocational drama courses which are based on the best practices of more than a hundred years of drama training, but which also recognise and embrace all the benefits of development and innovation.

Ian Kellgren is an award-winning theatre director. He started out as an assistant director at the Royal Court in London, rising to Literary Manager, before becoming Artistic Director of Durham Theatre Company and the longest-serving Artistic Director of the Liverpool Playhouse. Alongside his theatre and media work, he was NCDT Review Committee Chair until 2007.

The Essentials Guide

The essentials for excellence in vocational training for performing, production and technical careers – a joint initiative by leading Drama Schools.

If you are serious about a career in the performing arts then you will expect that your training, just like your ambition, will take over your life. Dance and Drama training in the UK has always been rigorous, inspirational and the envy of the world. This is a tradition that we, the schools that have created this document, believe in and want to sustain and develop. We urge you to make practical use of the following guidelines during your application and your training. They apply whatever the length of course you are following, whether this is one, two or three years, and whether you are training for acting, musical theatre, dance or production work.

This Guide is in two sections: *entitlements for you*, the applicant, and *signs of top quality* to look out for when you are deciding where to train.

Your entitlements

We believe you are entitled to:

1. **training that matches your ambition.** It needs to be your entire way of life for the duration of the course, not merely what you do only for part of each day. A student dancer was asked what she did. She replied: "I am a dancer. That's what I am, not what I do." An acting student would make the same reply.

2. **a minimum of 30 hours per week of 'class contact time'** – that is, being taught by, and in direct contact with, a tutor for all of each working day (not having private study time). You should usually expect at least 30 weeks of tuition during an academic year. There may be some exceptions in some weeks, but you will know if these are acceptable. In addition to the 30 hours, you should expect private practice, tutorials and extra rehearsal time.

3. **be taught by people who have been, or still are, working professionally in their specialist area of teaching, and whom you respect.** A school cannot train you to the highest vocational level unless its tutors have a thorough professional background and a passion for the future of the industry.

4. **an intensive focus on each individual student.** One clear indication that your school is getting the staff/student ratio right is that your tutors will know you very well. Tutors will not be able to do this if class and year group sizes are too large or if they come and go without commitment to the school and its students.

5. **a manageably sized group of final-year students.** The size of the graduating year group is extremely important; if it is too large, it will be impossible for the school to use its links with practising professionals to help you get the job that you want.

6. **a range of public performance opportunities.** You need to experience a productive variety of roles, audiences and venues as a core part of your training. At the right times in your training, according to your tutors' judgements, you need to be part of good-quality work in front of audiences.

7. **be provided with an environment in which you will be able to take artistic risks** and be encouraged to contribute towards the development of the art form.

8. **exposure to key professional 'gate-keepers', such as agents, casting directors, choreographers, musical directors, production managers and designers.** Different schools will do this in different ways, but you need, via showcases or other performance opportunities, to show such people your professional work.
9. **expert tuition to prepare you for life as an independent professional.** You need to be confident in running what will be, in effect, a one-person business.
10. **an environment in which a high level of challenge is matched with a high level of support.** You need to be supported by tutors, directors, choreographers and production managers who work well together and encourage you to extend the boundaries of your art form.
11. **expect that the first day of your training will be the first day of your career.** The rules and regulations, the working culture of the school, will echo as closely as possible what you will find in the profession.

Signs of top-quality training

To help you judge whether a school is right for you, you should ask to see the information listed below. Don't feel awkward about asking for these details; the schools who agree with the principles of this document will welcome your questions, because they want you to insist on the excellent training you deserve.

Timetable

This should give you information on exactly how many taught hours you will get per week.

Staffing list

This should make clear the balance between full-time, part-time and guest tutors, so you can get an accurate sense of the staff's professional background. Full-time staff provide understanding and continuity; part-time staff who are still working in the business keep everyone up-to-date. It is also important that there are sufficient senior managers in the school with direct professional experience that will guide their decisions.

Professional links

A detailed account of the links between the school and significant professionals (performers, directors, company artistic directors, choreographers, musicians, etc).

Public performances

A list of all public performances over the previous academic year, so you can see the range of venues, audiences and material performed.

Employment destinations

A list of the previous three years' employment destinations of graduating students, as far as they are known. Schools make considerable efforts to keep in touch with past students; it is very useful information for you as well as for the schools. You need to know the sort of jobs – range, quality – that students from the school have achieved

Deposits

A clear policy on any deposits the school requires from applicants. You should be told why the school charges a deposit, as well as how much it is and if/when it might be repaid to you.

Inspection reports

Copies of inspection and monitoring reports – for example, from HEFCE, Ofsted/the Adult Learning Inspectorate, NCDT or other professional bodies.

Informal but important quality indicators you should watch out for

The best schools will:

• have a very clear sense of a benchmark standard below which applicants will not be accepted on the course – that is, you will not be used merely to 'make up numbers'. These schools will only take you if they think you can fulfil your ambition to be a professional performer.

• encourage you to have the freedom to choose which school you want to go to. They will be happy that you may receive offers from more than one school, and will make clear to you the time period you have to make your final choice.

This Guide was the result of an initiative by The Oxford School of Drama in association with Bristol Old Vic Theatre School, Central School of Ballet, English National Ballet School, Guildhall School of Music & Drama, The London Academy of Dramatic Art (LAMDA), The Northern School of Contemporary Dance, Royal Academy of Dramatic Art (RADA) and The Royal Ballet School.

The Oxford School of Drama has Beacon Status from the Learning and Skills Council. The production and dissemination of this Guide is funded through the Beacon Innovation Project programme run by the Learning and Skills Improvement Service.

For further copies of this Guide, or a large print or audio version, please email **info@oxforddrama.ac.uk**, or see **www.theessentialsguide.co.uk**

Training

University acting-oriented courses

On the positive side, on one of these courses you'll have much more free time to 'do your own thing' than your drama school counterpart; on the negative side, most don't provide nearly enough vocational acting training for today's professional. However, one of these courses can be a viable option for those who simply wish to pursue drama as a career, but are not yet convinced that an actor's life is for them. Those who don't get drama school places (or funding) could also consider such a course. If, at the end, you decide that you want to be a professional actor, it is very important to get at least one year's vocational training on a recognised, 'postgraduate' acting course – some of which now offer the chance of also adding 'MA' after your name.

If you are determined to be a professional and choose the university route, it's also worth considering other subjects that might better enhance your earning-power when not in acting work. While one of these might not enhance your knowledge of dramatic literature, you will embark upon your postgraduate acting course uncluttered by the intellectual 'baggage' that can inhibit a complete connection with a vocational acting training. Instinctive impulses are probably more important than intellect in acting – and some people find it difficult to properly readjust the 'brain/gut balance' in the short space of a single year.

The following is a selected sample of university acting-oriented courses; more can be found from UCAS **www.ucas.ac.uk** and the Standing Conference of University Drama Departments **www.scudd.org.uk**.

Aberystwyth University

Department of Theatre, Film & Television Studies, Parry-Williams Building, Aberystwyth University, Penglais Campus, Aberystwyth SY23 3AJ
tel (01970) 622679 *fax* (01970) 622831
email nbs@aber.ac.uk
website www.aber.ac.uk
Key contact Nick Strong

Courses offered

Drama & Theatre Studies BA (Hons). The Drama & Theatre Studies course has been carefully designed to ensure a balance of academic and practical experience and a steady development of intellectual, performative and technical skills for students. In the first year students study a number of introductory modules, combining textual analysis and theatre history, as well as the skills of practical work – design, technical aspects and performance, taught in collaboration with the Scenography and Theatre Design degree scheme.

Anglia Ruskin University

Bishop Hall Lane, Chelmsford, Essex CM1 1SQ
tel 0845-271 3333 *fax* (01245) 251789
email answers@anglia.ac.uk
website www.anglia.ac.uk

Courses offered

The BA (Hons) Drama degree provides students with an understanding of the histories, practices, contexts and theories of drama, theatre and performance. This is balanced and supported by practical explorations, the acquisition of a range of performance techniques, and the creation of live performance events. An engagement with the processes and practices of theatre-making features as an important and integral part of the curriculum, and develops students as confident, versatile and exciting practitioners.

Bath Spa University

Newton Park, Newton St Loe, Bath BA2 9BN
tel (01225) 875875 *fax* (01225) 875444
email enquiries@bathspa.ac.uk
website www.bathspa.ac.uk

Courses offered

Performing Arts Hon BA (Hos). This intensive, highly practical course will develop your skills in acting, directing and production management, whilst at the same time exploring performance and its place in the world. Taught by highly experienced, internationally active staff, the course places a strong accent on exploration, adventure and innovation, and graduates should find themselves well equipped to carve out career paths in the performing arts or related fields.

De Montfort University, Leicester

Faculty of Humanities, Clephan Building, De Montfort University, Leicester LE1 9BH

tel 0116-250 6199 *fax* 0116-257 7199
email huadmiss@dmu.ac.uk
website www.dmu.ac.uk/faculties/humanities

Courses offered

BA (Hons) Drama Studies. Focuses on the study of theory through practice. Teaching staff are engaged in ongoing professional practice, devising and directing theatre at a national and international level; in addition, and in keeping with the university's professional and vocational ethos, the course includes contributions by well-known visiting professional practitioners.

There are also active links between Drama at De Montfort University and regional theatres and art centres. Students have opportunities to take part in full public productions in professional theatre spaces and at theatre festivals in Britain, including Cultural Exchanges, the faculty's own annual week of events.

Students are offered the chance to collaborate on productions with Drama departments across Europe and to show their own work in professional spaces abroad.

Doncaster College

The Hub, Chappell Drive, South Yorkshire DN1 2RF
tel (01302) 553610
email he@don.ac.uk
website www.don.ac.uk

Courses offered

The degree in Contemporary Performance Practice allows acting students to extend their skills and ideas about performance. Students have the opportunity to integrate digital technology into the creation of new and original work, as well as to be part of new developments in the theatre arts for the 21st century. Collaboration with other performing arts practitioners across the Faculty of Arts are positively encouraged.

Goldsmiths College, University of London

Drama Department, Goldsmiths College,
University of London, New Cross,
London SE14 6NW
tel 020-7919 7414 *fax* 020-7919 7413
email drama@gold.ac.uk
website www.goldsmiths.ac.uk/drama

Courses offered

• BA (Hons) Drama and Theatre Arts, Certificate in Performance Skills and Theatre Studies. Explores the theory and practice of performance across a range of media, with a strong focus on performance and production work.
• MA in Performance Making. Creative research is developed through classes and workshops in

performance, focusing on physical training methodologies drawn from a range of cultural forms. Work will address questions of performer-spectator relationships and the specific environments – community, cultural and architectural – for which they are created.

Kingston University

Student Information & Advice Centre,
Cooper House, 40-46 Surbiton Road,
Kingston upon Thames KT1 2HX
tel 020-8547 7053 *fax* 020-8547 7080
email aps@kingston.ac.uk
website www.kingston.ac.uk

Courses offered

Drama BA (Hons). This course enables students to explore the practice, history and theory of drama, in a range of contexts and settings. Students have the opportunity to work with leading professionals and to be actively involved in the productions. The Drama team has links with theatre and television, a close association with the town's new theatre, and is engaged in up-to-the-minute research. Students may also choose to study Drama as a joint Honours degree alongside another subject: see the course combinations section of the website for more information.

Lancaster University

The University, Lancaster, Lancashire LA1 4YW
tel (01524) 592029 *fax* (01524) 846243
email ugadmissions@lancaster.ac.uk
website www.lancs.ac.uk

Courses offered

Theatre Studies BA (Hons). Although it does not provide preparation specifically for a career in theatre, the university's approach includes a degree of training in theatre techniques and performance skills. These can be consolidated through a wide range of practical projects, including a vigorous programme of Outreach work and through regular workshops and residencies with professional theatre groups. Students also have opportunities to participate in community-based performance projects and in extra-curricular student theatre.

Liverpool Hope University College

Department of Drama,
Dance and Performance Studies,
Deanery of Arts and Humanities, Cornerstone,
Liverpool Hope University College, Liverpool L3 8QB
tel 0151-291 3000
website www.hope.ac.uk

Courses offered

The BA Drama programme offers an integrated programme of undergraduate study with a strong practical emphasis, and which is intended to prepare students for careers as Drama Practitioners or for postgraduate study.

Drama & Theatre Studies is also available as a pathway within the BA Combined Honours programme, in which it would be studied with another subject such as Dance, English Literature and Music.

Liverpool John Moores University

Roscoe Court, 4 Rodney Street, Liverpool L1 2TZ
tel 0151-231 5090 *fax* 0151-231 3462
email recruitment@ljmu.ac.uk
website www.ljmu.ac.uk

Courses offered

Drama BA (Hons). This programme aims to nurture the growth of both expressive and critical skills, through the practice and study of drama, to facilitate the greatest possible degree of artistic and intellectual independence of students at graduation.

London South Bank University

103 Borough Road, London SE1 0AA
tel 020-7815 7815 *fax* 020-7815 8273
email enquiry@lsbu.ac.uk
website www.lsbu.ac.uk

Courses offered

The Drama & Performance Studies BA (Hons) course provides a unique programme of study based on practical and theoretical approaches to the subject of drama and performance in all its forms. The ethos of the course is to encourage students to question the boundaries of theatrical disciplines, by exploring innovative ways of creating and thinking about drama and performance.

Manchester Metropolitan University

All Saints Building, All Saints, Manchester M15 6BH
tel 0161-247 2000 *fax* 0161-247 6390
email enquiries@mmu.ac.uk
website www.mmu.ac.uk

Courses offered

BA (Hons) Contemporary Theatre and Performance and BA (Hons) Theatre Arts (Acting). The Contemporary Theatre and Performance course offers a broad experience of practical work in both devised and scripted theatre and covers a variety of performing traditions. The Acting course develops the range of skills and abilities required for a career in acting, including voice, movement, acting, textual analysis and research. This programme is accredited by the National Council for Drama Training and students receive full Equity Cards upon graduation.

See entry under *Drama schools* for further information.

Newman University College Birmingham

Genners Lane, Bartley Green, Birmingham B32 3NT
tel 0121-476 1181 *fax* 0121-476 1196
email registry@newman.ac.uk
website www.newman.ac.uk

Courses offered

The Drama BA (Hons) course offers a variety of assessments to suit the experience of the module studied, and ranges from presentations, productions and written work, essays, reviews and log books. One of the main attractions for students on this course is the close personal attention they receive from tutors. As classes and workshops are held in small groups, the tutors can observe students' development and help them improve their skills on an individual basis. Lecturers have experience of both the academic and the theoretical side of drama in its practice; in addition, Newman has excellent links with a wide variety of industry practitioners, who advise students and know what is required to be successful in the theatre. The course is one of the few Drama degrees in the UK which is vocation-centred. Modules offered include the history of drama. Live theatre is seen as an essential aspect of the course, and the department usually makes a visit to the theatre at least once a term. There is a large element of practical work such as workshops, field trips and work experience to help students define their career plans and gain vital work experience in the theatre. In recent years Drama students have taken placements at the Birmingham Rep, the Birmingham Hippodrome and The Crucible Theatre in Sheffield, amongst others.

Queen Mary, University of London

School of English and Drama, Queen Mary, University of London, Mile End Road, London E1 4NS
tel 020-7882 3172 *fax* 020-7882 3357
email sedadmissions@qmul.ac.uk
website www.english.qmul.ac.uk

Courses offered

BA (Hons) Drama. Examines the theory and practice of performance across a range of social and historical contexts.

Roehampton University

Erasmus House, Roehampton Lane, London SW15 5PU
tel 020-8392 3232
website www.roehampton.ac.uk

Courses offered

BA/BSc Drama, Theatre & Performance Studies. Focuses on analysing the art of performance through integrated practical and theoretical study. Offers a wide range of emphases but is not designed for those wishing to pursue vocational actor training.

St Mary's University College

School of Communication, Culture & Creative Arts, Waldegrave Road, Twickenham TW1 4SX

tel 020-8240 4000
website www.smuc.ac.uk

Courses offered

- BA (Combined Hons) Drama
- BA (Single Hons) Drama & Applied Theatre
- BA (Single Hons) Drama & Physical Theatre
- BA (Single Hons) Drama & Theatre Arts
- MA Theatre Directing

Vocational courses which bring together University education and Drama School training, taught by academics and theatre practitioners.

The Arts Institute at Bournemouth

Wallisdown, Poole, Dorset BH12 5HH
tel (01202) 363225 *fax* (01202) 537729
email admissions@aib.ac.uk
website www.aib.ac.uk
Key contact Doug Cockle

Courses offered

The Acting BA (Hons) course provides those aspiring to be successful actors with key skills to be able to respond to the demands of the industry and to become creative, flexible and independent artists. Students study the history and development of the actor and the theatre, as well as exploring and developing the necessary skills and knowledge to become a good practitioner. There are opportunities to explore classical as well as contemporary playwrights and styles of acting.

The University of Northampton

Avenue Campus, St George's Avenue, Northampton, Northamptonshire NN2 6JD
tel (01604) 735500
website www.northampton.ac.uk

Courses offered

- BA (Hons) Drama. Students develop skills in improvisation, adaptation, physical and vocal technique, and critical analysis.
- BA (Hons) Acting. Professional actor training for stage and screen. Includes physical and vocal techniques, textual analysis, character creation and industry preparation.

University College Worcester

Department of Arts, Humanities and Social Sciences, University of Worcester, Henwick Grove, Worcester, WR2 6AJ
tel (01905) 855000
website www.worc.ac.uk

Courses offered

BA (Hons) Drama and Performance Studies, MA Performance Studies. Explore Drama and Performance through a variety of contexts and media, and develop practical performance skills.

University of Birmingham

Department of Drama and Theatre Arts, University of Birmingham, Edgbaston, Birmingham B15 2TT
website www.bham.ac.uk/drama

Courses offered

Drama and Theatre Arts as a Single, Joint or Minor Honours degree. Undergraduate degree programme integrates theoretical and practical approaches to theatre.

University of Bristol

Department of Drama, University of Bristol, Cantocks Close, Woodland Road, Bristol BS8 1UP
tel 0117-928 7833 *fax* 0117-928 7832
website www.bristol.ac.uk/drama

Courses offered

BA (Hons) Drama or Joint Honours with English or a modern language. Plays are studied in the light of their historical background as well as for their own interest as dramatic texts. Opportunities are provided for students to develop practical skills within areas such as acting and directing, design, lighting and stage management through workshop sessions and productions.

University of Central Lancashire

Preston, Lancs PR1 2HE
tel (01772) 201201 *fax* (01772) 894954
email admissions@uclan.ac.uk
website www.uclan.ac.uk

Courses offered

Acting BA (Hons). All the components of this core training are fully integrated into public performances and augmented with theoretical and contextual studies. In this way, as well as developing the contemporary actor, the course aims to develop the creative potential of each individual further, so that they can maximise their engagement with the huge variety of social and educational opportunities they will encounter while at this lively, vibrant and multi-cultural university.

University of Chester

Department of Performing Arts, Parkgate Road, Chester, Cheshire CH1 4BJ
tel (01244) 511000 ext. 3138 *fax* (01244) 511399
email performingarts@chester.ac.uk
website www.chester.ac.uk/performingarts

Courses offered

BA (Hons) Drama and Theatre Studies. Focus is on the study and practice of performance, with practical workshops, performances, lectures, seminars and research.

University of Chichester

Performing Arts Department, Bishop Otter Campus, College Lane, Chichester, West Sussex PO19 6PE

tel (01243) 816206
email J.Thurston@chi.ac.uk
website http://www.chiuni.ac.uk/performingarts/index.cfm

Courses offered

Performing Arts (Contemporary Performance Practice). The primary focus is on devised theatre with an emphasis on group and teamwork. This is developed within a vocational context that prepares students for graduate careers in the creative arts industries.

University of Cumbria

Fusehill Street, Carlisle, Cumbria CA1 2HH
tel (01228) 616234 *fax* (01228) 616235
website www.cumbria.ac.uk

Courses offered

Performing Arts BA (Hons). Drama is best studied in practice. Students spend much of their time exploring drama through practical, performance-based assessments. They are encouraged to pursue their own practical and academic interests, working in the studio with guidance from an experienced and supportive team of tutors. The Level 3 performance exams are currently staged at the Dukes Theatre, Lancaster – a professional theatre where students may also explore a variety of technical, administrative and production roles.

University of East Anglia

University of East Anglia, Norwich NR4 7TJ
tel (01603) 592280 *fax* (01603) 507728
email j.hyde@uea.ac.uk
website www.uea.ac.uk/lit/Drama
Drama Studio Administrator Jon Hyde

Courses offered

BA (Hons) Drama, BA (Hons) English Literature and Drama, and BA (Hons) Scriptwriting and Performance. UEA's programme in Drama has a strong practical emphasis on all aspects of dramatic production, and combines this with the study of the theory, history and social significance of drama. Students on all Drama programmes also study in other schools (for example, in Film & Television, and in American Studies).

University of East London

Docklands Campus, University Way,
London E16 2RD
tel 020-8223 2835 *fax* 020-8223 2979
email admiss@uel.ac.uk
website www.uel.ac.uk

Courses offered

Theatre Studies BA (Hons) is a relatively new academic discipline offered in many universities around the world. This discipline supports the study and research of all subjects related to theatre, including drama and performance. One of the essential questions that Theatre Studies asks is, 'What is theatre?' By addressing this question, students engage in both a theoretical and a practical understanding of the cultural significance of the theatre, providing them with a sound foundation for a professional career in the the theatre and performing arts industry.

University of Essex

Wivenhoe Park, Colchester CO4 3SQ
tel (01208) 873333 *fax* (01206) 873598
website www.essex.ac.uk

Courses offered

BA (Hons) Drama allows students to follow modules in drama that explore contemporary and classical texts, consider different ways in which theatre is made, and relate academic study to the practical experience of making and seeing theatre. Students benefit from the Lakeside Theatre, which is based on the university's Colchester Campus.

University of Exeter

Department of Drama, Thornlea, New North Road, Exeter EX4 4LA
tel (01392) 264580 *fax* (01392) 264594
email drama@exeter.ac.uk
website www.ex.ac.uk/drama

Courses offered

BA (Single Hons) Drama. Composed of a series of modules, all of which place emphasis on the social and aesthetic nature of theatre. The strong mutual relationship between theory and practice in teaching and learning is key. All drama students get equal opportunities to perform, act, direct, write and devise. Possible pathways include Applied Drama, Playwriting, Performance Art and New Media, Acting and Actor training, Music Theatre. Ranked top for student satisfaction in the National Student Survey 2008. PG programmes also offered.

University of Huddersfield

School of Music and Humanities, St Peter's Building, St Peter's Street, Huddersfield HD1 1RA
tel (01484) 478455 *fax* (01484) 478428
website www.hud.ac.uk/theatre

Courses offered

BA (Hons) Theatre Studies. A diverse range of modules is on offer, all of which combine studio-based practical work with theoretical study. Joint Honours with Media and Music also offered.

University of Hull

Drama Department, University of Hull,
Hull HU6 7RX

tel (01482) 466210
website www.drama.hull.ac.uk

Courses offered

BA (Hons) Drama. Introduces and develops key practical and theoretical approaches to the study of drama. Allows students to tailor the course to suit their specific academic and practical interests at a later stage.

University of Kent

School of Arts, Drama & Theatre Studies,
Eliot College, Canterbury, Kent CT2 7NS
tel (01227) 824274 or 827567
email D.Twomey@kent.ac.uk
website www.kent.ac.uk/sdfva/drama/ (please note that as of January 2010, the School will be moving to a new building on campus, and postal address and phone numbers may change; refer to the website for up-to-date information)

Courses offered

• MDrama. Kent offers one of the most exciting and popular Drama and Theatre courses in the UK, which was praised as 'innovative and leading' in the field by the external Periodic Review panel in 2008. "Drama means helping you develop creative competence for the theatre profession. We have our sights set firmly on theatre as it happens every day, in its various forms, from traditional text-based theatre to cutting-edge performance practice; from theatre management to community theatre." Close links with the profession are reflected in the regular guest lectures, workshops, and opportunities for placement learning leading to an excellent employment record. For this reason, the School offers a unique 4-year single honours course leading to the exclusive award of MDrama, an undergraduate master's degree. The programme has a final, pre-professional master's year where students focus on one selected professional specialism such as directing, producing, designing, applied theatre and theatre dramaturgy.
• BA Drama & another subject (3-year undergraduate joint honours programme)
• MA Theatre Dramaturgy. This taught postgraduate MA introduces the many shapes and fields of Dramaturgy in contemporary theatre, from production dramaturgy to PR work, from scholarly background to budgeting, producing and creative programming. Masters students of Theatre Dramaturgy will encounter, acquire skills in, and work in areas such as Venue Programming & Artistic Management, Production Research & Development, New Play Development, Educational Resources & Events, and Production Publicity.
• MA European Theatre. This taught postgraduate MA course offers a unique insight into European theatre practice, in Continental as well as in British contexts. Students will be able to participate fully in the activities of the European Theatre Research

Network, and there is the opportunity to spend a semester at one of the School's European partner universities, as well as to attend a summer school at the Avignon Festival, led by Professor Patrice Pavis.
• MA/MPhil/PhD by Research or Practice-as-Research

University of Lancaster

Lancaster Institute for Contemporary Arts,
Lancaster University, Lancaster LA1 4YW
tel (01524) 594156 *fax* (01524) 39021
email k.beale@lancaster.ac.uk
website www.theatre-studies.lancs.ac.uk

Courses offered

BA (Hons) Theatre Studies. Department has extensive links with professional performance, theatre and drama groups, and with individual practitioners, through its work in the Nuffield Theatre and other projects. *Also*: MA by Research in Theatre Studies; MPhil/PhD by Research.

University of Leeds

School of Performance and Cultural Industries,
Faculty of Arts, University of Leeds, Leeds LS2 9JT
tel 0113-343 9109
email enquiries-pci@leeds.ac.uk
website www.leeds.ac.uk/paci

Courses offered

BA (Hons) Acting. Combines technical work in voice, movement, singing and dancing with performance theory. Allows students to specialise in defined aspects of theatre, and to represent their talents in a number of professional contexts. *Note*: This course has been relocated to the main campus of the University of Leeds and is no longer at Bretton Hall.

University of Lincoln

University of Lincoln,
Brayford Pool, Lincoln LN6 7TS
tel (01522) 882000
email enquiries@lincoln.ac.uk
website www.lincoln.ac.uk/lishpa/performing_arts

Courses offered

BA (Hons) Drama. Provides sufficient time and space to explore and experiment with performance and the making of plays. The course offers lots of contact with faculty and guest artists to hone and direct students' creative instincts and skills.

University of Loughborough

Department of English and Drama,
Loughborough University, Loughborough,
Leicestershire LE11 3TU
tel (01509) 222967
email EandDundergraduate@lboro.ac.uk
website www.lboro.ac.uk/departments/ea

Courses offered

BA (Hons) Drama, BA (Hons) Drama with English. Examines the history and theory of performance, and develops students' practical and technical skills.

University of Manchester

Department of Drama, School of Music and Drama, University of Manchester, Oxford Road, Manchester M13 9PL
tel 0161-275 3347 *fax* 0161-275 3349
email drama@man.ac.uk
website www.art.man.ac.uk/DRAMA

Courses offered

BA (Hons) Drama, BA (Hons) Drama and Screen Studies, BA (Hons) Drama with English. Founded in 1961 following a gift from Granada Television, the Drama department aims to provide an academic study of theatre and drama based on history, theory and practical performance.

University of Middlesex

School of Arts, Middlesex University, Trent Park, Barnet, Hertfordshire N14 4YZ
tel 020-8411 5000
website www.mdx.ac.uk/arts

Courses offered

BA (Hons) Theatre Arts, BA (Hons) Theatre Arts (Performance), BA (Hons) Theatre Arts (Solo Performance), BA (Hons) Theatre Arts (Theatre Directing) and BA (Hons) Theatre Arts (Design & Technical Theatre).

Offers students with a theatre/performance background scope to develop broad-based skills and knowledge in Theatre Arts, focusing on specialist performance skills in years 2 and 3.

University of Northampton

Park Campus, Boughton Green Road, Northampton NN2 7AL
tel 0800-358 2232 *fax* (01604) 722083
email admissions@northampton.ac.uk
website www.northampton.ac.uk

Courses offered

BA (Hons) Acting. The Acting degree has been developed in collaboration with Northampton's prestigious Royal and Derngate theatre. It has 3 major strands: training; learning new skills; and performance practice. Training will cover the voice, the body, and acting with a text. Students will gain skills in a wide range of techniques, such as characterisation, textual analysis and improvisation, and the skills and techniques will be practised in a range of performance forms such as monologues, duologues, studio workshop productions, and full-scale productions. Third-year students will be

directed by an associate director at the Royal and Derngate, and the show will be staged in the main house of the Royal Theatre.

University of Salford

Faculty of Arts, Media and Social Sciences, University of Salford, Salford, Greater Manchester M5 4WT
tel 0161-295 5000 *fax* 0161-295 4704
website www.famss.salford.ac.uk

Courses offered

BA (Hons) Performing Arts and BA (Hons) Media and Performance. Performing Arts focuses on the development of creative performance skills to a professional level. Media and Performance allows students to combine key aspects of performance activity with practical media production and performance.

University of Staffordshire

School of Humanities and Social Sciences, Staffordshire University, College Road, Stoke-on-Trent ST4 2XW
tel (01782) 294415 ext. 4869
email a.dinnivan@staffs.ac.uk
website www.staffs.ac.uk/dta

Courses offered

BA (Hons) Drama and Theatre Arts. Develops knowledge and understanding of performance skills, theory, texts and contexts.

University of Sunderland

School of Arts, Design, Media & Culture, University of Sunderland, Priestman Building, Green Terrace, Sunderland SR1 3PZ
tel 0191-515 2182
email admcenquiry@sunderland.ac.uk
website www.sunderland.ac.uk

Courses offered

BA (Hons) Drama. Offers a programme of practical and theoretical work focusing on the development of collaborative work in a contemporary context.

University of the West of England, Bristol

St Matthias Campus, Oldbury Court Road, Fishponds, Bristol BS16 2JP
tel 0117-965 6261
website www.uwe.ac.uk

Courses offered

BA (Hons) Drama, BA (Hons) Drama and Education, BA (Hons) Drama and English and BA (Hons) Film Studies and Drama. The Drama programme is not intended to provide a vocational training for work in the theatre; rather, it offers a balance between practical, contextual and theoretical approaches to the study of theatre and has close links with the Bristol Old Vic.

University of Ulster at Coleraine

School of Media and Performing Arts,
University of Ulster, Northland Road, Londonderry,
Co. Londonderry BT48 7JL
tel 0870-040 0700
website www.arts.ulster.ac.uk

Courses offered

BA (Hons) Drama. Develops skills and knowledge associated with the various disciplines of drama, with particular emphasis on collaborative work.

University of Wales, Aberystwyth

Department of Theatre, Film & Television Studies,
Parry-Williams Building, University of Wales,
Aberystwyth, Penglais Campus, Aberystwyth,
Ceredigion SY23 3AJ
tel (01970) 622828 *fax* (01970) 622831
website www.aber.ac.uk/tfts

Courses offered

BA (Hons) Drama, BA (Hons) Drama and Performance Studies, BA (Hons) Drama and Film & Television Studies and BA (Hons) Drama and English. Focuses attention on a variety of different aspects of theatre as an artform and as a social phenomenon.

University of Warwick

School of Theatre,
Performance and Cultural Policy Studies,
University of Warwick, Millburn House,
Coventry CV4 7HS
tel 024-7652 3020 *fax* 024-7652 3297
email tsraj@warwick.ac.uk
website www.warwick.ac.uk/fac/arts/theatre_s

Courses offered

BA (Hons) Theatre and Performance Studies.

University of Winchester (formerly King Alfred's College)

Faculty of Arts, West Hill, Winchester,
Hants SO22 4NR
tel (01962) 841515 *fax* (01962) 842280
email course.enquiries@winchester.ac.uk
website www.wkac.ac.uk

Courses offered

BA (Hons) Drama Studies, BA (Hons) Performing Arts and BA (Hons) Drama, Community Theatre & Media.

The Drama Studies programme is designed to offer an experience of drama in its social, theoretical and practical contexts as well as a critical analysis of the relationships between practice and theory.

Performing Arts is an interdisciplinary programme looking to the role of performance in communities of the future. Work in theatre, dance and music is combined with approaches to live and virtual art, comedy, and innovation in performance technology and design.

Drama, Community Theatre & Media is split between the study of theatre and documentary. Encourages students to combine the mediums in innovative and creative ways. The emphasis of the drama element is on community/alternative forms of theatre, while the media part of the course focuses on researching and producing documentaries.

University of Wolverhampton

School of Sport, Performing Arts and Leisure,
Walsall Campus, Gorway Road, Walsall WS1 3BD
tel (01902) 322898 *fax* (01902) 322894
website www.asp.wlv.ac.uk

Courses offered

BA (Hons) in Drama and Performance, and MA in Drama and Performance. The Drama programme covers practical, creative and critical skills, allowing students to develop performance skills and learn from visiting professionals. It also offers practical and theoretical knowledge in a wide range of related areas, including community arts and teaching. The emphasis in the MA is on exploration and research in drama, theatre and performance.

York St John University

Lord Mayor's Walk, York YO31 7EX
tel (01904) 624624 *fax* (01904) 612512
email admissions@yorksj.ac.uk
website www.yorksj.ac.uk

Courses offered

BA (Hons) Theatre. Theory is integrated with practice at all points throughout the degree programme, and there are many opportunities to become involved in work placements, independent performance projects and the International Exchange Programme (IEP).

Training

Training

Short-term and part-time courses

This section lists both 'taster' opportunities for drama school aspirants and further training for professional actors.

Pre-drama school courses

Competition for drama school places seems to be growing even more ferocious, and many applicants will enhance their chances if they go on a pre-drama-school course. You may for example have done A level Drama, but the actual acting training on such courses is often limited – generally geared more towards the exam-passing university entrant than auditioning for drama school. Whatever your acting background, a 'taster' course (for just a week, for instance) can give you a good idea of what further help/training you need in order to prepare you properly for drama school auditions.

Additional skills

As well as the organisations listed below, there are periodic 'one-off' workshops around the country. These are usually 'trailed', and sometimes advertised, in *The Stage*. Equity occasionally subsidises such enterprises (some, away from the major cities), so it is worth checking with your local Branch/Organiser. Actors Centres are not just places to sharpen up your existing skills and develop new ones, but also great meeting places for actors to exchange ideas and information.

Academy of Creative Training

8/10 Rock Place, Brighton, East Sussex BN2 1PF
tel (01273) 818266
email info@actedu.org.uk
website www.actedu.org.uk
Principal/Director Janette Edisford *Key contact* Joanna Nash

All classes are in the evenings and at weekends to allow students to undertake actor training whilst maintaining their domestic and financial commitments. Entry onto both courses is via attendance on a 2-week intensive workshop (*Fee*: £60) held throughout the year and designed to "enhance creativity and explore acting skills, as well as offering an insight into the training that we offer". Students embarking on the Diploma in Acting training are invited to audition for a Scholarship that covers half of the tuition fees. The school operates an equal opportunities policy that includes disabled students, but there is limited physical access to the dance studio and washroom facilities.

Courses offered

• Diploma in Acting (2 years). For the 2006 intake there were 300+ applications for the 30 places offered. Course fee: £3525. *Minimum age*: 18.
Audition requirements: 2-week workshop, as above
• Intensive Foundation Course (1 year, 10 hours per week). For students aged 16+. Course fee: £1175.
Audition requirements: 2-week workshop, as above

The Academy of the Science of Acting & Directing

9-15 Elthorne Road, Archway, London N19 4AJ
tel 020-7272 0027 *fax* 020-7272 0026
email find@scienceofacting.org.uk
website www.scienceofacting.org.uk
Principal Helen Kogan

Courses offered

• Three Year Evening Acting Course. Applicants must be aged 16 or over. Course fee is £4160 p.a. Offers 14 places each year. *Audition requirements/fee*: see entry on page 6 for details)
• Two Year Evening Acting Course. Applicants must be aged 16 or over. Course fee is £4160 p.a. Offers 14 places each year. *Audition requirements/fee*: see entry on page 6 for details)
• Intensive Acting Course (33 weeks). Course fee is £1440 with 6 hours of classes per week. No audition required
• Spring Workshop (2 weeks). Course takes place in March and the fee is £500. No audition required
• Summer Workshop (2 weeks). Course takes place in July and the fee is £400. No audition required
• Autumn Workshop (2 weeks). Course takes place in March and the fee is £500. No audition required

Actors Centre (London)

1A Tower Street, Covent Garden,
London WC2H 9NP

tel 020-7240 3940
email act@actorscentre.co.uk
website www.actorscentre.co.uk
Artistic Director Matthew Lloyd

Full membership is open to Equity members, registered graduates from the Conference of Drama Schools in their first year of registration (must hold a student Equity card), and foreign actors holding an Equity letter of exemption. Members are entitled to a wide range of subsidised classes and workshops led by experienced directors and tutors who are active in the industry, plus full use of the centre, café facilities when available and a quarterly schedule. Fees are now £55 per year and £37.50 for 6 months (£5 discount for Equity members' first membership). Associate membership is also available for £25 per year; associates are entitled to observe designated workshops but not to participate in them. Provisional membership is open to applicants whose training/experience is not as substantial as that of the majority of members; this is available on the basis of an audition and is reviewed after a 6-month period.

Regular classes and workshops include Acting, Tool Box, TV and Film, Auditions, Advice, Labwork, Voice, Shakespeare, Stage Combat, Directing, Musical Theatre and Writing. In addition, members can book individual sessions to work on singing, acting, sight-reading, Alexander Technique, dialect, voice and movement. Contact the centre for a membership form or a current brochure.

Provisional Membership is offered to some applicants for membership at the Centre whose training and/or experience is not yet as substantial as the majority of our members. Provisional Membership is offered for an initial six-month period and entitles you to attend a range of classes targeted to your needs and to receive ongoing feedback and guidance sessions, use the Actors Centre café and bar facilities, use available studios on an ad hoc basis, sign in up to 4 guests, and receive a quarterly schedule and details of the Tristan Bates Theatre's programme.Towards the end of the six-month period your progress will be assessed to help us decide whether full membership can be offered at that stage. Provisional Membership Fees: £50.00 per six months.

Associate Membership is designed to allow members of related professions (eg directors, writers, producers) who are not actors to observe, but not participate in, selected classes. We accept applications for Associate Membership from members of Equity or affiliated unions (eg Directors Guild, Writers Guild) or from anyone working in the industry who has been nominated by a member or a tutor. This membership entitles you to use the cafe and bar facilities and available studios on an ad hoc basis, sign in up to 4 guests, and receive details of the Actors Centre's and Tristan Bates Theatre's programmes. Applicants should write to the Artistic Director explaining why they wish to take up Associate Membership and supply a CV that demonstrates their professional credentials. Associate Membership Fees: £25.00 per year.

All fees include 17.5%VAT.

Actors Centre North

21-31 Oldham Street, Manchester M1 1JG
tel 0161-819 2513 *fax* 0161-819 2513
email info@actorscentrenorth.co.uk
website www.actorscentrenorth.co.uk

Core provision of ongoing professional development for trained actors. Workshops for all Equity members, covering every aspect of an actor's toolbox and led by leading industry professionals. Equity members or professional actors with sufficient experience are eligible for membership. Membership fees £30 per year or £18 for 6 months. Graduates in the first year following graduation from an NCDT-accredited course are entitled to a reduced membership.

Regular workshops include Acting for Screen, Auditioning for TV & Theatre, Beginners' Meisner Technique, Tools for Learning an Accent, and Shakespeare Surgery, Advice, Voice, Stage Combat, Directing. Members can book individual sessions to work on any chosen area.

Actors Centre North East

Actors Centre North East closed in 2006 following funding problems.

Actors Temple

Studio Theatre, 13-14 Warren Street, London W1T 5LG
tel 020-3004 4537
email tanja@actorstemple.com
website www.actorstemple.com
Directors Mark Wakeling, Ellie Zeegen *Key contact* Tanje McGhie

Training and Production company specialising in the Meisner technique. Studio theatre in the West End.

Courses offered

• 5-week intensive 1st term; 5-week intensive 2nd term (20 weeks each). Fee for each is £1750
• Introduction week (monthly; Mon-Fri 5 x 4 hour classes). Fee is £350

"Unfortunately there are stairs to the basement studio, so not good for wheelchair-users; we do however have a disabled toilet. We have a very open policy towards those with disabilities."

Arts Ed London*

Cone Ripman House, 14 Bath Road, London W4 1LY
tel 020-8987 6666 *fax* 020-8987 6699
email receptionist@artsed.co.uk
website www.artsed.co.uk

Courses offered

• Foundation in Performance (1 year part-time). Course fee is £1000-1250 with 7.5 hours of classes per week. Entry is by audition

• Various short courses (10 weeks). Course fee is £150-250 with 2-3 hours of classes per week. Entry is in January, April, July and October. No audition required
• Intensive courses (1-2 weeks at Easter or in the summer). Course fee is £150-350 with 25-30 hours of classes per week. No audition required

Contact the school by telephone or email **ncussons@artsed.co.uk** for further details of the courses listed above.
• Post-Diploma BA (Hons) in performance, validated by City University. Course director is Terrie Fender (020-8987 6659, **fender@artsed.co.uk**). This is a 1-year part-time course to enable those with a diploma from NCDT- or CDET-accredited courses from 1995 onwards, or those who have undertaken vocational training of 3 years and can offer appropriate professional experience, to upgrade to a degree qualification.

Birkbeck College Faculty of Continuing Education

26 Russell Square, London WC1B 5DQ
tel 020-7679 1064 *fax* 020-7631 6688
email performance@fll.bbk.ac.uk
website www.bbk.ac.uk/ce/ps

The Faculty is a leading provider of part-time Higher Education courses in London. Its Performance Studies programme offers certificated courses in Acting, Dance, Opera and Concert Singing. It does not offer scholarships or bursaries. The college is committed to doing everything it can to support students with disabilities.

Courses offered

• Certificate of Continuing Education in Performance Studies: Acting (formerly the Foundation in Acting). The course lasts 96 hours (3 hours per week) and entry is by audition. Contact the college for details of fees
• Certificate of Higher Education in Performance Studies: Acting (formerly the Diploma in Acting). The course lasts 192 hours (6 hours per week) and entry is by audition. Contact the college for details of fees

Birmingham School of Acting*

Millenium Point, Curzon Street,
Birmingham B4 7XG
tel 0121-331 7200 *fax* 0121-331 7221
email info@bsa.uce.ac.uk
website www.bsa.uce.ac.uk
Principal Stephen Simms *Admissions Manager* Roger Franke

Courses offered

• Creative Drama (30 weeks part-time). Course fee is £306 with 3 hours of classes per week
• Acting Summer School. Course fee is £510 for 2 weeks in August

• Shakespeare Summer School. Course fee is £299 for 4 days in August
• Musical Theatre Week. Course fee is £350 for 6 days in August
• Musical Theatre Weekend. Course fee is £185 for 2 days in August

The Birmingham Theatre School

The Old Rep Theatre, Station Street,
Birmingham B5 4DY
tel 0121-643 3300 *fax* 0121-643 3300
email info@birminghamtheatreschool.co.uk
website www.birminghamtheatreschool.co.uk
Principal Chris Rozanski *Key contact* Andrea Cobham (Arts Admin Manager)

Courses offered

• Professional Diploma (Evenings & Weekends). Applicants must be aged 18 years or over
• Acting for Beginners (11 weeks). Covers the basics of character creation, voice, improvisation and performance discipline for acting beginners. Students participate in all aspects of the creative process from basic exercises to final presentations. Course fee is £79 per term; classes take place in the evening
• Creating Performance (11 weeks). Each term, students will create and perform using a variety of techniques and using both texts and devised work. All aspects of character creation and working with an audience will be explored. Suitable for people with previous experience in acting. Course fee is £79 per term; classes take place in the evening
• Pub Theatre (11 weeks). Provides students with the chance of experiencing exactly what working in a fringe theatre company is all about. Course fee is £89 per term; classes take place in the evening

The Bloomsbury Alexander Centre

Bristol House, 80A Southampton Row,
London WC1B 4BB
tel 020-7404 5348 or 020-8374 3184
email bloomsbury.alexandercentre@btinternet.com
Directors Stephen Cooper, Natacha Osorio

The centre specialises in teaching the Alexander Technique. Teachers are available for private lessons, with discounts available for students and actors. There are ongoing introductory workshops and courses, as well as drop-in vocal work for actors with experience of the AT. The introductory course runs for 4 weeks (1.5 hours a week) and costs £80. The drop-in AT vocal work classes are £15 per session. *Note for disabled actors*: "Our premises are on the ground floor with one step up onto the main entrance and one other just inside."

Boden Studios

99 East Barnet Road, New Barnet, Herts EN4 8RF
tel 020-8447 0909 *fax* 020-8449 5212
email info@bodenstudios.com
website www.bodenstudios.com
Director Adam Boden

Established in 1973. A part-time performing arts school offering 1 full scholarship each year.

Courses offered

• Acting Performance – 12 weeks, 1.5 hours per week. Course fee is £84
• Guildhall Drama Exams – 12 weeks, 1 hour per week. Course fee is £96

British Academy of Dramatic Combat

c\o 1 Stone Street, Faversham, Kent ME13 8PU
email enquiries@badc.co.uk
website www.badc.co.uk

Offers a Performance Certificate in Stage Combat at Foundation, Basic, Basic Level 2, Recommended and Advanced levels. Training is available in the following methods: Broadsword & Shield, Double Handed Broadsword, Quarterstaff, Rapier & Dagger, Rapier & Cloak, Rapier & Buckler, Smallsword, Unarmed Combat. Programmes of workshops are arranged throughout the country, and anyone with suitable venue spaces or wanting to be added to the workshop mailing list should email **workshops@badc.co.uk**.

British Military Fitness (BMF)

Unit 7B and C, 3/11 Imperial Studios,
Imperial Road, London SW6 2AG
tel 0870 241 2517
email barney@britmilfit.com
website www.britmilfit.com
Managing Director Robin Cope *Communications & Membership* Barney Larkin

The original 'military style' training provider. Set up in 1999 and now operating across the UK, BMF offers a great way to get fit while having fun in the great outdoors. Classes take place outdoors in parks throughout the country and throughout the year. Each class lasts for an hour and is divided into groups to cater for all levels of ability.

You can attend any class at any venue at any time, to suit your schedule (Equity card numbers must be provided). Actors' Yearbook have negotiated corporate rate membership for all Equity members. In London this is (at the time of writing) £38 per month; other regions vary between £26 and £34. BMF offers a free trial class for anyone interested in membership. After that, payment is by direct debit or by paying for sessions in a block. Membership can be suspended in the event that acting work makes attending classes impossible.

BMF is member of the Fitness Industry Association, has the backing of Sport England, and all instructors are either former or serving members of the armed forces with recognised fitness & adventure training qualifications. To find out where your nearest class is please see **www.britmilfit.com** or call the office on 0870-241 2517 for a chat.

BMF also organises adventurous events such as skiing, abseiling and mountaineering, as well as charity fundraising events and corporate training.

Central School of Speech and Drama*

64 Eton Avenue, London NW3 3HY
tel 020-7722 8183 *fax* 020-7722 4132
email enquiries@cssd.ac.uk
website www.cssd.ac.uk
Principal Gavin Henderson

Courses offered (a selection of courses offered in 2005/06)

• Saturday Drama Classes (1 term). Course fee is £145, entry is possible throughout the year. For ages 6-17
• Winter Introduction to Audition Speeches (3 days, January). Course fee is £275. Separate classes for ages 18+ and 16+
• Easter Scenes Workshop (9 days, April). Course fee is £380
• Introduction to Acting (2 evenings p.w., termly). Course fee is £385, entry is possible throughout the year. For ages 18+
• Introduction to Text (2 evenings p.w., termly). Course fee is £385, entry is possible throughout the year. For ages 18+
• Working Text (2 evenings p.w., termly). Course fee is £385, entry is possible throughout the year. For ages 18+
• Working Shakespeare (2 evenings p.w., termly). Course fee is £385, entry is possible throughout the year. For ages 18+
• Classical Theatre – Level 2 (2 evenings p.w., termly). Course fee is £385, entry is possible throughout the year. For ages 18+
• Introduction to Movement for Performance (2 evenings p.w., termly). Course fee is £385, entry is possible throughout the year. For ages 18+
• Movement for Perfomers – Level 2 (2 evenings p.w., termly). Course fee is £385, entry is possible throughout the year. For ages 18+
• Introduction to Voice for Performance (2 evenings p.w., termly). Course fee is £385, entry is possible throughout the year. For ages 18+
• Introduction to Acting for Camera (2 evenings p.w., termly). Course fee is £385, entry is possible throughout the year. For ages 18+
• Directed Scenes (Saturdays, termly). Course fee is £460
• Puppetry (2 evenings p.w., termly). Course fee is £385, entry is possible throughout the year. For ages 18+
• Singing (1 evening p.w., termly). Course fee is £165, entry is possible throughout the year. For ages 18+
• Central Theatre Group (1 evening p.w., termly). Course fee is £230, entry is possible throughout the year. For ages 18+

Summer School Courses

• Combat and Stage Fighting (1 week, July). Course fee is £440. For ages 17+
• Mask (1 week, July). Course fee is £440. For ages 17+

• Devising (1 week, July). Course fee is £740. For ages 17+
• Musical Theatre (1 week, July). Course fee is £870. For ages 17+
• Summer Shakespeare (1 week, July). Course fee is £870. For ages 17+
• Directed Scenes (1 week, August). Course fee is £740. For ages 17+
• Voice and Text (1 week, July). Course fee is £440. For ages 18+
• Actors' Auditions Pieces (1 week, July-August). Course fee is £550. For ages 17+
• Youth Theatre For Actors – 1 week (1 week, July). Course fee is £380. For ages 5-17
• Youth Theatre For Actors – 3 weeks (3 weeks, July-August). Course fee is £1140. For ages 5-17

The City Lit

Keeley Street, Covent Garden, London WC2B 4BA
tel 020-7430 0544 *fax* 020-7405 3347
email v.rochester@citylit.ac.uk
website www.citylit.ac.uk
Head of Drama, Dance & Speech Vivienne Rochester

The college offers an eclectic mix of activities – such as acting, movement, voice, mime, circus, stage fighting, magic, comedy, dance, self-presentation, accents, sight-reading and pronunciation – which develop vocational, social and personal skills. The John James Bursary is open to Access Course students and there are various other small access grants that might cover travel, books or child-care. Students may ring or come into the office for an interview between 12.30 and 1.30pm (Monday and Wednesday) or 5.30 and 6.30pm (Monday, Tuesday and Thursday).

The Rep Company was set up to train a company of actors to produce work of the highest professional standard, providing a platform for its members to hone their skills and display their talents. Directors, teachers and practitioners are invited and engaged to facilitate.

Its members are made up of a combination of graduates from the Access course, or from the advanced/professional provision in the Drama, Dance & Speech department's programme, and experienced practitioners who wish to further their experience with the college. Auditions are held annually.

The college has awarded associate status to a number of actors who have produced an excellent body of work with the company. All company members are eligible for the 3 productions staged each year, and are invited if appropriate to professional castings that are occasionally held at the Lit.

Courses offered

• Foundation course (1 year part-time). Applicants must be aged 19 or over. Entry is by audition
• Access course (1 year part-time). Applicants must be aged 19 or over. Entry is by audition
• Musical Theatre Diploma (1 year part-time). Applicants must be aged 19 or over. Entry is by audition

• Cacchetti Ballet School (1 year part-time). Applicants must be aged 19 or over. Entry is by interview
• Stage Fighting (1 year part-time). Applicants must be aged 19 or over. Entry is by interview

A range of acting, voice, movement and self-presentation classes is also available. Courses run for 12 weeks with entry at various points throughout the year.

Drama Studio London (DSL)*

1 Grange Road, London W5 5QN
tel 020-8579 3897 *fax* 020-8566 2035
email admin@dramastudiolondon.co.uk
website www.dramastudiolondon.co.uk
Director Peter Craze *Key contact* Sue Quelch-Woolls

Courses offered

• Summer Acting Course (4 weeks full-time). Course fee is £1200. Course starts in July/August

East 15 Acting School*

Hatfields, Rectory Lane, Loughton IG10 3RY
tel 020-8508 5983 *fax* 020-8508 7521
email east15@essex.ac.uk
website www.east15.ac.uk
Director Leon Rubin *Key contact* Linda Humphreys

Courses offered

All courses listed below take place in July:

• Introduction to Acting (1 week), fee is £220
• Approaches to Shakespeare and Jacobean Theatre (2 weeks), fee is £350
• Devised Theatre (3 weeks), fee is £500
• Audition Technique (1 week), fee is £220
• Physical Theatre (1 week), fee is £220
• Stage Combat (1 week), fee is £250 (includes BADC examination fee)

All of the above courses carry University of Essex credits. Applicants must be aged 17 years or over.

Equity (Wales and South West England Office)

Transport House, 1 Cathedral Road, Cardiff CF11 9SD
tel 029-2039 7971 *fax* 029-2023 0754
email info@cardiff-equity.org.uk
website www.equity.org.uk

In 2005, Equity ran 2 series of new workshops in Devon and Cornwall: a Creative Partnership Training Scheme based in Plymouth, and an Audition Skills Workshop in collaboration with the BBC. Workshops in the past have included improvisation, movement, working with text, puppetry, fooling, and taking direction; these have been offered at various points throughout the year. Contact the office to find out if and when more workshops are scheduled.

Exeter Dance Consultancy

Holly Tree Cottage, Clyst St George, Exeter EX3 0RB
tel (01392) 873683

email info@exedance.demon.co.uk

Offers 1:1 tuition in dance movement therapy for performing artists, specialist movement coaching for actors, and dance coaching for auditions. A 10% discount is available for Equity members, Spotlight members and students. To arrange an appointment, contact Jeanette Macdonald.

GSA Conservatoire* (formerly Guildford School of Acting)

Stag Hill Campus, Guildford GU2 7XH
tel (01483) 560701
website www.gsauk.org
Director Gerry Tebbutt

Courses offered

• Singing in the Theatre (1 week). A summer course designed for students over the age of 17 who wish to improve their singing. Other disciplines relating to the voice will also be explored. Entry is in July and the fee is £299
• Musical Theatre (2 weeks). Culminating in a performance in the Bellairs Playhouse, this course is open to students aged 17 or over and takes place in July/August. Course fee is £499
• Audition Techniques (1 week). Course takes place in August and is geared towards students aged 17 or over. Course fee is £198
• Intensive Musical Theatre Dance for Beginners (1 week). An intensive course to discover what your body is capable of doing. Explore the foundations of tap, jazz and ballet and get guidance and expert advice on what you need to work on and hopefully gain the confidence to compete in a dance class situation. The course takes place in August and is open students 17 years and over. Course fee is £295
• Acting for Camera (1 week). The course takes place in August and is open students 17 years and over. Course fee is £295

Summer Schools:

Courses are offered at a reasonable cost and provide either a stimulating refresher course or an introduction to basic theatre training. There is no audition procedure, and everyone is welcome. All courses are staffed by members of the GSA faculty.

July/August:
• Youth Theatre (9 days)
• Musical Theatre (2 weeks)
• Intensive Musical Theatre Dance (5 days)
• Intensive Musical Theatre Acting (5 days)
• Intensive Musical Theatre Singing (5 days)
• Audition Technique (2 x 5-day sessions)
• Directing a Musical (5 days)
• Acting for Camera (5 days)

For further information or to download an aplication form, please refer to the website, or telephone or email (**summerschool@gsauk.org**) for a brochure.

Guildhall School of Music & Drama*

Silk Street, Barbican, London EC2Y 8DT
tel 020-7628 2571 *fax* 020-7256 9438

email registry@gsmd.ac.uk
website www.gsmd.ac.uk
Director of Drama Wyn Jones

Founded in 1880, the Guildhall School is acknowledged internationally as a leading conservatoire for both music and drama.

Courses Offered

The 2 summer school courses in 2009 (Acting in Shakespeare & Contemporary Theatre; and Acting in Musical Theatre) will each offer 3 weeks of stimulating and inspiring training in acting. Both will include class work or workshops with many of the School's core staff.

• Acting in Shakespeare & Contemporary Theatre. 3 weeks of intensive tuition, workshops and rehearsals. Students have craft-based classes for half of the day; for the other half they work with a director and explore short scenes from Shakespeare and contemporary plays, investigating the texts through group exercises and improvisation. The aim is to demystify Shakespeare and provide a challenging insight into modern drama. The course concludes with a presentation of work-in-progress to students and staff (not open to the public) which may take the form of a workshop or open class.
• Acting in Musical Theatre. 3 weeks of intensive tuition, workshops and rehearsals. Students have craft-based classes for half the day; for the other half they work as an ensemble with a director on a musical project exploring a selection of scenes, songs and dances based around a theme. The focus of the course will be upon the craft of acting within the context of musical theatre. It will conclude with a presentation of work-in-progress to students and staff (not open to the public) which may take the form of a workshop or open class. The course is led by Guildhall School tutor Martin Connor, who directs the School's annual musical.

Craft-based classes for both courses include: Acting, Voice, Movement, Improvisation, Mask, Combat, Historical, Dance, Audition technique. At least 2 visits to attend performances in London theatres are included in the fees of both courses, which are set at £1600; there is a £350 non-refundable deposit. Applicants must be at least 18 years old by the start of the course; there is no upper age limit. A good standard of English is essential. Accommodation is available. Please consult the website (**www.gsmd.ac.uk/acting/summerschool**) for up-to-date information on fees, curriculum and application procdure, or telephone 020-7382 7183 for details of the application procedure. Email enquiries to **dramasummerschool@gsmd.ac.uk**

"There is no application deadline but, in view of the limited number of places, applicants are strongly advised to book early. If the summer school is full, you will be placed on a waiting list."

Hope Street Ltd

13a Hope Street, Liverpool L1 9BQ
tel 0151-708 8007 *fax* 0151-709 3242

email peter@hopestreet.org
website www.hope-street.org
Principal Peter Ward *Key contact* Alan Richardson

Provides actors with training for physical theatre and young people's theatre. Places are also available for trainee directors and workshop leaders. Courses culminate in 4 public performances directed by professionals. Fees stated below cover the 6-month course period and are applicable only to non-Merseyside residents. Merseyside residents may apply for an £80 weekly allowance.

Courses offered

• Physical Theatre (26 weeks full-time). Applicants must be aged 18 or over. Course fee is £2800. 8 places are offered each year
• Young People's Theatre (26 weeks full-time). Applicants must be aged 18 or over. Course fee is £2800. 4 places are offered each year

International School of Screen Acting

3 Mills Studios, Unit 3, 24 Sugar House Lane, London E15 2QS
tel 020-8555 5775
email office@screenacting.co.uk
website www.screenacting.co.uk
Key contact David Craik

Founded in 2001 to specialise in offering full-time training specifically in television and film acting, taking a holistic approach to creativity in relation to students' personal development. While the school is happy to receive applications from disabled students, there are currently significant access issues with the premises.

Courses offered

• Screen Acting (3 months for 3 nights a week). Course fee is £1200. No audition required
• 'Crash Course' – week-long course offered at various times throughout the year. Course fee is £295. No audition required
• Summer Course – week-long course offered in Aug/Sept. Course fee is £295. No audition required

London Academy of Music and Dramatic Arts (LAMDA)*

155 Talgarth Road, London W14 9DA
tel 020-8834 0500 *fax* 020-8834 0501
email enquiries@lamda.org.uk
website www.lamda.org.uk
Principal Peter James *Admissions Assistants* Amy Richardson, Elissa Perrau, Philip McDonnell

Courses offered

Short-term courses are offered on the following:

• Shakespeare and His Contemporaries (8 weeks)
• Shakespeare (4 weeks)
• Physical Theatre (2 weeks)
• Audition Technique (2 weeks)
• English Communication Skills Through Drama Workshop (EFL – 3 weeks)
• Introduction to Drama School (2 weeks)
• EFL in Audition Technique (2 weeks)
• Stage Management (2 weeks)
• Theatre Lighting (2 weeks)

With the exception of the Introduction to Drama School and Audition Technique courses, where the minimum age is 16, students on all other Summer Courses must be 18 years or above. For more information on all LAMDA's courses, including fees and deadlines, please visit the website.

London Academy of Radio, Film & TV

1 Lancing Street, London NW1 1NA
tel 0870-850 4994
website www.media-courses.com
Director of Courses Andy Parkin *Key contact* Estelle Burton

The academy has more than 30 teaching staff; around 1200 students take one or more of its 100+ courses. It is situated opposite Euston Station.

Courses offered

• Acting Masterclass (1 week – 30 hours). Course fee is £695. No audition required.
• Acting for Film & TV (9-week course – 9 x 3 hours). Course fee is £395. No audition required. (*Note*: 2 versions of this course exist – 1 on a weekday evening; 1 on a Saturday)

London Drama School

30 Brondesbury Park, London NW6 7DN
tel 020-8830 0074 *fax* 020-8830 4992
email enquiries@startek-uk.com
website www.startek-uk.com
Key contact Sarah Mann

Courses offered

• Saturday Drama Workshop (10 weeks). Course fee is £450 for 6 hours of classes per week, or £250 for 3 hours of classes per week
• Thursday Evening Workshop (10 weeks). Course fee is £185 for 2 hours of classes per week
• Advanced Drama Workshop (10 weeks). The course runs on Tuesday evenings for 2 hours and costs £195
• Developing Stage & TV Acting Skills (10 weeks). The course runs on Monday evenings for 2 hours and costs £225

Summer Courses

• Improvisation & Acting (July). 3-week intensive course. £875
• Comedy & Acting (July/Aug). 3-week intensive course. £875
• Acting & Screen Acting (August). 3-week intensive course. £875

The summer courses run consecutively. Course fees are reduced for students taking more than one course, thus: £1575 for 2 courses; £2230 for all 3 courses. 1-year courses are also available.

The Method Studio

Conway Hall, 25 Red Lion Square,
London WC1R 4RL
tel 020-7831 7335 *fax* 020-7831 8319
email info@themethodstudio.com
website www.themethodstudio.com

The Method Studio is a small drama school dedicated to the teaching of the 'Method', a system of acting first devised by Constantin Stanislavski, the original Director of the Moscow Arts Theatre, and continued by such American teachers as Sanford Meisner, Lee Strasberg, Stella Adler and Robert Lewis. It is registered with the Department of Education and Skills.

Offers a wide range of classes taught by working professionals and is located in central London, close to tube and bus links, and within easy walking distance of West End theatres and cinemas. It now offers a one-year Diploma Course.

The Studio works in a flexible way allowing students to plan a timetable to suit their individual needs.

Entry is by personal interview (not an audition) usually held between 10.00am and 4.00pm as arranged. You may telephone during office hours Monday to Friday to arrange an appointment. Students should be at least 18 years of age; there is no upper age limit.

Morley College Theatre School

61 Westminster Bridge Road, London SE1 7HT
tel 020-7450 1832
email keith-brazil@morleycollege.ac.uk
website www.morleycollege.ac.uk
Key contact Dominic Grant

Offers part-time acting classes which lead to London Open College Network accreditation. Classes are led by specialist acting tutors with extensive professional experience. An Access Hardship Fund and concessionary fees are available to some students.

Courses offered

• A range of evening and part-time acting skills courses are available, including: Actors' Voice Workshop, The Acting Business, Singing for Actors and Dancers, Absolute Beginners Drama Workshop, Developing Acting Skills, Introduction to Physical Theatre, and many different styles of Dance
• Intermediate Foundation Theatre Arts (1 year part-time). Covers Acting Techniques (including voice, improvisation, text work and scenes) and Dance Techniques (Jazz and Contemporary) leading to performances in term 3. Course fee is approximately £650 p.a. for EU students, with concessions and hardship grants available. Entry is by audition
• Acting Studies (1-year evening school). Develops improvisation, characterisation, voice and movement skills through a series of workshops and rehearsals. Course fee is approximately £400, with concessions and hardship grants available. Entry is by audition
• Morley Theatre School (1-year evening school). For those with ability and confidence as actors who want to consolidate their skills. Workshops explore different techniques and approaches, and lead towards performance at the end of the course. Entry is by audition

Mountview Academy of Theatre Arts*

Ralph Richardson Memorial Studios,
Clarendon Road, London N22 6XF
tel 020-8881 2201 *fax* 020-8829 0034
email enquiries@mountview.org.uk
website www.mountview.org.uk
Principal Sue Robertson

Courses offered

• Foundation Acting (1 year). Course fee is £1100 with 9 hours of classes per week. Entry is by audition
• Foundation Musical Theatre (1 year). Course fee is £1300 with 9 hours of classes per week. Entry is by audition
• Acting for Screen (2 terms). Course fee is £800 with 3 hours of classes per week. Entry is by audition
• Professional Masterclass, available from 1 day to 1 week during spring and autumn. Fees vary. No audition required
• Summer School Acting (2 weeks). Courses take place in July/August, fee is £550. No audition required
• Summer School Musical Theatre (2 weeks). Courses take place in July/August, fee is £550. No audition required
• Audition Technique (4-6 weeks). Courses take place in spring and autumn, fee is £180. No audition required
• Perform: Acting (2 terms). Course fee is £700 with 6 hours of classes per week. Entry is by audition
• Perform: Musical Theatre (2 terms). Course fee is £700 with 6 hours of classes per week. Entry is by audition

Oxford School of Drama*

Sansomes Farm Studios, Woodstock,
Oxford OX20 1ER
tel (01993) 812883 *fax* (01993) 811220
email info@oxforddrama.ac.uk
website www.oxforddrama.ac.uk
Principal George Peck *Executive Director* Kate Ashcroft

Courses offered

• 6-month Foundation Course in Acting which runs from September to March. Aimed at students aged 17 and over (most are 18-19 years old), the course covers acting methods and technique, movement, voice, singing, film and television, stage fighting and stage management. Course fee is £5,000 (2007/08)

with 32 hours of classes per week for 22 weeks. Entry is by audition
• 6-month Foundation Course in Musical Theatre, which runs from September to March. Aimed at students aged 17 and over (most are 18-19 years old), this course helps students develop a flexible, healthy voice and introduce them to the range of techniques required to act through song. Course fee is £5450 plus VAT (2009/10) with 32 hours of classes per week for 22 weeks. Entry is by audition

Pineapple Dance Studios

7 Langley Street, London WC2H 9JA
tel 020-7836 4004 *fax* 020-7836 0803
email studios@pineapple.uk.com
website www.pineapple.uk.com

Pineapple offers more classes than any other studio throughout Europe, and the widest variety of dance styles. The philosophy behind the creation of the Pineapple Dance Studios was to break down the elitist barriers surrounding dance, making it available to everyone – from the absolute beginner to the advanced and the professional dancer. All classes are open, so you do not need to book; you can just come along at any time and take a class. Everybody is welcome: Pineapple offers classes for all levels and all ages (from dancers who are 4 years of age to those in their 90s – its oldest member is currently 93!). Around 40 different varieties of dance styles are taught, at approx. 200 classes per week, ranging from classical ballet to street jazz, hip hop to Salsa, Egyptian dance to Bollywood grooves plus many more. *Opening hours*: Mon to Fri: 9am – 9pm; Sat: 9am – 6.30pm; Sun: 10am – 6pm.

The Questors Theatre Ealing

12 Mattock Lane, London W5 5BQ
tel 020-8567 0011 *fax* 020-8567 2275
email enquiries@questors.org.uk
website www.questors.org.uk
Principal David Emmet *Key contact* Andrea Bath, Executive Director

Provides part-time training for actors in the context of a working theatre. Financial support is available from a private trust fund for a limited number of students.

Courses offered

• Acting: Foundation and Performance (2 years). Course fee is £270 with 6 hours of classes per week. Entry is by audition
• Introduction to Acting (1 year). Age range for entry is 17-20. Course fee is £135 with 3 hours of classes per week. Entry is by audition

Richmond Drama School

Richmond Adult College, Parkshot,
Richmond TW9 2RE
tel 020-8439 8944

email Mark.Woolgar@racc.ac.uk
website www.richmonddramaschool.com
Key contact Mark Woolgar

Courses offered

Long-established Richmond Drama School Course incorporates an Access Course and sends many students on to Honours Degree Courses at top Drama Schools, while others go straight into the profession. Up-to-date details of all Courses from Mark Woolgar.

Rose Bruford College*

Lamorbey Park, Burnt Oak Lane, Sidcup DA15 9DF
tel 020-8308 2600 *fax* 020-8308 0542
email enquiries@bruford.ac.uk
website www.bruford.ac.uk
Principal Professor Michael Earley

Courses offered

• Acting Summer School (2 weeks). Designed for participants over the age of 18 (16+ for non-residential students), this programme includes classes, rehearsals and workshops on voice, movement, acting and improvisation.

Royal Academy of Dramatic Art (RADA)*

62-64 Gower Street, London WC1E 6ED
tel 020-7636 7076 *fax* 020-7323 3865
email enquiries@rada.ac.uk
website www.rada.org
Key contact Sally Power

Courses offered

• Acting Shakespeare (8 weeks). Designed for experienced actors, this course offers an opportunity to expand, explore and deepen awareness of Shakespeare's texts. Covers all aspects of vocal technique, with classes to develop the resonance and range of each student's voice. The last 2 weeks of the course are spent in full-time rehearsal for a workshop production culminating in 3 performances in a RADA theatre. Entry is deliberately restricted and places are awarded by competitive audition. Students below the age of 18 are not normally accepted; most students are in their 20s. Course fee is £4500 which includes breakfast, lunch and refreshments Monday-Friday. Course takes place in June and July. *Audition requirements*: 1 speech from Shakespeare and 1 from a modern play, each lasting no longer than 3 minutes. *Audition fee*: £33
• The RADA Summer School (4 weeks). Based on exploring Shakespeare from an actor's point of view, this course mixes rehearsing scenes and speeches with intensive classes in essential acting skills. Students below the age of 18 are not normally accepted; most students are in their 20s. Course fee is £2560 which includes breakfast, lunch and refreshments Monday-

Friday. Course takes place in July and August. No audition required

• Skill Development through Classical Acting (3 weeks). This course explores the acting skills required to handle the complex texts of the English Classical Theatre. Each week a director works on a different era in classical theatre: week 1 – Shakespeare; week 2 – Jacobean/Caroline tragedy; week 3 – Restoration comedy. Students also attend classes in voice and speech, movement, sword fighting and period dance. Students below the age of 18 are not normally accepted; there is no upper age limit. Course fee is £1750 which includes a light continental-style breakfast and lunch

• Musical Theatre (5 days). This course is designed for intermediate and advanced singer-actors who have already received some formal vocal training and are intending to pursue a career in musical theatre. During the course, guidance on casting and help with audition repertoire is given. Students work with a singing tutor, director, choreographer and musical director, both in groups and individually, to develop the necessary skills required by the successful singer-actor in today's musical theatre. At the end of the course there is an informal presentation of selected pieces for an invited audience, followed by individual feedback. Course fee is £725

• RADA Directing Course – How to Rehearse (2 weeks). This is an intensive course for 6 selected directors, focusing on the rehearsal period – what to do in it, how to shape rehearsals, and how to work with actors to discover the meaning and structure of the play. There is also the opportunity to work with designers and writers. Students study how to develop a method of work, and work on scenes with actors, with a presentation at the end of the course. Students

below the age of 18 are not normally accepted; there is no upper age limit. Course fee is £1400 which includes a light continental-style breakfast and lunch

• The RADA Contemporary Drama Summer School (10 days). This course provides the opportunity to work on modern or contemporary texts. Students work in groups led by a director, with support from a voice and a movement instructor. Other playwrights talk about their work during special evening sessions, describing their experience of working with actors and what they expect from them, following presentations of excerpts from their plays by RADA graduates. Students present rehearsed material and receive feedback from the director and the voice and movement teachers on the last day of the course. Students below the age of 18 are not normally accepted; there is no upper age limit. Course fee is £1250 which includes a light continental-style breakfast and lunch.

The School of the Science of Acting – now The Academy of the Science of Acting & Directing

Youngblood

Top Floor, 57 Paddington Street, Marylebone, London W1U 4HZ
tel 020-7193 3207
email info@youngblood.co.uk
website www.youngblood.co.uk

A company of fight directors and stage-combat teachers. Runs ongoing classes for professional actors in various locations around London. Also provides fight directors and trainers for film, television and theatre projects, including low-budget productions.

Training

Training

Private tutors and coaches

Acting Audition Success (Philip Rosch)

53 West Heath Court, North End Road,
London NW11 7RG
tel 020-8731 6686
email philiproschl@hotmail.com
website www.philiprosch.com

Specialises in Shakespeare; also offers expert career advice. Charges £50 per hour and gives generous extra time for free at the end of each lesson. Is happy to provide material for private students to use, and to answer minor follow-up queries. Teaches from home, about 3 minutes' walk away from Golders Green tube (bus routes 13, 82, 83, 102, 183, 210, 226, 240, 245, 260, 268, 328 and 460). "For more details about my work, the best thing is to call me so that I can explain in detail my working methods. I also send out extremely useful written information through the post." Has taught more than 1200 actors and aspiring actors over a 24-year period; is a highly experienced British-American actor (and acting tutor). Advises clients: "Truthful acting is simple and involves just two things: how your character feels, and what your character wants. My teaching methods are highly effective in bring actors to truthful performances."

Irene Bradshaw

Welbeck Mansions, Inglewood Road,
West Hampstead, London NW6 10X
tel/fax 020-7794 5721
email irene@irenebradshaw.fsnet.co.uk
website www.voice-power-works.co.uk

Specialises in audition technique, voice/production, RP and accents. Charges £40 per hour, which is a special rate for actors. Provides material for students to use, and all lessons are recorded to CD or memory stick. Is happy to answer minor follow-up queries. Teaches from home (unless a client is disabled, in which case will travel to theirs); the nearest tube is West Hampstead, a 5-minute walk. Bus routes are C11, 139 and 328.

Has taught "countless" actors and aspiring actors over 36 years. An actress for more than 20 years in film, television and theatre, she trained in the Linklater method of voice production at LAMDA with Kristin Linklater, sponsored by the Art Council of Great Britain. Has taught at the City Lit, the Actors Centre and most of the leading stage and drama schools, as well as running her own theatre company where she directed several plays in new writing as well as classics. Has trained numerous students for entry into drama school with considerable success, and has helped many actors find their voice.

Mel Churcher

mobile (07778) 773019
email melchurcher@hotmail.com
website www.melchurcher.com

Specialises in audition technique (stage and screen), voice (all aspects) and screen acting (teaching with camera, screen tests). Rates are negotiable – please ring or email to enquire. Happy to provide material for private students to use (except for teaching purposes), and to answer minor follow-up queries after a lesson.

Teaches at home, at the client's home, or at the Drill Hall/Actors Centre. The nearest tube is Northwood Hills (home) or Goodge Street (Drill Hall). More details are available from **www.imdb.com** and from own website.

Has taught thousands of actors and aspiring actors over 22 years. Has worked as an actor and theatre director; taught at the major Drama Schools and at the Actors Centre; run national and international workshops; and authored a book, *Acting for Film: Truth 24 Times a Second* (Virgin Books, 2003). Holds an MA in Performing Arts (Middlesex) and in Voice Research (CSSD). "I am happy to help with most aspects of auditioning and working in theatre and film. I can can advise on understanding the differences between film and theatre, film technique, and building confidence and overcoming nerves."

MJ Coldiron

54 Millfields Road, London E5 0SB
mobile (07941) 920498
fax 020-8533 1506
email jiggs@blueyonder.co.uk

Offers audition coaching for professional and aspiring actors; advice about theatre and performance training in the US and the UK; and coaching in acting technique, public speaking and presentation skills. Charges £40 per hour (3 sessions for £100). Occasional group workshops. Can provide material for clients and is happy to receive minor follow-up queries. Teaches from home, with the nearest rail station being Hackney Central Overground. Has taught hundreds of aspiring actors over 25 years: please make contact for more details. Advises clients: "The theatrical profession is very demanding and is not to be sought for fame or fortune. It is also very competitive and you must work hard, but if you have talent, desire and discipline I can help you to improve your technique and gain in confidence."

Jerry Cox

Flat 16, Aldermen Court, 4 Constable Close,
London N11 3GW
mobile (07957) 654027
email jerrymarwood@hotmail.com

Specialises in audition technique and voice. Charges £25 per hour or £40 for 2 hours. Is happy to provide material for private students to use, and to answer minor follow-up queries. Teaches from home or from the client's home. The nearest railway is Arnos Grove/New Southgate/Woodside Park – a 15-20 minute walk from the main teaching location. Bus routes are 221, 134, 43, 234 and 382. Further details of work can be found in *Contacts*. Has taught 300-500 actors and aspiring actors over 7 years, and worked as an actor, deviser and director; lots of film, theatre, TIE and touring experience. Advises clients: "To paraphrase Bella Merlin, get the process right, and the results look after themselves."

Bridget De Courcy
19 Muswell Road, London N10

Taught singing at the Actors Centre, Covent Garden for 19 years.

Patricia Doyle
19 Cranfield Road, Brockley, London SE4 1TN
tel 020-8691 2839 *mobile* (07941) 108942
email patricia.doyle@virgin.net

Has been teaching for more than 20 years. Specialises in audition technique and as a coach for young performers working or wishing to work in film. Offers career advice, guidance on how to approach looking for work, personal preparation for the profession, and honesty and encouragement. Rates are negotiable; cheque payments preferred. Happy to provide material for private students to use, and to answer minor follow-up queries after a lesson.

Teaches at home, at the client's home or at other locations. Brockley is the nearest railway station, approx. 4 minutes' walk away: trains go from Charing Cross and Leicester Square. Bus routes are 24, 171, 172.

Trained at RADA, an actress for over 25 years (RSC, NT, Royal Court). Has worked in film, radio and television, and as a director for professional companies and in Drama School and Dance training. Director and Co-director for Northern Ballet Theatre: the website **www.nbt.co.uk** offers links to further details and information.

Simon Dunmore
email Simon.Dunmore@btinternet.com
website www.Simon.Dunmore.btinternet.co.uk

Specialises in audition technique (primarily for Drama School entry) but also expert in other aspects of 'actor-promotion' – letter- and CV-writing, interview techniques and much more. Has a vast collection of audition speeches, a large library of plays and a wide knowledge of Drama Schools and the profession.

"Once I get to know you in person, I can help you:
– by commenting upon your current collection of speeches
– find speeches that are suitable for you
– with your choices of where to apply

– get the best from your chosen speeches
– with your overall presentation (believe me, this can make the difference between success and failure)."

Is happy to answer minor queries before and after meeting. Charges £40 per contact-hour, teaches at home, and lives just north of London – 20-30 minutes from King's Cross. Has taught around a thousand students over the last 15 years, in Drama Schools and privately. Also has 20 years' experience as a director in regional theatres, is author of *An Actor's Guide to Getting Work* and the *Alternative Shakespeare Auditions* series, and is the creator and Consultant Editor of *Actors' Yearbook*.

Diana Fairfax
62 Muswell Avenue, London N10 2EL
tel 020-8883 0817
email dianafairfax@gmail.com
website www.dianafairfax.co.uk

Specialises in audition technique. Offers "a high level of support and encouragement, always giving extra time at the end of the hour to discuss any questions arising from the session, or any acting or career issues". Charges £45 per hour. Is happy to provide material for private students to use, and to answer minor follow-up queries after a lesson.

Teaches at home, which is being made wheelchair-accessible – please enquire. The nearest tube/railway stations are Highgate and Bounds Green; a short bus ride on routes 104, 43 and 134. Has taught around 1000 actors over 15 years. Has wide classical and commercial experience in both stage and television, and has worked at the Actors Centre for many years. LGSM Drama Teacher's diploma.

Julia Gaunt
116 Nottingham Road, Selston, Notts NG16 6BX
tel (01773) 775156 *mobile* (07712) 624083
email joolsmusicbiz@aol.com
website www.joolsmusicbiz.com

Specialises in musical theatre, voice and performance; a subsidiary of Jools Music Biz. Charges a minimum of £30, and a maximum of £45, per hour, with discounted rates for block bookings. Happy to provide material for clients and to receive minor follow-up enquiries. Teaches from home, but will travel (if travel costs paid) for a company or group. The nearest railway station is Alfreton, and the house has stairs with a handrail. More information can be found on the music teachers' or LCPA websites. Has taught hundreds of aspiring actors both privately and in association with colleges and universities. Is a member of the British Voice Association and has run many workshops and masterclasses. Advises clients: "Remember the 3 Ds: Determination, Dedication and Discipline."

John Grayson
2 Jubilee Road, St Johns, Worcester WR2 4LY
mobile (07702) 188031

email jgtutor-performer@yahoo.co.uk
website www.JohnLGrayson.com

Specialises in audition technique, voice, accents, singing, public speaking and coaching. Charges £21 per hour. Can provide material for students and is happy to receive minor follow-up queries. Can teach from home or from a client's house. The nearest station is Worcester Foregate Street (there is a good service from Birmingham), from which the house is 10-15 minutes' walk. Has taught around 20 aspiring actors in about 6 years. Please see the website for more details. Is happy to advise students on how to survive when not working.

Martin Harris

32 Baxter Road, Sale, Manchester M33 3AL
tel 0161-969 1444 *mobile* (07788) 723570
email martin@auditioncoach.co.uk
website www.auditioncoach.co.uk

Specialises in audition technique and selection and direction of audition pieces. Offers group acting classes as well as one-to-one tuition for aspiring and professional actors. Also teaches sight reading and gives advice about CVs, agents and jobs. Charges £25 per hour, with a discount of 20% if the client pays for 10 sessions in advance. Accepts payment with cash or cheque, or via Internet banking.

Is happy to provide material for private students to use, and will answer minor follow-up queries at no extra charge. Teaches at home, or at the client's home (with a small extra charge). The home office is wheelchair-accessible. Sale metrolink is the nearest station, around 5 minutes' walk from the office (bus routes: 16, 18, 18A, 19, 41, 86, 99, 245, 263, 264, 266, 267, 268 and 272). Has taught more than 200 actor clients over 10 years. "I trained as an actor at Birmingham School of Acting, and have worked as an actor and director since 1995. I am the current Artistic Director of Rocket Theatre in Manchester."

Daniel Hoffmann-Gill

London
mobile (07946) 433903
email danielhg@gmail.com
website http://danielhg.blogspot.com

Specialises in actor confidence-building, improvisation technique, removing actors' blocks, audition technique, casting technique and various practitioner-centred methods such as Guskin, Meisner, Lecoq and Donnellan.

Has been a professional actor for more than 12 years, working in film, TV and theatre, and has taught actors for over 10 years. Focuses on one-to-one work aimed at enabling the actor to do themselves and their imagination justice – also, on practical assistance in audition technique and how to do the very best you can in any casting situation, "no matter how bizarre". Uses real casting briefs and exercises for students to try out their ideas. Currently teaches

at the Central School of Speech and Drama as a guest lecturer, and at the Actors Centre (previously at the Drill Hall), as well as for numerous London agents and their clients. References from previous students are available on request.

Charges £40 per hour, with special packages available for long-term work or working towards drama school entry: these are tailored on an individual basis, so please email for details. Works from home or from the client's home, and occasionally uses performance spaces, depending on the project. All locations used are wheelchair-accessible. The nearest stations are Wood Green or Bowes Park (bus routes 141, 329, 232 and 121). Has taught around 200 actors. Advises clients that "hard graft and positive attitude go a long way in a tough, tough industry".

Barbara Houseman

34 Shawbury Road, London SE22 9DH
mobile (07767) 843737
email barbarahouseman@hotmail.com

Specialises in audition technique and voice. Also teaches in the areas of confidence-building, presence, dealing with one's inner critic, acting, dealing with classical texts, and preparing for TV/film roles. Charges £60-100 per hour and may offer special packages for block bookings. Is happy to provide material for private students to use, and to answer minor follow-up queries afer a lesson.

Teaches at home, which is wheelchair-accessible. The nearest station is East Dulwich – a 10-15 minute walk. Bus routes are 176, 185 and 40. Has taught around 800 actors and aspiring actors over 29 years, and authored 2 books: *Finding Your Voice* and *Tackling Text and Subtext*. Worked as a Voice Coach for the RSC (1991-97) and as an Associate Director at the Young Vic. "I can advise on overcoming blocks, and becoming the actor you want to be."

Charlie Hughes-D'Aeth

22 Osborne Road, Brighton BN1 6LQ
mobile (07811) 010963
email chdaeth@aol.com

Charges £45 per hour; discounts are available for long-term students. Is happy to provide material for private students to use, and to answer minor follow-up queries. Teaches from home. The nearest station is Preston Park/Brighton, 10/25 minutes' walk away (bus route 5B). Has taught hundreds of actors and aspiring actors over 18 years. Is a director and playwright, and has been a performer and musician. Also teaches playwriting.

Desmond Jones

20 Thornton Avenue, London W4 1QG
tel/fax 020-8747 3537
email enquiries@desmondjones.com
website www.desmondjones.com

Specialises in physical audition techniques and mime and physical theatre. One of the founders of physical theatre; has run his own School of Mime and Physical Theatre for 25 years, with expertise in all aspects of movement. Charges are negotiable, with various packages and discounts available; please make contact for more information. Will provide clients with occasional worknotes and is happy to answer minor follow-up queries. Teaches out of home (a 3-minute walk from Turnham Green station, bus routes 94, 27, H91, 191, 267), or the home of the client – whichever is more suitable. Has taught more than 2500 aspiring actors over 40 years. Advises clients: "Do it now!"

Lawrence Lambert

c/o The Actors Centre, 1A Tower Street, London WC2
mobile (07962) 350229
email lawrielambo@yahoo.co.uk

Specialises in audition/creating character/improvisation/text/voice. Work detail can be for beginners, professionals or individuals returning to the profession. Charges £35 per hour with a discount for block bookings. Happy to provide material for private students to use, and to answer minor follow-up queries after a lesson.

Will teach at home, at the client's home, or at the Actors Centre; all are wheelchair-accessible. Nearbest tube/railway station is Arsenal (home) or Leicester Square (Actors Centre). Bus route is 19.

Has taught hundreds of actors and aspiring actors over 22 years of teaching. Experienced in stage, television and feature film, and is an East 15 graduate. "I cater for all types of experience – from novice to seasoned professional."

Martin McKellan

Neal Street, London WC2
mobile (07973) 372052
email martinmckellan@yahoo.co.uk

Specialises in auditions, acting classes and all aspects of voice work (accent and dialogue a particular area of expertise). Rates are negotiable and offers are available; please make contact for full details. Is happy to provide material for private students to use, and to answer minor follow-up queries at no extra charge. Will teach from home, from a client's home or at another location. Covent Garden is the nearest tube station, 3 minutes' walk away. Has taught thousands of actors and aspiring actors over the past 15 years, and has extensive experience as a freelance acting/voice coach working in the West End and in Regional Theatre and for both film and television.

Sally Mortemore

7 Groton Road, Earlsfield, London SW18 4ER
tel 020-8576 2192 *mobile* (07973) 835292
email mortemores@aol.com
website www.sallymortemore.com

Fully qualified voice coach and professional actress; specialises in Shakespeare and is very experienced in voice, audition coaching, text and accent softening. Charges £30 per hour or £40 for 1.5 hours. Offers a free half-hour consultation for new students, and a discounted rate of £20 per hour for drama school leavers in their first year as a professional. Is happy to provide material for students to use, and to answer minor follow-up queries. Teaches from home, which is wheelchair-accessible; the nearest station is Earlsfield, only 2 minutes away. Has taught 200+ actors and aspiring actors over 6 years. More details are available from *Contacts*.

Rebecca Semark

Epping, Essex
mobile (07956) 850330
email rebecca@semark.biz
website www.semark.biz

Specialises in audition technique, voice, and singing (to student level, not professional). Charges from £25 up to £40 per half hour, depending on whether the student is a child or working adult. Offers discounts to sibling groups. Fortnightly teaching is preferred, as this gives more time to do work and allows for other commitments. Is happy to provide material for private students to use, and to answer minor follow-up queries. Teaches from home; the closest station is Epping (Central Line) – a 5-10 minute walk. Has taught hundreds of actors and aspiring actors over a 19-year period. Since 1973 has worked extensively in theatre, especially in Musical Theatre (comedy).

Ros Simmons

120 Hillfield Avenue, Crouch End, London N8 7DN
tel 020-8347 8089
email info@realspeaking.co.uk
website www.realspeaking.co.uk

Specialises in accents, voice and auditions, as well as spoken English skills for those with Englsh as a second language. Charges £55 per hour with a reduction to £50 per hour if a block of 4 sessions is booked in advance. Student rate is £45 per hour. A one-off 1.5-hour accent coaching session is also available, at £75. Provides material for students' use and is happy to answer minor follow-up queries. Teaches from home, with Finsbury Park the nearest tube (overground, Hornsey Station on Tottenham Lane, just around the corner from the premises). Buses to Finsbury Park tube are the W3 to Tottenham Lane or the W7 to Crouch End Broadway. Has taught around 1000 actors and aspiring actors, in drama schools and privately, over a period of 9 years. Trained as an actor at the Polytechnic School of Theatre in Manchester, and has worked extensively in theatre, film, TV and radio.

Speak Good English Well

School of Economic Science Building, 11-13 Mandeville Place, London W1V 3AJ
mobile (07976) 805976
email neville@speakwell.co.uk
website www.speakwell.co.uk

Specialises in audition technique and voice. Dialogue coach, Shakespeare, musical comedy and lyrical interpretation. Services include coaching in elocution, communication techniques and self-awareness. Also the establishment of confidence and natural performance. Fee details are available on application. Offers special packages and coaching in stage, TV and radio techniques. Teaches from the Mandeville Place address, which is wheelchair-accessible. The nearest station is Bond Street underground, around 3 minutes' walk away (bus route 10). Has taught hundreds of actors and aspiring actors over 16 years. Advises clients: "Have complete faith and confidence in *yourself*. Continually work on voice and movement and penetration of Shakespeare – the greatest master teacher."

Giles Taylor
mobile (07973) 960681
email gilestaylor@ukgateway.net

Specialises in Shakespeare and audition speeches. Is a verse specialist, but works too on prose texts – classical and modern. Charges £40 per hour. Discounts are available: 3 sessions for £100, and students £30 per hour. Is happy to provide material for private students to use, and to answer minor follow-up queries after a lesson.

Teaches from home but other locations can be arranged (please note that these may incur travel costs). The nearest tube station is Highgate and bus routes are 43 and 134. Has taught more than 100 actors and aspiring actors over 6 years. "I have been in the business for nearly 20 years, working in theatre, music theatre, television, film and radio. I am a regular teacher at the Actors Centre."

Paul Todd
3 Rosehart Mews, London W11 3JN
tel 020-7229 9776
email paultodd@talk21.com

Specialises in audition technique and singing. Charges £33 per hour and offers discounts for block booking or lessons close together. Is happy to provide material for private students to use, and to answer minor follow-up queries after a lesson.

Teaches from home. The nearest tube station is Notting Hill and bus routes are 7, 70, 23, 28, 31, 328 and 17. More details about services offered are available via Google search. Has taught hundreds of actors and aspiring actors over 35+ years of tutoring. Has extensive experience as MD, arranger, actor, musician and writer.

Genevieve Walsh
37 Kelvedon House, Guildford Road, Stockwell, London SW8 2DN

mobile (07801) 948864

Specialises in coaching for auditions and public speaking (presentation technique). Charges £30 per hour (£20 for students). Happy to help in the selection of material for students' use, and to answer minor follow-up queries, time permitting. Teaches from home (nearest station is Stockwell, a 5-minute walk away; bus routes 2 or 88). Has taught dozens of actors and aspiring actors over a 35-year period, and has extensive experience as an actor, teacher and director. "Know your material inside out and all the background to the speech. It is very basic advice, but it is essential."

Tessa Wood
43 Woodhurst Road, London W3 6SS
tel 020-8896 2659 *mobile* (07957) 207808
email TessaRosWood@aol.com

Specialises in physical voice including centring, alignment, tension release, breath, articulation, range, projection, tone. Also Standard English, RP and period RP, and audition technique. Fee is negotiable and there is a 20% discount for students and sometimes for actors who aren't working. Can provide copies of audition material, but generally does not lend books as they never seem to be returned. Will give minor follow-up advice for no extra charge. Teaches from home or the client's home (for an additional charge). Nearest train link is the Silverlink (North London Line) and the station, Acton Central, is 5 minutes away. Acton Town (Piccadilly/District Lines) is about 15-minutes' walk, and Acton Mainline (1 stop from Paddington) is about 10 minutes away. Many of the buses from Shepherd's Bush going in the direction of Ealing pass within 5-6 minutes of the house (route 207 plus others).

Has taught well over 2000 actors and aspiring actors over a 15-year period. Pursued a full-time acting career for 15 years and still does some acting every year. Also directs the initial scene studios at Drama Studio London, and every year co-directs and voice-coaches an entry for the Sam Wannamaker Festival at The Globe. Has coached well-known TV presenters and actors on a one-to-one basis. "Whether or not an actor has full-time training (which I would highly recommend), they should keep up their process with classes, both one-to-one and in the form of group workshops."

An actor's toolkit

Compiled by Simon Dunmore

You need to organise the following essential items before you even get your first interview, let alone an agent and/or your first job. You should start planning for all these in good time before the end of your training – ready for your first public production.

1. Join Equity! You can join (very cheaply) as a student member (see **www.equity.org.uk/HowToJoin** and click on Student Membership) and for a small extra fee reserve your professional name: details of how to go about this are on the website.

2. A good, strong professional name. If you can't (or don't want to) use your real name, it's important to select an alternative that you're completely comfortable with.

3. Well-designed headed paper. Beatrice Warde, the passionate typography expert, said, "Typefaces are the clothes words wear." Find a typeface that 'dresses' your professional name well.

4. Secure and reliable telephone and Internet connections for professional use. *Note*: It is very important that your outgoing message and email address sound professional and not like hangovers from your adolescence.

5. A reliable computer with printer. *Tip*: Laser printers provide a much crisper quality when printing text – and laser toner is much cheaper, per page, than ink.

6. An up-to-date copy of *Actors' Yearbook*. *Tip*: It is worthwhile not only reading the rest of this book to get a feel for how different parts of the profession function, but also reading through websites.

7. A good set of photographs and sufficient copies. See Angus Deuchar's article and the introduction to Photographers and Repro Companies starting on page 406.

8. A well-laid-out and up-to-date CV. *Notes*: It's important to ensure that all spellings of proper names (directors, play titles, etc.) are correct. Also, to understand how to convert your CV into Portable Document Format (PDF) for email transmission.

9. A good standard letter that you can adapt for individual circumstances and use in emails, etc. See Ian Liston's article *Marketing Yourself – A Producer's Viewpoint* on page 133.

10. Half-a-dozen (or more) varied audition speeches. See my *Effective Audition Speeches* article on page 154.

11. Half-a-dozen (or more) varied audition songs. See Jennifer Reischel's article *Cattle Calls and How to Survive Them* on page 166.

12. A mental list of things (not just acting ones) you could talk about in order to respond to the almost inevitable question(s), "What have you been doing recently?" and/or "Tell me a bit about yourself."

13. An entry in *Spotlight* – details at **www.spotlight.com/join**. *Note*: Entry into *Spotlight* is strictly limited to professionally trained and/or professionally experienced performers, and applications are always vetted.

14. A reasonable selection of clothes for interviews and auditions. Essentially, you need to feel comfortable and appropriately dressed for each individual circumstance … and you will face a wide variety of such circumstances.

15. A budget. The costs of the above can accumulate quite quickly – before you've earned a penny. And there are many other minor things not listed: postage (see Postage Rates

on page 10), Equity entry fee and annual subscription, subscriptions to *The Stage* and other professional publications, travel costs to interviews, and so on. All the above items can easily add up to much more money than you might think: you need to calculate your potential professional expenses and budget for them. *Notes*: Although many of the above are allowable against tax (see Philippe Carden's article *Tax & National Insurance for Actors* on page 446), don't forget to include your potential tax bill! Also, at the outset of your career, consider carefully the cost-effectiveness of items like personal websites, showreels, etc.

16. Sources of non-acting income that are that are flexible enough for you to drop at 24 hours' notice. At an educated guess, only about 10 per cent of the profession earn a living *solely* from acting. And, even for those, incomes can be incredibly variable – £200 one year to over £20,000 the next, to quote just one example (see Andrew Piper's article *Between Engagements* on page 431).

17. A working knowledge of the nation's transport systems (especially London's): you will often not know where you might be required for audition/interview (even work) until very late in the day. *Tip*: As a general rule it is wise to double your estimated travelling time to allow for the almost inevitable foul-ups.

18. A great deal of patience, persistence, determination, cunning and resourcefulness.

19. A stoical source of solace for the bad times. *Tip*: Find another activity that absorbs you as much as acting does.

20. A copy of my *An Actor's Guide To Getting Work* for reading on the loo (published by A &C Black).

General points:

(a) Can you organise yourself? Acting can be an instant business. For days/weeks/months/ years nothing happens, and then a few minutes/hours/days/weeks/months/years later it can *all* be happening. You must always be ready but not constantly on tenterhooks. In spite of the popular image of the chaotic, dizzy actor, you have to be personally organised or you could significantly harm your employment prospects.

(b) As an actor you are your own business. You are not only your own work-force, but also your publicity and public relations office, accountancy division, transport manager, and – above all – your managing director. Of course, you may well have an agent, an accountant, etc., but none of these people can do anything unless you give them clear direction. You are finally responsible for your success or failure in the business.

Simon Dunmore has been directing productions for over 30 years – nearly 20 years as a resident director in regional theatres and, more recently, working freelance. In that time there have been more than 200 productions (of all styles, colours, shapes and sizes), most recently several Drama School Showcases, Maugham's *Home and Beauty* and new plays about sex, WB Yeats' up-and-down relationship with Maud Gonne, one set inside a pyramid, and another about Bismarck. Past favourites include: *The Promise* (Alexei Arbuzov), *Antigone* (Jean Anouilh), a seven-handed version of *Antony & Cleopatra* and too many others to mention. He also teaches acting and has worked in many drama schools and other training establishments around the country. He has written several books: *An Actor's Guide to Getting Work* (now in its fourth edition), the *Alternative Shakespeare Auditions* series, and is the Consultant Editor for *Actors' Yearbook*.

www.simon.dunmore.btinternet.co.uk

Agents and casting directors
Introduction

Actors have probably existed since before the invention of writing; actors' agents have only been around since the invention of the telephone, just over a century ago. Prior to this, work-seeking actors had to make themselves known in person to potential employers – for instance, certain hostelries in the Covent Garden area of central London were well-known 'talent-spotting' haunts. Actors would also 'catch a ride' with one of the touring companies in the hope of proving themselves to the manager – and then being put on the payroll. Others would pay managers to let them play small parts in the hope of being noticed. All this meant a lot of hard work and/or expense (let alone the time needed to earn his/her living by other means) for the pre-electronic-age actor. The invention of actors' agents seemed to fill a vital gap.

In the 1970s, a number of actors dissatisfied with the (by then) traditional agent system formed the first co-operative agencies (see page 99). This apparently simple idea – with all members taking turns to 'man' the office – took a while to become established. Like many 'simple ideas', the pioneers found that there were more complications involved than they'd initially envisaged, and employers were slow to accept the idea. Thirty years later, the best 'co-ops' have as much professional credibility as their conventional counterparts.

It used to be the case that only the biggest companies used casting directors. The administrative burden inherent in running such a company (let alone directing productions) meant that assistance in the casting process became essential. The 1990s saw a rise in the use of casting directors and in the number of freelancers working on short-term contracts: most of the latter work in a wide variety of fields.

The simple fact is that a significant proportion of properly paid acting work is 'brokered' by casting directors and agents.

Being an agent
Howard Roberts

There are a number of unfortunate stereotypes of agents, and – particularly among younger actors – misconceptions about an agent's role. Whilst popular belief would have us all enjoying long lunches between bouts of shark-like behaviour, the truth is somewhat more akin to that of any other hard-working facilitator.

What does an agent do?

There is no definitive job description for an agent; you will find that different agents have different styles and work in different ways. Broadly speaking, however, we can divide the agent's role into four broad aims, as follows: ·
* to maintain contacts across the industry, in order to secure work for their clients – most commonly in terms of obtaining casting information; ·
* to negotiate fees on behalf of those clients, in order to maximise rewards for the artist, and to ensure that those fees are paid; ·
* to manage the artist's diary in order not to miss the next job opportunity; and ·
* to advise the artist on their career choices and options.

Bear in mind that your agent is working for you all the time, even when you might not be earning. It is for this reason that you pay them commission for all performing work in which you are engaged whilst they represent you.

When you see agents at showcases and first nights, or when you hear that an agent is coming to your production, remember that this is usually after they have already worked a full day in the office. Attending these events is a key part of their business: it is their opportunity to network, to keep abreast of new developments and new performers, and to maintain good relationships – for example, with a casting director. The job of an agent can be immensely rewarding, but those rewards come as a result of long hours and hard work.

How do I get an agent?

Sadly, anyone can call themselves an agent, because there are no entry restrictions to the profession. In this book you will find more than 50 pages listing agents: some of them belong to the Personal Managers' Association (PMA), a body that requires members to have at least three years' trading in the industry prior to joining. However, many other established and reputable agents choose not to belong to the PMA. So take advice. Talk to other performers, to casting directors and to established industry advisers like John Colclough, and endeavour to establish a shortlist of suitable contacts.

A phone call or an email may establish whether an agency is currently considering new clients. Don't be too disheartened if they say that their list is full – persevere with other approaches. And do be careful with emailed requests: many agents now find themselves inundated with email traffic from actors seeking representation, and could choose not to respond.

If an agency asks you to send in your details, check what they require: this will usually be a current CV, a clear 10x8in head shot and a covering letter. See if they want a DVD showreel, or a CD voicereel, but be careful of sending these in unsolicited. I would suggest that you always send a correctly stamped and addressed envelope with your submission, as this will make it easier for the agent to respond.

The CV should contain your relevant professional experience, details of where you trained, and any other marketable skill(s) you may possess (for example, a clean driving licence, sports at which you are proficient, languages you might speak, musical instruments you can play, whether you can safely ride a horse, and anything else that might add to your performance).

Photographs should be clear and as up to date as possible. Remember, on the Spotlight site your photo will appear slightly smaller than a passport photo, so you want the best possible definition, at the smallest size. You are in an image-led profession and your picture is likely to be the first point of contact. Always go to a professional photographer, but be careful of spending too much money on photos until you have an agent; chances are, they might want something different. And always put your contact details on the back of your photo, as in a busy office it can get separated from your letter and CV

Keep your letter businesslike. Check to whom you are writing, date the letter and spell their name correctly. Finally, ensure that you use the correct postage: it will not improve your chances if the agent has to pay a surcharge on your letter. Of course, the agent might be happy to receive an emailed submission, using your Spotlight PIN number to access your details. Always ensure that your Spotlight entry is up to date with your correct playing age, latest credits and full list of marketable skills.

Interviews

Turn up on time – never late, but not too early either. Check where you are going in advance so that you don't arrive flustered. You are going to see a busy person, who may be in a position to help your career, so treat the meeting seriously. If you fail to attend at the agreed time, they may think that you will treat castings in a similar manner.

Before 'the day', have your questions ready and prepared in your mind. How long have you been established? How many agents work here? How many clients do you represent? What are your commission rates? (It is unusual for these to be higher than 15% – and be very wary of any agency who would charge you for joining them.) Are you VAT registered? (If so, remember that this means you will be paying VAT on top of your commission.) Where would you fit in with this agency, and would you clash with any of their existing clients?

This is all information that you need to glean – but at interview, do be careful *how* you ask your questions. Some agents might be more reticent than others; you will need to carefully judge the mood and tone of the meeting. The agent might want to make it clear that they are interviewing you, and not the other way round. Remember, agents will vary in their style and way of working: you must be sensitive and able to adapt.

Offers of representation

Agencies come in all shapes and sizes. Larger, well-established West End concerns certainly have the attraction of the star names they represent, and if they offer you a place it could work for you. They will have the first look at film scripts, and the international cachet. However, what are sometimes referred to as the 'boutique agencies' might also be advantageous: with them, you are likely to have direct access to the principal partners, and you are more likely to be important to them. Smaller agencies have the motivation to secure as much work as possible for their clients, for as much time as possible. They will not want 'passengers'.

If you do get an offer, or offers, of representation, take time to think about it and always seek advice. This is an important decision. Remember that you are entering into a business relationship, not looking for a new best friend. Of course, the best sort of actor to be is a working actor, and so the agency that works best for you is the one that helps you to keep working, irrespective of its size and location or how long it has been established.

Contracts

A contract should place your business relationship on a professional basis, clearly stating not just commission rates, but also such important issues as the required notice period for terminating your agreement. Don't be afraid of being contractually committed, but nor should you ever sign a contract on the spot. Take it away and get a second opinion, be it from another performer, from Equity, or from someone with specialist knowledge.

Problems?

How often do agents hear actors complain that their agent never puts them up for anything – or that they are not seen, even though they are ideal for a part? The harsh reality is that it is a buyer's market. You face vast amounts of competition for every job, and despite your agent's best efforts, the casting director still might not want to see you.

If you really do feel that the actor-agent relationship is not working, the first person you should talk to is your agent! Try to work out if there has been any misunderstanding about your skills, or playing age, or photo; often such issues can easily be resolved by honest discussion.

If there are irreconcilable differences, then try hard to part amicably. It's a small profession, and agents do talk to one another. Attempt to secure new representation before you move, but first check any obligations you have to your existing agent in terms of period of notice, or ongoing work, or work for which you have been submitted.

And finally ..

Always try and work with your agent. Establish how proactive they want you to be. If there are areas of work you do not wish to pursue, make sure that you let your agent know. Always ensure that you keep your agent fully aware of your availability – weekends and holidays included.

Remember: actors face huge amounts of competition, and it is the agent's job to improve the odds in a client's favour. It is a very tough profession, and experience often indicates that you have to work very hard just to be lucky.

Howard Roberts MSc is a partner in Sandra Griffin Management Ltd. He has been an actors' agent for more than 20 years, initially as an assistant and then as a co-director. Prior to this he was a lecturer in Economics and Politics in Further Education. He lives in West London.

Agents

A good agent understands contracts, knows the current rates in every field of work and – most importantly – has plenty of professional contacts and access to far more casting information than most individuals can ever possess. Directors and casting directors rely on the agents they know and trust to help with the filtering process of whom to interview. A good agent will work hard at promoting each of his/her clients; in return, it is not unreasonable that they charge commission on every contract they negotiate for you – generally, 10-20 per cent (plus VAT, if appropriate). A good agent will also (a) have only as many clients as they can reasonably handle, and (b) ensure that they have a good range of ages and types of actors to cover as many casting opportunities as possible.

When you are seeking representation, it is advisable to contact agents by post in the first instance – unless specifically informed otherwise. It is a good idea to include a separate 10x8in (25x20cm) photograph, and it is important that all your enclosures give your name and the best way to contact you (not a long list of confusing alternatives). Agents receive many requests for representation, and photographs can become separated from their accompanying letters and CVs, so proper labelling is essential.

Use the listings that follow to (a) target your submission as accurately as possible (by writing to a specific, named person, for example), (b) check for any details that could inform the content of your letter, and (c) find out whether each would be interested in any extras, like a showreel. Time spent checking details can save money and enhance your chances of being noticed more than the next person. Unless you have a good collection of professional credits, it is generally best to write to agents when there's an opportunity for them to see you in something.

If you are invited to meet an agent, that is often a good sign. You should approach the occasion in much the same way as you would an interview for a production. The major difference is that you should be prepared to ask (reasonable) questions – rates of commission, for instance.

When seeking representation, it can be a good idea to target only those agencies that you think might suit you. For instance, might you feel lost in a large agency, but feel more comfortable with a smaller one? On the other hand, some larger agencies have huge 'clout' and can be the first 'port of call' for the casting of prestigious productions.

When you've been taken on by an agent, it is important to establish how your working relationship will function. Be clear about any areas of work that you don't want to be suggested for, discuss your availability for auditions and interviews, agree how much promotion you should do for yourself, and so on.

These listings only contain agents who represent adult actors – there are many others who represent children, models, extras and so on.

21st Century Vaux Casting

The Corn Exchange, Fenwick Street,
Liverpool L2 7QS
tel 0151-258 1679 *fax* 0151-231 1067
email 21stcenturyvaux@beeb.net
Key personnel David Williamson

Established in 1991, the agency represents 20 actors.
Areas of work include theatre, television, film,
commercials, corporate and voice-overs.

Will consider attending performances at venues in
Greater London and the North West with at least 1
week's notice. Accepts submissions (with CVs and
photographs) from actors previously unknown to the
company sent by post or email. Will also accept
showreels, voice tapes, and invitations to view
individual actors' websites. *Commission*: 7.5%

A&J Management

242A The Ridgeway, Botany Bay, Enfield EN2 8AP
tel 020-8342 0542 *fax* 020-8342 0842
email info@ajmanagement.co.uk
website www.ajmanagement.co.uk
Managing Director Jackie Michael *Key
personnel* Joanne Michael, Hannah Liebeskind

Established in 1984. 3 agents represent actors. Areas
of work include theatre, musicals, television, film,
commercials, corporate and voice-overs.

Will consider attending performances at venues
within Greater London with a minimum of 2 weeks'
notice. Accepts submissions (with CVs and
photographs) from actors previously unknown to the
company if sent by post. Invitations to view
individual actors' websites are also accepted.
Commission: 15% plus VAT

June Abbott Associates

55 East Road, London N1 6AH
tel 020-7250 0520
email jaa@thecourtyard.org.uk
website www.thecourtyard.org.uk
Agent June Abbott *Assistant Agent* Tanya Parkin

Established in 1994. 2 agents represent 50 actors.
Areas of work include theatre, musicals, television,
film, commercials, corporate and voice-overs.

Attendance at performances is dependent on
potential client submissions/interviews. Accepts
submissions (with CVs and photographs) from actors
previously unknown to the company if sent by post.
Enclose an sae if a reply is required and for the return
of CVs and photographs. Showreels and voice tapes
should only be sent on request. Actors should only
apply if they have training, and will only be contacted
if the agency is interested. Recommends the
photographer Peter Simpkin (see entry under
Photographers and repro companies on page 418 for
further details). *Commission*: Theatre 10%; Voice-
Over and Radio 12%; Film and TV 15%

Access Artiste Management Ltd

PO Box 39925, London EC1V 0WN
tel 020-8505 1094 *fax* 020-8926 1273
email mail@access-associates.co.uk
website www.access-associates.co.uk
Manager Sarah Bryan

Established in 1999. Areas of work include theatre,
musicals, television, film, commercials, corporate.
Also represent Musical Directors.

Will consider attending performances in Greater
London and elsewhere with 1 month's notice.
Accepts submissions (with CVs and photographs)
from professional actors previously unknown to
them. Showreels, voice tapes and details of individual
actors' websites should only be sent upon request.
Follow up calls are welcomed. Welcomes enquiries
from disabled actors.

Acting Associates

71 Hartham Road, London N7 9JJ
tel 020-7607 3562 *fax* 020-7607 3562
email Fiona@actingassociates.co.uk
website www.actingassociates.co.uk
Agent Fiona Farley

Established in 1988. 1 agent represents 45-50 actors.

Will consider attending performances with 1 week's
notice. Accepts submissions (with CVs and
photographs) from actors previously unknown to the
company if sent by post. Recommends the
photographer Catherine Shakespeare Lane (see entry
under *Photographers and repro companies* on page 406
for further details). *Commission*: Theatre 10%; Other
15%

Actors International Ltd

Conway Hall, 25 Red Lion Square,
London WC1R 4RL
tel 020-7242 9300 *fax* 020-7831 8319
email mail@actorsinternational.co.uk
Agents Kay Potter, Ruth Robinson

Established in 2008. 3 agents represent around 80
actors. Areas of work include theatre, musicals,
television, film, commercials and corporate.

Will attend performances within Greater London
given as much notice as possible. Welcomes letters
(with CVs & photographs) from individual actors
previously unknown to the company sent by post or
email. *Commission*: Theatre 10%; TV, film and
commercials 15%

"Our office is at the top of a building with no lift, so
it is inaccessible to anyone with walking difficulties.
We would consider representing actors with
disabilities that would not prevent them from coming
to the office."

Actors Ireland

Crescent Arts Centre, 2-4 University Road,
Belfast BT7 1NH
tel 028-9024 8861 *fax* 028-9024 8861
email Geraldine@actorsireland.com
website www.actorsireland.com

Established in 2001. 2 agents represent 90 actors. Areas of work include theatre, musicals, television, film, commercials, corporate and voice-overs.

Will consider attending performances at venues in Northern Ireland. Accepts submissions (with CVs and photographs) from actors previously unknown to the company if sent by post. Will also accept invitations to view individual actors' websites. *Commission*: Theatre 5%; TV 10%

Actors World Casting

13 Briarbank Road, London W13 0HH
tel 020-8998 2579
email katherine@actors-world-production.com
Agent Katherine Pageon

Established in 2005. 1 agent represents 70 actors. Areas of work include theatre, musicals, television, film, commercials, corporate, voice-overs. *Commission*: Theatre 10%, Other 15%.

Will consider attending performances in Greater London with at least 2 weeks' notice. Notices of performances should be sent via email. Accepts submissions sent via email (with CVs and one photograph only) from actors previously unknown to them. Invitations to view individual actors' websites also accepted. Follow up calls are welcomed. Welcomes enquiries from disabled actors.

Actual Management

The Studio, 63a Ladbroke Road, London W11 3PD
tel 020-7243 1166 *fax* 0870-874 1149
email agents@actualmanagement.co.uk
website www.actualmanagement.co.uk

Established in 2002. 2 agents represent 50 actors. Areas of work include theatre, television, film and commercials.

Will consider attending performances at venues in Greater London with at least 2 weeks' notice. Accepts submissions (with CVs and photographs) from actors previously unknown to the company sent by post or email. Will also accept showreels, voice tapes, and invitations to view individual actors' websites.

The Agency

47 Adelaide Road, Dublin 2 Eire
tel 353-1661 8535 *fax* 353-1676 0052
email info@tagency.ie
website www.the-agency.ie
Directors Teri Hayden, Karl Hayden

Established in 1982. 2 agents represent 80+ actors in film, television, theatre and voice overs. *Commission*: 10%

Welcomes performance notices for shows in Dublin and London with 2 weeks' notice. Welcomes representations enquiries (with CV and photograph) by post or email. Happy to receive follow-up calls, showreels, invitations to view individual actors' websites, and enquiries from disabled actors.

Alexander Personal Management

Pinewood Studio, Pinewood Road, Iver Heath, Bucks SL0 0NH
tel (01753) 639204 *fax* (01753) 639205
email apm@apmassociates.net
website www.apmassociates.net

"For all your casting requirements." In-house casting services and personal management established in 1989, and representing British and International actors, singers, dancers and presenters with extensive film, television, commercial, voice-over and theatre credits. Will consider submissions with CVs and photographs.

All Talent UK

Central Chambers, 93 Hope Street, Glasgow G2 6LD
tel 0141-221 8887 *fax* 0141-221 8883
email enquiries@alltalentuk.co.uk
website www.alltalentuk.co.uk

Established in 2005. 2 agents represent 50-60 actors. Also represent other skills within the profession. Commission charges are 15%. Particular photographers are recommended to clients.

Will consider attending performances in Central London and Glasgow with at least 2-3 weeks' notice. Accepts submissions (with CV's and photographs) from actors previously unknown to them. Postal submissions preferred. Invitations to view showreels or voice tapes and individual actors' websites also accepted. Follow up calls are welcomed. Welcomes enquiries from disabled actors.

Anita Alraun Representation

5th Floor, 28 Charing Cross Road, London WC2H 0DB
tel 020-7379 6840 *fax* 020-7379 6865
Sole Proprietor/Agent Anita Alraun

1 agent represents a varying number of actors. Areas of work include theatre, musicals, film, television, commercials, radio drama, corporate and some voice-overs.

Attendance at performances is dependent on potential client submissions/interviews. Accepts submissions (with CV, photograph and sae – essential for reply) by post only from trained/experienced actors previously unknown to the company. Emailed submissions will not be considered. Showreels and voice tapes should be sent only if requested, following interview. *Commission*: Radio 10%; Theatre 10-12.5%; Film and TV 12.5%; Commercials 15%

Alvarez Management

33 Ludlow Way, London N2 0JZ
tel 020-8883 2206 *fax* 020-8444 2646

Established in 1990. 2 agents represent 55 actors. Areas of work include theatre, musicals, television, film, commercials, corporate and voice-overs.

Will consider attending performances at venues within Greater London with 3-4 weeks' notice.

Agents and Casting Directors

Accepts submissions (with CVs, photographs and sae) from actors previously unknown to the company if sent by post. "When you are on the phone, please introduce yourself." "Have a really decent photograph taken." *Commission*: Theatre and Radio 10%; Film and TV 12.5%; Commercials 15%

ALW Associates
1 Grafton Chambers, Grafton Place,
London NW1 1LN
tel 020-7388 7018 *fax* 020-7813 1398
email alweurope@onetel.com

Established in 1977 as Vernon Conway Ltd. Sole representation of 35 actors. Areas of work include theatre, musicals, television, film and commercials.

Will consider attending performances at venues within Greater London and occasionally elsewhere with 1 week's notice. Accepts submissions (with CVs and photographs) from actors previously unknown to the company sent by post or email. Also accepts invitations to view individual actors' websites. Showreels and voice tapes should only be sent on request. *Commission*: Theatre and Radio 10-12.5%; Film and TV 12.5%; Commercials 15%

Amber Personal Management Ltd
28 St Margaret's Chambers, 5 Newton Street,
Manchester M1 1HL
tel 0161-228 0236, 020-7734 7887 *fax* 0161-228 0235
email info@amberltd.co.uk
website www.amberltd.co.uk
Principal Agent Sally Sheridan *Agent* Jasmine Parris
Associate Agent Estelle Jenkins

Works in theatre, musicals, television, film, commercials, corporate and voice-over. 3 agents represent 90-100 actors. Recommends the photographer John Nicholls (**868online@googlemail.com**). Will consider attending performances in Manchester, Leeds and Liverpool if given a minimum of 2 weeks' notice.

Welcomes letters (with CVs & photographs) from individual actors previously unknown to the company if sent by post. Does not welcome email approaches or follow-up telephone calls. Encourages enquiries from actors with disabilities. Will accept showreels, voice tapes and invitations to view individual actors' websites. *Commission*: Recorded Media (TV/Film/Commercial) 15%; Theatre, Musicals, Corporate 10%

The American Agency
14 Bonny Street, London NW1 9PG
tel 020-7485 8883 *fax* 020-7482 4666
email americanagency@btconnect.com
Agent Ed Cobb

Areas of work include theatre, musicals, television, film, commercials, corporate and voice-overs. 2 agents represent 80 actors. Will consider attending performances within the Greater London area.

Accepts submissions (with CVs and photographs) from actors previously unknown to the agency if sent by post, but not by email. Invitations to view individual actors' websites, showreels and voice tapes are also accepted. Welcomes enquiries from disabled actors. *Commission*: Theatre 10%; Other 15%

Andrews Hamilton Ltd
BCM Box 3054, London WC1N 3XX
tel 020-8491 7904 *fax* 020-8551 3685
email info@andrewshamilton.com
website www.andrewshamilton.com
Agent Kelly Andrews

Established in 2003 and represents about 45 actors.

Accepts submissions (with CVs and photographs) from actors previously unknown to the company if sent by post only. Showreels and invitations to view individual actors' websites are also accepted. "If you require your material to be returned please enclose a stamped, self-addressed envelope of the correct size. Any material not returned will be destroyed."

Susan Angel & Kevin Francis Ltd
1st Floor, 12 D'Arblay Street, London W1F 8DU
tel 020-7439 3086 *fax* 020-7437 1712
email agents@angelandfrancis.co.uk
Director Kevin Francis

Established in 1976. 3 agents represent about 75 actors (including one disabled actor) and six major TV/film casting directors. Areas of work include theatre, television, film, and commercials.

Will consider attending performances at venues within Greater London and occasionally elsewhere (e.g. Leeds, Bristol, Manchester) with 2 weeks' notice. Accepts brief postal submissions (with CVs and photographs) from actors previously unknown to the company. Emailed applications are not considered due to the volume of mail. *Commission*: 10-12.5%

Christopher Antony Associates
The Old Dairy, 164 Thames Road, London W4 3QS
tel 020-8994 9952 *fax* 020-8742 8066
email info@christopherantony.co.uk
website www.christopherantony.co.uk
Agents Chris Sheils, Kerry Walker

Established in 2005 and represents about 35 actors. "We represent a small and diverse list of artistes in all areas of Theatre and Television and Film."

Accepts submissions (with CVs and photographs) from actors previously unknown to the company — sent by post or email. Suitable clients will be contacted to arrange a meeting or will be invited to attend one of their workshop auditions — "to select the right clients with whom we are confident we can work closely with creatively." "If you require your details to be returned, please enclose an sae".

APM Associates
Pinewood Studios, Iver Heath, Bucks SL0 0NH
tel (01753) 639204 *fax* (01753) 639205
mobile (07918) 166706

email apm@apmassociates.net
website www.apmassociates.net
Managing Director Linda French

Established in 1989. Represents around 65 actors. Areas of work include theatre, musicals, television, film, commercials, corporate and voice-overs. Also represents actor-writers, presenters and directors.

Will consider attending performances at venues within Greater London with 2 weeks' notice. Accepts submissions (with CVs and photographs) from actors previously unknown to the company if sent by post with sae. Will also accept showreels and voice tapes. Will consider looking at websites only if actor's CV is of interest. Welcomes applications from disabled actors. *Commission*: Brochure available upon offer of interview

Argyle Associates

St John's Buildings, 43 Clerkenwell Road, London EC1M 5RS
tel 020-7608 2095 *fax* 020-7608 1642
email argyle.associates@virgin.net
Director Richard Linford *Key personnel* Geraldine Pryor

Established in 1995. 2 agents represent 30 actors. Areas of work include theatre, musicals, television, film, commercials and corporate.

Will consider attending performances at venues in Sussex and Surrey (e.g. Eastbourne, Brighton, Guildford, Dorking, Windsor) with 2 weeks' notice. Accepts submissions (with CVs and photographs) from actors previously unknown to the company if sent by post. Invitations to view individual actors' websites are also accepted. "Be clear about what you think you have to offer the agency – your type and roles. Your photograph should look like you and be a high-grade holiday snap." *Commission*: Theatre and Radio 10%; TV 12.5%; Commercials, Film, Corporate and CD Rom 15%

Ash Personal Management

3 Spencer Road, Mitcham Common, Surrey CR4 15G
tel/fax 020-8646 0050
email ash-personal-mgmt@yahoo.co.uk
Agent Anthony Hyland

Established in 1986. 1 agent represents 15 actors working in theatre, musicals, television, film and commercials.

Will consider attending performances within Greater London and beyond, given 1-2 weeks' notice. Accepts submissions (with CVs and photographs) from actors previously unknown to the agency sent by post or email. Will also accept showreels, voice tapes and invitations to view an actor's website; follow-up telephone calls, however, are not welcomed. *Commission*: Stage 10%; Screen 15%

Asquith & Horner

The Studio, 14 College Road, Bromley BR1 3NS
tel 020-8466 5580 *fax* 020-8313 0443

website www.spotlightagent.info (view PIN 9858-0919-0728)
Senior Partner Anthony Vander Elst *Partner* Helen Melville

Established 1989. 2 agents represent 70 actors. Also represented are directors, choreographers, presenters, singers, dancers and commercial models. Areas of work include theatre, musicals, television, film, commercials, corporate and voice-overs. Will consider attending performances at venues within Greater London and elsewhere but requests as much notice as possible. Accepts submissions (CVs and photographs) from actors previously unknown to the company; also accepts showreels and voice tapes, and invitations to view actors' websites. "Unsolicited enquiries should always be accompanied by an appropriately stamped and addressed envelope for return of answer, photo, tape, etc." Email applications are discouraged.

Associated International Management (AIM)

Fairfax House, Fulwood Place, London WC1V 6HUT
tel 020-7831 9709 *fax* 020-7242 0810
email info@aimagents.com
website www.aimagents.com
Key personnel Derek Webster, Stephen Gittins, Lisa-Marie Assenheim, Amy Jenkins

An international management established in 1984. 3 agents represent around 90 actors. Areas of work include theatre, television, film and commercials. Also represents directors.

Will consider attending performances within the Greater London area with at least 3 weeks' notice. Accepts submissions (with CVs and photographs) from actors previously unknown to the agency if sent by post, but not by email. *Commission*: 12-15%

BAM Associates

Benets Cottage, Dolberrow, Churchill, Bristol BS25 5NT
tel (01934) 852942
email casting@ebam.tv
website www.ebam.tv

2 agents represent 60 actors. Areas of work include theatre, musicals, television, film, commercials, corporate and voice-overs.

Will consider attending performances at venues within Greater London and the South West, but requests as much notice as possible. Accepts submissions (with CVs and 10x8in black and white photographs) from actors previously unknown to the company if sent by post. Welcomes enquiries from disabled actors. *Commission*: Theatre 10%; Mechanical Media 15%

Gavin Barker Associates Ltd

2D Wimpole Street, London W1G 0EB
tel 020-7499 4777 *fax* 020-7499 3777

Agents and Casting Directors

email amanda@gavinbarkerassociates.co.uk
website www.gavinbarkerassociates.co.uk
Managing Director Gavin Barker *Associate
Director* Michelle Burke

Established in 1998. 2 agents represent 55 actors and
a handful of creatives. Areas of work include theatre,
musicals, television, film, commercials, corporate and
voice-overs. Also represents directors and
choreographers.

Will consider attending performances at venues in
Greater London given at least 3 weeks' notice.
Accepts submissions (with CVs and photographs)
from actors previously unknown to the company if
sent by post. Follow-up calls are not welcome. Happy
to receive showreels and voice tapes. "We do not
currently represent any disabled actors, but would
consider each applicant on a case by case basis."
Commission: 10-12.5%

Olivia Bell Ltd

189 Wardour Street, London W1F 8ZD
tel 020-7439 3270 *fax* 020-7439 3485
email info@olivia-bell.co.uk
Managing Director Xania Segal

Established in 2001. 2 agents represent 90 actors.
Areas of work include theatre, musicals, television,
film and commercials.

Will consider attending performances at venues
within Greater London with a minimum of 1 week's
notice. Accepts submissions (with CVs and
photographs) from actors previously unknown to the
company if sent by post. Invitations to view
individual actors' websites and showreels or voice
tapes are also accepted. *Commission*: 12.5-20%

Audrey Benjamin Agency

278A Elgin Avenue, Maida Vale, London W9 1JR
tel 020-7289 7180 *fax* 020-7266 4580
email a.benjamin@btconnect.co.uk
Director Audrey Benjamin

Established in 1985. Works in all areas; represents
around 45 actors. Will consider attending
performances within Greater London, given 2-3 days'
notice. Welcomes letters (with CVs & photographs)
from individual actors previously unknown to the
agency if sent by post, but not by email. Encourages
enquiries from actors with disabilities. Does not
welcome follow-up calls, showreels, voice tapes or
invitations to view individual actors' websites.
Commission: Theatre 10%; Film, TV, Commercials
15%

Better Chemistry

1st and 2nd Floors, 20 Stansfield Road,
London SW9 9RZ
tel 020-7737 5300 *mobile* (07905) 259060
email info@betterchemistry.co.uk
website www.betterchemistry.co.uk
Director Paul L Martin

Agency dedicated to cabaret, burlesque, circus and
variety acts. Corporate work, private parties, etc. for
already existing self-contained acts.

Jorg Betts Associates

Gainsborough House, 81 Oxford Street,
London W1D 2EU
tel 020-7903 5300 *fax* 020-7903 5301
email agents@jorgbetts.com

Established in 2001. Areas of work include theatre,
musicals, television, film, commercials and corporate.
Also represents directors and presenters.

Accepts submissions (with CVs and photographs)
from actors previously unknown to the company if
sent by post.

Billboard Personal Management

Unit 5, 11 Mowll Street, London SW9 6BG
tel 020-7735 9956 *fax* 020-7793 0426
email billboardpm@btconnect.com
website www.billboardpm.com
Agent Daniel Tasker

Established in 1985. 1 agent represents 55 actors.
Areas of work include theatre, musicals, television,
film, commercials, corporate and voice-overs.

Will consider attending performances at venues in
Greater London given a minimum of 2 weeks' notice.
Accepts submissions (with CVs and photographs)
from actors previously unknown to the company if
they are currently performing. *Commission*:
Commercials 16%; Film and TV 13.5%; Other 11%

Bishop Burnett Agency & Management

47 Dean Street, London W1P 5BE
tel 020-7734 9995 *fax* 020-7734 9996
email lara@mcslondon.com
Key personnel Keith Bishop, Lara James

Areas of work include theatre, musicals, television,
film, commercials, corporate and voice-overs. 3
agents represent 35 actors. Also represents models,
presenters, reporters, celebrities and celebrity
hairdressers. Will consider attending performances
within the Greater London area with at least 1
month's notice. Accepts submissions (with CVs and
photographs) from actors previously unknown to the
company (include an sae). Invitations to view
individual actors' websites, showreels and voice tapes
are also accepted. Welcomes enquiries from disabled
actors. *Commission*: Theatre 10-15%

Rebecca Blond Associates

69a Kings Rd, London SW3 4NX
tel 020-7351 4100 *fax* 020 7351 4600
email rebecca@rebeccablondassociates.com
Agent Rebecca Blond

Established in 1991, 2 agents represent around 60
actors in all areas of acting work; also represents
directors. Commission varies. Recommends the
photographers Wolf Marloh and Ruth Crafer.

Welcomes performance notices for shows within Greater London with two weeks' notice. Welcomes representation enquiries (with CV and photograph) by post or email, as well as showreels and invitations to view individual actors' websites. Does not welcome follow-up calls.

Bloomfields Management
77 Oxford Street, London W1D 2ES
tel 020-7493 4448 *fax* 020-7493 4449
email emma@bloomfieldsmanagement.com
website www.bloomfieldsmanagement.com
Director Emma Bloomfield

Established in 2004. Areas of work include theatre, musicals, television, film, commercials and corporate. 2 agents represent 40 actors. Will consider attending performances anywhere, given at least 2 weeks' notice. Accepts submissions (with CVs and photographs) from actors previously unknown to the company if sent by post, but not by email. Invitations to view individual actors' websites, showreels and voice tapes are also accepted. Welcomes enquiries from disabled actors.

Sandra Boyce Management
1 Kingsway House, Albion Road, London N16 0TA
tel 020-7923 0606 *fax* 020-7241 2713
email info@sandraboyce.com
Agent Sandra Boyce (MD)

2 agents represent 70 actors in all areas of acting work; directors also represented. Welcomes performance notices if given at least 2 weeks in advance, and is prepared to travel within the Greater London area. Happy to accept letters (by post, not email) with CV and photograph from individuals previously unknown to the company, but does not welcome follow-up calls. Encourages approaches from disabled actors. Also welcomes showreels and voice tapes. Advises those approaching the agency to "always include a stamped, addressed envelope (of correct size) for return of photos/showreels".

The Bridge Agency Ltd
PO Box 261, Loughton IG10 2WS
tel 0870-116 1388 *fax* 0870-116 1389
email the_bridge_agency@yahoo.co.uk
Agent Robert Stokvis

Established in 2002. 1 agent represents 10 actors. Areas of work include theatre, musicals, television, film, commercials, corporate and voice-overs.

Will consider attending performances at East 15 Acting School only, and with 2 weeks' notice. Accepts showreels and voice tapes from East 15 graduates. "Our agency is open to graduates of East 15 Acting School only. We aim to see all productions at East 15 and to intensify this cooperation." *Commission*: 8-18%. No unsolicited requests.

BROOD
High Street Buildings, 134 Kirkdale,
London SE26 4BB
tel 020-8699 1757
email broodmanagement@aol.com
website www.broodmanagement.com
Director Brian Parsonage Kelly

Established in 2003. 1 agent represents 40 actors. Areas of work include theatre, musicals, television, film, commercials and corporate. Also represents models.

Accepts submissions (with CVs and photographs) from actors previously unknown to the company if sent by post. *Commission*: Theatre 10%; Film 15%

Valerie Brook Agency
10 Sandringham Road, Cheadle Hulme,
Cheshire SK8 5NH
tel 0161-486 1631 *fax* 0161-488 4206
email colinbrook@freenetname.co.uk

2 agents represent 75 actors. Areas of work include theatre, musicals, television, film, commercials and corporate role-play.

Will consider attending performances at venues outside Greater London with 2 weeks' notice. Accepts postal submissions (with CVs and photographs) from actors previously unknown to the company. Invitations to view individual actors' websites are also accepted. *Commission*: Negotiated with clients individually

Brown & Simcocks
1 Bridgehouse Court, 109 Blackfriars Road,
London SE1 8HW
tel 020-7928 1229 *fax* 020-7928 1909
email mail@brownandsimcocks.co.uk
website www.brownandsimcocks.co.uk
Partners Carrie Simcocks, Peter Walmsley

Established in the 1970s; 2 agents represent 65-70 actors. Areas of work include theatre, musicals, television, film, commercials and corporate.

Will consider attending performances within the Greater London area given 2-4 weeks' notice. Accepts submissions (with CVs and photographs) from actors previously unknown to the company if sent by post. Unsolicited emails are not welcome. *Commission*: 10-15%

Brunskill Management Ltd
Suite 8A, 169 Queen's Gate, London SW7 5HE
tel 020-7581 3388 *fax* 020-7589 9460
email contact@brunskill.com
website www.brunskill.com
Agents Aude Powell, Geoff Stanton, Roger Davidson

Agency represents more than 100 actors. Areas of work include theatre, musicals, television, film, commercials, corporate and voice-overs. Also represents producers, directors and musical directors.

Will consider attending performances at venues in Greater London and occasionally elsewhere, but requests as much notice as possible. Accepts submissions (with CVs and photographs) from actors previously unknown to the company if sent by post. Enclose an sae of an appropriate size for the return of CVs and photographs. Emails are not encouraged, particularly if they include large attachments.

Bronia Buchanan Associates Ltd

1st Floor, 23 Tavistock Street, London WC2E 7NX
tel 020-7631 2004 *fax* 020-7631 2034
email info@buchanan-associates.co.uk
website www.buchanan-associates.co.uk
Agents Bronia Buchanan, Phil Belfield, Mark Ward

Sole representation of approximately 25 creatives and 150 actors. Areas of work include theatre, musicals, television, film and commercials.

Will consider attending performances at venues within Greater London and elsewhere, but requests as much notice as possible. Accepts submissions by post or email (with CVs and photographs) from actors previously unknown to the company. Showreels and voice tapes are also encouraged. Recommends the photographer Chris Baker (020-8441 3851). *Commission*: 10% plus VAT

Burnett Granger Crowther Ltd

3 Clifford Street, London W1S 2LF
tel 020-7437 8008 *fax* 020-7287 3239
email associates@bgcltd.org
website www.bgcltd.org
Agents Barry Burnett, Lindsay Granger, Lizanne Crowther

Established in 1965. 3 agents represent 140 actors.

Will consider attending performances at venues within Greater London, with 3 weeks' notice. Accepts submissions (with CVs, photographs and sae) from actors previously unknown to the company if sent by post. *Commission*: 10-12%

CADS Management

209 Abbey Road, Bearwood, Birmingham B67 5NG
tel 0121-420 1996 *fax* 0121-434 4909
email info@cadsmanagement.co.uk
website www.cadsmanagement.co.uk
Manager T Smith *Coordinator/Key contact* Rosina Chaudry *IT/Administration* Ben Steel

Established in 1990. Sole representation of 60-70 actors. Areas of work include theatre, musicals, television, film, commercials, corporate, voice-overs and role-play. Also represents directors and presenters.

Will consider attending performances at venues within Greater London and elsewhere with 3 weeks' notice. Accepts submissions (with CVs and photographs) from actors previously unknown to the company sent by post or email. Showreels and voice tapes are also accepted. Workshops are run in August each year, and contracts renewed in September. *Commission*: 20%

Jessica Carney Associates

4th Floor, 23 Golden Square, London W1F 9JP
tel 020-7434 4143 *fax* 020-7434 4175
email info@jcarneyassociates.co.uk

Established in 1950. Areas of work include theatre, television, films, commercials and musicals. Also represents technicians and directors.

Cannot consider actors for representation unless they can be seen in performance (not showcase) at a venue within Greater London. Requires 2-3 weeks' notice – or should have good mainstream TV credits. Accepts submissions (with CVs and photographs) from actors previously unknown to the company if sent by post; an sae must be included if a reply is required. Emails should only be sent with a sensible-sized photo & CV attached. Small client list so does not take many new clients on. *Commission*: 10%; *Commercials* 15%

Casting Couch Productions Ltd

213 Trowbridge Road, Bradford-On-Avon, Wiltshire BA15 1EU
tel (01225) 869212 *fax* (01225) 869029
mobile (07932) 785807
email moiratownsend@yahoo.co.uk
Key personnel Moira Townsend

Established in 1991. Sole representation of 25 actors. Areas of work include theatre, musicals, television, film, commercials, corporate and voice-overs.

Will consider attending performances at venues within Greater London and elsewhere, with 2-3 weeks' notice. Accepts submissions (with CVs and photographs, clearly stating age and nationality) from actors previously unknown to the company, preferably by email. An sae should be included for the return of hard-copy CVs and photographs. Actors will only be contacted if the agent would like to meet them. *Commission*: 15% across the board

See entry under *Casting directors* on page 115 for further details.

The Casting Department

277 Chiswick Village, London W4 DF
tel 020-7384 0388 *fax* 020-7736 2221
email jillscastingdpt@aol.com
website www.thecastingdept.co.uk
Key personnel Jill Searle

1 agent represents 400 actors. Areas of work include television and commercials.

Accepts submissions (with CVs and photographs) from actors previously unknown to the company if sent by post.

CFA Management

22 Church Street, Briston, Melton Constable, Norfolk NR24 2LE
tel (01263) 860650 *fax* (01263) 860650
email frances@cfamanagement.fsnet.co.uk
Key personnel Frances Ross

Established in 2000. 1 agent represents 30 actors. Areas of work include theatre, television, film and commercials.

Will consider attending performances in London and East Anglia with 2-3 weeks' notice. Accepts submissions (with CVs and photographs) from actors previously unknown to the company if sent by post. An invitation to telephone for further discussion and possible appointment will be offered if suitable. Items will be returned if an sae has been provided. *Commission*: Theatre 12.5%; Film and Television 15%; Commercials 20%

Chapman Agency

Millennium Point, Curzon Street, Birmingham B4 7XG
tel 0121-331 7220 *fax* 0121-331 7221
email chapmanagency@bsa.bcu.ac.uk
website www.bsa.bcu.ac.uk/graduates

Peter Charlesworth & Associates

2nd Floor, 68 Old Brompton Road, London SW7 3LQ
tel 020-7581 2478 *fax* 020-7589 2922
email petercharlesworth@tiscali.co.uk
Director Peter Charlesworth *Associate* Sharry Clark

Does not welcome unsolicited contact – including performance notices – from actors previously unknown to the company.

Cinel Gabran Management

PO Box 5163, Cardiff CF5 9JB
tel 0845-066 6605 *fax* 0845-066 6601
mobile (07958) 583718
email info@cinelgabran.co.uk
website www.cinelgabran.co.uk
Managing Director/Agent David Chance *Agent* Sioned James

Established in 1988. 2 agents represent 65 actors. Also represents presenters, singers who act, and actors who write. The company has a London client list, although 60% of clients are Wales-based and 75% bilingual. It works in both English and Welsh-language production.

Will consider attending performances at venues in Wales and Central London with 2 weeks' notice. Accepts submissions (with CVs and photographs) from actors previously unknown to the company if sent by post. An sae should be included with CVs and photographs. *Commission*: Varies according to type of work

"Our agency represents actors from any ethnic background, but also specialises in Welsh Language speakers – though not by any means exclusively."

Clic Agency

Rhoslwyn, Rhos Isaf, Cernarfon, Gwynedd LL54 7NF
tel (01286) 831001
email clic@btinternet.com
website www.clicagency.co.uk
Proprietor Helen Pritchard

Established in 2006. 1 agent represents around 50 actors in all areas of work.

Accepts submissions (with CVs & photographs) from actors previously unknown to the company sent by post or email. Encourages enquiries from disabled actors and welcomes showreels, voice tapes, follow-up calls and invitations to view individual actors' websites. *Commission*: varies, but not more than 15%

Cloud Nine Agency

96 Tiber Gardens, Treaty Street, London N1 0XE
tel/fax 020-7278 0029
email cloudnineagency@blueyonder.co.uk
website www.cloudnineagency.co.uk

Established in 1995; 2 agents represent around 80 actors working in theatre, musicals, television, film, commercials and corporate role-play.

Will consider attending performances in North London and the West End given 2 weeks' notice. Accepts submissions (with CVs, showreels, photographs and sae) from actors previously unknown to the agency if sent by post. Will also accept invitations to view an actor's website. Follow-up telephone calls and emails, however, are not welcomed. *Commission*: 20%

Elspeth Cochrane Personal Management

16 Old Town, Clapham, London SW4 0JY
tel 020-7819 6256 *fax* 020-7819 4297
email elspeth@elspethcochrane.co.uk

1 agent represents 40+ actors in theatre, musicals, TV, film, commercials and corporate work. Welcomes performance notices as far in advance as possible, and is prepared to travel to most venues in Greater London. Welcomes letters (by post or email) with CV and photograph from individuals (including disabled actors) previously unknown to the company. Also welcomes showreels. *Commission*: 12.5%

Cole Kitchenn Ltd

212 Strand, London WC2R 1AP
tel 020-7427 5680 (Switchboard)
tel 020-7427 5681 (Personal Management)
tel 020-7427 5682 (Production Department)
fax 020-7353 9639
email info@colekitchenn.com
website www.colekitchenn.com
Theatre/Creatives Agent Stuart Piper *TV/Film Agent* Paul Martin *Assistant* Jo Fell

The agency is a team of 4 representing a select list of actors and creatives, from directors and choreographers to designers and musical directors. Recommends LB Photography, Faye Thomas and John Clark – see separate entry under *Photographers and repro companies*.

Welcomes performance notices within Greater London given 2-3 weeks' notice. Happy to receive letters and emails (with CVs, photographs and showreels) from new actors, but prefers not to receive follow-up telephone calls.

Shane Collins Associates

11-15 Betterton Street, Covent Garden,
London WC2H 9BP
tel 020-7470 8864 *fax* 0870-460 1983
website www.shanecollins.co.uk
Agents Shane Collins, Polly Andrews

Established in 1986, the agency represents around 85 actors working in all areas of the industry.

Will consider attending performances within Greater London given as much notice as possible. Accepts submissions (with CVs and photographs) from actors previously unknown to the company; however, follow-up telephone calls, emails, showreels, voice tapes and invitations to view an actor's website are not welcomed. Photos, CVs and showreels will only be returned if the actor includes a stamped, addressed envelope.

Collis Management

182 Trevelyan Road, London SW17 9LW
tel 020-8767 0196 *fax* 020-8682 0973
email marilyn@collismanagement.co.uk
Agent Marilyn Collis

Established in 1992. 1 agent represents 60 actors working in theatre, musicals, television, film, commercial and corporate work. Will consider attending performances within the Greater London area with 3 weeks' notice. Welcomes letters, emails, showreels and invitations to view websites from actors previously unknown to the company, but not follow-up calls. *Commission*: 10-15%

Conway Van Gelder Grant

3rd Floor, 8-12 Broadwick Street, London W1F 8HN
tel 020-7287 0077 *fax* 020-7287 1940
Agents Jeremy Conway, Nicola van Gelder, John Grant, Liz Nelson

4 agents represent actors working in all areas of the industry.

Will consider attending performances within Greater London and occasionally elsewhere, given 3-4 weeks' notice. Accepts postal submissions (with CVs, photographs and sae to ensure reply) from actors previously unknown to the agency, along with invitations to view an actor's website. Showreels and voice tapes should only be sent if requested after initial contact has been made. Follow-up telephone calls and emails are not welcomed. *Commission*: Varies according to contract

Howard Cooke Associates (HCA)

19 Coulson Street, London SW3 3NA
tel 020-7591 0144
Managing Director/Senior Agent Howard Cooke
Associate Agent Bronwyn Sanders

2 agents represent 40 actors. Areas of work include theatre, musicals, television, film, commercials and corporate.

Will consider attending performances at venues within Greater London and elsewhere (if within easy travelling distance) with 3 weeks' notice. Hard-copy applications (with CVs, photographs and sae) from actors previously unknown to the company are welcome, but email submissions are not accepted. "Having trained as an agent at Frazer-Skemp Management, former actor Howard Cooke formed HCA in 1993. The company specialises in a very personal style of representation over a wide range of media, and is committed to handling a selective number of clients." *Commission*: 10-20% depending on type of engagement

Clive Corner Associates

3 Bainbridge Close, Ham, Richmond,
Surrey TW10 5JJ
tel/fax 020-8332 1910
email cornerassociates@aol.com
website www.cornerassociates.cwc.net
Key personnel Clive Corner, Duncan Stratton, Bill Upton

Established in 1988. 3 agents represent 75 actors. Areas of work include theatre, musicals, television, film, commercials and corporate.

Will consider attending performances at venues within Greater London with 3 weeks' notice. Rarely prepared to travel elsewhere. Accepts submissions (with CVs and photographs) from actors previously unknown to the company if sent by post. Showreels, voice tapes and invitations to view individual actors' websites are not accepted unless requested following receipt of CV/photograph. *Commission*: Theatre and Radio 10%; TV, Film and Corporate 15%; Commercials 20%

Coulter Management Agency

333 Woodlands Road, Glasgow G3 6NG
tel 0141-357 6666
email cmaglasgow@btconnect.com
Agent Anne Coulter

Areas of work include theatre, television, film, commercials, corporate and voice-overs.

Will consider attending performances at venues in Scotland with 3 weeks' notice. Accepts submissions (with CVs and photographs) from actors previously unknown to the company if sent by post. Showreels and voice tapes are also accepted. *Commission*: 7.5-15% (sliding scale)

Covent Garden Management

5 Denmark Street, London WC2H 8LP
tel 020-7240 8400 *fax* 020-7240 8409
email agents@coventgardenmanagement.com

Established in 2002. The agency represents around 30

actors. Areas of work include theatre, musicals, television, film, commercials, corporate and voice-overs. Also represents directors.

Will consider attending performances at venues within Greater London with 2 weeks' notice. Accepts submissions (with CVs and photographs) from actors previously unknown to the company if sent by post. *Commission*: 10-15%

CSM Artists

Honeysuckle Cottage, 93 Telford Way, Yeading, Middlesex UB4 9TH
tel 020-8839 8747
email csmartists@aol.com
Proprietor Angela Radford *Agent* Carole Deamer
Personal Assistant Anthea Francis

Personal management established in 1984. Sole representation of 40-50 actors. Areas of work include theatre, musicals, television, film, commercials and corporate.

Will consider attending performances at venues within Greater London with 3 weeks' notice. Accepts submissions (with CVs and photographs) from actors previously unknown to the company if sent by post. An sae must be included. *Commission*: 15%

Curtis Brown Ltd

Haymarket House, 28-29 Haymarket, London SW1Y 4SP
tel 020-7393 4400 *fax* 020-7393 4401
email info@curtisbrown.co.uk
website www.curtisbrown.co.uk
Agents Jacquie Drewe, Maxine Hoffman, Sarah MacCormick, Sarah Spear, Kate Staddon

One of Europe's oldest and largest independent literary and media agencies. Established over 100 years ago, there are now more than 20 agents within the Book, Media, Actors and Presenters Divisions, 5 of whom represent actors. Also represents writers, directors, playwrights and celebrities.

Submissions should be sent by post and addressed to 'Actors Agents'. They should include a covering letter with email address, CV, photograph, showreel on VHS (if actor has one) and sae for the return of the showreel. Tries to respond within 4-6 weeks. Does not meet potential clients before viewing their work. Does not accept email or faxed submissions. *Commission*: 12.5-15%

Lisa Dennis Management Ltd

Summit House, London Road, Bracknell RG12 2AQ
tel (01344) 707342
email agents@lisad.co.uk
website www.lisad.co.uk
Agent Lisa Dennis

2 agents represent 40-50 actors. Areas of work include theatre, musicals, television, film, commercials and corporate.

Will consider attending performances at venues within Greater London and sometimes elsewhere, given as much notice as possible. Accepts submissions (CV with photograph embedded is acceptable) from actors previously unknown to the company if sent by post. Applicants sending emails should ring first to let the agent know to expect them. Welcomes enquiries from disabled actors.

David Daly

Associates – see entry under Daly Pearson Associates

Daly Pearson Associates

586a King's Road, Chelsea, London SW6 2DX
tel 020-7384 1036 *fax* 020-7610 9512
email agent@dalypearson.co.uk
website www.dalypearson.co.uk
Agents Paul Pearson, Sophie Hurst

Established in 2005 by David Daly and Paul Pearson who merged the lists from their 2 respective companies.

Manchester office

16 King Street, Knutsford, Manchester WA16 6DL
tel 01565-631 999 *fax* 01565-755 334
email north@dalypearson.co.uk
Agents David Daly, Clare Marshall

Chris Davis Management

Tenbury House, 36 Teme Street, Tenbury Wells, Worcestershire WR15 8AA
tel (01584) 819005 *fax* (01584) 819076
email info@cdm-ltd.com
website www.cdm-ltd.com
Agent Kerry Foley

Areas of work are theatre, musicals, television, film, commercials and corporate. 2 agents represent 80 actors; directors, choreographers, designers and musical directors are also represented.

Will consider attending performances within Greater London and elsewhere, given as much notice as possible. Welcomes letters (with CVs & photographs) from actors previously unknown to the agency, sent by post or email. Does not welcome follow-up calls. Accepts showreels, voice tapes and invitations to view individual actors' websites. Encourages applications from actors with disabilities.

Davis Bishop Associates

Cotton's Farmhouse, 28 Whiston Road, Cogenhoe, Northamptonshire NN7 1NL
tel (01604) 891487
email admin@cottonsfarmhouse.freeserve.co.uk
Agents Lena Davis, John Bishop

Established in 1986. Number of actors varies. Areas of work include theatre, musicals, television, film, commercials, corporate, voice-overs. Also represent other skills within the profession. *Commission*: 10%-20%

Will consider attending performances in Greater London with plenty of notice. Accepts submissions (with CVs and photographs) from actors unknown to them. Follow-up calls and email submissions are not welcomed.

Caroline Dawson Associates

125 Gloucester Road, London SW7 4TE
tel 020-7373 3323 *fax* 020-7373 1110
email cda@cdalondon.com

3 agents represent 60 actors.

Will consider attending performances at venues within Greater London with 3 weeks' notice. Accepts submissions (with CVs and photographs) from actors previously unknown to the company if sent by post. Showreels, voice tapes and invitations to view individual actors' websites are also accepted. *Commission*: Variable

Felix de Wolfe

Kingsway House, 103 Kingsway, London WC2B 6QX
tel 020-7242 5066 *fax* 020-7242 8119

3 agents represent 100 actors. Areas of work include theatre, musicals, television, film, commercials, corporate and voice-overs. Also represents directors and producers.

Will consider attending performances at venues within Greater London and elsewhere, given 10 days' notice. Accepts submissions (with CVs and photographs) from actors previously unknown to the company if sent by post. *Commission*: Variable

Dealers Agency Belfast

22 North Street Arcade, Belfast BT1 1PB
tel 028-9031 1075
email info@dealersagency.co.uk
website www.dealersagency.co.uk
Agents Patrick Duncan, Philip Young

Established 1997 and represents about 250 clients.

DP Management

1 Euston Road, London NW1 2SA
tel 020-7843 4331 *fax* 020-7278 3466
email danny@dpmanagement.org
Agent Danny Pellerini

Founded in 2005, 1 agent represents 60 actors for all forms of acting work. Welcomes performance notices with as much notice as possible. Welcomes letters (with CV and photograph) from individuals previously unknown to the company, including disabled actors. Welcomes showreels and invitations to view individual's websites. *Commission*: 10-15%

DQ Management

Suite 2, Kingsway House, 134–140 Church Road, Hove, East Sussex BN3 2DL
tel (01273) 721221 *fax* (01273) 779065
email info@dqmanagement.com
website www.dqmanagement.com
Senior Partners Peter Davis, Kate Davis

Established in 2003. Areas of work include theatre, musicals, television, film, commercials and corporate. 2 agents represent 40 actors. Will consider attending performances within the Greater London area and elsewhere with at least 2 weeks' notice. Accepts submissions (with CVs and photographs) from actors previously unknown to the company if sent by post. Invitations to view individuals' websites, showreels or voice tapes are also accepted. Welcomes enquiries from disabled actors. *Commission*: Theatre 10%; West End 12.5%; TV/Film/Commercials 15%

Bryan Drew Ltd

Mezzanine, Quadrant House, 80-82 Regent Street, London W1B 5AU
tel 020-7437 2293 *fax* 020-7437 0561
email bryan@bryandrewltd.com
Managing Director Bryan Drew *Personal Assistant* Mina Parmar

Established in 1963. 2 agents represent 40 actors. Areas of work include theatre, musicals, television, film, commercials, corporate and voice-overs. Also represents writers. *Commission*: 12.5-15%

Kenneth Earle Personal Management

214 Brixton Road, London SW9 6AP
tel 020-7274 1219 *fax* 020-7274 9529
email kennethearle@agents-uk.com
website entertainment-kennethearle.co.uk

Established in 2000. 1 agent represents 10-15 actors. Areas of work include theatre, musicals, television, film, commercials, corporate and voice-overs.

Will consider attending performances at venues in Greater London and elsewhere with 1 week's notice. Accepts submissions (with CVs and photographs) from actors previously unknown to the company if sent by post. Follow-up telephone calls and invitations to view individual actors' websites are also accepted. Showreels and voice tapes should only be sent on request. *Commission*: 10-15%

Susi Earnshaw Management

The Bull Theatre, 68 High Street, Barnet, Herts EN5 5SJ
tel 020-8441 5010 *fax* 020-8364 9618
email casting@susiearnshaw.co.uk
website www.susiearnshawmanagement.com
Agents Susi Earnshaw, Melissa Gillespie, Jessie Tsang, Robin Parsons

Established in 1989. 4 agents and bookers represent 30 adult actors, 60 child performers, and various tribute bands. Areas of work include theatre, musicals, television, film, corporate, live entertainment, dance videos, radio and commercials.

Prefers submissions via email (with CVs and photos). *Commission*: Theatre 10%; TV, Film and Commercials 15%

Debbie Edler Management

Little Friars Cottage, Lombard Street, Eynsham, Oxon OX29 4HT

tel (01761) 436631 *fax* (01761) 436631
email dem2005@eircom.net
website www.dem.1colony.com
Directors Debbie Edler, David Edler

Established 2005. 2 agents represent 200 actors. Areas of work include theatre, musicals, television, film, commercials and corporate. *Commission*: between 5% and 15%.

Will consider attending performances in Greater London and elsewhere with plenty of notice. Accepts submissions (with CVs and photographs) from actors previously unknown to the agency. Follow-up calls are not welcomed. Preferred method for receiving CVs and photographs is via email. Invitations to view individual actors' websites and showreels are also accepted. Welcomes enquiries from disabled actors.

Annie Elliott Management
Top Floor, 19 Camden Passage, London N1 8ED
tel 020-7226 4863
email annieelliottmgmt@aol.com
Agent Clare Allen

Established in 2002. 1 agent represents 15 actors. Areas of work include theatre, musicals, television, film, commercials and corporate.

Will consider attending performances at venues within Greater London and occasionally elsewhere, given as much notice as possible. Accepts submissions (with CVs and photographs) from actors previously unknown to the company sent by post or email. Follow-up telephone calls, showreels, voice tapes and invitations to view individual actors' websites are also accepted. *Commission*: Theatre 5%; Technical 15%

June Epstein Associates
62 Compayne Gardens, London NW6 3RY
tel 020-7328 0864 (main number) or 020-7372 1928
fax 020-7328 0684
email june@june-epstein-associates.co.uk

Established in 1973; represents approximately 40 actors working in theatre, musicals, television, film commercials and corporate role-play. Recommends the photographers Jonathan Dockar-Drysdale (**fact-d@lineone.net**) and Peter Simpkin (**petersimpkin@aol.com**).

Will consider attending performances within Greater London given 2-3 weeks' notice. Accepts postal submissions (with CVs and photographs) from actors previously unknown to the agency. Welcomes voice tapes from singers, follow-up telephone calls and showreels, but prefers not to receive emails. *Commission*: 10%; Commercials 15%

Et-Nik-A Prime Management and Castings Ltd
30 Great Portland Street, London W1W 8QU
tel 020-7299 3555 *fax* 020-7299 3558
email info@et-nik-a.co.uk
website www.et-nik-a.co.uk
Managing Director Aldo Arcilla

Established in 2000. 3 agents represent 80 actors. Areas of work include theatre, musicals, television, film, commercials, corporate and voice-overs.

Will consider attending performances at venues within Greater London and occasionally elsewhere with 1-2 weeks' notice. Accepts submissions (with CVs and photographs) from actors previously unknown to the company if sent by post. Invitations to view individual actors' websites are also accepted. Showreels and voice tapes should only be sent on request. *Commission*: Theatre 10%; TV and Films 15%; Commercials 20%

Ethnics Artiste Agency
86 Elphinstone Road, Walthamstow, London E17 5EX
tel 020-8523 4242 *fax* 020-8523 4523
email info@ethnicsaa.co.uk
website www.ethnicsartisteagency.com
Managing Director Pauline Oni

Founded in 1997. 2 agents represent 60 actors in all areas of acting work. The company represents multicultural and international performers and artistes from across the globe, including actors, singers, dancers, musicians and martial artists from Asia, Africa and Europe, and performers of ethnic-minority British origin. Specialises in representation of performers of colour and those with fluent foreign-language skills. Welcomes performance notices 2-3 weeks in advance; will consider travelling to shows within Greater London. Welcomes letters (with CVs and photographs) from individuals previously unknown to the company if sent by post but not by email. Welcomes showreels, but not invitations to view individuals' websites. Welcomes representation enquiries from disabled actors.

– see entry under WIS Celtic Management on page 96

Stephanie Evans Associates (formerly Vocalworks International)
Rivington House, 82 Great Eastern Street, London EC2A 3JF
tel/fax 0870-609 2629
email steph@stephanie-evans.com
website www.stephanie-evans.com
Director Stephanie Evans

Established in 2003. 1 agent represents 60 actors. Areas of work include theatre, musicals, television, film, commercials and corporate.

Will consider attending performances in England and Wales with at least 1 month's notice. Accepts submissions (with CVs, photographs and showreels) from actors previously unknown to the company if sent by post. Invitations to view individual actors' websites are also accepted. Welcomes enquiries from disabled actors. *Commission*: 10%

Evolution Management
Studio 21, The Truman Brewery Building, 91 Brick Lane, London E1 6QB

tel 020-7053 2128 *fax* 020-7375 2752
email info@evolutionmngt.com
website www.evolutionmngt.com
Development Directors Loftus Burton, Henrik Bjork

Founded in 1999; 3 agents represent around 30 actors working in theatre, musicals, television, film and commercials. The agency also represents directors, make-up artists and presenters.

Welcomes performance notices within Greater London and occasionally further afield, given a minimum of 2 weeks' notice. Also accepts letters and emails with CVs and photographs, showreels and voice tapes. Always provide an sae if you wish your material to be returned. Advises actors to have monologues prepared when coming to see the agency – especially if agents have not had the opportunity to see their work beforehand. *Commission*: Theatre 10-15%; Commercials 20%

Feast Management

1st Floor, 34 Upper Street, London N1 0PN
tel 020-7354 5216 *fax* 020-7354 8995
email office@feastmanagement.co.uk
Agent Sadie Feast

3 agents represent actors. Areas of work include theatre, musicals, television, film, commercials, corporate and voice-overs.

Will consider attending performances in the London area if plenty of notice is given. Accepts submissions (with CVs and photographs) from actors previously unknown to them.

Colette Fenlon Personal Management

26 Hope Street, Liverpool LL1 9BX
tel 0151-707 7703 *fax* 0151-706 0838
email collettefenlon@hotmail.com
Director Colette Fenlon

Established in 1989, the agency represents 10 actors working in theatre, musicals, television, film and commercials.

Will consider attending performances within Greater London and beyond, given as much notice as possible. In general, does not welcome representation enquiries from actors unknown to the agency. *Commission*: 15-20%

First Act Personal Management

2 St Michaels, New Arley, Coventry CV7 8PY
tel (01676) 540285 *fax* (01676) 542777
email firstactpm@aol.com
website www.spotlightagent.info/firstact
Agent John Burton

Established in 2003. 1 agent represents 25 actors. Areas of work include theatre, musicals, television, film, commercials, corporate and voice-overs.

Will consider attending performances in England and Wales with at least 2 weeks' notice. Accepts submissions (with CVs and photographs) from actors

previously unknown to the company if sent by post. Invitations to view individual actors' websites, showreels or voice tapes are also accepted. Welcomes enquiries from disabled actors. "Always enclose an sae." *Commission*: 10-15%

Sharon Foster

15A Hollybank Road, Birmingham B13 0RF
tel 0121-224 7676 *fax* 0121-224 7677
email mail@sharonfoster.co.uk
website www.magnetmanagement.co.uk

1 agent represents around 40 actors working in theatre, musicals, television, radio, film, commercials and corporate role-play.

Will consider attending performances given sufficient notice. Accepts submissions (with CVs and photographs) from actors previously unknown to the agency sent by post or email. Follow-up telephone calls, showreels, voice tapes and invitations to view an actor's website are also accepted. *Commission*: 10-15%

Fushion

27 Old Gloucester Street, London WC1N 3XX
tel (08700) 111100 *fax* (08700) 111020
email info@fushion-uk.com
website www.fushionpukkabosh.com
Key personnel Lawrence Endacott, Judy Oliver

Established in 1998 and re-branded in 2004, Fushion Pukka Bosh is a sole management agency based in London and New York with an intimate portfolio of 25 leading performing and recording artistes. "As we deal only with featured established artistes, please – no unsolicited requests."

Hilary Gagan Associates

187 Drury Lane, London WC2B 5QU
tel 020-7404 8794 *fax* 020-430 1869
email hilary@hgassoc.freeserve.co.uk
Assistant Shiv Coard

3 agents represent approximately 100 actors. Areas of work include theatre, musicals, television, film, commercials, corporate, voice-overs. Also represent directors and choreographers.

Will consider attending performances in Greater London with at least 2 weeks' notice. Accepts submissions (with CVs and photographs with name on back of photograph) from actors previously unknown to the agency (include sae). Invitations to view individual actors' website, showreels and voice tapes are also accepted. Follow-up calls are welcomed. Welcomes enquiries from disabled actors. *Commission*: between 7.5% and 15%.

Galloways One

15 Lexham Mews, London W8 6JW
tel 020-7376 2288 *fax* 020-7376 2416
email hugh@gallowaysone.com
website www.gallowaysone.com

Directors Hugh Galloway, Jill Moore *Personal Assistant* Isabelle Desrochers

Established in 1971. Agency represents 150 actors. Areas of work include television, commercials, corporate and voice-overs, with the primary focus on commercials.

Will consider attending performances at venues within Greater London and occasionally elsewhere, given as much notice as possible. Accepts submissions (with CVs and photographs) from actors previously unknown to the company if sent by post. Enclose an appropriately sized sae for the return of personal details. *Commission*: TV 10%; Other 18%

Gardner Herrity (formerly Kerry Gardner Management)

24 Conway Street, London W1T 6BG
tel 020-7388 0088 *fax* 020-7388 0688
email info@gardnerherrity.co.uk
Key contact Andy Herrity

Areas of work include theatre, musicals, television and film. Will consider attending performances within the Greater London area with at least 3 weeks' notice. Accepts submissions (with CV and photograph) from actors previously unknown to the company if sent by post, but not by email. Also accepts showreels, voice tapes, and invitations to view individual actors' websites. Welcomes enquiries from disabled actors. *Commission*: 10%

Garricks

Angel House, 76 Mallinson Road,
London SW11 1BN
tel 020-7738 1600 *fax* 020-7738 1881
email megan@garricks.net
Key personnel Megan Willis

Established in 1981. Areas of work include theatre, television, film, commercials and corporate. Also represents directors and presenters.

Will consider attending performances at venues within Greater London and elsewhere with 2 weeks' notice. Accepts submissions (with CVs and photographs) from actors previously unknown to the company sent by post or email. Invitations to view individual actors' websites are also accepted. *Commission*: TV, Film and Theatre 10%; Commercials 15%

Gilbert & Payne Personal Management

Room 236, 2nd Floor, Linen Hall,
162-168 Regent Street, London W1B 5TB
tel 020-7734 7505 *fax* 020-7494 3787
email ee@gilbertandpayne.com
Director Elena Gilbert *Key personnel* Elaine Payne

Established in 1996. 2 agents represent 50 actors. Areas of work include theatre, musicals, television, film, commercials and corporate, with a particular emphasis on musical theatre. Also represents choreographers.

Will consider attending performances at venues in Greater London with a minimum of 1 week's notice. Accepts submissions (with CVs and photographs) from actors previously unknown to the company if sent by post. Follow-up telephone calls are also accepted. *Commission*: Theatre 10%

Global Artists

23 Haymarket, London SW1Y 4DG
tel 020-7839 4888 *fax* 020-7839 4555
email info@globalartists.co.uk
website www.globalartists.co.uk

A personal management company representing professional actors and actresses. Areas of work include theatre, musical theatre, television, film, commercials and corporate. Also represents a limited number of theatre designers, choreographers, directors and musical directors.

Accepts submissions from actors previously unknown to the company sent by post or email. Does not welcome telephone enquiries.

Grantham-Hazeldine

Suite 605, The Linen Hall, 162-168 Regent St,
London W1B 5TG
tel 020-7038 3737/8 *fax* 020-7038 3739
email agents@granthamhazeldine.com
website www.granthamhazeldine.com
Partners John Grantham, Caroline Hazeldine

Established in 1984. 2 agents represent 75 actors. Areas of work include theatre, musicals, television, film, commercials, corporate and voice-overs. Also represents writers and stunt co-ordinators.

Will consider attending performances at venues in Greater London and elsewhere with 1 month's notice. Accepts submissions (with CVs and photographs) from actors previously unknown to the company if sent by post. Will not accept showreels and voice tapes at the initial stage of contact. *Commission*: Theatre and Radio 10% plus VAT; TV and Film 15% plus VAT

Darren Gray Management

2 Marston Lane, Portsmouth, Hampshire PO3 5TW
tel 023-9269 9973 *fax* 023-9267 7227
email darren.gray1@virgin.net
website www.darrengraymanagement.co.uk
Managing Director Darren Gray

Established in 1994. 2 agents represent 60 actors in both England and Australia. Agency mainly represents Australian actors, the majority of whom come from Australian soap operas. Areas of work include theatre, musicals, television, film, commercials, corporate and voice-overs. Also represents directors, producers, writers and presenters.

Will consider attending performances at venues within Greater London and elsewhere at whatever notice possible. Accepts submissions (with CVs and photographs) from actors previously unknown to the company sent by post or email. Showreels, voice tapes and invitations to view individual actors' websites are also accepted. Welcomes enquiries from disabled actors. *Commission*: 10%

Joan Gray Personal Management

29 Sudbury Court Island, Sunbury-on-Thames, Middlesex TW16 5PP

1 agent represents a small number of actors. Areas of work include theatre, musicals, television, film, commercials, corporate and voice-overs. Not looking to take on any new actors at the moment. *Commission*: 10%

Grays Management Ltd

Panther House, 38 Mount Pleasant, London WC1X 0AP
tel 020-7278 1054 *fax* 020-7278 1091
email e-mail@graysmanagement.idps.co.uk
website www.graysman.com
Agent Mary Nelson

2 agents represent approximately 90 actors working in theatre, musicals, television, film, commercials and corporate role-play.

Will consider attending performances within Greater London given 1 week's notice. Advises actors to contact the agency only when currently appearing in a production, as the agency does not welcome general representation enquiries. *Commission*: Theatre 10%; Screen 15%

Katherine Gregor Associates

Colombo Centre, 34-68 Colombo Street, London SE1 8DP
tel 020-7261 9466 *fax* 020-7261 9466
email agent@katherinegregorassociates.co.uk
website www.katherinegregorassociates.co.uk
Key personnel Katherine Gregor

A personal management agency representing actors and directors. Areas of work include theatre, musicals, television, film, commercials and corporate. Accepts applications for representation by email only (please send CV, photo and covering letter). *Commission*: 12.5% for actors

Sandra Griffin Management Ltd

6 Ryde Place, Richmond Road, East Twickenham TW1 2EH
tel 020-8891 5676 *fax* 020-8744 1812
email office@sandragriffin.com
Key personnel Sandra Griffin, Howard Roberts

Established in 1989. Represents actors in theatre, musicals, television, film, commercial and corporate work.

Welcomes written enquiries from actors seeking representation (with CV, photograph and sae to

ensure reply), but does not accept unsolicited demo tapes, DVDs or showreels. Will consider seeing potential clients in current theatre productions, if in easily accessible locations. *Commission*: Varies according to contract

Louise Gubbay Associates

26 Westmore Road, Tatsfield, Kent TN16 2AX
tel (01959) 573080
email louise@louisegubbay.com
website www.louisegubbay.com
Managing Director Louise Gubbay

Founded in 2006. Works in theatre, musicals, television, film, commercials and corporate. 1 agent represents 40 actors. Will consider attending performances within Greater London given 2 weeks' notice. Welcomes letters (with CVs & photographs) from individual actors previously unknown to the agency if sent by post; encourages enquiries from actors with disabilities. Does not welcome unsolicited approaches by email. Accepts showreels, voice tapes, and invitations to view individual actors' websites. "LGA is an Associate Member of The Agents Association." *Commission*: Varies

Hall James Personal Management

PO Box 604, Pinner, Middlesex HA5 9GH
tel 020-8429 8111 *fax* 020-8868 5825
email info@halljames.co.uk
website www.halljames.co.uk
Directors Sam Hall, Stori James

Established in 2006. Areas of work include musicals, television, film, commercials and corporate. 2 agents represent around 50 actors; also represents theatre directors and choreographers. Welcomes performance notices, letters (with CVs) from individual actors previously unknown to the agency, and showreels. *Commission*: 10%

The Harris Agency

PO Box 308, Northwood, Middlesex HA6 2NT
tel (01923) 822744 *fax* (01923) 822253
mobile (07956) 388716
email theharrisagency@btconnect.com
Agent Sharon Harris

Established in 1977. 1 agent represents around 50 actors. Recommends Mad Photography (**www.mad-photography.co.uk**). Welcomes performance notices within Greater London, and elsewhere (seasonally, for example at Christmas) given at least 1 week's notice. Welcomes letters (with CVs & photographs) from actors previously unknown to the agency, sent by post or email. Also accepts follow-up calls, showreels, voice tapes, and invitations to view individual actors' websites. Encourages enquiries from actors with disabilities. *Commission*: Theatre 10%; TV, Film, Commercials 15%

Harris Personal Management Ltd

64-66 Millman Street, London WC1N 3EF
tel 020-7430 9890 *fax* 020-7430 9229

email agent@harrispersonalmanagement.co.uk
website www.harrispersonalmanagement.co.uk
Managing Director/Senior Agent Melanie Harris
Agents Georgina Coombs, Rosie Nimmo

Established in 2001; 2 agents represent up to 50 actors. Areas of work include theatre, television, film, commercials and corporate.

Will consider attending performances at venues within Greater London given as much notice as possible. Accepts submissions (with CVs, photographs and showreels if possible) from actors previously unknown to the company if sent by post. Enclosing an sae will ensure a reply. *Commission*: 12.5-15% depending on the type of work

Harrispearson Management Ltd – see entry under Daly Pearson Associates

Hatton McEwan

PO Box 37385, London N1 7XF
tel 020-7253 4770 *fax* 020-7251 9081
email info@thetalent.biz
website www.thetalent.biz

Established in 1988, the agency represents actors working in theatre, musicals, television, film, commercials and corporate. Other clients include directors, composers and designers.

Will consider attending performances within Greater London (but rarely elsewhere) given 4 weeks' notice. Accepts submissions (with CVs and photographs) from actors previously unknown to the company sent by post or email. Showreels, voice tapes and invitations to view an actor's website are also accepted, but follow-up telephone calls are not welcomed.

Henry's Agency

53 Westbury, Rochford, Essex SS4 1UL
tel (01702) 541413 *fax* (01702) 541413
email info@henrysagency.co.uk
website www.henrysagency.co.uk

Established in 1995; 1 agent represents 35 actors. Areas of work include theatre, musicals, television, film, commercials and corporate.

Will consider attending performances at venues within Greater London with 2 weeks' notice. Accepts submissions (with CVs and photographs) from actors previously unknown to the company if sent by post. Emails are accepted if attachments consist of Word documents or small jpeg files. Follow-up telephone calls, showreels and voice tapes are also accepted. Recommends the photographer Ash (**ash@ashphotomedia.com**). *Commission*: Variable

Edward Hill Management

Teddington Film and Television Studios, Broom Road, Teddington, Middlesex TW11 9NT
tel 020-8614 2678 *fax* 020-8614 2694

email hill@management.freeserve.co.uk

1 agent represents 40 actors. Will accept submissions (with CVs and photographs) from actors previously unknown to the company if sent by post. *Commission*: 10-15%

Elinor Hilton Associates

BAC, Lavender Hill, London SW11 5TF
tel 020-7738 9574 *fax* 020-7924 4636
email agent@elinorhilton.com
website www.elinorhilton.com

Represents actors for film, TV, radio and theatre. The agency was established in 2003, and currently has 60 actors.

Offers representation only after seeing an actor perform. This can either be in a theatre production or a showreel. Will consider attending shows with at least 2 weeks' notice. Showreels are accepted by email or post. Submissions to the agency are preferred via email, although postal applications are also considered. Welcomes enquiries from disabled actors. *Commission*: 12.5% across all disciplines

Dee Hindin Associates

9B Brunswick Mews, Great Cumberland Place, London W1H 7FB
tel 020-7723 3706 *fax* 020-7258 0651

Established in 1991. Represents 15-20 actors. Areas of work include theatre, musicals, television, film, commercials, corporate and voice-overs.

Recommends the photographer Chris Baker (020-8441 3851). *Commission*: 12.5-15% depending on the type of work

Liz Hobbs Group Ltd

65 London Road, Newark, Notts NG24 1RZ
tel 0870-070 2702 *fax* 0870-333 7009
email casting@lizhobbsgroup.com
website www.lizhobbsgroup.com
Managing Director Liz Hobbs MBE *Agent* Harriet Robson

2 agents represent 50-60 actors. Areas of work include theatre, musicals, television, film, commercials, corporate and voice-overs.

Will consider attending performances at venues in Greater London and elsewhere with 1-2 months' notice. Accepts unsolicited CVs / head shots, but not unsolicited show or voice reels. *Commission*: 10-15% depending on the type of work

Hobson's Actors

62 Chiswick High Road, Chiswick, London W4 1SY
tel 020-8995 3628 *fax* 020-8996 5350
website www.hobsons-international.com
Drama Agent Christina Beyer *Commercial Agent* Linda Sacks

Areas of work include theatre, musicals, television, film, commercials and corporate.

Will consider attending performances at venues within Greater London given 2 weeks' notice. Accepts submissions (with CVs and photographs) from actors previously unknown to the company if sent by post. Showreels are also accepted.

Hamilton Hodell Ltd

Fifth Floor, 66-68 Margaret Street,
London W1W 8SR
tel 020-7636 1221 *fax* 020-7636 1226
email info@hamiltonhodell.co.uk
website www.hamiltonhodell.co.uk

3 agents represent 80 actors, working in leading roles in film, television, theatre and radio productions.

Jane Hollowood Associates Ltd

Apartment 17, 113 Newton Street,
Manchester M1 1AE
tel 0161-237 9141 *mobile* (07801) 432842
email janehollowood@ukonline.co.uk
Agents Jane Hollowood, John Gully

Established in 1998; 2 agents represent approx. 75 actors working in many areas of the industry.

Will consider attending performances within Greater London and potentially elsewhere, depending on diary commitments and provided that 2-3 weeks' notice is given. Accepts postal submissions (with CVs and photographs) from actors previously unknown to the agency. Showreels and voice tapes should only be sent on request, and follow-up telephone calls and emails are unwelcome. *Commission*: Theatre 10%; Radio, Role-play and Voice-overs 12%; Television, Film and Commercials 15%

Amanda Howard Associates

21 Berwick Street, London W1F 0PZ
tel 020-7287 9277 *fax* 020-7287 7785
email mail@amandahowardassociates.co.uk
website www.amandahowardassociates.co.uk
Agents Amanda Fitzalan Howard, Mark Price, Darren Rugg, Kirsten Wright *Voice-over Agent* Annette Parnell

5 agents represent around 100 actors working in theatre, musicals, television, radio, film, commercials, corporate role-play and voice-overs. Other clients include writers, broadcasters, designers, directors and composers.

Will consider attending performances within Greater London given 2-3 weeks' notice. Welcomes submissions (with CVs, photographs, showreels, voice tapes and sae) from actors previously unknown to the agency if sent by post. Does not accept email applications or invitations to view an actor's website. *Commission*: 10-15% depending on the medium

Hunwick Hughes Ltd

Suite 2F, 45A George Street, Edinburgh EH2 2HT
tel 0131-225 3585 *fax* 0131-225 4535
email maryam@hunwickhughes.com
website www.hunwickhughes.com
Agent Maryam Hunwick *Assistant* Amanda Stewart

Personal management agency established in 1999. One agent represents actors in all media including several BAFTA and BIFA award-winning stage, screen and television artists.

Will consider attending performances at venues within Greater London and in Scotland given 4 weeks' notice. Accepts submissions (with CVs and photographs) from actors previously unknown to the company if sent by post. Will also accept showreels. *Commission*: Theatre 10%; TV and Broadcast Media 12.5%; Commercials 15%

Icon Actors Management

Tanzaro House, Ardwick Green North,
Manchester M12 6FZ
tel 0161-273 3344 *fax* 0161-273 4567
email info@iconactors.net
website www.iconactors.net
Agent Nancy Lang

Established in 2000. Areas of work include theatre, musicals, television, film, commercials, corporate and voice-overs.

Image Management

The Media Centre, 94 Roundhill Crescent,
Brighton BN2 3FR
tel 01273-695 290
email mail@imagemanagement.co.uk
website www.imagemanagement.co.uk
Agent Adam Campbell

"We are always interested to hear from experienced actors who are seeking new representation. However, in order to market you effectively it is essential that you have the following:

• A current Spotlight page
• Recent showreel on DVD
• Good quality recent 10x8in b&w headshots
• Recent professional feature film or terrestrial TV credits
• Voice clips on MP3 or disk.

Hard copy (only) applications should be sent to the address above. We treat each application with the utmost discretion. If you would like your material returned please enclose an sae."

Imperial Personal Management Ltd

102 Kirkstall Road, Leeds LS3 1JA
tel 0113-244 3222
email katie@ipmcasting.com
website www.ipmcasting.com
Managing Director Katie Ross

Established in 2007. 4 agents represent 30-50 actors working in television and film; also has a subsidiary company, IPM Crew. Recommends Imperial Photography (email: info@ipmcasting.com).

Welcomes performance notices within the Greater London and Northern areas (within 50 miles of the company's postcode), and prefers 1 month's notice if possible. Welcomes letters (with CVs and photographs) from individual actors previously unknown to the agency, sent by post or email. Accepts follow-up telephone calls, showreels and voice tapes, and welcomes invitations to view individual actors' websites. Encourages enquiries from actors with disabilities. *Commission*: 10-15%

Independent Talent Group Ltd (former ICM, London)

Oxford House, 76 Oxford Street, London W1D 1BS

11 agents represent actors. Areas of work include theatre, musicals, television, film, commercials, corporate and voice-overs. Also represents directors, writers, technicians and presenters.

Will consider attending performances at venues within Greater London. Accepts submissions (with CVs and photographs) from actors previously unknown to the company if sent by post. 10x8in photographs are preferred. *Commission*: 10%

Inter-City Casting

Portland Tower, Portland Street, Manchester M1 3LF
tel/fax 0161-238 4950
email intercitycasting@btconnect.com
website www.iccast.co.uk
Agent Caroline Joynt

Established in 1983. 2 agents represent approximately 60 actors. Areas of work include theatre, musicals, television, film, commercials and corporate.

Will consider attending performances at venues in Manchester and Liverpool. Accepts submissions (with CVs and photographs) from actors previously unknown to the company if sent by post. Showreels, voice tapes and invitations to view individual actors' websites also accepted. Recommends the photographer Michael Pollard (see entry under *Photographers and repro companies* on page 406 for further details). *Commission*: 10-12.5% plus VAT

International Artistes Ltd

4th Floor, Holborn Hall, 193-197 High Holborn, London WC1V 7BD
website www.intart.co.uk

7 agents represent approximately 220 actors. Also represents producers, directors, casting directors, presenters, light-entertainment artists and comedians. The company has a separate voice-over department. (Artists are represented by a total of 11 agents.)

Will consider attending performances at venues within Greater London and occasionally elsewhere, given 4 weeks' notice. Accepts submissions (with CVs and photographs) from actors previously unknown to the company if sent by post. Showreels, voice tapes and invitations to view individual actors' websites are also accepted. *Commission*: 10-12.5% plus VAT

International Theatre & Music Ltd

Garden Studios, 11-15 Betterton Street, Covent Garden, London WC2H

tel 020-7470 8786 *fax* 020-7379 0801
email info@it-m.co.uk
website www.it-m.co.uk
Managing Director Piers Chater-Robinson *Personal Assistant* Claire Lloyd *Assistant* Emma Brown

A team of 3 with musical backgrounds representing 70 actors and creatives. Areas of work include musicals, theatre, opera, TV and commercials. All artistes must have exceptional singing and/or instrumental skills. Will consider attending performances at venues in Greater London and occasionally elsewhere, given as much notice as possible. Accepts submissions (with CVs and photographs) from actors with the requisite skills if sent by post. Will also accept voice tapes/CDs of singing voices. *Commission*: Theatre 12.5%; Film and TV 15%

iPM Crew

102 Kirkstall Road, Leeds LS3 1JA
tel 0113-244 3222
email lee@ipmcasting.com
website www.ipmcasting.com
Head of Department Lee Johnson

Established in 2008; a subsidiary company of Imperial Personal Management Ltd. Main areas of work are television, film, commercials, corporate and voice-over. All skills required by professional crew are represented, and the agency welcomes relevant unsolicited approaches by post, email or telephone. Encourages enquiries from actors with disabilities. *Commission*: 10-20%

Alex Jay Personal Management

8 Higher Newmarket Road, Newmarket GL6 0RP
tel (01453) 834783 *fax* (01453) 834783
email alexjay@alex-jay-pm.freeserve.co.uk
Director Alex Jay

Established in 1992. 2 agents represent 30 actors. Areas of work include theatre, musicals, television, film, commercials, corporate and voice-overs.

Will consider attending performances in Greater London and elsewhere with 2 weeks' notice. Accepts submissions (CVs and photographs) from actors previously unknown to the agency. Encourages enquiries from disabled actors. Welcomes showreels and invitations to view actors' websites. *Commission*: 12-20%

JB Associates

4th Floor, Manchester House, 84 - 86 Princess Street, Manchester M1 1DN
tel 0161-237 1808 *fax* 0161-237 1809
email info@j-b-a.net
website www.j-b-a.net
Proprietor John Basham

Established in 1996. 2 agents represent 60 actors. Areas of work include theatre, musicals, television, film, commercials, corporate and voice-overs.

Agents and Casting Directors

Will consider attending performances at venues in the North and occasionally within Greater London, given 3-4 weeks' notice. Accepts submissions (with CVs and photographs) from actors previously unknown to the company if sent by post. Will also accept showreels, voice tapes, and invitations to view individual actors' websites. *Commission*: Theatre 10%; TV 15%

Jeffrey & White Management

16-19 Southampton Place, London WC1A 2AJ
tel 020-7745 7181
Partners Judith Jeffrey, Jeremy White *Key personnel* Laura Elgar

Established in 1986. 3 agents represent 85 actors. Areas of work include theatre, musicals, television, film, commercials and corporate.

Will consider attending performances given as much notice as possible. Accepts submissions (with CVs and photographs) from actors previously unknown to the company if sent by post. *Commission*: Theatre, Film and TV 12.5%; Commercials 15%

JGM

15 Lexham Mews, London W8 6JW
tel 020-7376 2414 *fax* 020-7376 2416
email mail@jgmtalent.com
website www.jgmtalent.com
Director Jilly Moore

Established in 1997. 3 agents represent 100-150 actors. Areas of work include theatre, musicals, television, corporate and voice-overs. Also represents directors, musical directors and choreographers.

Will consider attending performances within Greater London with at least 3 weeks' notice. Accepts submissions (with CVs and photographs) from actors previously unknown to the agency (please include sae). Invitations to view individual actors' websites are accepted, as are showreels and voice tapes. Welcomes enquiries from disabled actors.

JLM Personal Management

259 Acton Lane, London W4 5DG
tel 020-8747 8223 *fax* 020-8747 8286
email jlm.pm@btconnect.com
Agents Janet Malone, Sharon Henry

Established in 1978. 2 agents represent 80 actors. Areas of work include theatre, musicals, television, film, commercials, corporate and voice-overs.

Will consider attending performances at venues within Greater London given 2 weeks' notice. Showreels and voice tapes should only be sent on request. Welcomes letters (with CVs and photographs) from actors previously unknown to the company, including disabled actors. Does not welcome approaches via email. *Commission*: Theatre 10%; TV 15%

Johnston & Mathers Associates Ltd

PO Box 3167, Barnet, London EN5 2WA
tel 020-8449 4968 *fax* 020-8449 2386

email JohnstonMathers@aol.com
website www.johnstonandmathers.com
Key personnel Dawn Mathers, Suzanne Johnston

Established in 2001. Areas of work include theatre, musicals, television, film, commercials and corporate. 2 agents represent 65 actors.

Will consider attending performances within the Greater London area with at least 1 month's notice. Accepts submissions (with CVs and photographs) from actors previously unknown to the company sent by post or email. Invitations to view individual actors' websites are accepted, as are showreels and voice tapes. Welcomes enquiries from disabled actors.

JWS Associates Ltd

16-19 Southampton Place, London WC1A 2AJ
tel 020-7745 7181
email info@jwsassociates.co.uk
Agents Denise Silvey, Dean Harper

Founded in 2005. 2 agents represent 35 actors in theatre, musicals, television, film, commercials and corporate work. Also represents directors, MDs, presenters, lighting designers and production managers.

Welcomes performance notices and is prepared to travel within the Greater London area with at least 1 week's notice. Welcomes representation enquiries (with CVs and photographs) from individuals, whether submitted by post or by email, but does not encourage follow-up calls or enquiries from disabled actors. Does not welcome unsolicited showreels or invitations to view actors' websites. *Commission*: 12.5% to 15%

Also runs a production company called Cahoots Theatre Company from the same address. See entry on page 190.

KAL Management

95 Gloucester Road, Hampton,
Middlesex TW12 2UW
tel 020-8783 0039 *fax* 020-8979 6487
email kaplan222@aol.com
website www.kaplan-kaye.co.uk
Key personnel Kaplan Kaye

Established in 1982. Sole representation of approximately 25 actors. Areas of work include theatre, musicals, television, film, commercials, corporate and voice-overs.

Will consider attending performances at venues within Greater London given as much notice as possible. Accepts submissions (with CVs and photographs) from actors previously unknown to the company if sent by post. Showreels and voice tapes should only be sent on request. *Commission*: Theatre 10%; TV 15%

Roberta Kanal Agency

82 Constance Road, Twickenham,
Middlesex TW2 7JA

tel 020-8894 2277 *fax* 020-8894 7952
email roberta.kanal@dsl.pipex.com
Director Roberta Kanal

Established in 1972; 1 agent represents approximately 30 actors working in all areas of the industry.

Will consider attending performances within Greater London and occasionally elsewhere, given sufficient notice. Accepts submissions from actors (able-bodied or disabled) who have already checked that it is appropriate to do so. Follow-up telephone calls, emails, showreels, voice tapes and invitations to view an actor's website are not welcomed. "Courtesy is still important! Don't waste postage; ask first – and please do not expect items to be returned when postage has not been included. Take a simple approach: phone first; send a CV if requested, with a clear letter and 1 photograph along with an sae for their return. As with casting directors, only use email if requested. Unsolicited items will be ignored due to the growing number of applications becoming impossible to handle."

Karushi Management

Estilo, Unit 10, Wenlock Road, London N1 7SB
tel 0845-900 5511 0845-900 5522
email victoria@karushi.com
website www.karushi.com

Areas of work include theatre, television, film, commercials, corporate, voice-overs.

Will consider attending performances in Central London with at least 2 weeks' notice. Accepts submissions (with CV's and photographs) from actors previously unknown to the company. Will also accept CVs and photographs sent via e-mail. Invitations to view individual actors' website, showreels and voice tapes are also accepted. Follow up calls are not welcomed. Welcomes enquiries from disabled actors.

Keddie Scott Associates

Studio 1, 17 Shorts Gardens, Covent Garden, London WC2H 9AT
tel 020-7836 6802 *fax* 020-7147 1326
mobile (07786) 070543
email fiona@ks-ass.co.uk, anna@ks-ass.co.uk, alex@ks-ass.co.uk
website www.ks-ass.co.uk
Managing Director Fiona Keddie *Associate Agent* Anna Loose *Welsh Rep Agent* James Owen *Scottish Rep Agent* Paul Michael *Agents' Assistant* Alex Beuselinck

Keddie Scott Associates Ltd has been established since 2003 and became members of the Personal Managers' Association in 2007. Deals in practically every area of the performing industry, including TV, Film, Commercials, Theatre, Musical Theatre (Small/Mid/Large Scale) and Corporate Assignments of every nature. Please note that KSA operates on a Personal Exclusive Management basis.

Details for Welsh Book (KSA-Wales) and Scottish Book (KSA-Scotland):
Wales: Address c/o Head office (above)
tel 020-7836 6802 *fax* 020-7147 1326 *mobile* (07917) 272298
email wales@ks-ass.co.uk
website www.ks-ass.co.uk
Scotland: (0/1) 430 Tantallon Road, Langside, Glasgow G41 3HR
mobile (07980) 121728
fax 020-7147 1326
email scotland@ks-ass.co.uk
website www.ks-ass.co.uk

Kelly Management Ltd

11-15 Betterton Street, Covent Garden, London WC2H 9BP
tel 020-7470 8757
email assistant@kelly-management.com
website www.kelly-management.com

Established in 2006. 2 agents represent clients in musicals, theatre, television, film, radio and commercials. Recommends the photographer Steve Lawton (www.stevelawton.com). Will consider attending performances within Greater London, and at Repertory theatres nationally or Number 1 touring venues in the South East, given 4-6 weeks' notice. Welcomes letters (with CVs) from individual actors previously unknown to the agency, sent by post or email; showreels and/or voice tapes; and invitations to view individual actors' websites. *Commission:* Theatre 10%; Corporate & Radio 12.5%; TV & Film 15%

Steve Kenis & Co

Royalty House, 72-74 Dean Street, London W1D 3SG
tel 020-7434 9055 *fax* 020-7287 6328
email sk@sknco.com
Agents Steve Kenis, Tessa Glover

Founded in 2000. 2 agents represent 14 actors, as well as directors and technicians. Does not welcome any unsolicited contact from individuals unknown to the company. "As we are such a small agency, specialising in older, established actors, we will not take on any new clients." *Commission:* 10%

Tim Kent Associates

Pinewood Studios, Pinewood Road, Iver Heath, Bucks SL0 0NH
tel (01753) 655517 *fax* (01753) 655622
email casting@tkassociates.co.uk
Agents Tim Kent, Julie Fox

Established in 2002. 3 agents represent 20-30 actors. Areas of work include theatre, musicals, television, film, commercials, corporate. Also represents directors.

Will consider attending performances in Greater London with at least 2 weeks' notice. Accepts submissions (with CVs and photographs) from actors previously unknown to the agency. Follow-up calls are not welcomed. *Commission*: 12.5% for Film/TV and Theatre

Keylock Management

85 Rupert Avenue, High Wycombe, Bucks HP12 3NF
tel (01245) 321638
email agency@keylockmanagement.com
website www.keylockmanagement.com

1 agent represents 60 actors working in TV, film, commercial, theatre and corporate.

Will consider attending performances, given sufficient notice. Accepts sumissions (with CVs and photographs) from actors with professional training and previously unknown to the agency, if sent by post with sae. Showreels are also accepted.

Adrian King Associates

33 Marlborough Mansions, Cannon Hill, London NW6 1JS
tel 020-7435 4600/ 4700 *fax* 020-7435 4100
email akassocs@aol.com
Agent Adrian King *Assistant* Caroline Funnell

Established in 1989. 2 agents represents 48 actors. Areas of work include theatre, musicals, television, film, commercials and corporate. Also represents presenters and directors.

Welcomes showreels and letters from actors, as well as invitations to view individual actors' websites. May attend performances within the Greater London area, given 2 weeks' notice. *Commission*: 10%

Richard Kort Management

2-4 Clasketgate, Lincoln LN2 1JS
tel (01522) 526888 *fax* (01522) 511116
email richardkort@dial.pipex.com
website www.richardkortassociates.com

Established in 2005. 1 agent represents 50 actors. Areas of work include theatre, musicals, television, film, commercials, corporate and voice-overs. Also represents presenters.

Will consider attending performances within Greater London and elsewhere, with at least 2 months' notice. Accepts submissions (with CVs and photographs) from actors previously unknown to the agency; showreels, voice tapes and invitations to view individual actors' websites are also accepted. Welcomes enquiries from disabled actors. *Commission*: 15%

Ladida Management

Ladida Group, Cambridge Theatre, Earlham Street, London WC2H 9HU
tel 020-7379 6199 *fax* 020-7379 6198
email m@ladidagroup.com
website www.ladidagroup.com
Agent Jimmy Jewell *Assistant Agents* Eva Willis, Neal Wright

Established in 2005. Main areas of work are theatre, musicals, television, film and commercials. 2 agents represent 70 actors; also represented are directors, choreographers, musical theatre writers and musical directors.

Will attend performances in London only, if given at least 2 weeks' notice. Welcomes letters (with CVs & photographs) from individual actors previously unknown to the company if sent by post, but does not accept unsolicited emails, follow-up calls, or invitations to view individual actors' websites. Welcomes showreels and voice tapes, and actively encourages enquiries from actors with disabilities.

Laine Management

131 Victoria Road, Salford M6 8LF
tel 0161-789 7775 *fax* 0161-787 7572
email info@lainemanagement.co.uk
website www.lainemanagement.co.uk
Company Director Samantha Greeley

Areas of work include theatre, television, film, commercials and corporate. Will consider attending performances at venues in Manchester and the surrounding area with 2-4 weeks' notice. Accepts CVs and photographs from individuals previously unknown to the agency, but emails, showreels and invitations to view individuals actors' websites are not welcomed. *Commission*: 15%

Langford Associates Ltd

17 Westfields Avenue, Barnes, London SW13 0AT
tel 020-8878 7148
website www.langfordassociates.com
Key personnel Barry Langford, Simon Hayes

Established in 1987. 1 agent represents 40-45 actors. Areas of work include theatre, television, film, commercials, corporate and voice-overs.

Will consider attending performances at mainstream venues within Greater London given 2 weeks' notice. Accepts submissions (with CV and photo) by post or email, but not by fax. Email submissions should include no more than one small image (emails with multiple attachments will be deleted unread). 'Name' actors seeking representation may ring and speak to Barry Langford in complete confidence.

"I am always happy to receive details by post and I regularly meet with new actors. When writing, please include an sae if you would like your details to be returned. Please do not send unsolicited showreels. I prefer to receive 10x8in photographs, and would suggest that you use a good photographer and update your photo at least every 18 months. Make sure you are listed in Spotlight, as this is a prerequisite for all professional actors."

L'Brooke Personal Management

7 Malt House Place, High Street, Romford RM1 1AR
tel (01708) 723883 *fax* (01708) 723883
email lbrooke@btopenworld.com
Director Nancy Walker

Established in 2002. 1 agent represents 20 actors. Areas of work include theatre, musicals, television, film, commercials and corporate.

Will consider attending performances at venues within Greater London and elsewhere, given 2 weeks' notice. Accepts submissions (with CVs and photographs) from actors previously unknown to the company sent by post or email. Showreels, voice tapes and invitations to view individual actors' websites are also accepted.

Anna Lee Garrett Personal Management

24/26 Arcadia Avenue, Finchley Central, London N3 2JU
tel 020-8144 1142
email contact@annaleegarrett.net
website www.annaleegarrett.net
Agency Director Anna Lee Garrett *Associate Agents* Sandra Hughes, Nick Allan

Established in 2005. 3 agents represent 30-40 actors. Areas of work include theatre, musicals, television, film, commercials, corporate. Recommends the photographer Johnny Ball.

Will consider attending performances in Greater London with at least 2 weeks' notice. Accepts submissions (with CV's and photographs) from actors previously unknown to the agency. Follow-up calls are not welcomed. Welcomes enquiries from disabled actors, and older actors as well as up and coming talent. *Commission*: 10-15% (depending on whether theatre, film or commercials)

Lee Morgan Management

Cameo House, 11 Bear Street, London WC2H 7AS
tel 020-7766 5234 *fax* 020-7839 1900
email leemorganmgnt@aol.com
website www.leemorgan.co.uk

Established in 2005. Represents clients working in musicals, television, film and commercials.

Welcomes performance notices in the London areas, given 2 weeks' notice. Is happy to receive letters (with CVs and photographs) from individual actors previously unknown to the agency, sent by post or email. Accepts showreels and voice tapes, and encourages enquiries from actors with disabilities.

Jane Lehrer Associates

100a Chalk Farm Road, London NW1 8EH
tel 020-7482 4898 *fax* 020-7482 4899
email janelehrer@aol.com
Sole Proprietor Jane Lehrer *Agent* Caz Swinfield

Established in 1986. 2 agents represent 80 actors. Areas of work include theatre, musicals, television, film, commercials, corporate and voice-overs. Also represents presenters.

Will consider attending performances at venues in Greater London with 2-3 weeks' notice. Accepts

submissions (with CVs and photographs) from actors previously unknown to the company if sent by post. An sae must always be included with CVs and photographs. Showreels and voice tapes should only be sent on request.

Mike Leigh Associates

37 Marylebone Lane, London W1V 2NW
tel 020-7935 5500 *fax* 020-7486 5886
email mail@mikeleighassoc.com
website www.mikeleighassoc.com
Agents Mike Leigh, Janie Jenkins

Established in 2007. Works in all areas except voice-over. 2 agents represent 60 actors; also represented are presenters, comedians, DJs and writers. Recommends the photographer Steve Ullathorne (**steve@steveullathorne.com**). Will consider attending performances within Greater London given 1 month's notice. Welcomes letters (with CVs & photographs) from actors previously unknown to the agency sent by post, but not by email. Will accept showreels, voice tapes, and invitations to view individual actors' websites. *Commission*: 15%

Leigh Management

14 St David's Drive, Edgware HA8 6JH
tel 020-8951 4449 *fax* 020-8951 4449
email leighmanagement@aol.com

Established in 1989. 2 agents represent 75 actors. Areas of work include theatre, musicals, television, film, commercials and corporate. Also represents presenters.

Will consider attending performances at venues within Greater London given a minimum of 1 week's notice. Accepts submissions (with CVs and photographs) from actors previously unknown to the company if sent by post. Follow-up telephone calls and invitations to view individual actors' websites are also accepted. *Commission*: 10-15%

Lime Actors Agency & Management Ltd

Nemesis House, 1 Oxford Court, Bishopsgate, Manchester, M2 3WQ
tel 0161-236 0827 *fax* 0161-228 6727
email georgina@limemanagement.co.uk
Director Georgina Andrew

Established in 1999. 1 agent represents 70 actors. Areas of work include theatre, musicals, television, film, commercials, corporate and voice-overs. Also represents musical directors.

Will consider attending performances at venues within Greater London and elsewhere given 4 weeks' notice. Accepts submissions (with CVs and photographs) from actors previously unknown to the company sent by post. Follow-up telephone calls, showreels, voice tapes and invitations to view individual actors' websites are also accepted.

Linkside Agency

21 Poplar Road, Leatherhead KT22 8SF
tel (01372) 802374 or (01372) 378398
fax (01372) 801972

Established in 1986. 2 agents represent 40 actors. Areas of work include theatre, musicals, television, film, commercials, corporate and voice-overs.

Will consider attending performances at venues within Greater London given a minimum of 2 weeks' notice. Accepts submissions (with CVs and photographs) from actors previously unknown to the company if sent by post. An sae should be included for the return of CVs and photographs. Showreels and voice tapes are also accepted.

Eva Long Agents

107 Station Road, Earls Barton, Northants NN6 0NX
mobile (07736) 700849
fax (01604) 811921
email EvaLongAgents@yahoo.co.uk
Key personnel Eva Long

Established in 2003. 1 agent represents 40 actors. Areas of work include theatre, musicals, television, film, commercials, corporate and voice-overs.

Will consider attending performances within the Greater London, Midlands and East Anglia areas, with at least 1 month's notice. Prefers to receive submissions (with CVs and headshots) by email, rather than by post. Showreels, voice tapes and invitations to view individual actors' websites are also accepted. Welcomes enquiries from disabled actors. *Commission*: 15%

Longrun Artistes Agency

3 Chelsworth Drive, Plumstead Common, London SE18 2RB
tel (07748) 723228 *fax* 0871-522 7926
email gina@longrunartistes.co.uk
website www.longrunartistes.co.uk
Director Gina Pin

Established in 2006. Represents 20 actors. Areas of work include theatre, musicals, television, film, commercials, corporate and voice-overs. Recommends photographer Phil Conrad (**phil@ambercom.net**) for dancers and movement.

Will consider attending performances in Greater London with at least 10 days' notice. Accepts submissions (with CVs and photographs) from actors previously unknown to the agency. Follow-up calls are sometimes welcomed. Invitations to view showreels or voice tapes and individual actors' websites are also accepted. Welcomes enquiries from disabled actors. *Commission*: 15% for up to and including 31 days. 10% for 31 days plus.

"In January 2008 we took on business partner Irene Wernli, who is doing a great job specifically for actors. She can be contacted on (07983) 742022 or emailed at **irene@longrunartistes.co.uk**. We continue to take on a number of actors, and now have more than 50 on our books. Commission is now 20% for all television work; other commission remains the same."

Pat Lovett Associates

40 Margaret Street, London W1G 0JH
tel 020-7495 6400 *fax* 020-7495 6411
email London@pla-uk.com
Scottish office: 5 Union Street, Edinburgh EH1 3LT
tel 0131-478 7878 *fax* 0131-478 7070
website www.pla-uk.com
Key personnel Dolina Logan

Established in 1981. Areas of work include theatre, musicals, television, film, commercials, corporate and voice-overs.

Will consider attending performances at venues in Greater London and Scotland (handled by Scottish office) with 2-3 weeks' notice. Accepts submissions (with CVs and photographs) from actors previously unknown to the company if sent by post. Invitations to view individual actors' websites are also accepted.

LSW Promotions

181a Faunce House, Doddington Grove, London SE17 3TB
tel 020-7793 9755 *fax* 020-7793 9755
email lswpromos@hotmail.com
website www.londonshakespeare.org.uk
Executive Director Bruce Wall *Development Associate* James Croft

Established in 1998. 2 agents represent 20 actors. Areas of work include theatre, musicals, television and film.

Will consider attending performances at venues within Greater London and elsewhere, given 2 weeks' notice. Accepts submissions (with CVs and photographs) from actors previously unknown to the company sent by post or email. Invitations to view individual actors' websites are also accepted. *Commission*: 10% donation to charity (LSW Prison Project)

Dennis Lyne Agency

503 Holloway Road, London N19 DD
tel 020-7272 5020 *fax* 020-7272 4790
email info@dennislyne.com
Agent Dennis Lyne *Associate* Sharon Levinson

Established in 1995. 1 agent represents 50 actors. Areas of work include theatre, musicals, television, corporate.

Will selectively consider attending performances within Central London, given at least 2 weeks' notice. Does not welcome submissions from actors previously unknown to the agency – unless they are appearing in something. *Commission*: 10%; Commercials 15%

MacFarlane Chard Associates

33 Percy Street, London W1T 2DF
tel 020-7636 7750 *fax* 020-7636 7751
email enquiries@macfarlane-chard.co.uk
website www.macfarlane-chard.co.uk

Agents Theresa Hickey, Eamonn Bedford, Derick Mulvey

Founded in 1994. Works in all areas. 3 agents represent 120 actors, as well as directors, writers, producers, technicians and authors. Will consider attending performances in Greater London, given as much notice as possible. Welcomes letters (with CVs & photographs) from actors previously unknown to the agency if sent by post, and encourages enquiries from actors with disabilities. Does not welcome follow-up calls, invitations to view individual actors' websites, or unsolicited approaches by email. Will accept showreels and voice tapes. *Commission*: Varies

Magnolia Management

136 Hicks Avenue, Greenford, Middlesex UB6 8HB
tel 020-8578 2899 *fax* 020-8575 0369
email jaffreymag@aol.com
Proprietor Jennifer Jaffrey

Established in 1982. 2 agents represent 55-60 actors. Areas of work include theatre, musicals, television, film, commercials, corporate and voice-overs.

Will consider attending performances at venues within Greater London and occasionally elsewhere, given as much notice as possible. Accepts submissions (with CVs and photographs) from actors previously unknown to the company if sent by post. Photographs should have the actor's name written on the back, and sae(s) enclosed for the return of personal details. Follow-up telephone calls should only be made if the agency has shown an interest in the actor. Showreels, voice tapes and invitations to view individual actors' websites should only be sent on request. *Commission*: 10-15%

Management 2000

11 Well Street, Treuddyn, Flintshire CH7 4NH
tel (01352) 771231 *fax* (01352) 771231
email jackey@management-2000.co.uk
website www.management-2000.co.uk

Established in 2000. 1 agent represents 40 actors. Areas of work include theatre, musicals, television, film, commercials, corporate and voice-overs.

Will consider attending performances at venues within Greater London and elsewhere, given at least 1 week's notice. Accepts submissions (with CVs and photographs) from actors previously unknown to the company if sent by post. Follow-up telephone calls, showreels and voice tapes are also accepted. *Commission*: 10-15%

Andrew Manson Personal Management

288 Munster Road, London SW6 6BQ
tel 020-7386 9158
email post@andrewmanson.com
website www.andrewmanson.com

Established in 1988.

Will consider attending performances at venues within Greater London given as much notice as possible. Industry referrals are preferred. Follow-up telephone calls, showreels, voice tapes and invitations to view individual actors' websites are accepted. Advises actors to visit the Talent Room website (**www.talentroom.com**).

Marcus & McCrimmon

1 Heathgate Place, 75 Agincourt Road, London NW3 2NU
tel 020-7485 4040 *fax* 020-7485 5030
email info@marcusandmccrimmon.com
website www.marcusandmccrimmon.com

Founded in 1999. Main areas of works are theatre, musicals, film, commercials and voice-over. 3 agents represent around 60 actors; also represents presenters.

Will consider attending performances within Greater London given 4 weeks' notice. Welcomes letters (with CVs & photographs) from actors previously unknown to the agency if sent by post, but not by email. Encourages enquiries from disabled actors, and accepts showreels, voice tapes and invitations to view individual actors' websites.

Markham & Froggatt Ltd

4 Windmill Street, London W1T 2HZ
tel 020-7636 4412 *fax* 020-7637 5233
email admin@markhamfroggatt.co.uk
website www.markhamfroggatt.co.uk
Key personnel Pippa Markham, Alex Irwin, Stephanie Randall (Agents), Millie Chadbon (Voice-over and Commercials Agent)

Works in theatre, musicals, television, film, commercials, corporate and voice-overs.

Markham & Marsden

405 Strand, London WC2R 0NE
tel 020-7836 4111 *fax* 020-7836 4222
email info@markham-marsden.com
website www.markham-marsden.com
Agents John Markham, David Marsden

Areas of work include theatre, musicals, television, film, commercials, corporate and voice-overs. Consult the website for information about how to approach the agency with representation enquiries.

Ronnie Marshall Agency

66 Ollerton Road, London N11 2LA
tel 020-8368 4958

Established in 1980. 1 agent represents 25 actors. Areas of work include theatre, musicals, television, film, commercials, corporate and voice-overs.

Will consider attending performances at venues within Greater London with 2 weeks' notice. Accepts business-like submissions (with CVs and photographs) from actors previously unknown to the company if sent by post. Photographs should be a good likeness. Enclose an sae for return of personal details. Follow-up telephone calls and invitations to view individual actors' websites are also accepted. *Commission*: If instigated by client, 10%; otherwise 20%

Scott Marshall Partners

2nd Floor, 15 Little Portland Street, London W1W 8BW
tel 020-7637 4623 *fax* 020-7636 9728
email smpm@scottmarshall.co.uk
Agents/Company Directors Amanda Evans, Suzy Kenway, Manon Palmer

Areas of work include theatre, musicals, television, film, commercials, corporate and voice-overs. Also represents directors (theatre and TV) and sound designers.

Will consider attending performances at venues within Greater London if given as much notice as possible. Accepts submissions (with CVs and photographs) from actors previously unknown to the company if sent by post. No email submissions.

Cassie Mayer Ltd

5 Old Garden House, The Lanterns, Bridge Lane, London SW11 3AD
tel 020-7350 0880 *fax* 020-7350 0890
email info@cassiemayerltd.co.uk
Agents Cassie Mayer, Jayne Billington, Annalisa Gordon

Established in 1985. 3 agents represent 50-60 actors. Areas of work include theatre, musicals, television, film, commercials and corporate. Also represents directors, presenters and designers.

Will consider attending performances at Equity venues within Greater London if given 3 weeks' notice. Accepts submissions (with CVs and photographs) from actors previously unknown to the company sent by post or email. All artists' applications will receive an answer. *Commission*: PMA-recommended rates

MBA

Concorde House, 18 Margaret Street, Brighton BN2 1TS
tel (01273) 685970 *fax* (01273) 685971
email mba.concorde@virgin.net
website mbagency.fsnet.co.uk
Key personnel Bo Keller, Andrea Todd, Peter Stanford

Established in 1964. Sole representation of 85-90 actors. Areas of work include theatre, musicals, television, film, commercials and corporate.

Will consider attending performances at venues within Greater London and on the South Coast with 1 month's notice. Accepts submissions (with clearly written CVs and photographs) from actors previously unknown to the company if sent by post. Photographs should be of a good quality. Enclose an

sae for return of personal details. Showreels, voice tapes and invitations to view individual actors' websites are also accepted. *Commission*: 10-17% depending on the type of work

Alexandra McLean-Williams

14 Rathbone Place, London W1T 1HT
tel 020-7631 5385 *fax* 020-7631 3739
email info@mclean-williams.com

Established in 2002; 1 agent represents approximately 40 clients working in theatre, musicals, television, film, commercials and corporate role-play.

Will consider attending performances within Greater London given 2 weeks' notice. Welcomes submissions (with CVs, photographs, showreels and voice tapes) from actors previously unknown to the agency. Will also accept follow-up telephone calls, emails and invitations to view an actor's website.

Bill McLean Personal Management

23b Deodar Road, London SW15 2NP
tel 020-8789 8191 *fax* 020-8789 8192

Established in 1972.

Will consider attending performances in Greater London with sufficient notice. Accepts submissions (with CVs and photographs) from actors previously unknown to the company if sent by post. Follow-up telephone calls are also accepted. *Commission*: Theatre 10%; TV 12.5%; Commercials 15%

Ken McReddie Ltd

21 Barratt Street, London W1U 1BD
tel 020-7499 7448 *fax* 020-7408 0886
email ken@kenmcreddie.com
website www.kenmcreddie.com
Directors Ken McRreddie, Roger Charteries

5 agents represent actors for theatre, television, film, commercials and voice-overs. Also represents directors.

MCS Agency

47 Dean Street, London W1D 5BE
tel 020-7734 9995 *fax* 020-7734 9996
email info@mcs-group.freeserve.co.uk
Agent Keith Bishop

Established in 1994. 2 agents represent actors. Areas of work include theatre, musicals, television, film, commercials and voice-overs. Also represents presenters.

Will consider attending performances at venues within Greater London with 2 weeks' notice. Accepts submissions (with CVs and photographs) from actors previously unknown to the company if sent by post. Showreels, voice tapes and invitations to view individual actors' websites are also accepted. *Commission*: 15-20%

Mitchell Maas McLennan Ltd

29 Thomas Street, Woolwich, London SE18 6HU
tel 020-8301 8745

email agency@mmm2000.co.uk
website www.mmm2000.co.uk

Established in 2005. 2 agents represent approximately 60 actors. Areas of work include theatre, musicals, television, film, commercials, corporate. Also represents choreographers. Recommends the photographer John Clark (see entry on page 411).

Will consider attending performances in Greater London and elsewhere with at least 2-4 weeks' notice. Accepts submissions (with CV's and photographs) from actors previously unknown to the agency. Showreels, voice tapes and invitations to view individual actors' websites also accepted. Follow-up calls are welcomed. *Commission*: 10%.

MKA

11 Russell Kerr Close, London W4 3HF
tel 020-8994 1619 *fax* 020-8994 2992
email mka.agency@virgin.net
Key personnel Malcolm Knight

Founded under a different name in 1955, MKA was established under its present name in 1995. 2 agents represent 70 actors. Areas of work include theatre, musicals, television, film, commercials, corporate and voice-overs.

Will consider attending performances at venues within Greater London with 2 weeks' notice. Accepts submissions (with CVs and photographs) from actors previously unknown to the company if sent by post. *Commission*: 10-20% depending on the job

Morgan & Goodman

Mezzanine, Quadrant House, 80-82 Regent Street, London W1B 5RP
tel 020-7437 1383 *fax* 020-7437 5293
email mgl@btinternet.com
Proprietor Tanya Greep *Key personnel* Natalie Elliott

Established in 1981. 2 agents and 1 assistant represent 70-80 actors. Areas of work include theatre, musicals, television, film, commercials, corporate and voice-overs.

Will consider attending performances at venues within Greater London with 2 weeks' notice if an actor is playing a substantial role. Accepts submissions (with CVs and photographs) from experienced actors if sent by post. An sae must always be included for the return of CVs and photographs. Showreels and voice tapes should only be sent on request. *Commission*: 12.5%

Mrs Jordan Associates

Mayfair House, 14-18 Heddon Street, London W1B 4DA
tel 020-3151 0710 *fax* 0844-335 0881
email apps@mrsjordan.co.uk
website www.mrsjordan.co.uk
Associates Sean D Lynch, Guy Kean

Established in 2009. Areas of work include musicals, television, film, commercials, corporate and voice-

overs. Does not represent any walk-ons, extras, models or under-16s. 2 agents plus associates represent around 30 actors. Recommends the photographers Jon Campling (photo@joncampling.com) and Hayden Phoenix (hayden@phoeniximages.net). Will consider attending performances in London and the South East, given a minimum of 2 weeks' notice. Welcomes unsolicited CVs and photographs sent by email only – "no calls or letters, please" – and invitations to view individual actors' websites. Is happy to consider applications from actors with disabilities, on the understanding that, unfortunately, casting opportunities are very limited. Advises actors: "We have a very small client list and a strict 'no clash' policy. Check our website to see if you clash before you email us. We cannot consider people unless we have seen them perform." *Commission*: 10-15%

Elaine Murphy Associates

Suite 1, 50 High Street, London E11 2RJ
tel 020-8989 4122 *fax* 020-8989 1400
email elaine@elainemurphy.co.uk
Director Elaine Murphy

Established in 1990. 2 agents represent 50 actors. Areas of work include theatre, musicals, television, commercials, corporate and voice-overs. Will consider attending performances within Greater London with plenty of notice. Accepts submissions (with CVs and photographs) from actors previously unknown to the agency; showreels, voice tapes and invitations to view individual actors' websites are also accepted.

The Narrow Road Company

3rd Floor, 76 Neal Street, Covent Garden, London WC2H 9PL
tel 020-7379 9598 020-7379 9586 *fax* 020-7379 9777
email amy@narrowroad.co.uk
Agents Amy Ireson, Lisa Dennis, Richard Ireson

Established in 1986, the agency has 3 offices with each agent representing approximately 40 actors. Areas of work include theatre, musicals, television, film, commercials, corporate and voice-overs. In addition, the Surrey office represents writers, directors, lighting designers, fight directors and choreographers.

Will consider attending performances within the Greater London given 1-2 weeks' notice. Accepts submissions (with CVs and photographs) from actors previously unknown to the company if sent by post, but does not welcome email submissions. Showreels and voice tapes should be sent only if requested. "We always try to be helpful and informative, but callers should be aware of how busy we often are." *Commission*: 10-15%

Surrey office

182 Brighton Road, Coulsdon, Surrey CR5 2NF
tel 020-8763 9895 *fax* 020-8763 2558
email coulsdon@narrowroad.co.uk
Agent Richard Ireson

Manchester office
Grampian House, 4th Floor, 144 Deansgate, Manchester M3 3EE
tel 0161-833 1605 *fax* 0161-833 1605
email manchester@narrowroad.co.uk
Agent Elizabeth Stocking

Nelson Browne Management Ltd
40 Bowling Green Lane, London EC1R ONE
tel 020-7970 6010 *fax* 020-7837 7612
email enquiries@nelsonbrowne.com
website www.nelsonbrowne.com
Company Director Mary Elliott Nelson

Established in 2007. 2 agents represent 80-90 actors working in musicals, television, film, commercials, corporate and voice over; also represents directors and actor/musicians. Recommends the photographer maggie@davisonpictures.co.uk.

Welcomes performance notices within the Greater London area, given 2 weeks' notice. Welcomes letters (with CVs and photographs) from individual actors previously unknown to the agency, sent by post or email. Accepts follow-up telephone calls and invitations to view individual actrors' websites. No showreels or voice tapes. Encourages enquiries from actors with disabilities. *Commission*: Theatre 10%; TV and Film 15%

North West Actors
36 Lord Street, Radcliffe, Manchester M26 3BA
tel/fax 0161-724 6625
email info@northwestactors.co.uk
website www.northwestactors.co.uk
Proprietor Richard White

Established in 2007. Main areas of work are theatre, musicals, television, film, commercials, corporate and voce-overs. 1 agent represents 30 actors. Recommends the photographer Michael Pollard (info@michaelpollard.co.uk).

Will consider attending performances within the Greater Manchester area, given 2 weeks' notice. Welcomes letters (with CVs and photographs) from individual actors previously unknown to the agency, sent by post or email. Also accepts showreels, voice tapes and invitations to view individual actors' websites. "I don't actively seek out actors with disabilities, but it's never an impediment." *Commission*: 15%

Northern Lights Management
Dean Clough Mills, Halifax, Yorkshire HX3 5AX
tel (01422) 330101
Agents Maureen Magee, Angie Cowton

Established in 1998. 2 agents represent 40 Northern and Northern-based actors. Areas of work include theatre, musicals, television, film, commercials, corporate and voice-overs.

Will consider attending performances at venues within Greater London and elsewhere, given 2 weeks'

notice. Accepts submissions (with CVs and photographs) from actors previously unknown to the company if sent by post. Showreels and voice tapes are also accepted. Enclose an sae for the return of items sent. Telephone calls and emails with attachments are not accepted. Advises actors that the agency is small and rarely takes on new clients.

NS Artistes' Management
25 Claverdon House, Hollybank Road, Billesley, Birmingham B13 0QY
tel 0121-684 5607 *mobile* (07870) 969577
email nsmanagement@fsmail.net
website www.nsmanagement.co.uk
Managing Director Neale Stephen McGrath *Director* Arali Niamh McGrath

Founded in 2004, and representing 75 actors in all areas of acting work including role-play, presenting and training, the company also represents individuals for writing, consultancy, design, stage management, presenting, drama tutoring and fight arranging. "If you have a talent in the business, even if I have not mentioned it, then I am interested – no matter what age, creed or colour you are, or whether you are disabled or able-bodied."

Welcomes performance notices a fortnight in advance; will consider attending performances around the UK. Welcomes letters (with CVs and photographs) from actors previously unknown to the company if sent by post, but not by email. Does not welcome unsolicited showreels or invitations to view individual actors' websites. *Commission*: Theatre 12.5%; Stage Management 10%; Other 15%

Nyland Management Ltd
20 School Lane, Heaton Chapel, Stockport SK4 5DG

2 agents represent 60 actors. Areas of work include theatre, musicals, television, film, commercials, corporate and voice-overs.

Will consider attending performances at venues within Greater Manchester and the North West given at least 1 week's notice. Accepts submissions (with CVs, photographs and sae) from actors previously unknown to the company if sent by post. *Commission*: 15%

The Offstage Agency
No. 199, 2 Lansdowne Row, Mayfair, London W1J 6HL.
tel 020-7543 7780 *fax* 020-7493 4935
email info@theoffstageagency.com
website www.offstageagency.com
Managing Director Dean Salvara

Established in 2004. 2 agents represent 40 actors. Areas of work include television, film, commercials, corporate and voice-overs. Also represents presenters.

Accepts submissions (with CVs and photographs) from actors previously unknown to the company if sent by post. Also accepts showreels, voice tapes and invitations to view individual actors' websites. Welcomes enquiries from disabled actors.

On Screen Agency.com

No. 199, 2 Lansdowne Row, Mayfair, London W1J 6HL
020-7193 7547
email info@onscreenagency.com
website www.onscreenagency.com
Casting Agent Dean Salvara

Established in 2005. 2 agents represent around 20 actors. Areas of work include television, film, commercials, corporate and voice-over. Does not welcome performance notices, but letters (with CVs and photographs) from individual actors previously unknown to the company are accepted, sent by post or email. Welcomes showreels and voice tapes, and invitations to view individual actors' websites. Please note that showreels should be sent to the address on the website, **www.onscreenagency.com**. *Commission*: 15%.

David Padbury Associates

44 Summerlee Avenue, Finchley, London N2 9QP
tel 020-8883 1277 *fax* 020-8883 1277
email info@davidpadburyassociates.com
website www.davidpadburyassociates.com
Director David Padbury

2 agents represent 50-60 actors. Areas of work include theatre, musicals, television, film, commercials and corporate. Also represents presenters.

Will consider attending performances within Greater London with at least 1 week's notice. Accepts submissions (with CVs and photographs) from actors previously unknown to the agency. Invitations to view individual actors' websites are also accepted. Welcomes enquiries from disabled actors. Recommends the photographer Mark Davis, **mad.photo@onetel.net**. *Commission*: 15–20%

Pan Artists Agency

Cornerways, 34 Woodhouse Lane, Sale M33 4JX
tel 0161-969 7419
email panartists@btconnect.com
website www.panartists.co.uk

Established in 1973. Accepts submissions (with CVs and photographs, "which must be up to date") from actors previously unknown to the company – sent by post or email. Postal submissions "must be accompanied by an sae."

Parr & Bond

The Tom Thumb Theatre, Eastern Esplanade, Cliftonville, Kent CT9 2LB
tel (01843) 221791 *fax* (01843) 221791

Established in 1969. Sole representation of 12-20 actors. Areas of work include theatre, musicals,

television, film, commercials, corporate and voice-overs.

Will consider attending performances at venues within Greater London and elsewhere, given 2 weeks' notice. Accepts submissions (with CVs and photographs) from actors previously unknown to the company if sent by post. *Commission*: Theatre 10%; TV and Film 20%

Parsons & Brook

37 Berwick Street, London, W1F 8RS
tel 020-7434 0398 *fax* 020-7287 8016
email info@parsonsandbrook.co.uk
Partners Jeremy Brook, Grant Parsons

Originally Jean Clarke Management established in 1995. 2 agents represent 70 actors. Areas of work include theatre, musicals, television, film, commercials, corporate and voice-overs.

Will consider attending performances in Greater London with at least 2 weeks' notice. Accepts submissions (with CVs and photographs) from actors previously unknown to the agency. Will only accept showreels and voice tapes if they have been requested. Follow-up calls are not welcomed. *Commission*: Theatre 10%; TV/Film 12.5%; Commercials 15%

Pelham Associates

The Media Centre, 9-12 Middle Street, Brighton BN1 1AL
tel (01273) 323010 *fax* (01273) 202492
email petercleall@pelhamassociates.co.uk
website www.pelhamassociates.co.uk
Agents Peter Cleall, Dione Inman

Established in 1993. Areas of work include theatre, musicals, television, film, commercials, corporate and voice-overs.

Will consider attending performances at venues within Greater London and elsewhere, given at least 2 weeks' notice. Accepts submissions (with CVs and photographs) from actors previously unknown to the company if sent by post. *Commission*: 8-12.5%

Pemberton Associates Ltd

Express Networks, 1 George Leigh Street, Manchester M4 5DL
tel 0161-235 8440 *fax* 0161-235 8442
London office: 193 Wardour Street, London W1F 8ZF
tel 020-7734 4144 *fax* 020-7734 2522
website www.pembertonassociates.com

Established in 1989. 5 agents represent 150 clients. Areas of work include theatre, musicals, television, film, commercials, corporate and voice-overs.

Will consider attending performances at venues in the North West with 2-3 weeks' notice if looking for new clients. Accepts submissions (with CVs and photographs) from actors previously unknown to the company if sent by post.

Performers Directory

PO Box 29942, London SW6 1FL
tel 020-7610 6699 *fax* 020-7736 6088
email admin@performersdirectory.co.uk
website www.performersdirectory.co.uk
Directors Antonia Stratton, Clive Stevens

Established in 1995. 5 agents represent the actors.
Areas of work include theatre, musicals, television,
film, commercials and corporate.

Will consider attending performances at venues
within Greater London with 7-10 days' notice.
Accepts submissions (with CVs and photographs)
from actors previously unknown to the company if
sent by post. Also accepts follow-up telephone calls,
showreels, voice tapes and invitations to view
individual actors' websites. "We do not welcome
emails; however, feel free to enter your details on our
website, and call us to let us know they are there. We
also encourage companies to post audition or casting
information free of charge on the website."
Commission: 10-20%

See also entry under *The Spotlight, casting directories
and information services* on page 398.

PFD

Drury House, 34-43 Russell Street,
London WC2B 5HA
tel 020-7344 1010 *fax* 020-7836 9544
website www.pfd.co.uk

Please see website for latest details of actor-
representation.

Frances Phillips

89 Robeson Way, Borehamwood, Herts WD6 5RY
tel 020-8953 0303 *mobile* (07957) 334348
email derekphillips@talk21.com

Established in 1983 and representing 40 actors. Areas
of work include theatre, musicals, television, film,
commercials, corporate and voice-overs.

Will consider attending performances at mainstream
theatre venues within Greater London, with 4 weeks'
notice. The agency does not cover fringe work,
however. Accepts submissions (with CVs,
photographs and sae) from actors previously
unknown to the company if sent by post. No
submissions by email, please. Showreels and voice
tapes are also accepted. "Particularly interested in
artists with good CVs." *Commission*: 10-15%

PHPM

184 Bradway Road, Sheffield S17 4QX
tel 0114-235 3663
email philippa@phpm.co.uk
Key personnel Philippa Howell

Established in 1996. 1 agent represents 80 actors.
Areas of work include theatre, musicals, television,
film, commercials, corporate and voice-overs.

Will consider attending performances at venues
outside Greater London if given as much notice as

possible. Accepts submissions (with CVs and
photographs) from actors previously unknown to the
company if sent by post. Enclose an sae bearing the
correct postage. Showreels and voice tapes are also
accepted. Recommends the photographer Andrew
Chapman (see entry under *Photographers and repro
companies* on page 406 for further details).
Commission: Theatre, Radio and Voice-over 10%;
Film, TV and Commercials 15%

Piccadilly Management

23 New Mount Street, Manchester M4 4DE
tel 0161-953 4057 *mobile* (07930) 834891
email info@piccadillymanagement.com
website www.piccadillymanagement.com
Agent Peter Foster

Established in 1985. Main areas of work include
television, theatre, stage, commercials, corporate and
voice overs. Represents around 50 actors. Welcomes
approaches from actors previously unknown to the
company, sent by post or email. Accepts invitations
to view individual actors' websites and welcomes
enquiries from actors with disabilities.

Janet Plater Management Ltd

Floor D, Milburn House, Dean Street,
Newcastle upon Tyne NE1 1LF
tel 0191-221 2490
email magpie@tynebridge.demon.co.uk

Established in 1997. 1 agent represents approximately
50 actors. Areas of work include theatre, musicals,
television, film, commercials, corporate and voice-
overs.

Will consider attending performances at venues in
North East England with 1-2 weeks' notice. Accepts
submissions (with CVs and photographs) from actors
previously unknown to the company if sent by post.
Showreels and voice tapes should only be sent on
request. *Commission*: Maximum of 15%

PPM

73 Leonard Street, Shoreditch, London EC2A 4QS
tel 020-7739 7552 *fax* 020-7739 7552
Managing Director Polo Piatti

Established in 1996. Agency represents 3 actors and
works mainly in musicals/music videos.

Will consider attending performances at venues
within Greater London with 3-4 weeks' notice, if
complimentary tickets are provided. Accepts
submissions (with CVs and photographs) from actors
previously unknown to the company sent by post or
email. Showreels and voice tapes are also accepted.
"We will always consider actors wishing to expand
into music work, including pop music." *Commission*:
15-20%

Morwenna Preston Management

22 Streatham Close, Leigham Court Road,
London SW16 2NQ

tel/fax 020-8835 8147
email info@morwennapreston.com
website www.morwennapreston.com
– see also Take Flight Management

1 agent represents 45 actors for theatre, musicals, TV, film, commercials and corporate. Also represents some presenters and choreographers.

Welcomes performance notices 4 weeks in advance, and is prepared to travel within the Greater London area. Welcomes letters (by post or email) from individuals previously unknown to the company. Does not welcome follow-up calls. Encourages applications from disabled actors. Welcomes showreels and invitations to view individual actors' websites. *Commission*: 12.5%

Price Gardner Management
PO Box 59908, London SW16 5LL
Contact Sarah Barnfield

Television, film, theatre, musical theatre, commercials, radio, voice-over and corporate. Submissions can be made via the website **www.pricegardner.co.uk** or in writing to the office address. Please enclose correct postage, or material will not be returned.

Principal Artistes
4 Paddington Street, London W1U 5QE
tel 020-7224 3414 *fax* 020-7486 4668
email principalartistes@hotmail.com

Established in 1993. 2 agents represent 60 actors. Areas of work include theatre, musicals, television, film, commercials and corporate.

Will consider attending performances at venues in Greater London with at least 1 week's notice. Accepts submissions (with CVs and photographs) from actors previously unknown to the company if sent by post. Always enclose an sae bearing the correct postage for the return of photographs and CVs, and if a response is required. *Commission*: Theatre 10%; Other 15%

Profile Management
The Old Chapel, 9 West End, Ashwell,
Herts SG7 5TH
tel (01462) 743843 *fax* (01462) 742967
Agent George Perry

Agency represents 35 actors. Areas of work include theatre, television, film and commercials. Also represents physical theatre artists.

Will consider attending performances (particularly of physical theatre) at venues within Greater London and Hertfordshire, Cambridgeshire and Bedfordshire, given 3 weeks' notice. Accepts submissions (with CVs and photographs) from actors previously unknown to the company if sent by post. Showreels and voice tapes are also accepted. Does not welcome telephone calls.

Pure Actors Agency & Management Ltd
44 Salisbury Road , Manchester, M41 0RB
tel 0161-747 2377 *fax* 0161-746 9886

email enquiries@pure-management.co.uk
website www.pure-management.co.uk
Director Debbie Pine

Established in 2005. 1 agent represents 40 actors. Areas of work include Television, Film, Theatre, Commercials, Radio and Corporate.

Will consider attending performances within the Manchester area, given at least 6 weeks' notice. Recommends the photographer Michael Pollard (see his entry on page 416). Accepts submissions (with CVs and photographs) from actors previously unknown to the agency – but be sure to include an sae. Showreels, voice tapes and invitations to view individual actors' websites are also accepted. Welcomes enquiries from disabled actors. *Commission*: 15%

RBM Actors
3rd Floor, 168 Victoria Street, London SW1E 5LB
tel 020-7630 7733
email info@rbmactors.com
website www.rbmactors.com
Agent Rob Sandy

Works mainly in theatre, musicals, television, film and commercials. 2 agents represent around 20 actors, and some comedians/writers.

Will consider attending performances within Greater London, given 2-3 weeks' notice. Welcomes letters (with CVs and photographs) from individual actors previously unknown to the company, sent by post or email, but not follow-up calls. Accepts showreels and voice tapes, as well as invitations to view individual actors' websites. Encourages enquiries from actors with disabilities. "We advise you to contact us when you are appearing in something. We don't represent actors we don't know or haven't seen."

Randall Richardson Actors
2nd Floor, 145-157 St John Street, London EC1V 4PY
tel 020-7060 1645 *fax* 0870-762 3212
email mail@randallrichardson.co.uk
website www.randallrichardson.co.uk
Agent Juliet Fergus

Established in 2001. 2 agents represent 40 actors. Areas of work include theatre, musicals, television, film, commercials, corporate and voice overs.

Will consider attending performances within 1 hour's journey time from London, given at least 1 week's notice. Accepts submissions (with CVs and photographs) from actors previously unknown to the agency; also welcomes enquiries from disabled actors. *Commission*: 10%

RDF Management
22 Torrington Place, London WC1E 7HD
tel 020-7317 2251 *fax* 020-7317 2245
website www.rdfmanagement.com
Head of Agency Debi Allen

Established in 2002. 4 agents each represent approximately 25 actors. Areas of work include theatre, musicals, television, film, commercials and corporates. Also represents writers, presenters and stand-up comics.

Will attend performances at venues within Greater London, but requests as much notice as possible. Accepts submissions (with CVs, photographs and, if possible, showreels) from actors previously unknown to the company sent by post. Follow-up telephone calls and invitations to view individual actors' websites are also accepted. *Commission*: 15%

Redroofs Associates

Littlewick Green, Maidenhead, Berkshire SL6 3QY
tel (01753) 785444 *fax* (01753) 785443
email agency@redroofs.co.uk
website www.redroofs.co.uk

Established in 1947, the agency only represents Redroofs graduates and current students. It does not, therefore, welcome performance notices or representation enquiries from actors unknown to the school. Areas of work include theatre, musicals, television, film, commercials, corporate and voice-overs. *Commission*: 15%

Rhino Management

Studio House, Delamere Road, Cheshunt,
Herts EN8 9SH
tel/fax (01992) 893259
email info@rhinomanagement.co.uk
website www.rhinomanagement.co.uk
Owner/Head Booker J K Sands *Assistant Booker* Steve Day

Represents 72 actors (as well as 14 presenters and 10 voice-over artists) in all areas of acting work.

Will consider attending performances within Greater London and elsewhere, if given at least 1 week's notice ("the longer the better"). Welcomes letters (with CVs and photographs) from individuals previously unknown to the company sent by post or email. Happy to receive follow-up calls. Welcomes showreels, voice tapes and invitations to view individual actors' websites. Welcomes approaches from disabled actors. *Commission*: Up to 20%

Lisa Richards Agency

108 Upper Leeson Street, Dublin 4
tel 353 1 637 5000 *fax* 353 1 667 1256
email info@lisarichards.ie
website www.lisarichards.ie
Managing Director Lisa Cook *Agents (Actors)* Lisa Cook, Richard Cook, Jonathan Shankey
Administrator Lorraine Cummins

The Lisa Richards Agency was founded in 1989 by Lisa and Richard Cook. Originally established as a theatrical agency, Lisa Richards now provides representation for actors, comedians, voice-over artists, authors, playwrights, directors and designers.

The company employs a staff of 9 people across the different departments. 3 agents represent the 90-100 actors, and there is 1 voice-over agent, 1 comedy agent, and 1 literary agent.

Welcomes performance notices if sent 3 weeks in advance, and prepared to travel around Ireland. Welcomes letters (with CVs and photographs) from actors previously unknown to the company if sent by post, but not by email; does not welcome follow-up calls. Happy to receive showreels and invitations to view individual actors' websites. Welcomes enquiries from disabled actors.

Rossmore Management

10 Wyndham Place, London W1H 2PU
tel 020-7258 1953 *fax* 020-7258 0124
email agents@rossmoremanagement.com
website www.rossmoremanagement.com

Established in 1993. 4 agents represent 120 actors. Areas of work include theatre, musicals, television, film, commercials, corporate and voice-overs.

Will consider attending performances at venues within Greater London. Accepts submissions (with CVs and photographs) from actors previously unknown to the company if sent by post. Please include sae. *Commission*: Theatre and Radio 10%; Film, TV and Commercials 15% plus VAT

Royce Management

29 Trenholme Road, London SE20 8PP
tel/fax 020-8778 6861
email office@roycemanagement.co.uk
website www.roycemanagement.co.uk

Established in 1980. 1 agent represents 50-60 actors. Areas of work include theatre, musicals, television, film, commercials, corporate and voice-overs.

Will consider attending performances at venues within Greater London with a minimum of 1 week's notice. Accepts submissions (with CVs and photographs) from actors previously unknown to the company if sent by post. Include an sae if a reply is required. *Commission*: Commercials 15%; All other work 10%

RWM Management

The Aberdeen Centre, 22-24 Highbury Grove,
London N5 2EA
tel 020-7226 3311 *fax* 020-7226 3371
email rwm.mario-kate@virgin.net
Joint Partners Mario Renzullo, Kate Whaley

Established in 2000; 2 agents represent 40-50 actors working in all areas of the industry. The agency also looks after presenters.

Welcomes postal submissions (with CVs and photographs) from actors previously unknown to the agency, but does not accept emails or follow-up telephone calls. Showreels and voice tapes are accepted. *Commission*: 12.5%

St James's Management

19 Lodge Close, Stoke D'Abernon, Cobham,
Surrey KT11 2SG
tel (01932) 860666
Managing Director Jacqueline Leggo

Established in 1965. 1 agent represents approximately
40 actors. Areas of work include theatre, musicals,
television, film, commercials, corporate and voice-
overs.

Actors should approach the company by letter and
should enclose an sae.

Saraband Associates

265 Liverpool Road, London N1 1LX

2 agents represent actors. Areas of work include
theatre, musicals, television, film and commercials.

Will occasionally consider attending performances at
venues in Greater London, given 1 month's notice.
Accepts submissions (with CVs and photographs)
from actors previously unknown to the company if
sent by post. An sae should be included with CVs and
photographs. *Commission*: Varies

SCA Management

77 Oxford Street, London W1D 2ES
tel 020-7659 2027 *fax* 020-7659 2116
email agency@sca-management.co.uk,
scamanagement@aol.com

Established in 1980. 2 agents represent 50 actors.
Areas of work include theatre, musicals, television,
film, commercials and corporate.

Will consider attending performances within Greater
London given sufficient notice. Accepts submissions
(with CVs and photographs) from actors previously
unknown to the company if sent by post. Showreels
and voice tapes are also accepted. All submissions
must be sent with an appropriately sized sae for reply.
Commission: 15%

Tim Scott

PO Box 61776, London W1V UX
tel 020-7833 5733 *fax* 020-7278 9175
email timscott@btinternet.com

Established in 1988. Areas of work include theatre,
television, film, and commercials.

Accepts postal submissions (with CVs and
photographs) from actors previously unknown to the
company.

Dawn Sedgwick Management

3 Goodwins Court, London WC2N 4LL
tel 020-7240 0404 *fax* 020-7240 0415
email dawn@dawnsedgwickmanagement.com
website www.dawnsedgwickmanagment.com
Key personnel Dawn Sedgwick, Nicola Mason-
Shakspeare

Established in 1992. 1 agent represents 10 actors.
Areas of work include theatre, television, film,

commercials, corporate and voice-overs. Also
represents presenters, comedians and writers.

Accepts submissions (with CVs and photographs)
from actors previously unknown to the agency if sent
by post, but not by email. Showreels, voice tapes and
invitations to view individual actors' websites are also
accepted. Welcomes enquiries from disabled actors.
Commission: 10-15%

Vincent Shaw Associates

186 Shaftesbury Avenue, London WC2H 8JB
tel 020-7240 2927 *fax* 020-7240 2930
email info@vincentshaw.com
website www.vincentshaw.com

Sole representation of 100 actors. Areas of work
include theatre, musicals, television, film,
commercials and corporate.

Will consider attending performances at venues
within Greater London given sufficient notice.
Accepts submissions (with CVs and photographs)
from actors previously unknown to the company if
sent by post. Include an sae if a reply is required.
Showreels should only be sent on request.
Commission: 10-15%

Shepherd Management Ltd

13 Radnor Walk, London SW3 4BP
tel 020-7352 2200 *fax* 020-7352 2277
email info@shepherdmanagement.co.uk
Agent Christina Shepherd

2 agents and 1 junior agent represent 120 actors, 1
director and 1 designer. Areas of work include
theatre, musicals (occasionally), television, film,
corporate and voice-overs.

Will consider attending performances within Greater
London given as much notice as possible. Accepts
postal submissions (with CVs, photographs and sae)
from actors previously unknown to the agency.
Showreels and voice tapes will also be accepted.
Emails and follow-up telephone calls are not
welcomed.

Shepperd-Fox

5 Martyr Road, Guildford, Surrey GU1 4LF
tel 07957 624601
email info@shepperd-fox.co.uk
website www.shepperd-fox.co.uk
Agents Jane Shepperd, Sarah Fox

Established in 2005 and represents about 55 actors.
Areas of work include television, theatre, film,
commercials and radio.

Claire Sibley Management

15 Tweedale Wharf, Madeley, Telford,
Shropshire TF7 4EW
tel (01952) 588951
email claire@clairesibleymanagement.co.uk
website www.clairesibleymanagement.co.uk
Director Claire Sibley

Founded in 2007. Areas of work are theatre, musicals, television, film, commercials, corporate and voice-over. 1 agent represents 17 actors. Will consider attending performances throughout the UK, given at least 1 month's notice. Welcomes letters (with CVs & photographs) from actors previously unknown to the agency, sent by post or email. Also welcomes enquiries from actors with disabilities; also accepts follow-up calls, showreels, voice tapes and invitations to view individual actors' websites. *Commission*: 10-12%

Sandra Singer Associates

21 Cotswold Road, Westcliff-on-Sea, Essex SSO 8AA
tel (01702) 331616 *fax* (01702) 339393
email sandrasinger@btconnect.com
website www.sandrasinger.com
Key personnel Sandra Singer (MIEAM)

Main areas of work are feature films, film, TV, commercials and musical theatre. Also represents singers.

Will consider attending performances when looking for new clients to join the management. Accepts postal applications only with sae. No zip files, jpegs, or emails with large files unless requested. Showreels should only be sent on request. Enclose an sae for the return of material.

Soul Management

10 Coptic Street, London WC1A 1NH
tel 020 7580 1120
email thomas@soulmanagement.co.uk
website www.soulmanagement.co.uk

Represents about 35 actors. Accepts submissions (with CVs and photographs) from actors previously unknown to the company, sent by post or email.

Spire Casting

PO Box 372, Chesterfield S41 0XW
tel 0790 051 7707
email mail@spirecasting.com
www.spirecasting.com
Agents David Gilbrook

Established in 2001. Accepts submissions (with CVs and photographs) from actors previously unknown to the company, sent by post or email. "Applicants must be members of Equity and appear in the current edition of *Spotlight*; include an sae if you want your CV and photograph to be returned."

Paul Spyker Management

Works in all areas of the entertainment industry; also represents directors and choreographers. Recommends the photographer Jorge de Reval. Will consider seeing performances given a month's notice. Welcomes letters (with CVs) from individual actors previously unknown to the agency, sent by post or email, as well as invitations to view individual actors' websites. Encourages enquiries from actors with disabilities and currently represents, or plans to represent, disabled actors.

Helen Stafford Management

14 Park Avenue, Bush Hill Park, Enfield EN1 2HP
tel 020-8360 6329 *fax* 020-8482 0371
email Helen.Stafford@blueyonder.co.uk
Agent Helen Stafford

Established in 1991. Sole representation of 20 actors. Areas of work include theatre, musicals, television, film, commercials, corporate and voice-overs.

Will consider attending performances at venues within Greater London with 2 weeks' notice. Accepts submissions (with CVs and photographs) from actors previously unknown to the company if sent by post. Showreels and voice tapes should only be sent on request. "Hard work pays off – don't ever give up!" Recommends the photographer Mark Davis, MAD Photography (200 Gladbeck Way, Enfield Chase, Enfield EN2 7HS; *tel* 020-8363 4182). *Commission*: Commercials 15%; Other 10%

Stage & Screen Personal Management Ltd

20b Kidbrooke Grove, Blackheath, London SE3 0LF
mobile (07958) 684740
email info@stageandscreenpm.com
Agent Orit Sutton

Established in 2005. 2 agents represent 20 actors. Areas of work include theatre, musicals, film, commercials and corporate.

Books are now closed. Please do not send any CVs, photos or invitations.

Natasha Stevenson Management Ltd (NSM)

Studio 7C, Clapham North Arts Centre, Voltaire Road, London SW4 6DH
tel 020-7386 5333 *fax* 020-7385 3014
email nsm@netcomuk.co.uk
Agents Natasha Stevenson, Jennifer Withers, Pippa Godfrey

3 agents represent 85 actors. Areas of work include theatre, musicals, television, film, commercials, corporate and voice-overs.

Will consider attending performances at venues within Greater London with 2 weeks' notice. Actors should approach the company by post enclosing an sae. Showreels should only be sent on request.

Stiven Christie Management

1 Glen Street, Tollcross, Edinburgh EH3 9JD
tel 0131-228 4040 *fax* 0131-228 4645
email info@stivenchristie.co.uk
website www.stivenchristie.co.uk
Proprietor Douglas Stiven

Founded in 1983 (and incorporating The Actors Agency of Edinburgh); 1 agent represents actors for theatre, musicals, television, film, commercials, corporate and voice-overs.

John Strange Management
Film City, 401 Govan Road, Glasgow G51 2QJ
tel 0141-445 0444
email tracy@strangemanagement.co.uk
website www.strangemanagement.co.uk

John Strange Management represents around 50 actors. Areas of work include theatre, television, film, corporate, musicals, voice-overs and commercials.

Will consider attending performances in the West of Scotland, given a minimum of 1 week's notice. Welcomes letters (with CVs and photographs) from individual actors previously unknown to the company, but no follow-up calls or email submissions. Will accept showreels and invitations to view individual actors' websites. Encourages enquiries from actors with disabilities.

Take Flight Management
22 Streatham Close, Leigham Court Road, London SW16 2NQ
tel/fax 020-8835 8147
email info@takeflightmanagement.com
website www.takeflightmanagement.com
– see also Morwenna Preston Management

1 agent represents 35 actors for theatre, musicals, TV, film, commercials and corporate. Also represents some presenters and choreographers.

Welcomes performance notices 2 weeks' in advance, and is prepared to travel within the Greater London area. Welcomes letters (by post or email) from individuals previously unknown to the company. Does not welcome follow-up calls, and does not encourage applications from disabled actors. Welcomes showreels and invitations to view individual actors' websites. *Commission*: 12.5%

Talent Artists Ltd
59 Sydner Road, London N16 7UF
tel 020-7923 1119 *fax* 020-7923 2009
Director Jane Wynn Owen

Talent Artists Ltd represents actors working in all fields of the industry, with a particular emphasis on musical theatre. "No unsolicited enquiries, please."

Tavistock Wood
45 Conduit Street, London W1S 2YN
tel 020-7257 8725 *fax* 020-7240 9029
email info@tavistockwood.com
website www.tavistockwood.com
Agents Angharad Wood, Charles Collier

Represents about 30 actors and a few other directors and writers. Accepts submissions (with CVs and photographs) from actors previously unknown to the company by post only – these should be accompanied by a covering letter and an sae.

Brian Taylor Associates
50 Pembroke Road, London W8 6NX
tel 020-7602 6141 *fax* 020-7602 6301
email briantaylor@nqassoc.freeserve.co.uk
Director Brian Taylor

The agency was established in 1975 with 2 agents representing approximately 80 actors. Areas of work include theatre, musicals, television, film, commercials, corporate and voice-overs.

Will consider attending performances at venues within Greater London given 2 weeks' notice. Accepts submissions (with CVs and photographs) from actors previously unknown to the company, and will respond if an sae is enclosed. Showreels and voice tapes should only be sent if requested; email submissions are not welcomed. *Commission*: 10% and 15%

TCG Artist Management
14A Goodwin's Court, London WC2N 4LL
tel 020-7240 3600 *fax* 020-7240 3606
email info@tcgam.co.uk
website www.spotlightagent.info/tcgam

Established in 1998. 3 agents represent 60 actors. Areas of work include theatre, musicals, television, film, commercials and corporate role-play.

Will consider attending performances at venues within Greater London given as much notice as possible. Accepts submissions (with CVs and photographs) from actors previously unknown to the company if sent by post. Follow-up telephone calls, showreels and voice samples are also accepted. *Commission*: 10-15% depending on the job

Paul Telford Management
3 Greek Street, London W1D 4DA
tel 020-7434 1100 *fax* 020-7434 1200
email info@paultelford.net
website www.paultelford.net
Partner Paul Telford

Established in 1994. 2 agents represent around 70 actors. Areas of work include theatre, musicals, television, film, commercials and corporate.

Will consider attending performances at venues within Central London given at least 2 weeks' notice. Accepts submissions (with CVs and photographs) from actors previously unknown to the company if sent by post. Showreels and voice tapes are also accepted. Include sae for return of material. *Commission*: Variable

Katie Threlfall Associates
2a Gladstone Road, Wimbledon, London SW19 1QT
tel 020-8543 4344 *fax* 020-8543 7545
email katie@ktthrelfall.co.uk
Agent Katie Threlfall

Founded in 1996 as Hillman Threlfall; in 2006 changed its name to Katie Threlfall Associates. 1

Agents and Casting Directors

agent represents 90 actors in theatre, musicals, TV, film, commercials and corporate.

Will attend performances at venues within Greater London if given 1 month's notice. Accepts submissions from actors (CV and photographs) previously unknown to the company. Welcomes showreels and invitations to view individual actors' websites. "Address letters correctly to the agent. Only write in if you have a showreel, or with an invitation to a show: we do not take on or meet people whose work we do not know." *Commission*: Commercials 15%; Other 12.5%

Janice Tildsley Associates

47 Orford Road, London, E17 9NJ
tel 020-8521 1888 *fax* 020-8521 1174
email info@janicetildsleyassociates.co.uk
website www.janicetildsleyassociates.co.uk
Agents Janice Tildsley, Kathryn Kirton

Established in 2003. 2 agents represent 60-70 actors. Areas of work include theatre, musicals, television, film and commercials.

Will consider attending performances within the Greater London area. Accepts submissions (with CVs and photographs) from actors previously unknown to the agency if sent by post, but not by email. Welcomes enquiries from disabled actors. *Commission*: 10-15%

Total Vanity Ltd

15 Walton Way, Aylesbury, Bucks HP21 7JJ
mobile 07739 381788
email Teresa.Hellen@TotalVanity.com
website www.totalvanity.com
Agent Teresa Hellen

Established in 2000. 1 agent represents 50 actors. Areas of work include theatre, musicals, television, film, commercials, corporate and voice-overs. Also represents presenters.

Will consider attending performances within the Greater London area with at least 1 week's notice. Accepts submissions (with CVs and photographs) from actors previously unknown to the company if sent by post. Showreels, voice tapes and invitations to view individual actors' websites are also accepted. Welcomes enquiries from disabled actors. *Commission*: 20%

Two's Company

244 Upland Road, London SE22 0DN
tel 020-8299 4593 *fax* 020-8299 3714
email graham@2scompanytheatre.co.uk
Agent Graham Cowley

Founded in 2002; 1 agent represents 6 actors in all areas of acting work.

Recommends the photographer Philip Gammon (**philgammon@googlemail.com**). Does not welcome performance notices or any other unsolicited

approach from actors. The company "will definitely not be taking on any more actors". *Commission*: 10%; Commercials 12.5%

United Agents

12-26 Lexington Street, London W1F 0LE
tel 020-7166 5266 *fax* 020-7166 5282
email info@unitedagents.co.uk
website www.unitedagents.co.uk
Agents Ruth Cooper (Commercial & Voice-Over), Olivia Homan, Lindy King, Duncan Millership, Joanna Scarratt (Commercial & Voice-Over), Dallas Smith, Lisa Toogood, Maureen Vincent, Ruth Young

Established in 2007. Represents about 500 actors. The agency also represents writers, directors, producers, designers and other creatives.

Urban Talent

Nemesis House, 1 Oxford Court, Bishopsgate, Manchester M2 3WQ
tel 0161-834 0990 *fax* 0161-834 0014
email liz@nmsmanagement.co.uk
Key personnel Liz Beeley

Urban Talent represents 30-50 actors. Areas of work include theatre, television, film, commercials, corporate and voice-overs. Also represents presenters.

Will consider attending performances at venues in the North West with 2 weeks' notice. Accepts submissions (with CVs and photographs) from actors previously unknown to the company sent by post or email. Also accepts invitations to view individual actors' websites. *Commission*: 15%

UVA Management

118-120 Kenton Road, Harrow HA3 8AL
tel 0845-009 2988 *fax* 020-8909 9353
email info@uvamanagement.com
website www.uvamanagement.com
Head agent Wayne Berko

Established in 2004. Main areas of work are theatre, musicals, television, commercials and corporate. 2 agents represent around 8 actors; also represents presenters.

Welcomes letters (with CVs & photographs) from actors previously unknown to the company if sent by post or email, but prefers not to receive invitations to view individual actors' websites. Does not accept showreels or voice tapes. Welcomes enquiries from actors with disabilities. *Commission*: Theatre 10%; TV and Film 13%.

Roxanne Vacca Management

73 Beak Street, London W1F 9SR

2 agents represent 45 actors. Does not welcome performance notices, but will accept letters (with CVs & photographs) from individual actors previously unknown to the agency sent by post or email. Also accepts showreels, voice tapes, and invitations to view

individual actors' websites. *Commission*: Film & TV 12.5%; Theatre 10%; Commercials 15%

VisABLE People

PO Box 80, Droitwich WR9 0ZE
tel (01905) 776631
email louise@visablepeople.com
website www.visablepeople.com
Agent Louise Dyson

Founded in 1996, VisABLE is the UK's first agency representing only disabled people for professional engagements. It represents artistes with a wide range of impairments and in every age group, including children. 1 agent represents around 50 artistes in all areas of acting, including presenting.

Does not welcome performance notices: "Sorry, no time to get out and see them usually; existing clients only." Happy to receive other enquiries (with CVs and photographs) from disabled actors via email only. Showreels should always be accompanied by an sae for return. Also happy to receive invitations to view individual actors' websites. Recommends the photographer Derek Lee. *Commission*: 10-17%

Suzann Wade

9 Wimpole Mews, London W1G 8PB
tel 020-7486 0746 *fax* 020-7486 5664
email info@suzannwade.com
website www.suzannwade.com
Director Suzann Wade *Assistants* Andrew Simic, Martine Mercer

Areas of work include theatre, musicals, film, commercials, corporate and voice-over. 1 agent represents 19 actors. Welcomes performance notices for London venues (West End and Central) only, if received as hard copy by post with at least 2 weeks' notice. Welcomes letters (with CVs & photographs) from individual actors previously unknown to the company if sent by post with sae. No emails, follow-up calls or voice tapes, but will accept showreels if they are sent with an sae for return. Encourages enquiries from disabled actors sent by post, and currently represents, or plans to represent, actors with disabilities.

Waring & McKenna Ltd

31 Sackville St, Mayfair, London W1S 3DZ
tel 020-7734 7555 *fax* 020-7734 5050
email dj@waringandmckenna.com
Agents Daphne Waring, John Summerfield

Established in 1993. 2 agents represent approximately 80 actors. Areas of work include theatre, musicals, television, film, commercials, corporate and voice-overs.

Will consider attending performances at venues within Greater London and occasionally elsewhere, given at least 1 month's notice. Accepts postal submissions (with CVs and photographs) from actors previously unknown to the company. Follow-up

telephone calls are also accepted. Showreels and voice tapes should only be sent on request. *Commission*: Theatre 10%; TV and Low-Budget Films 12.5%; Commercials and Feature Films over £4 million 15%

Janet Welch Personal Management

Old Orchard, The Street, Ubley, Bristol BS40 6PJ
tel (01761) 463238
email info@janetwelchpm.co.uk

Established in 1990. Areas of work include theatre, musicals, television, film, commercials, corporate and voice-overs.

Will consider attending performances at venues within Greater London and sometimes elsewhere, given sufficient notice. Accepts submissions (with CVs and photographs) from actors previously unknown to the company if sent by post.

West End Management

The Penthouse, 42/17 Speirs Wharf, Glasgow G4 9TH
tel 0141-226 8941 *fax* 0141-226 8983
email info@west-endmgt.com
website www.west-endmgt.com
Agents Maureen Cairns, Martin Bristow

Established in 1996. 2 agents represent 50 actors.

Will consider attending performances at venues in Scotland with 3-4 weeks' notice. Accepts submissions (with CVs and photographs) from actors previously unknown to the agency, including disabled actors – but please do not submit by email. Showreels, voice tapes and invitations to view individual actors' websites are also accepted. *Commission*: 15%

Williamson & Holmes

9 Hop Gardens, St Martin's Lane,
London WC2N 4EN
tel 020-7240 0407 *fax* 020-240 0408
email info@williamsonandholmes.co.uk
Agents Jackie Williamson, Michelle Holmes *Voice-over Agent* Sophie Reisch, *Children's Agent* Danica Pickett

Established in 2004, the agency represents 70 actors and 30 voice-over artists. Areas of work include theatre, musicals, television, film, commercials, corporate and voice-overs.

Will consider attending performances at venues within Greater London with 2 weeks' notice. Accepts submissions (with CVs and photographs) from actors previously unknown to the company if sent by post. Showreels and voice tapes are also accepted with sae for their return. Emails with attachments will not be opened. *Commission*: Theatre 10%; TV, Film, Commercials and Radio 15%

Willow Personal Management

151 Main Street, Yaxley, Peterborough PE7 3LD
tel (01733) 240392
email office@willowmanagement.co.uk
website www.willowmanagement.co.uk
Director Peter Burroughs

Established in 1995. 1 agent represents more than 150 actors. Specialises in the representation of short actors (under 5ft) and tall actors (over 7ft). Areas of work include theatre, musicals, television, film, commercials, corporate and voice-overs.

Accepts submissions (with CVs and photographs) from actors previously unknown to the company if sent by post, but not by email. Showreels, voice tapes and invitations to view individual actors' websites are also accepted. Welcomes enquiries from disabled actors. *Commission:* 15%

Newton Wills Management

The Studio, 29 Springvale Avenue, Brentford, Middlesex TW8 9QT
tel (07989) 398381
email newtoncttg@aol.com
Managing Director Newton Wills
International Christopher Socci *Talent* Julia Hunt
Office Administrator Helene Barber

Established in 1963. 4 agents represent 50 actors. Areas of work include theatre, musicals, television, film and commercials. Also represents choreographers and location-finders.

Will consider attending performances at venues within Greater London and elsewhere, but requests as much notice as possible. Accepts submissions (with CVs and photographs) from actors previously unknown to the company sent by post or email. Showreels and voice tapes are also accepted. "Find out as soon as possible what an agent does. The relationship between actor and agent should be a partnership – work with your agent to develop your talents and add new ones to your repertoire." *Commission:* Theatre 10%; Film 15%

WIS Celtic Management

86 Elphinstone Road, London E17 5EX
tel 020-8523 4234 *fax* 020-8523 4523
email wis.celtic@ethnicsaa.co.uk
Managing Director Pauline Oni

Established in 2004, specialising in Welsh, Irish and Scottish actors. Areas of work include theatre, musicals, television, film, commercials, corporate and voice-overs. One agent represents 12 actors.

Will consider attending performances within Greater London with at least 3 weeks' notice. Accepts submissions (with CVs and photographs) from actors previously unknown to the agency if sent by post, but not by email. Welcomes showreels and voice tapes, and enquiries from disabled actors. *Commission:* Varies

Edward Wyman Agency

67 Llanon Road, Llanishen, Cardiff CF14 5AH
tel 029-2075 2351 *fax* 029-2075 2444
email edward.wyman@btconnect.com
website www.wymancasting.co.uk
Managing Director Edward Wyman *Casting/Accounts* Judith Gay *Casting* Audrey Williams

Established in 1969, the agency represents more than 200 actors. Areas of work include television, film, commercials, corporate and voice-overs. Also represents directors, singers, dancers, circus performers, models, look-alikes, extras and promotions people.

Accepts submissions from actors previously unknown to the company. Actors should download an application form from the website. All submissions should be sent by post only, and should include CVs, photographs and sae. "The large majority of our work is in the Welsh language and is filmed in the South Wales area, so Welsh actors are particularly welcome." Recommends the photographer Brian Tarr (6 Bangor Street, Cardiff CF24 3LR). *Commission:* OAPs 12.5%; Others 15%

Yellow Balloon Productions Ltd

Freshwater House, Outdowns, Effingham KT24 5QR
tel (01483) 281500 or (01483) 281501
fax (01483) 281502
email yellowbal@aol.com
Managing Director Mike Smith *Producer* Daryl Smith
Consultant Sally James

A management company established in 1974 and covering all aspects of clients' career and long-term development; represents around 10 actors. Areas of work include television, film, commercials, corporate and voice-overs. Also represents radio and TV presenters and sports stars.

Will consider attending performances at venues in Greater London and elsewhere, given 2-3 weeks' notice. Accepts submissions (with CVs and photographs) from actors previously unknown to the company sent by post or email. Also accepts showreels and voice tapes. Invitations to view individual actors' websites are only accepted if sent via email. Submitted CVs should be as complete as possible, and clearly separate professional experience from student productions. Applicants should always state if they have yet to acquire a professional role. *Commission:* 15-20% according to press, accountancy, and PR agreements

CPMA: the Co-operative Personal Management Association

Almost all actors' co-operative agencies belong to the CPMA, which was created in 2002 to promote co-op agencies in the profession, encourage the highest professional standards, and represent the interests of co-op agencies to outside bodies, such as Equity and Government departments.

Actors represented by co-operative agencies run the agency themselves, through a democratic structure, and work as unpaid agents for each other. Some co-ops employ a co-ordinator or administrator (who is not an actor). Co-op agencies are non-profit-making, and any surplus funds are put back into the business. Co-op agencies began in the UK in 1970, since when many more have been established and thrive. Co-ops access the same casting information as conventional agents and suggest actors for jobs, negotiate contracts and fees, take commission on jobs, and recommend and promote their clients to casting directors (CDs) and others. There is often a fee to join a co-op, which is refunded when you leave. Other, non-refundable, fees may be charged, and there could also be a voluntary monthly levy to cover office costs, co-ordinator's fees, etc. Co-op members work in the office (typically two to four times a month), attend business meetings (usually monthly) to discuss aspects of running the agency, oversee the work of other co-op members (often with CDs), and consider the work of applicants.

Belonging to a co-op has many advantages: ·
• You quickly learn how the industry works, which can be very useful for newcomers and those returning to the profession.
• You are in contact with many industry professionals, which could help you get work.
• You are supported by other actors in the agency, some of who will have a lot of experience.
• You know which jobs you have been suggested for, and can monitor them.
• You have more influence over how you are represented, and can be more pro-active in your career.
• You can say which type of work you will or won't do, without fear of being asked to leave the agency.
• Usually, more than one person decides whom to suggest for a job. Many CDs acknowledge that co-ops often know their clients much better, and can sell them with honesty and confidence.
• Co-ops have smaller lists of clients, tend to avoid clashes, and commission rates are lower.

However, you should be aware that there can be drawbacks to being part of a co-op. As with conventional agents, standards vary; a co-op is only as good and professional as its members. Can you be sure that other members are working as hard for you, as you are for them? Continuity can also be a problem, with so many people involved. Although co-ops with a co-ordinator may have an advantage in this respect, measures such as detailed note-taking and not changing negotiators on a contract still need to be taken. And CDs tend to send breakdowns for major TV and film roles to the top agencies in the industry – although other parts will be sent to good co-ops.

To join a co-op you need to be a good agent (not just a good actor), committed, reliable and keen to support fellow actors. You must be able to use a computer and learn the

Agents and Casting Directors

software the agency uses. You must be prepared to get on the phone, talk to CDs, and sell your clients with knowledge and conviction, making intelligent and credible suggestions for roles. Consider too your personal commitments, such as doing non-acting jobs to earn money, and expenses, such as travel to and from the office, and joining/training fees.

If you are thinking of applying to a co-op, first ask if applications are being considered – and if so, how they should be submitted. Many co-ops, like conventional agents, do not accept email applications. Check CVs and photos on the agency's website to identify potential gaps. Send your photograph and CV, saying why a co-op agency interests you and stressing skills and any contacts you have which could be useful. Co-ops usually want to see an applicant's work, so send a showreel or details of the show you're in (they tend not to go to drama school shows or showcases, unless someone has expressed interest).

To find out more about the agency, talk to current and former members. You might want to know when the agency was established, if any ex-members have returned, the extent of their contacts with CDs and with theatres, the range of casting information they receive, and whether they belong to the CPMA, which has a code of conduct (Equity particularly welcomed the creation of the CPMA for this reason). If the co-op is interested in your application, you will be interviewed by all available members. If offered a place, you will usually have a three- to six-month trial period. After discussion to see how both sides feel, you may be offered full membership.

Please visit **www.cpma.coop** for further information.

Co-operative agencies

Before making an approach, it is important to understand what being a member of one of these entails, and to be clear about your reason(s) for wanting to join.

21st Century Actors Management

E10 Panther House, 38 Mount Pleasant,
London WC1X 0AP
tel 020-7278 3438 *fax* 020-7833 1158
email mail@21stcenturyactors.co.uk

Co-operative management established in 1992. Represents 21 actors. Areas of work include theatre, musicals, television, film, commercials, corporate and voice-overs. Members are expected to work 3 days in the office per month.

Will consider attending performances at venues in and around London. Accepts submissions (with CVs and photographs) from actors previously unknown to the company if sent by post. Actors requesting representation should write stating why they wish to join a co-operative and outlining their casting type and skills. *Commission*: 10% for Theatre, TV, Commercials and Film

1984 Personal Management Ltd

Suite 508, Davina House, 137 Goswell Road,
London EC1V 7ET
tel 020-7251 8046 *fax* 020-7250 3031
email info@1984pm.com
website www.1984pm.com

Co-operative management (CPMA member) representing 22 actors. Areas of work include theatre, musicals, television, film, commercials, and corporate. Members are expected to work 4 days in the office per month unless paying commission.

Will consider attending performances at venues in Greater London with 1 month's notice. Accepts letters (with CVs and photographs) from actors previously unknown to the company following an initial telephone call. Actors should always enquire whether the agency is recruiting before sending CVs. Will also accept showreels and follow-up telephone calls. *Commission*: 10%

Actors Alliance

Disney Place House, 14 Marshalsea Road,
London SE1 1HL
tel 020-7407 6028 *fax* 020-7407 6028
email actors@actorsalliance.fsnet.co.uk

A co-operative group of actors established in 1976 to advance one another's careers. Currently there are 18 members, who are all in *Spotlight* and belong to Equity. Areas of work include theatre, musicals, television, film, commercials, corporates and voice-overs. Members are expected to work in the office at least 1 day a week.

When interested, and given a minimum of 2 weeks' notice, will attend an applicant's performance in Greater London. Apply (with CV and photograph) by post only, enclosing an sae for reply. Do not send a showreel unless requested to do so. Actors Alliance is not funded from commission.

Actors' Creative Team

Panther House, 38 Mount Pleasant,
London WC1X 0AN
tel 020-7278 3388 *fax* 020-7833 5086
email office@actorscreativeteam.co.uk
website www.actorscreativeteam.co.uk

Founded in 2001, the agency has 20 members working in theatre, musicals, television, film, commercials and corporate projects. Members are expected to work 4 days in the office each month.

Welcomes performance notices for events within Greater London (inside the M25), given 1 month's notice. Will also accept letters (with CVs and photographs) and follow-up telephone calls from actors previously unknown to the agency. Does not welcome emails, showreels or voice tapes. Is unlikely to look at an actor's website unless the agency has already shown interest. "Understand what a co-op is, and the financial/time commitment it involves, before you write to us. Make sure that this is the direction you want to pursue, and include your reasons in a covering letter." *Commission*: Theatre 10%; Media 12.5%

Actors Direct Ltd

Gainsborough House, 109 Portland Street,
Manchester M1 6DN
tel 0161-237 1904 *fax* 0161-237 1904
email actorsdirect@aol.com
Administrators Eilis Hetherington, Jonathan Byrne

Established in 1994. Co-operative management. Sole representative of approximately 25 actors. Areas of work include theatre, musicals, television, film, commercials, corporate and voice-overs. Members are expected to work 2-3 days in the office each month.

Will consider attending performances at venues in the North (Manchester, Leeds, and Liverpool areas) if given 2 weeks' notice. Accepts submissions (with CVs and photographs) from actors previously unknown to the company if sent by post. Also accepts showreels and voice tapes. Will consider applications from trained professional actors with excellent IT and communications skills and the ability to perform office duties to a high standard. "Actors Direct is constantly striving to maintain a high professional image and to provide a first-class service to casting directors." *Commission*: 10% for members

Actors Exchange Management (AXM)

308 Panther House, 38 Mount Pleasant,
London WC1X 0AN
tel 020-7261 0400 *fax* 020-7261 0408
email info@axmgt.com
website www.axmgt.com

Established in 1983. Co-operative management representing 20 actors. Areas of work include theatre, musicals, television, film, commercials, corporate and voice-overs. Members are expected to work 4 days in the office per month.

Will consider attending performances at venues in Greater London, given 1 month's notice. Accepts submissions (with CVs and photographs) from actors previously unknown to the company if sent by post. Showreels and voice tapes should only be sent on request following an interview. *Commission*: 10%

The Actors File

Spitfire Studios, 63-71 Collier Street, London N1 9BE
tel 020-7278 0364 *fax* 020-7278 0364
email mail@theactorsfile.co.uk
website www.theactorsfile.co.uk

Established in 1983. Co-operative management representing 20-25 actors. Areas of work include theatre, musicals, television, film, commercials, corporate and voice-overs. Members are expected to work 4 days in the office per month and to attend business meetings.

Will consider attending performances at venues in Greater London and occasionally elsewhere, if given a minimum of 3 weeks' notice. Accepts submissions (with CVs and photographs) from actors previously unknown to the company if sent by post. Will also accept showreels. *Commission*: 12% (negotiable on low fees)

The Actors' Group

21-31 Oldham Street, Manchester M1 1JG
tel/fax 0161-834 4466
mobile (07963) 832060
email enquiries@theactorsgroup.co.uk
website www.theactorsgroup.co.uk

Established in 1980. Co-operative management representing 20 actors. Areas of work include theatre, musicals, television, film, commercials, corporate and voice-overs. Members are expected to carry out various office duties.

Will consider attending performances at venues in the North West with 2-4 weeks' notice. Accepts submissions (with CVs and photographs) from actors previously unknown to the company if sent by post.

Will also accept follow-up telephone calls, showreels, voice tapes and invitations to view individual actors' websites.

Actors Network Agency

55 Lambeth Walk, London SE11 6DX
tel 020-7735 0999 *fax* 020-7735 8177
email info@ana-actors.co.uk
website www.ana-actors.co.uk
Coordinator and Administrator Sandie Bakker

Established in 1985. Co-operative management representing 20-30 actors. Areas of work include theatre, musicals, television, film, commercials and corporate. Also represents role-play. Members are expected to work 4 days in the office per month.

Will consider attending performances at venues in Greater London and occasionally elsewhere, given as much notice as possible. Accepts submissions (with CVs and photographs) from actors previously unknown to the company if sent by post. Will also accept showreels. "An interest in, and commitment to, this type of agency is essential." *Commission*: 10%; Commercials 12.5%

Actorum Ltd

9 Bourlet Close, London W1W 7BP
tel 020-7636 6978 *fax* 020-7636 6975
email actorum2@ukonline.co.uk
website www.actorum.com

Co-operative management representing 30 actors. Members are expected to work 4 days in the office per month.

Will consider attending performances at venues in Greater London and elsewhere, given 4 weeks' notice. Accepts postal submissions with CVs and photographs. "No applications by email, please." Showreels, voice tapes and invitations to view individual actors' websites accepted. *Commission*: Theatre 10%; TV, Commercials and Film 15%

Alpha Personal Management

Studio B4, 3 Bradbury Street, London N16 8JN
tel 020-7241 0077 *fax* 020-7241 2410
email alpha@alphaactors.com
website www.alphaactors.com

Established in 1983, the agency represents 25 actors in theatre, musicals, television, film, commercials and corporate work. Members are expected to work 4 days in the office each month.

Will consider attending performances within Greater London given as much as notice as possible. Welcomes submissions (with CVs and photographs) from actors previously unknown to the company sent by post or email. Will also accept invitations to view an actor's website. Follow-up telephone calls, however, are not appreciated. *Commission*: 10% with concessions for low paid work.

Arena Personal Management Ltd

E11 Panther House, 38 Mount Pleasant,
London WC1X 0AP

tel 020-7278 1661 *fax* 020-7278 1661
email arenapmltd@aol.com
website www.arenapmltd.co.uk

Co-operative management representing 20 actors. Areas of work include theatre, musicals, television, film, commercials, corporate and voice-overs. Members are expected to work 1 day in the office per week.

Will consider attending performances at venues in Greater London given 3-4 weeks' notice. Accepts submissions (with CVs and photographs) from actors previously unknown to the company if sent by post. Will also accept follow-up telephone calls, showreels, voice tapes and invitations to view individual actors' websites. *Commission*: Theatre 10%; Commercials 12.5%

Bridges: The Actors' Agency Ltd
St George's West, 58 Shandwick Place, Edinburgh EH2 4RT
tel 0131-226 6433
email admin@bridgesactorsagency.com
website www.bridgesactorsagency.com

Established in 2008. At present the only co-operative agency active in Scotland. Currently represents 14 member clients. Areas of work include theatre, television, film, commercials, radio and corporate. Members are expected to work 4 days in the office per month, and to attend fortnightly meetings; therefore all prospective member clients must be based a commutable distance from Edinburgh.

Accepts submissions via letters and emails: "Please outline any office skills you possess, explain your reasons for wanting to become part of a co-operative agency, and include a CV and headshot." Will also accept showreels, voice tapes and invitations to view individual actors' websites. Welcomes invitations to attend performances and showcases.

Entry to the agency is via audition. If successful, a stakeholder donation of £100 is required to join the agency. Prospective member clients must also be registered with Spotlight. *Commission*: Non-Electronic 10%; Electronic 12%

Cardiff Casting
Chapter Arts Centre, Market Road, Cardiff CF5 1QE
tel 029-2023 3321 *fax* 029-2023 3380
email admin@cardiffcasting.co.uk
website www.cardiffcasting.co.uk
Key personnel Co-operative Administrator

Established in 1981. Co-operative management representing 20-25 actors. Areas of work include theatre, musicals, television, film, commercials, corporate and voice-overs. Members are expected to work 2-3 days in the office per month.

Will consider attending performances at venues in Greater London, Cardiff, South West England and Wales given 2 weeks' notice. Accepts submissions

(with CVs and photographs) from actors previously unknown to the company if sent by post. Will also accept follow-up telephone calls, showreels, voice tapes and invitations to view individual actors' websites. Applicants are asked to state clearly why they have approached a co-operative. *Commission*: Theatre 8%; Mechanical Media 10%

Castaway Actors Agency
30-31 Wicklow Street, Dublin 2
tel 353-1671 9264 *fax* 353-1761 9133
email castaway@clubi.ie
website www.irish-actors.com

Established in 1989. A co-operative agency representing 29 actors. Members are expected to work 2 days a month. Areas of work include theatre, musicals, television, film, commercials, corporate, voice-overs. Also represent presenters.

Will consider attending performances in Dublin only with at least 1 week's notice. Accepts submissions (with CVs and photographs) from actors previously unknown to them. Will also accept CVs and photographs sent via e-mail. Invitations to view individual actors' websites, showreels and voice tapes are also accepted. Follow-up calls are welcomed.

CCM
Panther House, 38 Mount Pleasant, London WC1X 0AP
tel 020-7278 0507
email casting@ccmactors.com
website www.ccmactors.com

Secretary Jo Widdowson *Administrator* Suhayla Barton

Established in 1993. Co-operative management representing up to 30 actors. Areas of work include; theatre, film, television, musicals and commercials.

Members are expected to work up to 4 days in the office per month and need office skills. Members will consider attending performances, with notice. The agency accepts letters and emails (with photographs and CVs) from actors previously unknown to the membership. The agency will also accept invitations to view actors' personal websites.

Entry to the agency is via audition, which prospective members will be invited to attend. Actors must be aware of how co-operatives work and their role within them. Information is available from Equity and The Spotlight.

A Stakeholder fee of £250 (in 2 x 3-month instalments) is required to join the agency. Prospective clients must also be registered in *Spotlight*.

Central Line
11 East Circus Street, Nottingham NG1 5AF
tel 0115-941 2937
email www.the-central-line.co.uk

Established in 1984. Co-operative management

representing 15-25 actors. Areas of work include theatre, musicals, television, film, commercials, corporate and voice-overs. Also represents directors. Members are expected to work in the office as and when appropriate.

Will consider attending performances at venues in Greater London and elsewhere. Accepts submissions (with CVs and photographs) from actors previously unknown to the company sent by post or email. Will also accept follow-up telephone calls, showreels, voice tapes and invitations to view individual actors' websites. *Commission*: 10%

Circuit Personal Management Ltd

Suite 71 SEC, Bedford Street,
Stoke-on-Trent ST1 4PZ
tel (01782) 285388 *fax* (01782) 206821
email mail@circuitpm.co.uk
website www.circuitpm.co.uk

Established in 1988. Co-operative management representing 20-25 actors. Areas of work include theatre, musicals, television, film, commercials, corporate and voice-overs. Members are expected to work approximately 15 days annually and attend monthly meetings.

Will consider attending performances at venues in the West Midlands, North West and West Yorkshire, preferably with 3-4 weeks' notice. Accepts submissions (with CVs and photographs) from actors sent by post or email. Will also accept follow-up telephone calls.

City Actors' Management

Oval House, 52-54 Kennington Oval,
London SE11 5SW
tel 020-7793 9888 *fax* 020-7820 0990
email info@cityactors.co.uk
website www.cityactors.co.uk

Co-operative management representing 21 actors with 1 permanent, office-based rep. Areas of work include theatre, musicals, television, film, commercials and corporate. Members are expected to work 4 days in the office per month.

Will consider attending performances at venues in Greater London with a minimum of 2 weeks' notice. Submissions (with CVs and photographs) should be sent by post and not by email. Advises actors to contact the agency when appearing in a show, or with a showreel, as new members will not be admitted without their work being seen. Will also accept follow-up telephone calls. *Commission*: Theatre 10%/ 12.5% depending on income; Media 15%

Crescent Management

10 Barley Mow Passage, Chiswick, London W4 4PH
tel 020-8987 0191
email mail@crescentmanagement.co.uk
website www.crescentmanagement.co.uk

Established in 1991, the agency has 24 members working in theatre, musicals, television, film,

commercials and corporate drama. Members are expected to work 3 days in the office each month.

Will consider attending performances within Greater London given 2 weeks' notice. Accepts submissions (with CVs and photographs) from actors previously unknown to the agency if sent by post. Email applications are unwelcome. Will also accept follow-up telephone calls, showreels, voice tapes and invitations to view an actor's website. *Commission*: Theatre 10%; Television 12.5%; Film 15%

Denmark Street Management

Clarendon Buildings, Suite 425, Horsell Road, Highbury, London N5 1XL
tel 020-7354 8555 *fax* 020-7354 8558
email mail@denmarkstreet.net

Established in 1985. Co-operative management representing 15-25 actors. Areas of work include theatre, musicals, television, film, commercials, corporate and voice-overs. Members are expected to work 4 days in the office per month.

Will consider attending performances at venues in Greater London and elsewhere, given 1 month's notice. Accepts submissions (with CVs and photographs) from actors previously unknown to the company if sent by post. Showreels and voice tapes should only be sent on request. Applicants should state why they would like to join a co-operative. Ethnic-minority and older actors are particularly welcome. *Commission*: Theatre 10%; TV and Film 12.5%; Commercials 15%

Direct Personal Management

Park House, 62 Lidgett Lane, Leeds LS8 1PL
tel/fax 0113-266 4036
email daphne.franks@directpm.co.uk
St John's House, 16 St John's Vale, London, SE8 4EN
tel/fax 020-8694 1788
website www.directpm.co.uk

Established in 1984 (formerly Direct Line Personal Management). Co-operative management representing 35 actors. Areas of work include theatre, musicals, television, film, commercials, corporate, role-play and voice-overs. Members are expected to work 2 days in the office each month.

Will consider attending performances at venues within Greater London and elsewhere, with 1 month's notice. Accepts submissions (with CVs and photographs) from actors previously unknown to the company sent by post or email. Follow-up telephone calls, showreels, voice tapes and invitations to view individual actors' websites are also accepted. "Please consult our website before applying. Every applicant's enquiry is discussed at a monthly meeting. We do reply, but would appreciate it if actors enclosed an sae to help reduce our costs." *Commission*: 5-15%

IML

The White House, 52-54 Kennington Oval,
London SE11 5SW

tel 020-7587 1080 *fax* 020-7587 1080
email iml.london@btconnect.com
website www.iml.org.uk

Co-operative management established in 1980. Represents 22 actors. 2 members work in the office each day on a rotational basis. Areas of work include theatre, musicals, television, film and commercials. Members are expected to work 4 days in the office per month.

Will consider attending performances at venues in Greater London given 3 weeks' notice. Accepts submissions (with CVs and photographs) from actors previously unknown to the company if sent by post. Will also accept follow-up telephone calls. Showreels and voice tapes should only be sent on request. *Commission*: 5-15% depending on the job

Inspiration Management

Room 227, The Aberdeen Centre,
22-24 Highbury Grove, London N5 2EA
tel 020-7704 0440 *fax* 020-7704 8497
email applications@inspirationmanagement.org.uk
website www.inspirationmanagement.org.uk
Key contact Applications Team

Established in 1986, Inspiration is a co-operative management representing 20-25 actors. Principal areas of work include theatre, television, film and commercials; occasionally corporate, audio and role-play. Members work 3 days in the office per month, when not engaged in professional acting work, and attend regular meetings.

Actors should apply by post only, including a CV, 10x8in headshot and covering letter with land-line number and email address if available; do not send demos or showreels initially. Members are consulted on all applications and will interview candidates wherever possible. Actors are advised to consult the website to check for casting overlaps. As at least 2 members will need to see an applicant's work; a minimum of 3 weeks' notice is required for any forthcoming appearances. *Commission*: 10%

Links Management

34-68 Colombo Street, London SE1 8DP
tel 020-7928 0806 *fax* 020-7928 0806
email agent@links-management.co.uk
website www.links-management.co.uk
Office Manager John Holloway

Established in 1984. Co-operative management representing 25 actors. Areas of work include theatre, musicals, television, film, commercials and voice-overs. Members are expected to work 1 day in the office per week.

Will consider attending performances at venues within Greater London given 2 weeks' notice. Accepts submissions (with CVs and photographs) from actors previously unknown to the company if sent by post. Also accepts follow-up telephone calls, showreels and

voice tapes. *Commission*: Theatre 10%; TV and Film 12.5%

MV Management

Ralph Richardson Memorial Studios,
Kingfisher Place, Clarendon Road, London N22 6XF
tel 020-8889 8231 *fax* 020-8829 1050
email theagency@mountview.org.uk
website www.mvmanagement.co.uk

Represents actors in all areas of the industry –television, film, theatre, musicals, commercials, radio and voiceover. "MV Management is a co-operative agency exclusively for actors who attended and have graduated from Mountview Academy of Theatre Arts. Please do not contact the agency regarding representation unless you are a Mountview graduate."

North of Watford Actors Agency

Bridge Mill, Hebden Bridge, West Yorks HX7 8EX
tel (01422) 845361 *fax* (01422) 846503
email northofwatford@btconnect.com
website www.northofwatford.com
New Applications Coordinator Chris Orton

Established in 1992. Co-operative management representing 25-30 actors. Areas of work include theatre, musicals, television, film, commercials, corporate and voice-overs. Members are expected to work 3-4 days in the office per month.

Will consider attending performances at venues in Northern locations (Leeds, Manchester, etc.) but requests as much notice as possible. Accepts submissions (with CVs and photographs) from actors previously unknown to the company if sent by post. Will also accept follow-up telephone calls, showreels, voice tapes and invitations to view individual actors' websites. *Commission*: Varies depending on the work

North One Management

HG08 Aberdeen Studios, Highbury Grove,
London N5 2EA
tel 020-7359 9666 *fax* 020-7359 9449
email actors@northone.co.uk
website www.northone.co.uk

Established in 1987. Co-operative management representing 25 actors. Areas of work include theatre, television, film, commercials and corporate. Members are expected to work 3 days in the office per month.

Will consider attending performances at venues within Greater London given at least 1 week's notice. Accepts submissions (with CVs and b&w 10x8in photographs) from actors previously unknown to the company if sent by post. Will also accept follow-up telephone calls, showreels and voice tapes. Prefers to hear from actors when currently performing. Administration and technical skills are advantageous. Applications from non-European performers are particularly welcome. *Commission*: 10%

North West Actors

36 Lord Street, Radcliffe, Manchester M26 3BA
tel 0161-724 6625 *fax* 0161-724 6625

email info@northwestactors.co.uk
website www.northwestactors.co.uk
Manager Nigel Adams

Established in 2007, North West Actors is a vibrant and enterprising agency representing actors who originate from and/or have a base in the north west of England. The agency is run by Nigel Adams, himself an actor for 18 years, and comprises an exclusive and carefully selected list of actors of various ages, types and ethnicities. "We are open to applications from actors seeking representation: please submit your CV, photograph, covering letter and preferably a showreel of work and/or mention of any current show you can be seen in. Send an SAE for return."

Otto Personal Management Ltd

Office 2, Sheffield Ind. Film, 5 Brown Street, Sheffield S1 2BS
tel 0114-275 2592 *fax* 0114-279 5225
email admin@ottopm.co.uk
website www.ottopm.co.uk

Established in 1985. Co-operative management with a full-time co-ordinator, and representing approx. 45 actors. Areas of work include theatre, musicals, television, film, commercials, corporate and voice-overs. Also represents directors and presenters. Members are expected to work an average of 3 days per year in the office.

Will consider attending performances at venues in Yorkshire, the North Midlands, Manchester and the surrounding areas with approximately 1 month's notice. Accepts submissions (with CVs and photographs) from actors previously unknown to the company sent by post or email. Will also accept follow-up telephone calls, showreels, voice tapes and invitations to view individual actors' websites. "We mainly recruit actors living within a viable distance of Sheffield – Leeds to the North, Mansfield to Manchester." *Commission*: 10-13%

Our Company

Room 205, Channelsea House, Canning Road, Stratford, London E15 3ND
tel 020-8221 1151 *fax* 020-8221 1167
email info@our-company.co.uk
website www.our-company.co.uk
Company Directors Euan Winson, Anna Ecclestone
Head of Recruitment Kirsty Malyon

Established in 2006. Co-operative management representing 10-20 actors working in musicals, television, film, commercials, corporate and voice-overs. Members are expected to work 4 days in the office each month.

Will accept performance notices within the Greater London area only, with a minimum of 2 weeks' notice. Wecomes letters (with CVs and photographs) from individual actors previously unknown to the agency, sent by post or email; will also accept follow-up telephone calls, showreels, voice tapes, and invitations to view individual actors' websites. Encourages enquiries from actors with disabilities. *Commission*: 8% to Company; 2% to Member securing contract

Park Management Ltd

Unit C3, 62 Beechwood Road, London E8 3DY
tel 020-7923 1498 *fax* 020-7923 1422
email park_management@hotmail.com
Coordinator Stephen Leslie

Established in 1977. Co-operative management representing 20 actors. Areas of work include theatre, musicals, television, film, commercials and corporate. Members are expected to work 3-4 days in the office per month.

Will consider attending performances at venues within Greater London with 3 weeks' notice. Accepts submissions (with CVs and photographs) from actors previously unknown to the company if sent by post. Will also accept showreels, voice tapes and invitations to view individual actors' websites. "Only write if you are performing in something." *Commission*: Theatre 11%; TV and Film 13.5%

Performance Actors Agency

137 Goswell Road, London EC1V 7ET
tel 020-7251 5716 *fax* 020-7251 3974
email info@performanceactors.co.uk
website www.performanceactors.co.uk
Key personnel Lionel Guyett

Established in 1984. Co-operative management representing 30+ actors. Areas of work include theatre, musicals, television, film, commercials, corporate and voice-overs. Members are expected to work 4 days a month in the office.

Will consider attending performances at venues within Greater London and occasionally elsewhere, given as much notice as possible. Accepts submissions (with CVs and photographs) from actors previously unknown to the company if sent by post and enclosing sae. Will also accept showreels and voice tapes. " We only recruit new members when specific categories are required. Call first." *Commission*: 10%

RbA Management Ltd

37-45 Windsor Street, Liverpool L8 1XET
tel 0151-708 7273
email info@rbamanagement.co.uk
website www.rbamanagement.co.uk

Established in 1995 (as Rattlebag Management). Co-operative management representing more than 25 actors. Areas of work include theatre, musicals, television, film, radio, commercials, corporate and voice-overs. Many of the actors have other, additional skills. Members are expected to work a minimum of 4 full weeks within a 12-month period.

Will consider attending performances at venues in the North West (Manchester, Liverpool, North

Wales) and nationally with 3-4 weeks' notice. Accepts brief, straightforward submissions (with CVs and photographs) from actors previously unknown to the company if sent by post. Photographs should ideally be current b&w headshots. Showreels, voice tapes and invitations to view individual actors' websites are also accepted. "If invited to an audition or interview, it is always best to call in with a response – whether you wish to accept or not." *Commission*: 12.5%

Rogues & Vagabonds Management

The Print House, 18 Ashwin Street, London E8 3DL
tel 020-7254 8130
email rogues@vagabondsmanagement.com
website www.vagabondsmanagement.com

Co-operative management representing 28-30 actors. Areas of work include theatre, musicals, television, film, commercials and corporate. Members are expected to work in the office 3 days per month.

Will consider attending performances anywhere, if given at least 3-4 weeks' notice. Accepts submissions (with CVs and photographs) from actors previously unknown to the company if sent by post or email. Showreels, voice tapes and invitations to view individual actors' websites are also accepted. Welcomes enquiries from disabled actors. *Commission*: TV/Film 10% on first £200, 15% thereafter; Theatre 10%

Rosebery RM Management Ltd

Hoxton Hall, 130 Hoxton Street, London N1 6SH
tel 020-7684 0187 *fax* 020-7684 0197
email admin@roseberymanagement.com

Established in 1984. Represents 27 actors in theatre, musicals, television, film, commercials, corporate work and voice-overs. Rosebery has a full-time administrator who has seen auditions triple and revenue quadruple. Members are expected to work 2 days in the office per month, and pay 10% commission on all acting work.

Will consider attending performances at all venues within Central London. Only accepts submissions from actors seeking representation if sent by post. Submissions must include a 10x8in b&w photograph, a current CV and a covering letter explaining why

Rosebery is the right choice. Showreels, voice tapes and singing reels are also welcomed.

Stage Centre Management Ltd

41 North Road, London N7 9DP
tel 020-7607 0872 *fax* 020-7609 0213
email info@stagecentre.org.uk

Established in 1982. Co-operative management with Lead Agent representing 18-26 actors. Areas of work include theatre, musicals, television, film, commercials and corporate. Members are expected to work 1 day in the office per week when not acting.

Will consider attending performances at venues within Greater London and elsewhere, given at least 2 weeks' notice. Accepts submissions (with CVs and photographs) from actors previously unknown to the company sent by post or email. All applicants are advised to call asking for a specific contact name before applying. Will also accept follow-up telephone calls, showreels, voice tapes and invitations to view individual actors' websites. Applicants should not apply if they are unable to provide visible evidence of their work (e.g. performance notice, showcase or showreel). *Commission*: 10-15% depending on job

West Central Management

E4 Panther House, 38 Mount Pleasant,
London WC1X 0AP
tel 020-7833 8134 *fax* 020-7833 8134
email mail@westcentralmanagement.co.uk
website www.westcentralmanagement.co.uk

Established in 1984. Co-operative management representing 15-20 actors. Areas of work include theatre, musicals, television, film, commercials and corporate. Members are expected to work 4 days in the office per month.

Will consider attending performances at venues within Greater London with 2 weeks' notice. Accepts submissions (with CVs and photographs) from actors previously unknown to the company sent by post or email. Will also accept invitations to view individual actors' websites. "We would need to see an applicant's live performance or showreel, but only after an initial meeting/audition." *Commission*: 10%

Voice-over agents

This section lists agencies that specialise in voice-overs. Check the details of how each wishes to be approached, and refer to the 'Showreel & Voice-Demo Companies' section for more about getting a voice demo made. Some of the larger conventional agencies have their own voice-over departments – generally for their existing clients only.

Accent Bank
420 Falcon Wharf, 34 Lombard Road,
London SW11 3RF
tel 020-7223 5160
email enquiries@accentbank.co.uk
website www.accentbank.co.uk
Director Lisa Paterson

Areas of work include TV, film, commercials, audio books, radio, corporate and training material. 3 agents represent more than 200 clients. Has in-house facilities to produce voice reels for clients and other actors. See the website for current rates.

Accepts submissions from actors previously unknown to the agency. Will also accept submissions sent via email. Voice demos and invitations to view individual actors' websites are also accepted. Follow-up calls are welcome. Will consider representing disabled actors. *Commission*: 15%.

AD Voice
Oxford House, 76 Oxford Street, London W1D 1BS
tel 020-7323 2345 *fax* 020-7323 0101
email info@advoice.co.uk
website www.advoice.co.uk
Key personnel Susan Bartlett

1 agent represents more than 100 clients working in television and radio commercials, documentaries, corporate, animations and audiobook recordings.

Welcomes letters with CVs and voice samples from new actors, but strongly recommends that an sae is included for their return. Prefers not to be contacted by email.

Calypso Voices
25-26 Poland Street, London W1F 8QN
tel 020-7734 6415 *fax* 020-7437 0410
email calypso@calypsovoices.com
website www.calypsovoices.com
Manager Jane Savage

2 agents represent 80 clients for voice-over work. Areas of work include television and radio commercials, documentaries, animation, corporate, audio books and on-air promotions.

Cinel Gabran Management
PO Box 5163, Cardiff CF5 9JB
tel 0845-0666605 *fax* 0845-0666601
email info@cinelgabran.co.uk
website www.cinelgabran.co.uk
Managing Director/Agent David Chance

Represents actors from any ethnic background, but also specialises in Welsh-language speakers. See entry on page 67 for more details.

Conway Van Gelder Grant
18-21 Jermyn Street, London SW1 6HP
tel 020-7287 1070 *fax* 020-287 1940
email info@conwayvg.co.uk
website www.conwayvangelder.com
Agents Kate Pulmpton, Graeme Legg

Areas of work include animated film, commercials and audio books. 2 agents represent approximately 150 clients. Client list includes some disabled actors. *Commission*: 15%.

Cut Glass Voices
Studio 185, 181-187 Queens Crescent, Camden, London NW5 4DS
tel 020-8374 4701 *fax* 020-8374 4701
email info@cutglassproductions.com
website www.cutglassproductions.com
Agents Kerry Mitchell, Phil Corran

Voice-over agent dealing with all areas of voice work – commercials, documentaries, cartoons, audio books and radio. 45+ voices are represented by 3 agents.

"We provide a voice-over showreel service at Cut Glass Productions – for our own agency and others, and newcomers to the voice-over industry. For more details please visit our website."

Welcomes representation enquiries from actors not previously known to theagency, by post or email. "Please do not send large MP3s by email; send showreels by post." Happy to receive invitations to view individual actors' websites. Client list includes disabled actors and further enquiries are welcome. Happy to receive follow-up calls. Prefers actors to phone before sending their voice reel. *Commission*: 15%

Earache Voices
177 Wardour Street, London W1F 8WX
tel 020-7287 2291 *fax* 020-7287 2288
email alex@earachevoices.com
website www.earachevoices.com
Agent Alex Lynch-White

Provide voice-overs for commercials, documentaries, audio books and animation. One agent represents 85+ actors. Recommends Patrick Rowland at Angell

Sound (Top Floor, Film House, 142 Wardour Street, London W1F 8WX, 020-7478 7777).

Accept voice tapes (include sae). Will also accept voice reels sent via email. *Commission*: 15%

Foreign Versions
tel 0333 123 2001
email info@foreignversions.co.uk
website www.foreignversions.com
Directors Margaret Davies, Anne Geary *Project Manager* Bérangère Capelle

Works with advertising agencies for foreign markets, corporate clients, companies producing audio guides, and film and television companies.

As the agency specialises in foreign languages, all voices must be mother-tongue speakers. Voice samples should be sent on MP3 via email, together with a CV.

Hamilton Hodell Ltd
5th Floor, 66-68 Margaret Street, London W1W 8SR
tel 020-7636 1221 *fax* 020-7636 1226
email info@hamiltonhodell.co.uk
website www.hamiltonhodell.co.uk
Head of Voice and Commercials Louise Donald

Main areas of work are television, film, commercials and audio books. 1 agent in the Voice department and 4 in the Acting department represent around 124 clients in total.

Welcomes letters (with CVs) from individual actors previously unknown to the agency, sent by post only. Will accept follow-up telephone calls, unsolicited voice tapes, and invitations to view individual actors' websites. Currently represents, or plans to represent, actors with disabilities. *Commission*: 15%

Hobson's Voices
62 Chiswick High Road, London W4 1SY
tel 020-8995 3628 *fax* 020-8996 5350
email voices@hobsons-international.com
website www.hobsons-international.com
Managing Director Donna Lampton *Agents* Kate Davie (Head), Tania Edwards, Linda Spinetti, Ann Dawson, Maxine Burrows, Janet Ferguson-Lees

6 agents represent 160 artists. Welcomes submissions for representation. MP3s to submissions@hobsons-international.com, or CDs by post.

Lip Service
60-66 Wardour Street, London W1F 0TA
tel 020-7734 3393 *fax* 020-7734 3373
email bookings@lipservice.co.uk
Key personnel Susan Mactavish

4 agents solely represent 80 clients and a number of foreign clients. Areas of work include television, film, commercials and audio books.

Accepts submissions (with CVs and voice CDs) from individual actors previously unknown to the company sent by email or post. Please enclose an sae for their return.

Andrew Manson Personal Management Ltd
288 Munster Road, London SW6 6BQ
tel 020-7386 9158 *fax* 020-7381 8874
email post@AndrewManson.com
website www.AndrewManson.com

Works in musicals, television, film, commercials, audio books and radio.

Rabbit Vocal Management
2nd Floor, 18 Broadwick Street, London W1F 8HS
tel 020-7287 6466 *fax* 020-7287 6566
email info@rabbit.uk.net
website www.rabbit.uk.net
Founder Melanie Bourne *Managing Director* Rebecca Fuller *Agent* Lexi Cantacuzene-Speransky

3 agents represent 120 clients. Areas of work include television, film, commercials, audio books and radio.

Accepts submissions (with CVs) from actors previously unknown to the agency if sent by post, but not by email – and please always enclose an sae. Invitations to view individual actors' websites are also accepted. Represents disabled actors.

Red 24 Voices
Crown House, 72 Hammersmith Road, London W14 8TH
tel 020-7559 3611
email info@red24voices.com
website www.red24voices.com
Managing Director Pam Weedon

Main areas of work are television, commercials and radio. 2 agents represent around 30 clients. Recommends the company The Showreel for the production of voice tapes.

Welcomes letters (with CVs) from individual actors previously unknown to the agency, sent by post or email. Will accept unsolicited voice tapes and invitations to view individual actors' websites; currently represents, or plans to represent, actors with disabilities. *Commission*: 20%

Rhubarb Voices
1st Floor, 1a Devonshire Road, Chiswick, London W4 2EU
tel 020-8742 8683 *fax* 020-8742 8693
email johnny@rhubarbvoices.co.uk
website www.RhubarbVoices.co.uk
Key personnel Johnny Garcia

Leading UK voice talent agency with experience casting voices into all platforms of the spoken word, including commercials, continuity & promos, corporate pieces, animation, games, ADR/lip-synch and more. Represents around 90 exclusive UK and North American artists, and more than 100 foreign-language artists.

Actors seeking representation should email their CV (including any VO work to date), a photo and an mp3 showreel. Please note that the agency prefers not to receive follow-up calls.

Shining Management Ltd

12 D'Arblay Street, London W1F 8DU
tel 020-7734 1981 *fax* 020-7734 2528
Director Clair Daintree *Key personnel* Jennifer Taylor

2 agents represent 55 clients. Areas of work include voice-overs for television, film, commercials and audio books.

Accepts submissions (with CVs and voice CDs) from individual actors previously unknown to the company if sent by post. Include an sae for the return of submissions. "Please do not ring with submission enquiries." *Commission*: 15%

Speak Ltd

59 Lionel Road North, Brentford,
Middlesex TW8 9QZ
tel 020-8758 0666 *fax* 020-8758 0333
email info@speak.ltd.uk
website www.speak.ltd.uk
Key personnel Mou Mukherjee *Director* Abigail Wells-Hardy

Established in 1992. 3 agents represent more than 100 clients working in television and radio, commercials and channel idents, corporate, documentaries, IVRs, animation and CD-Rom games.

Submissions should be sent by post only, with CD, photo and CV; they must also enclose an sae. Does not welcome calls or emails and will only look at professionally recorded showreels. Advises actors to look at the 'Careers Advice' page on the website for information on how to proceed.

Recommends USP (24 Newman Street, London W1; 020-7927 6600) for production.

Speak-Easy Ltd

PO Box 648, Harrington, Northampton NN6 9XT
Voice-Overs & Corporate Agent Sarah Pickering
Television Agent Kate Moon (Director)

2 agents represent 80 clients. Areas of work include television, commercials and audio books.

Accepts submissions (with CVs and voice CDs) from individual actors previously unknown to the company if sent by post. Enclose an sae for reply.

Talking Heads

Argyll House, All Saints Passage, London SW18 1EP
tel 020-7292 7575 *fax* 020-7292 7576
email voices@talkingheadsvoices.com
website www.talkingheadsvoices.com
Key personnel John Sachs

4 agents represent 150 clients, including foreign-language voice-over clients. Areas of work include commercials, television, film, animation, corporate videos and audio books.

Accepts submissions (with CVs and voice CDs) from individual actors previously unknown to the company if sent by post. Invitations to view websites are also accepted. *Commission*: 15%

Sue Terry Voices Ltd

3rd Floor, 18 Broadwick Street, London W1F 8HS
tel 020-7434 2040 *fax* 020-7434 2042
email sue@sueterryvoices.co.uk
website www.sueterryvoices.co.uk
Managing Director Sue Terry

3 agents represent around 200 actors working in voice-overs only. Does not welcome unsolicited approaches by actors unknown to the company. *Commission*: 15%

Tongue & Groove

4th Floor, Manchester House, 84 - 86 Princess Street, Manchester M1 1DN
tel 0161-228 2469 *fax* 0161-237 1809
email info@tongueandgroove.co.uk
website www.tongueandgroove.co.uk
Producers Beverley Ashworth, John Basham

3 agents represent 47 clients. Areas of work include voice-overs for television, commercials and audio books.

Accepts submissions (with CVs and voice CDs) from individual actors previously unknown to the company if sent by post. Also accepts voice tapes and invitations to view individual actors' websites.

Vocal Point

25 Denmark Street, London WC2H 8NJ
tel 020-7419 0700 *fax* 020-7419 0699
email enquiries@vocalpoint.net
website www.vocalpoint.net
Agent Ben Romer Lee

Areas of work include: television, commercials and audio books. 2 agents represent approximately 85 clients.

Accepts submissions from actors previously unknown to them. Invitations to view individual actors' websites are also accepted. Follow-up calls are not welcomed. *Commission*: 15%.

Voice & Script International

Aradco House, 132 Cleveland Street,
London W1T 6AB
tel 020-7692 7700 *fax* 020-7692 7711
email info@vsi.tv
website www.vsi.tv
Voice-Over Coordinator Jenny Morris *Voice-Over Project Managers* Bea Potashnik, Isobel George *Key contacts* Maja Ludford-Thomas, Anna Jury

5 voice-over agents represent approx. 750-1000 foreign-language voice-over clients. Areas of work include voice-overs for television, film and commercials.

Accepts submissions (with CVs) from individual actors previously unknown to the company sent by post or email. Also accepts voice tapes and invitations to view individual actors' websites. "We only use mother-tongue foreign-language speakers."

Voice Bank Ltd

1st Floor, 100 Talbot Road, Old Trafford,
Manchester M16 0PG

tel 0161-874 5741 *fax* 0161-888 2242
email elinors@voicebankltd.co.uk
website www.voicebank.ltd.co.uk
Director Elinor Stanton

Works in all areas: musicals, television, film, commercials, audio books and radio. Represents 42 clients.

Welcomes unsolicited voice tapes and invitations to view individual actors' websites. Does not currently represent any actors with disabilities, but "this would not be a barrier to joining the company".

Voice Box Agency Ltd

Laser House, Waterfront Quay, Salford Quays, Manchester M50 3XW
tel 0161-874 5741
Manager Elinor Stanton

1 agent represents 40 clients. Areas of work include voice-overs for television, film, commercials and audio books.

Accepts voice tapes from individual actors previously unknown to the company. *Commission*: 15%

Voice Shop

First Floor, 1a Devonshire Road, London W4 2EU
tel 020-8742 7077 *fax* 020-8742 7011
email info@voice-shop.co.uk
website www.voice-shop.co.uk
Key contact Maxine Wiltshire

3 agents represent 44 clients working in television, film, commercials and audio-book recording.

Welcomes letters or emails with CD/MP3 audio samples from new actors, but prefers not to receive follow-up telephone calls or tapes. All submissions should include an sae with sufficient postage, and all audio samples should contain appropriate material and be professionally produced. *Commission*: 15%

Voice Squad

1 Kendal Road, London NW10 1JH
tel 020-8450 4451
email voices@voicesquad.com
website www.voicesquad.com
Director Neil Conrich

2 agents represent more than 70 clients. Areas of work include television, film, commercials and audio books.

Accepts submissions (with CVs and voice CDs) from individual actors previously unknown to the company if sent by post. Also accepts voice tapes. *Commission*: 15%

Voicebank, The Irish Voice-Over Agency

The Barracks, 76 Irishtown Road, Dublin 4, Eire
tel 01-668 7234 *fax* 01-660 7850
email info@voicebank.ie
website www.voicebank.ie
Company Manager Sharyn Hayden

Main areas of work include musicals, television, film, commercials, audio books and radio. 2 agents represent more than 80 clients. Welcomes letters (with CVs and photographs) from individual actors previously unknown to the agency, sent by post only. Accepts unsolicited voice tapes and invitations to view individual actors' websites. Currently represents, or plans to represent, actors with disabilites.
Commission: Varies

The Voiceover Gallery

Paragon House, 3rd Floor, 48 Seymour Grove, Salford, Manchester M16 0LN
tel 0161-881 8844 *fax* 0161-881 8951
email info@thevoicegallery.co.uk
website www.thevoicegallery.co.uk
Agents Marylou Thistleton-Smith, Rachel Knighting

Areas of work include corporate, documentary, new media, TV and radio advertising. 3 agents representing 60 English voices and multiple foreign voices. Recommends The Showreel.com (see entry on page 426) and Cut Glass (see entry on page 424).

For all representation enquiries and instructions for submissions to the agency, visit the 'our services' section of the website and click on 'artist services'. *Commission*: 15%.

Suzy Wootton Voices

72 Towcester Road, Far Cotton, Northampton NN4 8LQ
tel 0870-765 9660 *fax* 0870-765 9668
email suzy@suzywoottonvoices.com
website www.suzywoottonvoices.com

1 agent represents 38 clients. Areas of work include television, film, commercials and audio books.

Accepts submissions (with CVs) from individual actors previously unknown to the company sent by post or email. Also accepts follow-up telephone calls, voice tapes, showreels and invitations to view individual actors' websites. *Commission*: 15%

Yakety Yak All Mouth Ltd

7A Bloomsbury Square, London WC1A 2LP
tel 020-7430 2600 *fax* 020-7404 6109
email info@yaketyyak.co.uk
website www.yaketyyak.co.uk
Proprietor Jolie Williams

4 agents represent 155 clients. Areas of work include voice-overs for television, film, commercials, animation and audio books.

Accepts submissions (with CVs and voice CDs) from individual actors previously unknown to the company if sent by post. Include an sae for the return of submissions. Also accepts voice tapes – although CDs are preferred. "Please do not ring with submission enquiries." *Commission*: 15%

Presenters' agents

James Grant Media

94 Strand on the Green, London W4 3NN
tel 020-8742 4950 *fax* 020-8742 4951
website www.jamesgrant.co.uk

5 agents represent 21 presenter clients; also represents TV presenters and stage actors. Welcomes letters (with CVs and showreels) from individuals previously unknown to the agency, sent by post or email.

Jeremy Hicks Associates

114-115 Tottenham Court Road London W1T 5AH
tel 020-7383 2000 *fax* 020-7383 2777
email info@jeremyhicks.com
website www.jeremyhicks.com
Agents Jeremy Hicks, Sarah Dalkin *Agents' Assistant* Zarina Dick *Assistant* Julie Dalkin

2 agents represent 20 presenter clients. Also represents writers, comedians and chefs. Welcomes letters (with CVs and showreels) from individual presenters previously unknown to the company, sent by email only. *Commission:* 15% (10% for scriptwriters)

"Our only criteria is that someone is talented and we feel we can offer them something. We do not base any decision on gender, race, sexuality or disability status."

Sandra Singer Associates

21 Cotswold Road, Westcliff-on-Sea, Essex SS0 8AA
tel (01702) 331616 *fax* (01702) 339393
email sandrasingeruk@aol.com
website www.sandrasinger.com

2 agents represent 3 presenter clients. Also represents actors, choreographers and stylists. Will accept unsolicited CVs sent by email but not by post; showreels only upon request. Welcomes invitations to view individual presenters' websites. Will consider representing presenters with disabilities. *Commission:* 10-20% (depending on stage or television)

"When submitting showreels, remember it is you and your personality that are important. Some of the presenters that have made it in the industry submitted imaginative home-made showreels. Above all, be original."

Talent4 Media Ltd

Studio LG16, Shepherds Building Central, Charecroft Way, London W14 0EH
tel 020-7183 4330 *fax* 020-7183 4331
website www.talent4media.com

Jo Wander Management

110 Gloucester Avenue, London NW1 8HX
tel 020-7209 3777 *fax* 020-7209 3770
email jo@jowandermanagement.com
website www.jowandermanagement.com
Managing Director Jo Wander

1 agent represents 15-20 presenter clients. Welcomes letters (with CVs and showreels) from individual presenters previously unknown to the agency, sent by post or email; will accept invitations to view individuals' websites.

Paul Weedon / Red 24 Management

Crown House, 72 Hammersmith Road, London W14 8TH
tel 020-7559 3611
email info@red24management.com
website www.red24management.com
Managing Director Paul Weedon

1 agent represents 20 presenter clients. Also represents voice artists. Welcomes letters (with CVs and showreels) from individual presenters previously unknown to the company, sent by post or email, and accepts invitations to view individuals' websites. *Commission:* 20%

The working life of a theatre casting director

Sophie Marshall

Twenty-something years ago, when I became the first Casting Director for the Royal Exchange Theatre in Manchester, I inherited a four-drawer filing cabinet, stuffed with letters from actors who were keen to be seen by the directors. I had no idea how long the letters had been there, but soon found out that many actors had moved, others had become TV regulars, and one or two had even died. I realised then that casting is, and has to be, an 'in the moment' activity – circumstances change too much, too often.

The title Casting Director is perhaps a misnomer; s/he is more a facilitator, coordinator and encyclopaedia of information, rather than the final decision-maker – that has to be the director, at least in theatre. In television and film the process is much the same, in terms of selection for interview, although the readings and screen tests may often need to be more 'spot on'.

The process starts with a discussion between myself and the director about the play, from which can come a casting breakdown (which may be made accessible to actors and agents, or may be kept for us to work on in private). The director will generally have some actors in mind, or the project may be based on an element of 'lead' casting, and I will then add my own lists of ideas. About ten weeks before rehearsals begin I will then start on all the clerical back-up work – checking availabilities, sifting through the agents' and actors' submissions, setting up interviews. This is followed by the hands-on part: being at the auditions and probably reading-in, discussing the outcomes with the director, arranging recalls, offering and negotiating contracts.

Actors and agents sometimes assume that a casting breakdown is written in stone, and will not change, but this is very often only a starting point; in the ensuing weeks the ideas will develop throughout the audition process. When I was casting *A Midsummer Night's Dream*, we decided not to put out a breakdown; however, agents knew the production was happening, and submitted around 1000 CVs, and actors wrote too – probably about another 1000 letters. Everyone had an idea of how Oberon ought to look, how small Hermia should be, what regional accent Bottom could use. It can take literally hours to open all the envelopes, unfold the contents and read them, and it is even more time-consuming when the letters are badly typed or vague, the CVs uninformative, and the photos so bleached you can't distinguish any features.

In theatre it is by no means essential to have an agent, and even if you do, a letter from an actor is always interesting and the CV invariably more detailed. (In fact, it's a good idea to ask your agent for a copy of your CV, so you can see how they are promoting you. They are, after all, your representative and business partner.) When you write in for a particular production, by all means mention which role attracts you, and show a little of your personality in the letter; but your attached CV should tell all the truthful facts about your experience and skills, and your photo should look like you! The CV, photo and letter are a package, but one which should be altered according to the recipient. The CV and photo would most likely be fixed, but the letter would refer to the particular company or project. Don't repeat your whole CV in the text of the letter, but do refer to any specifically useful points. If you no longer look like your photo, get a new one! There may be instances where you are selected for interview because you resemble another member of the cast, for instance (lots of twins in Shakespeare!) – and if you turn up on the day and look nothing like the photo, the director's reaction could be very demoralising. It's harder to write for specific screen jobs, but the process of sending details to the casting director should be the same.

Silver pen on black paper, letters in rhyme, photos of you in a school production, camomile teabags ("to soothe you as you read my letter") ... all of these make you look a little desperate. Firm facts are better, and an approach such as, "I haven't had the opportunity to be in a Shakespeare play since I was at college, but I hope my music and movement skills will be of interest to you for the role of First Fairy," is much more positive and pertinent. It would show your interest, the fact that you've read the play, and make us look immediately at your CV to see which plays you covered at college, and what special skills you have – Result!

Some of the hardest auditions to deal with are those where we know the actor is terrific, but is so well-behaved in the interview – only speaking when spoken to, reading cautiously before getting some director input, and so on – that there is absolutely no personality and no sense of this being a two-way process. When we offer you an audition, it is not a charitable act – it's because we think you are worth it. So interact, be a part of it, ask questions, say what works for you. It's not an exam, so if you weren't happy with your speech or reading, for example, say so: that way, the director knows you are aware of what you are doing. It's worth remembering that if you get the job, you will be in a rehearsal room for a number of weeks with this person, so see what you can find out about him/ her, the production, the way of working.

Obviously a large part of our job is to watch shows, showcases, TV, films, even commercials. Sometimes the first half is enough – we're there for work, not fun, and may have five more nights out that same week. We sometimes hold general meetings with actors we know a little about, to discover more – especially for screen work, where you need to find out more about the actor's personality, their ability to cope without much rehearsal, and so on. Our knowledge of any actor is like a jigsaw puzzle, and putting another piece in it to complete the picture is helpful.

Of course, I remember some actors for the wrong reasons, such as the one who offered to knee-cap me if I didn't give him an interview, and the one who, in the course of doing a speech of adoration to a car engine, stripped down to a black leather jock-strap! I've had to cast cartoon characters, deadly sins, a statue, a pack of dogs, and the Marx Brothers, never mind all the run-of-the-mill roles. So really, there are jobs out there for all of you, if you just keep your cool and use your common sense. Good luck!

Sophie Marshall was born in Cheshire and joined the Royal Exchange Theatre Company in Manchester in 1973. She began as Secretary to the Project Manager for the building of the new theatre, and was able to see the company grow from a small part-time organisation (producing around three productions per year) to the nationally renowned company it is today, producing work on the main stage and in The Studio. Having seen the theatre built, bombed, and rebuilt, she left in 2004 to work freelance.

Casting for musical theatre

David Grindrod

The process of producing/casting a musical can be a very long and costly affair. Everyone is looking for the next *Phantom of the Opera* or *Mamma Mia!*; years of work can go into the production you see on stage today. Workshops have now become a necessity to see if a show 'has legs' without spending too much money. In consultation with the producer and creative team, I will assemble a group of actors who may not be totally right for the roles but who work well in a workshop situation. If the green light is given after the workshop presentation, the casting process – in conjunction with everything else – begins.

A casting breakdown is drawn up: this consists of all the details required by gents and artists about the characters, vocal ranges, etc. plus the proposed dates of the production. Open calls are sometimes organised for specific roles, but normally the breakdown gets sent to agents via The Spotlight Link, which reaches 500 agents/representatives at the touch of a button.

There is always a 'wish list' of actors whom producers would like in their production, but the bulk of submissions will come through agents in the form of photos and CVs. Unsolicited mail is also received; sometimes it is difficult to keep all this on file due to sheer number of submissions. Either I or my associates will also attend college shows and presentations to look for specific talent.

When preparing your photos and CVs, always remember that these are the calling cards with which you promote yourself! A good photograph is not 'artistic' (i.e. showing a face half in shadow); rather, it should always present a good full face that really does look like you. Your CV should ideally be just one page stapled to the back of your photograph. It should include all relevant details (*not* forgetting contact details) to show your skills. Make the information clear and precise. If you feel that you are suitable for musical casting, be very accurate and truthful about your vocal range: don't make it complicated – basically, tenor or soprano, with the top of your range noted. We can normally tell your style by the shows you have appeared in.

The audition process normally begins with artists performing two contrasting songs that show range and personality. Make an effort to pick a song that is suitable for the show – not pop, for example, when you are up for Rogers & Hammerstein. Nerves will take over; therefore, don't sing the song you learnt yesterday, but perform something tried and tested (something you would be happy singing naked in Trafalgar Square!). When we ask, "Have you got something else?" we don't want the answer, "My agent said you only wanted two songs,"; have your book of audition pieces with you and give us the chance to choose an alternative. Actors often ask whether I have favourite songs that I like to hear – or songs that I don't: I only really mind when they come in with completely the wrong song for the production.

If an actor is successful, they will receive a call-back for a dance/movement call. This normally causes concerns, but actually it is not usually that specific; we only want to see whether a person is happy with his/her body. If the audition is for a major dance show, hopefully you will know your limitations and either not audition at all, or be ready to throw yourself into the routine. Again, be honest: then you won't upset the creative team.

Further recalls take place with music and script from the show: the musical supervisor or associate director normally takes these calls. If you come in for the musical supervisor, come back with music prepared and your own song. *Always* bring your own song, it's a good reminder for the team. In addition to any script you are asked to read, you may get asked for a speech: have a couple of acting pieces prepared and again, nerves will take over, so make sure you know them properly. Remember that these speeches are also to allow the director to assess how well you can respond to direction, and how readily you can take a note.

The culmination of the casting process: 'the finals' – the most nerve-wracking experience even for a highly experienced artist. Bring everything with you that you have been given. You may not get *asked* for everything, but have it just in case. You may have been asked to dress in a certain way; always put some thought into that, as directors can be blinkered at times ... I have known artists to arrive with a couple of outfits and ask me to pick one! The panel will consist of the whole creative team and the producers. At this stage I can't do any more for you – though hopefully I can keep the atmosphere in the room happy and 'up'. Stay calm, don't change anything that you have been told, and audition to the best of your abilities.

Now the wait to see if you have the role. Always remember that you have got this far in the process because you can sing and act far better than anyone else. In the end, the decision could come down to height, look, hair colour; funnily enough it may not have anything to do with your singing/acting skills at this point. And you may not get an instant answer, you may have to wait until other meetings have taken place. You may get put on 'hold': normally that means you are not first on the list, but if somebody above you declines the offer you may move up. If you are lucky, the phone call will come with a straight offer. How exciting is that ... Contractual details are then advised and if all that is agreed, your date for first rehearsal is given. Always remember that you are a small part of the bigger picture – a small part of the jigsaw puzzle that goes together to form: The Musical.

David Grindrod founded David Grindrod Associates (DGA) with Stephen Crockett in January 1998, after 20 years' experience in the theatre in various roles ranging from assistant stage manager to general manager. Current West End casting includes *Chicago, Evita, The Lord of the Rings, Mamma Mia!* (worldwide), *Spamalot, The Sound of Music.* Films include *The Phantom of The Opera.* DGA are also casting consultants for *On The Town* and *Kismet* at the English National Opera, and belong to the Casting Directors Guild of Great Britain.

Casting directors

Essentially, casting directors take on the 'nitty-gritty' work involved in the casting process – it is usually the director, and sometimes the producer, who actually 'directs' the casting decisions. The crucial thing to remember is that each one is employed – by someone else. Some casting directors are employed on a full-time basis; a significant number work freelance and can be as concerned about where their next job is coming from as you are. Therefore, if one gets you to meet their director-employer, it is important that you live up to that casting director's expectations: carefully absorb any brief that s/he gives you. If you suddenly decide to take a radically different approach, s/he will be put into a difficult position with that director-employer.

Fundamental to the job of being a casting director is a wide knowledge of all kinds of actors. Therefore a good one is seeing as many productions as possible. Like squirrels storing nuts for the winter, they keep extensive notes and are continually adding to their collections of actor-profiles. An empathetic, intuitive and imaginative casting director has immeasurable value to both actors and director.

You should approach casting directors in much the same way as you would agents: however, it's even more important that there's something they can see you in. You can keep reasonably up to date with the activities of some casting directors by looking at the website of the Casting Directors Guild (CDG) – **www.thecdg.co.uk**.

Joanne Adamson Casting

Northern Spirit Creative Casting, PO Box 140, Leeds LS13 9BS
mobile (07787) 311270
email watts07@hotmail.com

Main areas of work are theatre, musicals, television, film and commercials. Casting credits include: *Flesh and Blood* and *Nice Guy Eddie* (BBC), and *Fat Friends II* (Rollem, Tiger Aspect and Yorkshire Television).

Will consider attending performances at venues in Greater London and elsewhere given 1-2 weeks' notice. Accepts submissions (with CVs and photographs) from actors previously unknown to the casting director if sent by post, but does not welcome email enquiries. Will also accept showreels. "I am eager to arrange general meetings with actors."

Pippa Ailion

3 Towton Road, London SE27 9EE

Main areas of work are theatre, musicals, television and commercials. West End: *The Drowsy Chaperone*; *Porgy and Bess*; *Wicked*; *Blue Man Group*; *Billy Elliot*; *We Will Rock You*; *The Lion King*. Current /recent Regional and tours: *The Sunshine Boys* (West Yorkshire Playhouse); *Acorn Antiques*; *My Fair Lady* (Denmark). *Jerry Springer The Opera*; *Tonight's the Night*; *The Lion King* (EuroDisney); *We Will Rock You* (Germany). West End/London credits include: *Generations*; *The Enchanted Pig* (Young Vic) *Six*

Dance Lessons in Six Weeks; *Acorn Antiques*; *The Postman Always Rings Twice*; *Simply Heavenly* (Young Vic and Trafalgar Studios); *Follow My Leader* (Hampstead); *Tonight's the Night*; Disney's *Beauty and the Beast*; *Rent*; *Japes*; *Wit*; *Prisoner of Second Avenue*; *All You Need is Love*; *Jackie*; *The Magistrate*; *Hair*; *All the Woods*; *Annie Get Your Gun*; *Forever Plaid*; *Blues Brothers*. Television: *Inquisition*; *Little White Lies*; *Breaking The Code* (multi-award winning); *Witness Against Hitler*; *The Bill*; *Mud*; *Space Vets*; *Grange Hill*; and *Hanger 17*.

Will consider attending performances at venues in Greater London and occasionally elsewhere (such as Chichester or Stratford) given 2-3 weeks' notice. Accepts submissions (with CVs and photographs) from actors previously unknown to the casting director if sent by post. Does not welcome email enquiries.

Dorothy Andrew Casting

Mersey TV, Campus Manor, Childwall Abbey Road, Childwall, Liverpool L16 OJP
tel 0151-737 4044 *fax* 0151-722 9079
email casting@merseytv.com

Casts mainly for television, film and commercials. Recent credits include: *Hollyoaks*, *Grange Hill* and *Court Room*.

Will accept postal submissions (with CVs and photographs) from actors previously unknown to the company, but unsolicited emails and showreels are not welcomed. "When writing, make your letter short and to the point. Always include a photograph (10x8in b&w) and a CV. Only send in a showreel if requested."

Ashton Hinkinson Casting

1 Charlotte Street, London W1T 1RD
tel 020-7580 6101 *fax* 020-7636 1657
email casting@ascasting.com
website www.ashtonhinkinson.com
Casting Directors Emma Ashton, Deborah Hinkinson

Areas of work include television, film and commercials. Recent credits include: *Brother* (commercial for Bacon, Copenhagen); *Galaxy* (commercial for RSA, London); *Hostel 1 & 2* (for International Production Co.).

Will consider attending performances in Greater London with at least 1 week's notice. Invitations to showcases are also welcomed. Accepts submissions (with CVs and photographs) from actors previously unknown to the company; invitations to view individual actors' websites are also accepted.

Derek Barnes CDG

BBC Drama Series Casting, BBC Elstree,
Room N221, Neptune House, Clarendon Road,
Borehamwood WD6 1JF
tel 020-8228 7096 *fax* 020-8228 8311
email derek@derek-barnes.com
website www.derek-barnes.com

Main areas of work are film and television. Casting credits include: *Casualty*, *Holby City*, *Doctors* (BBC Drama Series) and *Down To Earth* (Series V, BBC).

Beastall & North

41E Elgin Crescent, London W11 2JD
tel 020-7727 6496
email lesley@beastallnorth.co.uk
Casting Director Lesley Beastall

Works in commercials. Recent credits include: *Sunshine* (ITV1); *Built with You in Mind* (Thompson's Holidays); and voice-overs for The Natural Confectionary Company.

Does not welcome performance notices or unsolicited submissions by actors previously unknown to the company, but will accept invitations to view individual actors' websites. Any such approach should be made by email only.

Lauren Beauchamp Casting

34A Brightside, Billericay, Essex CM12 0LJ
mobile (07961) 982198
email laurenbeauchamp@tiscali.co.uk
Head Casting Director Lauren Beauchamp *Assistant Casting Director* Dee Atkins

Main areas of work are theatre, television, film and commercials. Recent casting credits include: *Itch*

(short film; Director, Antony Gallagher for Itchka Productions); and *Bacon Sandwich* (theatre; Director, Emily North for Interact Productions).

Will consider attending performances within the Greater London and Essex areas, given at least two weeks' notice. Welcomes unsolicited CVs and photographs sent by email only. Accepts showreels and invitations to view individual actors' websites.

Lucy Bevan CDG

Twickenham Film Studios, The Barons,
St Margaret's, Twickenham TW1 2AW
tel 020-8607 8888 *fax* 020 8607 8701
email lucy@lucybevan.com

Main areas of work are film, television, commercials, pop promos and theatre. Credits include: *His Dark Materials: The Golden Compass* (New Line Cinema); *The Libertine* (Mr Mudd/Weinstein Co.); *Dirty War* (BBC Films); and *Camera Obscura* (Almeida Theatre).

Sarah Bird CDG

PO Box 32658, London W14 0XA
tel 020-7371 3248 *fax* 020-7602 8601

Casts for film, television, theatre and commercials. Casting credits include: *You Don't Have To Say You Love Me*, directed by Simon Shore (Samuelson Productions); *Ladies in Lavender*, directed by Charles Dance (Scala Productions); *Fortysomething* (Carlton TV); and *Calico*, directed by Edward Hall (Sonia Friedman Productions).

Hanna Birkett Casting

26 Noko, 3-6 Banister Road, London W10 4AR
tel 020-8960 2848
email hannah@hbcasting.com
Casting Director Hannah Birkett *Casting Associate* Shae Potter

Areas of work include television, film, commercials, idents, pop promos, voice-overs. Recent credits include: Toyota, Coca Cola, Altoids, and *Beyond the Rave* (Hammer Horror).

Will consider attending performances within Greater London with reasonable notice. Accepts CVs and photographs via email. Hard copies are not usually kept.

Lucy Boulting CDG

22 Montreal Road, Brighton BN2 9UY
email lucy@boultingcasting.wanadoo.co.uk

Casts mainly for film. Casting credits include: *Besieged* (Bernardo Bertolucci); *Shadowlands* (Richard Attenborough); and *Sexy Beast* (Jonathan Glazer).

Siobhan Bracke CDG

Basement Flat, 22a The Barons, St Margaret's,
Middlesex TW1 2AP

Main area of work is theatre. Theatre credits include: Head of Casting for the RSC (1986-91); Shakespeare's Globe for Mark Rylance; Lyric Hammersmith for Neil Bartlett; Hampstead Theatre for Tony Clark/ Lucy Bailey; Cheek By Jowl for Declan Donnellan; Chichester – *Nicholas Nickelby* for Philip Franks; *I Am Shakespeare* for Mark Rylance; *When We Are Married* for Ian Brown, West Yorkshire Playouse. Television credits include: *A Doll's House* and *Measure for Measure* for David Thacker; *Buddha of Suburbia* and *Persuasion* for Roger Michell; *Cheek By Jowl*.

Will consider attending performances at venues in Greater London and occasionally elsewhere, given as much notice as possible (preferably 4-5 weeks). Accepts submissions (with CVs and photographs) from actors previously unknown to the casting director if sent by post. Does not welcome email enquiries.

Candid Casting

1st Floor, 32 Great Sutton Street, London EC1V 0NB
tel 020-7490 8882
email mail@candidcasting.co.uk
Casting Director Amanda Tabak CDG *Assistant* Georgina Harwood

Main areas of work are television, film and commercials. Casting credits include: *Kidulthood*, *Britain's Got the Pop Factor*, and *MI High*.

Will consider attending performances at venues in central London given at least 2 weeks' notice. Accepts submissions (with CVs and photographs) from actors previously unknown to the casting director if sent by post. Does not welcome email enquiries, unsolicited showreels or invitations to view individual actors' websites.

Cannon Dudley & Associates

43a Belsize Square, London NW3 4HN
tel 020-7433 3393 *fax* 020-7813 2048
email cdacasting@blueyonder.co.uk
Casting Director Carol Dudley CDG, CSA *Casting Associate* Helena Palmer

Main areas of work are film, theatre and television. Recent credits include: *The Third Mother – Mother of Tears* (Director: Dario Argento); *Master Harold and the Boys* (Director: Lonny Price); and theatre productions for Hampstead, Edinburgh and the West End.

Will consider attending performances at venues in Greater London given as much notice as possible. Accepts submissions (with CVs and photographs) from actors previously unknown to the casting director if sent by post. Does not welcome email enquiries. CVs which are not submitted for specific projects or with reference to current shows or television performances cannot be kept for future reference. Telephone enquiries about current casting projects or progress of mailed submissions are not welcomed.

John Cannon

BBC Elstree, (Rm N223) Neptune House, Clarendon Road, Borehamwood WD6 1JF
tel 020-8228 7122 *fax* 020-8228 8311
email john.cannon@bbc.co.uk, john@johncannon.co.uk

Former Resident Casting Director for the Royal Shakespeare Company, now working for BBC Drama. Recent credits include: *The Bill* (ITV); *Presence* by Doug Lucie (Plymouth Drum); *See How They Run* (No. 1 Tour); *Hedda Gabler* (West Yorkshire Playhouse/Liverpool Playhouse); and *Yellowman* (tour for Liverpool Everyman).

Welcomes performance notices with at least 2 weeks' notice. Also happy to receive letters and emails (with CVs and photographs) from actors, as well as invitations to view individual actors' websites. Does not welcome unsolicited showreels.

Anji Carroll CDG

tel (01270) 250240
email anji@anjicarroll.tv

Main areas of work are film and television. Casting credits include: *The Cup* (BBC); *Number 10*, political drama series (BBC R4); *The Sarah Jane Adventures*, hour-long pilot (Dr Who Productions for BBC); *Mrs Ratcliffe's Revolution* (feature film directed by Bille Eltringham); *The Bill* (Talkback Thames); four films shot by first-time drama directors (IWC Media for C4); *The Knock*, 4 x 90 minute eps. (LWT); *London's Burning*, 32 x 60 minute eps. (LWT); *Out of Depth* (feature film directed by Simon Marshall); *The Jolly Boys' Last Stand* (feature film directed by Chris Payne); various commercials for home and abroad. Theatre credits: 8 shows for the Bristol Old Vic, 5 for the Northcott Theatre, Exeter, and 1 co-production for Ludlow Festival and Northcott Theatre.

The Casting Angels (London and Paris)

Suite 4, 14 College Road, Bromley BR1 3NS
fax 020-8313 0443
Director Michael Ange
Key personnel Michael *(Big Decisions)*, Gabriel *(Announcements)*, Raphael, Uriel *(The Daily Grind)*, Lucifer *(Special Consultant)*

Main areas of work are television, musicals, film and commercials with "casting across the board". Casts for the UK and other countries within Europe.

Will consider attending performances at venues in Greater London and elsewhere, given as much notice as possible. Accepts showreels.

Casting Couch Productions Ltd

213 Trowbridge Road, Bradford-on-Avon, Wiltshire BA15 1EU
mobile (07932) 785807
email moiratownsend@yahoo.co.uk
Casting Director Moira Townsend

Agents and Casting Directors

Main areas of work are television, film and commercials. Casting credits include: *Who Killed Tutankhamen?* (documentary) and advertisements for DVLA and Lunn Poly.

Will consider attending performances at venues in Greater London and elsewhere (especially Bath/Bristol area), given 2-3 weeks' notice. Accepts submissions from actors previously unknown to the casting director if sent by email. Actors will only receive a response if the casting director is able to attend a performance.

See entry under *Agents* on page 59 for further details of the company's work.

Casting UK

26-34 Emerald Street, London WC1N 3QA
tel 020-7580 3456
email drew@castinguk.com
Casting Director Andrew Mann

Casts mainly for film and commercials. Casting credits include: commercials for Bacardi, Acuview, DFS, ASDA and Maltesers; and pop videos for Placebo, Sugababes and Busted.

Will consider attending performances at venues in Greater London given 2 weeks' notice. Accepts submissions (with CVs and photographs) from actors previously unknown to the casting director if sent by post. Does not welcome email enquiries.

Suzy Catliff CDG

PO Box 39492, London N10 3YX
tel 020-8442 0749
email soose@soose.co.uk

Casts mainly for television, film and theatre. Most recent credits include: for television, *Lifeline* (BBC1), *Empathy* (BBC1), *Silent Witness* (Series IX & X), *Blitz* (Channel 4), *D-Day* (BBC 1), and *Sir Gadabout* (ITV); for film, *Stormbreaker* (associate), *The Swimming Pool* (assistant), *Sense and Sensibility* (assistant), and *Wilde & Hackers*; and for theatre, *Life X 3* (No. 1 tour), *The Play What I Wrote*, *Ducktastic* (associate).

Urvashi Chand CDG

115a Kilburn Lane, London W10 4AN
tel 020-8968 7016 *fax* 020-8960 3167
email urvashi@cinecraft.biz

Main area of work is film. Recent credits include: *Daylight Robbery* (directed by Barry Leonti), and *Red Mercury* (directed by Roy Battersby).

Will consider attending performances within the Greater London area and elsewhere with at least 2 weeks' notice. Accepts submissions (with CVs and photographs) from actors previously unknown to the agency by email. Showreels, voice tapes and invitations to view individual actors' websites are also accepted.

Alison Chard CDG

23 Groveside Court, 4 Lombard Road,
London SW11 3RQ

tel 020-7223 9125
email alisonchard@castingdirector.freeserve.co.uk
website www.thecdg.co.uk

Main areas of work are theatre, television and film. Casting credits include: *M.I.T.* and *The Bill* (television). Formerly cast for the Royal National Theatre and the Royal Shakespeare Company.

Will consider agents' invitations to performances at venues in Greater London given good notice. Accepts submissions (with CVs and small photographs) from actors sent by post. Only CVs may be emailed. Showreels are accepted if they are on DVD, accompanied by an sae and of good quality (does not welcome filmed stage pieces). Invitations to view individual actors' websites are unnecessary; ensuring that *Spotlight* entries are up-to-date is more useful. Advises actors to: "Target performance notices in accordance with the location of the recipient. Avoid unnecessary expense and disappointment by doing your research; find out what they are working on, who they are working with and if they are familiar with your work."

Charkham Casting

Suite 361, 14 Tottenham Court Road,
London W1T 1JY
tel 020-7927 8335 *fax* 020-7927 8336
email info@charkhamcasting.co.uk
Casting Directors Beth Charkham, Gary Ford

Areas of work include theatre, musicals, television, film and commercials. Recent credits include: *Charlie and the Chocolate Factory*, *Silent Witness* and *The Bill*.

Andrea Clark Casting

PO Box 28895, London SW13 0WG
tel 020-8876 6869
website www.aclarkcasting.com
Casting Director Andrea Clark

Works mainly in film, television, commercials and theatre. Recent credits include: *Mutant Chronicles*, *Keeping Mum*, and *7 Lives*.

Will consider attending performances in London only, given a minimum of 2-3 weeks' notice. Welcomes letters (with CVs & photographs) from individual actors previously unknown to the company if sent by post, but not by email. Accepts showreels and invitations to view individual actors' websites. "Sorry but I am unable to return unsolicited showreels and photos. When an actor has an agent I prefer contact to be made via the agent."

Jayne Collins

4th Floor, 20 Bedford Street, London WC2E 9HP
tel 020-7422 0014 *fax* 020-7422 0015
email info@jaynecollinscasting.com
website www.jaynecollinscasting.com

Areas of work include theatre, musicals, television, film and commercials. Will consider attending performances within the Greater London area and elsewhere, given at least 1 week's notice. Accepts submissions (with CVs and photographs) from actors previously unknown to the company if sent by post, but not by email. Welcomes showreels.

John Connor CDG

See entry for Jane Davies Casting Ltd.

Lin Cordoray

66 Cardross Street, London W6 0DR

Main areas of work are television and commercials.

Will consider attending performances at venues in Greater London. Accepts submissions (with CVs and photographs) from actors previously unknown to the casting director if sent by post. Does not welcome email enquiries.

Irene Cotton Casting

25 Druce Road, Dulwich Village, London SE21 7DW
tel 020-8299 1595 *fax* 020-8299 2787
email irenecotton@btinternet.com
Director Irene Cotton CDG

Recent credits include: *The Bill* (ITV), *The Countess* (Criterion Theatre, London), *Panorama* (BBC), and *Caffe Latte* commercial (Home Productions). Welcomes performance notices as far in advance as possible, and is prepared to travel to performances within Greater London. Does not welcome any other unsolicited form of approach, including CVs, photographs, showreels or invitations to view individual actors' websites. Advises actors to make contact only to inform the casting director "when [she] can see their work – TV, film or stage".

Margaret Crawford

92 Castelnau, London SW13 9EU

Casts mainly for television. Casting credits include: *Bad Girls* (Series 2-8), *Footballers' Wives* (Series 1-5), *Footballers' Wives Extra Time* (Series 1 & 2), *Waterloo Road* (Series 1) and *Bombshell* (Series 1).

Will consider attending performances at venues in Greater London and occasionally elsewhere, given as much notice as possible. Accepts submissions (with CVs and photographs) from actors previously unknown to the casting director if sent by post. Does not welcome email enquiries. Also accepts showreels, voice tapes and invitations to view individual actors' websites.

Crocodile Casting

9 Ashley Close, Hendon, London NW4 1PH
tel 020-8203 7009 *fax* 020-8203 7711
website www.crocodilecasting.com
Casting Directors Tracie Saban, Claire Toeman

Established in 1996 with the aim of constantly accessing new faces and fresh talent. The company casts mainly for commercials, pop videos and corporate work; sometimes holds general auditions to meet new actors and models.

Jane Davies Casting Ltd

PO Box 680, Sutton, Surrey SM1 3ZG
tel 020-8715 1036 *fax* 020-8644 9746
email info@janedaviescasting.co.uk
Casting Directors Jane Davies CDG, John Connor CDG

Casts mainly for television. Casting credits include: *My Family*, *The Green Green Grass*, and *Black Books*.

Will consider attending performances of light drama, and particularly of comedies, at venues in Greater London.

Gary Davy CDG

1st Floor, 55-59 Shaftesbury Avenue, London W1D 6LD

Casts for film and television. Casting credits include: Steve McQueen's 2008 Cannes-winning *Hunger*; Nick Love's *The Business*, *Outlaw* and upcoming *The Sweeney*; *Revengers Tragedy* (Alex Cox); Nick Cave's *The Proposition* (John Hillcoat); *44 inch Chest* (Malcolm Venville); and the comedy *Faintheart* (Vito Rocco). Television credits include: *He Kills Coppers*, *My Boy Jack*, *Sweeney Todd*, *Mr Eleven*, *Mistresses II*, and UK Casting on *Band of Brothers*.

Gabrielle Dawes CDG

PO Box 52493, London NW3 9DZ
tel 020-7435 3645
email gdawescasting@tiscali.co.uk

Gabrielle Dawes is Associate for Casting at Chichester Festival Theatre, and a freelance Casting Director.

Theatre includes: *The Norman Conquests*, *All About My Mother*, *New Voices 24-Hour Plays* (Old Vic); *Cat on a Hot Tin Roof*, *Three Days of Rain*, *Treasure Island* (West End); Rupert Goold's *Macbeth* (Chichester/West End/Broadway); *Wallenstein*, *The Grapes of Wrath*, *Separate Tables*, *Hay Fever*, *Aristo*, *Funny Girl*, *The Circle*, *Taking Sides / Collaboration* (and West End); *Hobson's Choice*, *The Waltz of the Toreadors*, *Twelfth Night* (all Chichester); *The English Game* (Headlong Theatre); *The Elephant Man* (Sheffield); *As You Like It* (Watford).

As Deputy Head of Casting at the National Theatre 2000-2006, award-winning productions included *Caroline, or Change*, *His Dark Materials*, *Elmina's Kitchen*, *The Pillowman*, and *Coram Boy*.

Television credits include: Harold Pinter's *Celebration*, and *Elmina's Kitchen* by Kwame Kwei-Armah. Films include *Perdie* (BAFTA award for Best Short Film) and *The Suicide Club*.

Stephanie Dawes

13 Nevern Square, London SW5 9NW
tel 020-7261 3509 *fax* 020-7737 8541

Works mainly for television. Recent credits include: casting for *Crime Monthly* and *Most Wanted* (LWT); children and extras casting for *Spaced* (LWT/Paramount Comedy Channel for Channel 4); and *Johnny and the Dead* (LWT).

See entry for Granada under *Independent television* on page 331 for further details.

Kate Day CDG

Pound Cottage, 27 The Green South, Warborough, Oxfordshire OX10 7DR

Main areas of work are television, film and commercials.

Will consider attending performances at venues in Greater London and occasionally elsewhere, given as much notice as possible. Accepts submissions (with CVs and photographs) from actors previously unknown to the casting director if sent by post. Does not welcome email enquiries.

Paul De Freitas

PO Box 4903, London W1A 7JZ
tel 020-7486 5407 *fax* 020-7486 181 7
email info@pauldefreitas.com
website www.pauldefreitas.com

Main areas of work are film, television and commercials. Casting credits include: *Dog Boy* (BBC2); *Lazarus & Dingwall* (BBC2); *Bernard & The Genie* (Talkback/Attaboy); *The Princess Academy* (Weintraub Productions); and *What Larry Says* (Platypus Productions).

The Denman Casting Agency

Burgess House, Main Street, Farnsfield, Notts NG22 8EF
Key personnel Jack Denman FEAA

Main areas of work are theatre, musicals, television, film and commercials. Casting credits include: *Peak Practice*, *Doctors*, and *Crimewatch* (television); and videos for PC World and Boots. Awarded Preferred Agents status by the BBC for supporting artists and walk-ons.

Accepts submissions (with CVs and photographs) from actors previously unknown to the casting director if sent by post. Does not welcome email enquiries. No short film enquiries.

Lee Dennison CDA

Fushion, 27 Old Gloucester Street, London WC1N 3XX
tel 0870-011 1100 *fax* 0870-011 1020
email leedennison@fushion-uk.com
website www.ukscreen.com/crew/ldennison
website www.leedennisonassociates.com
Casting London/New York Lee Dennison, Chuck Harvey, Ram Tucker *Casting London/Paris* Lee Dennison, Will Baker, Jamie Lowe *Assistant* Dean Saunders

Casts mainly for film and television features as well as commercials and music promos. Recent credits include: *Vacancy* (Screen Gems), *Buttermilk Sky* (Charles R Leinenweber), *Echo Park LA* (Sony), *United 93* (Universal), and *Standoff* (Fox).

"As we deal only with featured established artistes, please, no unsolicited requests."

Malcom Drury CDG

34 Tabor Road, London W6 0BW
tel 020-8748 9232

Casts mainly for television. Casting credits include: *The Bill*, *Heartbeat*, *The Beiderbecke Affair* and Laurence Olivier's *King Lear*.

Carol Dudley CDG, CSA

See entry for Cannon Dudley & Associates.

Maureen Duff CDG

PO Box 47340, London NW3 4TY
tel 020-7586 0532 *fax* 020-7681 7172

Main areas of work are film, television and theatre. Credits include: *Closing The Ring* (Richard Attenborough); *The History of Mr Polly* (Granada Media); *Poirot* (several episodes for Granada Media); and *Dancing At Lughnasa* (and several other productions for the Northcott Theatre, Exeter).

Julia Duff CDG

73 Wells Street, London W1T 3QG
tel 020-7436 8860 *fax* 020-7436 8859

Casts mainly for television. Casting credits include: *New Tricks*, *Hotel Babylon*, *Secret Diary of a Call Girl*, *Persuasion*, *Monarch of the Glen*, and *The Amazing Mrs Pritchard*.

Jennifer Duffy CDG

11 Portsea Mews, London W2 2BN
tel 020-7262 3326
email casting@jennyduffy.co.uk

Main areas of work are film and television. Credits include: *Life 'n' Lyrics* (Fiesta Productions, BBC Films, Universal), *Wallace & Gromit: The Curse of the Wererabbit* (Aardman/Dreamworks), *Macbeth* (BBC) and *Dunkirk* (BBC2, Huw Wheldon BAFTA Award 2005).

Irene East Casting CDG

40 Brookwood Avenue, Barnes, London SW13 0LR
tel 020-8876 5686 *fax* 020-8876 5686
email IrnEast@aol.com

Main areas of work are theatre and film. Casting Director for Love and Madness Productions. Theatre credits include: *Macbeth*, *Ajax* (dir. Jack Shepherd), *A Skull in Connemara*, *The Tempest*, *The Playboy of the Western World*, *Murder in Paris*. Features include: *A Distant Mirage*, *The Problem with Pets*, *Big Claus*, *Little Claus*.

Will attend performances at venues in Greater London and occasionally elsewhere, given a couple of days' notice. Showreels should only be sent on request.

EJ Casting

150 Tooley Street, London SE1 2TU
tel 020-7564 2688
email info@EJCasting.com
Director Edward James

Casts for theatre, musicals, film, commercials and corporate work. Casting credits include: *Into the Woods* and *Sweet Charity* (theatre); commercials for AOL, Lloyds Bank, Sony BMG, Universal Music, and Cadbury's Fingers; and *Air on a G String* (film).

Will consider attending performances at venues in Greater London and occasionally elsewhere. Accepts showreels containing work that has been broadcast. Due to the overwhelming number of CVs sent, is unable to accept general enquiries. "Please only send an application if it is a performance notice or in response to a specific breakdown."

Richard Evans CDG

10 Shirley Road, London W4 1DD
tel 020-8994 6304
email info@evanscasting.co.uk
website www.evanscasting.co.uk
Key personnel Richard Evans CDG

Main areas of work are theatre, musicals, television, film and commercials. Casting credits include: *The Rat Pack – Live From Las Vegas* (theatre).

Will consider attending performances at venues in Greater London and occasionally elsewhere, given sufficient notice. Requests 1-2 weeks before the opening night for theatre productions, and 2-3 days prior to transmission for television shows. Accepts follow-up telephone calls after a production has opened. Welcomes submissions (with CVs and photographs) from actors previously unknown to the casting director if sent by post. Does not welcome email enquiries. Showreels should only be sent on request. Advises actors to: "Be specific, find out about current projects and suggest yourself for particular roles. Always ensure that the part you are playing is worth casting personnel coming to see. Offer complimentary tickets. It is worth keeping in touch as your career progresses."

Bunny Fildes Casting CDG

56-60 Wigmore Street, London W1U 2RZ
tel 020-7935 1254 *fax* 020-7298 1871

Casts mainly for theatre, television, film and commercials.

Will consider attending performances within Greater London given 2 weeks' notice. Accepts postal submissions (with CVs and photographs) from actors previously unknown to the company. Unsolicited emails and showreels, however, are not welcomed.

Sally Fincher CDG

tel 020-8347 5945
email sallyfincher@btinternet.com

Main area of work is television. Credits include: *Murder In Suburbia, Sweet Medicine, Barbara, Kiss Me Kate, Outside Edge* and *The Upper Hand.*

Janie Frazer CDG

ITV/Granada, London Television Centre, Upper Ground, London SE1 9LT
tel 020-7261 3848 *fax* 020-7737 8541

Casts mainly for television (drama and comedy, serials and one-offs); currently Resident Casting Director at ITV (Granada). Casting credits include: *Coronation Street, Vincent, Murder in Suburbia, Blue Murder, Island at War, City Lights* and *Spaced.*

See entry for ITV under *Independent television* on page 331 for further details. Also see See Janie's article on page 327 for advice on television casting.

Caroline Funnell

25 Rattray Road, London SW2 1AZ
tel 020-7326 4417

Areas of work include theatre and musicals. Will consider attending performances within the Greater London area with at least 2 weeks' notice.

Artistic Director of Sixteenfeet Productions (25 Rattray Road, London SW2 1AZ, info@sixteenfeet.co.uk).

Tracey Gillham CDG

Room 4018, BBC TV Centre, Wood Lane, London W12 7RJ
tel 020-8225 8648 *fax* 020-8576 4414
email tracey.gillham@bbc.co.uk

Main areas of work are film and television. For recent credits, please see *Spotlight* or the CDG website.

Nina Gold CDG

117 Chevening Road, London NW6 6DU
tel 020-8960 6099 *fax* 020-8968 6777

Main areas of work are film, television and commercials. Casting credits include: *Vera Drake,* directed by Mike Leigh (Thin Man Films); *The Life and Death of Peter Sellers,* directed by Stephen Hopkins; *The Jacket,* directed by John Maybury (Warner Bros); *Daniel Deronda,* directed by Tom Hooper (BBC TV); *Amazing Grace* and *Rome* both directed by Michael Apted; *Starter for Ten* directed by Tom Vaughan; *The Illusionist* directed by Neil Burger; and *Brothers of the Head* directed by Keith Fulton and Louis Pepe.

Miranda Gooch

102 Leighton Gardens, London NW10 3RP

Casts mainly for feature films. Recent credits have included: *True Story* and *Tooth.*

Will consider attending performances within Greater London given as much notice as possible. Accepts submissions (with CVs and photographs) from actors previously unknown to the company sent by post or email. Showreels are also accepted.

Jill Green CDG

PO Box 56927, London N10 3UR
tel 0845-478 6343

Casts for theatre, musicals and film. Casting credits include: *Jersey Boys* (Prince Edward Theatre); *The Producers* (Drury Lane Theatre); *Thoroughly Modern Millie* (Shaftesbury Theatre); *Contact* (Queens Theatre); and *Beyond the Sea* (film directed by Kevin Spacey).

Will consider attending performances within Greater London and occasionally elsewhere, given a minimum of 2 weeks' notice. Accepts postal submissions (with CVs and photographs) from actors who are currently appearing in a production, but does not welcome blanket mailings, unsolicited emails or showreels (unless an sae is enclosed for their return).

Marcia Gresham CDG

3 Langthorne Street, London SW6 6JT
tel 020-7381 2876 *fax* 020-7381 4496
email marcia@greshamcast.com

Main area of work is television. Casting credits include: *Britz, The Government Inspector, Warriors,* and *The Project* – all projects directed by Peter Kosminsky for television.

Will consider attending performances at venues in Greater London given 1 month's notice. Accepts submissions (with CVs and photographs) from actors previously unknown to the casting director if sent by post, but does not welcome email enquiries. Showreels and voice tapes (with sae for return) are also accepted.

David Grindrod CDG

4th Floor, Palace Theatre, Shaftesbury Avenue, London W1D 5AY
tel 020-7437 2506 *fax* 020-7437 2507
email dga@grindrodcasting.co.uk

Casts for musicals and films. Film credits: Dance casting *Nine*, Ensemble casting *Mamma Mia!* and *The Phantom of the Opera*. West End casting: *Chicago, Mamma Mia!, Ghost, Hairspray, Love Never Dies, Sister Act*.

Will consider attending performances within Greater London and possibly elsewhere, given as much notice as possible. Does not welcome unsolicited submissions from actors. Casting breakdowns are released via The Spotlight, therefore actors should only write in with reference to specific productions. See also David's article *Casting for musical theatre* on page 113.

Janet Hall

69 Buckstones Road, Shaw, Oldham OL2 8DW

Main areas of work include television, film and commercials. Casting credits include: AXA commercial, and *The Sound of Music* (theatre).

Will consider attending performances at venues in Greater London and in Manchester, Liverpool and Leeds, given 1 week's notice. Accepts submissions (with CVs and photographs) from actors previously unknown to the casting director sent by post or email. Also accepts showreels, voice tapes and invitations to view individual actors' websites.

Louis Hammond

6 Brewer Street, London W1F 0SD
tel 020-7734 1880

Main areas of work are theatre, television and film. Casting credits include: *Mirrormask* and *Arsene Lupin* (films); *The Bill* (TV); *Rock 'N' Roll* (Royal Court/West End); *The Member of the Wedding* (Young Vic); *The Importance of Being Earnest* (West End); and *Testing the Echo* (Tricycle).

Will consider attending performances. Accepts submissions (with CVs and photographs) from actors previously unknown to the casting director. "When sending submissions, I suggest a photograph built into the CV. 10x8in photographs may not be retained by the casting director."

Gemma Hancock CDG

North Lodge, Weald Chase, Staplefield Road, Cuckfield, West Sussex RH17 5HY
tel (01444) 441398 *fax* (01444) 441398

Main areas of work are theatre, television and film. Casting credits include: *The Bill* (Talkback Thames); Peter Ackroyd's *London* (BBC 2); *Blithe Spirit* (West End and tour); and *The Dresser* (Bath Theatre Royal and tour).

Judi Hayfield CDG / Judi Hayfield Ltd

6 Richmond Hill Road, Gatley, Cheshire SK8 1QG
mobile (07919) 221873
email judi.hayfield@hotmail.co.uk

Polly Hootkins CDG

PO Box 52480, London NW3 9DH
tel 020-7233 8724 *fax* 020-7828 5051
email phootkins@clara.net
website www.thecdg.co.uk
Key personnel Polly Hootkins

Will consider attending performances at venues in Greater London and occasionally elsewhere, given as much notice as possible. Accepts submissions (with CVs and photographs) from actors previously unknown to the casting director if sent by post. Does not welcome email enquiries. Showreels, voice tapes and invitations to view individual actors' websites are also accepted.

Hubbard Casting

14 Rathbone Place, London W1T 1HT
tel 020-7631 4944 *fax* 020-7636 7117
Casting Directors John Hubbard, Ros Hubbard, Dan Hubbard, Amy Hubbard

Casts mainly for film, television, theatre and commercials. Casting credits include: *United 93, The Damned United, Lord of the Rings, The Bourne Ultimatum,* and *Ben-Hur* (mini series).

Sarah Hughes

Room 4018, BBC Television Centre, Wood Lane, London W12 7RJ

Former Resident Casting Director for the Stephen Joseph Theatre, Scarborough.

International Collective (INC)

9-13 Grape Street, London WC2H 9ED
tel 020-7484 5060 (London office)
tel 0113-219 2896 (Leeds office)
email joadamson@internationalcollective.co.uk
email casting@internationalcollective.co.uk
website www.internationalcollective.co.uk
Key personnel Jo Adamson CDG, Christopher Manoe

Area of works include television, theatre, film, musicals and commercials. Recent work includes: *The War of The Worlds* (UK National Tour); *That's Amore* (UK National Tour); *Fat Friends* (ITV/ Tiger aspect); *The Bill* (Talkback Thames) and *Touchdown* (Findaway Films).

Will consider attending performances within the Greater London area, in the North of England and elsewhere, given at least 1 week's notice. Welcomes invitations to view actors' showreels and websites.

Sue Jackson

53 Moseley Wood Walk, Leeds LS16 7HQ

Freelance casting director.

Trevor Jackson CDG

1 Bedford Square, London WC1B 3RA
tel 020-7637 8866 *fax* 020-7436 2683

Casts mainly for musicals produced by Cameron Mackintosh Ltd. Casting credits include: *My Fair Lady, Les Miserables, Miss Saigon, Phantom of the Opera, Mary Poppins, Avenue Q* and *Oliver!.*

Will consider attending performances at venues in Greater London given as much notice as possible. Accepts submissions (with CVs and photographs) from actors previously unknown to the casting director if sent by post, but does not welcome email enquiries. Showreels, voice tapes and invitations to view individual actors' websites are also accepted.

Janis Jaffa Casting

67 Starfield Road, London W12 9SN
tel 020-7565 2877 *fax* 020-8743 9561

email janis@janisjaffacasting.co.uk

Works mainly in television, film and commercials. Recent credits include: *The Bill.* Will consider attending performances within Greater London. Welcomes letters (with CVs & photographs) from individual actors previously unknown to the agency sent by post, but not by email. Will accept showreels and invitations to view individual actors' websites.

Jennifer Jaffrey

The Double Lodge, Pinewood Studios, Pinewood Road, Iver Heath, Bucks SL0 0NH
tel 020-8578 2899 *fax* 020-8575 0369
Key personnel Jennifer Jaffrey *(Proprietor)*

Main areas of work are theatre, musicals, television, film and commercials. Casting credits include: *Cross My Heart, Ten Minutes Older* and *Such a Long Journey.*

Will consider attending performances at venues in Greater London given as much notice as possible. Accepts submissions (with CVs and photographs) from actors previously unknown to the casting director if sent by post, but does not welcome email enquiries. Photographs should have the actor's name written on the back and an sae must be included for the return of material. Showreels should only be sent on request.

Lucy Jenkins CDG

74 High Street, Hampton Wick, Kingston on Thames, KT1 4DQ
tel 020-8943 5328 *fax* 020-8977 0466

Casts mainly for film, television, theatre and commercials. Casting credits include: *Babyfather* (BBC), *The Bill* (television), *Top Dog* (short film) and *Emma* (theatre).

Marilyn Johnson CDG

11 Goodwin's Court, London WC2N 4LL
tel 020-7497 5552 *fax* 020-7497 5530
email marjoncast@aol.com

Main area of work is television. Credits include *Our Mutual Friend, Holding On, Murphy's Law, Nature Boy* and *Inspector Morse.*

Doreen Jones

PO Box 22478, London W6 0WJ
tel 020-8746 3782 *fax* 020-8748 8533

Casts mainly for television and film. Recent credits include: *Fingersmith, Prime Suspect, Elizabeth, The Palace* and *Wallander.*

Will consider attending performances within Greater London and occasionally elsewhere, given as much notice as possible. Unsolicited submissions and enquiries from actors are not welcome.

Sam Jones CDG

7B Trinity Church Square, London SE1 4HU
tel 020-7378 0222

Agents and Casting Directors

email get@samjones.fsnet.co.uk

Former Head of Casting for the Royal Shakespeare Company. Other credits include: *Journey's End* (West End and tour); *After Mrs Rochester* (for Shared Experience); *Abigail's Party* (Hampstead Theatre/ West End); *Trial & Retribution* (for La Plante Productions/ITV); and *Human Cargo* (for CBC/Force Four – nominated for 17 Gemini Awards).

Sue Jones CDG

24 Nicoll Road, London NW10 9AB
tel 020-8838 5153 *fax* 020-8838 1130

Main areas of work are film, television, theatre and commercials. Casting credits include: *The Virgin of Liverpool*, starring Ricky Tomlinson and Imelda Staunton (MOB Films); *The Sound of Thunder*, with Ed Burns, Ben Kingsley and Catherine McCormack; *The Origins of Evil* (CBS/Alliance Atlantis); *Messiah* and *Coriolanus* (both plays directed by Stephen Berkoff); *The Vicar* (BBC television); and *The Politician's Wife* (Channel 4).

Kate and Lou Casting

The Basement, Museum House, 25 Museum Street, London WC1A 1JT
mobile (07976) 252531
website www.kateandloucasting.com

Casts for commercials. Recent credits include: Tilda Rice, Macdonalds, Lotto, and Doritos.

Does not welcome performance notices. Will accept letters (with CVs and photographs) from individual actors previously unknown to the company, and unsolicited CVs and photographs sent via email. Does not welcome showreels or invitations to view individual actors' websites.

Anna Kennedy Casting

8 Rydal Road, London SW16 1QN

Welcomes performance notices, for productions within the Greater London area, with 2 weeks' notice. Will accept letters, but not emails, with CVs and photographs from individuals previously unknown to the casting director; also welcomes showreels and invitations to view actors' websites.

Beverley Keogh

29 Ardwick Green North, Ardwick, Manchester M12 6DL
tel 0161-273 4400 *fax* 0161-273 4401
email Beverley@beverlykeogh.tv

Main areas of work are television, film and commercials. Casting credits include: *Fat Friends*, *Clocking Off* and *Second Coming*.

Accepts submissions (with CVs and photographs) from actors previously unknown to the casting director sent by post or email.

Jerry Knight-Smith CDG

Royal Exchange Theatre, Manchester, M2 7DH
tel 0161-615 6761

website www.royalexchangecasting.co.uk

Resident Casting Director for the Royal Exchange Theatre, Manchester. See entry under *Producing theatres* on page 147 for further details.

Suzy Korel CDG

20 Blenheim Road, St John's Wood, London NW8 0LX

Will consider attending performances at venues in Greater London given as much notice as possible. Accepts submissions (with CVs and photographs) from actors previously unknown to the casting director if sent by post, but does not welcome email enquiries. Invitations to view individual actors' websites are also accepted.

Larca Ltd

Ynyslas Uchaf Farm, Blackmill, Bridgend CF35 6DW
tel (01656) 841841 *mobile* (07779) 321954
email leigh-annregan@btconnect.com
website www.leigh-annregancasting.co.uk

Works in theatre, musicals, television, film and commercials. Recent credits include: *Y Pris* (21-part television drama series); and *Caerdydd* (5-year television series, S4C).

Will consider attending performances within Greater London and elsewhere, given 2 weeks' notice. Welcomes letters (with CVs and photographs) from individual actors previously unknown to the company, sent by post only; also welcomes showreels.

Sharon Levinson

30 Stratford Villas, London NW1 9SG

Main areas of work are theatre, television, film and commercials. Casting credits include: *Two Thousand Acres of Sky* and *A Christmas Carol* (television).

Will consider attending performances at venues in Greater London and occasionally elsewhere, given 2 weeks' notice. Not currently casting.

Karen Lindsay-Stewart CDG

PO Box 2301, London W1A 1PT

Main areas of work are television and film. Casting credits include: *Sylvia*, *Harry Potter and the Chamber of Secrets* and *Cambridge Spies*.

Will consider attending performances at venues in Greater London with sufficient notice. Accepts submissions (with CVs and photographs) from actors previously unknown to the casting director if sent by post, but does not welcome email enquiries. Do not send sae(s) for replies.

Maggie Lunn

Resident Casting Director for the Almeida and Chichester Festival theatres. See entries for respective theatres under *Producing theatres* on page 136.

Kay Magson Casting

PO Box 175, Pudsey, Leeds LS28 7LN
tel 0113-236 0251

email kay.magson@btinternet.com
Casting Director Kay Magson

Recent credits include *Bollywood Jane, Twelfth Night, Alice in Wonderland, Duchess of Malfi* (West Yorkshire Playhouse), National Tours of *Singin' In the Rain, Aspects of Love, Round the Horne...Revisited* and *Dracula, Noises Off, Billy Liar, The Flint Street Nativity, The Electric Hills* (Liverpool), *A Model Girl* (Greenwich), *One Last Card Trick, Aladdin* (Watford), *Merrily We Roll Along, Importance of Being Earnest, As You Like It* (Derby), *The Way of the World, Follies* (Northampton), *East Is East* (York/Bolton), *Rosencrantz & Guildenstern Are Dead, Much Ado About Nothing* (Manchester Library).

Will consider attending performances within the Greater London area and elsewhere, with at least 4 weeks' notice. Accepts submissions (with CVs and photographs) from actors previously unknown to the casting director via email only.

Lisa Makin

Resident Casting Director for the Royal Court Theatre. See entry under *Producing theatres* on page 136 for further details.

Andrew Mann

See entry for Casting UK.

John Manning

4 Holmbury Gardens, Hayes, Middlesex UB3 2LU
tel 020-8573 5463

Works in theatre and musicals. Recent credits include: *The 39 Steps* (Criterion Theatre); *Turandot* (Hampstead); and *An Inspector Calls* (national tour).

Will consider attending performances within the Greater London area, and regularly attends regional theatre – but does request 4 weeks' notice. Welcomes letters (with CVs and photographs) from individual actors previously unknown to the company, sent by post only; will also accept invitations to view individual actors' websites.

Carolyn McLeod

PO Box 26495, London SE10 0WO
tel + 44 (0)704 4001720
email actors@cmcasting.eclipse.co.uk

Main areas of work are film, television and promos. Casting director credits include: *WMD, Starship Troopers 3, Pumpkinhead 3: Ashes to Ashes, Pumpkinhead 4: Blood Feud, The Bill* (2006-2008), and *Power Rangers: Operation Overdrive*. Promos for: Lemar, Oasis, and The Feeling.

Will consider attending performances at venues in Greater London and occasionally elsewhere, given 2-3 weeks' notice. Accepts submissions (with CVs and photographs) from actors previously unknown to the casting director sent by post or email. Showreels, voice tapes and invitations to view individual actors' websites are also accepted. Applicants should only submit their details once. Advises actors that: "As most casting directors have little capacity for storing CVs, it may be worth telephoning to check whether they are accepting submissions – though do be warned that some people may not appreciate the phone call. If you already have an agent, ask them to contact us on your behalf."

Chrissie McMurrich

16 Spring Vale Avenue, Brentford, Middlesex TW8 9QH

Main areas of work are theatre and television. Recent casting includes: the tour of *Scooby Doo and the Pirate Ghost Live on Stage*; the Ludlow Festival/Exeter Northcott Theatre production of *Romeo and Juliet*; *Original Sin, The Blue Room, A Christmas Carol* and *Cyrano de Bergerac* for the Haymarket Basingstoke; and the tour of *Thomas the Tank Engine and Friends*.

Will consider attending performances at venues in Greater London given 2 weeks' notice. Accepts submissions with performance notices (containing photos and CVs) from actors previously unknown to the casting director if sent by post. No unsolicited emails are accepted. "Please be aware of the new postage rates for A4 envelopes. Not everyone will pay the Royal Mail handling charge to get unsolicited photos and CVs."

Anne McNulty

Resident Casting Director for Donmar Warehouse. See separate entry under *Producing theatres* on page 136.

Sooki McShane CDG

8a Piermont Road, East Dulwich, London SE22 0LN
tel 020-8693 7411 *fax* 020-8693 7411

Works mainly in theatre, film and television. Casting credits include: *Rainbow Room* (Granada television); *My Brother Rob* (feature film); and casting for the Warehouse Theatre Croydon.

Currently Resident Casting Director for the Nottingham Playhouse. See entry under *Producing theatres* on page 136 for further details.

Carl Proctor CDG

3rd Floor, 76 Neal Street, London WC2H 9PL
tel 020-7379 6200 *mobile* (07956) 283340
email carlproctor@btconnect.com
website www.carlproctor.com

Casts mainly for film, television, theatre and commercials. Casting credits include: *Mrs Palfrey at the Claremont, Something Borrowed* and *Dead Cool*.

Performance notices, submissions, showreels and unsolicited emails are not welcomed. Advises that CVs and photographs are no longer kept on file as these details are available on Spotlight Interactive.

Andy Pryor CDG

Suite 3, 15 Broad Court, London WC2B 5QN
tel 020-7836 8298 *fax* 020-7836 8299

Casts mainly for film and television. Casting credits include: *Glorious 39* (a film directed by Stephen Poliakoff); and *Doctor Who* and *Life on Mars* (for BBC Television).

Gennie Radcliffe

Casting Director for *Coronation Street*. See entry for Granada under *Independent television* on page 331 for further details.

Leigh-Ann Regan

Ynyslasuchaf Farm, Blackmill, Bridgend LF35 6DW
tel 01656-841 841 *fax* 01656-841 815
email leigh-annregan@btconnect.com

Areas of work include television, film, commercials and theatre. Resident casting director at Clwyd Theatr Cymru (see entry under *Producing theatres* on page 138). Recent credits include: 21 part drama series for S4C/Fiction Factory (Ypris), 4 years casting *Caerdydd* for S4C/Fiction Factory.

Will consider attending performances in Greater London and elsewhere with at least one week's notice. Accepts submissions (with CVs and photographs) from actors previously unknown to the casting director.

Samantha Relph CDG

email srelph@derbyplayhouse.co.uk

Resident Casting Director for the Derby Playhouse. See entry under Producing theatres on page 139 for further details.

Simone Reynolds CDG

60 Hebdon Road, London SW17 7NN

Main areas of work are film, television, theatre and commercials. Casting credits include: *The 39 Steps* (Olivier Award for Best Comedy); *The Vicar of Dibley* and *Turning Points: Emma's Story* (both for BBC television); *Jack and Sarah* (film for Granada); *Shining Through* (film for Twentieth Century Fox) and *Quicksand* (film).

Will consider attending performances at venues in Greater London and elsewhere, given as much notice as possible. Accepts postal submissions (with CVs and photographs) from actors previously unknown to the casting director, but does not welcome email enquiries. Advises actors to: "Keep CVs clear (separate out the part from the director and venue) and keep covering submissions brief."

Danielle Roffe Casting

71 Mornington Street, London NW1 7QE

Works in film and television. Recent credits include: *The Upside of Anger*, *She's Gone*, and *Holy Cross*.

Welcomes performance notices and is prepared to travel within Greater London. Does not welcome unsolicited CVs, photographs or showreels, but is happy to receive invitations to view individual actors' websites.

Jane Salberg

86 Stade Street, Hythe, Kent CT21 6DY
tel (01303) 239277
email janesalberg@aol.com

Works in theatre and musicals. Recent credits include: UK Casting Director for Jean Ann Ryan (Cruise Musicals); *Horrid Henry Live and Horrid* (UK tour); and *The Wizard of Oz* (Royal Festival Hall).

Prefers not to receive performance notices or unsolicited submissions, but will consider invitations to view individual actors' websites.

Laura Scott CDG

56 Rowena Crescent, London SW11 2PT
tel 020-7978 6336 *fax* 020-7924 1907
email laurascottcasting@mac.com

Main areas of work are film, television, theatre and commercials. Casting credits include: *Bonekickers* (BBC TV), *William and Mary* (Series 1-3, TV), *Trial and Retribution XIV* (TV), and *The Time of Your Life* (TV).

The Searchers

70 Sylvia Court, Cavendish Street, London N1 7PG
Directors Wayne Waterson, Ian Sheppard

Casts mainly for television, film and commercials. Recent credits include: commercials for Pepsi, Nike, Kellogg's and Royal Mail. Has worked for directors including Terry Gillingham, Tarsem and Earl Morris.

Will consider attending performances within Greater London given 1 week's notice. Accepts submissions (with CVs, showreels and photographs) from actors previously unknown to the company, but does not welcome unsolicited emails or invitations to view an actor's website.

Phil Shaw

Suite 476, 2 Old Brompton Road, South Kensington, London SW7 3DQ
tel 020-8715 8943
email shawcastlond@aol.com

Main areas of work are theatre, television, film and commercials. Casting credits include: *Deckies* (TV series pilot); *Days in the Trees* (BBC Radio); *Body Story* (BBC doc/drama series); *Romans 12:20* (short); *Winter Fiction* (NFTS); *The Turn of the Screw* (theatre); *The Last Post* (film – BAFTA nominated); and *Love and Virtue* (feature).

Will consider attending performances at venues in Central London given a minimum of 2 weeks' notice. Accepts postal submissions (with CVs and photographs) from actors previously unknown to the casting director, but does not welcome unsolicited showreels or email enquiries.

Michelle Smith CDG

220 Church Lane, Woodford, Stockport SK7 1PQ
tel 0161-439 6825 *fax* 0161-439 0622

Main areas of work are film, television and commercials. Casting credits include: *Steel River Blues* (ITV); *Max and Paddy* (Channel 4); *Phoenix Nights* (Channel 4); and *Cold Feet* (Series 1-5 – Granada).

Suzanne Smith CDG

33 Fitzroy Street, London W1T 6DU
tel 020-7436 9255 *fax* 020-7436 9690

Main areas of work are film, television, theatre and musicals. Casting credits include: UK casting for *Alien vs Predator* (directed by Paul Anderson for 20th Century Fox); *The Dark* (directed by John Fawcett for Impact Pictures); UK casting for *Black Hawk Down* (directed by Ridley Scott); and *Band of Brothers* (for television – HBO/Dreamworks).

Wendy Spon CDG

c/o National Theatre, South Bank, London SE1 9PX

Main areas of work are film, television, theatre and musicals. Until recently, Head of Casting at Talkback Thames (*The Bill*), and now Head of Casting at the National Theatre (see entry under *Producing theatres* on page 143). Casting credits include: *The Graduate* (theatre, directed by Terry Johnson); *Oklahoma* and *Oh What a Lovely War* (both for the National Theatre); and *Shadow Man* (short film).

Emma Stafford

Royal Exchange, St Ann's Square,
Manchester M2 7BR
tel 0161-833 4263 *fax* 0161-833 4264
email info@emmastafford.tv
website www.emmastafford.tv

Areas of work include television, film and commercials. Recent credits include: *200 Magazine*, Co-op Bank, Robinsons, *If I Were a Butterfly*.

Will consider attending performances within the North West area with at least 2 weeks' notice. Accepts letters (with CVs and photographs) from actors previously unknown to the agency; will also accept CVs and photographs sent by email, and view showreels.

Gail Stevens Casting CDG

Greenhill House, 90-93 Cowcross Street, London EC1M 6BF

Main areas of work are television, film and commercials. Casting credits include: *Twenty-Eight Days Later*, *Calendar Girls* and *Spooks*.

Sam Stevenson CDG

email sam@hancockstevenson.com
website www.hancockstevenson.com

Main areas of work are television, theatre and film. More details are available on the website.

Liz Stoll

BBC Elstree, Room N223 Neptune House,
Clarendon Road, Borehamwood WD6 1JF
tel 020-8228 8285 *fax* 020-8228 8311
email liz.stoll@bbc.co.uka

Has worked in all areas of actor casting and has been casting BBC1 drama for the past 7 years. Credits include: *Holby City*; 5 series of *Judge John Deed*; 5 series of *Down To Earth*; various episodes of *Waking the Dead* and *Dalziel & Pascoe*; *Magnificent Seven* (a film for BBC2); *A View from a Hill* (a film for BBC4); and 6 Afternoon Plays for BBC1.

Happy to receive performance notices at least 2 weeks in advance, and is prepared to travel within Greater London (sometimes further, work permitting) to see shows. Welcomes letters (but not emails) with CVs and photographs from actors previously unknown to the casting director; does not welcome unsolicited showreels, but is happy to receive invitations to view individuals' websites.

Emma Style CDG

1 Overton Cottages, Kings Lane, Cookham, Maidenhead SL6 9BA
Main areas of work are film and television. Credits include: *Scenes of a Sexual Nature* (feature film), *Mansfield Park* (ITV drama), *Callas Forever* (Callynta Films, Franco Zeffirelli), *Tea With Mussolini* (Universal, Franco Zeffirelli), *Prime Suspect V* (Granada Television) and *Our Friends In The North* (episodes 5-9, BBC2).

Syson Grainger Casting

1st Floor, 33 Old Compton Street, London W1D 5JT
tel 020-7287 5327 *fax* 020-7287 3629

Recent feature films include: *Children of Men*, directed by Alfonso Cuaron; *Syriana*, directed by Stephen Gagan; *Batman Begins*, directed by Chris Nolan; *Troy*, directed by Wolfgang Petersen; *Snatch*, directed by Guy Ritchie; *Spygame*, directed by Tony Scott; and *Fifth Element*, directed by Luc Besson.

Amanda Tabak CDG

See entry for Candid Casting.

Topps Casting

The Media Centre, 7 Northumberland Street, West Yorkshire HD1 1RL
tel (01484) 511988 *fax* (01484) 483100
email nicci@toppscasting.co.uk
website www.toppscasting.co.uk
Casting Director Nicci Topping

Works in television, film and commercials. Recent credits include: AA TVC, Iceland TVC, and Global Stories. Welcomes performance notices within Greater London and elsewhere (Manchester, Leeds, Sheffield) if given 2 weeks' notice. Accepts letters (with CVs & photographs) from individual actors previously unknown to the agency, sent by post or email.

Moira Townsend

See entry for Casting Couch Productions Ltd.

Jill Trevellick CDG

92 Priory Road, London N8 7EY
tel 020-8340 2734 *fax* 020-8348 7400

Main areas of work are film and television. Casting credits include: *The Ruby In The Smoke*, *North and South*, and *The Canterbury Tales* (all BBC); *Primeval* (ITV); and *The Queen's Sister* and *The Hamburg Cell* (both Channel 4).

Sarah Trevis CDG

PO Box 47170, London W6 6BA
tel 020-7602 5552 *fax* 020-7602 8110

Main areas of work are television and film. Recent casting credits include: work for Granada television, the BBC and Twentieth Century Fox.

Will consider attending performances given 2 weeks' notice. Accepts submissions (with CVs and photographs) from actors previously unknown to the casting director if sent by post. Does not welcome email enquiries.

Sally Vaughan CDG

2 Kennington Park Place, London SE11 4AS
tel 020-7735 6539

Main area of work is theatre. Credits include: *Porridge* (No. 1 UK tour); *'Allo, 'Allo* (No. 1 UK tour); *Dad's Army – The Lost Episodes* (No. 1 UK tour); *Sweet Charity* (Victoria Palace Theatre), *Of Thee I Sing* and *Sweeney Todd* (Bridewell Theatre); and *Anna Weiss* (Whitehall Theatre).

Vital Productions

PO Box 26441, London SE10 9GZ
tel 020-8316 4497 *fax* 020-8316 4497
email mail@vital-productions.co.uk
Key personnel Melissa Waudby

Main areas of work are theatre and television. Casting credits include: *BBC Crimewatch* and *The Great Dome Robbery* (television).

Will consider attending performances at venues in Greater London and elsewhere, given 1 month's notice. Accepts submissions (with CVs and photographs) from actors previously unknown to the casting director if sent by post. Does not welcome email enquiries. "Because of time pressure, we tend to use *Spotlight* and specific agents or individual suggestions rather than CVs and photographs submitted to us."

Anne Vosser CDG

PO Box 408, Aldershot GU11 9DS
tel 020-7427 5684 *mobile* (07968) 868712
email anne@vosser-casting.co.uk

Main areas of work are theatre and musicals. Casting credits include: *Romeo and Juliet* and *Taboo* (both in the West End); *Fame* and *Saturday Night Fever* (West End and tour).

June West

Resident Casting Director at Granada. See entry under *Independent television* on page 331 for further details.

Matt Western

150 Blythe Road, London W14 0HD
tel 020-7602 6646
email matt@mattwestern.co.uk

Main areas of work are film, television and commercials. Casting credits include: *Affinity* (ITV1), *Coup!* (BBC2), *Roman Mysteries* (2 series for BBC1), *55 Degrees North* (2 series for BBC1), and *Class of '76* (ITV1).

Toby Whale CDG

80 Shakespeare Road, London W3 6SN
tel 020-8993 2821 *fax* 020-8993 8096
website www.whalecasting.com

Head of Casting at the National Theatre 2003-06. Main areas of work are film, television and theatre. Casting credits include: *The History Boys*; *East is East* (Assassin Films/FilmFour); *The French Film* (Slingshot); *True Dare Kiss* (BBC); *Spoonface Steinberg* (BBC Films); *Wire in the Blood* (Series 1 & 2 – Coastal/ITV); and more than 40 theatre productions for the Royal Court Theatre, Out of Joint, the Almeida Theatre, English Touring Theatre and Sheffield Crucible, among others.

Tara Woodward

Top Flat, 93 Gloucester Avenue, Primrose Hill, London NW1 8LB
tel 020-7586 3487 *fax* 020-7681 8574

Main areas of work are film, television, theatre and commercials. Casting credits include: *The Early Days*, *Post* and *Hello Friend* (all for Shine/Film Four Lab); *Chasing Heaven* (for Venice Film Festival); *The Browning Version* and *Romeo and Juliet* (theatre); and commercials for Parmalat Aqua and Royal Danish Post. Has worked as Casting Assistant to Nina Gold on films including *All Or Nothing* (directed by Mike Leigh) and *Love's Labour's Lost* (directed by Kenneth Branagh).

Jeremy Zimmermann Casting

36 Marshall Street, London W1F 7EY
tel 020-7478 5161 *fax* 020-7437 4747

Main areas of work are film and television. Recent casting work includes: the films *Keeping Mum*, *The Contract*, *Van Wilder 2*, *Dog Soldiers* and *Blood And Chocolate*.

Will consider attending performances at venues in Greater London and elsewhere. Accepts postal submissions (with CVs and photographs) from actors previously unknown to the casting director, but does not welcome email enquiries. Invitations to view individual actors' websites are also accepted.

Theatre
Introduction

Theatres and theatre companies/managements abound in all kinds of different forms, and paid opportunities for live performance are not restricted to putting on productions. The days of the permanent repertory company are almost gone, but there is a much wider diversity of work available. The larger companies/managements often use casting directors (see page 115), who should usually be your first port of call with your letter, CV and photograph. However, it can be worth exploiting any personal contacts that you may have.

For all approaches, it is important to send your submissions to the person named – unless you have a personal contact.

Some organisations have regular casting patterns – see The Casting Calendar on page 299 for details.

A director's life

Jeremy Raison

So I've just finished directing *Therese Raquin*, my first show as Artistic Director of the Citizens' Theatre. Well, 'finished' is a misnomer. There's still work to be done, but we've had the press night and any work now can only be minimal, as all the stage management and some of the cast have moved on to the next show. And an actor asks the inevitable question: "What do you do now the show's opened?"

Well, what I'd really like is to take a nice long holiday somewhere hot. But I won't. Not yet ...

First I have 188 emails waiting for me on my computer. I also have a pile of letters three-and-a-half inches high. Then there's work to do on a major capital development for an innovative new creative learning centre at the Citizens'. A vision, a business plan and architectural plans all need to be formulated within an incredibly short period of time. I have to attend meetings at the Scottish Arts Council, with the City Council, with the architects, and with the consultants. The deadline is looming fast.

The Citizens' also has to make a submission to the Cultural Commission, which is looking at all cultural provision in Scotland in order to come up with a blueprint for the future, and could prove incredibly important to the future of the Arts here. Set up by the Scottish Executive, the Citizens' Theatre's response needs serious and considered thought.

I have three workshops to do on the show I've just directed, as well as a post-show discussion. I try to attend as many performances of the show as possible, and to make sure I'm here to meet the many people who come to see it.

I need to work on the design for the Christmas show which I am directing. Study the script. Make cuts. Find an assistant director – my original one having just pulled out. Finalise casting and also find three Acting ASMs, all of whom will go on, so must be of a high standard. Casting has mainly taken place in June, when we held a week of auditions in Glasgow and in London. The Citizens' has long worked with a pool of actors: in the early days of the Havergal/Prowse/Macdonald regime, open auditions were held at the Roundhouse in London and 600 people would turn up before nine o'clock in the morning. All would be seen for five minutes, and interesting ones brought back later. Gradually this built up a group of inspiring actors who have worked regularly at the Citizens'; this pool is added to each year. So I am seeing some regulars whom I don't yet know; some new people I have seen in other shows, or been told about, or had some connection with; some actors I've worked with before; and, very occasionally, some I've just seen a picture of.

Deciding whom to audition from a huge pile of CVs is an impossible process. If a particular skill is required – such as the ability to play a particular musical instrument – well, it is much easier to whittle actors down to a number that can be seen. However, if the part is open to interpretation, it is much more difficult. You can't see everyone. Pictures are misleading. I do look to see which directors an actor has worked with; but the best way to get work is to work, undoubtedly. To be seen in shows, to put on shows, anything to get your face noticed. And suppose you get that audition, what then?

As a director, you are desperate to find the right person, and always hope that the next actor will be 'the one'. But they look wrong, or can't speak well enough, or don't move well, or can't sing, or they're the wrong age, or a couple wouldn't pair well together, or they're late without reason, or simply unprepared ... You must know the play you're coming to audition for; ideally, know the director's work; know the Theatre's work; be curious, and *be pleasant*. Some actors I simply won't cast, no matter how good they seem, because they are unpleasant and will cause havoc.

I often ask people to read. As far as is possible, pages will be sent to actors beforehand – but sometimes I may ask them to read different pages. At this stage, if you can't read for any reason (particularly dyslexia), just say. It won't go against you, but if you read badly you can look unintelligent, and I always looks for intelligence in actors, even if it is an instinctive intelligence rather than an academic one. I always look for people who have lots of ideas, who are sparky, who think in different ways. I want to have a buzzy rehearsal period with fascinating people, all of whom challenge each other to go that bit further.

The Citizens' often asks people to do speeches. It is a test, but it is curiously revealing: it shows up laziness and lack of technique very quickly. All trained actors should be able to speak Shakespearean verse well. Nowadays, many actors can't: basic technique is lacking, and it affects not just Shakespeare but every part they will play, particularly on a main stage, and even in a house as acoustically good as the Citizens' Main Theatre.

I cast the final actors in the Christmas show. So what next? I need to programme the spring, and have meetings with designers, directors and actors I am chasing. Book children's shows – a new regular Saturday afternoon slot. And book the other visiting shows. Liaise with Celtic Connections and the Comedy Festival about possible slots. Organise workshops for the spring.

I need to see someone else's shows for a change, to get a perspective on what else is happening outside my own brick walls. There is a list of shows opening that I would like to see. And I need to see the Citizens' own shows: as well as my production in the main house, we have a season of five plays performed by six actors, four of whom are directing in our circle studio. A unique but extremely rewarding experiment which produces incredibly polished results, but ideally I should attend at least one dress rehearsal and also the press night of each. And I need to touch base with our Education and Outreach department, in order to catch up and also discuss future plans at a time when the department's three-year funding is running out.

I have another meeting at Glasgow City Council about our capital plans; am asked to attend the Deacon Convenor's Dinner at the Trades Hall of Glasgow – White Tie, and Carriages at 10.20pm; and the Chancellor's dinner at the University of Glasgow. I'm also asked to be a judge for the short film category of the Scottish BAFTAs.

I need to prepare a speech for a Corporate Citizens' night.

And ... view tapes people have sent me; talk to staff, and deal with any problems; oversee the director coming in to direct the next show. Talk to the cast of my show most days, tell my artistic collaborators how the show has gone and thank them for their work. Do interviews for the newspapers. Organise trips to London and Dublin to see work.

And ... get a haircut. Bank some cheques. Answer my personal mail. Buy birthday presents for my sister, my niece, my brother. Book flights for Christmas. Do my tax return. Send flowers to a friend. Lead a 'normal' life. See my wife and children. Go to a movie. Have a day off without thinking about the Theatre at all.

I love my job. I love its variety. I love the way it plugs you into a culture, shows a side of this city I wouldn't otherwise see. I love the privilege of putting on shows. Expressing a

Theatre

vision. Developing this great theatre and its audience. The challenge of engaging with an increasingly multi-cultural Glasgow. It's a job that's never finished. Things always move on. One project completed always means there's something else to do. It's easy to see why artistic directors tend to burn out.

I only have 34 emails to answer now. My letters are down to a thin pile. I have read 15 plays in the past month. The spring season is just about taking shape. The last visiting show will soon be in place. The copy needs checking, proofing. The look of the publicity will need discussing: what are we trying to sell, and how? But already I'm back in rehearsal and the whole cycle is starting again.

Sooner or later another actor will ask: "And what do you do now the show's opened?"

Oh. And I still need that nice long holiday somewhere hot.

Jeremy Raison is Artistic Director of the Citizens' Theatre in Glasgow. He was previously Artistic Director of Chester Gateway Theatre, for which he won a TMA Award for Special Achievement in Regional Theatre. He has worked in many regional theatres, and at the National, with actors such as Sir Dirk Bogarde, Ralph Fiennes and Robert Carlyle. He has also worked in television and film. Awards and nominations include: Best Young Playwright Radio 4; Plays and Players Best Children's Play; and Manchester Evening News/Liverpool Post Best Production (twice).

Marketing yourself: a producer's viewpoint

Ian Liston

Anything and everything an actor does in his or her working life is about presentation. A sloppy, badly rehearsed performance is not going to win prizes, let alone get you more work. You may have spent a couple of years or more – and invested many thousands of pounds – developing your talent with a lifelong career in mind, so why risk the good work you've done already by not marketing yourself properly? Hopefully you regard yourself as an actor of some quality, so why jeopardise your potential by failing to promote yourself in a 'quality' way?

Whether you've had formal training or never had a day's tuition in your life, it is still going to take a lot of effort and hard work on your part to find work and ensure that the time and heartache already invested has been worth it. It's inadvisable to rely solely on an agent, no matter how good they may be, to find you work. If you don't have an agent, in order to get one you will have to impress them as much as any other director or company you want to contact – and the ability to market yourself properly and create a good impression is even more essential.

Your most important asset will be your CV. Using even the simplest word processing programme makes it easy to keep this up to date. Not only will your CV contain ideally a couple of contrasting recent photographs, but you should also have the ability to 'drop in' a particular photograph that may be more suited to the part you are applying for.

It's worth spending as much as you can afford to obtain decent photographs. Even though you may a have a friend who knows how to use a digital camera, they're unlikely to have the skill and experience of a professional photographer, who will have the expertise to produce pictures that will get you noticed.

Published yearly by The Spotlight, *Contacts* provides many and varied examples of the work of specialist photographers; you can also find out more details about individual photographers starting on page 406 of this book. Most have websites, which can help you choose someone who appeals to you.

As with photographs, don't skimp on materials: invest in some decent paper – 100gsm at the very least. CVs usually get passed around various interested parties and, while they may arrive in good condition, for a few pence extra you can enclose them in a plastic folder to prevent them from becoming dog-eared when passed around a busy casting or production office. Most people prefer to print on white paper, but a tint or subtle colour can make your CV stand out even more and make it easier to locate at a hectic casting session.

In terms of layout, a neat listing of your credits in chronological order is essential. As a producer I much prefer to see credits categorised into separate sections of Stage, TV, Film, plus other relevant categories (e.g. Radio, Opera, etc.). Most actors are in *Spotlight*, which has a neat and efficient layout in its online publication that is worth adopting.

You should list the year of performance followed by the medium (i.e. Stage, TV, etc.) and then the character name, the title of the piece, the production company and the director. If the productions were at drama school or were unpaid or amateur, make that clear.

Every producer / director will look for their own 'tell-tale' clues in a CV: I put great emphasis on directors and companies with whom an actor has worked. Make sure you spell the names correctly. There's nothing more indicative of a sloppy actor than inaccurate spelling, be it a play title, director or character's name, and poor grammar. Don't be tempted to pad out your CV or fabricate plays, parts and directors, as you can be sure your sins will find you out!

You may have a wealth of leading roles under your belt before you became a professional actor: much better to list them as 'non-professional', 'training' or 'unpaid' work. Sadly there still seems to be a stigma surrounding the word 'amateur' when, in truth, much good work comparable with the best of fringe or profit-share is performed by amateur companies.

Let's assume that you've done all your groundwork. You will have familiarised yourself with the various casting services that are available (several offer free trials) and you are developing a network of your own to find out about the possibilities of work. You are reading the trade press (e.g. *The Stage*, which can now be accessed online on a daily basis) and you have invested in a copy of *Contacts* (and this yearbook, of course) so that you have all the names and contact addresses to hand of just about anyone who is anybody.

Now starts the slog – and it's not going to be a one-off afterthought on a Friday afternoon after the phone hasn't rung about work for yet another week. Treat it as a business: your business. Research the market. Identify the companies whose work most interests you – or who might be most interested in you. A simple telephone call is usually sufficient to find the name of the person to contact. It could be a producer, director or casting director, but getting an individual's name will better your chances. It's useless writing to ask for a general audition or interview if the company never holds any.

To maximise your chance of success write your short, to-the-point letter and send it with your CV to the identified contact. A brief comment to acknowledge the company's work doesn't go amiss and gives you a better chance of engaging someone's interest ... but don't be smarmy, smart-assed or clever. There is nothing more annoying to a producer than someone who 'desperately wants to work for your company' when plainly they have no real idea of what the company does.

Avoid gimmicks. I've never forgiven the sender of the childishly folded letter which, when opened, spilled a heap of stars and glitter that took months to get out of clothes and carpet. I may not have forgotten the gimmick about wanting to be a star, but I've certainly forgotten the name!

If you're sending a photo with your CV then you must remember to *put your name and contact details on the back of the photo*! It never ceases to amaze me how many people omit to do such a simple thing. For at least 50% of the hundreds of applications we receive each year we have no means whatsoever of identifying the photo – so if it gets separated from a CV, as can often happen, it will have been a total waste of time and money.

First impressions count. You wouldn't (would you?) attend an audition or interview looking scruffy and unkempt. Some people do, but that's another story. Take care with your spelling and grammar and avoid using exclamation marks at the end of every sentence. A neatly addressed, handwritten letter using quality paper certainly grabs my attention:

they're such a rarity these days. Keep it brief and to the point, without being verbose. If you have 'doctors' handwriting', use simple typed labels and a neatly typed letter but, at the very least, handwrite the salutation and the signature. Mass-produced mail-shot letters are easy to spot and they usually end up straight in the bin. Unless a stamped addressed envelope is enclosed (and I only speak for myself) I would not usually offer the courtesy of a reply and the return of a photograph.

There is an increasing tendency these days to include a DVD or similar visual medium as part of the submission. This should be of the highest possible quality and capable of being played on any equipment; and it should comprise a personal introduction from your good self together with a selection of video clips / photographs from recent work. It should *not* be a replacement for the letter and CV. As with every element of your submission, make sure your contact details are clearly marked.

A major factor to get right is the postage. Since the new method of sizing, weighing and pricing for postage came into force in 2007, it's amazing how few people still bother to check they have the right amount of stamps. Too few, and your recipient will have to fork out a few pounds to get something he or she hasn't expected and will likely bin; too many and you're wasting your own hard-earned cash. Useful advice on this matter is included in Simon Dunmore's introduction to this *Yearbook*.

Email is being used increasingly as a method of contact and every recipient has their own way of dealing with it. It can be particularly useful if a potential work opportunity comes to your attention at short notice. It's faster than the post and nothing is more effective than striking whilst the iron is hot – but make sure any files you send are as small as possible. Include your Spotlight link and, if you have a website, the link to that as well.

In similar fashion, always make sure you have ready a good supply of your photographs and CVs, although it's pointless printing too many at one time as the real worth of a good CV is the fact that it's absolutely up to date. If you're suggesting that your correspondent can look up your entry in *Spotlight*, make sure that too is up to date. In 2007 an agent suggested I look up his client in *Spotlight*; a pointless exercise since the actor's most recent credits were for 1998!

Success is so often a matter of luck. A letter / CV arriving in the right hands, just when a producer / director is looking for someone like you, can open untold doors, but it's astonishing how few actors bother to spend that little bit of extra time and effort getting it right.

Always remember the wise words of Ivor Novello, one of the most successful actor / managers of the 20th century: "If you want to be a success, look it!" – and that goes for your correspondence as well as your appearance.

Good luck! I look forward to hearing from you.

Ian Liston is an actor and producer whose career covers over 40 years' experience as an actor in feature films, on TV and on the stage. His company, Hiss & Boo Ltd, is one of the UK's leading producers of pantomime and revue and its productions are frequently seen on the UK touring circuit and overseas.

Theatre

Producing theatres

Included in this section are the national and regional building-based companies that mount their own productions – sometimes in co-operation with others, and sometimes sending out tours. (Almost all also receive touring productions.) The majority are subsidised by the national and regional Arts Councils (and use Equity's regional theatre contract), but a few are not (and use Equity's commercial theatre contract), and a few have their own contractual arrangements. Almost all have websites which can be very useful for keeping track of their activities. A little extra insight – beyond that listed on the following pages – into a theatre might just tip the balance in your favour.

In real terms, rates of pay are better than they were a decade and more ago, but they are still only 'adequate' – especially if you are incurring the extra costs of living away from home. However, rehearsing and performing a production in such a theatre can be an exhilarating experience. A well-run theatre has a wonderful 'family' atmosphere, and in the close-knit working environment you can often make friendships which sustain for many years afterwards – as well as contacts who might be useful in years to come. It is well worth checking each theatre's 'casting procedures' very carefully as there are significant variations between them. It is also worth familiarising yourself with their programmes of productions via *The Stage* and/or their websites.

Almeida Theatre

Almeida Street, London N1 1TA
tel 020-7288 4900 *fax* 020-7288 4901
email info@almeida.co.uk
website www.almeida.co.uk
Artistic Director Michael Attenborough *Associate Director* Howard Davies *Artistic Associate* Jenny Worton *Executive Director* Neil Constable *General Manager* Ros Brooke-Taylor

Production details

The Almeida is committed to staging British and international drama presented to the highest possible standards, and productions which reveal classic plays in a new light. Embraces international classics, foreign classics in newly commissioned versions, and new plays – in addition to an annual Opera season of specially commissioned operas, music theatre pieces and concerts of contemporary music. Stages approximately 6 productions each year. Recent productions include: *Big White Fog, Dying For It, There Came A Gypsy Riding, The Lightning Play,* and *Tom and Viv.*

Casting procedures

Productions are cast by external freelance casting directors on a project by project basis. Uses the TMA/ Equity Subsidised Rep contract and subscribes to the Equity Pension Scheme. Actively encourages applications from disabled actors and promotes the use of inclusive casting.

Yvonne Arnaud Theatre

Millbrook, Guildford, Surrey GU1 3UX
tel (01483) 440077 *fax* (01483) 564071
website www.yvonne-arnaud.co.uk
Artistic Director James Barber

Production details

The Yvonne Arnaud Theatre is a busy producing and receiving house, creating shows in Guildford and touring nationally, with many transferring to the West End. On both the main stage and in the Mill Studio an eclectic mix of classical and contemporary work is staged by new, lesser-known and established writers.

The Youth and Education facility offers an exciting mix of activities for young people and adults all year round. The Yvonne Arnaud opened the 80-seat Mill Studio in 1993 to provide a venue for work that would not otherwise be seen in Guildford. It also forms the base for the Youth Theatre's activities. Recent productions include: *Aladdin, Drowning on Dry Land* and *Telstar.*

Belgrade Theatre

Belgrade Square, Coventry CV1 1GS
tel 024-7625 6431
email admin@belgrade.co.uk
website www.belgrade.co.uk
Theatre Director & Chief Executive Hamish Glen
Associate Director Gadi Roll

Production details

After closure for refurbishment, the Belgrade re-opened in late 2007. Recent productions include: *One Night in November* (about the Coventry Blitz), *Scenes from a Marriage* (directed by Trevor Nunn), and 'legendary' annual pantomimes.

Birmingham Repertory Theatre

Centenary Square, Broad Street, Birmingham B1 2EP
tel 0121-245 2000
website www.birmingham-rep.co.uk
Artistic Director Rachel Kavanaugh *Associate Director (Literary)* Ben Payne *Executive Director* Stuart Rogers *Associate Director Learning & Participation* Steve Ball *Casting Co-ordinator* Alison Solomon

Production details

Stages 15 productions in the main house each year and 6 in the studio. Also runs Outreach, Community and Education programmes.

Casting procedures

"The play's director, a casting director and sometimes a producer handle casting for all Main House and Door productions. We currently make use of freelance casting directors, specific to each production, administrated by our in-house Casting Co-ordinator."

Birmingham Stage Company (BSC)

Suite 228, 162 Regent Street, London W1B 5TB
tel 020-7437 3391 *fax* 020-7437 3395
email info@birminghamstage.net
website www.birminghamstage.net
Actor/Manager Neal Foster *Chief Executive* Philip Compton *General Manager* Sally Humphreys *Administrator* Michael Throne

Production details

Founded in 1992, the BSC stages 5 shows each year, 4 of which tour nationally. Produces a range of plays with particular emphasis on new writing, and is recognised for its children's shows which visit 60 venues around the UK. Recent productions include: *Proof* (West End), *Horrible Histories* (UK tour), *The Jungle Book* (UK Tour), *Treasure Island* (UK Tour), *Danny the Champion of the World*. Offers TMA/Equity approved contracts and subscribes to the Equity Pension Scheme.

Casting procedures

Uses freelance casting directors and sometimes holds general auditions. Casting breakdowns are published on their website, and in *Spotlight*, *SBS* and *PCR* (see entry under *The Spotlight, casting directories and information services* on page 398). Submissions by hardcopy only – no phonecalls. "Do as much research as you can before submitting." Actively encourages applications from disabled actors.

Bristol Old Vic

King Street, Bristol BS1 4ED
tel 0117-949 3993 *fax* 0117-949 3993
email admin@bristol-old-vic.co.uk
website www.bristol-old-vic.co.uk
Artistic Director Tom Morris *Executive Director* Emma Stenning

After a closure for refurbishment, the theatre re-opened in 2009.

The Bush Theatre

Shepherds Bush Green, London W12 8QD
tel 020-7602 3703 *fax* 020-7602 7614
email info@bushtheatre.co.uk
website www.bushtheatre.co.uk
Artistic Director Josie Rourke *Executive Producer* Fiona Clark

Production Details

Founded in 1972, The Bush specialises in developing and producing new writing to the highest professional standard. It stages 5-8 productions a year, totalling around 280 performances. Also tours productions to up to 8 venues, although the bulk of performances are at The Bush itself. Up to 6 actors are employed on each production, and the company offers TMA/Equity approved contracts. Recent productions include: *Monsieur Ibrahim & The Flowers of The Qur-an* and *When You Cure Me* (Bush Theatre); *Mammals* (national No. 1 tour); and a number of rehearsed readings.

Casting procedures

Casts in-house and does not hold general auditions or issue public casting breakdowns. Welcomes letters (not emails) from actors previously unknown to the company. Does not welcome showreels or invitations to view individual actors' websites. Actively encourages applications from disabled actors and promotes the use of inclusive casting.

Byre Theatre

Abbey Street, St Andrews KY16 9LA
tel (01334) 475000 *fax* (01334) 475370
email enquiries@byretheatre.com
website www.byretheatre.com
Chief Executive Officer Jacqueline McKay

Production details

Founded in 1933, the Byre moved into a new state-of-the-art theatre in 2001, where it presented a mixed programme of in-house and guest productions. From July 2007 the Byre refocused its programme, presenting a range of touring theatre as well as co-producing with a range of partners.

Casting procedures

Please see the website **www.byretheatre.com** for current casting procedures.

Theatre

Chichester Festival Theatre

Oaklands Park, Chichester PO19 6AP
Artistic Director Jonathan Church *Casting Director* Maggie Lunn *Executive Director* Maggie Saxon

Production details

Consists of the main house set in parkland, the Minerva Studio, and a multipurpose auditorium. In-house plays and musicals are produced in the main house during the festival season (April-September), and family shows at Christmas. The Minerva Studio places emphasis on new and experimental work during the festival and also stages an in-house Christmas production. 4 productions are staged both in the main house and the Minerva Studio each year. Also runs TIE, Outreach and Community programmes (contact Alison Roden). Recent productions include: *The Merchant of Venice, Pinocchio, The Seagull* and Gilbert & Sullivan's *The Gondoliers.*

Casting procedures

Occasionally holds general auditions. Actors should write in December or January requesting inclusion. Welcomes submissions (with CVs and photographs) sent by post or email.

Citizens Theatre

Gorbals, Glasgow G5 9DS
tel 0141-429 5561 *fax* 0141-429 7374
website www.citz.co.uk
Artistic Directors Guy Hollands, Jeremy Raison *Company Manager* Jacqueline Muir

Production details

Internationally renowned producing theatre, producing work in Glasgow and on tour as well as a pioneering year-round Citizens Learning and TAG programme for participants of all ages. Stages 7 productions a year, and undertakes 2 tours per annum. Offers TMA/Equity approved contracts.

Casting procedures

Does not use freelance casting directors. Holds limited general auditions once a year in June, and specific casting for individual shows as and when required. Welcomes emails from actors (with CVs and photographs), which should be submitted to **jackie@citz.co.uk.**

Clwyd Theatr Cymru

Mold, Flintshire CH7 1YA
tel (01352) 756331 *fax* (01352) 701558
email mail@clwyd-theatr-cymru.co.uk
website www.clwyd-theatr-cymru.co.uk
Artistic Director Terry Hands *Associate Director* Tim Baker *Casting Director* Leigh-Ann Regan

Production details

The major drama-producing company in Wales. Although most work is presented in English, some pieces are performed in Welsh. Stages 5-6 shows in the main house and 5-6 in the studio each year, with some mid/large-scale productions touring Wales and England. Also runs TIE programmes. Recent productions include: *Mary Stuart, Noises Off, Great Expectations* and *A History of Falling Things.* Offers TMA/Equity approved contracts and subsribes to the Equity Pension Scheme.

Casting procedures

Welcomes enquiries from actors: these should be sent to Leigh-Ann Regan at the above address. (More information about Leigh-Ann Regan can be found under Casting directors on page 126.) Will consider applications from disabled actors to play characters with disabilities.

Coliseum Theatre

Fairbottom Street, Oldham OL1 3SW
tel 0161-624 1731 *fax* 0161-624 5318
email mail@coliseum.org.uk
website www.coliseum.org.uk
Artistic Director Kevin Shaw *Administrative Director* Liz Wilson *Administrator* Joanne Moss

Production details

A traditional repertory theatre producing 8 shows each year, with additional incoming tours and one-off special events. Also runs TIE, Outreach and Community programmes (contact Jodie Lamb). Recent productions include: *Look Back in Anger, How the Other Half Loves, Return to the Forbidden Planet, Women on the Verge of HRT.*

Casting procedures

Does not use freelance casting directors. Sometimes holds general auditions. Casting breakdowns are available through postal application (with sae). Welcomes letters and email submissions (with CVs and photographs). Also accepts invitations to view individual actors' websites. Offers TMA/Equity approved contracts and subscribes to the Equity Pension Scheme. Will consider applications from disabled actors to play characters with disabilities.

Contact Theatre

Oxford Road, Manchester M15 6JA
tel 0161-274 3434 *fax* 0161-274 0640
website www.contact-theatre.org
Artistic Director John McGrath *Executive Producer* Jon Morgan *Associate Director* Cheryl Martin *Administrative Officer* Katie Taylor (casting enquiries) *Head of Creative Development* Ekua Bayunu

Production details

Since re-opening in 1999, Contact has emphasised its work with young adults (aged 13-30), putting participation at the heart of its ethos and activities. Contact is also one of the most culturally diverse theatres in the country; it was awarded the inaugural ECLIPSE award for cultural diversity, as well as the Arts Council's ART04 Award Northwest for 'outstanding achievement in the arts'.

Contact has striven to rewrite the rulebook on what 'theatre' can be. A wide range of touring theatre, music, dance and mixed-media work complements the theatre's in-house productions. The huge variety of participatory work with young people is integrated as closely as possible with the company's 'professional' programme. High quality and innovation are key to Contact's participatory work; leading companies working with young people at Contact have included: Frantic Assembly, RJC Dance, Quarantine, and Nitro – as well as a huge range of artists from hip hop to forum theatre and from verse drama to contemporary dance. Recent productions include: *Perfect* (Kaite O'Reilly and Paul Clay); *Slamdunk* (Felix Cross, Benji Reid with Nitro); *Dancing within Walls* (by Rani Moorthy with Rasa); *Dreaming of Bones* (with Red Ladder).

Casting procedures

Uses freelance casting directors and does not advertise casting breakdowns publicly. Welcomes letters (with CVs and photographs) from actors but warns that it is unable to reply to unsolicited submissions. The theatre prefers not to receive showreels, emails and invitations to view actors' websites. Offers TMA/Equity approved contracts. Actively encourages applications from disabled actors and promotes the use of inclusive casting.

Crucible Theatre

55 Norfolk Street, Sheffield S1 1DA
tel 0114-249 5999 *fax* 0114-249 6003
email info@sheffieldtheatres.co.uk
website www.sheffieldtheatres.co.uk
Chief Executive Louise Timothy *Artistic Director* Daniel Evans

Closed for major refurbishment until February 2010.

Curve

Halford Street, Leicester LE1 1SB
tel 0116-253 0021 *fax* (0870) 7065241
email enquiries@leicestertheatretrust.co.uk
website www.curveonline.co.uk
Artistic Director Paul Kerryson *Associate Director* Adel Al-Salloum *Chief Executive* Ruth Eastwood *Executive Producer* Ian Gillie

Production details

A new state-of-the-art theatre designed by world-renowned architect Rafael Vinoly. Has 2 auditoria, one with 750 seats and the other providing a 350-seat flexible smaller space. "A stunning glass facade encloses a magnificent foyer and mezzanine walkway, with views onto the cafe, bars, dressing rooms and workshop areas. The stage is placed at street level between the 2 auditoria."

Casting procedures

Uses both in-house and freelance casting directors. Holds general auditions; actors may write in for casting breakdowns as soon as productions are announced. Does not welcome unsolicited approaches by post or by email, showreels, or invitations to view individual actors' websites. Offers Equity-approved contracts as negotiated through TMA. Actively encourages applications from disabled actors and promotes the use of inclusive casting.

Derby Playhouse

Theatre Walk, Eagle Centre, Derby DE1 2NF
tel (01332) 363271 *fax* (01332) 547200
website www.derbyplayhouse.co.uk
Artistic Director Stephen Edwards

Following the withdrawal of its Arts Council funding, the theatre closed in January 2008. Derby Playhouse is currently developing 4 of its past productions for the West End and International Touring: *Moon Landing*, *Christmas Carol*, *Master Class* and *Treasure Island*. See the website for the latest details.

Donmar Warehouse

41 Earlham Street, London WC2H 9LX
tel 020-7240 4882
website www.donmarwarehouse.com
Artistic Director Michael Grandage *Executive Producer* Lucy Davies *General Manager* James Bierman *Development Director* Kate Mitchell *Casting and Creative Associate* Anne McNulty

Production details

Independent producing house located in Covent Garden. The building originally served as a vat room and hop warehouse for the local brewery. In 1961 it was purchased by Donald Albery and converted into a rehearsal studio for the London Festival Ballet, which he formed with ballerina Margot Fonteyn. The theatre takes its name from them.

In the 1990s the Donmar was redesigned. The current theatre space retains the characteristics of the former warehouse while incorporating a new thrust stage. Recent productions include: *The Chalk Garden*, *Othello*, *Parade*, *The Wild Duck*, and *Mary Stuart*.

Casting procedures

Casting breakdowns are not publicly available. Offers TMA/SOLT/Equity approved contracts. Rarely has the opportunity to cast disabled actors.

The Dukes

Moor Lane, Lancaster LA1 1QE
tel (01524) 598505 *fax* (01524) 598579
website www.dukes-lancaster.org
Director Joe Sumison *Theatre Secretary* Jacqui Wilson

Production details

A producing theatre with an independent cinema. Stages 5 shows each year in the main house (313

Theatre

seats) and 1 in the studio (178 seats), with a focus on contemporary drama and outdoor site-specific productions. Also runs a Youth Arts programme. Recent productions include: *Blue Remembered Hills*, *Betrayal*, *Under Milk Wood*, *The Accrington Pals*, and *Tom Thumb and Other Giant Stories* (outdoor production).

Casting procedures

Does not use freelance casting directors. Casting breakdowns are obtainable through the website, postal application (with sae), Equity Job Information Service and *PCR*. Welcomes letters (with CVs and photographs) but not email submissions. Showreels and invitations to view individual actors' websites are also accepted. Offers TMA/Equity approved contracts. Actively encourages applications from disabled actors and promotes the use of inclusive casting.

Dundee Repertory Theatre

Tay Square, Dundee DD1 1PB
tel (01382) 227684 *fax* (01382) 228609
website www.dundeerep.co.uk
Artistic Director James Brining

Production details

Producing theatre housing Dundee Repertory Ensemble – Scotland's only permanent acting company. Stages 6 shows each year in the main house. Also runs TIE, Outreach and Community programmes (contact James Brining). Recent productions include: *Peter Pan* and *Twelfth Night*.

Casting procedures

Does not use freelance casting directors. Welcomes letters (with CVs and photographs) but not email submissions. Actors should write in the spring.

Gate Theatre

Above Prince Albert Pub, 11 Pembridge Road, London W11 3HQ
tel 020-7229 0906 *fax* 020-7221 6055
email gate@gatetheatre.freeserve.co.uk
website www.gatetheatre.co.uk
Artistic Directors Natalie Abrahami, Carrie Cracknell
Producer Evanna Meehan *General Manager* Cath Longman *Education & Access Manager* Lynne Gagliano

Production details

Presents new writing and undiscovered classics from around the world in original and visually imaginative productions. Stages 5-6 shows each year. Also runs a Community/Education programme. Recent productions include: *Things Of Dry Hours* by Naomi Wallace, *Ghosts* by Henrik Ibsen, *The Chairs* by Eugene Ionesco.

Casting procedures

Does not accept unsolicited CVs/submissions. "Individual directors tend to cast from their own lists

– contact with the director is the best way to ensure that your application is considered. The Gate Theatre Company is committed to promoting theatre as an activity for all."

Greenwich Theatre

Crooms Hill, Greenwich, London SE10 8ES
tel 020-8858 4447 *fax* 020-8858 8042
email info@greenwichtheatre.org.uk
website www.greenwichtheatre.org.uk
Executive Director James Haddrell

Production details

Currently mainly receiving touring productions, but occasionally produces shows in-house. Specialises in musical theatre and produces showcases, semi-staged readings and cabarets at different points of the year which often involve professional performers. Recent productions include: *Longitude* (play with music), and *Sleeping Beauty* (pantomime). The theatre also runs a year-round programme of training for 14-19 year-olds (the Greenwich Musical Theatre Academy) including a full-time course. Offers TMA/Equity approved contracts and subscribes to the Equity Pension Scheme.

Casting procedures

Generally uses freelance casting directors. "Please don't send unsolicited applications, as we can't maintain a sensible filing system. Please do look at the casting section on the website, as we aim to provide advance information on our future productions and answer standard questions. Most casting is concerned with the pantomime so the best time to enquire is between May and July. We are keen to hear from locally based musical performers and especially anyone that has experience of working with young people." Does not have a specific policy on casting disabled actors, as the stage is not wheelchair-accessible: "It depends on the actor's particular needs."

Hampstead Theatre

Eton Avenue, London NW3 3EU
tel 020-7449 4200 *fax* 020-7449 4201
email info@hampsteadtheatre.com
website www.hampsteadtheatre.com
Artistic Director Anthony Clark (until January 2010)
Literary Director Frances Poet *Education Director* Eric Dupin

Production details

Hampstead Theatre identifies and produces important new writers. It aims to challenge established writers and seek out the best international work to bring to London. Plays are sometimes provocative, always intelligent and often full of laughter. The auditorium has been built for writers who understand actors, and The Space will provide a dedicated arena for a rich and varied education and workshop programme. Presents 7 shows in the main house each year and a varying number in the studio. Recent productions include: *In The Club* by Richard Bean; *Glass Eels* by Nell Leyshon; *Taking Care Of Baby* by Dennis Kelly

Casting procedures

Uses freelance casting directors; suggests that actors write 2 months before each season starts. Casting breakdowns are sometimes available by postal application (with sae) or email, depending on the director.

Harrogate Theatre

Oxford Street, Harrogate, North Yorks HG1 1QF
tel (01423) 502710 *fax* (01423) 563205
email info@harrogatetheatre.co.uk
website www.harrogatetheatre.co.uk
Chief Executive David Bown

Production details

Stages 3 productions annually in the main house; also works in Outreach and Community (key contact, Hannah Draper). Recent productions include: *Absolutely Frank*; *Blithe Spirit*; *Aladdin*.

Casting procedures

Uses freelance casting directors and sometimes holds general auditions. Offers Equity approved contracts as negotiated through TMA, and participates in the Equity Pension Scheme. Will consider applications from disabled actors to play characters with disabilities. "We have no resident Artistic Director and so unsolicited approaches are not welcome. Please check the website for any casting opportunities."

Haymarket Theatre

Wote Street, Basingstoke RG21 7NW
tel (01256) 323073
email www.haymarket.org.uk

The Haymarket Theatre is now a receiving house and no longer delivers in-house productions.

Hull Truck Theatre

50 Ferensway, Hull HU2 8LB
tel (01482) 224800 *fax* (01482) 581182
email admin@hulltruck.co.uk
website www.hulltruck.co.uk
Creative Director John Godber *Artistic Director* Gareth Tudor Price *Operations Director* Paul Marshall *Associate Director* Nick Lane *Casting Enquiries* to Administration Department

Production details

In operation since 1971, Hull Truck has established a national/international reputation for excellence. Hull Truck moved into a brand new purpose-built theatre in April 2009, which houses 2 auditora. It presents a mix of new writing, classic adaptations and one-night comedy/music events. The theatre also works on TIE, Outreach and Community projects for which Mark Rees is the lead contact. Stages approximately 14 productions each year, touring to more than 70 venues including theatres, educational and community venues. Roughly 2-6 actors are used in each production. Recent productions include: *Studs, Teachers, Bouncers, Beef, Lucky Sods* and *Funny Turns* by John Godber; *The Flags* by Bridget O'Connor; *Honeymoon Suite* by Richard Bean; *Ladies Down Under* and *Amateur Girl* by Amanda Whittington; *My Favourite Summer* and *A Christmas Fairytale* by Nick Lane; *A Kick in the Baubles* by Gordon Steel; *Confessions of a City Supporter* by Alan Plater; *Every Time it Rains* by Rupert Creed; and *Say it with Flowers* by Jane Thornton.

Casting procedures

Casting is done in-house. Casting breakdowns are advertised on the website and in *PCR* and *The Stage*, and are also available by postal application. Welcomes letters (with CVs and photographs) from actors, but prefers not to receive showreels. Actively encourages applications from disabled actors and promotes the use of inclusive casting.

Key Theatre

Embankment Road, Peterborough, Cambridgeshire PE1 1EF
tel (01733) 552437
email michael.cross@peterborough.gov.uk
website www.peterboroughkeytheatre.co.uk
Artistic Director Michael Cross *Youth Theatre/TIE Officer* Paul Collings

Production details

Mainly a receiving house with occasional in-house productions including an annual pantomime and TIE tours. Stages 4 shows each year. Recent productions include: *The Full Monty, Bad Blood* and *Cinderella*.

Casting procedures

Does not use freelance casting directors. Occasional general auditions. Unsolicited communications are not advised. Casting requirements are sometimes available through the website, but usually through professional casting services, Spotlight Link, *PCR* and *The Stage*. "Actors working in the area (and especially touring to the Key) are always encouraged to make contact with the Artistic Director and introduce themselves. Invitations to see artists working in productions are always welcome – and wherever possible accepted!" Offers TMA/Equity contracts and does not subscribe to the Equity Pension Scheme. Rarely (or never) has the opportunity to employ disabled actors.

Library Theatre Company

St Peter's Square, Manchester M2 5PD
tel 0161-234 1913 *fax* 0161-274 7055

email ltcadmin@manchester.gov.uk
website www.librarytheatre.com
Artistic Director Chris Honer

Production details

Regional producer of contemporary drama and
modern classics; also produces a play for families and
children at Christmas. Stages 5-6 shows each year,
and runs an Education programme (contact Liz
Postlethwaite). Recent productions include: *If I Were
You, Frozen, Waiting for Godot, Tom's Midnight
Garden, Faith Healer*, and *Private Lives*. Offers TMA/
Equity approved contracts.

Casting Procedures

Uses freelance casting directors; casting breakdowns
are available from the website. Also holds a limited
number of general auditions/interviews in the
Summer. Actors requesting inclusion in these are
advised to write in March or April. Encourages
applications from actors with disability, and
promotes inclusive casting.

Live Theatre

Broad Chare, Quayside,
Newcastle upon Tyne NE1 3DQ
tel 0191-261 2694 *fax* 0191-232 2224
email info@live.org.uk
website www.live.org.uk
Artistic Director Max Roberts *Associate
Directors* Jeremy Herrin, Paul James

Production details

New writing theatre established in 1973. Produces 8-
10 shows each year in the main house. Also runs TIE,
Outreach and Community programmes (contact Paul
James).

Casting procedures

Does not use freelance casting directors. Welcomes
submissions (with CVs and photographs) sent by
post or email. Actors may write at any time.
Showreels and invitations to view individual actors'
websites are also accepted. Offers ITC/Equity
approved contracts. Actively encourages applications
from disabled actors and promotes the use of
inclusive casting.

Liverpool Everyman and Playhouse Theatres

13 Hope Street, Liverpool L1 9BH
tel 0151-708 3700 *fax* 0151-708 3701
email info@everymanplayhouse.com
website www.everymanplayhouse.com
Artistic Director Gemma Bodinetz

Production details

The Liverpool Playhouse focuses primarily on
imaginative interpretations of classic drama, from
ancient to modern, while new writing forms the core
of the programme at the Everyman. The theatre also
hosts touring companies from around the country;
runs a busy Literary Department, working to nurture
the next generation of Liverpool playwrights; and has
an active Community Department which takes work
to all corners of the city and surrounding areas.
Recent productions include: *King Lear, Ten Tiny Toes*
and *The Hypochondriac*.

Lyric Theatre

Admin offices: 88A Stranmillis Road,
Belfast BT9 5AD
email clare@lyrictheatre.co.uk
website www.lyrictheatre.co.uk
Chief Executive Ciaran McAuley *Artistic
Director* Richard Croxford *Admin Manager* Clare
Gault

Production details

*(please note that the Lyric is currently closed for the
rebuild of a new £18.5m theatre; re-opening 2011)*

Northern Ireland's leading full-time producing house
for professional theatre. Presents a distinctive,
challenging and entertaining programme of new
writing as well as contemporary and classic plays by
Irish, European and American writers. Currently
offsite whilst new theatre being built, and producing
4 productions a year as well as a full education and
outreach programme. Recent productions include:
*The Homeplace, Be My Baby, Pump Girl, The Parker
Project*.

Casting procedures

Does not use freelance casting directors. Welcomes
submissions (with CVs and photographs) sent by
post or email – actors may write in at any time.
Advises actors to check the website for its future
programme. Offers TMA/Equity approved contracts.
Will consider applications from disabled actors to
play characters with disabilities.

Lyric Theatre Hammersmith

King Street, London W6 0QL
tel 0870-050 0511 *fax* 020-8741 5965
email enquiries@lyric.co.uk
website www.lyric.co.uk
Artistic Director Sean Holmes *Executive
Director* Jessica Hepburn

Production details

Produces and co-produces original theatre for a wide
audience. Recently completed work which
redeveloped the theatre, creating 2 new spaces – a
purpose-built rehearsal studio, and an education/
training room. The theatre runs an extensive
Education programme and focuses on working with
disadvantaged communities and young people in the
local area. For further information, contact the

Education Administrator, Herta Queirazza. Recent productions include: *Don Juan* and *The Firework-Maker's Daughter*.

Casting procedures

Different directors cast their own productions using freelance casting directors.

Manor Pavilion Theatre

Manor Road, Sidmouth, Devon EX10 8RP
tel 020-7636 4343 *fax* 020-7636 2323
email cvtheatre@aol.com
Artistic Director Charles Vance *Associate Director* Imogen Vance

Production details

Summer repertory theatre with a 3-month season (July-September). Stages 12 shows each year in the main house.

Casting procedures

Welcomes letters (with CVs and photographs) but not email submissions. Actors should write in February sending application to: Summer Play Festival, Hampden House, 2 Weymouth Street, London W1W 5BT.

Mercury Theatre

Balkerne Gate, Colchester, Essex CO1 1PT
tel (01206) 577006 *fax* (01206) 769607
email info@mercurytheatre.co.uk
website www.mercurytheatre.co.uk
Artistic Director & Chief Executive Dee Evans *Artistic Director* Gregory Floy *Associate Directors* Adrian Stokes, Sue Lefton

Production details

A regional repertory theatre which opened in 1972, producing 3 ensemble shows each season. Stages 6 shows each year in the main house and 1-2 in the studio. Also runs a Community programme (contact Elaine Leppard). Recent productions include: *Wagstaffe the Wind-Up Boy*, *The Lonesome West*, *A Chorus of Disapproval* and *David Copperfield*.

Casting procedures

Each show is cast by the director from within an ensemble company which has evolved over the past 6 years. It is preferred for actors to build up a relationship with the artistic team rather than to approach by letter or email. A knowledge of the Mercury's work is essential. For all casting enquiries please email Hannah Love (**hannahl@mercurytheatre.co.uk**).

The Mill at Sonning Theatre

Sonning Eye, Reading RG4 6TY
tel 0118-969 6039
email admin@millatsonning.com
website www.millatsonning.com
Artistic Director Sally Hughes

Production details

Popular 'dinner theatre' venue, producing a range of plays for audiences to watch while eating a meal. Recent productions include: *French Without Tears*, *Time to Kill*, and *It Runs in the Family*.

Casting procedures

Forthcoming productions are listed on the website. Actors should send their details, along with specific casting suggestions, to the Artistic Director 2 months before each show.

National Theatre

South Bank, London SE1 9PX
tel 020-7452 3335 *fax* 020-7452 3340
email info@nationaltheatre.org.uk
website www.nationaltheatre.org.uk
Artistic Director Nicolas Hytner *Head of Casting* Wendy Spon CDG

Production details

A National Theatre was first proposed in 1848. In 1951 a foundation stone was laid by the Royal Festival Hall, and in 1962 Sir Laurence Olivier was appointed the National's first director, based at London's Old Vic Theatre. Finally, in 1976, the new NT officially opened with a production of *Hamlet*. Today, the National stages a range of classics, musicals, new plays and entertainment "for all the family". It comprises 3 theatres: the Olivier (open-stage, capacity 1120 people); the Lyttleton (proscenium arch, capacity 890); and the Cottesloe (studio theatre on 3 levels with flexible staging, capacity 300).

Casting details

The National Theatre's casting team works with approximately 10 directors a year casting NT shows. Actors known to the theatre may be approached directly, but casting is predominantly carried out through agents. The NT will first approach agents to check actors' availability, then audition a shortlist. New talent is actively sought out and the casting team sees several performances a week within London and (less frequently) outside. It also attends drama schools' showcases and will sometimes approach other casting directors known to the NT.

National Theatre of Scotland (NTS)

Atlantic Chambers, 45 Hope Street, Glasgow G2 6AE
tel 0141-221 0970 *fax* 0141-248 7241
email info@nationaltheatrescotland.com
website www.nationaltheatrescotland.com
Artistic Director & Chief Executive Vicky Featherstone *Executive Producer* Neil Murray *Casting Director* Anne Henderson

Production details

The National Theatre of Scotland launched to the public in February 2006. It has no building and

Theatre

instead takes theatre all over Scotland and beyond, working with new and existing venues and companies to create and tour theatre of the highest quality. This theatre takes place in the great buildings of Scotland, but also in site-specific locations, community halls and drill halls, car parks and forests. To date over 130,000 people have seen or participated in its work. NTS has produced 28 pieces of work in 62 locations, from the Shetlands to Dumfries, and from Belfast to London. In 2007/8 NTS toured to the USA and Australasia.

Scottish theatre has always been for the people, led by great performances, great stories and great playwrights. The National Theatre of Scotland exists to build a new generation of theatre-goers as well as reinvigorating the existing ones; to create theatre on a national and international scale that is contemporary, confident and forward-looking; to bring together brilliant artists, designers, composers, choreographers and playwrights; and to exceed expectations of what and where theatre can be.

Offers actors in-house ITC/Equity approved contracts and does not subscribe to the Equity Pension Scheme.

Casting procedures

Each casting process is led by the Director of each production with advisory support from the NTS Artistic Team and Casting Director. When casting for specific shows, the Casting Director puts out a call to agents through *Spotlight*.

The NTS Artistic team makes every effort to see every theatrical production produced in Scotland, maximising the number of actors that NTS sees. The team also responds to individual requests to go and see actors' work. All actors' CVs and headshots that NTS receives are acknowledged and kept on file in the NTS office. The NTS Casting Director reviews these files at regular intervals and Directors are encouraged to go through these files before casting their productions. In addition, NTS holds an annual 2-day casting workshop to connect with actors who have sent in CVs but whose work it has been unable to see during the year. Actively encourages applications from disabled actors and promotes the use of inclusive casting.

New Vic Theatre

Etruria Road, Newcastle-under-Lyme ST5 OJG
tel (01782) 717954 *fax* (01782) 712885
email admin@newvictheatre.org.uk
website www.newvictheatre.org.uk
Artistic Director Theresa Heskins *General Manager* Nick Jones

Production details

Purpose-built theatre-in-the-round with a full programme of in-house drama, concerts and occasional touring productions. Stages 10 shows each

year in the main house. Also very active with Outreach and Education programmes (contact Sue Moffat and Jill Rezzano respectively). Recent productions include: *Sweeney Todd, My Night with Reg, The Duchess of Malfi, Kes* and *The Marriage of Figaro*.

Casting procedures

Does not use freelance casting directors. Casting breakdowns are obtainable by postal application (with sae), and up-to-date casting information is posted on the casting section of the website. Welcomes letters (with CVs and photographs), but not email submissions. Submissions should be specific and referenced to a particular role. Also accepts invitations to view individual actors' websites.

Northcott Theatre

Northcott Theatre, Stocker Road, Exeter EX4 4QB
tel (01392) 223999
website www.northcott-theatre.co.uk
Creative Director Rebecca Manson Jones

Production details

The Northcott produces or co-produces a varied programme of 10-11 shows each year, with runs of between 10 days and 3.5 weeks (the Christmas show being the only one that runs for approximately 6 weeks). Over the last 2 years the theatre has been developing links with other theatre companies, and hopes to build on this – leading to more joint ventures with repertory companies across the country.

In addition the theatre runs active Community and Education departments, giving people of all ages a chance to be involved in shows, workshops, masterclasses and trips. Recent productions include: *Humble Boy, Dancing at Lughnasa, Jack and the Beanstalk* and *Harry in the Moonlight*.

Northern Stage (formerly Newcastle Playhouse)

Barras Bridge, Newcastle NE1 7RH
tel 0191-232 3366 *fax* 0191-261 8093
email directors@northernstage.co.uk
website www.northernstage.co.uk
Chief Executive/Artistic Director Erica Whyman
Associate Director Neil Murray

Production details

Northern Stage is the largest producing theatre company in the North East of England. Following a £9m redevelopment programme, the company's new home – formerly Newcastle Playhouse and Gulbenkian Studio – re-opened in summer 2006 as Northern Stage. The new building has 3 stages and presents and produces a wide repertoire of UK and international theatre. Staging 6 shows a year, the company also works on participatory projects, with

Kylie Lloyd as the lead contact. Recent productions include: *Great Expectations, Son of Man, The Little Prince, Thumbelina, 1001 Nights Now, Ruby Moon, Our Friends in the North, A Christmas Carol, Tattercoats*, and *A Doll's House*. Offers TMA/Equity-approved contracts and subscribes to the Equity Pension Scheme.

Casting procedures

Casting breakdowns, when available, are published on the website. Actively encourages applications from disabled actors and promotes the use of inclusive casting.

Nottingham Playhouse

Wellington Circus, Nottingham NG1 5AF
Artistic Director Giles Croft *Casting Director* Sooki McShane *Director of Roundabout & Education* Andrew Breakwell

Production details

Nottingham Theatre Trust was founded in 1948 and moved to its current location in 1963. Stages 10 shows each year in the main house and 3 Roundabout productions. Also runs TIE, Outreach and Community programmes. Recent productions include: *Burial at Thebes, On the Waterfront, Vertigo, Whale's Tooth, Can You Whistle Johanna?*.

Casting procedures

Does not use freelance casting directors. Casting breakdowns are available from the casting director, Sooki McShane. Welcomes letters (with CVs and photographs) but not email submissions. Showreels and invitations to view individual actors' websites are also accepted.

Nuffield Theatre

University Road, Southampton SO17 1TR
tel 023-8031 5500 *fax* 023-8031 5511
email info@nuffieldtheatre.co.uk
website www.nuffieldtheatre.co.uk
Artistic Director Patrick Sandford *Associate Director* Russ Tunney *Administrative Director* Kate Anderson

Production details

A regional theatre performing a range of classic plays and new writing. Stages 5-7 shows each year in the main house, and 3-4 in the studio. Also runs TIE, Outreach and Community programmes. Recent productions include: *Hamlet, Nelson* (new play by Pam Gems) and *Wizzil* (touring primary schools). Offers ITC and TMA/Equity approved contracts and subscribes to the Equity Pension Scheme.

Casting procedures

Uses freelance casting directors. Holds local auditions for actors in the Southampton area. Actors may write

at any time requesting inclusion. Casting breakdowns are sometimes available through *PCR* or Equity Job Information Service. "We consider applications from disabled actors in exectly the same way as applications from able-bodied actors."

Octagon Theatre

Howell Croft South, Bolton BL1 1SB
tel (01204) 529407 *fax* (01204) 556502
email info@octagonbolton.co.uk
website www.octagonbolton.co.uk
Artistic Director David Thacker *Executive Director* John Blackmore *Head of Production* Lesley Chenery *Head of Administration* Lesley Etherington

Production details

Stages 8-9 shows each year in the main house and 18 in the studio. Also runs TIE, Outreach and Community programmes (contact Activ8 Department). Recent productions include: *All My Sons; A Midsummer Night's Dream; Rafta Rafta;* and *The Hired Man*.

Casting procedures

Does not use freelance casting directors. Actors may write requesting inclusion in the company at any time and should enclose an sae. Accepts invitations to view individual actors' websites.

The Old Vic

The Cut, London SE1 8NB
tel 020-7928 2651 *fax* 020-7261 9161
email ovtcadmin@oldvictheatre.com
website www.oldvictheatre.com
Artistic Director Kevin Spacey

Production details

After a number of years as a receiving house, The Old Vic's Chief Executive (Sally Greene), Artistic Director (Kevin Spacey) and Producer (David Liddiment) launched The Old Vic Theatre Company in 2004, with the aim of revitalising the theatre and making it a destination as a producing house once again. Recent productions have included: *Aladdin*, with Ian McKellen as Widow Twankey; *The Philadelphia Story* with Jennifer Ehle; and *Richard II*, for which Trevor Nunn directed Kevin Spacey in the title role.

Casting procedures

"We're not able to accept CVs or speculative applications for employment."

Open Air Theatre

Inner Circle, Regent's Park, London NW1 4NR
website www.openairtheatre.org
Artistic Director Timothy Shaeder *Executive Director* William Village *Casting Director* freelance

Production details

Stages 4 shows each year in the main house, including one family show. Recent productions include: *Much*

Theatre

Ado About Nothing; *The Tempest* re-imagined for everyone aged 6 or over; *The Importance of Being Earnest*; and *Hello, Dolly!*.

Casting procedures

Uses freelance casting directors who send full casting breakdowns to agents as required for each production. "Unfortunately we are unable to consider unsolicited CVs."

Orange Tree Theatre

1 Clarence Street, Richmond TW9 2SA
tel 020-8940 0141 *fax* 020-8332 0369
email admin@orangetreetheatre.co.uk
website www.orangetreetheatre.co.uk
Artistic Director Sam Walters

Production details

"The Orange Tree Theatre is wholly concerned with the performance of quality live theatre, and with reaching as wide an audience as possible with its work. Over the 30 years of its existence it has established a reputation for being the leader in its field and is the only permanent theatre-in-the-round in London." Presents a mixture of new writing, classic plays, comedies and musicals. Education and Community work forms a major area of activity. Stages 7 shows each year.

Casting procedures

Does not use freelance casting directors. Welcomes letters (with CVs and photographs) but not email submissions. Write in June for the new season. Also accepts invitations to view individual actors' websites. Offers TMA/Equity approved contracts. Actively encourages applications from disabled actors and promotes the use of inclusive casting.

Perth Theatre at Horsecross

185 High Street, Perth PH1 5UW
tel (01738) 472700 *fax* (01738) 624576
email info@horsecross.co.uk
website www.horsecross.co.uk
Creative Director Ian Grieve *Administrator* Elaine White *Associate Director – Youth Theatre* Jennifer McGregor

Production details

Scotland's oldest theatre company with a mixed programme of in-house and guest productions throughout the year, including drama, musical theatre and pantomime. Produces 4 shows each year. Also runs Outreach and Community programmes. Recent productions include: *A Streetcar Named Desire*; *The Snow Queen*; *Tom O'Shanter*; and *The Mystery of Irma Vep*.

Casting procedures

Casts in-house. Welcomes submissions (with CVs and photographs) sent by post, or by email to casting@horsecross.co.uk. Actors should write in the spring. Also accepts invitations to view individual actors' websites.

Pitlochry Festival Theatre

Port-Na-Craig, Pitlochry PH16 5DR
tel (01796) 484600 *fax* (01796) 484616
email admin@pitlochry.org.uk
website www.pitlochry.org.uk
Artistic Director & Acting Chief Executive John Durnin
Community and Education Director Drew Scott

Production details

Founded in 1951, Pitlochry Festival Theatre is a producing and presenting theatre located in the Perthshire Highlands. Comprises the main house (capacity 544), an extensive production facility, and Explorers: The Scottish Plant Hunters Garden, containing a number of open-air performance spaces. Between April and October each year a 20-strong acting ensemble presents a season of 6 major productions performed in day-change repertoire. Visiting theatre, music, dance, opera and other activities are presented during the winter months. Also runs TIE and Community programmes. Recent productions include: *Habeus Corpus*; *Arcadia*; *Outlying Islands*; *Whisky Galore – A Musical!*; *Good Things*; and *The Prime of Miss Jean Brodie*. TMA/Equity contracts are offered.

Casting procedures

Does not use freelance casting directors. Recruits new members of the acting ensemble each autumn and winter, with a detailed casting breakdown published each September. The closing date for applications is usually in mid-November; auditions are then held in London and Edinburgh in November, December and January. Casting breakdowns are obtainable by postal application (with sae) from September. Submissions at any other time – or not in response to the casting breakdown – will not be considered. The theatre actively encourages applications from disabled actors and promotes the use of inclusive casting.

Queen's Theatre

Billet Lane, Hornchurch, Essex RM11 1QT
website www.queens-theatre.co.uk
Artistic Director Bob Carlton *Associate Director* Matt Devitt *Education Manager* Patrick O'Sullivan
Administrative Director Thom Stanbury

Production details

Has been a producing theatre since it was first established in 1953. Currently works with actor-musicians in a permanent repertory company model. Stages 9 shows each year in the main house. Also runs TIE, Outreach and Community programmes. Recent productions include: *A Midsummer Night's Dream*, *Jane Eyre* and *Return to the Forbidden Planet*.

Casting procedures

Does not use freelance casting directors. Holds general auditions; actors should write in April or May requesting inclusion. Welcomes letters (with CVs and photographs) from actor-musicians only.

Rose of Kingston

24-26 High Street, Kingston-upon-Thames, Surrey KT1 1HL
tel 020-8546 6983
email admin@rosetheatrekingston.org
website www.rosetheatrekingston.org
Artistic Director Stephen Unwin *Executive Director* David Fletcher *General Manager* Jerry Gunn *Director Emeritus* Sir Peter Hall *Life President* David Jacobs

The Rose Theatre, Kingston opened its doors to the public in January 2008 with English Touring Production's production of *Uncle Vanya*, directed by Sir Peter Hall. The design of the theatre was inspired by the Elizabethan Rose on London's Bankside; Kingston's Rose has the same horse-shoe shaped auditorium and an open lozenge stage, creating a sense of intimacy between actors and audiences. The Rose auditorium has a capacity of more than 850 across 3 tiers of seating, including a pit area where audiences can sit on cushions for just £7. In addition to the main space there is a studio, capacity 120, and a gallery, capacity 60. These spaces host a variety of talks and workshops led by theatre writers and practitioners. The theatre also has a strong connection with Kingston University, where it facilitates the University's MA in Classical Drama.

The Rose presents a combination of home-produced drama and received work. Since opening, it has produced *Love's Labour's Lost*, directed by Sir Peter Hall; *A Christmas Carol* and *The Winslow Boy*, directed by Stephen Unwin; and a rep season which included *Bedroom Farce* and *Miss Julie*.

Royal & Derngate Theatres

Guildhall Road, Northampton NN1 1DP
tel (01604) 626222 (Admin) or (01604) 627566 (TIE)
website www.royalandderngate.com
Artistic Director Laurie Sansom *Associate Director* Dani Parr

Recently the subject of a £15 million redevelopment project, the theatre offers 2 auditoria and 'Underground', a creativity centre that is home to the Youth Theatre and a wide range of workshops and projects for the local community. The theatre's annual pantomime is produced by Qdos (see entry under *Pantomime producers* on page 237).

Royal Court Theatre

Sloane Square, London SW1W 8AS
tel 020-7565 5050 *fax* 020-7565 5001
email info@royalcourttheatre.com
website www.royalcourttheatre.com
Artistic Director Dominic Cooke *Casting Director* Amy Ball

Production details

Since 1956 the English Stage Company at the Royal Court has focused on developing, funding and producing new writing. Productions frequently transfer to the West End and Broadway. Stages 6 productions each year in the Jerwood Theatre downstairs and 8 upstairs. Also presents programmes of rehearsed readings (contact Lisa Makin). Recent productions include: *The Seagull*, *Drunk Enough to Say I Love You?* by Caryl Churchill and *Rock 'n' Roll* by Tom Stoppard. Offers SOLT/TMA/ Equity approved contracts and does not subscribe to the Equity Pension Scheme.

Casting procedures

Welcomes submissions (with CVs and photographs) by post or email all year round. Will consider applications from disabled actors to play disabled characters.

Royal Exchange Theatre

St Ann's Square, Manchester M2 7DH
tel 0161-833 9833
website www.royalexchange.co.uk
Artistic Directors Greg Hersov, Braham Murray, Sarah Frankcom *Casting Director* Jerry Knight-Smith *Casting Associate* Katherine Lawson *Education Director* Amanda Dalton

Production details

Manchester's leading producing theatre company, comprising a main theatre and studio space. Presents 8-9 productions, on average, in the main theatre and 4-5 in the studio each year. Also runs Education and Community programmes involving schools, young people, community groups and theatre enthusiasts of all ages. Work is based around the theatre's repertoire and its unique building. Where possible the department leads sessions in the theatre and frequently works with other departments around the building to give participants an insight into how theatre, and particularly the Royal Exchange, works. Recent productions include: *The Glass Menagerie*, *Three Sisters*, *Antigone*, and *A Taste of Honey*.

Casting procedures

Has a casting department of 2 who coordinate casting for each show. Actors are contracted for individual plays rather than for a season of work. Releases advance production information to around 200 agents on the website. Detailed casting breakdowns are only available for some shows.

Will consider attending performances at venues in the North West and London with sufficient notice. Accepts submissions (with CVs and photographs), but actors should bear in mind that the department expects to receive more than 2000 CVs and photos each season – and more in the summer months following graduation at the drama schools. All submissions are considered but they are not kept on file indefinitely.

Royal Lyceum Edinburgh

Grindlay Street, Edinburgh EH3 9AX
tel 0131-248 4800 *fax* 0131-228 3955
email info@lyceum.org.uk
website www.lyceum.org.uk
Artistic Director Mark Thomson

Production details

The Royal Lyceum is one of Scotland's largest producing theatre companies with a season of in-house drama productions running from September to May. In addition the theatre stages a children's show every Christmas. Occasionally tours in Scotland and abroad, limited hosting of touring companies and runs an ambitious and acclaimed Education Department. Recent productions include: *Mary Rose*; *The Lion, the Witch and the Wardrobe*; *The Man Who Had All the Luck*; *Curse of the Starving Class*; and *Copenhagen*.

Casting procedures

Does not offer general auditions. "Casting depends on individual directors' choices."

Royal Shakespeare Company (Casting Department)

1 Earlham Street, London WC2H 9LL
tel 020-7845 0500 *fax* 020-7845 0505
website www.rsc.org.uk
Artistic Director Michael Boyd *Head of Casting* Hannah Miller

Production details

One of the best-known theatre companies in the world, the RSC has been operating under its present name since 1961, a year after Peter Hall was appointed director. The repertoire was widened at this time to include modern writing and classics other than Shakespeare. Over the next 30 years the company continued to expand under the artistic directorships of Peter Hall, Trevor Nunn, Terry Hands and Adrian Noble. Michael Boyd succeeded Adrian Noble as Artistic Director in 2003. The RSC is committed to an ensemble approach to theatre, with actors most often being contracted to perform in several productions for 1-3 years.

Casting procedures

Welcomes performance notices 2-6 weeks in advance, and is prepared to travel around the UK dependent on workload. Welcomes submissions with CV and photograph of some kind – original 10x8 not required – and showreels via post, and preferably in relation to specific productions.

Salisbury Playhouse

Malthouse Lane, Salisbury SP2 7RA
tel (01722) 320117
email casting@salisburyplayhouse.com
website www.salisburyplayhouse.com
Artistic Director Philip Wilson *Casting Coordinator* Nicholas Gall

Production details

Stages 9 productions each year in the main house, alongside a studio programme. Also runs an Outreach programme.

Casting procedures

Casting breakdowns are available by postal application (with sae). Welcomes submissions (with CVs and photographs) by post only. Actors should write in May or October. Also accepts invitations to view individual actors' websites. Offers TMA/Equity approved contracts. Actively encourages applications from disabled actors and promotes the use of inclusive casting.

Shakespeare's Globe

21 New Globe Walk, Bankside, London SE1 9DT
tel 020-7902 1400 *fax* 020-7902 1401
email info@shakespearesglobe.com
website www.shakespeares-globe.org
Artistic Director Dominic Dromgoole *General Manager* Lotte Buchan *Executive Producer* Conrad Lynch *Theatre & Projects Officer* Jasmine Lawrence

Production details

A reconstruction of Shakespeare's Globe, the theatre has a repertoire which includes the work of Shakespeare, his contemporaries and new writing. The season runs from May to October with up to 6 productions staged each year. Also runs Outreach and Community programmes (contact Deborah Callan on 020-7902 1430). Recent productions include: *Othello*, *The Merchant of Venice*, *Love's Labour's Lost*, *Rome & Juliet* - UK Tour, *In Extremis* by Howard Brenton, *Holding Fire!* by Jack Shepherd, *We the People* by Eric Schlosser.

Casting procedures

Welcomes letters (with CVs and photographs) but not email submissions. Actors should write to the Theatre & Projects Officer in December and early January. Offers actors Equity approved contracts through an in-house agreement. Actively encourages applications from disabled actors and promotes the use of inclusive casting. The website has more information about casting procedures.

Sheringham Little Theatre

2 Station Road, Sheringham, Norfolk NR26 8RE
tel (01263) 822117
email enquiries@sheringhamlittletheatre.com
website www.sheringhamlittletheatre.com
Artistic Director Debbie Thompson

Production details

A professional seaside repertory summer season which runs for 10 weeks from July to September, comprising 5 plays which are traditional comedies, farces, thrillers and classics.

Casting procedures

Holds general auditions. Actors should write between Jan and March sending a CV and *recent* photograph. Email submissions not welcome. "As a small venue we are non-Equity, but we do work with Equity to pay a realistic wage; we also pay for accommodation and towards travel costs." Actively encourages applications from disabled actors and promotes the use of inclusive casting.

Sherman Cymru

Senghennydd Road, Cardiff CF24 4YE
tel 029-2064 6901 *fax* 029-2064 6902
website www.shermantheatre.co.uk
Director Chris Ricketts

Production details

Stages 4 shows each year and specialises in work for young audiences. Often uses actor-musicians.

Casting procedures

Does not use freelance casting directors. Sometimes holds general auditions. Welcomes letters (with CVs and photographs) but not email submissions. Also accepts invitations to view individual actors' websites.

Soho Theatre

21 Dean Street, London W1D 3NE
tel 020-7287 5060 *fax* 020-7287 5961
website www.sohotheatre.com
Artistic Director Lisa Goldman *Executive Director* Mark Godfrey *Casting* Nadine Rennie

Production details

Soho Theatre is a producing theatre dedicated to new work and presenting a year-round programme of new plays, comedy and cabaret from its own central London theatre with 2 performance spaces. It also houses the Writers' Centre, running an extensive writers' development programme of readings, workshops and other events; and a community and education programme entitled Soho Connect.

Casting procedures

Casting is carried out in-house by Nadine Rennie.

Southwold & Aldeburgh Summer Theatre

14 York House, Upper Montagu Street, London W1H 1FR
tel 020-7724 5432 *fax* 020-7724 3210
Artistic Director Jill Freud Co-director Anthony Falkingham *Production Coordinator* Peter Adshead

Production details

Summer theatre with an extensive programme. Stages 5 productions each year. Recent productions include:

Arsenic and Old Lace, Dick Barton – Special Agent, One for the Pot, Climbing the Wall, Private Lives, and 6 guest Children's shows.

Casting procedures

Does not use freelance casting directors. Holds general auditions; actors should write in November requesting inclusion. Does not issue casting breakdowns. Welcomes letters (with CVs and photographs) but not email submissions, and advises that it is not possible to see everyone who writes in. Offers non-Equity contracts. Rarely (or never) has the opportunity to cast disabled actors.

Stephen Joseph Theatre

Westborough, Scarborough YO11 1JW
tel (01723) 370540 *fax* (01723) 360506
email enquiries@sjt.uk.com
website www.sjt.uk.com
Artistic Director Chris Monks *Executive Director* Stephen Wood

Production details

Stages 6-7 productions each year with lunchtime shows, late nights, rural and national touring. Most work is new writing. Recent productions include: *Improbable Fiction, Playing God*, and *Villette*.

Casting procedures

Sometimes holds general auditions; actors may write at any time requesting inclusion. Welcomes submissions (with CVs and photographs) by post or email. Also accepts showreels and invitations to view individual actors' websites. Offers TMA/Equity approved contracts. Will consider applications from disabled actors to play characters with disabilities.

"Casting Director Sarah Hughes is not resident at the SJT. Casting normally only takes place 2-3 times a year. Please note that unsolicited CVs/photos/showreels will only be returned with an sae to the same value as the original."

Theatre By The Lake

Lakeside, Keswick, Cumbria CA12 5DJ
website www.theatrebythelake.com
Artistic Director Ian Forrest *Associate Director* Stefan Escreet *Artistic Coordinator* Sophie Curtis

Production details

Each year, Theatre by the Lake produces a Summer Season of 6 plays in repertoire, an Easter production / Spring Season, and a Christmas production. Also promotes a touring programme of visiting professional work across all artforms, and runs Education and Outreach programmes. Recent productions include: *A Chorus of Disapproval; Blackbird; The Memory of Water*; and *A Midsummer Night's Dream*. Offers TMA / Equity approved contracts and subscribes to the Equity Pension Scheme.

Theatre

Casting procedures

Auditions are held 3 times a year. All casting is in-house; does not use freelance casting directors. Casting breakdowns can be obtained by postal application with SAE. Does not accept general submissions from actors. Further information about the casting process can be found on the website.

Theatre Royal & Drum Theatre Plymouth

Royal Parade, Plymouth PL1 2TR
tel (01752) 668282 *fax* (01752) 230499
website www.theatreroyal.com
Artistic Director Simon Stokes

Predominantly a receiving house, but produces some shows (especially musicals) which transfer to the West End.

Theatre Royal, Bury St Edmunds

Westgate Street, Bury St Edmunds, Suffolk IP33 1QR
email sharron.stowe@theatreroyal.org
website www.theatreroyal.org
Artistic Director Colin Blumenau *Artistic Co-ordinator* Sharron Stowe

Production details

Seating capacity 358. Built in 1819, the theatre is the only surviving Regency theatre in the country. Produces an annual pantomime at Christmas and produces two other shows a year – a rural tour in the Spring (2007 production was Ayckbourn's *Intimate Exchanges*) and an in-house production in the autumn, often from or about the Regency period. Offers non-Equity contracts.

Casting procedures

Casting is done in-house by Sharron Stowe. Casting breakdowns are published via *Spotlight* only. Actors wishing to be considered for the pantomime should write to the theatre in August. (The Spring and Autumn shows are cast in January/February and June/July respectively). Only welcomes letters and emails (with CVs and photographs) from actors previously unknown to the company during these casting periods. Does not welcome showreels but is happy to receive performance notices. Rarely or never has the opportunity to cast disabled actors.

Theatre Royal Stratford East

Gerry Raffles Square, London E15 1BN
tel 020-8534 7374 *fax* 020-8534 8381
email theatreroyal@stratfordeast.com
website www.stratfordeast.com
Artistic Director Kerry Michael *Associate Director* Dawn Reid *Executive Director* Vanessa Stone

Production details

Committed to work which portrays the experiences of different social and ethnic communities, the theatre is constantly striving to present shows which resonate with its diverse local audiences. Stages 8 shows each year. Also runs TIE, Outreach and Community programmes. Recent productions include: *The Harder They Come*, *Pied Piper* and *Township Stories*.

Casting procedures

Casting opportunities are advertised on the website. Welcomes submissions (with CVs and photographs) sent by post. Advises actors to research the theatre's work before writing, and to think carefully about their own suitability. Invitations to view individual actors' websites also accepted. Actively encourages applications from disabled actors and promotes the use of inclusive casting.

Theatre Royal Windsor

Thames Street, Windsor SL4 1PS
tel (01753) 863444 *fax* (01753) 831673
website www.theatreroyalwindsor.co.uk
Chief Executive Bill Kenwright *Theatre Director* Simon Pearce

Production details

A long-standing, non-subsidised producing theatre. Shows run for 2-3 weeks. Stages 15 productions each year with some going on to tour. Recent productions include: *Stepping Out*, *Lord Arthur Saville's Crime* and *A Man for All Seasons*.

Casting procedures

Does not use freelance casting directors. Welcomes letters (with CVs and photographs) but not email submissions. Offers TMA/Equity approved contracts. Will consider applications from disabled actors to play characters with disabilities.

The Tobacco Factory

Raleigh Road, Southville, Bristol BS3 1TF
tel 0117-902 0345 *fax* 0117-902 0162
email theatre@tobaccofactory.com
website www.tobaccofactory.com
Artistic Director Dan Danson *Theatre Manager* David Dewhurst

Production details

Stages 2 productions a year in the theatre space, and also works with the local community. Does not offer Equity approved contracts.

Casting procedures

Casts in-house and does not hold general auditions. Casting breakdowns are available from the website, via postal application (with sae), and via *SBS*. Welcomes letters (by post and email) from actors previously unknown to the company, but does not welcome showreels or invitations to view individual actors' websites. Actively encourages applications from disabled actors and promotes the use of inclusive casting.

Torch Theatre

St Peter's Road, Milford Haven SA73 2BU
tel (01646) 694192 *fax* (01646) 698919
email info@torchtheatre.co.uk
website www.torchtheatre.co.uk
Artistic Director Peter Doran *PA to Artistic Director* Lynn Muir *Casting Director* Christine O'Reilly

Production details

Stages 4-5 productions each year. Recent productions include: *Macbeth, One Flew Over the Cuckoo's Nest* and *Blue Remembered Hills.*

Casting procedures

Sometimes holds general auditions; actors should write in June requesting inclusion. Casting breakdowns are available by postal application (with sae) and Equity Job Information Service. Welcomes submissions (with CVs and photographs) sent by post or email. Showreels and invitations to view individual actors' websites are also accepted. Advises actors to join the mailing list so they know what is being planned 6 months in advance. Offers TMA/ Equity approved contracts. Actively encourages applications from disabled actors and promotes the use of inclusive casting.

Traverse Theatre

Cambridge Street, Edinburgh EH1 2ED
tel 0131-228 3223 *fax* 0131-229 8443
email philip@traverse.co.uk
website www.traverse.co.uk
Artistic Director Dominic Hill *Associate Director* Lorne Campbell

Production details

Scotland's only theatre committed to new writing. Presents a mixed programme of in-house and guest productions. Stages 4 shows each year in the main house and 2 in the studio. Also runs Outreach and Script Development programmes (contact Neil Coull). Recent productions include: *People Next Door* by Henry Adam; *Dark Earth* by David Harrower; *Iron* by Rona Munro; and *Outlying Islands* by David Greig.

Casting procedures

Does not use freelance casting directors. Welcomes letters (with CVs and photographs) but not email submissions. Actors should write in January, June or September. Particularly interested to hear from Scottish actors. Invitations to view individual actors' websites are also accepted.

Tricycle Theatre

269 Kilburn High Road, London NW6 7JR
tel 020-7372 6611 *fax* 020-7328 0795
email admin@tricycle.co.uk
website www.tricycle.co.uk
Artistic Director Nicolas Kent *General Manager* Mary Lauder

Production details

Since opening in 1980, the Tricycle has striven to produce a challenging and innovative programme of theatre, cinema and visual arts reflecting the cultural diversity of its neighbourhood – and in particular plays by Irish, African-Caribbean, Jewish and Asian writers – as well as responding to contemporary issues and events with its ground-breaking 'tribunal' plays. The new Tricycle now comprises a 230-seat theatre, a 300-seat cinema, a large rehearsal studio, a visual arts studio for educational use, a smaller theatre/workshop space, an Art Gallery, and a new room called the Creative Space for educational/social exclusion workshops. The Tricycle maintains a comprehensive Youth and Education programme in Brent schools, and a thriving youth theatre reaching more than 20,000 children and young people each year through access schemes and community work. The theatre stages 5 plays each year. Recent productions have included: the premières of Harold Pinter's *The Dwarfs* and Athol Fugard's *Sorrow and Rejoicings*; 2 plays about the political situation of Northern Ireland – *As the Beast Sleeps* by Gary Mitchell, and *10 Rounds* by Carlo Gebler; and a collaboration with the Royal National Theatre of Zinnie Harris's *Further than the Furthest Thing.*

Casting procedures

Uses freelance casting directors but also occasionally posts casting breakdowns on the noticeboard section of the website. Does not welcome casting enquiries and submissions from actors unknown to the company. The Tricycle does however keep files on Black/Asian actors for its own information and as a resource for others; in these cases a photograph and CV are welcome.

Tron Theatre

63 Trongate, Glasgow G1 5HB
tel 0141-559 3748 *fax* 0141-552 6657
email casting@tron.co.uk
website www.tron.co.uk
Artistic Director Andy Arnold *General Manager* Anne McCluskey *Outreach* Lisa McIntosh.

The Tron is one of Scotland's leading producing and presenting venues delivering a vital and engaging programme of creative, popular and contemporary theatre by both Scottish-based and international artists and companies. The Tron also provides a supportive environment for emerging and established direction talent, nurturing the future voices of Scottish Theatre. Seating Capacity: Main House 230, Studio 60.

Production details

6 productions are staged annually in the Main House (including co-productions) and 1 production is

Theatre

staged annually in the Studio. Other areas of work include Outreach. Recent productions include: *The Patriot* by Grae Cleugh, *The Boy's Own Story* by Peter Flannery, *Wullie Whittington* by Gordon Dougall and Fletcher Mathers and *The Tempest*.

Casting procedures

Casting is done by liaising with show director and casting directors, and using details of actors on file. Actors can write at anytime to request inclusion as their submissions will be kept on file. Accepts submissions (with CV's and photographs) from actors unknown to the company. Actors are employed under Equity approved contracts, and the theatre participates in the Equity Pension Scheme. Encourages applications from disabled actors and promotes the use of inclusive casting.

Warehouse Theatre

Dingwall Road, Croydon CR20 2NF
tel 020-8681 1257 *fax* 020-8688 6699
email info@warehousetheatre.co.uk
website www.warehousetheatre.co.uk
Artistic Director Ted Craig *Administrative Director* Evita Bier *Education Manager* Rose-Marie Vernon

Production details

New-playwriting producing theatre for South London, presenting a mixed programme of in-house and guest productions. Recent productions include: the *Dick Barton* series; *Femme Fatale*; *Blowing Whistles*; and *Woody Allen's Murder Mysteries*.

Casting procedures

Uses freelance casting directors. Welcomes postal submissions at any time (with CVs and photographs) with sae for reply, but not email submissions. Offers ITC/Equity approved contracts. Encourages applications from disabled actors, although the building is not wheelchair accessible.

Watermill Theatre

Bagnor, Nr Newbury RG20 8AE
tel (01635) 45834 *fax* (01635) 523726
website www.watermill.org.uk
Artistic and Executive Director Hedda Beeby *Associate Directors* John Doyle, Edward Hall *Outreach Director* Ade Morris

Production details

A producing theatre where actors live onsite. Stages 6 shows each year with runs of 6-8 weeks, and 2 Outreach tours. Recent productions have included: Shakespeare, Music Theatre, New Writing and Classics.

Casting procedures

Does not use freelance casting directors. Casting breakdowns are available by postal application (with

sae), but actors should call first. Welcomes letters (with CVs and photographs) with reference to specific castings only. Offers TMA/Equity approved contracts and subscribes to the Equity Pension Scheme. Will consider applications from disabled actors to play characters with disabilities.

Watford Palace Theatre

20 Clarendon Road, Watford WD17 1JZ
tel (01923) 235455 *fax* (01923) 819664
email enquiries@watfordpalacetheatre.co.uk
website www.watfordpalacetheatre.co.uk
Artistic Director and Chief Executive Brigid Larmour
Executive Director Matthew Russell

Production details

Producing theatre built in 1908 and recently refurbished, it currently stages 8 shows each year. The theatre presents a varied programme but with an emphasis on new plays and adaptations. Also involved in Education and Community theatre, for which Kirsten Hutton (Head of Learning & Participation) is the lead contact. Offers TMA/Equity approved contracts and does not subscribe to the Equity Pension Scheme.

Casting procedures

Uses freelance casting directors and is unable to respond to individual CVs. Will consider applications from disabled actors to play disabled characters.

West Yorkshire Playhouse

Playhouse Square, Quarry Hill, Leeds LS2 7UP
tel 0113-213 7800 *fax* 0113-213 7250
website www.wyp.org.uk
Artistic Director Ian Brown *Producer* Henrietta Duckworth

Production details

Founded in 1990, the West Yorkshire Playhouse has 2 auditoria – the Quarry (750 seats), and the Courtyard (350 seats). Works include new writing, classics, Shakespeare and musicals, as well as guest productions from incoming touring companies. Also runs TIE, Outreach and Community programmes (contact Gail McIntyre): the schools company tours 3 times a year. Stages 15-17 productions each year across both theatre spaces. Recent productions include: *The Lion, the Witch and the Wardrobe*; *Othello*; *Animal Farm*; *The Hounding of David Oluwale*; *When We Are Married*; and *Peter Pan*. Offers TMA/Equity contracts and does not subscribe to the Equity Pension Scheme.

Casting procedures

Currently the West Yorkshire Playhouse casts through agents' submissions, and works with casting directors on productions on a show-by-show basis. Replies to individual actors can only be sent on receipt of sae. Casting breakdowns are only available to agents. "The West Yorkshire Playhouse is an equal opportunities employer in relation to casting."

The New Wolsey Theatre

Civic Drive, Ipswich IP1 2AS
tel (01473) 295911 *fax* (01473) 295910
email info@wolseytheatre.co.uk
website www.wolseytheatre.co.uk
Artistic Director Peter Rowe

Production details

Mixed producing/receiving house, staging 4-5 productions a year in the main house and 2 in the studio. Also works in Creative Learning and Community Outreach; the contact for this is Rob Salmon. Recent productions include: *Angel House, The Glass Menagerie, The Doubtful Guest, Spies*, and *Laurel & Hardy*.

Casting procedures

Uses freelance casting directors and does not hold general auditions. Casting breakdowns are available via postal application (with sae). Does not welcome unsolicited approaches from actors, unless in response to a casting breakdown. Offers TMA/Equity approved contracts. Actively encourages applications from disabled actors and promotes the use of inclusive casting.

York Theatre Royal

St Leonard's Place, York YO1 7HD
tel (01904) 658162 *fax* (01904) 550164
website www.yorktheatreroyal.co.uk
Artistic Director Damian Cruden *Chief Executive* Daniel Bates

Production details

One of the oldest theatres in the country; seats 867 in the main theatre and 102 in the studio. Productions include classics, new writing and the famous York pantomime every Christmas. Also hosts touring companies, premières and has a partnership with Pilot Theatre Company who are resident at the theatre. Also runs Outreach and Community programmes (contact Julian Olline). Recent productions include: *Terms of Endearment, Enjoy, Twinkle Little Star, Patient No. 1, The Reading Room,* and *A Man for All Seasons*.

Casting procedures

Occasionally uses freelance casting directors; submissions from actors may be sent in directly to Katy Nelson.

Young Vic

66 The Cut, London SE1 8LZ
email info@youngvic.org
website www.youngvic.org
Artistic Director David Lan *Associate Artistic Director* Sue Emmas

Production details

During 2005/6 the Young Vic's home in The Cut was redeveloped. From the new building, it now runs TIE, Outreach and Community programmes (contact Sue Emmas). Recent productions include: *Skellig* by David Almond (directed by Trevor Nunn); *Hobson's Choice* adapted by Tanika Gupta (directed by Richard Jones); *Simply Heavenly* by Langston Hughes (directed by Josette Bushell-Mingo); and *Cruel and Tender* by Martin Crimp (directed by Luc Bondy).

Casting procedures

Uses freelance casting directors. Does not welcome direct submissions from actors. Offers TMA/Equity approved contracts. Actively encourages applications from disabled actors and promotes the use of inclusive casting.

Effective audition speeches
Simon Dunmore

Audition speeches may be a fundamental part of the actor's 'toolkit', but a surprising number of otherwise good actors are not very good at doing them – and many make poor choices of material to use. It's true that most castings involve a reading, but sometimes audition speeches are asked for in advance (see Jeremy Raison's article on page 130), and occasionally you'll get, "We'd just like to see something else; what can you show us?" It would be very silly to be caught out because you haven't done an audition speech since drama school.

Essentially, audition speeches should be self-contained, well chosen, well researched, well staged and well gauged for the space you are in and for whoever is watching you – just like a good production of a play. In fact an audition speech should be a 'mini-production' (of a 'mini-play') in its own right.

Essential parameters
Length
An audition piece should be no more than two or two-and-a-half minutes long (that's roughly 300 words, depending on pace). Two minutes (or less) can be very effective provided that it contains all the parameters listed elsewhere in this article.

How many?
The important thing is to have a good range of audition material so that you've got a library to choose from to suit each given circumstance. I suggest at least half a dozen.

What types?
Your collection should consist of a good variety of characters you could credibly play. They should be within your 'playing range' and appropriate to your appearance: an audition speech is not an acting exercise; it's part of your marketing portfolio.

You should also aim to find material that rarely (if ever) appears elsewhere on the audition circuit. Judging acting is a highly subjective business, so it is generally better to find 'original' material to heighten your chances of not being compared to others. I suggest that you only use material that is popular if you feel sure you can perform it (them) extremely well – on a bad day ...

Don't neglect to include at least one Shakespeare – you will find lists of 'popular' Shakespeare speeches on my website. I will not attempt a similar list of modern speeches as these change constantly; you'll have to ask around to discover whether a speech is currently in this category.

NB There are some wonderful monologues written by well-known writer-performers like Victoria Wood and Alan Bennett. It is generally better to avoid these, as they were specifically written to be performed by the writer or another well-known performer. It is very, very hard for the viewer not to compare your rendition with the original.

It is also probably better to avoid any character who is generally remembered through a specific performance. As an example, Rita (*Educating Rita*) will remain associated with Julie Walters for a very long time to come.

Accents

If you choose to do a speech written in a regional accent, make sure you can do that accent well enough to convince a native. (It is important to have at least one in your repertoire that features your own accent if it is a strong and 'characterful' one.) Some people choose to 'translate' a speech into an accent with which they are more comfortable, and this can work. However, watch that in doing this you are not sacrificing too much of the quality of the original language. Some directors can be quite purist about this, and will only countenance speeches done in their original accents, particularly well-known ones.

Sources of speeches

Don't just rely on plays that you know; you should be steadily expanding your knowledge of dramatic literature. Seeing, reading, sitting in libraries and bookshops (especially, second-hand ones); even picking up an audition book to find inspiration for a playwright (previously unknown to you) whom you could explore further.

Look in novels, less well-known films, and good journalism (for instance) for material that could be made into good 'drama'. For example, Shakespeare copied (almost word-for-word) Queen Katherine's wonderful speech beginning "Sir, I desire you do me right and justice ..." (*Henry VIII*, Act II, Scene 4) from the court record.

It's generally inadvisable to write your own speech(es). This rarely works because very few actors are good playwrights. If you do decide to use a self-written piece, it can be a good idea to use a *nom de plume;* you're selling yourself as an actor; not a playwright. You should also be prepared to talk about the whole play, even if you haven't written it yet.

Finding 'original' speeches

It can be hard to know where to start when faced with all those shelves full of plays. Try focusing on the writers of speeches (from an audition speech book, for instance) that you've enjoyed. they almost certainly wrote other plays.

It is possible to find out-of-print plays via libraries or book-finding services and by combing second-hand book shops. Some publishers (even a few playwrights' agencies) will organise a photocopy, for a fee. Also, The British Library (in theory) has a copy of every play ever performed in this country (although there can be complications in actually getting hold of a copy). Start with your local library if you're determined to find a specific play; if they don't have it, they may well be able to get it from another library (via the 'inter-library loan' system), but be prepared for it to take a long time.

NB There is a list of playwrights worth exploring for audition material on my website.

Content

Too many people fail because they choose to do an indifferent speech. Even if they do it well, it somehow doesn't have much impact because of indifferent writing, lack of depth, and so on. Essentially you should go for pieces that have good 'journeys' – just like a good play.

It can be useful to find speeches that enable you to show your special skills (singing or juggling, for instance), but don't try to cram so much in that the sense is lost in a firework display of technical virtuosity. At the other extreme, avoid something that requires performance at one pace or on one note.

And, never set out to shock deliberately through content and/or crude language. That is not to say don't do 'shockers'; rather, don't set out with the specific idea of shocking

Theatre

your interviewer(s) as many people seem to intend. We've heard most of it before. I cannot describe how mind-numbingly tedious audition-days can become when peppered with such speeches.

Warning: There is now a lot of free audition material available on the Internet. Much of it is indifferently written; however, I have come across the occasional 'gem'.

Shape

Make sure that each of your pieces has a decent shape. In a sense it should be like a good play, with a beginning, middle and ending. Even if the character ends up back where he/she started, so long as he/she has travelled a 'journey' then that's fine.

Editing

It is possible to make a complete speech by 'stringing together' short speeches from a piece of dialogue and/or taking a section out of a novel or a newspaper article (etc.), but does it (a) make sense and (b) sound like spoken language? It often isn't simply a question of cutting out the other person's lines or removing phrases like "she explained". You usually need to make some other detailed edits. Once you think that you've completed an edit, type it out. Trying to get a proper perspective on a page full of crossings-out and word changes is nigh-on impossible.

Shakespeare and the classics

Traditionally you have to have at least one of these in your armoury. The fact is that most people perform them indifferently. Too many renditions seem as dead as their writers. The problem is that they are remote – in language and in content – from our direct experience, and therefore usually require much more research, thought and preparation than a modern speech.

NB It's very tedious to see comedy Shakespeare speech done in a 'cod' West Country accent. If you can genuinely do one of the many variants of this accent, then that's fine, but his language works in every other regional accent in which I've heard it done.

'Trying on'

Try reading any speech that looks good to you (on the page) out loud in front of someone else before you start rehearsing it. If you do this, you'll get an even better idea of whether each speech really suits (and 'grabs') you. It's a bit like buying clothes: you see a pair of trousers (say) that look good on the hanger; sometimes you will feel completely different about them when you try them on. The opposite can also occur: you feel indifferent about a speech on the page; you read it out loud and it feels much, much better.

Rehearsing your speeches

'What are you bringing on stage?'

You must bring your character's life history (gleaned from the play and supplemented by your imagination) into your performance. [As the character (i.e. in the first person), write notes of all the bits of information (big and small) that you find in order to build his/her life.] Most of what you 'bring' won't be obvious to your auditioner(s). However, it will be immediately obvious if that 'life history' is not present. Just as 90% of an iceberg is underwater, a similar proportion of a good performance is also hidden ... but must be there, underneath, to support that performance.

It is particularly important to be clear about what actually provokes the character to start speaking – the 'ignition' that kicks your 'engine' into life. Try running a brief 'film' in your imagination, culminating in the event (for instance, a statement or a gesture from someone else) that is your cue.

Your invisible partner(s)

If you choose a speech addressing another character, then it is vital that that other person (and how they are reacting through the speech) is clear to you. It is generally better to imagine an adaptation of someone you know rather than to 'borrow' someone you've only seen on a flat screen. There can be a huge difference in how we perceive others between two and three dimensions.

It's not just them (and how they are reacting); it's also important to be clear about your relationship. As well as imagining what your character's lover looks like (for instance), you must also know the feel of their touch, their smell, and so forth – and many more personal aspects.

It is also important that any other people, places and events mentioned in the speech are similarly 'clear' in your imagination.

Your invisible circumstances

You should also bring the setting, clothes and practical items with you – in your imagination. (NB I could have written 'set, costumes and props', but I believe that it's important to think of everything being 'real' and not items constructed for a production.) I believe that actors neglecting these is the cause of a high proportion of failed and indifferent speeches. It's not just the visual images, it is also what the other senses give you: the 'brush' of a summer breeze across your face, for instance. Plays are not performed in 'real' rooms (there will be at least one wall missing) and every play has at least one non-appearing character mentioned. These absences are filled by the actors' imaginations. Do the same with these 'absences' in the audition circumstances.

It isn't just the major features that you should think about, but also the apparently minor details – for instance, that mark on a wall that suddenly catches your character's eye. It can be a good idea to draw a map (or groundplan) so that the whole 'geography' of your 'circumstances' is clear for you. Then fill out your imaginary location with as much detail as possible.

Journey

There will often be some variations between characters as they appear in the play and as they appear in your speech when it has been separated from the play. The journey travelled in that speech within the context of the play will be different from the journey you have to travel when doing the speech on its own.

Interpretation

As you are creating a 'mini-production' of a 'mini-play' (the 'child' of its 'parent-play'), I believe that it's legitimate to make changes to the given circumstances of the speech when it occurs in the play, especially if such changes enhance your audition performance. [After all, a 'child' can never lose the genetic code of its 'parents', but he/she will evolve their own personality, which will be different.] However, be prepared to justify it – and don't get defensive. There's usually no harm in honest disagreement.

That voyage of discovery

Be aware of the 'voyage of discovery' that shapes your speech. Don't anticipate the end at the beginning. This is a common fault in rehearsal, which is easily corrected – but a remarkable number of people fall into this trap when performing their audition speeches.

Theatre

It can be very useful to write out a speech with each sentence (or even each phrase) on a separate line. It then appears less of a 'block' of words on the page and more a series of separate, but connected, thoughts and ideas. It is also a good idea to leave sufficient space between each line to write notes on what the impulse is to go on to say the next thing, and the next, and ...

Beginnings

If you start your speech nebulously, your interviewer probably won't take in what you are doing for the first few seconds and may miss vital information that could make the rest of it a complete puzzle to them. You need to find a way of starting your speech that will grab their attention from the very beginning. This doesn't mean that the beginning has to be loud, simply that it should be positive and effective – almost as if the house lights were faded down and the curtain rising on ... You!

NB It can also be very useful to incorporate a simple movement to start a speech; a turn of the head, for instance.

Endings

It's also important to be clear as to why a character stops speaking after talking for two minutes. You need to be clear what your character's final thought is – crucially stopping his/her flow.

Finally

Ask yourself: "Is my speech and my presentation of it a good piece of 'Theatre'?"

Some practical considerations

Staging

Once you've done all the work set out in the previous paragraphs, you need to think carefully about how you stage each piece. Too many people seem inclined to put in extraneous moves either to compensate for the lack of the other character(s), or because they think the speech is boring if it doesn't contain enough movement. If you are properly 'connecting' to character and 'circumstances', the moves will follow naturally from each 'impulse'. However, much of the effect of your performance will be dissipated if your auditioners don't see enough of your face, and especially your eyes. In general (unless it is an address to the audience), they should be able to see three-quarters of your face for at least half the duration of the speech. To achieve this, orientate the other character(s) and 'circumstances' to suit the audition circumstances. For instance, place the imaginary person to whom you're talking at around 45 degrees to left or right in front of you. If your map (or groundplan) is clear in your mind, then it should be simple to angle it appropriately.

There is no point in placing a chair specifically to mark another character – or even the hat-stand which I once saw used as the object of some singular passions. If you do use such objects you'll usually find yourself concentrating on that object rather than your 'partner(s)'. They should be clearly lodged in your imagination so that the interviewer can 'see' them through you. Also, don't think that you have to stare at one place continually just to make it clear that he or she is there.

Chairs

A warning about chairs. There is a common variety of chair, as familiar as the bollard is to the motorway, that inhabits many popular audition venues. It can serve all kinds of functions as well as the simple one of being sat upon. However, don't rely on the well-known weight and balance of these plastic and steel functionaries for crucial elements of your well-prepared speech. You may suddenly find only chairs with arms or a room filled with wobbly ones. Be prepared to adapt to whatever form of seating is available.

Tip 1 Do a brief check on the mechanics of your audition-chair before you start your speech. For instance, you don't want to be thrown by the fact that the back is lower than that of the chair you rehearsed with ...

Tip 2 If your audition-chair represents a different type of seat (a low, backless bench, for instance), sit on the chair as though you're sitting on that 'bench'.

Props

Avoid using props. As you haven't got a proper set, costume or lighting, too much of the visual emphasis goes on to the prop and consequently away from you. It is amazing how riveting even a small piece of paper produced for one of the numerous 'letter' speeches can become.

Props can be mimed: that mime doesn't need to be brilliant. And think how much easier it is to put down an imaginary glass on an imaginary table, without making a sound at the wrong moment. In using any imaginary prop, remember not just the shape as you 'hold' it in your hand but also its weight and its impact on your sense of touch.

The only exception to this can be a prop introduced briefly and then quickly discarded. Even then, make sure its impact doesn't take the focus from the rest of the speech. Some find it useful to have some kind of 'token' secreted on their person to help 'connect' with the character.

New speeches

It is essential to try a new piece in front of someone else first. If you don't have a friendly director to help you (and even if you have, be wary: directing a play is different from directing an audition speech), almost anybody else in the profession will do as a first-time audience. A speech always feels different when done in front of an audience – just like a play.

A six-month service and an MOT

Be careful your speeches don't go stale. (The better the writing, the more chance of them staying fresh; there will always be more layers of that 'subtextual onion' to peel off.) Audition speeches, like cars, need regular servicing or reassessment. If a favourite old banger has done you good service in the past, make sure it's still road-worthy before you bring it out again. If not, trade it in for something new.

Essentially, each time you do a speech it should still have that freshness, that need to communicate and that willingness to give blood that personifies a first night. A second-night performance will not do. It is no excuse to blame the cold ambience of the room you are doing it in.

The last-minuter

Don't try to get a new speech together at the last minute. An audition speech, like a performance, needs a good gestation period to come to full fruition. The rehearsal-time needed varies from person to person, and from speech to speech, but the 'last-minuter' rarely succeeds. A half-known, half-prepared speech, however suitable, will waste everybody's time and put you right out of the running. I would suggest that a new speech needs at least a month's – conscious and subconscious – preparation before its first airing in the 'field'.

'Should I take a copy of my speech with me?'

Some like to carry a copy of their speech with them as a security blanket. Most directors won't want to know about it. In fact, offering one can label you an 'amateur' with all the dreadful prejudices that professionals have against that group. However, I have heard of occasions when one has been asked for, usually when the speech is obscure. So it can be handy to have a copy of such a speech with you; even better, take the complete play with you.

Performing your speeches

Each presentation of a speech has to have the raw energy of a first performance. Unlike a first night, where the only new factor (in theory, at least) is the audience, you have to face numerous new and possibly unexpected factors when doing your audition speech. You need to be not only well rehearsed but also well prepared for how to cope with all the peripherals that are other people's responsibilities when you are actually doing a production. You are your own stage-management, wardrobe department, front-of-house manager, and so forth.

'Act in here?'

I don't think any audition-room is entirely satisfactory. They can be dirty and unkempt, too hot or too cold, too big or too small, have inconvenient echoes, have barely adequate waiting facilities and/or be hard to find down a maze of corridors. You'll be very fortunate if the whole session has only road traffic as a background noise. You have to be prepared to adjust the presentation of your speech(es) to each context – by fractionally slowing down and enhancing your diction slightly if there's an unavoidable echo, or scaling down your movement in a small room, for instance.

It's your space

You should regard the space in which you are doing your speech as your stage with which to do whatsoever you wish – as long as you have due reverence for the fabric of the building, for your interviewers and their goods and chattels. Move the chairs if you need to, take your shoes off if that's necessary, and so on ... but don't ask if it's 'all right' to do so. It can get very tedious for an interviewer if you keep on asking permission every time you want to change something. Providing it doesn't affect your audience directly, just get on with what is necessary for your performance.

Don't ask where to stand; your actor's instinct should tell you the optimum place for what you are about to do. Especially, don't ask permission to start, even if it's only with one of those pathetic little enquiring looks – another way of undermining yourself in your interviewer's eyes. Once you've been given your cue, it's all yours and in your own time.

Natural hazards

Be aware of natural hazards in the room: for example, a low afternoon sun pouring through the windows that blinds you as soon as you happen to turn into it. Don't, on the other hand, stand in the deepest shadow; nobody wants an actor who cannot find his or her light.

Your interviewer will probably be sympathetic if the unexpected suddenly interrupts you, but it really is your responsibility to spot this kind of thing beforehand and adjust accordingly. If it is something impossible to anticipate, then aim to recover as quickly as possible and get back into your speech. After all, if something goes wrong during a performance, you don't just stop until it's put right; you continue as best you can, and 99.9% of the time nobody in the audience will notice that anything went wrong.

Explanations

Minimise explanations about your speech. Ask yourself if you need them at all. In fact the best speeches are self-contained and don't need explanation beyond the character's name and possibly the title and the writer of the play. Whatever their individual faults, most directors do know a lot of plays, the characters within them and who wrote them. Be careful not to insult directors by telling them what they already probably know. (For example, 'Hamlet from *Hamlet* by William Shakespeare.') On the other hand, make sure you know the title and writer of more obscure plays and be prepared to discuss them.

Sometimes, in the process of getting inside the character, actors forget to give these basic details. I don't think this matters (I enjoy trying to work them out for myself), but some directors have a nasty habit of interrupting actors' preparations with demands like "What are you doing, then?" If you do forget and are so interrupted, don't be so thrown that you rush into your speech.

Your interviewer as the other character

Some people try to use their interviewer as the other character for the purposes of their speech. This is not necessarily a good idea. It can work but is fraught with pitfalls.

First of all, do you need to ask permission beforehand? Politeness dictates that you should. After all, you are asking the auditioner to do the job of being in your play. He or she may say, 'Yes, of course', but has probably been asked the same question in every other session of the day; it can get very tedious. Even if it is all right, the auditioner is probably not an actor, will become self-conscious in the process, not react in the way you anticipated, may well want to drop out of character to write notes and consequently won't be a consistent partner.

'You choose'

Actors often come up with several alternatives on being asked: "Well, what speeches have you got?" That's good – they are well prepared – but they often trip up when they cannot make up their minds which one to do. This may not matter; the auditioner may enjoy choosing one for you to do. However, don't then suddenly say: "I don't feel like doing that." If a speech is not going to feel right for that particular ambience, don't suggest it. Be crisp and positive about the decision-making.

Preparation

Do give yourself a moment to position and check your chair and to check the 'geography' of your performance in this particular space.

A pause for thought

Then, also do give yourself that moment of thought before starting a speech – a moment to immerse yourself within your character and circumstances. Almost everybody understands that it can be hard to change gear from chatting to acting. Don't think that you are wasting time; it'll only be a few seconds, and your interviewer will almost certainly have something else to write down before concentrating on you again. (For most actors a 'few seconds' feels much, much longer in these stressed circumstances.)

However, don't take too long to wind up into your speech with lots of heavy breathing or pacing about or even just standing quietly in a corner. That may be what you have to do before you go on stage, but most directors, however understanding, will begin to wonder what kind of lunatic you are and are you going to take up precious rehearsal-time with these warm-ups? Your 'pause for thought' should be as brief as you can make it without showing your inner turmoil. Properly done, this can be riveting to watch.

Starting

One of the hardest aspects of doing a speech is starting it from cold. If you are onstage at the beginning of a stage-production (especially on a first night), you'll experience an immense, and for some, terrifying, feeling of excitement and power as the audience goes quiet. You should aim to recreate this feeling just before you start your speech. It'll give you tingles up your spine and put a real 'kick' into your speech. This will 'communicate' to your auditioners and make them really look at you – even if they've had their heads down scribbling in the preceding seconds.

Tip To help stimulate this process, get the smell of dust into your imagination – it's the pervading smell of any theatre.

Communication

You may well 'feel' your speech, but are you communicating it? Just because you are in a small room with only one person watching, don't mutter your speech at below conversation-level. How do I know you can fill a stage, however small, if you are not filling the room we're in? You have to make that room your stage, the interviewer(s) your audience. Think of them as being in the best seats in the stalls (the ones reserved for the critics on a first night) and aim just beyond the limits of the space. Only a lazy actor will give a smaller performance on stage just because there is a small audience.

Don't blast your interviewer out of his seat, either. Measure the acoustics: a lot of audition-rooms are part of church-hall complexes and tend to have high ceilings with the inevitable echo.

The 'need'

There is a 'need' that drives any speech; two minutes is a long time for someone to keep on talking. A long speech is a series of connected thoughts and ideas; underneath there has to be the 'need' to talk at such length. We all know people who 'go on' too much in everyday life – the odd person is able to sustain attention because of the energy and 'need' to communicate. The same is true on stage and in the audition.

Also, remember that your character hasn't usually planned to say so much. Essentially, the circumstances provoke the 'need' for them to add more, and more, and...

Your whole body

Another trait of auditionees is to forget about their bodies. Maybe it's because of the 'artificiality' of the situation and they wouldn't do it on stage – but how is the auditioner to know that? Just because you haven't got the proper costume, props and furniture it doesn't mean your body isn't part of your speech.

Stopping

If you do need to stop during a piece – you've dried or it's started badly – do it positively and calmly, and do it without a grovelling apology. You may feel terrible but you have to get yourself out of the mess without becoming embarrassing. You can even capitalise on having handled it well. A brief (and positive) "I'll start again" or whatever won't be held against you. If you dry or make a mistake significantly into a speech, just pause briefly and find your way back, just as you would in a public performance.

Bear in mind that most interviewers do not know how acting works. So if, say, your breathing starts going haywire, that's not a reason to stop unless it really is affecting the speech badly. You have left your teachers behind at drama school.

Finishing

When you finish you should keep the final thought in your mind and gently freeze for a moment, just as you would if you're left onstage at the end of a scene in a play. Then fade the imaginary stage-lighting (and close the curtains) at a suitable rate. (That 'moment' should last about a second. If you're unsure, say a multi-syllable word like 'Mississippi' in your head.) Then – without looking your interviewer(s) in the eye – relax back to your normal self, ready to move on to whatever your interviewer wants to do next. Many find the not 'looking your interviewer(s) in the eye' difficult, and a few even think that it might seem rude. However, if you do make eye contact at that crucial moment, you'll probably start to feel very vulnerable – and give out the 'vibe' that you're unconfident about your performance. Whatever you may really feel about that performance, there's nothing else that you can now do, except wait.

There may be a silence; your interviewer(s) may well want to write notes on what you've done. Just settle down and let them get on with it. Don't be thrown by that aching pause; you should quietly wait. The 'ball' is now very definitely in the interviewer's 'court' to restart the conversation.

'Thank you' (a)

There may be a vague 'Thank you' or 'Right', even 'Mmmm' from the interviewer at the end of your speech. Don't read anything in to these vague expostulations. If you do you'll start to undermine yourself. We directors are usually thinking about what we're going to write down about your efforts. That thinking process is dominant and what comes out of our mouths is merely our acknowledgement that you've finished – an attempt at politeness that doesn't come out quite right. (I hear myself doing this constantly, but have never found a way round it.)

'Thank you' (b)

Some actors opt for a 'Thank you', or 'That's it', at the end. Sometimes this sounds pathetic; on others it comes across as sheer arrogance (watch the way some actors do curtain calls). If you've got a good enough 'ending', you've given the cue. The director may not respond to it immediately, but you should have clearly established that the 'ball' is now firmly in his or her 'court'. It's much better to say nothing.

Switching off

It is respected that it can take a few seconds to come back to reality, particularly if it's a very emotional speech. But it's fundamental to acting that just as you can 'switch on', you can 'switch off' with apparent ease. I will never forget a woman who did a wonderfully passionate speech from Arnold Wesker's *Four Seasons* and ended up in buckets of tears. She had done it extremely well but when it was over she simply could not stop crying and had to be taken from the room and given time to recover. What would have happened if she'd had to get similarly emotional on stage and then immediately go on to do a comic scene, as can occur? This is an extreme example which exemplifies the need to look very carefully at how you change back to reality.

'Why did you choose that speech?'

This is probably one of the most common of questions afterwards. Often, it's simply the interviewer's way of continuing the conversation. Whatever the motivation, it's much better to have some positive explanation beyond the often limp, 'I like it' or 'My teacher suggested it.'

'Why don't you try that again? This time standing on your head'

Don't get so stuck into a way of doing a speech that you cannot do it in any other way put to you. Some directors like to work on speeches. You should understand the insides of each speech so well that you could do it 'standing on your head'.

'That was dreadful'

It is rare for interviewers to tell you exactly what they thought of your efforts – even rarer for somebody to say: "That was dreadful." If you know, without paranoia, that you've done your speech (or reading) badly – and know you are capable of doing it very well – and the director is on the verge of saying "Next, please", try to find a way of discussing your failure positively. This is very hard to judge properly, but it is worth looking for the opportunity without seeming pushy or paranoid. (There may even be time to do it again.) You could climb some way back into their esteem.

Another speech?

If there's time, and the interviewer is inclined, you might be asked to do another speech. Some actors come in with the idea that this will automatically be the case. Not necessarily! A director may well feel that he or she has learnt enough from just the one — this is not necessarily a bad sign and can in fact bode well. Anyway, it will take up more precious time.

If you are asked to do another speech, make sure it's sufficiently contrasting. If the idea isn't mentioned, don't suggest it! And don't, as I have seen several people do, go straight from one to another with hardly a pause between – let alone asking whether the second was wanted or not.

Tip If you are asked to do a second speech it's a good idea to make the staging as different as possible from your first effort.

Advice

Some directors give constructive advice. In general, take that as a compliment, even if they are critical. Nobody will waste time and energy giving notes if they didn't at least like some aspect of you and your work. However, one director's constructive notes can become another's criticisms. In rehearsal an actor will take a note and try it out. Sometimes it doesn't work, and the moment has to be looked at again. Maybe it was only half-right. In an audition there is usually no time to rehearse that note to see if it works for you. So, when you do try it, and it perhaps doesn't quite work, you have no recourse to its originator for further amplification. Take such notes as suggestions to be utilised or discarded as suits you and your speech. That's how rehearsals should be anyway.

Final note
Working on audition speeches can be a wonderful way of keeping your 'acting juices' flowing through periods of unemployment.

Simon Dunmore has been directing productions for over 30 years – nearly 20 years as a resident director in regional theatres and, more recently, working freelance. In that time there have been over 200 productions (of all styles, colours, shapes and sizes) – recently: several Drama School Showcases, Maugham's *Home and Beauty* and new plays about sex, WB Yeats' up-and-down relationship with Maud Gonne, one set inside a pyramid and another about Bismarck. Past favourites include: *The Promise* (Alexei Arbuzov), *Antigone* (Jean Anouilh), a seven-handed version of *Antony & Cleopatra* and too many others to mention. He also teaches acting and has worked in many drama schools and other training establishments around the country. He has written several books: *An Actor's Guide to Getting Work* (now in its fourth edition), the *Alternative Shakespeare Auditions* series and is the Consultant Editor for *Actors' Yearbook*. **www.simon.dunmore.btinternet.co.uk**

Theatre

Cattle calls and how to survive them

Jennifer Reischel

Standing in the same spot for hours in the cold at 7am. Listening to endless renditions of the same songs. Finally, being herded into a small studio with 50 others to try and dance a routine from *Cats* in the back row without kicking the person next to you. Sound familiar? These are all experiences you may encounter when attending the infamous 'cattle calls', also known as open auditions ...

Why are open auditions held?

These 'mass viewings' are often the only possibility for newcomers to the industry and performers without the required contacts, to get a foot in the audition system door, as literally anyone can attend. Casting directors and production teams use opens to spot those who do not have agent representation, are not fully professional (therefore not found in *Spotlight*, etc.), and those professionals they may have missed in their jam-packed audition schedule. Usually held for large-scale musicals, such as *Les Miserables*, *Phantom* or the recent production of *My Fair Lady*, most open auditions tend to take place for West End shows, although there are also examples of opens for touring productions. As an educated guess, I would say that musicals hold at most around half-a-dozen adult calls (for properly paid work), each year. Other types of open auditions include searches for children and teenagers for musicals, film and television shows, such as *Harry Potter* and *Billy Elliott* (film and musical version), as well as very occasional open auditions for adult parts in screen and stage ventures. Cruise ship auditions also tend to be open calls, as do searches for pop/rock band members and solo music artists for recording deals and similar projects.

How do I find out about when/where they take place?

Opens are usually advertised in the weekly newspaper *The Stage*, and sometimes in *PCR* (*Production Casting Report*) and other casting services such as Castweb and Castnet. Auditions for children and large nationwide searches are also often found in daily newspapers such as *The Guardian* or in local papers sold in the town hosting the audition. Common audition venues tend to be large theatres, dance studios (such as Pineapple and Danceworks in London), grand buildings such as The Welsh Trust Centre in London, and similar locations that are capable of hosting sizeable numbers of waiting and queuing hopefuls.

Cattle calls ads: what are they actually looking for?

Ads for opens in newspapers tend to be quite general and vague. "Looking for excellent singers and dancers" is a favourite, as are "come prepared to dance and sing", "young, sexy and funny", or "hip, trendy and cool". How do you judge if your particular skills are up to scratch or your look is right? First of all, be honest. Can you really hit that top C like your favourite musical theatre performer? Can you really pass for 25 if you are actually 40? If in doubt, ask an industry professional. The truth about opens is that most of the time, the panel will make up their minds within 10 seconds of seeing you walk in – based on first impressions of your appearance, general persona and whether you fit the general look of the part/show. You have very little control over this process, but you can make sure that you start your audition with the right attitude. Be open, friendly, and full of positive 'ready to perform' energy (a smile always helps). Make sure that your 'hello' or similar greeting is clearly audible. Just be yourself, and be proud of who you are and what you have to offer. After all, if you are not confident in your own abilities, how can you expect anyone else to believe in you?

Being recalled – the next step in the process– often depends purely on whether you have the right look or not, although singing range (which should be indicated on your CV), sometimes where you trained, and whether your dance technique is up to scratch during the few minutes they see you leaping around the room can also affect your chances. A lot of it is gut feeling, and whoever the panel feels drawn to or stands out for them at that particular moment. They usually have a pretty definite view of what they are looking for, and make decisions very quickly as lack of time forces them to do so.

NB Some open calls may involve members of the casting team going through the queue of waiting hopefuls, telling people then and there to go home/stay to be seen. This often happens if the auditions are running late or they know that they will not be able to see everyone queuing that day.

Physical and age restrictions

Some ads mention size and height restrictions. Most of the time, the panel will stick to these and you may be sent home while queuing if they see that you are not in the required bracket. There are always exceptions, of course, and sometimes an inch or two may not be noticed. Music groups tend to be stricter, especially if they are replacing band members. Children/teenage auditions seem to take height restrictions very seriously. As regards age, if you are underage and the ad specifically states that you should be 18 or over, or 16 or over, there is little point in attending this open call as the age limit has been given for legal reasons.

The procedure on the day – and how to prepare

Preparing for an open calls starts with one important point – having an EARLY night the day before. You will be up at the crack of dawn heading to the particular audition venue so you can be there at least two hours before the official start time given in the ad. If you do not turn up early, a) you may have to wait for up to eight hours or b) you may not get seen at all. For example, if the queue officially opens at 9am, get there at 7am. Some auditions will involve you literally queuing until you get seen by the panel, while other opens will give you a number and ask you to return at a specific time to audition with another 50 or so people in the queue. It is impossible to tell beforehand. While you are waiting, your CV and photo will be collected by an assistant and they may also sometimes take a Polaroid of you and ask you to fill out a form. Most open calls will tell you straight after your audition whether you were successful or not, and say that they will be in contact for any recall.

Musicals

Depending on the ad, you will have been asked to prepare to sing, dance or both. Even if the ad only asks for one of these, be prepared for both. You may turn up at *My Fair Lady* thinking you will be giving your best 16-bar rendition of 'I could've danced all night', but once you are in the building you discover that you will actually be dancing to 'Get me to the church on time'. It is best to be prepared for everything. Remember that if your open call is the 'queuing until you get seen' kind, you will not have time to find somewhere to

Theatre

warm up. You will have to warm up beforehand and/or in the queue, dancing and singing. Dance auditions often take place in small, crowded dance studios with anything between 20 and 50 people at a time. You are normally given about 10 minutes to learn a routine (sometimes two routines) taught by the dance captain, and then have to perform this to the panel (who will be in the same room watching as you rehearse) with the entire audition group (and then in smaller groups, usually of four or six). In terms of singing, you will very probably not get past 16 bars (I have been to opens where they cut people off after eight bars). In most cases you will be able to choose your own song and will be required to bring your own sheet music. Do NOT sing anything from the show you are auditioning for unless requested to do so in the ad. The ad will usually ask for material "in the style of the show" or to "show off your vocal range/style" – this is particularly popular if the open is for a new musical. Some opens hold both dance and singing auditions on the same day. Remember this if you are taking time off work, as if you are successful in the first part they may well require you to stay on for a second round. The panel will not excuse you or make arrangements for you to come back on another day. They are usually unsympathetic when it comes to work commitments.

Children

Auditions for child roles often require accompaniment by an adult, height measurements, and proof of age. Sometimes they may involve group auditions/workshops to put children at ease and encourage them to perform to the best of their best abilities.

Cruise ship opens

These are quite similar to open calls for musicals, although it is common to be asked to sing two contrasting songs here. It pays off to bring a selection and let the panel choose, especially for Disney cruises. For cruise ship auditions it is also sometimes acceptable to bring backing tracks instead of sheet music – to be on the safe side, bring both unless the ad definitely states which kind of accompaniment to use. Again, be prepared to sing and dance on the same day, which is common for cruise ship calls.

NB Your audition may be videotaped for later use.

Music groups/solo artists

With no existing production to refer to, these cattle calls can often be the hardest. Ads sometimes state the genre that they are looking for, e.g. "in the style of Beyonce/Michael Jackson/Sugarbabes", etc. – but most of the time you will literally have to turn up and just present what shows you and your talents/skills off best. Again, prepare sheet music and backing tracks if you can. Note that for music auditions your style of dress is very important, as image and look can be a large part of your appeal. Don't be afraid to be yourself. Don't copy anyone or try to sound exactly like anyone referred to in the ad. Use you own style and bring your own interpretation to a piece of music. Feel free to bring along a guitar, etc. if you feel that this represents you and/or the kind of band you are going for.

Plays, soaps, films, other

In this kind of open audition you may be asked to sight-read, meaning you will be given a piece of text in the queue or in a waiting room to study (not learn by heart) and then read in front of a camera and/or the panel once it is your turn to be seen. Auditions for screen productions may also involve a screen test, which simply consists of you saying your name (and sometimes an interesting random fact about yourself) in front of a camera and turning your head from right to left so they can take shots of your profile.

The open call survival guide

• Take along a large bottle of water. You may not be able to get out of the queue for an entire day and the last thing you need is to have a dry throat and 'stick-together' lips when you finally get your 30-second chance to sing!

• Bring easily digestible food. Comfort food such as your favourite takeaway chicken tikka masala may clog up your throat and make you feel too heavy to stand, let alone dance.

• Bring a friend. They really can be lifesavers at opens. It is best if they are also auditioning, as you can share experiences of open calls or warm up together ... and most importantly, they can hold your place in the queue while you go to the toilet at a nearby M&S.

• Buy a reliable alarm clock! There is nothing worse than waking up hours too late because yours failed to wake you.

• Take something to distract you. iPods are good to drown out chatter, tears, screaming fits, family feuds and unbearable warm-up exercises by fellow queue members. If you are able to read surrounded by lots of noise, a book can come in handy.

• Remember to take a copy of your CV and photo! Keep the CV to one page, type it out and follow a professional format. Your photo should be a 10 x 8 inch black and white professional headshot if you are a professional. For children's auditions, other photos may do.

• Have details of your agent and personal details like your measurements, etc. listed somewhere, as you may need them to fill out forms handed to you.

• Take a pillow. This is very useful for sitting on the kerb when standing becomes too tiring. Or to hit annoying queue members with if their singing becomes too aggravating.

• Take your demo CD and/or a showreel. Vital for any aspiring recording artists – but also handy for musical theatre and cruise ship auditions, especially if they run out of time and simply collect CVs and photos and say they will be in touch with anyone who looks interesting.

• Choose your dance wear/movement wear carefully. ALWAYS bring these along to a musical theatre/cruise ship cattle call, even if dance is not mentioned in the initial ad. Remember to bring various types of dance footwear (ballet, jazz, capezios, tap, character shoes or 'heels').

• Dress comfortably. Wear a warm coat, scarf, boots, anything to keep you warm and your voice protected if it is cold. You can always take these off once you get inside the actual building. Standing outside for long periods of time can make weather seem much colder than it actually is. Don't invest in expensive make up, clothes or hair styling; it is not needed.

• Use sunscreen on a hot summer's day. You don't want to suffer burns from queuing in the blazing sun and look like a tomato when you finally get seen!

• Whatever you do, do NOT forget your sheet music/backing tracks! Have your sheet music photocopied, neat and taped together , and with any key changes, etc. highlighted. Do not bring books (especially if they are new) as these will just fall off the piano once opened and cause delays and embarrassment.

• A mobile phone with free minutes/free text messages is a must-have at an open call queue.

Do's and don'ts for cattle calls

Do ...

• Chat to other people in the queue. Everyone is in the same boat and you may meet some like-minded people and make new friends.
• Warm up physically and vocally beforehand.
• Turn up EARLY.
• Remain friendly and polite at all times. You never know who may be watching.
• Make sure your hair is out of your face so the panel/camera can actually see you.

Don't ...

• Take a family member with you (unless you are underage). Most of the time they will not understand the process and will get impatient, cold/hot, worried or embarrass you with overprotective care. This is your audition and you need to deal with it by yourself. It's part of the process of being a professional. (Not to mention the fact that an entourage of family members simply clogs up the queue even further.)
• Wait until you get into the queue to learn/choose your song. Choose and rehearse a couple of songs that are appropriate BEFOREHAND; take all required sheet music/backing tracks along with you and make your final choice when you get into the audition situation (think about it while waiting). There is nothing worse than an audition hopeful panicking because they have not learnt a song/learnt the words, and rehearsing it at the top of their voice for hours in the queue.
• Dress the part. You turning up in Maria von Trapps' nun's habit, Eponine's rags or the Phantom's mask will do you no favours whatsoever and only cause a lot of giggling and pitiful looks. Equally, don't dress as Britney, Snoop Dogg or a member of ABBA. This is not a fancy dress party. Very occasionally, dressing as the part is specified in the advertisement – this is the only time dressing in costume is appropriate.
• Be put off by someone singing 'your song'. The panel will probably hear the song that you selected a hundred times that day, and for opens your choice of song is not that vital as long as it suits your voice, range and the production they are casting for.
• Practise your song full blast in the queue. It's just annoying for everyone else around you and will not help you. Hum to yourself quietly after a thorough warm-up at home.

Originally of German heritage, **Jennifer Reischel** was raised predominantly in the Far East, schooled in various languages, and following her passion for the performing arts, graduated from the three-year musical theatre course at Mountview Academy in 2002. Professional experience includes musical theatre productions in London and other parts of the country, acting stage work touring the UK, cabaret and jazz solo singing engagements in London and Singapore, as well as filming a television pilot at Pinewood Studios. Born into a family of professional writers, she is pleased to carry on this tradition, having recently also completed her first book, *So You Want to Tread the Boards*, available through Robson Books. After several years of experiencing the pit falls and difficulties first hand, Jennifer decided to compile her experiences in the form of a practical, non-nonsense and to the point guide, including specifically advice on a career in musical theatre. She hopes her experiences and research will assist fellow and aspiring performers to create work and audition opportunities, as well as remaining financially and emotionally afloat in a difficult and uncertain industry with no rules to follow to guarantee success.

Independent managements/theatre producers

This section mostly lists commercial organisations that mount West End and touring productions to larger-scale venues – some of which originate in the subsidised sector. Most such productions will be led by well-known actors, but they will usually need supporting actors who can also understudy those leads. (In long-running West End productions, the understudies get a chance to do their own performance – a useful opportunity to 'showcase' for agents and casting directors.) Sometimes, such a production will tour to try it out before (hopefully) coming into the West End; at others, a management will tour to 'milk' further profits from a West End success.

On tour, apart from 'Acting ASMs' (assistant stage managers who also understudy), you shouldn't be asked to do any of the graft of get-ins and get-outs – unlike on smaller-scale touring. However, if you are also understudying, you will be expected to do an understudy rehearsal every week until the last stages of the tour. This rehearsal will probably be taken by the company manager (rarely, the director) and the whole ambience will feel very unsympathetic to good acting. Despite this, it is very important to be as fully prepared as possible for the chance that the 'name' you are understudying will be unavoidably delayed one night. Touring is fraught with potential delays, and a reputation for being able to 'deliver the goods' at very short notice will enhance future employment prospects. The downside of playing small parts and understudying is that you can become stuck doing this – a good agent will be able to advise in this area.

Touring is not for everyone: long periods away from home, wide variations in the quality of digs (often costing more in holiday resorts during the 'season'), and the fact that you could miss opportunities to be seen for other work are some of the potential disadvantages. On the plus side, contracts for large-scale tours are usually at least three months with a minimum of a week in each venue, and you should have time to see some of the most beautiful sights in the UK (if not Europe and further afield).

Although not as expensive as major films, such productions do cost a lot of money to mount, and productions have been known to collapse suddenly without any warning. When accepting work in this area it is important to have a proper Equity contract.

Ambassador Theatre Group (ATG)

Duke of York's Theatre, 104 St Martin's Lane, London WC2N 4BG
Head of Production Meryl Faiers *Head of Group Casting* Neil Rutherford

Production details

ATG is the second-largest theatre owner and operator in the UK, with 22 venues (11 in the West End and 11 regionally). It produces across the UK, Japan, Europe and New York. Anywhere between 3 and 30 actors work on each production. Recent productions include: *Guys and Dolls*, *Sweeney Todd*, Matthew Bourne's *Nutcracker* and *Highland Fling*, *The New Statesman* and *The Rocky Horror Show*. Offers Equity approved contracts and is "happy to make contributions [to the Equity Pension Scheme] on behalf of any members of the scheme that we employ".

Casting procedures

Uses freelance casting directors. Welcomes letters (with CVs and photographs), but not email submissions. Actors may write at any time, but prefers contact to be made via an agent and preferably during pre-production. Advises actors against sending expensive photos 'on spec', especially

Theatre

if unaccompanied by a letter. Actively encourages applications from disabled actors and promotes the use of inclusive casting.

Anthony Vander Elst Productions

The Studio, 14 College Road, Bromley BR1 3NS
tel 020-8466 5580
Director Anthony Vander Elst

Established in 1977. Produces 1-2 productions per year touring the UK. Recent productions include: *Appearances* (Mayfair Theatre, London); *The Teddy Bears Picnic* (Chester Gateway Theatre); and *Last of the Red Hot Lovers* (London). Unsolicited approaches from actors are discouraged. Offers TMA/Equity approved contracts.

Andy Barnes Productions

Ambassadors Theatre, West Street,
London WC2H 9ND
tel 020-7395 5460
email andy@andybarnesproductions.com
website www.andybarnesproductions.com
Director Andy Barnes *Associate Producer* Wendy Killian

Production details

Founded in 2005. Primarily a producer of new musicals with Fringe and West End experience; also produces small plays. Founder and producer of Perfect Pitch Musicals Ltd – a development network for musical theatre. Stages 2 to 3 productions each year at the same number of venues, which include arts centres and theatres. Number of actors going on tour varies, and regions covered include London, the South East and New York. Recent productions include: *Days of Hope* (King's Head); *Departure Lounge* (Arts Theatre); and *Someone Who'll Watch Over Me* (Gene Frankel, NY).

Casting procedures

Uses freelance and in-house casting directors. Holds general auditions; actors should write in March and September to request inclusion. Casting breakdowns are available on the website and via Spotlight, and are published in *The Stage* and *PCR*. Welcomes letters (with CVs and photographs) from individual actors previously unknown to the company. Also welcomes email submissions and showreels but will not accept invitations to view individual actors' websites. "We only look for musical theatre performers, so singing ability is essential."

Nick Brooke Ltd

The Penthouse, 7 Leicester Place, London WC2H 7RJ
tel 020-7851 0393 *fax* 020-7734 7185
email info@nickbrooke.com
Directors Nick Brooke, Philip Noel

Production details

Founded in 2002 as an independent theatre production company, Nick Brooke Ltd stages 2

productions each year, averaging an annual total of about 280 performances. Tours to approximately 30 theatres throughout England and Wales annually. In general 6-10 actors work on each production. Recent productions include: *Corpse* and *The Shell Seekers*.

Casting procedures

Occasionally employs freelance casting directors. Also holds general auditions; actors should write in January and in the early summer to request inclusion. Casting breakdowns are publicly available via the website and postal application. Welcomes submissions (with CVs and photographs) from actors previously unknown to the company if sent by post, but does not welcome email enquiries. Also accepts invitations to view individual actors' websites.

Cole Kitchenn Ltd

212 Strand, London WC2R 1AP
tel 020-7427 5680 (Switchboard)
tel 020-7427 5681 (Personal Management)
tel 020-7427 5682 (Production Department)
fax 020-7353 9639
email info@colekitchenn.com
website www.colekitchenn.com
Key personnel Stuart Piper, David Cole, Guy Kitchenn

Production details

Production company established in 1970; personal management established in 2005. Has produced more than 60 productions in the West End over the past 35 years. Offers Equity approved contracts. Recent London productions include: *The Female of the Species* (Vaudeville Theatre) with Eileen Atkins; *Lifecoach* (Trafalgar Studios) with Phill Jupitus; *Daddy Cool* (Shaftesbury Theatre) with Javine & Michelle Collins. Current personal management clients include: Helen Lederer (*Ab Fab*), Paul McEwan (*Emmerdale*), Stephen Uppal (*Hollyoaks*), Jess Robinson (*Headcases/Dead Ringers*), Sarah Lark (*I'd Do Anything*), and award-winning West End stars Paul Baker, Graham Bickley, Kim Criswell, Frances Ruffelle, Robyn North, Jimmy Johnston and Caroline O'Connor.

Casting procedures

Casting breakdowns available from *SBS*, Spotlight and Castweb. Welcomes letters (with CVs and photographs) from actors previously unknown to the company sent by post or email. Invitations to view individual actors' websites and showreels are accepted. Rarely has the opportunity to cast disabled actors.

Ray Cooney Plays

Everglades, 29 Salmons Road, Chessington KT9 2JE
Director Ray Cooney *General Manager* Alan Osman

Occasionally directs, but no longer produces, plays.

CV Productions Ltd

Hampden House, 2 Weymouth Street,
London W1W 5BT

tel 020-7636 4343 *fax* 020-7636 2323
email cvtheatre@aol.com
Director Charles Vance

Production details

Regional touring theatre company.

Casting procedures

Does not use freelance casting directors. Sometimes holds general auditions. Casting breakdowns are not publicly available. Welcomes submissions (with CVs and photographs) sent by post or email. Invitations to view individual actors' websites are also accepted.

Paul Elliot Ltd

1st Floor, 18 Exeter Street, London WC2E 7DU
tel 020-7379 4870 *fax* 020-7379 4860
email info@paulelliott.ltd.uk
Director Paul Elliott *General Manager* David Bownes

Production details

Large-scale theatre producers, touring no. 1 venues across the UK with plays and musicals. Stages 2-4 productions a year, touring from between 6 weeks to 2 years or more. May use from 3 to 30 actors in each production. Offers TMA SOLT/Equity approved contracts and subscribes to the Equity Pension Scheme. Recent credits include: *Stones in his Pockets*.

Casting procedures

Casts in-house and also uses freelance casting directors. Actors may write at any time requesting inclusion in auditions. Casting breakdowns are published in *The Stage, PCR* and *SBS*, and included in Spotlight Link. Happy to receive CVs and photographs, by post or email, from actors previously unknown to the company. Also happy to receive showreels and invitations to view individual actors' websites. Will consider applications from disabled actors to play characters with disabilities.

Andrew Fell Ltd

4 Ching Court, 49-51 Monmouth Street,
London WC2H 9EY
tel 020-7240 2420 *fax* 020-7240 2499
email hq@andrewfell.co.uk
Directors Andrew Fell, Sally Hoskins

Production details

Theatre production company and general management. Recent productions include: *The Producers; Romeo and Juliet; The Lieutenant of Innishmore* and *Taboo*.

Casting procedures

Uses freelance casting directors.

Vanessa Ford Productions Ltd

Upper House Farm, Upper House Lane,
Shamley Green GU5 0SX

tel (01483) 278203 *fax* (01483) 271509
email vfpltd@btinternet.com
website www.vfpltd.com
Managing Director Vanessa Ford

Production details

Founded in 1979. Tours to approximately 30 theatres throughout the UK each year. On average, 14 actors work on each production. Recent productions include: *The Hobbit, A Christmas Carol* and *Shirley Valentine*. Offers ITC/Equity approved contracts and does not subscribe to the Equity Pension Scheme.

Casting procedures

Occasionally uses freelance casting directors, and sometimes holds general auditions. Casting breakdowns are available on the website and through *Spotlight*. Welcomes submissions (with CVs and photographs) by post and email. Invitations to view individual actors' websites are also accepted. Will consider applications from disabled actors to play disabled characters.

Robert Fox Ltd

6 Beauchamp Place, London SW3 1NG
tel 020-7584 6855 *fax* 020-7225 1638
email info@robertfoxltd.com
website www.robertfoxltd.com
Director Robert Fox

Production details

Founded in 1980. Theatre and film production company specialising in large-scale theatre productions and musicals as well as feature films. Performances are staged in the West End and on Broadway. Recent theatre productions include: *The Breath of Life, The Boy from Oz* and *Gypsy*. Also recently produced the feature films *The Hours* and *Iris*.

Casting procedures

Employs casting directors for specific projects and does not welcome unsolicited submissions from actors. Casting breakdowns are available on the website, and details of casting directors are sometimes posted there as well.

Sonia Friedman Productions

Duke of York's Theatre, 104 St Martin's Lane,
London WC2N 4BG
tel 020-7854 7050 *fax* 020-7854 7059
email queries@soniafriedman.com
website www.soniafriedman.com
Producer Sonia Friedman *General Manager* Diane Benjamin *Creative Producer* Lisa Makin *Head of Production* Pam Skinner *Associate Producer* Matthew Gordon

Production details

Sonia Friedman Productions is one of the West End's most prolific and significant theatre producers, responsible for some of the most successful theatre productions in London over the past few years. West End and Broadway Theatre includes: *Dumb Waiter* by Harold Pinter; *Boeing-Boeing* by Marc Camoletti; *Love Song* by John Kolvenbach; *Bent* by Martin Sherman, directed by Daniel Kramer, starring Alan Cumming; *Rock 'n' Roll* by Tom Stoppard, directed by Trevor Nunn; *Eh Joe* by Samuel Beckett, directed by Atom Egoyan, starring Michael Gambon; *Faith Healer*, by Brian Friel, directed by Jonathan Kent, starring Ralph Fiennes, Cherry Jones and Ian McDiarmid (Broadway).

Fresh Glory Productions

59 St Martin's Lane, London WC2N 4JS
tel 020-7240 1941
email info@freshglory.com
website www.freshglory.com

Production details

Established in 2007. Stages 2-3 productions annually, with 175-200 performances in 28-30 arts centres and theatres across England. In general 6-7 actors are involved in each production. Offers Equity-approved contracts as negotiated through TMA and ITC. For recent productions, please consult the website.

Casting procedures

Uses freelance casting directors. Casting breakdowns are available through Castweb and Spotlight Link. Welcomes letters (with CVs and photographs) from individual actors previously unknown to the company, but prefers hard copy to email. Actively encourages applications from disabled actors and promotes the use of inclusive casting.

Ian Fricker (Theatre) Ltd

3rd Floor, 146 Strand, London WC2R 1JD
tel 020-7836 3090 *fax* 020-7836 3078
email mail@ianfricker.com
website www.ianfricker.com
Producer Ian Fricker *Associate Producer* Louise Toeman

Production details

Founded in 2004. West End and touring producer. Stages 4-8 productions each year, with approximately 100 performances in 20 theatres across the UK. In general 1-15 actors go on tour. Offers Equity approved contracts as negotiated through TMA. Recent productions include: *Brief Lives* (Richmond, Brighton, Lincoln, Windsor); *Visiting Mr Green* (13-week tour and West End); Noel Coward's *A Song at Twilight* (10-week tour).

Casting procedures

Uses in-house casting directors; sometimes holds general auditions, and actors should write to request inclusion when advertised in *Spotlight*. Welcomes letters (with CVs & photographs) from actors previously unknown to the company sent by post, but not by email. Accepts showreels and invitations to view individual actors' websites. Rarely (or never) has the opportunity to cast disabled actors.

Gareth Johnson Ltd

Plas Hafren, Eglwysrw, Crymych, Pembrokeshire SA41 3UL
tel (01234) 891368 *mobile* (07779) 007845
email gjltd@mac.com
Director Gareth Johnson

Production details

Founded in 2000, this general management company produces (for a client) up to 6 shows a year, including West End, UK and European tours. Recent productions have included: *The Far Pavilions* (Shaftesbury Theatre); *Jus' Like That!* (Garrick Theatre and tour); *Songs My Mother Taught Me* (Lorna Luft at the Savoy Theatre); and a UK tour of *The Merchant of Venice*. Offers Equity contracts.

Casting procedures

Uses freelance casting directors and does not welcome unsolicited contact of any kind from actors. Policy on disabled actors "depends on the client".

David Graham Entertainment Ltd

72 New Bond Street, London W1S 1RR
tel 0870-321 1600 *fax* 0870-321 1700
email info@david graham.co.uk
website www.davidgrahamentertainment.com
Director David Graham

Production details

Theatre producer and concert promoter. Stages around 8 productions in 70-80 theatres and concert halls on an annual basis, with more than 300 performances per year. Countries covered include Britain, Holland, Germany, Canada, Spain, Norway and Ireland. In general, 12 performers work on each production. Recent productions include: *The Real Monty, The Wonderful West End* and *Hold Tight, It's 60s Night*.

Casting procedures

Does not use freelance casting directors or hold general auditions. Casting breakdowns are available via the website, *PCR* and advertisements in *The Stage*.

The Derek Grant Organisation

13 Beechwood Road, West Moors, Dorset BH22 0BN
tel (01202) 855777
email admin@derekgrant.co.uk
website www.derekgrant.co.uk
Director Derek Grant *Administrative Director* Michael Jones

Production details

Producer of nationwide theatre tours, children's shows, comedy, concerts and plays. On average stages

3-4 projects annually, with around 80 performances in arts centres, theatres and community venues across the UK. In general 6 actors are involved in each production. Recent productions include: Hans Andersen's *The Snow Queen* (13 performances at Lichfield Garrick Theatre), *Pinocchio* (at Bolton Albert Halls), Vince Hill in Concert (at North Pier Blackpool); and *Goldilocks and the Three Bears* (nationwide tour).

Casting procedures

Does not use freelance casting directors. Sometimes holds general auditions and actors are advised to write in September and January requesting inclusion. Welcomes letters (with CVs and photographs) from individual actors previously unknown to the company, sent by post or email. Accepts showreels and will consider invitations to view individual actors' websites. Considers applications from disabled characters to play characters with disabilities. "We treat all our artistes with respect and have a high reputation in the business."

Hiss & Boo Theatre Company

Nyes Hill, Wineham Lane, Bolney,
West Sussex RH17 5SD
tel 01444-881707 *fax* 01444-882057
email email@hissboo.co.uk
website www.hissboo.co.uk
Artistic Director Ian Liston

Production details

Established in 1977. Pantomime producers also specialising in touring plays and revues in the UK and overseas.

Casting procedures

Works with a known pool of performers. Casting and auditions are only available via Spotlight Interactive Casting. Does not welcome unsolicited CVs. Offers actors TMA/Equity approved contracts.

Paul Holman Associates

Morritt House, 58 Station Approach, South Ruislip,
Middlesex HA4 6SA
tel 020-8845 9408 *fax* 020-8582 2557
email enquiries@paulholmanassociates.co.uk
website www.paulholmanassociates.co.uk
Directors Paul Holman, Adrian Jeckells, John Ogle
Associate Producer Andrew Lynford

Production details

Established in 1990. Produces pantomimes, summer shows and one-night attractions. See entry under *Pantomime producers* on page 236 for more details.

Thelma Holt Ltd

Noel Coward Theatre, 85 St Martin's Lane,
London WC2N 4AU
tel 020-7812 7455 *fax* 020-7812 7550
email Thelma@dircon.co.uk
website www.thelmaholt.co.uk
Managing Director Thelma Holt *Executive Director* Malcolm Taylor

Production details

Founded in 1990. Theatre producer of classic plays in the West End, on tour and internationally (particularly Japan). Stages 4-5 productions annually with a total of 250 performances. Tours 6 theatres across the UK each year. On average, 18 actors work on each production. Recent productions include: *Hamlet, The Taming of the Shrew, All's Well that Ends Well, Othello, Pericles, Titus Andronicus* and *Kean*. Offers Equity/TMA/SOLT approved contracts and subscribes to the Equity Pension Scheme.

Casting procedures

Uses freelance casting directors. Does not hold general auditions. Advises that the company does not encourage unsolicited approaches with letters or photographs, as they will be ignored if not in production. When casting, requirements are made well known via casting directors. "I have employed disabled actors and will continue to do so – not necessarily to play characters with disabilities. When an actor's good, it's horses for courses."

Hull Truck Theatre

See entry under *Producing theatres*.

Image Musical Theatre

23 Sedgeford Road, Shepherd's Bush,
London W12 0NA
tel 020-8743 9380 *fax* 020-8749 9294
email brian@imagemusicaltheatre.co.uk
website www.imagemusicaltheatre.co.uk
Composer/Lyricist Robert Hyman

Production details

Founded in 1988. Stages 4 productions annually, with around 900 performances in 70 venues including arts centres, theatres, schools and other educational venues throughout the UK. In general 3-4 actors are involved in each production. *Recent productions* include: *The Jungle Book, The Secret Garden, Tom's Midnight Garden, The Snow Queen, The Wind in the Willows*, and *Alice in Wonderland*.

Casting procedures

Sometimes holds general auditions. Actors should write in June, October and late January to request inclusion. Casting breakdowns are publicly available via the website, from Equity Job Information Service, in *PCR*, and from Castnet and Castweb. Welcomes letters (with CVs & photographs) from individual actors previously unknown to the company only if sent by post. No emails and no showreels, but will

Theatre

accept invitations to view individual actors' websites. Rarely (or never) has the opportunity to cast disabled actors.

Colin Ingram Ltd

Suite 526, Linen Hall, 162-168 Regent Street, London W1B 5TE
tel 020-7038 3905 *fax* 020-7038 3907
email info@coliningramltd.com
website www.coliningramltd.com
Director Colin Ingram *Production Associate* Simon Ash

Production details

Theatrical producers and general managers. The company offers Equity-approved contracts and participates in the Equity Pension Scheme. "Please see the website for details of recent productions and venues."

Casting procedures

Uses freelance casting directors. Does not welcome unsolicited approaches from individual actors previously unknown to the company.

International Theatre & Music Ltd

Garden Studios, Betterton Street, Covent Garden, London WC2H 9BP
tel 020-7470 8786 *fax* 020-7379 0801
email info@it-m.co.uk
website www.it-m.co.uk
Managing Director Piers Chater Robinson *Marketing* Richard Thomas *Management* Thomus Kohut *Director* Steve Johnstone

Production details

Established in 1994. "Management of artistes with strong singing, dancing and / or instrumental skills; co-production, publishing and composition. We mostly license productions and have issued more than 1000 licences internationally. For more information, please see the website (in development)."

Casting procedures

Uses freelance casting directors and sometimes holds general auditions. Casting breakdowns are available from Spotlight. Welcomes letters (with CVs and photographs) from individual actors previously unknown to the company, sent by post or email. Rarely, or never, has the opportunity to cast disabled actors.

Bruce James Productions

68 St George's Park Avenue, Westcliff-on-Sea, Essex SS0 9UD
tel/fax (01702) 335970
email info@brucejamesproductions.co.uk
website www.brucejamesproductions.co.uk
Artistic Director Bruce James

Production details

Produces dramas, comedies, thrillers, pantomimes, children's shows and 'summer schools' for many theatres all over the UK. Stages around 12 productions a year. Between 2 and 14 actors are involved in each production. Does not offer Equity-approved contracts. Recent productions include *Mother Goose* (Pomegranate Theatre, Chesterfield); *Babes in the Wood* (Tyneside Theatre); and UK tours of *Dry Rot* (farce) and *The Case of the Frightened Lady* (thriller).

Casting procedures

Casts in-house and holds general auditions. Actors should write in January, May and September to request inclusion. Casting breakdowns are published via *SBS*, Castcall and Castweb. Welcomes letters (by post, not by email) with CVs and photographs from individuals previously unknown to the company. "Do not, under any circumstances, send unsolicited emails containing large [file-sized] photographs." Does not welcome showreels, but is happy to receive invitations to view individuals' websites. Will consider applications from disabled actors to play characters with disabilities. Advises actors: "Never give up or stop trying to get seen!"

Andy Jordan Productions Ltd

Studio D, 413 Harrow Road, Maida Vale, London W9 3QJ
mobile (07775) 615205
email andy@andyjordanproductions.co.uk
Director Andy Jordan

Production details

Founded in 2000. Commercial production company, largely producing new plays of all genres. Stages 2-4 productions annually with 50-100 performances per year. Performs annually in 4-10 theatres across the UK, including Northern Ireland and Eire. Also tours overseas. On average, 3-7 actors work on each production. Recent productions include: *Lies Have Been Told: An Evening with Robert Maxwell* (two seasons in West End, 2006), *2Graves* (West End 2006), *Worlds End* (Edinburgh Festival), *Escaping Hamlet* (Edinburgh Festival). Usually offers Equity approved contracts (either TMA or ITC)

Casting procedures

Uses freelance casting directors. Actors may write at any time requesting inclusion. Casting breakdowns are published on Spotlight Link. Welcomes submissions (with CVs and photographs) sent by post and email. Rarely has the opportunity to cast disabled actors but will consider submissions to play disabled characters.

Richard Jordan Productions Ltd

Mews Studios, 16 Vernon Yard, London W11 2DX
tel 020-7243 9001 *fax* 020-7213 9667

email Richard.Jordan@virgin.net
Director Richard Jordan

Production details

Founded in 1998. Produces theatre in the West End, throughout the UK and internationally. Main area of work is new writing and revivals of plays; occasionally produces musicals. Company also works as general managers and consultants for a wide range of producers and theatres in the UK and abroad. Stages 5-10 productions annually with 300 performances during the course of the year. Recent productions include: *The Twits*, *Single Spies* and *The Lady in the Van*.

Casting procedures

Uses freelance casting directors. Sometimes holds general auditions. Casting breakdowns are sometimes publicly available in *PCR*. Welcomes letters (with CVs and photographs) but not email submissions. Applications are particularly welcome if actors are currently in a production that the company can go and see. Advises that applicants should have an awareness of the type of work produced by the company before sending CVs.

Bill Kenwright Ltd

BKL House, 1 Venice Walk, London W2 1RR
tel 020-7446 6200 *fax* 020-7446 6222
email info@kenwright.com
website www.kenwright.com

Production details

Commercial producing management presenting revivals and new works for the West End and for touring theatres. Recent (or current) productions include: in the West End – *Blood Brothers*, *Hay Fever*, *Joseph & The Amazing Technicolor Dreamcoat*, *Whistle Down the Wind*, *The Crucible*, and *A Man for All Seasons*; on tour – *Blood Brothers*, *Festen*, *The Hollow*, and *This Is Elvis*.

Casting procedures

Uses freelance casting directors, but does some casting in-house. Welcomes letters (with CVs and photographs) sent to Josh Andrews.

Limelight Entertainments

Unit 4, The Gateway, 2a Rathmore Road, London SE7 7QW
tel 020-8858 6141 *fax* 020-8805 2684
email enquiries@limelightents.co.uk
website www.limelightents.co.uk
Artistic Director Richard Lewis *Executive Producer* Martin Ronan

Production details

Established in 1996. Stages 2-3 productions annually, touring to 50 theatres and arenas. Roughly 4-6 actors used in each production. Recent productions include: *Sing-A-Long-A-ABBA*, *The Fimbles*, *Love Shack* and *Fully Committed*. Equity approved contracts.

Casting procedures

General auditions are usually held in September. Encourages applications from disabled actors and promotes the use of inclusive casting.

Cameron Mackintosh Ltd

1 Bedford Square, London WC1B 3RB
tel 020-7637 8866 *fax* 020-7436 2683
Chairman Cameron Mackintosh *Managing Director* Nicholas Allot *Casting Director/Associate Producer* Trevor Jackson

Production details

Stages musical theatre productions worldwide. Recent productions include: *Les Miserables*, *Miss Saigon* and *The Phantom of the Opera*.

Casting procedures

In-house casting. Does not hold general auditions. Welcomes letters (with CVs and photographs) but not email submissions. Also accepts showreels and invitations to view individual actors' websites.

Christopher Malcolm Productions Ltd

11 Claremont Walk, Bath BA1 6HB
tel (01225) 445459 *fax* (01225) 458077
email cm@christophermalcolm.co.uk
Director Christopher Malcolm *Other key personnel* Judith Lloyd

Production details

Founded in 1980, the company works in both licensing and production. Theatre producer for the West End, UK touring and European touring. Stages 2-3 productions annually with 200 300 performances during the course of the year. Tours on average 30-40 UK venues, and 100-150 European venues annually. 13-25 actors are involved in each production. Recent productions include: *The Rocky Horror Show* and *Footloose*. Offers TMA/Equity approved contracts and does not subscribe to the Equity Pension Scheme.

Casting procedures

Uses freelance casting director, Debbie O'Brien. Sometimes holds general auditions. Actors should write to the casting director only, requesting inclusion. Advises actors to use their agents as a means of contact with the casting director. Unsolicited letters and photographs are not considered. Actively encourages applications from disabled actors and promotes the use of inclusive casting.

Johnny Mans Productions Ltd

PO Box 196, Hoddesdon, Herts EN10 7WG
tel (01992) 470907 *fax* (01992) 470516

Theatre

email johnnymansagent@aol.com
website www.johnnymansproductions.co.uk
Key contact Johnny Mans

Production details

Founded as a limited company in 1989. Activities include producing and promoting one-night stands, celebrity concerts, musicals and touring productions; casting for television, pantomime and cruise ships; and artiste and personal management for Sir Norman Wisdom OBE, Max Bygraves, Jeremy Spake, Jess Conrad, Leah Bell, Gerry George and many others. Stages about 30 productions annually, totalling around 250 performances during the course of the year. Tours concert productions to more than 300 different theatres and arts centres across the UK and Ireland each year. Recent productions include: *Calamity Jane; Beatlemania; The Spirit of Pavarotti; Yesterday Once More; Don't Laugh At Me;* and *Rock Shock Horror.*

Casting procedures

In the first instance, contact johnnymansagent@aol.com by email, or write in with photograph and CV / biography to the address given above. Prospective future clients will then be contacted accordingly. Johnny Mans Productions offers Equity-approved contracts.

Middle Ground Theatre Co

3 Gordon Terrace, Malvern Wells,
Malvern WR14 4ER
tel (01684) 577231 *fax* (01684) 574472
email middleground@middlegroundtheatre.co.uk
website www.middlegroundtheatre.co.uk
Artistic Director Michael Lunney *Production Manager* Mat Larkin

Production details

Theatre company producing drama to tour No. 1 UK theatre venues and arts centres. Stages 1 or 2 productions a year with 180 performances across around 25 venues. Covers the whole of Britain and Northern Ireland. Size of cast varies from show to show. Offers actors non-Equity contracts and does not participate in the Equity Pension Scheme. Recent productions include: *Meeting Joe Strummer; The Importance of Being Earnest; Billy Liar; Dial M for Murder;* and *Tunes of Glory.*

Casting procedures

Casts in-house. Casting breakdowns are not publicly available (Spotlight only). Welcomes submissions from actors (with CV and photograph) if sent by post or email. Also welcomes showreels and invitations to view individual actors' websites. Will consider applications from disabled actors to play disabled characters.

Millionth Muse Productions

1st and 2nd Floors, 20 Stansfield Road,
London SW9 9RZ

tel 020-7737 5300 *mobile* (07905) 259060
email info@millionthmuse.com
website www.millionthmuse.com
Director Paul L Martin

Eleven-year-old production house for cabaret and variety shows. Runs a useful database for performers to join free of charge. Previous regular shows produced for Old Vic Pit Bar, Soho Revue Bar, CellarDoor, The Arts Theatre, The Leicester Square Theatre, Theatre Museum and many others.

Norwell Lapley Productions Ltd

Tenbury House, 36 Teme Street, Tenbury Wells,
Worcestershire WR15 8AA
tel (01584) 819005 *fax* (01584) 819076
email info@cdm-ltd.com
website www.cdm-ltd.com
Director Chris Davis *Artist Manager* Kerry Foley

Production details

Produces theatre in the West End and touring productions. Stages 4-5 productions annually and gives 40-50 performances during the course of the year at theatres nationwide. Recent productions include: *Zipp.* Offers TMA/SOLT/Equity approved contracts and subscribes to the Equity Pension Scheme.

Casting procedures

Uses freelance casting directors and does not deal directly with actors. Rarely has the opportunity to cast disabled actors.

Pendle Productions

Bridge Farm, 249 Hawes Side Lane, Blackpool,
Lancashire FY4 4AA
tel (01253) 839375 *fax* (01253) 792930
email admin@pendleproductions.co.uk
website www.pendleproductions.co.uk
Director TS Lince

Production details

Touring professional theatre company. Stages between 10 and 15 productions each year, with 600 performances nationally in 300 venues of all types. Recent productions include: *Cinderella, Sinbad,* and *Treasure Island.*

Casting procedures

Sometimes holds general auditions; actors should write in April-June requesting inclusion. Casting breakdowns are publicly available via the usual channels. Welcomes letters (with CVs & photographs) from individual actors previously unknown to the company sent by post or email. Accepts showreels but prefers not to receive invitations to view individual actors' websites. Actively encourages applications from disabled actors, and promotes the use of inclusive casting.

Popular Productions Ltd

18B Hornsey High Street, London N8 7PB
email info@popularproductions.com
website www.popularproductions.com
Directors Lucy Blakeman, John Payton

Production details

International theatre producer. Stages 4-6
productions annually, with around 80 performances
in 4 theatres in the UK and Dubai. Anything from 2
to 100 actors may be involved in each production.
Recent productions include: *Annie* (International;
Middle East Premiere); *Woman in Black* (Dubai).

Casting procedures

Uses freelance casting directors. Sometimes holds
general auditions. Casting breakdowns are available
from *PCR*, Castweb and Casting Call Pro. Does not
welcome unsolicited approaches by actors unknown
to the company, but will consider invitations to view
individual actors' websites. Rarely, or never, has the
opportunity to cast disabled actors.

David Pugh & Dafydd Rogers

Wyndhams Theatre, Charing Cross Road,
London WC2 0DA
tel 020-7292 0390 *fax* 020-7292 0399
Directors David Pugh, Dafydd Rogers

Production details

Theatre production company staging 2-3 productions
annually in the West End and Broadway, and touring
to theatres throughout the UK. Recent productions
include: *Art*, *The Play What I Wrote* and *Blues
Brothers*.

Casting procedures

Sometimes holds general auditions. Actors should
address requests for inclusion to Sarah Bird CDG (see
entry under *Casting directors* on page 115), who is
responsible for all casting.

PW Productions Ltd

2nd Floor, 80-81 St Martins Lane,
London WC2N 4AA
tel 020-7395 7580 *fax* 020-7240 2947
email info@pwprods.co.uk
Chief Executive Peter Wilson

Production details

The company, which Peter Wilson founded in 1983,
specialises in the production, general management
and bookkeeping/accountancy for theatre
presentations. Recent productions include: *The
Woman in Black*, Stephen Daldry's production of *An
Inspector Calls*, and *Honour* at The Wyndham's
Theatre London, starring Dame Diana Rigg, Martin
Jarvis OBE and Natasha McElhone.

The Really Useful Group Ltd

22 Tower Street, London WC2H 9TW
tel 020-7240 0880 *fax* 020-7240 1204
website www.reallyuseful.com

Production details

The Really Useful Group (RUG) was founded in 1977
by Andrew Lloyd Webber. It is an international
entertainment company actively involved in theatre
ownership and management, theatrical production,
film, television, video and concert productions,
merchandising, records and music publishing.

Rho Delta Ltd

26 Goodge Street, London W1T 2QG
tel 020-7436 1392 *fax* 020-7436 1395
email info@ripleyduggan.com
Director Greg Ripley-Duggan

Production details

Founded in 1991. Produces West End and touring
commercial theatre. Stages 1 production annually
which tours to 6 theatres. Recent productions
include: *The Old Masters*, *Life x 3* and *The Memory of
Water*. Offers actors TMA/SOLT/Equity approved
contracts and subscribes to the Equity Pension
Scheme.

Casting procedures

Uses freelance casting directors and does not deal
directly with actors. Will consider applications from
disabled actors to play disabled characters.

Suzanna Rosenthal Ltd

PO Box 40001, London N6 4YA
tel 020-8340 4421 *fax* 020-8340 4421
email admin@suzannarosenthal.com
website www.suzannarosenthal.com

Production details

Founded in 2001, the company produces Off-West
End shows. Stages 3-5 productions annually with 100
performances over the year in theatres and outdoor
venues across London. In general 5-15 actors are
involved in each production. Recent productions
include: *Henry VIII* and *The Resistible Rise of Arturo
Ui*, *Victor/Victoria* and London's Free Open-Air
season at The Scoop.

Casting procedures

Uses freelance casting directors. Sometimes holds
general auditions. Actors should only write
requesting inclusion in response to advertisements.
Casting breakdowns are available via the website,
PCR and advertisements in *The Stage*.

Showcase Entertainments Productions Ltd

2 Lumley Close, Newton Aycliffe,
Co. Durham DL5 5PA

Managing Director / Executive Producer Geoffrey JL Hindmarch *Director / Choreographer* Paul W Morgan

Production details

A professional theatrical touring company. Stages 5 productions annually, with around 100 performances in 60 theatres across England, Scotland and Wales. In general 10 actors are involved in each production. Recent productions include: *Musical Magic* starring Paul Daniels and full showcase company (Harlow Playhouse, Litchfield Garrick, Palace Theatre Mansfield).

Casting procedures

Sometimes holds general auditions; actors may write at any time to request inclusion. Welcomes letters (with CVs and photographs) from individual actors previously unknown to the company, sent by post or email. Also welcomes showreels. Rarely, or never, has the opportunity to cast disabled actors.

Marc Sinden Productions Group of Companies

1 Hogarth Hill, London NW11 6AY
tel 020-8455 3278
website www.sindenproductions.com,
www.onenightbooking.com,
www.uktheatreavailability.co.uk,
www.montecarlotheatre.co.uk
Director Marc Sinden

Production details

A West End and touring theatre producer, reaching theatres and arts centres across the UK and Europe. For details of recent productions, please consult the website. Also runs the UK Theatre Availability System (**www.uktheatreavailability.co.uk**) which allows touring companies to check the availability and suitability of theatre spaces.

Casting procedures

Uses freelance casting directors and does not welcome casting enquiries and submissions from actors.

Adam Spiegel Productions

Stage Entertainment Ltd, 6th Floor, Swan House, 52 Poland Street, London W1F 7NQ
tel 020-7025 6970 *fax* 020-7734 2613

Please note that Adam Spiegel Productions is now part of Stage Entertainment UK Ltd (**www.stage-entertainment.com**).

Squaredeal Productions Ltd

24 De Beauvoir Square, London N1 4LE
tel 020-7249 5966 *fax* 020-7275 7553
email jenny@jennytopper.com
website www.jennytopper.com
Director Jenny Topper

Production details

Established in 2003. An independent theatre producer staging on average 2-3 productions annually and performing in the West End and 20 theatre venues across the UK. Recent productions include: *The Clean House* (10-week tour); *Martha, Josie and Chinese Elvis* (12-week tour); *Duet for One* (West End).

Casting procedures

Does not hold general auditions. Will accept letters (with CVs and photographs) from actors previously unknown to the company, sent by post or by email. Offers Equity-approved contracts as negotiated through TMA. Rarely has the opportunity to cast disabled actors.

Barrie Stacey UK Productions

Flat 8, 132 Charing Cross Road, London WC2H OLA
tel 020-7836 6220/4128 *fax* 020-7836 2949
email hopkinstacey@aol.com
Director Barrie Stacey *Stage Director* Tony Joseph

Production details

Founded in 1966. Specialises in children's musicals and songbook concerts. Stages 24 productions annually with 100 performances during the course of the year. Tours to 8 different theatres in Southern England, including the London area. In general 8 actors are involved in each production. Recent productions include: *West End to Broadway* and *Movie Memories.* Offers non-Equity contracts and does not subscribe to the Equity Pension Scheme.

Casting procedures

All casting is done in-house. Holds general auditions. Casting breakdowns are available on request. Welcomes letters (with CVs and photographs) but not email submissions. Advises actors: "Don't be grand when just starting." Actively encourages applications from disabled actors and promotes the use of inclusive casting.

Stage Further Productions Ltd

Westgate, Stansted Road, Eastbourne BN22 8LG
tel (01323) 739478 *fax* (01323) 736127
email info@stagefurther.co.uk
Director Garth Harrison *Producer* David Nott *Artistic Director* Keith Myers

Production details

Founded in 1985. Produces plays and pantomimes for its repertory seasons and national tours. Also provides entertainment and shows to the cruise industry. Stages 10 productions annually and performs in around 18 different venues, including arts centres and theatres nationwide and cruise vessels. In general 6 actors are involved in each production. Recent productions include: *Anybody for Murder* and *Dead of Night*.

Casting procedures

Holds general auditions. Casting breakdowns are available via *PCR*, *The Stage* and from agents. Welcomes letters (with CVs and photographs) but not email submissions. Invitations to view individual actors' websites are also accepted.

Stanhope Productions Ltd

4th Floor, 80/81 St. Martins Lane,
London WC2N 4AA
020-7240 3098 020-7504 8656
email admin@stanhopeprod.com
Director/Producer Kim Poster *Assistant General Manager* Brad Fitt

Production details

Founded in 2001. Theatrical producing company. Stages 4-5 productions annually and gives 576 performances during the course of the year. Tours to 2-4 different theatres, primarily in the West End and London area. In general 18 actors are involved in each production. Recent productions include: *A Woman of No Importance*, *Epitaph for George Dillon*, *Summer and Smoke*, *Fiddler on The Roof* and *Brand*. Offers SOLT/Equity approved contracts and does not subcribe to the Equity Pension Scheme.

Casting procedures

Uses freelance casting directors. Holds general auditions. Casting breakdowns are available via Equity Job Information Service. Will consider applications from disabled actors to play disabled characters.

Tenth Planet Productions

Medius House, 2 Sheraton Street, London W1F 8B
tel 020-7297 9474 *fax* 020-7439 3584
email admin@10thplanetproductions.com
website www.10thplanetproductions.com
Artistic Director Alexander Holt *Literary Manager* Mark Underwood *Associate Directors* Susan Harriet, Alex Scrivenor

Production details

Founded in 1998, the company has produced more than 30 productions to date. Stages 4-6 productions annually and presents 100-150 performances during the course of the year. Tours to 2-6 different regional theatres in the UK; also tours internationally in association with Sh! Productions Co (its sister company), performing dinner theatre in the Emirates. Performs in site-specific locations such as the Rose Theatre in London. For the past few years the company has been resident Upstairs at the Gatehouse in London. In general 4-8 actors are involved in each production. 2005-2007 productions

included: *Trestle At Pope Lick Creek* (in association with the Royal Exchange); *Kafka's Dick*; *Absurd Person Singular*; *Bedroom Farce*; *Playhouse Creatures*; *Keeler* (in association with Paul Nicholas). 2007/8 productions include: *Black Ajax*; *Our Boys*; *Les Liaisons Dangereuses*; *Keeler* (tour). Offers non-Equity contracts and does not subscribe to the Equity Pension Scheme.

Casting procedures

Holds general auditions. Actors should write in response to advertisements only, or consult the website for information on forthcoming productions. Casting breakdowns are available via *SBS*, *PCR*, CastNet and Castweb (see entry under *The Spotlight, casting directories and information services* on page 398). Showreels and invitations to view individual actors' websites are also accepted. Advises that the company principally casts NCDT-trained actors or well-established actors with demonstrable experience. As it is unable to retain submissions on file, actors should only write in when casting is advertised, or telephone first. Will consider applications from disabled actors to play disabled characters.

UK Productions

Churchmill House, Ockford Road, Godalming,
Surrey GU7 0NB
tel 01483-423600 *fax* 01483-418486
email mail@ukproductions.co.uk
website www.ukproductions.co.uk
Directors Martin Dodd, Peter Frosdick *Production Manager* Andy Batty *Administrator/Casting Assistant* Derek Raper

Production details

Established 1995. Produce pantomimes and musicals for No. 1 touring. (See entry under *Pantomime producers* on page 238.) Produces 3 musicals a year, each touring around the UK and Ireland to large scale theatres for 30-35 weeks. Cast size is around 27-30 performers. Offers non-Equity contracts ("roughly in line with Equity") and does not subscribe to the Equity Pension Scheme. Recent productions include: *Seven Brides for Seven Brothers*, *42nd Street*, *Disney's Beauty & The Beast*, *South Pacific*.

Casting procedures

Casting is done in-house. Does not hold general auditions. Casting breakdowns are distributed via Spotlight or direct to agents. Welcomes performance notices but not any other unsolicited form of correspondence. "Unsolicited CVs are generally a waste of time." Will consider applications from disabled actors to play characters with disabilities.

West End International

17 Leighton Place, London NW5 2QL
tel 020-7428 0555 *fax* 020-7428 0577

website www.westendinternational.com
Director Martin Yates *General Manager* Alison Price
Administrator Annie Rose

Production details

"West End International has been producing first-class entertainment throughout the world since its inception in 1995. Our unique practice of engaging artists of the highest calibre has resulted in unprecedented success and respect on a worldwide basis." Stages 50 productions each year and tours to about 30 theatres/outdoor venues around the world.

The average cast size is 5. Recent productions include: *Fascinatin' Rhythm* (Symphony Hall, Birmingham); *The Best of West End* (Glasgow Royal Concert Hall); and *Beatlemania!*

Casting procedures

Will accept casting enquiries and letters (with CVs and photographs) from actors previously unknown to the company provided that these are posted and not emailed. Does not welcome unsolicited showreels.

Mounting a production without a base theatre

Graham Cowley

So. There's a play you're desperate to do, but you have no theatre. You're in one of two situations: either you are a funded company with good relationships with producing or touring theatres, or it's just you on your own.

Out of Joint started ten years ago. Max Stafford-Clark was about to leave the Royal Court after 13 years; he'd spent all his working life up until then producing new plays, and needed an environment in which that work could continue. As the former Artistic Director of The Traverse, Joint Stock and the Royal Court, and with an international reputation, he could have been forgiven for assuming that funding would be readily available for a new venture such as this. But the fledgling Out of Joint was in competition for the meagre Arts Council project funds along with everyone else, and its early years were as hand-to-mouth as those of any new company. There was no office, so Max and Sonia Friedman, the company's first producer, set up productions and booked tours from their front rooms; blind eyes were turned as small quantities of Royal Court stationery disappeared; and friends were persuaded to give help and advice for no payment.

Financially, the early years were a balancing act between Arts Council Touring grants, stretched as far as they would go, and co-production deals with producing theatres. For the first few shows this was the Royal Court, but since then Out of Joint has co-produced with other theatres as well: Hampstead, the Young Vic, the Soho Theatre, the National, the Liverpool Everyman and Playhouse, and the Abbey, Dublin. Out of Joint co-productions usually take a straightforward form. Both partners agree a pre-production budget, covering the rehearsal costs, wages and fees, building the set, acquiring costumes and props and generally assembling the show. They agree to split this cost in some fashion – either 50/50 or in a ratio reflecting how long each company will have use of the play. If Out of Joint is touring for eight weeks and the run at the Soho Theatre is four weeks, there is a case for an unequal split of the cost of mounting the play. Then, each partner takes full responsibility for the running costs and income while the show is under its management. In Out of Joint's case, this means we pay the wages and all other costs while the show is touring, and our co-producer does the same while it plays in London (or Liverpool, or Dublin).

This way of working has many virtues. For both parties, it represents an opportunity to get more value from a pre-production budget – either by saving money, or, more commonly, by enhancing the total budget available. For the company, it brings not only financial stability but also a temporary home. Having an office and a rehearsal room is all very well, but theatre people like to belong to a theatre. For the theatre, it means that their programme is enhanced by a play or project which would not otherwise have been available to them. And whoever was the initiator, both parties feel an ownership of the play. This is vital, although it involves a good deal of give and take on each side. Where will you rehearse? Who builds the set? Can the theatre contribute a stage manager? All these things are important in encouraging a feeling of joint ownership.

Now, happily, Out of Joint receives regular funding from the Arts Council, and has its own office and photocopier. But early habits of frugality remain: the company has tiny overhead costs, employs only five full-time staff and still enjoys co-producing. A touring company cannot run up substantial debts: with the only tangible assets being some lighting equipment and an ageing van, there is no security for an overdraft. So preserving financial security is crucial.

Financial security can seem like a pipe dream for those at the sharper end of producing. Together with some good friends, I have been putting on plays independently for several years, under the banner of Two's Company. This year we received a small Arts Council grant, for the first time. But by then we had established a way of working with some of London's small theatres which enabled us (just) to operate.

So – you have a play. The first thing is to secure the rights. For an existing play in a small theatre, all you'll get is a licence for your production dates. This may well mean that you need to have a theatre. The first question to ask is, where should it ideally go? It's by no means unknown for plays with epic themes and huge casts to be seen in tiny pub theatres, but perhaps this one needs more space, more facilities? Or is this three-hander capable of filling 250 seats? Maybe we should keep it to 70 ... *Time Out* and *Contacts*, between them, have the most complete lists of the theatres available. How many do you know? It's easier to have a view about a theatre if you've seen a show there. If you don't think your play will fit the policies and criteria of the Bush, Hampstead, the Almeida or the Royal Court, or you don't want to wait (sometimes) a long time for them to tell you that, you can approach one of the fringe theatres. If you've thought carefully about the match between your play and the theatre, you'll have a better chance of securing a suitable venue.

Most theatres are unfunded, so if they show interest, and have a production slot that fits your dates, they will charge you a weekly rent. At this point you'll need to finalise your budget. You know how many actors you need and how much you can pay them. The budget for a set, costumes and props – well, how long is a piece of string? Priorities are all-important. If your play needs army uniforms, you'll almost certainly have to hire them, so allow enough for that. On the other hand, to secure a clever designer, it's often worth sacrificing some money from the physical budget to add to his/her fee – inventiveness can add huge value to your budget.

Clarity about exactly what you can expect from the theatre in return for your rent is important to establish. What hours can you use it for? Can you work all night on the get-in, or are there neighbours who object? What staff, if any, will work with you, and what will they do? How long does it take to move the seating, and who knows how it all works? And almost most important of all, what marketing support will the theatre provide? There might be a season brochure, but how many are produced and where do they go? How does the box office operate, and what figures will you get? And so on. Theatres vary enormously in what they can offer, how much they will support you and how welcoming they are.

Even the smallest show needs some sort of funds to operate with. Even though the box office receipts will be an important source of income (you hope), you can't expect the theatre to pay the takings over until they are very sure you've paid everything that you owe them, so you'll need enough money to keep cash flowing. Nothing demoralises a cast of actors more than being told you can't pay them yet. And while a lot can be done with the beg/borrow/steal method, there are some things you just have to pay for. So you apply to the Arts Council, charitable trusts, businesses, ask friends and relations to give you money. This all takes a long time, so start as soon as you can. Please don't remortgage your house.

In London, particularly, press reviews can be of enormous importance as to whether or not your production is a success. It's really worth engaging a press rep who knows his/her stuff. That, by the way, is a very difficult judgement to make until you've worked with somebody, so see if you can get some informed opinions about the person you're contemplating hiring. If s/he can get you advance press publicity, that's wonderful, but what you really need is for the critics to come, and to come early – it's no use their appearing after the run is over. Some shows take off like a rocket; some burn slowly for a bit before catching alight; and lots more need an audience to be laboriously reached and persuaded to come. Sometimes, it seems, one by one. But whichever it is, your job isn't over until every seat is sold.

So why do it? Because there is a play you believe in, a director of genius, stunningly talented actors – or at least, some of those things. I firmly believe that if you're going to produce a play, you've got to love it. The response of the critics and the audience is personal, and therefore unpredictable – so it's important to be able to say at the end, "Well, I liked it." And, of course, there is nothing like the feeling you get when you look round the theatre bar, or the dressing room, or indeed the auditorium, and think, "All these people are here because I brought them together." Good luck!

Graham Cowley is Producer with Out of Joint, and also Two's Company. He was previously with the Theatre of Comedy Company, the Royal Court Theatre (on whose behalf he transferred a string of hit plays to the West End), the Half Moon Theatre, and Joint Stock Theatre Group.

Theatre

Middle and smaller-scale companies

This section covers a huge range of companies: from the very prestigious, often subsidised (like Out of Joint), which usually only perform in theatres with around 500 seats (or more), to the very small, which frequently have little or no public subsidy and perform wherever they can find a paying audience. The bigger companies operate much like the commercial 'big boys' in the previous section – except they tend to have longer rehearsal periods. The smaller companies rarely use casting directors, tend to do only one or two performances in each venue, and often pay below Equity rates – and it's probable that you'll have to help with get-ins and get-outs. It's very hard work and you have to rise to the peak of performance every time in spite of travelling in cramped vans, sharing unsatisfactory digs and rarely, if ever, being seen by anyone who could advance your career. However, some very prestigious companies have grown from such very small beginnings – and a number of now highly respected directors, playwrights and actors have started this way. It is important to assess the potential quality of the product (as well as the pay, and terms and conditions) before accepting such a job.

As such companies tend to come and go with great rapidity, the listings only contain companies that have been in existence for three years or more.

Note Some of the companies listed are members of the Independent Theatre Council (ITC) – **www.itc-arts.org**.

7:84 Theatre Company Scotland

Film City Glasgow, 4 Summertown Road,
Glasgow G51 2LY
tel 0141-445 7245
email admin@784theatre.com
website www.784theatre.com
Artistic Director Lorenzo Mele

Production details

Founded in 1973. Recent productions include: *Futured: Our Journey, Into the Daldorch Woods*, and *As Others See Us*. "Our aims for the future are to develop forms of political theatre and its ability to affect policy making decisions, and to increase the company profile in Scotland, the UK and abroad."

20 Stories High Theatre Company

6 Marmaduke Street, Liverpool L7 1PB
tel 0151-260 5185
email info@20storieshigh.org.uk
website www.20storieshigh.org.uk
Directors Julie Samuels, Keith Saha *Projects Co-ordinator* Tessa Buddle

Production details

Established in 2006. Creates dynamic, challenging theatre which attracts new audiences, artists and participants. Stages 2 projects annually, with around 80 performances in 60 arts centres, theatres, and educational and community venues in the North West and nationally. In general 2-4 actors are involved in each production. Offers Equity-approved contracts as negotiated through ITC. Also participates in the Equity Pension Scheme. Recent productions include: *Babul and the Blue Bear* by Keith Saha (co-production with Contact Theatre and Horse & Bamboo – national tour); and *Slow Time* by Roy Williams (North West tour).

Casting procedures

Holds general auditions; actors may write in May and October to request inclusion. Casting breakdowns are available from the website, Equity Job Information Service and *PCR*. Welcomes letters (with CVs and photographs) from individual actors previously unknown to the company, sent by post or email, and is happy to consider invitations to view individual actors' websites. Actively encourages applications from disabled actors and promotes the use of inclusive casting.

Actors of Dionysus (AOD)

14 Cuthbert Road, Brighton BN2 0EN
tel/fax (01273) 692604
email info@actorsofdionysus.com
website www.actorsofdionysus.com
Artistic Director Tamsin Shasha *Development Officer* Alice Booth

Production details

National and international touring company founded in 1993. A member of the ITC and Arts & Business, it currently receives no regular funding. Specialises in performing new adaptations of Ancient Greek drama through a fusion of poetry, music and movement. Has a strong educational focus and runs international summer schools. Stages 1-2 productions each year with an average annual total of 120-150 performances. Venues include arts centres, theatres (including Greek and Turkish theatres), and educational venues across the UK, Eire and Turkey. Also performs on cruise ships. In general 4-6 actors work on each production. Recent productions include: *Trojan Women* (2005), *Hippolytus* (2004), and *Oedipus* (2003 & 2006).

Casting procedures

Does not use freelance casting directors. Holds general auditions; actors should write to request inclusion in August and December. Casting breakdowns are available through the website and *PCR*. Does not welcome general submissions from actors but will accept invitations to view individual actors' websites. Offers non-Equity contracts. Actively encourages applications from disabled actors and promotes the use of inclusive casting.

Actors Touring Company (ATC)

Malvern House, 15-16 Nassau Street, London W1W 7AB
tel 020-7580 7723 *fax* 020-7580 7324
website www.atc-online.com
Artistic Director Bijan Sheibani *Executive Producer* Hannah Bentley

Production details

Established in 1979. 2 productions are staged annually, touring to arts centres and theatres and employing roughly 4-6 actors. Offers ITC/Equity approved contracts. Recent productions include: A *Brief History of Helen of Troy* (UK tour).

Casting procedures

Encourages applications from disabled actors and promotes the use of inclusive casting. Unsolicited approaches from actors are discouraged.

Admiration Theatre

PO Box 50255, London EC3A 5WA
tel 0870-765 1584 *fax* 0870-765 1594
email admiration@admirationtheatre.co.uk
website www.admirationtheatre.co.uk
Director Jon Hewitt

Production details

Founded in 2001, the company stages 3-4 productions each year with an average annual total of 30 performances across theatres in London. Cast size varies from 2-8 actors. In September 2006, Admiration organised a residential theatre retreat in Gascony, in the south of France. An international group of actors was invited to spend 2 weeks in the countryside, working in a natural environment away from the distractions of the big city. The group's work was research into the creativity of the actor, in creating new material and characters, as well as work on more traditional text. Recent productions include: *Ubu Roi* (Courtyard Theatre, London) and *Seasons of Purity* (Theatro Technis, London).

Casting procedures

Uses freelance casting directors but sometimes holds general auditions. Welcomes letters and emails (with CVs and photographs) from actors previously unknown to the company. Will also accept showreels and invitations to view actors' websites.

ARC Theatre Ensemble

PO Box 1146, Barking, Essex IG11 9WB
tel 020-8594 1095
email carole@arctheatre.com
website www.arctheatre.com
Chief Executive Officer/Artistic Director Carole Pluckrose *Creative Director* Clifford Oliver (Olly) *Associate Directors* Joss Bennathan, Jim Dunk, Thierry Lawson, Neville Lawrence OBE

Production details

Founded in 1984, Arc has built a strong core Management and Associate team bringing together an exceptional range of creative skills, educational experience and business and social expertise. The company is governed by an equally diverse and committed Board of Management. "We also benefit from a first-class pool of highly skilled, trained actors, storytellers, facilitators, workshop leaders, production managers and designers who are individually hand-picked to suit each programme or bespoke project." See the website for more details of its work.

Casting procedures

"To register your interest in working with Arc, please submit your details via the website. We will keep your details on record and contact you when a suitable opportunity arises. Alternatively you can email your details to our General Manager, Nita Bocking: **nita@arctheatre.com**."

Attic Theatre Company

Mitcham Library, 157 London Road, Mitcham CR24 2YR
tel/fax 020-8543 7838
email info@attictheatre.com
website www.attictheatre.com
Artistic Director Jenny Lee *Associate Director* Merhdad Seyf *Administrator* Teun Timmers *Booking & Finance Manager* Victoria Hibbs *Production Manager* Kate Reynolds

The company was formed in 1987 to produce high-quality theatre and develop audiences for new plays,

Theatre

musicals, reworked clasics and contemporary plays with a cutting edge. Work is presented at Wimbledon Studio Theatre and other venues, and the company tours on average 1 production each year. Tours up to 15 venues across the UK annually; these include arts centres, theatres, educational venues and community venues. Cast size varies from 1-6 actors. For recent productions, refer to the website **www.attictheatre.com**.

Community work is an integral part of the company's vision. In recent years it has developed *Ma Kelly's Doorstep*, an entertaining show with a serious message on the topic of bogus callers, which tours to day centres and lunch clubs in London boroughs. The sequel is a show on home safety – *Ma Kelly Plays it Safe*. In 2004 the company produced a show celebrating age, with music, dance and drama – *It's the Ritz!*; in 2005, it collaborated with Croydon Clocktower on *Dancing in The Dark* – a celebration of the lives of Croydon people during World War II.

Attic Theatre Young People's Company holds workshops for 11-15 year olds who meet every Wednesday evening in term time.

Casting procedures

Uses freelance casting directors. Does not hold general auditions and does not welcome casting enquiries or submissions from actors.

Badapple Theatre Company

PO Box 57, Green Hammerton, York YO26 8WQ
tel (01423) 339168
email office@badapple.freeserve.co.uk
website www.badapple.freeserve.co.uk
Director Kate Bramley

Production details

Founded in 1998. Specialises in new comedy and biography-based drama as well as documentary drama commissions. Stages between 2 and 5 productions per year at a local rural touring level or national arts centre/small-mid scale theatre level. Recent productions include: *An Honorary Yorkshireman* (which brought the stories of James Herriot to the stage for the first time ever); and *Laurel and Charlie* (based on the early lives of Stan Laurel and Charlie Chaplin). Uses 6-8 actors per year.

Casting procedures

Does not use freelance casting directors. For open castings uses Equity Job Information Service, *PCR* and advertisements in *The Stage*. Actors should write by post or email in response to casting breakdowns only. Directors prefer to see actors in performance prior to castings, so welcomes updates of performances in the Yorkshire region that company directors would be able to attend.

Benchtours Productions Ltd

Bonnington Mill, 72 Newhaven Road,
Edinburgh EH6 5QG

tel 0131-555 3585
email info@benchtours.com
website www.benchtours.com
Co-directors Peter Clerke, Catherine Gillard *General Manager* Ben Walmsley

Production details

Founded in 1991, Benchtours is Scotland's leading international touring ensemble. The company seeks to extend the boundaries of theatre and open it up to new and diverse audiences, and is committed to new writing, highly visual theatre, rural touring and disability work. Normally stages 2 productions each year with an average annual total of 40 performances. Tours to approximately 25-30 theatres, arts centres, educational venues and community venues across Scotland (including islands and Highlands) and Northern England each year. Benchtours also tours internationally – recently, to Poland and the USA. Recent national tours include: *The Emperor's Opera* and *Crowhurst*.

Casting procedures

Holds casting workshops in December each year, which the artistic directors invite selected actors to attend. Actors are advised to email CVs and cover letters in October/November. Benchtours offers Equity ITC contracts to all performers and actively encourages applications from disabled actors as part of its integrated casting policy.

Big Telly Theatre Company

Town Hall, The Crescent, Portstewart,
Londonderry BT55 7AB
tel 028-7083 6473 *fax* 028-7083 2588
email info@big-telly.com
website www.big-telly.com
Director Zoë Seaton

Production details

Big Telly Theatre Company is Northern Ireland's longest established professional not-for-profit theatre company, formed in 1987 and based in Portstewart on the North Coast. The company produces theatre, interactive workshop programmes and community creativity projects, which mainly tour throughout Northern and Southern Ireland and international markets. It concentrates on the visual potential of theatre through fusion with other art forms such as dance, music, circus, magic and film to create a unique sense of spectacle. "Big Telly's work is driven by a determination to offer audiences entertainment that surprises, stimulates and ignites the imagination."

Casting procedures

Does not use freelance casting directors. Casting breakdowns are available through the website and Equity Job Information Service, and are also released to agents. Welcomes submissions (with CVs and photographs) from actors previously unknown to the company sent by post or email. Invitations to view individual actors' websites are also accepted. Offers ITC/Equity contracts, and endeavours to employ disabled actors when casting for disabled characters.

Boilerhouse

Gateway Theatre, The Arts Quarter, 40-44 Elm Row, Edinburgh EH7 4AH
tel/fax 0131-556 5644
email paul@boilerhouse.org.uk
website www.boilerhouse.org.uk
Director Paul Pinson *Producer* Chloe Dear *General Manager* Jon Clarke

Production details

Founded in 1992, Boilerhouse is an Edinburgh-based performance company which has developed a reputation as a leading creator of exciting, high-quality work in non-theatre spaces. Over the last 12 years, work has been produced in clubs, car parks, warehouses, Pacific ocean-front wharves, London's Docklands, derelict buildings, churches and under a motorway bridge. Boilerhouse aims to create performance events of spectacle and meaning. We work with artists from an extensive range of disciplines in the development of medium- to large-scale outdoor and street-theatre productions. Work has involved collaborations with award-winning novelists (including Irvine Welsh, Alan Warner and Duncan McLean), poets, playwrights, dancers, performers, composers, designers, choreographers, musicians, metal sculptors, pyro-technicians, DJs, trapeze artists and car mechanics.

The company normally stages 2 productions each year totalling approximately 15-30 performances, and tours to a variety of venues across the UK, Europe and New Zealand. The cast size can be anything from 2 to 12 actors. Recent productions include: *The Bridge* (large-scale outdoor show, with aerial choreography, live and pre-recorded film, pyrotechnics and performed in Scotland and France – with audiences of up to 10,000 per show); and *Running Girl* (large-scale indoor promenade production with a cast of 8, including a performer running throughout the show, moving film-screens and live music).

Casting procedures

Does not use freelance casting directors; actors may write requesting inclusion in the next round of auditions at any time. Will accept letters, emails, showreels, CVs and photographs from actors previously unknown to the company, but advises all applicants to do their research first and only to send details if they are sure that they are right for Boilerhouse's style of work.

Border Crossings

13 Bankside, Enfield EN2 8BN
tel 020-8829 8928 *fax* 020-8366 5239
email BorCross@aol.com
website www.bordercrossings.org.uk
Director Michael Walling

Production details

Established in 1995. International company working in theatre and combined arts that creates dynamic performances by fusing many forms of world theatre, dance and music. Stages 1 or 2 productions per year touring to up to 15 venues including arts centres and theatres. Roughly 4-9 actors used in each production. Recent credits include: *The Dilemma of a Ghost* (2007); *Bullie's House* (Riverside Studios); *Orientations* (Oval House); *Dis-Orientations* (Riverside Studios) and *Double Tongue* (UK tour). "We don't offer Equity contracts, although our own contracts are modelled on the ITC/Equity contract, and we usually pay above the minimum." Does not subscribe to the Equity Pension Scheme.

Casting procedures

Welcomes letters (with CVs and photographs) from actors previously unknown to the company if sent by post, but not by email. Invitations to view individual actors' websites and showreels are accepted. Actively encourages applications from disabled actors and promotes the use of inclusive casting.

Borderline Theatre Co.

North Harbour Street, Ayr KA8 8AA
tel (01292) 281010 *fax* (01292) 263825
email enquiries@borderlinetheatre.co.uk
website www.borderlinetheatre.co.uk
Producer Edward Jackson

Production details

Founded in 1974, the company stages 2-3 productions each year with an average annual total of 60-90 performances. Each tour normally runs for 31 performances across 13 different venues. Venues include arts centres and theatres across Scotland. In general 4 actors work on each production. Recent productions include: *Tally's Blood, Women on the Verge of HRT* and *Angel's Share*.

Casting procedures

Does not use freelance casting directors. Currently releases casting breakdowns to agents, but may publish these on the website in future. Welcomes submissions (with CVs and photographs) from actors previously unknown to the company sent by post or email. Also accepts showreels.

Bottlefed Ensemble

13 Sydney Road, London N10 2LR
(07751) 420344
email info@bottlefed.org
website www.bottlefed.org
Artistic Directors Kathrin Yvonne Bigler, Rebeca Fernandez Lopez

Production details

A London-based physical theatre ensemble founded in 2004 and co-run by Kathrin Yvonne Bigler (writer/director) and Rebeca Fernandez Lopez (choreographer/performer), who merge their European tanztheatre background with British approaches to improvisation and physical theatre practice. "The ensemble's creative process is rooted in durational improvisation and telling stories through the performers' bodies without a big emphasis on technical support."

In recent years Bottlefed has been run as a laboratory for regular research, development and experimentation, and as a platform for cross-art-form collaborations. In each project the company works with a defined group of international artists who commit to the ensemble as freelance collaborators on a long-term basis. Also works in Education and Corporate, delivering creative workshops and performance projects for professional performers, young people and adults in school and community settings, theatres and universities across the UK and internationally. Recent projects include: *Return to Reason* (London & Edinburgh Fringe Festival, 2007; nominated for the 'Total Theatre Award for Best Original Work by an Ensemble'); and *Camille* (London, 2006; nominated for 'Best Direction' at the Lost Theatre Festival in the same year).

Casting procedures

Holds general auditions; actors may write at any time, and are invited to join the mailing list for information about upcoming auditions and workshops. Welcomes letters (with CVs & photographs) from individual actors previously unknown to the company if sent by post or email; also accepts showreels but prefers not to receive invitations to view individual actors' websites. Rarely (or never) has the opportunity to cast disabled actors. "We cast performers to join the ensemble on a long-term basis (which includes regular training, public improvisation events and performances) and not just for individual productions."

Bridge House Theatre

Myton Road, Warwick CV34 6PP
tel (01926) 776437
email ask@warwickschool.org
website www.bridgehousetheatre.co.uk
Director Alison Sutcliffe *Performing Arts Manager* Bronwyn Robertson

Production details

Founded in 2005. Professional theatre-in-residence twice-yearly at Warwick School's purpose-built theatre. Stages 2 productions annually with around 35 performances. Up to 10 actors are involved in each production. Recent productions include: *The Tempest, An Inspector Calls, Educating Rita, Macbeth, As You Like It, Death of a Salesman.*

Casting procedures

Casting breakdowns are occasionally available from Spotlight Interactive. Welcomes letters (with CVs and photographs) from individual actors previously unknown to the company, sent by post only; will consider invitations to view individual actors' websites. Rarely, or never, has the opportunity to cast disabled actors. "We prefer Midlands-based actors for logistical / financial reasons."

Cahoots Theatre Company

Suite 1803, 16-19 Southampton Place,
London WC1A 1AJ
tel 020-7240 7000
email denise@cahootstheatre.co.uk
Artistic Director Denise Silvey

Production details

Founded in 1999. Produces theatre, cabaret and CD recordings, as well as acting as a general management and press agent. (See also Silvey Associates' entry under Agents). Stages 3-4 productions a year, with 100 performances over 15 venues (arts centres, theatres and cabaret venues) in London, Edinburgh and New York. Productions may have from 1 to 17 performers involved. Does not offer Equity-approved contracts. Recent credits include: *A Clockwork Orange, Rain Pryor in Concert,* and *The Translucent Frogs of Quuup.*

Casting procedures

Uses freelance casting directors. Also publishes casting breakdowns on the Equity JIS and *PCR*. Welcomes letters (but not emails) with CVs and photographs from individuals previously unknown to the company. Does not welcome showreels, but is happy to receive invitations to view actors' websites. Will consider applications from disabled actors to play characters with disabilities.

Cambridge Shakespeare Company

11 Crossways House, Anstey Way, Trumpington, Cambridge CB2 9JZ
tel (01223) 842293
email cambridgeshakespeare@hotmail.co.uk
website www.cambridgeshakespeare.com
Artistic Director Dr David Crilly *Associate Directors* Simon Bell, David Rowan

Production details

The Festival Company was established in Oxford in 1988 by Artistic Director Dr David Crilly. The main focus for the Company is the annual Cambridge Shakespeare Festival, which runs throughout July and August. Situated in the gardens of the Colleges of Cambridge University, its pastoral setting is one of the loveliest in the world.

Cardboard Citizens

26 Hanbury Street, London E1 6QR
tel 020-7247 7747 *fax* 020-7650 0002

email mail@cardboardcitizens.org.uk
website www.cardboardcitizens.org.uk
Artistic Director Adrian Jackson *Associate Director*
Sarah Levinsky

Production details

The UK's only homeless people's professional theatre company. Specialises in making forum theatre, but has broadened its scope to the provision of a range of performance-based cultural actions with, for and by homeless and previously homeless people.
Productions include: *Woyzeck* – national tour; *Timon of Athens* – national tour with RSC; *Visible* – national tour, 'down and out' community production.

Casting procedures

Uses in-house casting directors. Holds general auditions; actors may write at any time requesting inclusion. Casting breakdowns are publicly available. Welcomes letters, CVs and photographs from individual actors previously unknown to the company, sent via post or email. Also welcomes showreels and invitations to view individual actors' websites. Offers Equity approved contracts. Actively encourages applications from disabled people and promotes the use of inclusive casting.

The Castle Players

PO Box 17, Barnard Castle, Co. Durham DL12 9YS
tel 0800-074 7080 *fax* (01325) 321473
email fred.traice@googlemail.com
website www.castleplayers.org.uk
Artistic Director Simon Pell *Associate Director* Jill Cole
Commercial Director Frederick Traice

Production details

A community theatre company limited by guarantee. Established in 1987. Undertakes major open-air summer productions in specially constructed tiered-seat theatre. Stages 1 outdoor production and 1 touring production annually. Recent productions include: *Measure for Measure*, *The Two Gentlemen of Verona* and *Twelfth Night* in the main house; and *Wind in the Willows*, *Shakespeare – the Cabaret* and *Dracula Revamped* in the studio.

Casting procedures

Uses in-house casting directors and holds general auditions; actors should write in January to request inclusion. Will accept unsolicited CVs and photographs sent by email only. Rarely or never has the opportunity to cast disabled actors.

Cavalcade Theatre Company

57 Pelham Road, London SW19 1NW
tel 020-8540 3513 *fax* 020-8540 2243
Directors Graham Ashe, Kim Joyce, Carol Crowther
Touring Manager Colin Agate

Production details

Founded in 1972. Stages an average of 5 productions each year – an annual total of around 200 performances. Tours approximately 20 venues per year, including arts centres, theatres, and outdoor, educational and community venues throughout the UK and Ireland. Also performs at conferences and exhibitions and covers publicity and PR events. In general 8 actors work on each production. Recent productions include: *Alice in Wonderland*, *The Adventures of Brer Rabbit*, pantomimes, musicals and some small-scale plays.

Casting procedures

Does not use freelance casting directors. Sometimes holds general auditions; actors may write at any time to request inclusion. Casting breakdowns are available in *PCR*, *The Stage* and through agents. Welcomes submissions (with CVs and photographs) from actors previously unknown to the company if sent by post, but does not welcome email enquiries. Also accepts invitations to view individual actors' websites.

Chain Reaction Theatre Company

3 Mills Studios, Sugar House Yard,
Sugar House Lane, London E15 2QS
tel 020-8534 0007 *fax* 020-8534 0007
email mail@chainreactiontheatre.co.uk
website www.chainreactiontheatre.co.uk
Key personnel Tuhina Ahmed (Administrator), Anjali Rundle (Project Manager)

Production details

Established in 1994. An award-winning theatre company producing informative, entertaining and thought-provoking theatre, workshops and video productions for people of all ages. Aims to create quality accessible theatre experiences, and engage audiences with writing and performances that explore contemporary issues and perceptions of everyday life. Currently has 12 educational shows in its repertoire, each designed for a specific age range from 5 to 16 years. Performances tackle sensitive and controversial topics including drugs awareness, sexual health, bullying, healthy eating and exercise, and emotional wellbeing. Also designs bespoke pieces of theatre and video productions for a range of professionals, which may be used at corporate workshops, training events and conferences, and works too in TIE and Outreach.

Since 2003 has produced original musical theatre for adult audiences. Its first production, *Everyone Loves Me*, won an award for best musical and its most recent production, *Pretty Please*, premiered in London in 2007.

Tours up to 4 shows each year. Recent productions include: *Food 4 Thought*; *It's Your Body*; *Movin' On Up*; and *Totally Together*. For more information, contact Sarah Choppen.

Casting procedures

Uses freelance casting directors and sometimes holds general auditions. Actors may write in July to request inclusion.

Theatre

Chalkfoot Theatre Arts (formerly Channel Theatre Company)

36 Park Place, Margate CT9 1LE
tel (01843) 280077 *fax* (01843) 280088
email info@chalkfoot.org.uk
website www.chalkfoot.org.uk
Director Philip Dart *Outreach Director* Claudia Leaf
Administrator Edward de Souza

Production details

A creative production company making work for many different venues and communities. Artistic programme is subject to funding.

Casting procedures

"We regret that we are unable to hold general auditions or see actors outside of designated casting periods (unless local to Kent). Agents' information services such as *SBS* or Castweb are normally supplied with casting breakdowns. We cannot mail individuals with submissions. Please send an sae if you would like us to return your photo."

Cheek by Jowl

Stage Door, Barbican Theatre, Silk Street, London EC2Y 8DS
email info@cheekbyjowl.com
Artistic Directors Declan Donnellan, Nick Ormerod

Production details

The company was founded in 1981 by Declan Donnellan and Nick Ormerod. The name conveys an intimacy between the actors, the audience and the text; the phrase 'cheek by jowl' is quoted from *A Midsummer Night's Dream* ("Follow! Nay, I'll go with thee cheek by jowl" (Act III Sc II)) Recent productions include: *Cymbeline* and *Three Sisters*.

Casting procedures

"Like the vast majority of other British theatre companies, our actors are on fixed-term contracts. However, many actors come back regularly to work with us. For each new Cheek by Jowl production, a Casting Director is appointed. Please do not send unsolicited CVs as we are unable to accept them."

Cherub Company London

9 Park Hill, London W5 2JS
tel 020-8723 4358 *fax* 020-8248 0318
email mgieleta@cherub.org.uk
website www.cherub.org.uk
Director Michael Gieleta *Producer* Rebecca Miller

Production details

Founded in 1973, Cherub stages an average of 3 productions a year, with 40 performances across 5 theatre venues in the South East region. Roughly 10 actors are employed for each production. Does not offer Equity approved contracts.

Casting procedures

Uses freelance casting directors; also holds general auditions from time to time. Casting breakdowns are available by sending the company an sae. Welcomes letters (with CVs and photographs) from actors previously unknown to the company, but does not welcome these by email. Happy to receive both showreels and invitations to view actors' websites. Actively encourages applications from disabled actors and promotes the use of inclusive casting.

Chicken Shed Theatre

Chase Side, Southgate, London N14 4PE
tel 020-8351 6161 *fax* 020-8292 0202
email info@chickenshed.org.uk
website www.chickenshed.org.uk
Artistic Director Mary Ward *Associate Director of Music* David Carey *Associate Director & Education Manager* Jonathan Morton *Director of Education & Outreach* Paul Morrall *Artistic Development Director* Louise Perry *Director of Dance* Christine Niering *Key personnel* John Bull (Executive Consultant), Jo Collins (Director of Music), David Balcombe (Chief Executive)

Production details

An inspirational theatre company that produces "beautiful and memorable" performances by working on the basis that everyone should be included, regardless of background, age, race or ability. Runs a Children's and Youth Theatre for 800 young people, operates 3 nationally accredited Education courses, engages in community Outreach projects, and has established a growing network of satellite 'Sheds' across the country (plus 2 in Russia).

Produces on average 3 productions in the main house (seats 300) and 4 in the studio theatre (seats 100). Recent productions include: *A Christmas Carol*; *"as the mother of a brown boy ... "*; *Vanity Fair*; *Tales from the Shed*; and *Seachange*.

Casting procedures

Uses in-house casting directors. Does not hold general auditions; actors may write at any time to request inclusion. Welcomes letters (with CVs & photographs) from actors previously unknown to the company if sent by post or email, but no showreels please. Accepts invitations to view individual actors' websites. Offers Equity approved contracts. Actively encourages applications from disabled actors, and promotes the use of inclusive casting.

Clean Break

2 Patshull Road, London NW5 2LB
tel 020-7482 8600 *fax* 020-7482 8611
email general@cleanbreak.org.uk
website www.cleanbreak.org.uk
Executive Director Lucy Perman *Administrative Producer* Helen Pringle

Production details

Clean Break was founded in 1979 by 2 women prisoners at HMP Askham Grange. The company commissions professional writers to produce new work looking at issues faced by women with experience of the criminal justice system. The company generally stages 1 production, presenting 35 performances each year. Tours to around 5 theatres and prisons across England and Scotland annually. The average cast size is 3-4. Recent productions include: *Black Crows* by Linda Brogan (Arcola Theatre), *Mercy Fine* by Shelley Silas (Southwark Playhouse, Birmingham Rep, York Theatre Royal, Salisbury Playhouse) and *Compact Failure* by Jennifer Farmer (Arcola Theatre, Contact Manchester, York Theatre Royal, Traverse Edinburgh). Offers ITC/Equity approved contracts and does not subscribe to the Equity Pension Scheme.

Casting procedures

Uses freelance casting directors but also holds general auditions in Oct/Nov. Casting breakdowns are available via the website, Equity Job Information Service, *PCR* and *The Stage*. Welcomes letters, CVs and photographs from actors, but prefers not to be contacted by email and does not accept unsolicited showreels. "Clean Break only employs women (section 7(2)(a) of the Sex Discrimination Act applies). We also actively seek to work with artists with an offending background." Actively encourages applications from disabled actors and promotes the use of inclusive casting.

Clod Ensemble

Unit 1-2 Crown Works, Temple Street,
London E2 6QQ
tel 020-7749 0555 *fax* 020-7749 0597
email admin@clodensemble.com
website www.clodensemble.com
Artistic Directors Suzy Willson, Paul Clark *General Manager* Anneliese Graham

Production details

A small to midscale company established in 1996. Creates theatre, music and performance events, workshops and courses in London, the UK and internationally. Stages on average 1 production each year in the main house; also works in Outreach and Community. Recent productions include: *Red Ladies* and *Greed*.

Casting procedures

Producer does the casting. Sometimes holds general auditions and actors should write in winter and spring to request inclusion. Welcomes unsolicited CVs and photographs if sent by email. Also accepts invitations to view individual actors' websites. Offers Equity approved contracts as negotiated through ITC. Actively encourages applications from disabled actors and promotes the use of inclusive casting.

Close for Comfort Theatre Company

34 Boleyn Walk, Leatherhead, Surrey KT22 7HU
tel (01372) 378613
email close4comf@aol.com
website www.hometown.aol.com/close4comf
Director Janet Gill *Co-director* Glenn Johnson

Production details

Founded in 2001. "Takes theatre to living rooms across the country." Stages 3-4 productions each year, averaging an annual total of 30-40 performances in the same number of private homes in the South East, South West and the Midlands. 2 actors work on each production. Recent productions include: *Dossier: Ronald Ackerman in a House in Bristol*.

Casting procedures

Does not use freelance casting directors or hold general auditions.

Cloud Nine Theatre Productions

5 Marden Terrace, Cullercoats,
North Shields NE30 4PD
tel 0191-253 1901
email ironpress@blueyonder.co.uk
website www.cloudninetheatre.co.uk
Artistic Director Peter Mortimer *Associate Director* Colette Stroud

Production details

Established in 1997. Dedicated to commissioning and producing new work from Northern playwrights. Has produced plays by more than 20 Northern dramatists, in leading North-East venues. On average stages 2 productions in the main house and 1 in the studio each year. Recent productions include: *Selkie – A Modern Myth with Live Sea Music* by Valerie Laws (The Sage, Gateshead then touring the North); *The Laughter Factory* (2007, Touring Sketch Show).

Casting procedures

Uses in-house casting directors. Holds general auditions and actors may write at any time requesting inclusion. Casting breakdowns are available from the website; also from the company's quarterly newsletter. Welcomes letters (with CVs and photographs) from actors previously unknown to the company if sent by post, but not by email. Does not accept showreels or invitations to view individual actors' websites. Offers Equity approved contracts as negotiated with ITC. Will consider applications from disabled actors, but opportunities to cast disabled actors are rare. "As a North East based company, we tend to cast with actors from this region, and generally would not encourage other actors to apply unless specifically requested."

Company of Angels

126 Cornwall Road, London SE1 8TQ
tel 020-7928 2811

Theatre

email info@companyofangels.co.uk
website www.companyofangels.co.uk
Director John Retallack *General Manager* Vanessa
Fagan

Production details

Established in 1999. New and experimental work for
young audiences, with a particular focus on new
European writing. Stages 1-4 productions annually,
performing in arts centres, theatres, educational and
community venues throughout the UK. In general 4-
6 actors are involved in each production. Offers
Equity-approved contracts as negotiated through
ITC. Recent productions include: *Truckstop*
(Edinburgh Festival and 3-month small- to mid-scale
tour); Theatre Cafe Festival (venues including
Unicorn Theatre and Southwark Playhouse); and
Sense (Southwark Playhouse).

Casting procedures

Sometimes holds general auditions, and actors may
write at any time to request inclusion. Casting
breakdowns are available from the website, *The Stage*,
SBS, the Arts Council mailing list, and ITC.
Welcomes letters (with CVs and photographs) from
individual actors previously unknown to the
company, sent by post only. Also welcomes showreels
and invitations to view individual actors' websites.
Actively encourages applications from disabled actors
and promotes the use of inclusive casting.

Compass Theatre Company

St Jude's Parish Hall, 175 Gibraltar Street,
Sheffield S3 8UA.
tel 0114-275 5328 *fax* 0114-278 6931
email neil@compasstheatrecompany.com
website www.compasstheatrecompany.com
Artistic Director Neil Sissons

Production details

The company's credo is: "Theatre is at the heart of a
vibrant society. People are interdependent and have a
common responsibility. Theatre expresses our
commonality and resists the notion that we are
separate and alone. It has faith in human beings. It
acknowledges our weaknesses and failings but
believes in our possibilities. It offers the possibility of
redemption and satisfies the overwhelming human
urge for renewal. It addresses the question of how we
should live. It connects the everyday with the
eternal." Recent productions include: *The Price* by
Arthur Miller, *Happy Days* by Samuel Beckett, and
Peer Gynt by Ibsen.

Complicite

14 Anglers Lane, Kentish Town, London NW5 3DG
tel 020-7485 7700 *fax* 020-7485 7701
email email@complicite.org
website www.complicite.org

Artistic Director Simon McBurney *Producer* Judith
Dimant *Education & Marketing* Natasha Freedman

Production details

Award-winning theatre company founded in 1983.
Constantly evolving its ensemble of performers and
collaborators. Work ranges from entirely devised
pieces to theatrical adaptations and revivals of classic
texts. On average presents 2 productions annually.
The average cast size is 7 but can be up to 18. Recent
productions include: *The Elephant Vanishes, Measure
for Measure* and *A Disappearing Number*. Contracts
vary: some are TMA/Equity approved; some (as for
The Elephant Vanishes) are non-Equity.

Casting procedures

Occasionally uses freelance casting directors.
Welcomes letters (with CVs and photographs) sent
by post rather than email. "We are always more
inclined to meet actors previously unknown to us if
they are familiar with our work (i.e. if they have seen
a Complicite show or participated in an Open
Workshop). Complicite's Education Department
programmes up to 2 Open Workshop seasons for
actors each year. Contact us to join the Open
Workshop mailing list." Actively encourages
applications from disabled actors and promotes the
use of inclusive casting.

Comyns Carr and Tyger's Heart

18 St Ann's Terrace, London NW8 6PJ
tel 020-7586 5252 *fax* 020-7722 1945
email tygersheart@comynscarr.fsnet.co.uk
website www.comynscarr.co.uk
Artistic Director Melissa Holston *Associate
Producer* Victoria Walker

Production details

Originally founded in 1995, Comyns Carr now
includes a new division, Tyger's Hart, founded in
2003. Stages 1-4 productions each year, averaging an
annual total of 40-70 performances. Tours up to 22
venues per year, including arts centres, theatres, and
outdoor, educational and community venues
throughout London and the South East. In general 5-
8 actors work on each production. Recent
productions include: *Fair Maid of the West* and *The
Way of the World*.

Casting procedures

Uses freelance casting directors. Actors should only
write to request inclusion when auditions have been
announced. Casting breakdowns are available
through Equity Job Information Service and *PCR*.
Welcomes letters (with CVs and photographs) from
actors previously unknown to the company, but not
email submissions. Also accepts invitations to view
individual actors' websites.

Concordance

Finborough Theatre, 118 Finborough Road,
London SW10 9ED

tel 020-7244 7439 *fax* 020-7835 1853
email admin@concordance.org.uk
website www.concordance.org.uk

Production details

Concordance is a theatrical production company, founded by Neil McPherson in 1981, and is resident at the Finborough Theatre, London – see entry under *Fringe theatres* on page 265. The company presents new writing, revivals of neglected work and music theatre. "We currently offer non-Equity contracts but sometimes at Equity minimum rates." Actively encourages applications from disabled actors and promotes the use of inclusive casting.

Cragrats Theatre

Cragrats Mill, Dunford Road, Holmfirth, West Yorkshire HD9 2AR
tel (01484) 686451 *fax* (01484) 686212
email lauren@cragrats.com
website www.cragrats.com
Director Mark Greenop *Head of Casting* Lauren Tritton

Production details

Established in 1989. Cragrats is a theatrical communications company that uses performance to inspire learning. It is a values-driven creative organisation, offering an immense variety of work in TIE, corporate training and in its in-house venue. 300+ productions per year are performed in Educational venues, touring in the UK, France and the Middle East. Offers Equity approved contracts. Roughly 4 actors are used in each production.

Casting procedures

Casting breakdowns are available on the website, and in *PCR* and *The Stage*. Welcomes letters (with CVs and photographs) from actors previously unknown to the company, sent by post and email. Accepts invitations to view individual actors' websites and showreels. Actively encourages applications from disabled actors.

Note: Cragrats went into receivership in June 2009. However, as this book was going to press, a bidder was lined up to purchase parts of the company. See the website for the latest situation.

Creation Theatre Company

2nd Floor, Kennett House, 108-110 London Road, Headington, Oxford OX3 9AW
tel (01865) 761393 *fax* (01865) 245745
email enquiry@creationtheatre.co.uk
website www.creationtheatre.co.uk
Director David Parrish

Production details

Produces site-specific Shakespeare. Stages 2-5 productions annually in unusual, non-traditional theatre venues (e.g. open air shows in parks, factory spaces, and a spiegletent) with approximately 150 performances per year, mostly in Oxford. 8 actors work on each production. Recent productions include: *The Snow Queen* and *King Lear*.

Casting procedures

Does not use freelance casting directors or hold general auditions. Casting breakdowns are available by postal application (with sae) and via *PCR* and Castfax. Welcomes letters and emails (with CVs and photographs) from actors previously unknown to the company at any time of year.

Dead Earnest Theatre

Applied Theatre Specialists, Sheffield Design Studios, 40 Ball Street, Sheffield S3 8BD
tel 0114-321 0450
email info@deadearnest.co.uk
website www.deadearnest.co.uk
Artistic Director Ashley Barnes *Drama Project Leaders* Vic Roberts, Stacey Sampson, Charlie Barnes
Administration Manager Greg Morrall *Administrative Assistant* Agnes Wolinska

Production details

Dead Earnest is an applied theatre company, using theatre techniques to pursue social goals and in particular to impact on how people act and interact. The main focus of activity is in 3 key areas: Creative Learning (working with schools and universities and developing new techniques); Health and Well-being (CPD with health professionals and service user delivery focused on mental well-being); and Changing Communities (community consultation and looking at issues such as equality and diversity). The company works through forming strong partnerships with clients in the Public, Voluntary and Community sectors in order to bring creative thinking and theatre techniques to their specific needs. Clients are spread the length and breadth of the country. There is also a strong link to Sheffield Hallam University, where Artistic Director, Ashley Barnes, teaches in Applied Theatre.

Stages around 30 productions each year (mainly forum theatre), which all rehearse in Sheffield but are shown throughout the country, and supplies roleplay simulators to local hospitals. Does not offer Equity approved contracts and does not subscribe to the Equity pension scheme.

Casting procedures

Uses freelance casting directors. Sometimes holds general auditions. Welcomes postal or email submissions (with CVs and photographs) from actors previously unknown to the company. Applicants should live locally or have a local base, since company resources do not often extend to assistance with accommodation. The company aims to employ 1 new

Theatre

actor per project. Actively encourages applications from disabled actors.

Debut Theatre Company

New Greenham Arts, 113 Lindenmuth Way,
New Greenham Park, Berkshire RG19 6HN
mobile (07979) 541964
email info@debut-theatre.org.uk
website www.debut-theatre.org.uk
Artistic Director Elizabeth Park *Associate Directors*
Ciaran McConville, Daniel Weyman

Production details

Aims to create the best possible theatre, specialising in new writing and adaptations. Work has a narrative, ensemble quality, addressing 20th- and 21st-century ideas and challenging audiences. Focuses on "telling the story". To date has created 11 productions – 1-2 on average each year, most recently *Snowbound* by Ciaran McConville at Trafalgar Studios (London, April 2008; Critics' Choice, *The Independent*).

Casting procedures

Sometimes uses a casting director; actors are invited to write in at any time to request inclusion. Casting breakdowns may be publicly available, via Castweb and Castnet and in *PCR*. Welcomes unsolicited letters from actors, especially if they have seen a Debut production, but prefers not to receive emails or showreels. Will accept invitations to view individual actors' websites.

DV8 Physical Theatre

Toynbee Studios, 28 Commercial, London E1 6AB
tel 020-7655 0977 *fax* 020-7247 5103
email dv8@artsadmin.co.uk
website www.dv8.co.uk
Artistic Director Lloyd Newson

Production details

Stages 1 production annually in the main house. Recent productions include: *To Be Straight With You* (Verbatim Theatre production); *Just for Show* (stage production); *The Cost of Living* (film); *Living Costs* (stage production); *Enter Achilles* (film/stage); *Strange Fish* (film/stage).

Casting procedures

Uses in-house casting directors. Actors should write in when advertised. Does not welcome unsolicited approaches but will accept showreels and invitations to view individual actors' websites. Offers Equity approved contracts as negotiated through ITC, and participates in the Equity Pension Scheme. Actively encourages applications from disabled actors and promotes the use of inclusive casting.

Eastern Angles Theatre Company

Sir John Mills Theatre, Gatacre Road,
Ipswich IP1 2LQ
tel (01473) 218202 *fax* (01473) 384999
email info@easternangles.co.uk
website www.easternangles.co.uk
Director Ivan Cutting *General Manager* Jill Streatfield

Production details

Founded in 1982, the company tours theatre productions around East Anglia. New writing and a flavour of the region colour all of its original work. Stages 4-5 pieces each year, with an average annual total of 200 performances at 80 different venues. These include arts centres and theatres, educational and community venues, and site-specific locations. Tours mainly to East England but also nationally on occasion. In general 6 actors work on each production. Recent productions include: *The Anatomist, Birds Without Wings, Peapickers* and *Truckstop*. Offers ITC/Equity contracts; does not subscribe to the Equity Pension Scheme but uses the ITC Stakeholder Pension.

Casting procedures

Does not use freelance casting directors or hold general auditions. Casting breakdowns are not currently publicly available but may, in future, be posted on the website. Welcomes letters (with CVs and photographs but not saes); no email submissions please. Advises applicants to consult the website to get an idea of the sort of work the company produces. Applicants should only write once and should specify in their letter if they are local or native to the region. Will consider applications from disabled actors to play characters with disabilities.

Ed Stephenson Productions

7 Hawthorn Road, Little Sutton, Cheshire CH66 1PR
tel 0151-339 6145
email roger@edstephensonproductions.co.uk
website www.edstephensonproductions.co.uk
Company Administrator Diane Barker

Production details

Founded in 2004. Stages on average 1 production every 1-2 years; plans to stage shows in historic buildings in the future. Recent productions include: *The Charnwood Sisters* and *Wrens at War*.

Casting procedures

Uses in-house casting directors. Sometimes holds auditions; actors should write in prior to each show, as advertised on the Equity Job Information Service. Welcomes letters (with CVs & photographs) from individual actors previously unknown to the company, sent by post or email. Accepts showreels and invitations to view individual actors' websites. Will consider applications from disabled actors to play characters with disabilities. "Our contracts are heavily based on ITC/Equity contracts."

English Chamber Theatre

6 St Simon's Avenue, London SW15 6DU
mobile (07951) 912425

email jane@janemcculloch.com
website www.englishchambertheatre.co.uk
Artistic Director Jane McCulloch *President* Dame Judi
Dench

Production details

A theatre company "without a building". There are
25 productions on the list, which go wherever they
are requested. Mainly biographical plays and
entertainments with small casts and star actors in
leading roles. Recent productions include: a tour of
Irish castles with *Dearest Nancy, Darling Evelyn* – the
dramatised letters of Evelyn Waugh and Nancy
Mitford, with Fenella Fielding.

Casting procedures

Uses only in-house casting directors. Will not
consider unsolicited submissions: "Casting is always
done when the drama is being written, and roles are
tailored for particular actors." Rarely or never has the
opportunity to cast disabled actors.

English Touring Theatre

25 Short Street, London SE1 8LJ
tel 020-7450 1990 *fax* 020-7633 0188
email admin@ett.org.uk
website www.ett.org.uk
Director Rachel Tackley

Production details

As one of England's foremost theatre companies, ETT
creates emotionally and intellectually engaging
theatre of outstanding quality, imagination and
ambition. The company works with the country's
leading directors and practitioners to produce
artistically ambitious theatre that is vigorous, popular
and challenging, and tours to large-scale venues
nationwide. 4-15 actors are involved in each
production. Offers ITC/Equity contracts and
subscribes to the Equity Pension Scheme.

Casting procedures

Uses freelance casting directors and does not
welcome unsolicited submissions from actors.

European Theatre Company

39 Oxford Avenue, London SW20 8LS
tel 020-8544 1994 *fax* 020-8544 1999
email admin@europeantheatre.co.uk
website www.europeantheatre.co.uk
Directors Adam Roberts, Jennie Graham

Production details

Founded in 1992, the company produces French-
language theatre which tours the UK. Stages 3 or
more productions a year, with around 250
performances in arts centres, theatres, schools and
community venues. Normally employs 5 actors for
each production.

Casting procedures

Casts in-house, and publishes its casting breakdowns
via *PCR* and *SBS*. Welcomes letters (not emails) with
CVs and photographs from French-speaking actors
previously unknown to the company.

Feather Productions Ltd

137 Sheen Road, Richmond, Surrey TW9 1YJ
tel 020-8439 9848
email info@featherproductions.com
website www.featherproductions.com
Artistic Directors Tim Whitnall, Anna Murphy

Production details

Has produced 2 new plays at the Old Red Lion,
Islington. Welcomes scripts from new writers.

Casting procedures

Uses in-house casting directors. Sometimes holds
general auditions; actors should write in Jan-Feb to
request inclusion. Welcomes letters (with CVs &
photographs) from individual actors previously
unknown to the company sent by post or email. Also
accepts showreels and invitations to view individual
actors' websites. Offers Equity approved contracts as
negotiated through PACT. Will consider applications
from disabled actors to play characters with
disabilities.

Forbidden Theatre Company

20 Rupert Street, London W1D 6DF
tel 0845-009 3084
email info@forbidden.org.uk
website www.forbidden.org.uk
Education Co-ordinator Linda Baker *Ensemble
Production Team* Steve Brownlie, Erica Lowe, Mark
Reid

Production details

Physical and visual theatre company. Produces small-
scale productions of adaptations of classics and
devised work. Stages 1 production annually and gives
approximately 40 performances per year. Tours 2
venues on average and performs in arts centres and
theatre venues in London and Scotland. In general, 4-
6 actors work on each production. Recent
productions include: *Goddess, Stung,* and *Mrs Wobble
the Waitress and Friends.*

Casting procedures

Does not use freelance casting directors. Sometimes
holds general auditions. Actors can write at any time
requesting inclusion. Welcomes letters (with CVs and
photographs) but not email submissions. Advises that
the company will only reply to actors if inviting them
to audition. CVs are kept on file.

Forced Entertainment

The Workstation, 15 Paternoster Row,
Sheffield S1 2BX

tel 0114-279 8977 *fax* 0114-221 2170
email fe@forcedentertainment.com
website www.forcedentertainment.com
Key personnel Tim Etchells (Artistic Director), Robin Arthur, Richard Lowden, Claire Marshall, Cathy Naden, Terry O' Connor

Production details

Since forming the company in 1984, the 6 core members of the group have sustained a unique artistic partnership for 25 years, confirming their position as "trailblazers in contemporary theatre". The company's substantial canon of work reflects an interest in the mechanics of performance, the role of the audience, and the machinations of contemporary urban life. Its work, framed and focused by Artistic Director Tim Etchells, is distinctive and provocative, delighting in disrupting the conventions of theatre and the expectations of audiences. Forced Entertainment's trademark collaborative process – devising work as a group through improvisation, experimentation and debate – has made them pioneers of British avant-garde theatre, and touring all over the world has earned them an unparalleled international reputation. Vist the website for a full archive of work.

Forest Forge Theatre Co

The Theatre Centre, Endeavour Park,
Crow Arch Lane, Ringwood, Hants BH24 1SF
tel (01425) 470188 *fax* (01425) 471158
email info@forestforge.co.uk
website www.forestforge.co.uk
CEO/Artistic Director Kirstie Davis *Administrative Director* Karen Jeffries *Associate Director* David Haworth

Production details

Forest Forge Theatre Company was founded in 1981 with a grant from Manpower Services. In 1996 the company was awarded a grant enabling a new operational base to be built in Ringwood, which comprises of a studio, offices and a workshop. The company tours 3 productions a year into studios, village halls and arts centres, and has a large Creative Learning programme attached. Recent productions include: a new play about the Romany embankment in the New Forest entitled *A Clearing* by Dan Allum; and *Stamping, Shouting and Singing Home* by Lisa Evans.

Forkbeard Fantasy

PO Box 1241, Bristol BS99 2TG

Production details

Founded in 1974; an artist-led, multimedia film and performance company. Stages 1-2 productions and performs about 50 times per year. Tours to 10 venues both nationally and internationally on an annual basis. As this is an artist-led company, actors are only occasionally involved in productions. Performed recently at the Blackpool Puppet Festival, Warwick Arts Centre and The Lowry, Salford.

Casting procedures

Never holds general auditions. Advises actors that the company usually performs with artists who are already in the core team.

Found Theatre

c/o Packhorse Cottage, Crowdecote,
Buxton SK17 0DB
tel (01298) 883167 *fax* (07967) 648136
email found_theatre@yahoo.co.uk
website www.foundtheatre.org.uk
Artistic & Casting Director Simon Corble
Administrator Judy Meetham

Production details

Small-scale touring and site-specific theatre.

Casting procedures

Sometimes holds general auditions; actors should write in August to request inclusion. Welcomes unsolicited CVs and photographs sent via email, and invitations to view individual actors' websites. Does not accept showreels or approaches by post. Rarely (or never) has the opportunity to cast disabled actors.

Foursight Theatre

Newhampton Arts Centre, Dunkley Street,
Wolverhampton WV1 4AN
tel (01902) 714257 *fax* (01902) 428413
email admin@foursighttheatre.co.uk
website www.foursighttheatre.co.uk
Co-Artistic Director Frances Land, Sarah Thom
Administrator Abigail Prosser

Production details

National touring theatre company. Emphasises the need for "total theatre" combining word, movement and music. Specialises in biographical plays about women in history and runs a strong education programme. Stages 1 production annually in addition to its regional and education work. Performs at arts centres, theatres and educational venues. Cast size varies according to production needs. Recent productions include: *Can Any Mother Help Me?*, *The Corner Shop, Six Dead Queens & An Inflatable Henry* and *Thatcher The Musical!*. Offers ITC/Equity approved contracts and does not subscribe to the Equity Pension Scheme.

Casting procedures

Casting breakdowns are not publicly available. Actors are advised to keep an eye on the website for information posted prior to productions. Welcomes submissions (with CVs and photographs) by post and email. Invitations to view individual actors' websites are also accepted. Actively encourages applications from disabled actors and promotes the use of inclusive casting.

Frantic Assembly

31 Eyre Street, London EC1R 5EW
tel 020-7841 3115
email admin@franticassembly.co.uk
website www.franticassembly.co.uk
Artistic Directors Scott Graham, Steven Hoggett
Company Administrator Vicki Middleton

Production details

Established in 1994. Produces "thrilling, energetic and uncompromising theatre". The company's work reflects contemporary culture and attracts new audiences. In collaboration with a wide variety of artists, the Artistic Directors create new work that places equal emphasis on movement, design, music and text. Has toured extensively throughout the UK and abroad, building a reputation as one of the country's most exciting companies.

Casting procedures

Does not hold open auditions. Actors interested in working with the company are advised to send a CV by post to the Administrator. All CVs are read by the Artistic Directors. "We recommend that you attend our public workshops, which give you the opportunity to meet and work with the Artistic Directors. These workshops are not auditions, but do give the company a chance to spot talented performers."

Frantic Theatre Company

32 Wood Lane, Falmouth TR11 4RF
tel (01326) 312985 *fax* (01326) 312985
email info@frantictheatre.com
website www.frantictheatre.com

Production details

Founded in 1990. Stages 2 productions annually with around 1500 performances in 1500 venues throughout the UK and Ireland every year. Venues include arts centres, village halls, theatres, outdoor venues, educational and community venues, private homes and hospitals. On average 4 actors work on each production. Recent productions include: *Can I Do You Now, Sir?* and *Don't Dilly Dally*.

Casting procedures

Holds general auditions. Actors should write in May and November to request inclusion. Casting breakdowns are available by postal application (with sae), Equity Job Information Service, *PCR* and advertisements in *The Stage*. Welcomes submissions (with CVs and photographs) by post or email. Showreels and invitations to view individual actors'

websites are also accepted. Actors are advised not to telephone, and to send their details only when they have researched the company's very specific work and can explain their suitability.

Freedom Studios

Bradford Design Exchange, 34 Peckover Street, Little Germany, Bradford BD1 5BD
tel (01274) 730077 *fax* (01274) 730044
email hello@freedomstudios.co.uk
website www.freedomstudios.co.uk
Director Madani Younis *General Manager* Deborah Fox

Production details

Established in 2007. A national touring, devising theatre company. Stages 1 production annually in around 6 venues (arts centres, theatres and outdoor venues) across Yorkshire, the Midlands and London. In general 2-4 actors are involved in each production. Offers Equity-approved contracts as negotiated through ITC. Recent productions include: *Happy & Married?* (national tour). Also holds the Asian Theatre School for a 15-week period each year, for aspiring Yorkshire British Asian Artists; and Unit 4, "a twice-yearly platform event for some of the most exciting voices in the UK contemporary arts scene".

Casting procedures

Sometimes holds general auditions. Welcomes letters (with CVs and photographs) from individual actors previously unknown to the company, sent by post or email; also accepts showreels and invitations to view individual actors' websites. Will consider applications from disabled characters to play characters with disabilities.

Full Body & The Voice

Lawrence Batley Theatre, Queen's Street, Huddersfield HD1 2SP
tel (01484) 484441 *fax* (01484) 484443
email fullbody@lbt-uk.org
website www.fullbody.org.uk
Key contact Jon Palmer

Production details

Established in 2000. Production company exploring a range of projects that include actors with learning disabilities and promote inclusive working practices. Approximately 1 production per year touring to 10-15 venues, including arts centres and theatres in Yorkshire, the North West and internationally. Roughly 5-8 actors are used in each production.

Casting procedures

Occasionally uses freelance casting directors. Does not welcome unsolicited CVs. Actively encourages applications from disabled actors and promotes the use of inclusive casting. Offers Equity approved contracts.

Theatre

Gagged Theatre

11 Wheatsheaf Court, Off Kendall Road, Colchester,
Essex CO1 2BU
tel (01206) 525712
email gag@fsmail.net
website www.gaggedtheatre.com
Director Lucy Traube

Production details

A new writing company established in 2002 and
funded by Arts Council England. The company stages
1-2 productions with approximately 35 performances
each year. Has toured to theatres and arts centres
across the Eastern region, London and the Edinburgh
Festival. Cast sizes are normally somewhere between
1 and 6 actors. Recent productions include: *Shot*
(Colchester Arts Centre, Hemel Old Town Hall and
Ipswich's Pulse Festival); and *Again* (Mercury
Theatre, Colchester, Edinburgh Festival and Upstairs
at the Gatehouse, London).

Casting procedures

Uses freelance casting directors, but actors may write
with CVs and photographs and their details will be
kept on file until the company is next auditioning.
Will also accept showreels, emails and invitations to
view websites. The company runs a comprehensive
workshop programme and therefore particularly
welcomes actors with this kind of experience.

Galleon Theatre Company Ltd

Greenwich Playhouse, Greenwich Station Forecourt,
189 Greenwich High Road, London SE10 8JA
tel 020-8858 9256
email boxoffice@galleontheatre.co.uk
website www.galleontheatre.co.uk
Artistic Director Alice de Sousa *Theatre Director* Bruce
Jamieson

Production details

Founded in 1990. Stages 12-14 productions annually
and presents 282 performances at its own venue,
Greenwich Playhouse. Has toured throughout Britain
in previous years. On average 15 actors work on each
production. For recent productions, please see the
website. Also has a film company, Galleon Films Ltd,
which is developing a slate of 4 feature films.

Casting procedures

Uses in-house casting director. Holds general
auditions; actors should write to request inclusion
when the company is casting for a specific project.
Casting breakdowns are available through *PCR*, *SBS*,
Castnet and advertisements in *The Stage*. Welcomes
letters (with CVs and photographs) but not email
submissions. Showreels and invitations to view
individual actors' websites are also accepted.

David Glass Ensemble

96 Teesdale Street, London E2 6PU
tel 020-7734 6030 *fax* 020-7734 0365
email matthew@davidglassensemble.com
website www.davidglassensemble.com

Production details

Founded in 1990, the company tours nationally and
internationally, especially in South East Asia – recent
productions have toured to Cambodia, Vietnam and
Korea, as well as performing at the Portsmouth New
Theatre Royal and the Battersea Arts Centre in
London. Stages 2 productions a year, and tours to
roughly 10 theatre venues, with a company of around
5 actors. Offers ITC/Equity approved contracts.

Casting procedures

Does not issue casting breakdowns. Welcomes CVs
and photographs from actors whose work is not
known to the company, and also welcomes showreels
and invitations to view actors' websites. The company
actively encourages applications from disabled actors
and promotes the use of inclusive casting.

Godot Company

operating from the Bookshop Theatre, 51 The Cut,
Waterloo, London SE1 8LF
tel 020-7633 0599
email info@godotcompany.com
Administrator John Calder

Production details

An actors' cooperative performing at theatres and
other suitable venues, including its own headquarters
in Waterloo (behind the Calder Bookshop, opposite
the Young Vic) and at British, Irish and European
theatres and festivals. Stages between 10 and 30
productions in the main house, and the same in the
studio, each year. Also works in TIE, Outreach and
Community: contact John Calder for details. Recent
productions include: many plays by Beckett and
similar authors; also readings and adaptations.

Casting procedures

Uses in-house and freelance casting directors.
Sometimes holds general auditions; actors may write
at any time to request inclusion. "Policy, repertory,
casting etc. is the joint decision of the cooperative,
which votes when necessary."

Graeae Theatre Company

Bradbury Studios, 138 Kingsland Road,
London E2 8DY
tel 020-7613 6900 *fax* 020-7613 6919
email info@graeae.org
website www.graeae.org
Artistic Director Jenny Sealey

Production details

Founded in 1980. Produces theatre made by disabled
people (actors, directors and other theatre
practitioners) with physical and sensory impairments.

Stages 3 productions annually and gives 70 performances at 50 venues each year. Venues include arts centres and theatres in England, Scotland, Wales and Ireland. 3-6 actors are involved in each production. Recent productions include: national tour of *Blasted* by Sarah Kane, and *Whiter Than Snow* by Mike Kenny, which was a co-production with Birmingham Rep. Graeae/New Wolsey Theatre co-produced *Flower Girls* by Richard Cameron in Autumn 2007, and Graeae/Suspect Culture co-produced a new play in Spring 2008.

Casting procedures

Sometimes holds general auditions. Welcomes postal or email submissions (with CVs and photographs) from actors with physical and sensory impairments. Also accepts showreels and invitations to view individual actors' websites. Offers ITC/Equity approved contracts.

Into The Scene is a new Arts Council England initiative led by Graeae. Works with leading drama schools on inclusive practice to encourage drama schools to recruit more disabled actors onto their training courses.

Scene Change is a Graeae initiative working with venues, drama schools and colleges offering taster workshops to encourage more young people to apply to drama schools.

The company offers Continued Professional Development workshops for actors. Past workshops have included Comedy Acting with director Gordon Anderson (ATC/Catherine Tate), and Singing with Barb Jungr.

Grassmarket Project

1 Harley Street, London W1G 9QD
tel 020-7307 8734
email info@grassmarketproject.org
website www.grassmarketproject.org
Artistic Director Jeremy Weller

Production details

Founded in 1989. Independent theatre company producing new work in theatres across Europe, USA and the UK. Stages 2 productions annually and gives 30-40 performances every year. On average, 5-6 actors work on each production. Recent productions include: *De Andre (The Others)*; *Fathers & Sons* (Betty Nansen Theatre, Copenhagen); *Bus Stops* (Glasgow); and *The Foolish Young Man* (Roundhouse Theatre, London).

Casting procedures

Productions are cast by freelance casting directors or the company's artistic director. Sometimes holds general auditions. Employs a mixture of trained and untrained actors. Welcomes letters (with CVs and photographs) by post or email. Showreels and invitations to view individual actors' websites are also accepted. Offers non-Equity contracts. Will consider applications from disabled actors to play characters with disabilities.

Grid Iron Theatre Company

85 East Claremont Street, Edinburgh EH7 4HU
Director Ben Harrison *Producer* Judith Doherty
General Manager Claire Robb

Production details

Founded in 1995. Produces new writing and site-specific theatre. Stages 1-3 productions annually and gives 20-50 performances every year. Performs in theatres, outdoor and site-specific venues in Scotland, England and Northern and Southern Ireland. 2-8 actors work on each production. Recent productions include: *Variety*, *Decky Does A Bronco* and *Those Eyes, That Mouth*.

Casting procedures

Sometimes holds general auditions. Actors may write requesting inclusion at any time throughout the year. Welcomes submissions (with CVs and photographs) sent by post and email. Showreels and invitations to view individual actors' websites are also accepted.

Handstand Productions

13 Hope Street, Liverpool L1 9BH
tel 0151-708 7441 *fax* 0151-709 3515
email info@handstand-uk.com
website www.handstand-uk.com
Director Han Duijvendak *Producer* Nicholas Stanley
Co-producer Lucy Dossor

The company is now working almost exclusively in documentary, film, TV and video production. Rarely requires actors, so please do not submit anything unless a specific casting requirement has been made available on the website.

Headlong Theatre

Chertsey Chambers, 12 Mercer Street, London WC2H 9QD
tel 020-7438 9940 *fax* 020-7438 9941
email info@headlongtheatre.co.uk
website www.headlongtheatre.co.uk
Artistic Director Rupert Goold *Key contact* Henny Finch

Production details

Formerly Oxford Stage Company. Established in 1974. National touring theatre company dedicated to new ways of making theatre by exploring revolutionary writers and practitioners of the past, present and future. Stages 4-6 projects annually, performing 24-32 weeks of the year. Tours nationally to arts centres and theatres. Recent productions include: *The English Game* (UK Tour); *The Last Days of Judas Iscariot* (Almeida); *Rough Crossings* (UK

Theatre

Tour); *Faustus* (UK Tour); and *Angels in America* (UK Tour).

Casting procedures

Accepts submissions (with CVs and photographs) from actors previously unknown to the company sent by post or email. Invitations to view individual actors' websites are accepted, as are showreels. Offers TMA/Equity approved contracts.

Hidden Talent Productions Ltd

109 Drakefell Road, Brockley, London SE4 2DT
mobile (07905) 175934
email info@hiddentalent.org.uk
website www.hiddentalent.org.uk
Artistic Director Adam Linsson *Associate Directors* Evan Regueira, Alex Hughes, Ben Wiles *Casting Directors* Adam Linsson, Evan Regueira, Alex Hughes, Ben Wiles *Key personnel* Ben Wiles (Resident Musical Director), Samantha Zoe-French (Resident Choreographer)

Production details

Established in 2006 as a not-for-profit, small-scale theatre producing company. Stages primarily musical theatre productions and cabarets. Aims to raise the profile of musical theatre in the community as a recognised art form, by producing new works alongside established 'classic' musicals. Tours to small fringe venues and halls, and provides interactive performances in local schools and other education establishments across the UK. Offers closed workshop performances and readings through to fully staged musical productions in larger theatres. Stages on average 1 production in the main house and 2 in the studio each year. Also works in TIE and Community, for which the key contact is Adam Linsson. Recent productions include: *Heaven Sent, A New Musical Comedy* (Workshop); *Nights on Broadway* (Cabaret); and *Changing Direction* (TIE).

Casting procedures

Uses in-house casting directors. Sometimes holds general auditions; actors may write in at any time, but preferably when the company is casting specific projects. Casting breakdowns are available via the website or on postal application with an sae. Welcomes letters (with CVs & photographs) from individual actors previously unknown to the company sent by post or email. Accepts showreels and invitations to view individual actors' websites. Will consider applications from disabled actors to play characters with disabilities.

Highly Sprung Performance Company

49 Abercorn Road, Chapelfields, Coventry CV5 8EE
tel 020-7667 0141
email mail@sprunghq.fsnet.co.uk
website www.highlysprungperformance.co.uk

Artistic Director Sarah Hunt *Company Director* Mark Worth

Production details

Founded in 1999. Aims to create original and innovative performances exploring the relationship between dance, text and physical theatre. Also runs community and educational activities alongside productions. Stages 1 production annually with 25 performances every year. Tours 10-15 venues annually: these include arts centres, theatres, outdoor and educational venues in the West Midlands, London, Manchester and Edinburgh. On average 2-8 actors work on each production. Recent productions include: *Pretend I'm Not Here* and *More Than Kisses*.

Casting procedures

Holds general auditions. Actors should send CVs and photographs by post or email. These will be kept on file for future auditions. Casting breakdowns are available on the website, by postal application and via Equity Job information Service and advertisements in *The Stage*. Showreels and invitations to view individual actors' websites are also accepted.

Hijinx Theatre

Wales Millennium Centre, Bute Place, Cardiff CF10 5AL
tel 029-2030 0331 *fax* 029 2063 5621
email info@hijinx.org.uk
website www.hijinx.org.uk
Artistic Director Gaynor Lougher *Associate Director* Louise Osborn *Administrative Director* Val Hill

Production details

Founded in 1981, the company stages at least 2 professional productions a year on a one-night-stand basis across Wales and England, for community and theatre venues. In general the Spring show is aimed at a learning disabled audience and their communities, while the Autumn and Winter tours target the general public.

The company has developed a strong commitment to new writing over the years, commissioning plays from many of Wales' leading playwrights. On average 4 actors work on each production, which includes a strong musical element. Recent productions include: *Chasing Rainbows* (touring day centres, gateway clubs, community centres and colleges); and *The Other Woman* (Wales Millennium Centre, Torch Theatre and community venues). Offers ITC/Equity approved contracts and does not subscribe to the Equity Pension Scheme.

Casting procedures

Shows are cast by the artistic and associate director. Welcomes letters, CVs and photographs from actors previously unknown to the company. Does not accept emails or showreels. Welcomes applications from disabled and non-disabled actors.

Historia Theatre Co

8 Cloudesley Square, London N1 0HT
tel 020-7837 8005 *fax* 020-7278 4733
email kate@kateprice.org
website www.historiatheatre.com
Artistic Director Catherine Price

Production details

Established in 1997. "Historia presents plays that
have their source or inspiration in history." 1
production annually with 20-30 performances.
Touring productions visit theatres, arts venues,
National Trust houses, museums, churches, schools
and village halls both nationally and in London.
Roughly 6-8 actors are used in each production.
Recent productions include: *An African's Blood* (2007,
and a limited season in 2008; Tour); *Five Eleven or the
Powder Treason* (2005; Tour), and *Evelina* (2004;
Pentameters Theatre). Offers ITC/Equity rates where
possible.

Casting procedures

Does not use freelance casting directors or hold
general auditions. Breakdowns are published via *PCR*,
SBS, Equity's Job Information Service and via
Spotlight Link. Unsolicited approaches from actors
are discouraged. "Watch *PCR/SBS*/JIS and apply
accordingly." Will consider applications from
disabled actors when casting for characters with
disabilities.

Hoipolloi Theatre

Office F, Dale's Brewery, Gwydir Street,
Cambridge CB1 2LJ
tel/fax (01223) 322748
email info@hoipolloi.org.uk
website www.hoipolloi.org.uk
Director Shôn Dale-Jones *Associate Director* Stephanie
Müller *Production Manager* Richard Couldrey

Production details

Founded in 1994, the company creates visually and
physically dynamic, imaginative and comic work
which tours to small- and middle-scale theatres and
arts centres throughout the UK. In 2005 the company
worked in overseas locations such as the USA and
Europe; it is also involved in educational work. Stages
1-2 productions annually, presenting 100
performances every year at 60-70 venues. On average
4-5 actors work on each production. Recent
productions include: *My Uncle Arly*.

Casting procedures

Sometimes holds general auditions. Actors may write
at any time requesting inclusion. Welcomes letters
(with CVs and photographs) but not email
submissions. Invitations to view individual actors'
websites are also accepted. Advises actors
approaching the company to have some knowledge
of its work.

Hollow Crown Productions Ltd

2 Norfolk Road, London E17 5QS
mobile (07930) 530948
email enquiries@hollowcrown.co.uk
website www.hollowcrown.co.uk
Artistic Director Peter Adshead *Associate Directors*
Andrew Jarvis, Carl Jacobs

Production details

"A theatrical production company with a difference.
Provides an extension to the young graduate actor's
training through the professional production
experience." Offers ongoing vocational support to
develop and enhance the foundation skills conferred
through recognised drama school training, so that
each company member may achieve their full
potential. Stages 3 productions (Classical, Modern
Classics) annually.

Casting procedures

Uses in-house casting directors. Sometimes holds
general auditions via workshops; actors may write in
at any time. Casting breakdowns are available from
the website, in *PCR*, and from CastNet. Welcomes
letters (with CVs and photographs) from actors not
previously known to the company if sent by post; no
email submissions. Does not accept showreels. Offers
own contract based on Equity Fringe/TMA. Will
consider applications from disabled actors to play
characters with disabilities. "The company is
especially keen to hear from actors whose
philosophy/approach to text resonates with its artistic
policy, and who would be keen to explore often
neglected classical texts – including Shakespearean
texts in their quarto/folio forms." Consult the website
for more details.

Horse and Bamboo Theatre

The Horse and Bamboo Centre, Waterfoot,
Rossendale, Lancashire BB4 7HQ
tel (01706) 220241 *fax* (01706) 831166
email info@horseandbamboo.org
website www.horseandbamboo.org
Key personnel Richard Hall, Alison Duddle

Production details

Established in 1978. A visual touring theatre using
masks, puppetry, video and movement in theatre.
Produces approximately 3 productions per year,
touring to 60 venues including arts centres and
outdoor venues in the UK, Europe and the USA.
Performers must have mask/puppetry or dance
experience to a professional level. Offers non-Equity
contracts and does not subscribe to the Equity
Pension Scheme. Members of ITC.

Casting procedures

Welcomes letters (with CVs and photographs) from
actors previously unknown to the company if sent by

Theatre

post, but not by email. Invitations to view individual actors' websites are also accepted. Will consider applications from disabled actors to play characters with disabilities.

Ibsen Stage Company

434 Hornsey Road, London N19 4EB
tel 020-7281 4322
email ask@ibsenstage.com
website www.ibsenstage.com
Director Terje Tveit *Company Co-ordinator* Rosalind Stockwell

Production details

Productions are characterised by a "different and revitalised" approach to Ibsen. Stages 1-2 productions each year, plus workshops and readings, with 40-60 performances annually in theatres in London and Europe. In general, 5-15 actors are involved in each production. Does not offer actors Equity-approved contracts, but will pay Equity rates when funding allows. Recent productions include: *Little Eyolf* (Riverside Studios); *Peer Gynt* (Pleasance Theatre, Islington); *A Doll's House* (National Theatre, Oslo); and *The Nightingale Mystery* (Rosemary Branch Theatre).

Casting procedures

Holds general auditions; actors may write at any time to request inclusion. Casting breakdowns are publicly available via the website, *PCR*, Casting Call Pro and CastNet. Welcomes letters (with CVs and photographs) from actors previously unknown to the company sent by post or email. Is happy to receive showreels and invitations to view individual actors' websites. Rarely (or never) has the opportunity to cast disabled actors.

Icarus Theatre Collective

105 Bell Street, London NW1 6TL
tel 020-3239 7033
email info@icarustheatre.co.uk
website www.icarustheatre.co.uk
Artistic Director Max Lewendel *Associate Director* Rosa Wyatt

Production details

"Explores the the harsh, brutal side of contemporary and classical drama." Aims to produce 2 mid-scale and 3 professional fringe productions of theatre every 2 years, using new writing and under-appreciated classics in diverse performance formats. Teams artists from the international community with British artists, and experienced artists with promising young professionals. Also works in TIE, Outreach & Community, for which the key contact is Rosa Wyatt. Recent productions include: *The Lesson* by Eugene Ionesco; *Albert's Boy* by James Graham; *Othello* by William Shakespeare; and *Vincent in Brixton* by Nicholas Wright.

Casting procedures

Uses in-house casting directors. Holds general auditions; actors should write in when advised to do so by the company's newsletter. Casting breakdowns are available from the website and are advertised in *PRC* and *SBS*. Welcomes letters (with CVs & photographs) sent by post, but not email, and does not accept showreels or invitations to view individual actors' websites.

Ichiza Theatre Company

2 Bradford Court, Bloxham, Oxon OX15 4RA
tel (01295) 720500 *fax* (01295) 722118
email office@ichiza.co.uk
website www.ichiza.co.uk
Artistic Director Togo Igawa *Associate Director* Masumi Kako *Administrator* Nao Miyauchi

Production details

Established in 2007. Produces Japanese plays, from traditional theatre to contemporary works, in collaboration with artists from different backgrounds. Recently completed its first production, *The Face of Jizo* by Hisashi Inoue, at Arcola Theatre, to acclaim from wide audiences. Plans to start work in TIE/Outreach in the near future.

Casting procedures

Uses in-house casting directors and holds general auditions; actors are advised to write in only when auditions are announced. Casting breakdowns are available from Equity Job Information Service, *PCR* and *The Stage*. Does not welcome unsolicited approaches by email, but will accept letters (with CVs and photographs) and showreels sent in response to specific, announced auditions. Actively encourages applications from disabled actors and promotes the use of inclusive casting.

Incisor

Flat 1, 5 York Avenue, Hove BN3 1PH
mobile (07979) 498450
fax 020-8830 4992
email sarahmann7@hotmail.co.uk
website www.theatre-company-incisor.com
Artistic / Casting Director Sarah Mann *Associate Director* James Madden

Production details

Recent productions include: *Abigail's Party* and *Blithe Spirit*.

Casting procedures

Uses in-house casting directors and does not hold general auditions. Casting breakdowns are published in *PCR* and available from Casting Call Pro / Castweb / Castnet. Welcomes letters (with CVs and photographs) from actors previously unknown to the company, sent by post or by email. Does not accept showreels but will respond to invitations to view individual actors' websites. Actively encourages applications from disabled actors and promotes the use of inclusive casting. "Incisor's style is big and bold, especially as a lot of our work is outdoors. Large characters and voices needed."

Indigo Entertainments

Tynymynydd, Bryneglwys, Corwen,
Denbighshire LL21 9NP
tel (01978) 790211
email info@indigoentertainments.com
website www.indigoentertainments.com
Director Emma Hands

Production details

Founded in 2000. Takes existing small-scale theatre productions, usually with a literary theme, and tours them around the UK and internationally. Stages 5-10 productions annually with 50 performances in 50 venues every year. These include arts centres, theatres, outdoor and educational venues, community venues and hotels all over the UK and in the Middle East and Far East. On average 1-3 actors work on each production. Recent productions include: *The Tale of Beatrix Potter, Testament of Youth, Hic! The Entire History of Wine (Abridged), Red Wings, Richard Bucket Overflows, Emily Dickinson & I, My Darling Clementine,* and *How Pleasant to Know Mr Lear.* Offers non-Equity contracts and does not subscribe to the Equity Pension Scheme.

Casting procedures

Does not welcome unsolicited CVs. Will accept showreels if they demonstrate productions of interest and are not just an actor's general showreel. Advises that the shows presented are usually intelligent, light, witty commercial pieces rather than experimental work.

Jasperian Theatre Company

29 Harvard Court, Honeybourne Road,
London NW6 1HL
tel 020-7813 4362 *fax* 020-7435 4246
email jasperiantheatre@mac.com
Artistic Director Tony Jasper *Production Directors* Ken Pickering, Peter Moreton, Harry Gostelow, Clare Davidson

Production details

Founded in 1992, JTC specialises in straight plays and revues that have a religious underpinning and/or deal with the human condition. The company is a member of ITC and casts all shows on artistic ability – not on any religious affiliation. Normally stages 3-5 productions each year with a total of around 100 performances. Tours to a variety of different venues including theatres, churches and private houses

across the UK. In general 3-7 actors work on each production. Recent productions include: *Charles Wesley 1707* (100 venues), and *Stories of Grace,* dealing with race, gender and the hospice movement.

Casting procedures

Uses freelance casting directors. Actors may write requesting inclusion in the next round of auditions at any time, but the beginning of February, June and September are normally good times. Casting breakdowns are available through *SBS* and CastNet. Prefers actors to send in their details by post but will accept the occasional email. Showreels are also accepted. Advises actors to read audition notices carefully and only come if suitable and available over the time period specified. A member of ITC, offers non-Equity contracts; however: "Apart from usually £220-£320 I also offer all accommodation and meals paid, and in some instances this is better than a basic Equity contract. I attempt to cast only Equity members. In 17 years, no-one has been owed money [by me]." Actively encourages applications from disabled actors and promotes the use of inclusive casting.

Kabosh

The Old Museum Arts Centre,
7 College Square North, Belfast BT1 6AR
tel 028-9024 3343 *fax* 028-9023 1130
email kabosh@dircon.co.uk/info@kabosh.net
website www.kabosh.net
Artistic Director Karl Wallace *Company Touring Manager* Azucena Avila

Production details

Founded in 1994. Produces innovative physical and visual theatre for local, national and international touring and site-specific work. Stages 2-4 productions annually with 56 performances during the course of the year. Tours to around 30 venues annually, including arts centres and theatres, and site-specific locations. In general 2-6 actors are involved in each production. Countries covered include Northern Ireland, Republic of Ireland, England (including London), Scotland, Wales, parts of Europe and North America. Recent productions include: *Rhinoceros* and *Todd.*

Casting procedures

Auditions are by invitation only. Actors should write requesting inclusion in July (for autumn productions) and November (for spring productions). Welcomes applications (with CVs and photographs) sent by post and email. Also accepts invitations to view individual actors' websites. Any actor known to the company is welcome to send a CV and headshot (which will be kept on file), and to notify the director of performances where their work may be seen. The director will endeavour to see new actors. Any unseen actor who has sent a CV will be notified of open auditions, should they arise.

Kali Theatre Company

20 Rupert Street, London W1 6DF
tel 020-7494 9100
email info@kalitheatre.co.uk
website www.kalitheatre.co.uk
Artistic Director Janet Steel *General Manager* Chris Corner

Production details

Founded in 1990 to encourage, support and promote new writing by Asian women. "We focus on content and ideas as much as style, aiming to present memorable theatre events based on challenging and innovative ideas." Stages on average 1 production in the main house and 1 in the studio each year, playing to audiences that are increasingly diverse. Nurtures novice playwrights through its Kali Shorts and Kali Futures initiatives, and has worked with writers such as Tanika Gupta, Rukhsana Ahmad, Gurpreet Bhatti and Shelley Silas among others. Recent productions include: *Azmeen*, *Another Paradise* and *Bhena*. The company also runs a regional Outreach programme and a Talk Back Festival for Asian Women – consult the website for further details.

Casting procedures

Welcomes letters (with CVs & photographs) from actors previously unknown to the company if sent by post, but not by email. Does not accept showreels or invitations to view individual actors' websites. Rarely (or never) has the opportunity to cast disabled actors.

"Phone to find out what we are casting before sending CVs and photos."

Kaos Theatre

39-41 North Road, Islington, London N7 9DP
tel 020-7700 3885 *fax* 020-7700 3885
email admin@kaostheatre.com
website www.kaostheatre.com
Director Xavier Leret

Production details

Founded in 1994. Working ensemble of actors, musicians, designers and artists working with text-based theatre. Stages both new writing and contemporary adaptations of existing work (classic and modern). Receives funding from Arts Council England. Stages 1-2 productions annually with 80 performances during the course of the year. The company tours on average to 30 different venues across the UK (excluding the Highlands and Islands) each year. Recent productions include: *Titus Andronicus* and *The Kaos Importance of Being Earnest*.

Casting procedures

In-house casting. Does not hold general auditions. Casting breakdowns are publicly available via the website, postal application (with sae), Equity Job Information Service, *PCR* and advertisements in *The Stage*. Sometimes welcomes letters (with CVs and photographs) but not email submissions. Accepts invitations to view individual actors' websites. Advises that the company mainly works with a regular ensemble of performers and only occasionally meets or auditions newcomers. Members of the ensemble come from a diverse training background (rarely straight from drama school). Does not welcome over-persistent enquiries; the company will make contact if interested in an applicant.

Kneehigh Theatre

14 Walsingham Place, Truro, Cornwall TR1 2RP
Artistic Director Emma Rice

Production details

Stages 3 productions annually with 130 performances during the course of the year. On average tours to 15 venues annually. Performs in arts centres, theatres, outdoor and "out of the ordinary" indoor venues across the UK and internationally. Recent productions include: *A Matter of Life and Death*, *Cymbeline*, *Rapunzel*, and *Brief Encounter*. Offers ITC/Equity approved contracts but does not subscribe to the Equity Pension Scheme.

Casting procedures

Does not hold general auditions. Advises that the company works with a pool of performers, but is interested in meeting new actors – either by personal recommendation or by seeing their work. Actively encourages applications from disabled actors and promotes the use of inclusive casting.

LipService

The Comedy Suite, 116 Longford Road, Manchester M21 9NP
tel 0161-881 0061 *fax* 0161-881 0061
email info@lip-service.net
website www.lipservicetheatre.co.uk
Joint Artistic Directors Sue Ryding, Maggie Fox

Production details

Over the past 20 years, LipService has established itself as one of the leading comedy touring companies, producing shows for the theatre which have a strong base in popular culture. These include: *Jane Bond* (blonde and dangerous; a spoof of all things Bond); *Very Little Women* (a comic version of Louisa May Alcott's *Little Women*); *Hector's House* (an epic tale of togas and taramasalata); *The Importance of Being Earnest* (a trivial comedy for serious people); *Women on the Verge* (a hilarious look at romantic women's fiction); *Move Over Moriarty* (an impenetrable case for Sherlock Holmes and Doctor Watson); and *Withering Looks* (a slice of life with the Bronte Sisters).

LipService attracts audiences from a wide social mix and age range. Based in Manchester, the company has built up a solid touring circuit in the North of England and throughout the rest of Britain. Challenges its audience by setting up a recognisable form and subverting it. This is partly achieved by two women playing all the characters, but also by ingenious theatrical surprises. "Along with the National Theatre of Brent, LipService is one of our great 2-person ensembles." (*The Guardian*)

Casting procedures

Uses casting directors of co-producing venue. Does not hold general auditions. Actors should write requesting inclusion when extra performers are needed for a new production. Casting breakdowns are available direct from the co-producing theatre; details of these are available via the website. Welcomes invitations from actors to view their work, and information from actors familiar with the company's work. Offers TMA/Equity approved contracts. Rarely (or never) has the opportunity to cast disabled actors.

London Actors Theatre Co

Unit 5a, Spaces Business Centre, Ingate Place, London SW8 3NS
tel 020-7978 2620 *fax* 020-7978 2631
email latchmere@fishers.org.uk

Production details

Founded in 1987 and normally stages 1-2 productions annually, employing 6-8 actors on non-Equity contracts.

Casting procedures

Casting breakdowns are published in *PCR* or *The Stage*. Any approaches not relating to a specific breakdown are discouraged.

London Bubble Theatre Co

5 Elephant Lane, London SE16 4JD
tel 020-7237 4434 *fax* 020-7231 2366
email admin@londonbubble.org.uk
website www.londonbubble.org.uk
Artistic Director Jonathan Petherbridge *Associate Director, Community* Sylvan Baker *Associate Director, Education* Sonia Hyams *Associate Director, New Projects* Karen Tomlin

Production details

The company's mission is "to attract and involve a wide range of audiences and participants, particularly those experiencing theatre for the first time, to inventive and unpredictable events that reflect the diversity of our city and its people".

To this end, the company has the following aims:

• To work particularly with and for people who do not normally have access to theatre for geographical, financial or cultural reasons
• To encourage and enable people to develop their own theatre and related skills
• To work to create a popular theatre form which is open, exciting and accessible
• To produce events which demonstrate and celebrate the creative abilities of all those taking part
• To examine issues of common concern to all those involved through the choice of material for workshops, projects and professional performances
• To challenge prejudice and bigotry through the company's organisation, working processes and final product
• To achieve a diversity of influence that is discernible throughout the company's work and consciousness

Recent productions include: *Spangleguts*, *Metamorphoses*, *Myths, Rituals And Whitegoods*, *Jumping The Gap* and *My Home.*

Mad Dogs and Englishmen

The Old Post Office, Green Lane, Quidenham, Norfolk NR16 2AP
tel (01953) 888499 *fax* (01953) 888499
email info@mad-dogs.org.uk
website www.mad-dogs.org.uk
Director Ann Courtney *Administration* Jacqui Merryweather

Production details

Founded in 1995. Theatre company based in Norfolk, whose policy is to provide well-balanced, entertaining and educational drama. Main areas of work are new writing, adaptations and classical work. Stages 2 productions annually with 70 performances during the course of the year, plus 30 workshops for schools. Tours to rural venues (churches, public houses) as well as arts centres, theatres, outdoor venues, educational venues, and community venues. On average 4-9 actors are involved in each production. Recent productions include: *As You Like It* and *Outrageous Nonsense.*

Casting procedures

Sometimes holds general auditions. Audition criteria are published in *PCR* at the appropriate times of the year. Welcomes letters (with CVs and photographs) but not email submissions.

Magnetic North Theatre Productions

18 Brandon Terrace, Edinburgh EH3 5DZ
tel 0131-556 3299 *fax* 0131-556 3299
email mail@magneticnorth.org.uk
website www.magneticnorth.org.uk
Director Nicholas Bone

Production details

Founded in 1999. Commissions and produces new plays: 5 full productions and 1 film have been produced. Also produces 'Rough Mix', a creative development programme for writers and other practitioners. Stages 1-2 productions annually and gives 20-40 performances during the course of a year. Tours on average to 12 venues annually. About 5 actors are involved in each production. Recent productions include: *After Mary Rose, Walden* and *My Old Man*.

Casting procedures

Sometimes holds general auditions. Actors should write to request inclusion when productions are announced on the website. Casting breakdowns are publicly available through the website, postal application (with sae) and *PCR*. Welcomes submissions (with CVs and photographs) sent by post or email. Also accepts invitations to view individual actors' websites. Advises that the company has a low turnover of productions and a small staff, and finds it difficult to respond to general enquiries about available work.

Manchester Actors Company

c/o Administration, PO Box 54,
Manchester M60 7AB
tel 0161-227 8702 *fax* 0161-227 8702
email s.s.boyes@btinternet.com
website www.manactco.org.uk
Artistic Director Stephen Boyes *Administrator* Brian Lavers

Production details

Established in 1980 and now the North West's leading provider of theatre in schools. "We are emphatically *not* a TIE company." Reaches well over 80,000 young people each year with around 6 touring productions. Recent productions include: *The Tempest, Of Mice and Men, The Pirate Queen, Much Ado About Nothing*, and *Poetry in Motion*.

Casting procedures

Uses in-house casting directors and sometimes holds general auditions. Actors may write in June/July requesting inclusion. Casting breakdowns are available via Equity Job Information Service and specific casting websites, for example **www.castingcallpro.com**. Welcomes letters (with CVs and photographs) from individual actors previously unknown to the company, sent by post or email; also welcomes showreels and invitations to view individual actors' websites. Actively encourages applications from disabled actors and promotes the use of inclusive casting. "We give priority to formally trained actors who have completed recognised courses at drama school. We like actors who can face the rigours of touring with good humour!"

Guy Masterson Productions

Millfield House & Theatre, Silver Street, Edmonton,
London N18 1PJ
Director Guy Masterson

Production details

For more than a decade, a successful producer of small- to mid-scale work. Stages 4-6 productions annually with 400 performances during the course of the year. Tours on average to 350 different national and international venues, including arts centres, theatres, and outdoor, educational and community venues. Recent productions include: *Twelve Angry Men, Animal Farm* and *Under Milk Wood*.

Casting procedures

Sometimes holds general auditions. Only works with actors seen on a previous occasion, and then only by invitation.

Meeting Ground Theatre Co

4 Shirley Road, Nottingham NG3 5DA
tel 0115-962 3009
website www.meetingground.org.uk
Director Tanya Myers

Production details

At the heart of the company's artistic policy and vision is the theatrical exploration of what the company calls "the politics of the imagination". Work is based on the belief that, by taking artistic work across barriers and frontiers – whether they be national, psychological, intellectual, cultural, spiritual or disciplinary – new sources of energy and creativity can be engendered.

Since 1985 Meeting Ground has been celebrating the meeting of artists from different disciplines and cultures. Building a strong international reputation for new production work of the highest innovative standards and qualities, the company has toured extensively throughout Germany, Poland, Italy and the UK, also appearing at numerous festivals.

Casting procedures

Offers ITC/Equity contracts and does not subscribe to the Equity Pension Scheme. Actively encourages applications from disabled actors and promotes the use of inclusive casting.

Midland Actors Theatre (MAT)

25 Merrishaw Road, Northfield,
Birmingham B31 3SL
tel 0121-608 7144 *fax* 0121-608 7144
email news@midlandactorstheatre.co.uk
website www.midlandactorstheatre.co.uk
Director David Allen *Associate Director* Gillian Adamson *Secretary* Judith Aston

Production details

Founded in 1999. Produces classics and new work. Stages 2-3 productions annually with 90 performances during the course of the year. Tours on average to 75 different theatres, schools, and other venues in the West Midlands, East Midlands, and nationally each year. Around 4-5 actors are involved in each production. Recent productions include: *Macbeth*, *Prospero's Island*, *The Children* and *The Mothers*. Offers ITC/Equity approved contracts and does not subscribe to the Equity Pension Scheme.

Casting procedures

Sometimes holds general auditions. Actors should write requesting inclusion when auditions are advertised; general casting enquiries are most welcome in January and June. Casting breakdowns are publicly available via Equity Job Information Service and *PCR*. Advises that the company is primarily interested in actors who are Midlands-based. Actively encourages applications from disabled actors and promotes the use of inclusive casting.

Mikron Theatre Company

Marsden Mechanics, Peel Street, Marsden, Huddersfield HD7 6BW
tel (01484) 843701 *fax* (01484) 843701
email admin@mikron.org.uk
website www.mikron.org.uk
Artistic Director Richard Povall *Associate Director* Mike Lucas *General Manager* Peter Toon

Production details

Has been touring for 38 years: "a little touring company with the reputation for tackling large-scale subjects and turning history into vivid and dramatic entertainment". Tours on Tyseley, the company's Narrowboat, on the inland waterways of Britain in the summer, and by road in the autumn months. Almost unique in writing and presenting 2 new plays with original music and songs each year. Tours to every conceivable type of venue, reaching audiences that other companies cannot. Recent productions include: *Married to the Job* and *The Lacemakers* (2007); *Debtonation* and *Fair Trade* (2008).

Casting procedures

Uses in-house casting directors and does not hold general auditions. Actors may write in Dec/Jan to request inclusion, and are strongly advised to keep an eye on the website. Casting breakdowns are publicly available from the website, via Equity Job Information Service and Castweb, and in *PCR*. Welcomes letters (with CVs & photographs) from individual actors previously unknown to the company if sent by post, but not by email, and does not accept showreels. Welcomes invitations to view individual actors' websites. Rarely (or never) has the opportunity to cast disabled actors "because of the nature of our tour – however, our Artistic Director is disabled". Asks actors to "please bear in mind that this is a hard tour: boating all day and shows and get-ins every night. Do consult the website before applying".

Mokita Productions

54 Canning Road, London N5 2JS
mobile (07980) 564849
email mail@mokitaproductions.org
website www.mokitaproductions.org
Artistic Director Emily Agnew *Associate Director* Jane Lesley *Other key personnel* Alfie Talman (Assistant Producer), Lucy Leigh (Funding Manager)

Production details

Established in 2007 "to promote work of an exciting, raw, passionate and original nature". Specialises in new writing and developing work with new and emerging writers; also aims to encourage new and emerging practitioners in directing, producing, design, technical theatre and acting. In general stages 6 productions each year; also works in TIE (contact: Emily Agnew). Recent productions include: *Involution* by Rachel Welch (Pacific Playhouse, London; Pleasance Theatre, Edinburgh); *Pluto* (co-produciton, Blue Elephant Theatre); and Pages (co-production, Pacific Playhouse, London).

Casting procedures

Uses in-house casting directors. Sometimes holds general auditions; actors may write in at any time and details filed for future reference. Casting breakdowns are available from the website, *PCR*, *The Stage*, Castnet, Castweb and Castingcallpro. Welcomes letters (with CVs & photographs) from individual actors previously unknown to the company sent by post, but not by email. Accepts showreels and invitations to view individual actors' websites. Will consider applications from disabled actors to play characters with disabilities.

MonStar Productions

65A Huddleston Road, London N7 0AE
email monstar@fsmail.net
website www.monstarproductions.co.uk
Artistic Director Monique Briggs

Production details

A freelance producer (own shows, co-productions and sole producer). Also works in TIE. Recent productions include: *Love & Human Remarks* by Brad Fraser, directed by Dominic Leclerc at the Warehouse Theatre.

Casting procedures

Uses in-house casting directors. Holds general auditions; actors should write when a casting call goes out. Casting breakdowns are usually available via agents, or by direct email. Welcomes letters (with CVs & photographs) from actors previously unknown to the company sent by post, but not by email. Prefers not to receive invitations to view individual actors' websites, although may accept showreels. Actively encourages applications from

Theatre

disabled actors, and promotes the use of inclusive casting. Offers Equity approved contracts as negotiated through ITC. "An agent is advised."

Mu-Lan Theatre Company

The Albany, Douglas Way, London SE8 4AG
tel 020-8694 0557 *fax* 020-8694 0618
email mailbox@mu-lan.org
website www.mu-lan.org
Director Paul Courtenay

Production details

Founded in 1988. Stages 1 production annually and gives 30 performances during the course of the year. Tours have covered the North West, South and South West England. About 8 actors are involved in each production. Recent productions include: *Sun is Shining, Romeo and Juliet* and *Takeaway*.

Casting procedures

Uses freelance casting directors. Does not hold general auditions. Casting breakdowns are publicly available via *PCR*. Welcomes submissions (with CVs and photographs) sent by post or email. Also accepts invitations to view individual actors' websites.

New Perspectives Theatre Co

Park Lane Business Centre, Park Lane, Basford, Nottingham NG6 0DW
tel 0115-927 2334 *fax* 0115-927 1612
email info@newperspectives.co.uk
website www.newperspectives.co.uk
Artistic Director Daniel Buckroyd *Key personnel* Chris Kirkwood (General Manager), Emma Morley (Administrator), Mandy Ivory-Castile (Production Manager)

Production details

Founded in 1972. A leading East Midlands touring theatre company; also tours nationally. On average stages 3-4 productions each year, giving 200 performances in 190 arts centre and community venues in the East and West Midlands, Wales, London, the South West, and the North. Offers Equity approved contracts as negotiated through ITC. Recent prodcutions include: *On Saturdays This Bed Is Poland* (Lakeside Arts Centre); *The Iron Man* (Darlington Arts Centre; Riverhead Theatre, Louth); *Saturday Night and Sunday Morning* (Lakeside Arts Centre).

Casting procedures

Does not welcome unsolicited approaches. Actively encourages applications by disabled actors and promotes the use of inclusive casting. "Casting breakdowns are available through Spotlight Link and from the website."

NITRO

6 Brewery Road, London N7 9NH
tel 020-7609 1331 *fax* 020-7609 1221
email info@nitro.co.uk
Artistic Director Felix Cross *Executive Producer* Matthew Jones *Administrator* Laura Tomlinson

Production details

Founded in 1978; formerly known as Black Theatre Co-operative Ltd. National touring theatre company that generates and produces contemporary black musical theatre. First established to provide training for black writers, directors and artists. Aims to explore ways of using black music as a means of attracting new audiences to theatre. Stages 1-2 productions annually with 1-2 performances during the course of the year. Recent productions include: *Nitrobeat* and *A Nitro at the Opera*.

Casting procedures

Sometimes uses agents when casting. Also holds general auditions; actors should write at the start of the year to request inclusion. Welcomes submissions (with CVs and photographs) sent by post or email. Accepts invitations to view individual actors' websites. Advises that the company keeps an up-to-date catalogue of black actors and would particularly welcome CVs from actors of different ethnic backgrounds. Offers TMA/Equity approved contracts and does not subscribe to the Equity Pension Scheme. Actively encourages applications from disabled actors and promotes the use of inclusive casting.

No Limits Theatre

Dundas Street, Monkwearmouth, Sunderland SR6 0AY
tel 0191-565 3013 *fax* 0191-565 3015
email info@nolimitstheatre.org.uk
website www.nolimitstheatre.org.uk
Artistic Director/Chief Executive Janet Nettleton
Technical Director Alan Parker

Production details

Founded in 1995, No Limits is a touring theatre company that works with adults with and without learning disabilities. Aims to produce high-quality, devised work that challenges traditional perceptions of theatre and disability, staging 1 production in 20 different venues across the UK each year. It also has a strong commitment to outreach and development work. In general 5-8 actors work on each production. Recent productions include: *I Catch Your Breath* (The Lowry, Manchester); *Silver Street* (The Maltings, Berwick) and *Wall of Whispers* (Blackfriars, Boston).

Casting procedures

Welcomes letters, CVs and photographs from actors previously unknown to the company, but does not accept emails or unsolicited showreels. Advises that the company already has a core acting team but often takes on new actors in workshop training sessions.

Northern Broadsides

Dean Clough, Halifax HX3 5AX
tel (01422) 369704 *fax* (01422) 383175
website www.northern-broadsides.co.uk
Artistic Director Barrie Rutter *Associate Director*
Conrad Nelson

Production details

Formed in 1992 by Artistic Director Barrie Rutter, Northern Broadsides is a multi-award winning touring company based in the historic Dean Clough Mill in Halifax, West Yorkshire. The company has built up a formidable reputation performing Shakespeare and classical texts with an innovative, popular and regional style, often in unconventional locations (The Tower of London, cattle markets, churches, indoor riding stables, Victorian mills). As well as touring extensively in the UK, the company has delighted audiences across the world, touring to India, Brazil, the USA, Greece, Cyprus, the Czech Republic, Poland, Germany, Austria and Denmark.

The company repertoire consists mainly of Shakespeare and classical texts. These plays possess a timeless resonance and their universal exploration of the human condition has currency in any day and age, appealing directly to the soul, the emotions and the imagination. Northern Broadsides are dedicated to interpreting the classics in a manner which makes what is often regarded as 'difficult' work extremely accessible. Their lively 'no frills' approach, with simple storytelling and minimal sets, has not only won the company many plaudits and awards, but enabled both established and new audiences to enjoy Shakespeare regardless of language or theatrical convention.

Northern Broadsides' work is characterised by its vitality and humour; the passion of the performers, whose acting style is far less 'mannered' than conventional theatrical productions; an ensemble style which adds coherence to the performances (the result of working with a group of actors over a period of time, in some cases many years) and precise direction which results in work of remarkable clarity.

NOT the National Theatre

116 Dalberg Road London SW2 1AW
tel 020-7771 0009
email info@notthenational.com
website www.notthenational.com
Artistic Directors Pete Colley, Lilian Evans, Michael Fry and Daniel Leatherdale

Production details

The company was founded in 1984 by 3 National Theatre actors, with the aim of presenting contemporary plays to varied audiences across the UK and beyond. The productions have always been sufficiently flexible to be performed in both conventional and non-conventional theatre spaces in a repertoire which mixes new plays with revivals of modern classics.

The company has now played over 300 venues nationally and internationally. It has toured on consecutive days from the Swan in Stratford to Holloway Jail, and in consecutive weeks from Brazilia to Bucharest. NOT The National Theatre was the first British company to visit Communist Romania and Czechoslovakia, and the first company to play in Argentina after the Falklands War.

Most tours now play between 30 and 50 dates throughout Britain and Ireland on the small and middle-scale circuits. The company has established strong relationships with theatres and audiences across the UK and beyond, which has allowed it widen the scope and boldness of its programming.

In recent years the company has focused on the second productions of new plays that may have had only a limited first run, or the work of a new or established playwright whose work has not been seen on the national circuit. NOT The National Theatre produced the first national tours of (among others) *Hysteria, Two, The Beauty Queen of Leenane, Not a Game for Boys* and *My Mother Said I Never Should*.

NTC Touring Theatre Company

The Playhouse, Bondgate Without, Alnwick, Northumberland NE66 1PQ
tel (01665) 602586 *fax* (01665) 605837
email admin@ntc-touringtheatre.co.uk
website www.ntc-touringtheatre.co.uk
Director Gillian Hambleton *General Manager* Anna Flood *Tour Administrator* Hilary Burns

Production details

Founded in 1978 as Northumberland Theatre Company. Small-scale touring theatre company performing at village halls, small theatres and community venues in predominantly rural areas. Main areas of work are new writing and ensemble physical theatre pieces. Stages 3-4 productions annually with more than 120 performances during the course of the year. Tours on average to 120 different venues nationally. 5 actors are usually involved in each production. Recent productions include: *Bedazzled, Great Expectations* and *Alex, The Warrior & The Winter Star*. Offers ITC/Equity approved contracts but does not subscribe to the Equity Pension Scheme.

Casting procedures

Sometimes holds general auditions for locally based actors (best time to write is early June or September), but most casting is done through agents via *SBS*. Casting breakdowns are available on request via postal application (with sae) and on the website. Welcomes submissions (with CVs and photographs) sent by post. Also accepts invitations to view individual actors' performances and will always reply to individual actors. Particularly interested in locally based actors or actors with local origins, and will keep details on file for future reference unless requested to do otherwise. Actively encourages applications from disabled actors and promotes the use of inclusive casting.

Off the Cuff Theatre Company Ltd

91A Rivington Street, London EC2A 3AY
tel 020-7739 2857 *fax* 020-7739 3852
email otctheatre@aol.com
Artistic Director Paul Dubois

Production details

Stages 1-2 productions annually, with around 30 performances in 2 arts centres and theatres in the UK and internationally. In general, 4-6 actors are involved in each production. Offers Equity-approved contracts as negotiated through ITC, and participates in the Equity Pension Scheme. See the website for details of recent productions.

Casting procedures

Holds general auditions; actors may write in January to request inclusion. Casting breakdowns are available via the website. Welcomes letters (with CVs and photographs) from individual actors previously unknown to the company, sent by post or email. Also welcomes showreels, but prefers not to receive invitations to view individual actors' websites. Actively encourages applications from disabled actors, and promotes the use of inclusive casting.

The Okai Collier Company Ltd

The Bell Tower, St Barnabas Church, Grove Road, Bow, London E3 5TG
tel 020-8981 6511 *fax* 020-8983 0858
email info@okaicollier.co.uk
website www.okaicollier.co.uk
Artistic Director Omar F Okai

Production details

The Okai Collier Company was formed in 1994 by artistic director Omar F Okai and producer Simon James Collier to explore and push the boundaries of everyday ideas, opinions and opportunities in the creative arts: music, theatre, dance, painting and the written word. Using a variety of media including IT, the company aims to break down contemporary social barriers and encourage new talent by developing a range of projects in this field. These projects include award-winning theatrical productions, opera, creative writing with young people, exhibitions for new artists and community arts projects, as well as its innovative publishing division. Okai Collier is committed to maintaining a balanced portfolio of work, divided between the commercial and charitable spheres and drawing on a diverse range of people and disciplines.

Open Clasp Theatre Company

Level 2, 36 Lime Street, Ouseburn Valley, Newcastle upon Tyne NE1 2PQ
tel 0191-230 1698 *fax* 0191-261 7144
email info@openclasp.plus.com
website www.openclasp.org.uk
Artistic Director Catrina McHugh *Company Development Manager* Roma Yagnik

Production details

In 1998 Open Theatre Company began with a simple idea: to use theatre and drama to give a voice to women of all ages. Since then the company has worked in partnership with other community groups, running issue-based drama workshops with women's and girls' groups to create theatre that is taken to community and mainstream venues across the North East. "We work with many women whose voices have never before reached the stage, and whose stories are worth telling. They share them with us, and we create new stories that reflect those experiences and bring them back to the community. We make sure everyone involved has a great time and a good laugh." On average stages 1 touring production per year, usually in Feb-March, with 16-35 performances in 16-30 arts centres, theatres, and educational and community venues in North East UK, Scotland, North West UK and Yorkshire. Recent productions include: *Stand 'N' Tan*, and *A Twist of Lemon*.

Casting procedures

Sometimes holds general auditions; actors requesting inclusion should write in September. Casting breakdowns are available from the website, by postal application with sae, and from online casting services such as www.starnow.co.uk. Welcomes letters (with CVs and photographs) from individual actors previously unknown to the company, sent by post or email, but does not accept showreels. Will consider invitations to view individual actors' websites if accompanied by a full CV. Will also consider applications from disabled actors to play characters with disabilities. "It is paramount that our actors share the ethos of the company. Open Clasp ensures that casting is representative of the diverse groups we work with, the issues explored, and the characters they have created."

The Original Theatre Company

Dovedon Hall, Chedburgh Road, Whepstead, Bury St Edmunds, Suffolk IP29 4UB
tel (01284) 735447
email info@originaltheatre.com
website www.originaltheatre.com
Director Alastair Whatley *Technical Manager* Alan Valentine

Production details

Established in 2004. Stages 3-4 productions annually, with 120-150 performances in 40-50 arts centres, theatres and outdoor venues across the UK. In general 8-13 actors are involved in each production. Offers Equity-approved contracts. Recent productions include: *Vincent in Brixton* (Yvonne Arnaud, Theatre Royal Windsor, Northcott Exeter); *Othello* (Harrogate Theatre, Buxton Opera House).

Casting procedures

Sometimes holds general auditions; actors may write in March and July to request inclusion. Casting breakdowns are available from the website, by postal application with sae, and from Spotlight. Welcomes letters (with CVs and photographs) from individual actors previously unknown to the company, sent by post only. Also welcomes showreels and invitations to view individual actors' websites. Actively encourages applications from disabled actors and promotes the use of inclusive casting.

Out of Joint

7 Thane Works, Thane Villas, London N7 7PH
tel 020-7609 0207 *fax* 020-7609 0203
email ojo@outofjoint.co.uk
website www.outofjoint.co.uk
Director Max Stafford-Clark *Administrator and Education Manager* Natasha Ockrent *Producer* Graham Cowley

Production details

Stages 2 productions annually with approximately 230 performances during the course of the year. Tours both nationally and internationally playing to around 12-15 arts centres and theatres each year. Recent productions include: *Duck, The Permanent Way, Macbeth* and *Talking to Terrorists.*

Casting procedures

Welcomes letters (with CVs and photographs) but not email submissions. Also accepts performance notices from individual actors. Offers Equity approved contracts. Will consider applications from disabled actors to play characters with disabilities.

Ovation Productions

Upstairs at The Gatehouse, Highgate,
London N6 4BD
tel 020-8340 4256
website www.ovationtheatres.com
Director John Plews *Casting Director* Katie Plews

Production details

Founded in 1985. Owns and operates Upstairs at the Gatehouse, a fringe theatre in North London (see entry under *Fringe theatres* on page 263). Recent productions include: *Into the Woods* and *Cooking with Elvis.*

Casting details

Casting breakdowns are publicly available via *PCR* and advertisements in *The Stage*. Welcomes letters (with CVs and photographs) and email submissions. "Castings are always posted on **www.upstairsatthegatehouse.com**." Offers non-Equity contracts. Will consider applications from disabled actors to play characters with disabilities.

The Oxford Shakespeare Company

3 Gunter Grove, London SW10 0UN
tel 020-7351 5417
email info@oxfordshakespearecompany.co.uk
website www.oxfordshakespeare.company.co.uk
Directors Kevin Hosier, Charlotte Windmill, Nick Green

Production details

Founded in 2001. Took over from Bold and Saucy (established in 1992), staging Shakespeare plays in Wadham College Gardens, Oxford. Also has a residency at North Garden, Lincoln's Inn, London. Stages 3 productions with 90-100 performances during the course of the year. 9-10 actors are involved in each production. Tours have reached Oxford, London and Basingstoke. Recent productions include: *Merry Wives of Windsor* and *Macbeth.*

Casting procedures

Actors requesting inclusion should write in March or April. Casting breakdowns are released to agents and are available via *PCR*. Welcomes letters (with CVs and photographs) but not email submissions. Actors applying should be able to demonstrate experience of Shakespeare and the rigours of open-air performing.

Oxford Stage Company – now Headlong Theatre

Oxfordshire Theatre Company

The Annexe, SS Mary & John School, Meadow Lane, Oxford OX4 1TJ
tel (01865) 249444
website www.oxfordshiretheatrecompany.co.uk
Artistic Director Karen Simpson *Administrative Director* Louise Wiggins

Production details

Tours high-quality, challenging, entertaining and accessible theatre to audiences in Oxfordshire and beyond. The company has a unique reputation for taking theatre to non-theatre venues, especially in rural areas. Creates a minimum of 3 productions each year, each of which has a resonance with both adults and younger audiences. The autumn production appeals to families with young children; the spring show embraces narratives that challenge, engage and excite adult audiences. From 2009 the company is producing a summer production that will actively encourage young people and older people to become a more prominent part of its audience.

Casting procedures

The company casts by audition. Breakdowns are published on the website as well as in *PCR, SBS,*

Theatre

Castcall, and Casting Call Pro, among others. Is unable to consider unsolicited submssions at other times. Actively encourages applications from disabled actors and promotes the use of inclusive casting.

Paines Plough

4th Floor, 43 Aldwych, London WC2B 4DN
tel 020-7240 4533 *fax* 020-7240 4534
email office@painesplough.com
website www.painesplough.com
Artistic Director Roxana Silbert *General Manager* Anneliese Davidson *Literary Director* Tessa Walker *Administrative Assistant* Clare Martynski

Production details

Founded in 1974, the company is dedicated to producing new writing. Stages 3-4 productions annually across the UK and internationally. Recent work includes: Mark Ravenhill's *Shoot/Get Treasure/Repeat*, and Steve Thompson's *Roaring Trade*.

Casting procedures

Uses freelance casting directors. Does not accept unsolicited CVs or photographs, as there is no facility to store such information.

Pentabus

Bromfield, Ludlow, Shropshire SY8 2JU
tel (01584) 856564 *fax* (01584) 856254
email john@pentabus.co.uk
website www.pentabus.co.uk
Development Director John Moreton *Artistic Director* Orla O'Loughlin

Production details

Founded in 1974, Pentabus is a national touring company focused on the development and production of new writing. Stages 1-2 productions annually and gives 20-60 performances during the course of the year. In general 5 actors are involved in each production. Tours annually to about 10 different arts centres, theatres and outdoor venues. Recent productions include: *Silent Engine* by Julian Garner; *Precious Bane* by Bryony Lavery. Actors are also used in writing development workshops as well as in productions.

Casting procedures

Occasionally uses freelance casting directors. Casting breakdowns are available via Equity Job Information Service, *PCR* and the website. Welcomes letters (with CVs and photographs) but not email submissions.

People Show

Pollard Row, London E2 6NB
tel 020-7729 1841 *fax* 020-7739 0203
email people@peopleshow.co.uk
website www.peopleshow.co.uk
Steering Group Chahine Yavroyan, Mark Long,

George Khan, Gareth Brierley, Sadie Cook, Fiona Creese, Jessica Worral *General Manager* David Duchin

Production details

The longest-running experimental theatre company in the UK, touring nationally and internationally for 43 years. In general stages 1-2 productions each year, with 20-40 performances at 10 venues including arts centres, theatres, and outdoor and site-specific venues. Anything from 3 to 65 actors are involved in each production. Offers Equity-approved contracts as negotiated through ITC. Recent credits include: *People Show 118: The Birthday Tour* (Northern Stage, Contact Theatre, Arena Theatre, Lighthouse, Tobacco Factory, New Cut Arts Centre, Alsager Arts Centre, Gardner Arts Centre, Windsor Arts Centre, Unity Theatre); and *People Show 119: Ghost Sonata* (site-specific show commissioned for Liverpool Capital of Culture at Sefton Park Palm House, Liverpool).

Casting procedures

Does not use freelance casting directors or hold general auditions. Welcomes letters (with CVs and photographs) from actors previously unknown to the company sent by post and email. Is happy to receive showreels and invitations to view individual actors' websites. Actively encourages applications from disabled actors and promotes the use of inclusive casting. "People Show is an ensemble company with a core group of 8 artists, and an extended network of 45+."

Pilot Theatre Co

York Theatre Royal, St Leonards Place, York YO1 7HD
tel (01904) 635755 *fax* (01904) 656378
email info@pilot-theatre.com
website www.pilot-theatre.com
Artistic Director Marcus Romer

Production details

Pilot Theatre Company is a national touring theatre company based in Yorkshire. The company was launched in 1981 by a group of students from Bretton Hall College and established itself in Wakefield. Throughout the 1980s worked as a devising collective responding reactively to requests for work. The projects that followed ranged from playscheme activities to workshop sessions to touring issue-based work in schools. In 1994, underwent an internal restructuring which resulted in the appointment of a new Artistic Director, Marcus Romer.

"Between 1994 and 1997 Pilot developed its touring circuit nationally. The last 3 schools' touring shows showed an increase of earned income by 600% and an increase in audiences from 5000 to over 18,000 per tour. *Lord of the Flies*, our first midscale touring project, reached an audience of 50,000 per tour. Collaborating with nationally significant venues the Theatre Royal York and the Lyric Theatre Hammersmith, the project has enabled Pilot to reach more young people than ever before, with a full workshop programme available to every tour venue, and teacher resources available to every teacher through the Pilot website."

Casting procedures

The company regularly posts casting information online. "Please try and avoid sending surface mail for casting, as we are trying to minimise wastage and energy usage." Please email your details to: **casting@pilot-theatre.com**.

Playbox Theatre (Generator)

The Dream Factory, Shelly Avenue, Warwick CV34 6LE
tel (01926) 419555 *fax* (01926) 411429
email stewart@playboxtheatre.com
website www.playboxtheatre.com
Artistic Director Stewart McGill *Directors* Emily Quash, Mary King

Production details

Established in 1986, Generator is the professional acting company of Playbox Theatre, reworking classic drama for contemporary audiences. 2 productions staged annually, touring nationally to arts centres, theatres, outdoor venues and educational venues. Based in Warwick. Up to 12 actors used in each production. Offers Equity approved contracts. Recent productions include: *A Doll's House*, and *Henry VI – The Wars of the Roses*.

Casting procedures

Accepts submissions (with CVs and photographs) from actors previously unknown to the company sent by post or by email. Actively encourages applications from disabled actors and promotes the use of inclusive casting.

Point Blank

Unit 2, 67 Earl Street, Sheffield S1 4PY
tel 0114-249 3650/51 *fax* 0114-249 3655
email info@pointblank.org.uk
website www.pointblank.org.uk
Directors Liz Tomlin, Steve Jackson *Company Manager* Bianca King

Production details

Established in 1999. Small-scale national touring theatre producing new work, devised, physical theatre and new writing. Stages 1 production annually. 30-60 performances per year touring 18 venues which include art centres, theatres, outdoor venues, educational and community venues. Regions covered include North, North West, Yorkshire, West

Midlands, South East, London, Scotland, Ireland and Wales. 2-4 actors are involved in each production. Actors are employed under Equity approved contracts negotiated through ITC. Recent productions include: *Operation Wonderland* (15 venues including The Crucible, Latchmere and The Traverse); *Roses and Morphine* (18 venues including The Crucible, Royal Exchange and Aberystwith Arts Centre); and *Last Orders* (Sheffield, site-specific).

Casting procedures

Casting is carried out by in-house casting director. Hold general auditions. Actors can write at anytime to request inclusion; details will be kept on file. Casting breakdowns are obtainable via casting websites. Accepts submissions (with CVs and photographs) from individual actors previously unknown to the company. Applications from disabled actors are considered to play disabled characters whereever possible.

"Research the company first to check it's appropriate. We will get back with details of shows as appropriate. Yorkshire-based actors are particularly welcome to apply."

Prime Productions

54 Hermiston Village, Currie, Midlothian EH14 4AQ
tel/fax 0131-449 4055
email primeproductions@talktalk.net
website www.primeproductions.co.uk
Artistic Director Martin Heller

Production details

Founded in 1985, operates small-scale touring of mainstream drama throughout Scotland; project funded by Scottish Arts Council. 1 production is staged each year, touring around 30 venues – arts centres, theatres, educational and community venues. Between 4 and 10 actors are involved in each production. Recent productions include: *Great Expectations, Further than the Furthest Thing, Romeo & Juliet, Mary Queen of Scots Got Her Head Chopped Off* and *Sunset Song*.

Casting procedures

Casts in-house. Casting breakdowns are not publicly available, and the company does not welcome unsolicited approaches from actors, although it is happy to receive invitations to view individual actors' websites. "We stage productions with very specific casting requirements, which we seek at the time."

Primecut Productions

285A Ormerth Road, Belfast BT7 3GG
tel 028-90645101 *fax* 028-90645101
email info@primecutproductions.co.uk
website www.primecutproductions.co.uk

Production details

An independent touring company based in Belfast and bringing the best of contemporary international

Theatre

playwrights to Irish audiences. Recent productions include: a double bill of *The Mercy Seat*, and *Ashes to Ashes* at the Belfast Lyric; and touring productions of Caryl Churchill's *A Number* and Owen McCaffery's *Cold Comfort*. The company stages 2-3 productions per year and tours to 10-15 venues across Northern and Southern Ireland.

Casting procedures

Does not publish casting breakdowns, but welcomes CVs and photographs from individual actors whose work is previously unknown to the the company; also welcomes invitations to view actors' websites. Will consider applications from disabled actors when casting for characters with disabilities. Offers ITC/Equity approved contracts.

Proteus Theatre Co

Queen Mary's College, Cliddesden Road,
Basingstoke, Hants RG21 3HF
tel (01256) 354541 *fax* (01256) 350186
email info@proteustheatre.com
website www.proteustheatre.com
Artistic Director Mary Swan

Production details

Established in 1981. Touring theatre company operating in the South. Stages 2-3 productions annually touring to 80 venues including arts centres, theatres, outdoor venues, educational and community venues and churches. Recent credits include *Peter Pan* and *Whatever Happened to Bette and Joan?*

Casting procedures

Casting breakdowns available via the website, Equity Job Information service and *PCR*. Does not welcome unsolicited CVs. Actively encourages applications from disabled actors and promotes the use of inclusive casting. Offers ITC/Equity approved contracts.

Purple Fish Productions

197 Goldhawk Road, London W12 8EP
mobile (07976) 809693
email info@purplefishproductions.co.uk
website www.purplefishproductions.co.uk
Directors Michelle Seton, Luan de Burgh

Production details

Founded in 2001. Aims to produce both established work and exciting devised pieces for adults and children. Michelle Seton and Luan de Burgh both trained in London and at Le Coq in Paris. Stages 3 productions with 75 performances during the course of the year. Tours to 20 different arts centres, theatres, educational and community venues annually. Tours have covered Greater London, Ireland and Canada. In general 2 actors are involved

in each production. Recent productions include: *Told by a Dodo* and *The Two of Us*.

Casting procedures

Casting breakdowns are available via *PCR* and the website. Welcomes letters (with CVs and photographs) but not email submissions. Actors should write only when the company advertises. Invitations to view individual actors' websites are also accepted.

Pursued by a Bear

The Maltings, Bridge Square, Farnham,
Surrey GU9 7QR
email pbab@pbab.org

Production details

Theatre company touring new writing across the UK. Stages 2 productions annually and gives 60 performances during the course of the year. Tours to around 10 different arts centres, theatres, educational and community venues each year. Tours have covered the East, North East, South East, South West and London. In general 2 actors are involved in each production. Recent productions include: *Double Helix, You Don't Kiss* and *All Fall Away*.

Casting procedures

Welcomes submissions (with CVs and photographs) sent by post or email.

Raised Eyebrow Theatre Company

Low Hall Cottage, Carr Lane, Brompton,
Scarborough YO13 9DH
tel/fax (01723) 850538
email admin@raisedeyebrow.co.uk
website www.raisedeyebrow.co.uk
Artistic Director Lizi Patch *Associate Director* Jon Stokes

Production details

A community and TIE company staging 2-3 productions each year and presenting approximately 220 performances in schools and community venues across England. The company also runs youth theatres and workshops. In general 5 actors work on each production. Recent productions include: *Farmer Charles*, Raised Eyebrow Youth Theatre; *Destination 2014*, for Capacity Builders conference in Birmingham; *The Street Never Ends* and *The Wave*, Filey Festival; *The Past on Your Doorstep*, Chaddeston Park and Osmaston Park, Derby; *A Midsummer Murder*, The Old Mill, Langtoft Abbey House (in partnership with Derbyshire-based Orange Box Design); *Space Pirates – Adventures on Planet Maths*, Tour; *Spike* (in partnership with Scarborough Safer Communities); and *A Midsummer Night's Dream* (Raised Eyebrow Youth Theatre).

Casting procedures

Casting is done in-house and with the help of freelance casting directors. Casting breakdowns are available by postal application (with sae), and in *PCR* and *The Stage*. Welcomes letters and emails (with professional CVs and 10x8 photographs) from actors previously unknown to the company. Will also accept showreels and emails. Advises that professional applications will be given priority over photocopies, passport photos and holiday snaps.

Real Circumstance Theatre Company

100 Lexden Road, West Bergholt,
Colchester CO6 3BW
email info@realcircumstance.com
website www.realcircumstance.com
Artistic Director Dan Sherer *Creative Producer* Anna Bewick *Key personnel* Suresh Patel, Ruth Brock

Production details

Established in 2006 with 3 aims: to produce innovative theatre consisting of new writing by emergent authors, and new plays created by the Company through long-term real-time improvisation; to help young theatre-practitioners develop their crafts (both before and after professional training) and investigate new ways of working; and to raise the profile of Essex and the Eastern Region as a national centre of creative artistic work. Tours 1 Studio Production each year, to the community. Recent productions include: *LIMBO* by Declan Feenan, and *Lough/Rain* by Declan Feenan and Clara Brennan (both co-produced with York Theatre Royal).

Casting procedures

Uses in-house casting directors. Sometimes holds general auditions; actors may write at any time to request inclusion. Welcomes letters (with CVs and photographs) from actors previously unknown to the company, and accepts submissions by email. Welcomes showreels and invitations to view individual actors' websites. Offers Equity approved contracts negotiated through ITC.

Red Ladder Theatre Co

3 St Peter's Buildings, York Street, Leeds LS9 8AJ
tel 0113-245 5311 *fax* 0113-245 5351
email rod@redladder.co.uk
website www.redladder.co.uk
Artistic Director Rod Dixon

Production details

Red Ladder's mission is to make theatre which celebrates, inspires and challenges young people, developing in them the desire and ability to express ideas and strengthen social and cultural cohesion. The company, founded in 1968 in London, has a colourful history. It spans 40 years, from the radical socialist theatre movement in Britain known as agitprop, to its current position.

The company moved to Leeds in the 70s and is still based in the city. During the 80s it redefined itself,

changing its cooperative structure to a hierarchy and specialising in targeted work for youth audiences. Acknowledged today as one of Britain's leading national touring companies producing high-quality new plays for youth audiences.

Recent productions include: *Where's Vietnam?* by BAFTA-nominated writer Alice Nutter, and *Forgotten Things* by Emma Adams.

The Red Room

Garden Studios, 11-15 Betterton Street,
Covent Garden, London WC2H 9BP
tel 020-7470 8790 *fax* 020-7379 0801
email info@theredroom.org.uk
website www.theredroom.org.uk
Artistic Director Topher Campbell *Producer* Bryan Savery *Administrator* Claire StanleyTanya Campbell

Production details

Founded in 1995. Produces new theatre & film work which frees the imagination to challenge the status quo. Creates groundbreaking collaborations between writers, artists and communities to provoke and influence wider social debate. Engages in cultural activism, including bi-monthly RRPlatform events. Stages 1-2 productions annually with 25-50 performances during the course of the year. Tours to international and national locations. In general, fewer than 5 actors (often with ability to work in a devised way) are involved in each production. Recent productions include: *Unstated*, July 2008 (sold out at the Southwark Playhouse, London), *Journeys to Work*, *Hoxton Story*, *Animal*, *The Bogus Woman* and *Stitching*.

Casting procedures

Accepts emailed CVs and photographs - no letters or telephone enquiries please. Offers ITC/Equity approved contracts where possible. Does not subscribe to Equity pension scheme. Actively encourages applications from disabled actors and promotes the use of inclusive casting.

Red Rose Chain

1 Fore Hamlet, Ipswich, Suffolk IP3 8AA
tel (01473) 288886 *fax* (01473) 288682
email info@redrosechain.com
website www.redrosechain.com
Directors Joanna Carrick, David Newborn, Jimmy Grimes

Production details

A film and theatre company which spends every summer outdoors with its theatre-in-the-forest event. Runs workshops and develops new writing. "Our diverse work all serves to underpin Red Rose Chain's aim: to use theatre and film to challenge thinking and make connections with those who are normally ignored or avoided by mainstream arts." Stages 4 productions annually, with 50 performances in 20 venues including arts centres, theatres, and outdoor, educational and community venues in East Anglia. In general 3-12 actors are involved in each production. Recent productions include: *A Winter's Tale* (Rendlesham Forest); *Slide Down the Rainbow* (Nowton Park); and *I love Kitkats* (Red Rose Chain).

Casting procedures

Sometimes holds general auditions; casting breakdowns are available via the website. Welcomes letters (with CVs and photographs) from individual actors previously unknown to the company, sent by post or email. Also welcomes showreels and invitations to view individual actors' websites. Actively encourages applications from disabled actors and promotes the use of inclusive casting.

Red Shift Theatre Company

PO Box 60151, London SW19 2TB
tel/fax 020-8540 1271
email jonathan@redshifttheatreco.co.uk
website www.redshifttheatreco.co.uk
Artistic Director Jonathan Holloway

Production details

Red Shift is a London-based company which tours nationally to small-scale theatres (under 300 seats) and middle-scale (300+ seats) venues throughout the UK. The company also plays London, and has an enviable reputation established over many years as successful participants in the Edinburgh Festival. The company has toured abroad to Alexandria, Cairo, Santiago de Chile and Hong Kong, under the auspices of the British Council. Red Shift has a very distinctive style which has evolved out of the interests of its founding director, Jonathan Holloway.

Casting procedures

Casting breakdowns are advertised on the company's website. Submissions should be made in writing including CV, photo (not returnable) and covering letter stating why you want to work with Red Shift. Applicants must possess a full clean driving licence and be prepared to drive company vehicles. "Bulk submissions from agents not welcome."

Rejects Revenge Theatre Company

The Annexe, 15 Hope Street, Liverpool L1 9BH
tel 0151-708 8480 *fax* 0151-708 8480
email rejects.revenge@virgin.net
website www.rejectsrevenge.com
Director Ann Farrar *Administrator* Adrian Watts

Production details

Founded in 1990. Tours physical comedy to small and midscale venues in the UK and abroad. Stages 1-3 productions annually with 60-90 performances during the course of the year. Tours to 50-70

different arts centres, theatres, educational and community venues across the UK each year. In general 3-4 actors are involved in each production. Recent productions include: *Peasouper* and *Bicycle Bridge*.

Casting procedures

Uses freelance casting directors. Sometimes holds general auditions. Casting breakdowns are available via Equity Job Information Service and the website. Welcomes letters (with CVs and photographs) but not email submissions. Invitations to view individual actors' websites are also accepted.

Reveal Theatre Company

40 Pirehill Lane, Walton, Stone,
Staffordshire ST15 0JN
tel (01782) 745386
email robert.marsden@revealtheatre.co.uk
website www.revealtheatre.co.uk
Artistic Director Robert Marsden *Associate Director* Andrew Raffle *Designer* Laura Clarkson

Production details

Established in 1999. A professional small to middle-scale producing company for touring and residency. Also has a strong Outreach deparment. Stages on average 4 productions each year. Recent productions include: *Game On* and *The Most Dangerous Man in England*.

Casting procedures

Uses in-house casting directors; casting breakdowns are available via the website and in *PCR*. Actors may write at any time requesting inclusion. Welcomes submissions (with CVs and photographs) sent by post, but not by email. Also welcomes showreels, and invitations to view individual actors' websites. Offers Equity approved contracts as negotiated through ITC. Will consider applications from disabled actors to play characters with disabilities.

Richmond Productions

47 Moor Mead Road, St Margaret's,
Twickenham TW1 1JS
Director Alister Cameron

Production details

Founded in 1993. International touring company producing small-cast comedies. Stages 2 productions annually. Tours to hotels in the Middle East and Eastern Europe. Offers non-Equity contracts. Rarely (or never) has the opportunity to cast disabled actors.

Casting procedures

Advises that the company only uses actors already known to it.

Riding Lights Theatre Company

Friargate Theatre, Lower Friargate, York YO1 9SL
tel (01904) 655317

website www.ridinglights.org
Artistic Director Paul Burbridge *Artistic Associates* Sean Cavanagh, Bridget Foreman

Production details

Initially a community theatre project founded in York in 1977, today Riding Lights is touring up to 3 diverse companies simultaneously throughout the UK and abroad. The company is recognised both as a pioneer in reinstating the value of theatre in Christian communication and for significant original and artistic achievement. Recent productions include: *Flight Cases* and *African Show* (co-production with York Theatre Royal).

Rifco Arts

The West Wing Arts Centre, Stoke Road, Slough, Berkshire SL2 5AY
tel (01753) 570700
website www.rifcoarts.com
Director Pravesh Kumar

Production details

An international multicultural touring theatre company that "wants audiences to deal with contemporary and at times taboo subjects whilst still being able to laugh at the world we live in". Stages 1 production annually, with around 70 performances in 6 arts centres and theatres in the UK and Pakistan. In general 2-17 actors go on tour. Offers Equity-approved contracts as negotiated through ITC. Recent productions include: *Where's My Desi Soulmate* (Theatre Royal Stratford East; Arts Depot, North London); and *It Ain't All Bollywood* (Alhambra Studio, Arts Depot).

Casting procedures

Sometimes holds general auditions; advises actors to keep an eye on the press for casting calls. Welcomes letters (with CVs and photographs) from individual actors previously unknown to the company, sent by post or email; also accepts showreels and invitations to view individual actors' websites. Will consider applications from disabled actors to play characters with disabilities.

Rocket Theatre

32 Baxter Road, Sale, Manchester M33 3AL
tel 0161-969 1444 *mobile* (07788) 723570
email martin@rockettheatre.co.uk
website www.rockettheatre.co.uk
Director Martin Harris

Production details

Rocket Theatre was set up in 1995 and for 10 years produced work in Manchester and toured throughout the North of England with regional premieres of work originally staged by some of London's new-writing venues (particularly the Royal Court, the Bush and the National). The company has also produced some completely new plays and has won various awards for its work over that time. Previous productions inlcoude: *I Licked a Slag's Deodorant* by Jim Cartwright; *Howie the Rookie* by Mark O'Rowe; *A Skull in Connemara* by Martin McDonagh; and *Dealer's Choice* by Patrick Marber – as well as several new plays by Jim Burke. The company is currently looking to re-launch with several new projects over the next few years: see the website for details. Rocket Theatre is interested in hearing of any interesting collaboration opportunities with other companies or individuals.

Casting procedures

Casting breakdowns are available on the Rocket website and through various industry casting resources. Does not welcome applications from actors unless casting is called for specific parts. No emailed applications.

Scamp Theatre Ltd

44 Church Lane, Arlesey, Bedfordshire SG15 6UX
tel (01462) 734843 *fax* (01462) 730878
email admin@scamptheatre.com
website www.scamptheatre.com
Directors Jennifer Sutherland, Louise Callow

Production details

Established in 2003. An independent production company staging 4 shows annually, with more than 100 performances in the same number of theatres across the UK. In general 3 actors are involved in each production. Offers Equity-approved contracts as negotiated through ITC. Recent productions include: *Private Peaceful* by Michael Morpurgo (West End, Edinburgh); and *Aesop's Fables* (UK, Australia & New Zealand tour).

Casting procedures

Uses freelance casting directors. Welcomes unsolicited CVs and photographs sent by email only, and accepts invitations to view individual actors' websites. Will consider applications from disabled actors to play characters with disabilities.

Scarlet Theatre

Studio 4, The Bull, 68 High Street, Barnet EN5 5SJ
tel 020-8441 9779 *fax* 020-8447 0075
email admin@scarlettheatre.co.uk
website www.scarlettheatre.co.uk
Director Grainne Byrne

Production details

A touring theatre company founded in 1982 which stages between 2 and 6 productions each year. On average the company tours to 10 venues across the UK, Ireland and the rest of Europe annually, with anywhere between 2-10 actors working on each production. Recent productions include: *The Chair Women* (Riverside Studios and Traverse Theatre) and *The Wedding* (Southwark Playhouse).

Casting procedures

Casting is done in-house and actors are welcome to write or email with their CVs and photographs. The company prefers not to receive showreels unless it has requested them.

Sgript Cymru

Chapter, Market Road, Canton, Cardiff CF5 1QE
tel 029-2023 6650
email sgriptcymru@sgriptcymru.com
website www.sgriptcymru.com
Director Simon Harris *Administrative Director* Mai Jones

Production details

Founded in 2000 and funded by the Arts Council of Wales, Sgript Cymru is a strategic new writing theatre company. Stages 3 productions annually and gives 75 performances during the course of the year. Tours to 25 different arts centres, theatres, and community venues in Wales, Scotland, London and the North West. In general 5 actors are involved in each production. Recent productions include: *Crossings* by Clare Duffy and *The Life of Ryan... and Ronnie* by Meic Povey.

Casting procedures

Uses freelance casting directors. Welcomes letters (with CVs and photographs) but not email submissions. Offers ITC/Equity approved contracts. Will consider applications from disabled actors to play characters with disabilities.

Shakespeare at The Tobacco Factory

Raleigh Road, Southville, Bristol BS3 ITF
tel 0117-936 3054
email office@sattf.org.uk
website www.sattf.org.uk
Artistic Director Andrew Hilton *General Manager* Sophie Jerrold

Production details

Established in 2000. 2 productions staged annually with 80 performances. Up to 18 actors used in each production. Performances in Bristol and London. Recent productions include: *Julius Caesar* and *Antony and Cleopatra*.

Casting procedures

Casting breakdowns available via the website. Accepts submissions (with CVs and photographs) from actors previously unknown to the company if sent by post and via email. Invitations to view individual actors' websites are also accepted. Actors writing to request inclusion should make contact in Oct/Nov. Rarely has the opportunity to cast disabled actors.

Shared Experience

13 Riverside House, 27-29 Vauxhall Grove, London SW8 1SY
tel 020-7587 1596 *fax* 020-7735 0374
email admin@sharedexperience.org.uk
website www.sharedexperience.org.uk
Joint Artistic Directors Nancy Meckler, Polly Teale
Administrative Producer Jon Harris

Production details

An award-winning theatre company founded during the 1970s, Shared Experience stages 2-3 productions annually and tours to different arts centres and theatres in the UK and abroad. In general 6-10 actors are involved in each production. Recent productions include: *The Caucasian Chalk Circle*, *A Passage to India*, *Jane Eyre*, *Kindertransport* and *War and Peace*.

Casting procedures

Uses freelance casting directors. Advises that actors should contact Hanna Osmolska by phone to enquire about the current casting director. "Please do not send unsolicited mail." Offers TMA/Equity approved contracts. Actively encourages applications from disabled actors and promotes the use of inclusive casting.

Sphinx Theatre Company

13 Riverside House, 27/29 Vauxhall Grove, London SW8 1SY
tel 020-7587 1596
email info@sphinxtheatre.co.uk
website www.sphinxtheatre.co.uk
Artistic Director Sue Parrish *Administrator* Louisa Fitzgerald

Production details

Established 30 years ago, the company specialises in writing, directing and developing roles for women. Recent productions include: *Blame* by Judith Jones and Beatrix Campbell, and *The Berlin Cabaret*.

Casting procedures

Casting breakdowns are available via email and/or postal application (with CVs and photographs). Offers Equity approved contracts. Will consider applications from disabled actors to play characters with disabilities.

Suspect Culture

CCA, 350 Sauchiehall Street, Glasgow G2 3TD
tel 0141-332 9775 *fax* 0141-332 8823
email info@suspectculture.com
website www.suspectculture.com
Director Graham Eatough *Administrative Producer* Purni Morell

Production details

Suspect Culture was formed in 1990 by Graham Eatough, David Greig and Nick Powell. Early productions include: *One Way Street* (1995), *Airport* (1996), *Timeless* (1997) and *Mainstream* (1999). The company is based in Glasgow and tours 1-2 productions throughout Scotland and internationally each year. Generally uses 2-6 actors on each production. Recent productions include: *8000m* (Tramway, Glasgow) and *One-Two* (Traverse, Edinburgh; Contact Theatre, Manchester; MAC, Birmingham; Tron, Glasgow; Byre Theatre, St Andrews; Lemon Tree, Northampton; Tolbooth, Stirling and Paisley Arts Centres).

"To us, a collaborative approach means giving text, design, music and performance equal weight in all our work. The director, writer, designer and composer are involved from the very beginning of each new idea, which is then developed through a long process of workshops and rehearsal before being presented to an audience. This emphasis on collaboration is reflected in the way we credit artists and assign authorship, which is always shared among the artistic team."

Casting procedures

Suspect Culture does not hold formal auditions, but rather open workshops which are by invitation. This gives the company a chance to meet practitioners it hasn't worked with before (and vice versa). The company welcomes letters, emails, showreels, invitations to view actors' websites, CVs and photographs from actors – but asks all applicants to gain a full understanding of Suspect's particular working methods before writing. Only rarely employs actors who have not seen at least some of Suspect's work.

TABS Productions

57 Chamberlain Place, London E17 6AZ
tel 020-8527 9266
email adrianmljamcs@aol.com
website www.tabsproductions.co.uk
Directors Adrian Lloyd-James, Karen Henson

Production details

Founded 15 years ago, the company stages approximately 6 productions each year totalling around 300 performances. It has produced No 1 and middle-scale tours and has co-produced with repertory theatre companies. Generally tours to about 45 different arts centres, theatres and outdoor venues across the UK annually. The average cast size is 4-8 actors.

Casting procedures

Welcomes letters, CVs and photographs from actors previously unknown to the company, but does not accept emails or showreels. Actors should only write when a job has been advertised to agents through *SBS*. Occasionally offers Equity approved contracts. Rarely (or never) has the opportunity to cast disabled actors.

Taking Flight Theatre Company

79 Kings Road, Canton, Cardiff CF11 9DB
tel 029-2064 5505
email takingflighttheatre@yahoo.co.uk
website www.takingflighttheatre.com
Directors Beth House, Elise Davison *Chair* Clark Baim

Production details

Established in 2007. Holds residential workshops with physically disabled adults. Accessible, professional promenade productions with integrated casts / support teams. Stages 1-2 productions annually, with around 15 performances in 5 outdoor venues across South Wales. In general 6-10 actors are involved in each production. Recent productions include: *A Midsummer Night's Dream* (National Trust, National Botanical Gardens, CADW, Afan Forest).

Casting procedures

Sometimes holds general auditions and actors may write at any time to request inclusion. Casting breakdowns are publicly available via the website, Equity Job Information Service and Casting Call Pro, as well as from the Disability Arts Cymru site. Welcomes letters (with CVs and photographs) from individual actors previously unknown to the company sent by post or email, as well as showreels and invitations to view individual actors' websites. Actively encourages applications from disabled actors and promotes the use of inclusive casting. "We are very eager to hear from disabled and / or deaf actors."

Talawa Theatre Company

Ground Floor, 53-55 East Road, London N1 6AH
tel 020-7251 6644 *fax* 020-7251 5956
email hq@talawa.com
website www.talawa.com
Director Patricia Cumper *Interim CEO* Nadia Stern

Production details

Founded in 1986, Talawa is one of Britain's leading Black Theatre companies. "We give voice to the Black British experience and we nurture, develop and support talent. We cultivate Black audiences for Black work. In doing so we enrich British theatre." Offers ITC/Equity contracts and does not subscribe to the Equity Pension Scheme.

Casting procedures

Welcomes submissions (with CVs and photographs) sent by post or email. Actively encourages applications from disabled actors and promotes the use of inclusive casting.

Tamasha Theatre Company

Unit 220 Great Guildford Business Square,
30 Great Guildford Street, London SE1 0HS
tel 020-7633 2270 *fax* 020-7021 0421

email info@tamasha.org.uk
website www.tamasha.org.uk
Artistic Directors Kristine Landon-Smith, Sudha
Bhuchar *Executive Director* Alex Darbyshire

Production details

Founded in 1989. Produces "untold stories" in
mainstream theatre venues. Stages 2-3 productions
annually and gives approximately 60 performances
during the course of the year. Tours annually to
small- and mid-scale theatre venues in London and
regionally (e.g. Yorkshire, the Midlands and the
South West). In general 2-15 actors are involved in
each production. Recent productions include: *A Fine
Balance*, *The Trouble with Asian Men* and *Strictly
Dandia*.

Casting procedures

Only holds auditions when casting for a specific
production. Tends to use own files when inviting
people to audition plus possibly *SBS* breakdown.
Welcomes CVs and headshots by post at any time;
these will be kept on file and looked at afresh during
each casting process. Also runs professional artist
development scheme – Tamasha Developing Artists.
Actors requesting inclusion should write in the run-
up to productions – suggests 3 months in advance.
Offers ITC/Equity approved contracts.

Tara Arts Group

356 Garratt Lane, London SW18 4ES
tel 020-8333 4457 *fax* 020-8870 9540
email tara@tara-arts.com
website www.tara-arts.com
Artistic Director Jatinder Verma

Production details

"Positioned between East & West, the company
champions creative diversity through the production,
promotion and development of work that defies all
barriers to the imagination. The creative health of
modern diverse humanity demands *no passports*.

• *No passports* for the stories we tell
• *No passports* for the artists we work with
• *No passports* for our audiences."

Founded in 1977, the company tours vibrant
adaptations of European and Asian classics, develops
new writing and brings the great stories of the world
to children in junior schools. The company tours
annually to England, Scotland and Wales, and has
also toured the Netherlands, Ireland, France,
Belgium, Spain, Turkey, Egypt, Hong Kong,
Singapore, Japan and Australia. Recent productions
include *The Genie of Samarkand*, *When the Lights
Went Out* and *A Taste For Mangoes*.

The People's Theatre Co

12E High Street, Egham TW20 9EA
tel (01784) 470439 *fax* (01784) 470439

email admin@ptc.org.uk
website www.ptc.org.uk
Director Steven Lee

Production details

Established in 2003. 4 productions are staged
annually. All work is new and original, and the
company has built an international reputation for its
unique brand of sophisticated pop musicals. Stages
120 performances per year, touring across the
country to Receiving Houses and number 1/number
2 venues. The company does *not* play to educational
or community venues ("Please do not apply to us for
TIE."). 7 actors are generally involved in each
production. Recent productions include: the award-
winning *Head*; *The Witch's Bogey*; *Bink and the Hairy
Fairy*; and *Bink and the Riddle of the Sphinx*.

Casting procedures

Casting is done in-house. Hold general auditions.
Actors should only write requesting inclusion in
response to casting calls. Actors can also register on
PTC's website for first alerts to castings. Casting
breakdowns are obtainable via Castweb, Casting Call
Pro, CastNet and through the PTC mailing list.
Accepts submissions (with CVs and photographs)
from individual actors previously unknown to them.
Submissions sent by email are also accepted.
Invitations to view showreels and individual actors'
websites are welcomed. Applications from disabled
actors are considered to play disabled characters.

"We want a well-presented CV with personal
information, training, experience and detailed skills –
particularly singing, as most of our work is musicals.
New actors and recent graduates welcome."

theatre-rites

The Warehouse, 12 Ravensbury Terrace,
London SW18 4RL
tel 020-8946 2236 *fax* 020-8946 0965
email info@theatre-rites.co.uk
website www.theatre-rites.co.uk
Artistic Director Sue Buckmaster *Associate Artist*
Sophia Clist *General Manager* Natalie Highwood

Production details

Founded in 1995, theatre-rites is versatile in its
approach, creating theatre shows which tour the UK
and abroad and pieces set in unusual spaces such as
an old tidal mill, a disused corner shop and an empty
ward of a real working hospital. theatre-rites also
creates interactive exhibitions and installations in
galleries, museums and other public spaces. Drawing
on a rich fusion of performance, installation art,
puppetry, video and sound, theatre-rites creates
work, which stirs the imagination of children and
adults alike. Recent productions include:
Hospitalworks, *The Thought that Counts* (part of the
Young Genius season at the Barbican), and a national
re-tour of *In One Ear*.

Casting procedures

Welcomes letters (with CVs and photographs) from actors previously unknown to the company. "Multi-disciplined performers are always very welcome." Offers ITC/Equity approved contracts.

Theatre Absolute

I.C.E., Parkside, Coventry CV21 2QR
tel 024-7615 8340
email info@theatreabsolute.co.uk
website www.theatreabsolute.co.uk
Artistic Director Chris O'Connell *Producer* Julia Negus

Production details

Founded in 1992, the company develops, produces and tours new plays. Its development arm, the Writing House, works with writers, actors and directors on new scripts. Stages 1 production annually with 30-40 performances during the course of the year. Tours to around 20 arts centres and theatres in the North West, West Midlands, East Midlands, London and the South East. In general 6 actors are involved in each production. Recent productions include: *Zero*, *Hang Lenny Pope*, and *Street Trilogy*.

Casting procedures

Actors should consult the website for details of the next project and for casting breakdowns and information. Welcomes letters (with CVs and up-to-date photographs) but not email submissions. Advises actors not to send blanket letters and CVs. "Find out about our work first – we always see actors who have seen our work if they're suitable for the role offered." Also happy to give advice to new/emerging actors.

Theatre Alibi

Northcott Studio Theatre, Emmanuel Road, Exeter EX4 1EJ
tel/fax (01392) 217315
email alibi@eclipse.co.uk
website www.theatrealibi.co.uk
Artistic Director Nikki Sved *Marketing Director* Annemarie Macdonald *Administrative Director* Jenny Lawrence

Production details

Founded in 1982, the company works with existing and commissioned stories to create work that is physically and visually inventive and often enriched by other art forms – original music, film, puppetry, dance and photography, for instance. Stages 2 productions a year, with a total of around 130 performances. Tours 20 theatres and arts centres as well as schools and community venues, although the nature of the venue depends on the individual show. There are generally 5 actors in each show, and the company offers ITC/Equity approved contracts.

Past work includes: *Birthday* (based on the work of Marc and Bella Chagall, which was nominated for a Fringe First); *Little White Lies* (*Time Out* Critics' Choice); and *Shelf Life*. Recent productions include: *The Crowstarver* (mid-scale national tour for 8-13 year-olds); *Bonjour Bob* (tour of South West for 5-10 year olds and their families); and *One in a Million* (national tour of small-scale venues aimed at adults).

Casting procedures

Casts in-house. Does not publish casting breakdowns, but welcomes letters (not emails) with CVs and photographs from individuals previously unknown to the company at any time of year. Does not welcome showreels or invitations to view individuals' websites. Actively encourages applications from disabled actors and promotes the use of inclusive casting.

Theatre Babel

PO Box 5103, Glasgow G78 9AR
tel 0141- 16 0051
email admin@theatrebabel.co.uk
website www.theatrebabel.co.uk
Director Graham McLaren *General Manager* Kate Bowden *Producer and Casting Director* Rebecca Rodgers

Production details

Founded in 1994, the company stages 1-2 classical theatre productions each year which tour to 10 venues across the UK and internationally. Normally presents approximately 60 performances annually with an average of 8 actors working on each production. Recent productions include: *Macbeth*, *A Doll's House*, *Thebans* and *Uncle Vanya*.

Casting procedures

Welcomes letters, CVs and photographs from actors previously unknown to the company, but does not accept email applications or showreels.

Theatre Hebrides

71-77 Cromwell Street, Stornoway, Isle of Lewis HS1 2DG
tel (01851) 701193
email info@theatrehebrides.com
website www.theatrehebrides.com
Artistic Director Muriel Ann Macleod *Administrator* Donnie Macdonald

Production details

Works mainly in film and multimedia. Commissions new plays and devises scripts. All work is based on Western Isles historic and contemporary culture. Also works as a TV production company and is currently producing comedy drama. Recent productions include: *The Callanish Stoned* by Kevin Macneil; *Kinoch ... Somewhere* by Eric John Macdonald (1-man show); and *Lostbost* by Billy Matheson.

Theatre

Casting procedures

Uses in-house casting directors and holds general auditions. Actors may write in at any time requesting inclusion. Casting breakdowns are available via Equity Job Information Service or by postal application with sae. Welcomes letters (with CVs and photoraphs) sent by post, but not by email. Will accept showreels and invitations to view individual actors' websites. Offers Equity approved contracts as negotiated through ITC and PACT. Actively encourages applications from disabled actors and promotes the use of inclusive casting. "We are working in Gaelic and English at present, and are also developing international collaborations. Check the website for details."

Theatre Is

The Innovation Centre, College Lane,
Hatfield AL10 9AB
tel (01279) 461607 *fax* (01279) 506694
email info@theatreis.org
website www.theatreis.org

Production details

Established in 2006. Challenging and creating new models of live performance by, with and for young audiences across the East of England and beyond. 3 productions are staged annually touring East of England, London, Midlands, North West and Wales. 50 performances per year at an average of 20 venues. Types of venue include: arts centres, theatres, outdoor venues, educational and community venues. 4 actors are generally involved in each production. Actors are employed under ITC/Equity approved contracts. Recent productions include: *Master Juba* (Hackney Empire, Norwich Playhouse); *Claytime* (New Wolsey Theatre, Lyric Hammersmith, Unicorn Theatre).

Casting procedures

Casting is done by an in-house casting director. Casting breakdowns are only available to agents via the Spotlight Link. Does not welcome individual submissions from actors. Actively encourages applications from disabled actors and promotes the use of inclusive casting in new writing productions.

Theatre Lab Company

76 St Dunstan's Avenue, London W3 6QJ
mobile (07958) 4048806
email anastasia@theatrelab.co.uk
website www.theatrelab.co.uk
Director Anastasia Revi

Production details

Established in 1997. Stages 1 production annually, with around 20 performances in 3 theatres in the Midlands and South East, and abroad. In general 4-6 actors are involved in each production. Offers Equity-approved contracts as negotiated through ITC "when funded". Recent productions include: *Velvet Scratch* (Prague Festival 2007; Edinburgh Festival 2007; Greek tour 2008; New York Fringe Festival 2008).

Casting procedures

Uses freelance casting directors. Holds general auditions, and actors may write to request inclusion when advertised. Casting breakdowns are available from the website, by postal application (with sae), and in *PCR* and *The Stage*. Welcomes letters (with CVs and photographs) from individual actors previously unknown to the company, sent by post or email. Also welcomes showreels and invitations to view individual actors' websites. Will consider applications from disabled actors to play characters with disabilities.

Théâtre Sans Frontières

Queen's Hall, Beaumont Street, Hexham,
Northumberland NE46 3LS
tel (01434) 652484 *fax* (01434) 607206
email admin@tsf.org.uk
website www.tsf.org.uk
Artistic Directors Sarah Kemp (CEO), John Cobb
Administrator Sue Maltby *Finance Officer* Gabby
Keaveny *Marketing & Development Officer* Alison
Maw

Production details

Founded in 1991. Set up by former students of Philippe Gaulier and Monika Pagneux. Specialises in physical theatre and stages texts in different languages for adults and children using international performers. Stages 2-3 productions annually with 60-100 performances in venues including arts centres, schools and theatres. In general 3-6 actors are involved in each production. Recent productions include: *Como Agua Para Chocolate* (*Like Water for Chocolate*); *Lipsynch* (co-produced with Robert Lepage and Ex Machina, touring internationally); and *La Pelota Magica*, an engaging introduction to Spanish for children aged 6 to 11 years. Touring nationally: autumn 2009 – *Les Trois Mousquetaires*; UK schools January to March 2010 – *Contes Dores* (for childred aged 8 to 12 years); June/July 2010 – *La Pelota Magica*.

Casting procedures

Sometimes holds general auditions. Actors may write at any time requesting inclusion. Casting breakdowns are available on request. Welcomes submissions (with CVs and photographs) sent by post or email. Invitations to view individual actors' websites are also accepted. "We are usually looking for actors who have languages other than English (especially French, Spanish or German), and who have a clear physical theatre training (i.e. Le Coq, Gaulier, Pagneux or Complicite)."

Theatre Set-up

12 Fairlawn Close, Southgate, London N14 4JX
website www.ts-u.co.uk
Charitable Director Wendy Macphee

Production details

Founded in 1976. Presents Shakespeare productions in historic and beautiful sites. Stages 1 production annually with 55 performances over the course of the year. Tours to 35 different outdoor venues annually in the UK, Norway, the Netherlands and Belgium. In general 8 actors are involved in each production. Recent productions include: *The Winter's Tale.* Offers non-Equity contracts and does not subscribe to the Equity Pension Scheme.

Casting procedures

Actors should write in February requesting auditions. Welcomes letters (with CVs and photographs) but not email submissions. Advises actors that "the tour is rigorous and not for the faint-hearted".

Theatre Without Walls

Forwood House, Forwood, Gloucestershire GL6 9AB
mobile (07976) 204044
email hello@theatrewithoutwalls.org.uk
website www.theatrewithoutwalls.org.uk
Directors Jason Maher, Genevieve Swift

Production details

Established in 2002. Award-winning theatre company specialising in forum, education and new writing. Productions represent only one-fifth of its output; also produces television and corporate films. 2 productions are staged annually with 60 performances per year, touring to 20 venues including arts centres, theatres and outdoor venues. Tours cover the UK, Ireland and Europe. 3 actors are involved in each production. Actors are employed under ITC/Equity approved contracts. Recent productions include: *Don Quixote* (Banbury Mill); *The Hold* (Cheltenham Everyman); and *The Plant Hunters* (National Trust).

Casting procedures

"We cast mostly through agents and our own knowledge/word of mouth/recommendations. We sometimes post casting information via Equity JIS and other 'freely available resources'. We never use casting services which actors have to pay for, except for The Spotlight. Any information obtained via paid-for services has simply been copied from another source. Please don't send us any information (such as photos, CVs, showreels, etc.) unless we have requested it. We regularly hold actors' labs and often cast from them." Theatre Without Walls is a member of ITC and most of its work is undertaken using Equity contracts. Those working with vulnerable adults or children must have a current enhanced Criminal Record Bureau/Police Check and hold full insurance equal or greater than that provided by Equity for its members." Considers applications from disabled actors to play disabled characters.

See also the company's entry under *Role-play companies* on page 318.

Theatre Workout

13A Stratheden Road, Blackheath, London SE13 7TN
tel 020-8144 2290
email enquiries@theatreworkout.co.uk
website www.theatreworkout.co.uk
Director Adam Milford

Production details

Established in 2006. West End workshops, schools workshops, corporate training and productions. Stages 1 production annually with 30 performances in 1-10 venues. Offers Equity-approved contracts. Recent productions include: *English Theatre in Venice.*

Casting procedures

Sometimes holds general auditions; actors may write at any time to request inclusion. Casting breakdowns are publicly available from casting breakdown services. Welcomes letters (with CVs and photographs) from individual actors previously unknown to the company, sent by post or email, and will consider invitations to view individual actors' websites.

Theatre Workshop

34 Hamilton Place, Edinburgh EH3 5AX
tel 0131-225 7942 *fax* 0131-220 0112
email afleming@twe.org.uk
website www.theatre-workshop.com
Artistic Director Robert Rae *Company Manager* Anne Fleming

Production details

Founded in 1965; stages 4 productions a year with around 60 performances across 2 theatre venues. Occasionally tours internationally. Employs an average of 5 actors on each production, using ITC/Equity approved contracts. Recent productions include: *The Jasmine Road* (No Limits International Theatre Festival, Berlin); and *The Threepenny Opera* (Edinburgh Festival Theatre & Tramway, Glasgow).

Casting procedures

Casting breakdowns are available from the website and Equity Job Information Service. Welcomes letters and emails (with CVs and photographs) from individuals previously unknown to the company. Also happy to receive showreels and invitations to view individuals' websites. Encourages applications from disabled actors and promotes the use of inclusive casting. "Theatre Workshop casts both

Theatre

disabled and non-disabled actors in all our productions."

Tinderbox Theatre Company

Imperial Buildings, 22 High Street, Belfast BT1 2BE
tel 028-9043 9313 *fax* 028-9032 9420
email info@tinderbox.org.uk
website www.tinderbox.org.uk
Artistic Director Michael Duke *General Manager* Kerry Woods

Production details

Founded in 1988. Produces, develops and stages new work which interrogates life in Northern Ireland. Stages 2-3 productions and tours to 12 different venues annually, including arts centres, theatres and site-specific locations in Ireland, England and Scotland. In general 6 actors are involved in each production. Recent productions include: *Revenge* and *Family Plot*.

Casting procedures

Sometimes holds general auditions. Welcomes letters (with CVs and photographs) but not email submissions. Invitations to view individual actors' websites are also accepted. Offers ITC/Equity approved contracts; only contributes to the Equity Pension Scheme for permanant staff. Encourages applications from disabled actors and promotes the use of inclusive casting.

Told by an Idiot

The Print House, 18 Ashlin Street, London E8 3DL
tel 020-7978 4200 *fax* 020-7978 5200
email ggranger@dial.pipex.com
website www.toldby.dircon.co.uk
Directors Hayley Carmichael, Paul Hunter, John Wright *General Manager* Ghislaine Granger *Associate Producer* Nick Sweeting

Production details

Founded in 1992, the company tours to arts centres and theatres throughout England.

Casting procedures

Sometimes holds general auditions. Actors may write at any time throughout the year. The company will make contact if and when a relevant project arises. Welcomes submissions (with CVs and photographs) sent by post or email. Invitations to view individual actors' websites are also accepted. Offers ITC/Equity contracts. Actively encourages applications from disabled actors and promotes the use of inclusive casting.

TOSG Gaelic Theatre Company

Sabhal Mor Ostaig, Sleat, Isle of Skye IV44 8RQ
tel (01471) 888542 *fax* (01471) 888542
email tosg@tosg.org
website www.tosg.org.uk

Artistic Director Simon Mackenzie *General Manager* Janet Ward

Production details

Founded in 1996. Professional Gaelic Theatre Company producing theatre for both adults and children. Also runs a new writing scheme. All productions are performed in Gaelic. Stages 2 productions annually and gives 50 performances per year. Tours to 30 different venues annually, including arts centres, theatres, educational and community venues in Scotland. In general 5 actors are involved in each production.

Casting procedures

Sometimes holds general auditions. Gaelic-speaking actors can write in May requesting inclusion. Welcomes letters (with CVs and photographs) but not email submissions. Invitations to view individual actors' websites are also accepted.

Trestle Theatre Company

Trestle Arts Base, Russet Drive, St Albans AL4 0JQ
tel (01727) 850950 *fax* (01727) 855558
email admin@trestle.org.uk
website www.trestle.org.uk
Artistic Director Emily Gray *Executive Director* Alison Young

Production details

Founded in 1981 as a touring theatre company, now also with a home venue (Trestle Arts Base) and national workshop programme (Taking Part). Performers/facilitators used across all 3 areas of the company. All projects concentrate on new, devised or commissioned work, incorporating text, physical theatre, dance and other movement forms, storytelling, puppetry, music and song. 1 small to mid-scale tour annually, to 50 venues including arts centres and theatres in Britain, Europe and other international locations. In general 2-5 performers are involved in each project. Offers ITC/Equity contracts.

Casting procedures

Rarely holds general auditions. Does not welcome on-spec CVs. Will consider invitations to see actors in shows if the performance style is relevant to the way in which Trestle works. If looking for suggestions, casting breakdowns will be posted on the website. Usually casts actors with strong physical/ visual theatre acting training or experience. Actively encourages applications from disabled actors and promotes the use of inclusive casting.

Triangle Theatre Company Ltd

c/o The Herbert, Jordan Well, Coventry CV1 5QP
tel (02476) 294730/1 *fax* (02476) 294790
email office@triangletheatre.co.uk
website www.triangletheatre.co.uk

Joint Artistic Directors Carran Waterfield, Richard Talbot

Production details

Since 2001, company-in-residence at The Herbert Art Gallery & Museum. Won the UK Museums & Heritage Award for excellence and the Roots & Wings Award for performance and interactive projects in response to museum collections. Runs performances and talks for conferences, schools and colleges as well as collaborations with academics and researchers contributing to the ongoing dissemination of Trangle's method of extended and immersive play with character, personal biography and history. Stages on average 2 major original productions each year, including studio and site-specific situations. Studio work is actor-centred and scripted from lengthy, devised rehearsals. Site-specific work is experimental and participatory, and developed in partnership with universities and local authorities. Recent productions include: *The Last Women* and *Knickers and Vests* (part of the Cultural Olympiad to London 2010).

Casting procedures

Casting and contracts agreed by Artistic Directors. Triangle holds frequent ensemble auditions and training workshops to develop material, generate ideas and employ associate artists. Actors are advised to consult the website for detailed information and to approach the company regarding specific, relevant projects. Does not welcome unsolicited submissions by post or by email, or showreels, but will accept invitations to view individual actors' websites. Offers independent contracts based on ITC. Actively encourages applications from disabled actors and promotes the use of inclusive casting.

UK Arts International

2nd Floor, 6 Shaw Street, Worcester WR1 3QQ

Production details

Stages 1 production annually which tours to approximately 70 different venues, including arts centres, theatres, education and community venues across the UK.

Casting procedures

Does not hold general auditions and does not welcome submissions from actors previously unknown to the company.

Unlimited Theatre

Studio 11, Aire Street Workshops, 30-34 Aire Street, Leeds LS1 4HT
tel 0113-234 5400
email unlimited@unlimited.org.uk
website www.unlimited.org.uk
Artistic Director Jon Spooner *Development Director* Liz Margree

Production details

Founded in 1997. Creates work intended to "explore how personal experience can illuminate political debate, and which puts marginalised voices centre-stage". Stages 1-2 productions annually with 50-100 performances. Tours to 10-20 different venues each year, including arts centres and theatres throughout the UK (including Glasgow, Edinburgh and Belfast) and overseas. In general 4-6 actors are involved in each production. Recent productions include: *Safety*, *Neutrino* and *Zero Degrees and Drifting*.

Casting procedures

Sometimes holds general auditions. Welcomes letters (with CVs and photographs) but not email submissions. Invitations to view individual actors' websites are also accepted. "We are a small- to middle-scale organisation and only occasionally employ freelance actors. We are always interested in hearing from potential new collaborators." Offers ITC/Equity approved contracts. Actively encourages applications from disabled actors and promotes the use of inclusive casting.

Vaya Naidu Company Ltd

Unit LFB2, Lafone House, The Leathermarket, 11-13 Leathermarket Street, London SE1 3HN
tel 020-7378 0739
email vayu.naidu@vayunaiducompany.org.uk
website www.vayunaiducompany.org.uk
Artistic Director Vayu Naidu *Associate/Casting Director* Chris Banfield *Key personnel* Rebekah Cross (General Manager), Emily Parrish (Storyteller in Education & Outreach)

Production details

The only performing arts company in the UK dedicated to promoting Storytelling Theatre. Seeks to establish a unique base from which a multi-racial cast of theatre writers, musicians, dancers, storytellers and performers can collaborate, bringing together various art forms to create "contemporary, enriching and diverse cultural experiences". Stages on average 3 productions each year: these can take place in traditional performance venues utilising technical resources, or in workshop settings in schools, colleges, libraries and museums. Creates new works to tour mainstream venues, as well as small-scale programmes 'in repertoire' and tailor-made for specific events. Also works in TIE, Outreach and Community, for which the key contact is Emily Parrish. Recent productions include: *Mistaken* (Annie Besant in India); *Nine Nights* (stories from the Ramayana); and *License to Tell* (pub-storytelling evenings.)

Casting procedures

Holds general auditions; actors may write at any time to request inclusion. Welcomes letters (with CVs &

photographs) from actors previously unknown to the company if sent by post; no emails please. Accepts showreels and invitations to view individual actors' websites. Offers Equity approved contracts as negotiated through ITC. Will consider applications from disabled actors to play characters with disabilities.

Volcano Theatre Company

Swansea Metropolitan University, Townhill Road, Swansea SA2 0UT
tel (01792) 281280
email paul@volcanotheatre.co.uk or claud@volcanotheatre.co.uk
website www.volcanotheatre.co.uk
Directors Paul Davies, Fern Smith *General Manager* Carys Shannon *Marketing Manager* Claudine Conway

Production details

Original theatrical productions and site-specific events. Small-scale national and international touring company based in Wales. Devised and collaborative work, physical theatre, new writing, adaptations/deconstructions of classics. Stages 2-4 productions and gives 50-80 performances each year. Venues include arts centres and theatres in the UK, Europe and worldwide. Usually 2-8 performers per production. Recent productions include: *i-witness*, *Dead Cat Bounce*, *A Few Little Drops*.

Casting procedures

There are no casting breakdowns. Performers are selected through workshops and invited auditions. Unsolicited admissions are read but not held on record.

Keith Whitall

25 Solway, Hailsham BN27 3HB
tel (01323) 844882
Director Keith Whitall

Production details

Founded in 2000. Produces revues, small-scale musicals and occasionally plays and one-person shows. Stages 2-3 productions annually with 20 or more performances in theatres in Brighton and the South East. So far has only toured to 1 arts centre. In general 9-10 actors are involved in each production. Recent productions include: *Broadway Calling.*, *The Pleasure of Your Company* and *Noel Coward & Cole Porter Revisited*. Offers non-Equity contracts and does not subscribe to the Equity Pension Scheme.

Casting procedures

Sometimes holds general auditions. Actors may write at any time requesting inclusion. Casting breakdowns are usually made available to casting directors or actors seen in a production. Welcomes letters (with

CVs and photographs) but not email submissions. "In my revues I usually use 3-4 experienced artistes plus new young artistes in whom I am especially interested." Musical theatre experience is preferable. Rarely has opportunity to cast disabled actors, but "possible in future depending on backstage access".

Wildcard Theatre Company

PO Box 267, High Wycombe, Bucks, HP11 2WB
tel 0870-760 6158 *mobile* (07092) 024967
website www.wildcardtheatre.org.uk
Creative Producer Jo Salkilld

Production details

Recent productions include: *Titus Andronicus*, *Wicked* and *Greek*.

Casting procedures

Casting information is published on the website.

The Wrestling School

42 Durlston Road, London E5 8RR
tel 020-8442 4229
website www.thewrestlingschool.co.uk
Director Howard Barker

Production details

Founded in 1988. "Develops ways of presenting complex ideas in the theatre through the work of Howard Barker." Stages 1 production annually; in general 5-7 actors are involved in each production.

Casting procedures

Sometimes holds auditions. Welcomes letters when casting (with CVs and photographs) but not email submissions. Actors should telephone in late July, or consult the website, to find out if the company is casting.

Y Touring Theatre Co

One KX, 120 Cromer Street, London WC1B 8BS
tel 020-7520 3090 *fax* 020-7520 3099
email info@ytouring.org.uk
website www.ytouring.org.uk
Artistic Director Nigel Townsend *General Manager* Martin Ball *Tour Producer* David Jackson *Associate Director, Creative Learning* Jenny May While

Production details

Y Touring is Central YMCA's award winning professional touring theatre company for young people and adults. Produces 2-4 tours per year in the UK. Offers ITC/Equity approved contracts and does not subscribe to the Equity Pension Scheme.

Casting procedures

Uses freelance casting directors and publishes casting breakdowns through various agencies including,

PCR, *SBS*, Castcall, etc. Does not hold general auditions. Will accept CVs and photos by post at any time of year to be held on file for consideration. Please do not send showreels or unsolicited scripts. Will consider applications from disabled actors to play characters with disabilities.

Yellow Earth Theatre

20 Rupert Street, London W1 6DF
tel 020-7734 5988 *fax* 020-7287 3141
email admin@yellowearth.org
website www.yellowearth.org
Artistic Director David Tse Kashing

Production details

Founded in 1995. An award-winning Asian theatre company touring nationally and internationally with work that embraces Eastern and Western theatrical traditions and dramatic languages. Stages 1-2 productions each year, with around 40 performances at 10 arts centre and theatre venues. Regions covered include all of the UK, China, Hong Kong and Malaysia. In general 3-10 actors are involved in each production. Offers Equity approved contracts as negotiated through ITC. Recent productions include: *Typhoon 4* (Soho Theatre), *Chinese Two-Step 1925-2005* (Trafalgar Square), and *King Lear* (Shanghai and UK Tour).

Casting procedures

Casts in-house. Sometimes holds general auditions; the best time to write requesting inclusion is in the Spring. Welcomes letters (not emails) with CVs and photographs from East Asian actors only. Accepts invitations to view individual actors' websites, but not showreels. Actively encourages applications from disabled actors and promotes the use of inclusive casting. "As an East Asian company, we only keep on file details of actors with East Asian backgrounds (everywhere east of India, for example China, Japan, Korea, Philippines, etc."

Theatre

Pantomime is not just for Christmas – it's for life!

Nigel Ellacott

From the audience's point of view, Pantomime is a perennial entertainment, unique to this country, and it happens over the Festive Season when the nights draw in, and the Yule logs crackle by an open fire.

The audience knows it is a "safe" place to take the family – the kids, Gran and Granddad. They know it will always be there. Warm and comforting, and that it will never change.

Ah! But of course it does change, and it has changed over its peculiar development into one of Great Britain's intrinsic art forms. It is our art form, even though we stole a bit here and there to make it so. If Pantomime didn't change, I doubt it would be one of the all time money-spinners and popular entertainments we have today. Pantomime has constantly changed. It has evolved and adapted, and in doing so it has ensured audiences for the future, made managements and theatres a fair bit of profit and, in some cases has enabled theatres to fund the forthcoming rep season well into the summer months.

This Panto season alone, over 360 professional pantomimes will be staged in this country, and a great many actors, musicians and technicians will be employed for periods of up to eight or nine weeks in many cases. Annually it provides regular work for an army of artistes and techies, it employs musicians (although it has to be said in ever decreasing numbers) writers, directors, choreographers and a vast army of outworkers – scenic artists, wardrobe and prop makers, footwear suppliers and wig makers. Pantomime monopolises the transport industry as pantechnicans travel the length and breadth of the land collecting wardrobe boxes, crystal coaches and giant inflatable beanstalks!

The preparation for the annual onslaught from Fairyland begins, on average while the current pantomime is half-way through. The Pantomime "Giants" are not looking for Daisy the Cow to make a Daisy-Burger; they are the "Big Boys" who control the largest number of productions around the country. In this year of writing Qdos hold the poll position as pantomime employers.

Qdos produced twenty pantomimes this season, with two in Scotland, one in Belfast and three in Wales, and the others ranging from The Hippodrome Birmingham to The Alhambra Bradford.

First Family Entertainment, a recent newcomer to Pantoland produced nine major productions. FFE is the combined umbrella of Ambassadors Theatre Group and Live Nation (formerly Clear Channel).

UK Productions has Eleven pantomimes around the country, the same number as PHA (Paul Holman Associates), whilst Evolution, Hiss & Boo, Duo Productions, John Spillers and Pantoni are just a few of the many producing managements providing pantomimes around the UK.

A helpful place to search out these companies would be on the diary section of my website: **www.its-behind-you.com**. Every pantomime in the UK is listed there.

If you consider that Qdos will employ on average ten principals, six to eight dancers, six musicians, a director, choreographer, company manager, three stage management in each of their twenty venues – the numbers begin to mount up. In addition the venue will provide a stage crew, electricians, sound and wardrobe staff, as well as the combined efforts of in house marketing, publicity, box office and FOH staff.

Pantomime is often the longest running show in the provinces during the year. Seasons can run between four to nine weeks. The Grand Theatre Wolverhampton runs until February 4th, as does a smaller venue like The Kenneth More Theatre in Ilford.

Major star names adorn the posters. The Managements increasingly trying to outdo their rivals with bigger names, more lavish productions – with standards constantly rising, panto is no longer the poorer relation of the theatre world. Admittedly there was a lull somewhere in the 1960's and 70's when it seemed as if an air of complacency had settled in pantoland, but over the past few decades the genre has taken on a new lustre.

The newspapers were delighted to announce that a Theatrical Knight, one Ian McKellan was to don the skirts of Widow Twankey and perform panto at the Old Vic no less! The lure of the Golden Egg has brought soap stars from Australia and Hollywood stars to strut their stuff on the stages of Richmond and Milton Keynes.

There's nothing new in this – Panto has simply done what it does best. It has constantly taken on board the new, the novel the "Now" and the "Wow" factors to keep its position as our premier family entertainment.

Augustus Harris employed the "star" system at the Drury Lane Pantomimes of the 1890's. Pantomime sucked in Music Hall stars and the odd sporting celebrity in the Edwardian era just as today it might embrace a Big Brother "Celebrity" or a bone fide classical actor from the RSC.

Desmond Barritt, much loved at the RSC was performing as Dame many years before Sir Ian McKellan. Sir George Robey was doing the same sixty years before.

Pantomime has always had its stars – from Dan Leno to Danny La Rue. It has always had its impresarios, from Augustus Harris, Francis Laidler and Emile Littler to Paul Elliott. It has also been a home to many artistes starting out in the business, and still remains so today. In this day and age it may be difficult " to solve a problem like" a first job, but with pantomime as a major employer of actors, singers and dancers, it is "a very good place to start!"

Pantomime is the place to specialise. The traditional characters of the plots are tailor made for this. There are the comics – the younger comedians who follow the origins laid down in commedia d'ell arte – those of Harlequin who evolved into "Buttons" or "Muddles" or "Simple Simon". There are the Principal Girls, who, like Columbine before them are expected to be the epitome of femininity, but unlike Columbine are expected nowadays to have a "belter" of a voice – sweet ballads have evolved into this year's "Girls Aloud" hit!

The Dame role appeals to both the older comic and the character actor, the "Sisters" to character actors with a penchant for villainy and high camp. Sadly today the role of Principal Boy is more likely to be cast as a male. Up until Norman Wisdom played "Dick Whittington" at the London Palladium, the role seemed safely held by the ladies. However, things change, and eventually we might see the resurgence of the fishnets and swagger that personified the role. For now the requirements are Hollyoaks looks and a strong singing voice.

Pantomime is not ageist. As well as encouraging the newcomer, it welcomes the elder statesmen of theatre. There are roles for Villains, Kings, Fairy Queens and of course Dames, as well as Wicked Queens and Baronesses. Maturity, and the well crafted skills learnt in a lifetime of performing and observing are more than welcome in Pantoland.

The route to appearing in a pantomime production is the usual "double edged sword" that newcomers to the business face constantly. It used to be that if you wanted to be a member of Equity you had to have a job. To get a job you had to be a member of Equity. This may no longer apply, but often managements casting for pantomime prefer artistes who have previously appeared in a pantomime.

"Word of mouth" is employed very often by pantomime producers. They visit many productions (not just their own) during the panto season, and will note down artistes who they are interested in. They will look at a track record of where an artiste was the previous year, and will most likely make enquiries to see how they fared in the last pantomime before making a decision on the next one.

Panto producers rarely (if ever) employ a casting director. Some have their own in house casting department, but mostly they employ their artistes through agents, and, on some occasions they will hold auditions – these are often secured via agents rather than an "open" audition.

For pantomime dancers the audition process is somewhat different. The panto companies frequently hold auditions, generally in the early autumn. These are usually advertised in *The Stage* a few weeks beforehand. At these auditions dancers will often be asked to dance first, and then sing. The managements are often looking for "covers" and understudies at the same time as ensemble. Certainly it helps both dancers and actors to be general "all rounders".

Securing a job as a dancer and understudying a leading role will certainly add to a pantomime CV for the following year. This is often a door of opportunity that will open to allow the transition from ensemble to lead role in a future production.

If you want to pursue a pantomime contract it helps to know into which category you want to be placed. In the past an actress who stood over five foot six knew that her height and a fine singing voice would earmark her as a Principal Boy. Nowadays these female to male roles are rare. You need to know your strengths- comic ability and timing would make for a role as Henchman or Chinese Policeman. A tall character actor would be aiming at Abanazar or the Sheriff of Nottingham. Pantomime by its very nature places you into one of these traditional and stereotype roles, and knowing what roles you are most suited for enhances the audition process. Having secured the part, what else do you need?

If I had to use just one word to describe the chief requirement a performer needs in Panto, it would be this: energy.

Energy is required both in performance on stage, and if it is well controlled and paced, off stage as well. The audience is young. The attention span of the average child is getting shorter. Panto has evolved to meet this new challenge. The pace is faster, the dialogue sharper, the effects more transfixing. However – woe betide the performer who lacks energy. The children will not be fooled by a lack of energy, and a lack of truth. Truth is the second requirement.

Pantomimes may be lavish and spectacular. They should be comical and magical, but the entire structure is based on one solid and immovable thing – the plot. It is the story that will transfix the audience. It is what drives the pantomime onward through to its inevitable conclusion. That good will always overcome evil.

That simple retelling of what is essentially a morality play can only be held together by truth. If the performer believes in their character – be it good or evil, then the audience, and the child in every audience will believe in it too. In panto we have no "Fourth Wall". We talk directly to the audience at times (well, certain characters can, others shouldn't). Barriers you find in plays are broken down. Direct contact is encouraged. A pantomime is, after all, the original "Interactive" game.

To create the magic that IS pantomime, we onstage must believe in that magic. We must do it with a truth and a great deal of energy if that magic is to work.

Pantomime is larger than life. When we are on that stage we become almost cartoon characters. Gestures are broad, expressions are big, and the excitement of the storyline is expressed by our excitement in performing it. Twice a day. Every day. Six days a week. Twelve shows a week for perhaps eight weeks. That energy must be controlled and it must be paced. Above all, every word that you speak must sound as if it is the first time you have ever spoken it. After all, the audience have never heard it before. That audience of children must be nurtured. If their pantomime experience is a joyful and enlightening one, then they will continue to come to the pantomime. In time they will bring their own children, then their grandchildren...you see..

Pantomime is not just for Christmas – it's for life. OH YES IT IS!

Nigel Ellacott began his career with the Welsh Drama Company (part of Welsh National Opera) having trained as a Drama Teacher. He has worked in theatre and in television for the past thirty-five years. Nigel has performed in over thirty pantomimes across the country. Until Christmas 2008 he spent a happy 27 years as Ugly Sister with his stage partner Peter Robbins – for both E&B Productions (Paul Elliott) and Qdos Entertainment. They have appeared in theatres around the UK from Aberdeen to Plymouth, and recently completed the record breaking season of "Cinderella" with Brian Conley at the Hippodrome Birmingham. Nigel has written over twenty-two pantomime scripts. Each year he writes for the Kenneth More Theatre, and in addition has written pantomime scripts for companies both in Great Britain and in Canada, America and South Africa. He established "The Pantomime Roadshow" ten years ago. This production tours schools, taking the "Magic of Pantomime" to three thousand school children in a week. The show aims to attract young audiences to the theatre, and to pantomime in particular, and apart from entertaining, it reveals some of the history and traditions of British Panto. He created the pantomime website **www.its-behind-you.com** a few years ago. This site aims to encourage new audiences for the genre, as well as providing a current data base for performers, and a resource for pantomime and theatre historians. This website is currently sponsored by Qdos. Nigel was the feature of a Channel 4 documentary "Pantoland – The Biz", produced by Iambic Productions, and, together with Peter Robbins became the faces of the Royal Mail Christmas Campaign throughout the UK.

Theatre

Pantomime

This section lists some of the major pantomime producers and some of the theatres and arts centres that produce their own pantomimes. These latter (often subsidised by a local authority) largely present touring and (sometimes) amateur productions. However, a number of these do mount their own professional pantomimes and it can be useful to look through the Theatres & Provincial/Touring section of *Contacts* to check which. Many have websites.

Another way of finding out is to check through the listings and reviews in *The Stage* every Christmas. (Also look at **www.its-behind-you.com** which lists forthcoming pantomimes.) Pantomimes in such theatres will often be directed by the resident director and usually cannot afford the services of a casting director.

Some of these theatres occasionally produce their own shows throughout the year, especially as part of the work of their Education departments. Where possible we have included this information in each entry, but it is also worth visiting the theatre's website for further details.

PANTOMIME PRODUCERS

Chaplins Ltd
Chaplins House, The Acorn Centre, Roebuck Road, Hainault, Essex IG6 3TU
tel 020-8501 2121 *fax* 020-8501 3336
email fun@chaplinspantos.co.uk
website www.chaplinsentertainment.co.uk
Directors Mr J Weborne, Mr J Holmes *Productions Manager* Emma Newland

Production details
A touring pantomime and theatre-in-education company which also works in film and television production. Stages 28 productions annually, performing in small theatres, schools, social clubs and community centres.

Casting procedures
Uses freelance casting directors and holds general auditions; actors requesting inclusion are asked to write from August until the end of October only. Casting breakdowns are publicly available from the website, by postal application (with sae), in *The Stage* and via Casting Call Pro. During the period specified, the company welcomes letters (with CVs and photographs) from individual actors previously unknown to them, sent by post or email, and will accept showreels and invitations to view individual actors' websites. Rarely or never has the opportunity to cast disabled actors.

Duggie Chapman Associates
The Old Coach House, 202 Common Edge Road, Blackpool FY4 5DG
tel (01253) 691823 *fax* (01253) 691823
email duggie@chapmanassociates.fsnet.co.uk
website www.duggiechapman.co.uk
Director Duggie Chapman *Artiste Bookings* Kim Holmes

Production details
Established in 1970. Producers of pantos, concerts and plays. Annually produces 6 resident pantos including Billingham (Forum Theatre), Blackburn (Thwaites Empire Theatre), Bolton (Albert Halls), Boston (Blackfriars), Barrow-in-Furness (Forum 28) and Bedworth (Civic), plus tours.

Casting procedures
Casting is carried out by in-house casting director. Occasionally holds general auditions. For the pantos, actors should write from March onwards to request inclusion. Casting breakdowns are obtainable through *PCR* and *The Stage*. Accepts submissions (with CVs and photographs) from individual actors previously unknown to the company. Invitations to view showreels and individual actors' websites are welcomed. Rarely has the opportunity to cast disabled actors.

Duo Entertainment
5 Market Place, London W1W 8AE
tel 020-7580 9070 *fax* 020-7580 9060
email office@duo.uk.net
website www.duo.uk.net
Directors Barrie C Stead, Richard Cadell, Carina Skinner *Administrator* Brian Sandford

Produces pantomimes for The Ashcroft Theatre, Croydon; Grove Theatre, Dunstable; Ipswich Regent Theatre; and Embassy Centre, Skegness.

Evolution Productions

Hampton Lodge, 183 Hanworth Road,
Hampton TW12 3ED
tel 020-8941 2227 *fax* 020-8255 4273
email emily@evolution-productions.co.uk,
paul@evolution-productions.co.uk
website www.evolution-productions.co.uk
Directors Emily Wood, Paul Hendy

Production details

Founded in 2004 and run by husband-and-wife team,
Emily Wood and Paul Hendy. Produces pantomimes
and occasional musicals (recently produced *Oliver!* at
The Central Theatre, Chatham). Stages 5
pantomimes a year: The Marlowe Theatre,
Canterbury; The Central Theatre, Chatham; Yvonne
Arnaud Theatre, Guildford; Lyceum Theatre,
Sheffield; and Gordon Craig Theatre, Stevenage.
Offers non-Equity, in-house contracts ("Equity
equivalent") and does not subscribe to the Equity
Pension Scheme.

Casting procedures

Casts in-house – all casting enquiries should be
addressed to Paul Hendy. Holds general auditions;
the best time to write to request inclusion is March/
April. Casting breakdowns are published via Spotlight
and Castweb, and current casting requirements can
be found on the website. Welcomes letters (with CVs
and photographs) and performance notices from
actors previously unknown to the company, sent by
post or email. Happy to receive appropriate showreels
and invitations to view individual actors' websites.
Will consider applications from disabled actors to
play disabled characters.

Extravaganza Productions

PO Box 25, Boston, Lincolnshire PE21 8YE
tel (01205) 355978 *fax* (01205) 354094
email chandler@extravaganza.wanadoo.co.uk
website www.panto-mime.co.uk
Directors David Vickers, Richard Chandler *Casting*
Mike Holoway

Production details

Established in 1995, and associated with Mike Fisher
Associates. Presenting Pantomimes for The Plaza,
Stockport and Middlesborough Theatre. Number of
productions staged annually varies.

Casting procedures

Casting is carried out by in-house casting director
Mike Holoway. Actors can write at any time to
request inclusion. Accepts submissions (with CVs
and photographs) from individual actors previously
unknown to the company. Will also accept CVs and
photographs sent via email, invitations to view
individual actors' websites, and showreels.
Applications from disabled actors are considered to
play disabled characters.

First Family Entertainment

Fortune Theatre, Russell Street, London WC2B 5HH
tel 020-7010 7890 *fax* 020-7010 7899
email casting@ffe-uk.com
website www.ffe-uk.com
Chief Executive Kevin Wood *Casting Consultant* Scott
Mitchell *Production Co-ordinator* Jamie Taylor

Production details

Produces large-scale pantomimes. Venues include:
Theatre Royal, Brighton; Churchill Theatre, Bromley;
The King's Theatre, Glasgow; Milton Keynes Theatre,
Richmond Theatre, Regent Theatre, Stoke on Trent;
New Wimbledon Theatre; New Victoria Theatre,
Woking; Opera House, Manchester; Sunderland
Empire. Offers Equity-approved contracts and
subscribes to the Equity Pension Scheme.

Casting procedures

In-house casting director is Scott Mitchell. Does not
hold general auditions: only write in response to a
specific breakdown. Breakdowns are published in
February on Castweb, CastNet and direct to agents.
Welcomes letters (with CVs and photographs) from
actors previously unknown to the company if sent by
post, but not by email. ("Please do not phone!")
Happy to receive appropriate showreels, invitations
to view individual actors' websites and performance
notices. Actively encourages applications from
disabled actors and promotes the use of inclusive
casting.

Hammond Productions

211 Piccadilly, London W1J 9HF
tel 020-7917 2767
email hftm@btopenworld.com
website www.hammondproductions.co.uk
Director Paul Hammond *Casting* Ruth Langridge

Production details

Produces 4 pantomimes: Victoria Theatre, Halifax;
Hazlitt Theatre, Maidstone; Pavilion Theatre,
Worthing; and Drayton Manor Big Top. Offers actors
non-Equity contracts and does not subscribe to the
Equity Pension Scheme.

Casting Procedures

Casts in-house. Actors should write to or email Ruth
Langridge (with CVs and photographs) between
February and July. Casting breakdowns are published
in *The Stage, SBS*, Castweb and Entsweb. Welcomes
CVs and photographs from actors previously
unknown to the company. Happy to receive
appropriate showreels, invitations to view individual
actors' websites and performance notices. Will
consider applications from disabled actors to play
disabled characters.

Hiss & Boo Theatre Company

1 Nyes Hill, Wineham Lane, Bolney,
West Sussex RH17 5SD

Theatre

tel (01444) 881707 *fax* (01444) 882057
email email@hissboo.co.uk
website www.hissboo.co.uk
Artistic Director Ian Liston

Production details

Established in 1977. Pantomime producers also specialising in touring plays and revues in the UK and overseas. Pantomime venues include: The Riverfront Theatre, Newport; The Corn Exchange, Newbury; Hall for Cornwall, Truro; Queens Theatre, Barnstaple; Garrick, Lichfield. Actors are employed under TMA/Equity-approved contracts. The company subscribes to the Equity Pension Scheme. See also entry under *Independent managements/theatre producers* on page 175.

Casting procedures

Casting is done in-house. Casting breakdowns are only available to agents via Spotlight Interactive. Does not welcome unsolicited CVs and photographs. Rarely has the opportunity to cast disabled actors.

Paul Holman Associates

Morritt House, 58 Station Approach, South Ruislip, Middlesex HA4 6SA
tel 020-8845 9408 *fax* 020-8839 3124
email enquiries@paulholmanassociates.co.uk
website www.paulholmanassociates.co.uk
Directors Paul Holman, Adrian Jeckells, John Ogle
Associate Producer Andrew Lynford

Production details

Produces Pantomimes, Summer Seasons, Tours and other commercial projects. Stages between 10-15 productions annually. Venues where productions are staged include: Bridlington, Aylesbury (Civic), Catford (Broadway) Derby (Assembly Rooms), Leeds (Carriageworks), Newark (Palace), Redditch (Palace), Weston Super Mare (Playhouse). Summer Seasons: The Pier Theatre (Bournemouth), Princess Theatre (Hunstanton). Offers non-Equity (Variety) contracts and does not subscribe to the Equity Pension Scheme.

Casting procedures

Casting is done by in-house casting director. Occasionally hold general auditions; Spring is the best time to write requesting auditions. Casting breakdowns are available on Castweb and *SBS*. Accepts submissions (with CVs and photographs) from individual actors previously unknown to the company, sent by post or email. Invitations to view showreels and to attend other productions are also accepted. Will consider applications from disabled actors to play disabled characters, but in practice rarely has the opportunity to cast disabled actors.

Imagine Theatre Ltd

Unit F4-F6, Little Heath Industrial Estate, Old Church Road, Coventry CV6 7ND

tel 024-7668 8122
email casting@imaginetheatre.co.uk
website www.imaginetheatre.co.uk
General Manager Stephen Boden *Office Manager* Sarah Boden

Production details

Imagine Theatre (since 2009; formerly Wish Theatre) produces pantomimes and children's theatre for No. 1 tours, including *The Tweenies* and *Fun Song Factory*. Venues for pantomime include: Grand Pavilion, Porthcawl; Eden Court, Inverness; Victoria Theatre, Halifax; Belgrade Theatre, Coventry; Lyceum Theatre, Crewe; Palace Theatre, Kilmarnock; Town Hall, Loughborough; Roses Theatre, Tewksbury. Offers in-house contracts ("enhanced Equity") and does not subscribe to the Equity Pension Scheme.

Casting procedures

Casts mainly in-house. Hold general auditions; actors should email the company in March-May to request inclusion. Casting breakdowns are not published except on Spotlight. Welcomes CVs and photgraphs from actors previously unknown to the company; prefers these to be emailed rather than posted. Will consider applications from disabled actors to play disabled characters. "Panto isn't a cop-out: it's a serious business. We use actors who can engage with the audience and have fun. It is really useful if actors can indicate their location/home town, which helps with accents and knowing if an individual is local to one of our pantomime venues. Please do not send showreels or invitations to view websites, as unfortunately we just don't have time to deal with them."

Bruce James Productions Ltd

68 St George's Park Avenue, Westcliff-on-Sea, Essex SS0 9UD
tel/fax (01702) 335970
email info@brucejamesproductions.co.uk
website www.brucejamesproductions.co.uk
Directors Bruce James, Martin Roddy

Production details

A touring and repertory company that plays musicals and thrillers together with numerous pantomimes since 1995. Stages on average 8-12 productions annually, touring to a range of venues (pantomime at Thameside Theatre, Grays, and Pomegranate Theatre, Chesterfield). Offers Equity approved contracts; does not subscribe to the Equity Pension Scheme.

Casting procedures

Uses in-house casting directors. Holds general auditions and actors should write in to request inclusion in January, June and October. Casting breakdowns are available from the website, by postal application with sae, or from *Spotlight*. Welcomes letters (with CVs & photographs) from individual actors previously unknown to the company, sent by post or email. Also accepts showreels and invitations to view individual actors' websites. Will consider applications from disabled actors to play characters with disabilities. "Please do not email large photo or CV files (i.e. over 1MB) as they just clog up our system."

Owen Money Productions

4 Westgate Close, Porthcawl CF36 3NP
tel (07896) 258893
email owen.money@btinternet.com
Director Owen Money *Company Manager* Roger Bell

Production details

Established in 2000. Produces 3-4 family pantomimes a year, touring to 7-8 theatres and community venues around Wales between the end of November and the end of February. Also produces a Brian Rix-style 'adult' panto in April (2007 production was *Buttons Undone*). Offers non-Equity contracts and does not subscribe to the Equity Pension Scheme.

Casting procedures

Casts in-house. Casting notices are published in *The Stage*. Actors wishing to audition for the company should write (with CV and photograph) between November and January. Does not welcome unsolicited CVs and photographs by email. Happy to receive appropriate showreels and invitations to view individual actors' websites. Will consider applications from disabled actors to play disabled characters.

New Pantomime Productions

27 Shooters Road, Enfield, Middlesex EN2 8RJ
tel 020-8363 9920
email simonbarry@nppltd.freeserve.co.uk
Director Simon Barry

Production details

Produces pantomimes at 7 venues: Theatr Colwyn, Colwyn Bay; Brindley Arts Centre, Runcorn; Southport Theatre; Kings Theatre, Southsea; Princess Theatre, Torquay; Grand Opera House, York. Offers non-Equity contracts and does not subscribe to the Equity Pension Scheme.

Casting procedures

Casts in-house. Holds general auditions; actors should write in July to request inclusion. Casting breakdowns are not publicly available. Welcomes emails only (with CVs and photographs) from actors previously unknown to the company. Does not welcome showreels or invitations to view individual actors' websites. "Make sure you're suitable for the job you're applying for. We have employed disabled actors – and not just to play disabled characters. So long as the actor is good, that's all that matters."

Pantoni Pantomimes

205 Bexhill Road, St. Leonards on Sea,
East Sussex TN38 8BG
tel (01424) 443400 *fax* (01424) 714847
email david@pantoni.com
website www.pantoni.com
Directors David Lee and Rita Proctor

Produces pantomimes for the Doncaster Civic Theatre; Empire Theatre, Consett, New Floral Pavilion, New Brighton; The Leatherhead Theatre; Library Theatre, Luton; and Octagon Theatre, Yeovil.

The Proper Pantomime Company

6 Empress Avenue, Farnborough,
Hampshire GU14 8LX
tel (01252) 547547
email chris@properpantomime.com
website www.properpantomime.com
Producers Chris Lillicrap, Paul Harvey *Choreographer* Nicola Miles

Production details

Produces pantomimes for: Hexagon Theatre, Reading; Dorking Halls; The Connaught Theatre, Worthing. Also produces children's shows (TIE) and corporate entertainment. Offers actors non-Equity contracts and does not subscribe to the Equity Pension Scheme.

Casting procedures

Casts in-house. Holds general auditions; actors should write or email (with CV and photograph) in Feb/March to request inclusion. Casting breakdowns are published in *SBS* only. Happy to receive letters (with CVs and photographs) from actors previously unknown to the company, but prefers emails. Happy to receive showreels and invitations to view individual actors' websites, but does not welcome performance notices. Will consider applications from disabled actors to play disabled characters, especially for the TIE tours.

Qdos Entertainment (Pantomimes) Ltd

Qdos House, Queen Margaret's Road,
Scarborough YO11 2SAT
tel (01723) 500038
email info@qdosentertainment.plc.uk
website www.qdosentertainment.co.uk
Producer Jonathan Kiley

Production details

The largest of the commercial pantomime producers with 21 pantomimes across the UK: His Majesty's, Aberdeen; Grand Opera House, Belfast; Hippodrome Theatre, Birmingham; The Alhambra, Bradford; New Theatre, Cardiff; The Hawth, Crawley; Civic Theatre, Darlington; The Orchard, Dartford; Kings Theatre, Edinburgh; Beck Theatre, Hayes; Wycombe Swan, High Wycombe; Hull New Theatre; Venue Cymru,

Llandudno; Theatre Royal, Newcastle upon Tyne; Derngate Theatre, Northampton; Theatre Royal, Nottingham; Theatre Royal, Plymouth; Cliffs Pavilion, Southend; Alban Arena, St Albans; Wyvern Theatre, Swindon; Grand Theatre, Wolverhampton. Offers Equity-approved contracts and subscribes to the Equity Pension Scheme.

Casting procedures

Actors should send CVs and photographs by post to Jonathan Kiley in March (star-casting only in February). Welcomes performance notices. Send to: Qdos Entertainment (Pantomimes) Ltd, 1st Floor, 18 Exeter Street, London WC2E 7DU (020-7379 0405)

Spillers Pantomimes

The Old Post Office, Honey Tye, Leavenheath, Suffolk CO6 4NX
tel (01473) 810100
email jkspillers@talktalk.net
Managing Director John Spillers *Casting* (Mr) Bev Berridge

Production details

Established 1989. Produces pantomimes for Alexandra Theatre, Bognor Regis; Epsom Playhouse; Woodville Hall Theatre, Gravesend; Motherwell Theatre; Majestic Theatre, Retford; Civic Theatre, Rotherham; The Music Hall, Shrewsbury; Pavilion Theatre, Weymouth. Offers actors non-Equity contracts and does not contribute to the Equity Pension Scheme.

Casting procedures

Casting is done in-house. Holds general auditions. Best time for actors to write (with CV and photograph) to request inclusion is March/April. Casting breakdowns are published in *PCR* and *The Stage*. Welcomes CVs and photographs from actors previously unknown to the company sent by post or email. Will consider applications from disabled actors to play disabled characters.

UK Productions

Lime House, 78 Meadrow, Godalming, Surrey GU7 3HT
tel (01483) 423600 *fax* (01483) 418486
email mail@ukproductions.co.uk
website www.ukproductions.co.uk
Directors Martin Dodd, Peter Frosdick *Production Manager* Andy Batty *Administrator/Casting Assistant* Derek Raper

Production details

Established 1995. Produce pantomimes and musicals for No. 1 touring. (See entry under *Independent managements/theatre producers* on page 181.) Pantomime venues include: The Anvil Theatre, Basingstoke; Bath Theatre Royal; The Grand Theatre,

Blackpool; The Pavilion Theatre, Bournmouth; Mansfield Palace Theatre; Malvern Festival Theatre; The Pavilion Theatre, Rhyll, The Grand Theatre, Swansea; The Assembly Hall Theatre, Tunbridge Wells. Offers non-Equity contracts and does not subscribe to the Equity Pension Scheme.

Casting procedures

Casting is done in-house. Does not hold general auditions. Casting breakdowns are distributed via Spotlight or direct to agents. Welcomes performance notices but not any other unsolicited form of correspondence. "Unsolicited CVs are generally a waste of time. Very occasionally suggestions for a specific character – e.g. Dame – can be useful." Will consider applications from disabled actors to play characters with disabilities.

IN-HOUSE PANTOMIMES

Buxton Opera House

Water Street, Buxton, Derbyshire SK17 6XN
tel (01298) 72050 (admin) *fax* (01298) 27563
email admin@boh.org.uk
website www.buxtonoperahouse.org.uk
Chief Executive Andrew Aughton *Theatre Secretary* Pat Russell

Production details

A receiving theatre presenting around 450 performances each year including dance, comedy, children's shows, drama, musical concerts, pantomime and opera as well a Fringe Theatre and Community and Education Programme. Edwardian theatre designed by Frank Matcham, restored in 2001.

Casting procedures

Commissioned Channel Theatre to produce its 2007 annual pantomime, and it is anticipated that this arrangement will continue. Philip Dart, the artistic director of Channel Theatre, is responsible for casting. Please see the entry under *Middle and smaller-scale companies* on page 192.

Cambridge Arts Theatre

6 St Edwards Passage, Cambridge CB2 3PJ
tel (01223) 578903 *fax* (01223) 578929
email slowe@cambridgeartstheatre.com
website www.cambridgeartstheatre.com
Theatre Administrator Sue Lowe

Production details

Seating capacity 665. A receiving theatre which presents a wide range of work, including children's theatre, music, dance and drama. Produces in-house panto annually.

Casting procedures

Engages a freelance director who, together with the producer and choreographer, is responsible for casting the panto. Actors should contact the theatre to request an audition for the pantomime in March/April. These submissions will be forwarded to the director. Submissions should be marked for the attention of Sue Lowe. Actors are employed under Equity approved contracts. Invitations to see actors in other productions are only welcomed from actors in whom the director has already shown interest. Will consider applications from disabled actors to play disabled characters.

The Capitol

North Street, Horsham, West Sussex
tel (01403) 756080 *fax* (01403) 756092
website www.thecapitolhorsham.com
Artistic Director Michael Gattrell

Production details

Seating capacity 423. Produces a professional pantomime each year. Offers TMA/Equity approved contracts.

Casting procedures

Uses in-house casting director. Optimum time to write requesting an audition is in Spring/Summer. Casting breakdowns are publicly available on the website, in *SBS* or by postal application (with sae). Accepts letters (with CVs and photographs) from individual actors previously unknown to the company, sent by post or email. Also welcomes invitations to view showreels and to attend other productions. Will consider applications from disabled actors to play disabled characters.

The Theatre, Chipping Norton

2 Spring Street, Chipping Norton,
Oxfordshire OX7 5NL
tel (01608) 642349 *fax* (01608) 642324
email administration@chippingnortontheatre.com
website www.chippingnortontheatre.com
Director John Terry *General Manager* Christopher C Durham *Community & Education Officer* Anneke Hay

Production details

The Theatre is a pivotal part of the artistic life of the area, and takes care to programme as diverse a range of performances – theatre, film, dance, comedy and opera – as possible. Its Community & Education programme takes film and opera out to village halls.

An intimate space, it seats 217 (including 4 wheelchair spaces) in either proscenium (end-on) or in-the-round configurations. While predominantly a receiving house, The Theatre produces an annual pantomime which runs for around 80 performances over the Christmas period, as well as occasional smaller ventures. Recent productions include: *Mother Goose* and *Puss in Boots*, new pantomimes by Simon Brett; and *Taste*, a new play which toured Normandy.

The Theatre offers TMA/Equity approved contracts and subscribes to the Equity Pension Scheme.

Casting procedures

Does not use casting directors. Welcomes unsolicited CVs and photographs from actors unknown to the company, as well as invitations to view actors' websites. Casting breakdowns for the pantomime are available from mid-summer – via the website, postal application (with sae), the Equity Job Information Service, and occasionally *The Stage*; this is the best time to write to request inclusion. Actively encourages applications from disabled actors, and promotes the use of inclusive casting.

City Varieties

Swan Street, Leeds LS1 6LW
tel 0113-391 7777 *fax* 0113-234 1800
email info@cityvarieties.co.uk
website www.cityvarieties.co.uk
Artistic Director Peter Sandeman

Production details

Seating capacity 531. Grade II listed building, built in 1865. World-famous as the home of BBC TV's *Good Old Days*. Produces a professional pantomime each year, running from the end of November to mid-January. Also continues to produce *Good Old Days* music hall entertainment. Actors are employed under Equity approved contracts and the theatre subscribes to the Equity Pension Scheme.

Casting procedures

Optimum time to write requesting an audition is between February and May. Accepts submissions (with CVs and photographs) from individual actors previously unknown to the company. Invitations to attend other productions are also welcome, depending on distance. Rarely has the opportunity to cast disabled actors (the venue is not currently wheelchair accessible).

Connaught Theatre

Union Place, Worthing, West Sussex BN11 1LG
tel (01903) 231799
website www.worthingtheatres.co.uk
Admin Officer Rosie Gray

Production details

Seating capacity 506 with 6 wheelchair spaces. The Connaught Theatre was built in 1914, but was originally called the Picturedrome. For 20 years it was an early cinema, until 1935 when the Worthing Repertory Company outgrew its own premises and came into the venue, bringing with it the name Connaught Theatre.

Casting procedures

A receiving theatre, but from 2007 has been co-producing its annual panto with The Proper

Theatre

Pantomime Company (see entry on page 237.) Casting enquiries should be through Chris Lillicrap at The Proper Pantomime Company.

The Courtyard

The Courtyard Centre for the Arts, Edgar Street, Hereford HR4 9JR
tel (01432) 346500 *fax* (01432) 346349
email martyn.green@courtyard.org.uk
website www.courtyard.org.uk
Artistic Director Martyn Green *Administrator* Mel Langford

Production details

Seating capacity 436. The Courtyard opened in September 1998 and was the first Lottery-funded theatre to be built in England. It provides "an eclectic programme of work, from produced to received, and offers something for the whole community". Produces a professional pantomime each year, from end November to mid January. Provides actors with Equity-approved contracts as negotiated through TMA.

Casting procedures

Uses in-house casting directors; actors may write in June to request an audition. Casting breakdowns are available from the website, in *PCR*, or via CastNet Ltd, Castweb and SBS. Welcomes letters (with CVs and photographs) from individual actors previously unknown to the company, sent by post or email. Also accepts showreels and invitations to visit other productions. Actively encourages applications from disabled actors and promotes the use of inclusive casting.

Cumbernauld Theatre

Kildrum, Cumbernauld, Glasgow G67 2BN
tel (01236) 737235 *fax* (01236) 738408
email info@cumbernauldtheatre.co.uk
website www.cumbernauldtheatre.co.uk
Artistic Director Ed Robson

Production details

Established in 1978. A year-round producing theatre with a broad range of artist development and creative learning programmes. Produces a professional pantomime each year, together with other in-house plays, musicals and 'seasons'. Recent productions include: *The Wasp Factory* by Iain Banks.

Casting procedures

Casting is done by the Artistic Director. Auditions are held all year round; actors should obtain casting breakdowns from the website only. Welcomes letters (with CVs and photographs) from individual actors previously unknown to the company sent by post or email. Will consider invitations to visit other productions, but requests that no showreels be submitted. Actively encourages applications from disabled actors and promotes the use of inclusive casting.

The Everyman Theatre

Regent Street, Cheltenham, Gloucestershire GL50 1HQ
tel (01242) 572573 *fax* (01242) 224305
email admin@everymantheatre.org.uk
website www.everymantheatre.org.uk
Director of ReachOut Paul Milton (new writing)
Production Assistant Deb Dovinson

Production details

Seating capacity: main house 668, studio 60. Built in 1891. A receiving theatre which presents a wide range of work, from stand-up comedy to children's theatre and including live music, dance and drama. Also works with many emerging and established theatre companies from Gloucestershire and beyond, creating partnerships and productions that are performed at the Everyman and on tour across the county. Produces in-house panto as well as promoting new writing.

Casting procedures

A freelance director is engaged to direct the panto. The director is responsible for the casting process and will choose how and where the casting breakdowns are made available. Actors should write requesting auditions for the panto in February, as auditions are held in March and April. Submissions (photos & CVs) are welcomed from actors previously unknown to the company for both panto and new writing projects; these should be marked for the attention of Deb Dovinson. The Everyman also runs an Actor's Lab, providing professional training and opportunities to meet and work with established directors. The Everyman Theatre is an equal opportunities employer and gives due consideration to applications from all sectors of the community.

The Gatehouse

Eastgate Street, Stafford ST16 2LT
tel (01785) 253595
website www.staffordgatehousetheatre.co.uk
Artistic Programme Manager Derrick Gask

Production details

Celebrated its silver jubilee in 2007. A receiving theatre which presents a wide range of work, from stand-up comedy to children's theatre and including live music, dance and drama. Usually produces its own in-house panto; however in 2007/8 the panto was a co-production with The New Wolsey Theatre, Ipswich (see entry under *Producing theatres* on page 0).

Casting procedures

Casting is done by freelance casting directors. Breakdowns are available via Spotlight to agents only.

Will consider applications from disabled actors to play disabled characters.

The Gatehouse also produces the Stafford Festival Shakespeare. See entry under *Festivals* on page 308.

Hackney Empire

291 Mare Street, London E8 1EJ
020-8510 4500 020-8510 4530
email susie.mckenna@hackneyempire.co.uk
website www.hackneyempire.co.uk
CEO Simon Thomsett *Associate Director &*
Pantomime Producer Susie Mckenna

Production details

Grade II listed Frank Matcham theatre built in 1901. Recently renovated and refurbished. Provides a wide range of productions for the local community and London as a whole. Seating capacity is up to 1280. Produces an immensely popular and critically acclaimed traditional pantomime, eschewing 'celebrities' in favour of the core elements of traditional pantomime: a well-conceived narrative line, spectacular sets and costumes, magical spectacle, music, dance and slapstick comedy. Offers TMA/Equity approved contracts.

Casting procedures

Casting breakdowns are not publically available, but actors wishing to audition for the pantomime should contact Susie Mckenna, by post or email, in August/September. Happy to receive appropriate showreels and invitations to view individual actors' websites. Actively encourages applications from disabled actors and promotes the use of inclusive casting.

Kenneth More Theatre

Oakfield Road, Ilford, Essex IG1 1BT
tel 020-8553 4464 *fax* 020-8553 5476
email kmtheatre@aol.com
website www.kmtheatre.co.uk
Manager and Artistic Director Vivyan Ellacott

Production details

Seating capacity 365. Ilford's civic theatre, the Kenneth More, opened on the very last day of 1974 with a preview of *The Beggar's Opera*. The official opening was on January 3rd, 1975.

Balances its commitment to amateur theatre by providing 26 weeks each year for local amateur companies. The remaining half of the programme consists of visiting professional shows and the professional in-house panto production.

Casting procedures

Casting for the panto is done in-house. There is a regular team of actors who perform in the panto but any additional casting is done through preferred agents. The best time to write requesting an audition

for the panto is August and September. Welcomes submissions (CVs and photo) from actors previously unknown to them. Actors applying should have song and dance or previous panto experience. Will consider invitations to see actors in other productions on 'word of mouth' recommendations. Has employed disabled performers but the theatre building has a number of accessibility issues for disabled actors. "We will always consider young local performers."

macrobert

University of Stirling, Stirling FK9 4LA
tel (01786) 467155 *fax* (01786) 466600
email info@macrobert.org
website www.macrobert.org
Artistic Director Liz Moran *Operations Director* Bill Armitage

Production details

A busy multi-venue arts centre seating 472, with particular emphasis on work with and for young people. Produces a professional pantomime each year, in November and December. Offers Equity approved contracts as negotiated through TMA. Subscribes to the Equity Pension Scheme.

Casting procedures

Uses freelance and in-house casting directors; actors may write in April and May to request inclusion. Welcomes letters (with CVs and photographs) from individual actors previously unknown to the company, sent by post or by email. Accepts showreels and invitations to visit other productions. Rarely (or never) has the opportunity to cast disabled actors.

Millfield Theatre

Silver Street, Edmonton, London N18 1PJ
tel 020-8887 7301
website www.millfieldtheatre.co.uk
Arts Centre Manager and Producer Ralph Dartford

Production details

Produces panto in-house. Has been a receiving theatre but is now starting to co-produce a couple of productions each year with partners such as Face Front Inclusive Theatre (**www.facefront.org**).

Casting procedures

Casting is done by liaising with show director and in-house producer. Breakdowns for the panto are sent out to agents via Spotlight Link. Contracts offered are negotiated directly with actors or their agents. Actors can write requesting an audition for the panto in May, addressing their submission to Ralph Dartford. At present only welcomes submissions (with CVs and photographs) from actors previously unknown to the company at the time of casting the panto (May). As co-productions are still relatively new to the theatre, is considering developing the website to include a casting page. Will only view showreels if they have been requested. Welcomes invitations to see actors in other productions in the Greater London area. Will consider invitations to shows at The Edinburgh Festival. Encourages applications from disabled actors and promotes the use of inclusive casting.

The Customs House Trust Ltd

Mill Dam, South Shields, Tyne & Wear NE33 1ES
tel 0191-454 1234 *fax* 0191-456 5979
email mail@customshouse.co.uk
website www.customshouse.co.uk
Executive Director Ray Spencer

Production details

Seating capacity 441. Established in 1994 as an arts centre, gallery, cinema and theatre. Produces approximately 6 in-house shows each year, and is a member of the North East Theatre Consortium. Stages a professional pantomime in early December which runs through to the first week in January, as well as new writing and occasional new musicals. Provides actors with Equity-approved contracts as negotiated through TMA.

Casting procedures

Uses both in-house and freelance casting directors. The pantomime is cast in June, and CVs are received all year. Casting breakdowns are available from *PCR*. Welcomes letters (with CVs and photographs) from individual actors previously unknown to the compay, sent by post or email. Also accepts invitations to visit other productions. Advises actors to "find out about the venue via our website. Mention our work; it makes us feel important and makes you look as if you care!".

Theatre Royal, Bury St Edmunds

Westgate Street, Bury St Edmunds, Suffolk IP33 1QR
email sharron.stowe@theatreroyal.org
website www.theatreroyal.org
Artistic Director Colin Blumenau *Artistic Co-ordinator* Sharron Stowe

Production details

Seating capacity 358. Built in 1819, the theatre is the only surviving Regency theatre in the country. Produces an annual pantomime at Christmas and produces two other shows a year – a rural tour in the Spring (2007 production was Ayckbourn's *Intimate Exchanges*) and an in-house production in the autumn, often from or about the Regency period. Offers non-Equity contracts.

Casting procedures

Casting is done in-house by Sharron Stowe. Casting breakdowns are published via *Spotlight* only. Actors wishing to be considered for the pantomime should

write to the theatre in August. (The Spring and Autumn shows are cast in January/February and June/July respectively). Only welcomes letters and emails (with CVs and photographs) from actors previously unknown to the company during these casting periods. Does not welcome showreels but is happy to receive performance notices. Rarely or never has the opportunity to cast disabled actors.

Theatre Royal, Margate

Addington Street, Margate, Kent CT9 1PW
tel 0845-130 1786 (Box Office)
tel (01843) 293397 (Admin)
email admin@theatreroyalmargate.com
website www.theatreroyalmargate.com
Artistic Director Will Wollen *General Manager* Art Hewitt

Production details

Seating capacity 440. "A dynamic theatre which re-opened in September 2007 under the leadership of Will Wollen. Receives 2 seasons of professional work and produces its own high-quality actor-musician Christmas show." As well as producing a professional pantomime in December each year, the company is developing new work with Associate companies from the South East.

Casting procedures

Uses in-house casting directors. Actors may write in June and July to request inclusion. Casting breakdowns are sometimes available, obtained via Spotlight, Equity Job Information Service and CastNet Ltd. Welcomes unsolicited approaches (by post – letters, CVs and photographs) from actors previously unknown to the company, only if those actors are actor-musicians and/or Kent-based. No emails, please. Will accept showreels (although "these are not necessary") and invitations to visit other productions. Actively encourages applications from disabled actors, and promotes the use of inclusive casting.

Theatre Royal, Norwich

Theatre Street, Norwich NR2 1RL
tel (01603) 598500 *fax* (01603) 598501
email j.walsh@theatreroyalnorwich.co.uk
website www.theatreroyalnorwich.co.uk
Programming Manager Jane Walsh

Production details

Seating capacity 1300. Produces an annual pantomime each Christmas and is a receiving house for the rest of the year. Offers ensemble actors Equity approved contracts (principals are on buy-out contracts) and subscribes to the Equity Pension Scheme.

Casting procedures

Casts in-house. Actors wishing to audition for the pantomime should contact Jane Walsh in Feb/March.

Casting breakdowns are not published. Uses *SBS* to recruit chorus/ensemble; principals will generally be star names or performers that the theatre already has some relationship with. Welcomes letters and emails (with CVs and photographs) from actors not previously known to the company. Does not welcome showreels or performance notices. Will consider applications from disabled actors on the same basis as for non-disabled actors. "Take time to research the theatre's needs before sending your CV. Lots of CVs and photographs are wasted because they are sent at a time when they are not required."

Theatre Royal, Nottingham

Theatre Square, Nottingham NG1 5ND
tel 0115-989 5500 *fax* 0115-950 3476
email enquiry@royalcentre-nottingham.co.uk
website www.royalcentre-nottingham.co.uk
Managing Director & Pantomime Executive Producer
Jimmy Ashworth

Production details

Seating capacity 1186. Produces in-house commercial pantomime each year as well as occasional children's shows and community theatre. Offers actors Equity approved contracts but does not subscribe to the Equity Pension Scheme.

Casting procedures

Casts in-house. Actors wishing to request an audition should contact Jimmy Ashworth in April/May.

Casting breakdowns are not publicly available. Welcomes letters and emails (with CVs and photographs) from actors previously unknown to the company. Happy to receive appropriate showreels and performance notices. Actively encourages applications from disabled actors and promotes the use of inclusive casting.

Theatre Royal, Winchester

Jewry Street, Winchester, Hampshire SO23 8SB
tel (01962) 844600 *fax* (01962) 810277
website www.theatre-royal-winchester.co.uk
Chief Executive Fiona Burn

Production details

Seating capacity 400. A receiving theatre which presents a wide range of work, from stand-up comedy to children's theatre and including music, dance and classic plays. The theatre was re-opened in 2001 following a major refurbishment. Produces panto in-house.

Casting procedures

Casting is done by the Director of the show. Breakdowns are available publicly mid-June through *PCR*. Only welcomes submissions (with CVs and photographs) from actors previously unknown to the company in response to a casting breakdown. Encourages applications from disabled actors and promotes the use of inclusive casting.

Starting your own theatre company

Pilar Ortí

The first question you should ask yourself before starting a theatre company is – do you really need to set up a company, or do you just want to put on a show? In order to put on a show you don't need to go through all the hassle of setting up a company. If you *do* want to set up a company – why? In some cases this might be as difficult a question to answer as, "Why do you want to act?", but it's worth having an idea of why you want to invest so much time and energy in setting up and running an organisation rather than looking for acting work. Whatever your answer, be honest with yourself. And the clearer you can be, the better, as this will affect the kind of organisation you end up creating.

Of course, many companies emerge after a group of actors produce a show together: at some point, someone decides that as a company of people, you are worth keeping together. If this is the case, then you are ready to run a company of your own. But there are many ways of making theatre, as you well know, and the range of theatre produced is also vast. What kind of work do you want to do? At this point it is worth bearing in mind your 'artistic policy', and coming up with a couple of sentences that describe the work you do. I know that 'policy' sounds dry, but if you end up constituting yourself as a non-commercial organisation and applying to public funds (or trusts and foundations), you will need to learn a whole new vocabulary which seems to have little to do with your art. You should never lose sight of your artistic dreams and ambitions – but you may need to talk about them in terms of policy, objectives, qualitative evaluation, benefits, management structure, cultural diversity, contingency ... the list goes on and on. This article is meant to inspire you, not send you off to sleep, so don't despair: learn the language and then use it in a creative way that makes sense to you.

Allow yourself to dream

Long-term plans are necessary – so learn to dream. (Okay, give it a try in the first instance by putting on a show. Then, if you enjoy it, carry on!) Plans, of course, can change along the way: I suggest that you have an absolutely ambitious dream plan and a let's-try-and-see-what's-possible-now plan. Opportunities arise when you least expect them, and if you know where you are heading, you can grab them without letting them throw you off-course.

I view running a theatre company rather like directing a show: the more theatre you watch, the stronger the idea you will have of what *you* want the show to be, what is unique about it, and what you can realistically achieve. So, if you, like me, trained as an actor or actress and suddenly find yourself running a company, seek advice and look at how others operate. If you consider how other people do things, you will be able to adapt the bits you like and which make sense to you. In a sector such as ours, it is not difficult to find those pleased to help – and the freshness of people just starting out reminds us all of how much can be achieved when we don't know our limitations.

Seek help

There is an awful lot of free/cheap advice out there. During the year in which we focused on building the administrative foundations for our company, my colleague and I talked to as many consultants, local authority officers, venue managers, etc. as we could. Some of these conversations came about through informal meetings; others, by taking part in official programmes. We found out what funders were really looking for, and what other companies were doing in our area; we learnt to draw up business plans with budgets covering three and five years; and we discovered what our strengths and weaknesses were, and what threats and opportunities exist 'out there'.

A word of warning: take *all* advice (including that which I am giving you now) with a pinch of salt, especially from those who hardly know you and your work. Follow your gut instinct. When we were in pre-production for *Antigone*, a business consultant suggested that we invite Funeral Services to advertise in our programme, "seeing as how they all die in the end". Mmm.

The best consultancies are those which have been carefully structured so that the consultant spends time with you, getting to know you and your plans, and then helps you find your own answers by providing their expertise. Arts & Business's 'Business in the Arts' programme is worth checking out, although you need to have a very definite idea of what you need help with. (To see what else Arts & Business do, check out their website, **www.aandb.org.uk**.)

Making it 'proper'

Once you have decided on the work you want to do and how you want to go about producing it, you will need to find a legal structure for your company. This shows outsiders that you are serious, and it also makes monetary transactions easy.

Forbidden's first show was produced in Edinburgh: the only 'proper' thing the company had was a bank account (and a name!). We then registered the name and became a limited company, and after our first London show, became a registered charity. This was a good idea as our income mainly comes from trusts and foundations (most of which require you to be a charity to receive their grants, for tax purposes); it also allows us to claim Gift Aid when we receive donations from individuals. (Gift Aid is great: the donor claims their donation as tax-deductible, and you receive an extra 23 per cent from the Inland Revenue.)

Setting up a charity still allows you to pursue your own artistic programme: making theatre for the public is considered to 'advance education', which is a charitable objective. So you can still run your company as a business, drawing salaries, etc. and making sure that any annual profits stay within the company.

Just like a limited company, a registered charity is governed by a Board. The main difference between the two set-ups is that those who sit on a charity's Board (the Trustees) do so on a voluntary basis. It therefore would make no sense for *you* to be part of the Board (although there is talk of a possible change in the law to allow Trustees to be remunerated for their work). This means that, in theory at least, you are putting the fate of your company in the hands of other people. So choose your Trustees very carefully and try to include people who have some knowledge of legal matters and accountancy.

This set-up has worked for Forbidden, as we have been extremely lucky: we have managed to find experienced individuals with integrity and a passion for what we do. You might prefer a different kind of set-up which gives you more legal control: banks and Business Links offer free advice on the different options. If you want some focused advice and have a bit of cash to spare, you might attend the Independent Theatre Council's (ITC) seminar on 'Starting a Theatre Company' … and when you have a bit more cash, you might want to join the ITC – membership is bound to come in handy when questions on legal matters start to arise. (Have a look at the website, **www.itc-arts.org.uk**.)

Learn as you go along

Know your strengths and weaknesses. Setting up a theatre company will involve doing ten thousand things you might never have done before; however, a lot of it can be learnt along the way, and much of it is common sense. It won't take you long to discover those things you are useless at, and those that you absolutely hate. You then have two choices: do them anyway, or find someone else to do them for you/with you.

If there are more than two of you running the company, decide who will be in charge of what. Certain things like fundraising might be too daunting for one person to do on their own, but you can break it down into more manageable pieces: someone might have a clearer head for numbers and can prepare the budget, and someone else can write the description of the show and why it will make a huge contribution to theatre in this country.

Let's talk about money

And seeing as I've come to fundraising, I shall dwell on it. You can't escape it. No matter how much your company grows, no matter how successful you are, no matter how large your staff is – if you are in charge, you will worry about it, so learn to enjoy it. I know that this sounds perverse ... but fundraising applications are your chance to enthuse someone else about what you do. To tell them about your plans – about what you want to do and why you want to do it. Tell them how you want to make a difference; about *why* you think it's different; about how it will help you, and others, grow. And yes, you will need to learn some new vocabulary and be able to distinguish between qualitative and quantitative evaluation, but it helps if you see this as a game with which you have to keep up. (At the last ITC annual general meeting, I found out that 'well-being' is a new way of convincing funders that theatre is necessary to people's lives!) What's really important is to convince funders that you really want to do the work, and that you want to do it well. (When I talk about funders, I am referring to anyone who might want to donate to or invest in your company. I have no experience of commercial deals, but I imagine that these work in a similar way: you find out what it is that people want in return for their money, and then convince them that you can provide it – as well as putting on a really good show.)

This is also where having long-term plans comes in handy: funding applications usually take between six weeks and three months to be assessed. Sometimes, even more: our first successful application for an Education Officer took more than one year from the date on which I sent it to the day the letter of acceptance came through. While I'm on the subject of those who will give you money – *nurture your relationships with them*. We have found that those trusts, foundations and individuals who are willing to help us out once, are likely to do so again.

I have also discovered that funding applications help you plan in detail how you are going to realise a production or a project. Good funding applications might come in useful even if you don't get the money – they will probably provide a good description of your plans which you can then show others interested in your work. (For books and directories on Fundraising, check out the Directory of Social Change's website, **www.dsc.org.uk**. They also have a small bookshop in Stephenson Way, near Euston Square in London NW1.)

Final words

I have left the most important thing until last. *Treat those working with you well, especially your actors.* Make working with you an enjoyable experience. If you hold auditions, make them worthwhile for those attending. When you are able to pay your personnel, pay them on time. Treat them like the professionals that they are. And when things go wrong, as they inevitably will, take responsibility for your company and make up for the hassle with a gesture, however small – custard creams work for me!

When I first started running Forbidden, I kept hearing that I should treat it like running a business. What I have discovered is that it is an exercise in people management. Forbidden exists because people have believed in our work and are willing to invest their time and money in what we do. Different organisations work in different ways: I hope these words have helped you find one that will work for you.

After running Forbidden Theatre Company as Artistic Director for seven years, **Pilar** now uses her people management skills to facilitate learning in leaders and in teams. She is director of Unusual Connections, a company which uses theatre-based training to deliver Leadership Programmes and Strategic Team-Away days. She also freelances as workshop leader and voce-over artist, and can be contated via **info@unusualconnections.co.uk**

Finding funding for projects
Sinead Mac Manus

Finding funding for projects is an essential part of the subsidised theatre scene. Unless you are working in the commercial sector, most theatre productions do not generate enough income to cover their costs. Fundraising provides the shortfall. The funding landscape in the UK is wide and varied and can seem to the beginner to be an impossible terrain to navigate. However, as with most things there are tricks of the trade that you can learn and the process *does* get easier with practice.

Starting points

There are two good starting publications that I would recommend for fledging arts fundraisers: the first entitled 'Guide to Arts Funding in England', is an excellent overview of arts funding available to download for free from the Department for Culture, Media and Sport (DCMS) website (**www.culture.gov.uk/what_we_do/Arts/funding_for_the_arts**). Also recommended is Susan Forrester's & David Lloyd's *The Arts Funding Guide* published by the Directory of Social Change in 2002 (**www.dsc.org.uk**), which may be available in your local library. These guides take the user through the areas where you can find funding for projects, such as Government grants including Arts Council funding, Lottery funding, funding from your Local Authority, grants from charitable trusts and foundations, and bursaries.

Research, research, research

Successful fundraising is all about research and matching available funds to your projects. If you approach fundraising creatively you should be able to adapt projects to available funds while still retaining your artistic integrity. So how do you find out what is out there? Get on the arts mailing lists to find out about new rounds of funds. Research the funding bodies and their criteria. Talk to your local Council about what funds they can offer you and your project. Find out what venues support new work with bursaries or support in kind such as free space. Find out what trusts and foundations there are and who they give money to. Look up fundraising directories in your local library or one of the resource centres at organisations such as CIDA in east London (**www.cida.co.uk**), the Directory of Social Change (**www.dsc.org.uk**) or Arts and Business (**www.aandb.org.uk**).

The Funder Finder website (**www.funderfinder.org.uk**) features downloadable resources including a handy budget tool and grant application tool. Their cd-rom with details of hundreds of grants can be found in some resource centres or libraries for free use. They also have a free comprehensive advice pack on their website which has downloadable leaflets on areas such as budgeting, planning a funding strategy and tips for successful applications. The website also has a comprehensive A–Z list of trusts and foundations that have available funds.

It is important to research the funder that you are applying to, to find the 'essence' of the funder. This is essential so that you can match your projects to the relevant funder. For example, a Lottery Funding scheme such as Awards for All (**www.awardsforall.org.uk**) distributes public money for the benefit of local communities. Therefore any application to them must be for a project that demonstrates clear benefit to an identified community or body of people.

Similarly, the Arts Councils of England, Wales, Scotland and Northern Ireland all distribute public funds so they have to be very open and transparent about how their funds are distributed.

Arts Council England (ACE) is the development and funding agency for the arts in England. You can apply to ACE as an individual for funding between £200 to £30,000. Organisations can receive up to £100,000. You can apply any time and there are no deadlines. A decision will be forthcoming with six weeks for grants under £5,000 and twelve weeks for grants over £5,000. ACE set aims every three years which form the basis of their grant making policy so it is important for applicants to think about how their project will fit into these aims. As with any funding body, building a relationship is paramount. Even before you approach ACE for funding, you should be inviting them to your productions and telling them about your projects. Full details of how to apply including guidance notes are on the website (**www.artscouncil.org.uk**).

The Arts Council of Wales (**www.artswales.org.uk**) has a similar funding system and structure to England but there are regular funding deadlines throughout the year. The Scottish Arts Council (**www.scottisharts.org.uk**) has a slightly more complicated funding system with deadlines for different funding streams. The Arts Council of Northern Ireland (**www.artscouncil-ni.org**) has different funding schemes for individuals and organisations and different closing dates for individual schemes.

In contrast to the Arts Councils in the UK, many charitable trusts and foundations only distribute funds to limited companies, and in some cases, registered charities. Some can fund individuals but they are not many. When applying to trusts and foundations, it is important to remember they were usually set up to address an issue or problem. You will need to identify what this is and ensure that your project addresses this.

Find out what you can about the funding body that you are applying to and what their funding priorities are. Make sure you fit into their guidelines and that you are eligible to apply. Remember that all funders have agendas – they do not give money away for nothing. For example, many Local Authority arts funding schemes usually look for local projects that impact on the community and have public benefit. View researching and applying for funding as you would looking for a job. You would not apply to a company if you did not think you were qualified. Similarly, you are wasting your time and theirs if you apply for funding that you are not eligible to get, e.g. your theatre company is not a registered charity or they only fund work with older people and you work with children.

The proposal

An easy to read guide on writing funding proposals is Tim Cook's *Avoiding the Wastepaper Basket – A practical guide to applying to Grant Making Trusts* (LVSC, 1998). The book is written from the perspective of the funding body and looks at examples of good and bad funding proposals.

If there is no application form, write a clear and concise (2 x A4 page) proposal. Write in plain English and do not use jargon. Find what the 'grain' of the funding body is. Do their work for them. Show in your funding application exactly how you meet their criteria and fit into their funding policy. Again to use the analogy of applying for a job, use the exact wording of the guidelines in your application when you are talking about your project, much in the way you would use the wording in the Person Specification when you are applying for a job. You can even highlight their criteria in bold or italics to make it stand out.

Theatre

Follow the guidelines of the fund to the letter – supply all the information that they require but do not add in additional information if it is not requested. If you have something that you think may be of interest to them, mention that this is available on request in your application. Convey your enthusiasm and passion for your project and your belief in yourself and/or your company. Show how the project will be successful. Funders like to back winners.

When you are finished, show your finished application to a non-arts person and ask them to read it for clarity. If you do get a grant, remember to say thank you! Start to build a relationship with the funder and keep them updated on progress with the project. If you are not successful, ask for feedback from the funder on why.

Business sponsorship

Business sponsorship can be a useful way of raising funds for projects if you are not eligible to apply for grant project funding. Business sponsorship is where a company gives your organisation or project cash, or support in kind, in exchange for publicity for their product or service. It is important to remember that businesses will not give you money or support for nothing – they will require something in return. Sponsorship is essentially a commercial deal between yourself and the business and therefore there should be a clear exchange of benefits, e.g. advertising benefit for the company and monetary benefit for the arts organisation, and there should be a value to the benefit given or received.

Arts & Business is the leading agency for bringing business and the arts together in the UK. Their website provides valuable information about building relationships between the arts and business including details of investment schemes such as *Read* and *Invest*. They also publish an essential guide to business sponsorship entitled *Arts Business Sponsorship Manual* which is included when you book on their Arts & Business Sponsorship Seminar which is held regularly around the UK. The guide and other resources on sponsorship can also be read at their free resource centre in London (**www.aandb.org.uk**).

Income generation

An important part of finding funding for projects is generating your own income. Income can be earned or generated from a number of different sources: venues can pay you a fee or share the box office receipts of a production with you. They can also commission or co-produce a work. You can sell merchandise at your events such as programmes, t shirts or postcards. You can generate income through education work including fees for workshops and residencies. Individuals can give you money for your projects (angels) or they can invest in your work and expect (or not!) a return. You can also raise funds through events ranging from theatre related events such as benefit performances and cabarets to 'fun' events such as sponsored walks to parachute jumps.

Creative thinking

When you are starting out, it can be difficult to see where you are going to get the money for projects. The Arts Council do prefer to fund artists or organisations with a track record and therefore you may have to find alternative funding initially for your productions or projects. Trusts and foundations tend to only fund limited companies or registered charities and so again this may not be an area of funding that you can tap into straight away.

Therefore it is important to think of ways of funding your work outside of the traditional funding system. In many cases, this may mean that you have to fund your work yourself and hope that you can get a return on it or at least break even. This is how the majority of companies fund their Edinburgh Fringe Festival run – by investing the money upfront in the hire of the venue, the accommodation and travel and the cost of the production and hoping that the take at the box office will cover these costs and give everyone involved in the production some wages. If you are using your own money to mount a production, you need to be able to assess what level of risk you are willing to accept and think of ways of lessening this risk. Take your budget and see where you can reduce or cut costs. You could try to get free rehearsal space from a local school in exchange for workshops or use a local printer for your flyers in exchange for advertising in your programme. Consider sharing your venue with another company for a double bill (check that this is acceptable to the venue in advance) to halve the costs of the venue hire. Book a venue in your local area that you know so that you can at least invite friends and family to have a guaranteed audience. Ask friends and family to invest small amounts of money in your production. This can be done as a gift or on an investment and return basis e.g. an individual invests £100 and is guaranteed a return of £75 or an amount above £100 depending on how well the show does. Offer credits for purchase in the production as gifts – purchasers get credit in the publicity material and an invitation to a performance.

There are many examples of artists and companies that have used creative ways to get their projects up and running. One company sold performances in the customer's sitting room on EBay for cash. Another company raised the money for a string of rural performances by doing a sponsored walk from venue to venue. Another company raised the money for a production by offering to do up a local community centre – they got free rehearsal space and a venue as part of the deal.

Remember that you are a creative individual! Use some of that creativity to think outside the box when it comes to find money for projects.

Sinead Mac Manus has worked for a wide range of arts organisations, including Frantic Assembly, Tall Stories and Mimbre. She is currently a freelance creative business consultant and trainer, and has many years of experience working with and training creative entrepreneurs. She is the author of *eVolve Graduate Handbook: a practical guide to producing performance*, and founder of **StartaTheatreCompany.com** – an online guide to starting a performing arts company. Her activity in developing new business models around the idea of e-learning for creative entrepreneurs using web 2.0 tools and social media led her to be chosen this year as one of the Courvoisier: Future 500 to watch.

Theatre

English-language European theatre companies

This small section seems to be populated by companies set up by enthusiasts who have kept on going with very little subsidy – and sometimes with none at all. Although living away from home and isolated from auditions, it can be fun working for such companies. It is important to note that the work often involves educational projects and/or touring.

ACT Company
25 Avenue du Marechal Leclerc, 92240 Malakoff, France
tel (33) 1 4656 2050
email andrew@actheatre.com
website www.actheatre.com
Artistic Director Andrew Wilson *Administrator* Anne Wilson *Secretary* Marie Christine Bento

Founded in 1981. An English-language theatre company focusing on research and development to make theatrical experiences in English accessible to a non-native-speaking public. Runs theatre in Education projects, workshops, performing for adults and young French native speakers learning English. Takes a physical approach to theatre - regularly working with actors from L'Ecole Internationale de Théâtre Jacques Lecoq. See the Act website for recent and present productions. "As we are based in France we do not follow the Equity system of salaries. However, our system of payment follows the recognised system here in France paying actors by the performance. This 'French system' however requires actors to be registered here in France, so casting is mainly with French registered bilingual actors."

Casting is during the months of May and June and CVs (by post) are welcome just before this period. "Please note we are a small company and engage no more than eight actors per season. We are completely open to casting disabled actors, but please note that we are a touring company and a reasonable arrangement needs to be made between us and the actor concerning travel arrangements."

Dear Conjunction Theatre Company
6 Rue Arthur Rozier, 75019 Paris, France
tel (33) 1 4241 6965
email dearconjunction@wanadoo.fr
Artistic Directors Leslie Clack, Patricia Kessler

Founded in 1991, this bilingual company is composed of professional actors, directors and writers who are resident in Paris and who present productions in both French and English. Past productions include: Pinter's *Ashes to Ashes* and *The Hothouse*; and *Someone Who'll Watch Over Me* by Frank McGuinness. Welcomes letters and emails

(with CVs and photographs) from actors previously unknown to the company. Contact Leslie Clack for more information.

The English Speaking Theatre Oslo (TESTO)
Jacob Aalls Gate 30, 0364 Oslo, Norway
tel (47) 22 466248
email testo-no@online.no
website home.tiscali.no/testo.no
Artistic Director Simon Lay *Director* Kristin Zachariassen

Founded in 1996 by actors Simon Lay and Kristin Zachariassen. Main focus of work is Theatre in Education. Produces theatre adaptations targeted at Norwegian students but also appealing to the general Norwegian public. Recent productions include: *How High Is Up?*, *Too Much for Punch and Judy*, *Pygmalion* and *The Woman in Black*.

The English Theatre Company Ltd
Nybrogatan 35, 114 39 Stockholm, Sweden
tel (46) 8 662 4133 *fax* (46) 8 660 1159
email etc.ltd@telia.com
website www.englishtheatre.se
Artistic Director Christer Berg

Founded in 1981. Stages 2 productions annually. Recent productions include: *Shirley Valentine* and *A Christmas Carol*. Uses freelance casting directors. Holds general auditions; actors requesting inclusion should write between August and September. Casting breakdowns are not publicly available. Welcomes postal enquiries from actors previously unknown to the company.

English Theatre Frankfurt
Kaiserstrasse 34, D-60329 Frankfurt, Germany
tel (49) 69 242 31615 *fax* (49) 69 242 31614
email mail@english-theatre.org
website www.english-theatre.org
Artistic Adviser Clive Paget *Managing Director* Daniel Nicolai

Founded in 1979. Presents contemporary plays, musicals and classics. 5 productions performed in the main house each year, totalling 260 performances.

Uses London-based freelance casting directors. Does not hold general auditions. Actors should write requesting inclusion in the company in April. Casting breakdowns are only available via Spotlight.

The English Theatre of Copenhagen

The London Toast Theatre, Kochsvej 18, 1812 Fred C, Copenhagen, Denmark
tel (45) 3322 8686
email mail@londontoast.dk
website www.londontoast.dk
Artistic Director Vivienne McKee *Administrator* Soren Hall

Founded in 1982. The largest English-speaking theatre company in Northern Europe. Presents theatre productions and provides corporate entertainment, stand-up comedy and Murder Mystery shows in Scandinavia and abroad. The company's voice-over bureau, 'Speaker's Corner', provides English and American voices for films and commercials. Recent productions include: *Dracula – A Pain in the Neck!* and *The Importance of Being Earnest.*

The English Theatre of Hamburg

Lerchenfeld 14, 22081 Hamburg, Germany
tel (49) 40 227 7089 *fax* (49) 40 229 5040
email ETHamburg@onlinehome.de
website www.englishtheatre.de
Contact Robert Rumpf, Clifford Dean

Founded in 1976 by 2 Americans, Robert Rumpf and Clifford Dean, who originally trained and worked professionally in the USA. They share general management responsibilities, plan the artistic programme and direct productions. Since 1981 the theatre has occupied its present premises at Mundsburg in 22081 Hamburg. Performs 8 times per week from September to June. A typical season at the English Theatre includes a classic American or British drama, a comedy and a thriller. Recent productions include: *Over the River and Through the Woods, I Ought To Be in Pictures, Educating Rita* and *When the Reaper Calls.* Also runs Education programmes.

Light Nights – The Summer Theatre

Baldursgata 37, IS-101 Reykjavik, Iceland
tel (354) 551 9181 *fax* (354) 551 5015
website www.lightnights.com
Artistic Director Kristín G Magnús

Runs a summer theatre show at the Idnó Theatre in Reykjavik. Previous productions have included: *Light Nights* and *On The Way to Heaven.*

Sometimes holds general auditions. The best time to write requesting inclusion is February/March. Casting breakdowns are not publicly available. Welcomes letters (with CVs and photographs) from actors previously unknown to the company, but not via email. Does not welcome showreels, but is happy to receive invitations to view actors' websites. Offers

non-Equity contracts; rarely (or never) has the opportunity to cast disabled actors.

Merlin International Theatre

1052 Budapest, Gerloczy Utca 4, Hungary
tel (36) 1 317 9338 *fax* (36) 1 266 0904
email angol@merlinszinhaz.hu
website www.szinhaz.hu/merlin/english
Director Laszlo Magacs *Associate Director* Emma Vidovsky

Founded in 1991; Hungary's first and currently its only international theatre. Recent productions include: *The Importance of Being Earnest, Don't Drink the Water, Stones in His Pockets* and *Twelfth Night.* Resident companies at the Merlin Theatre are the Atlantis Company, Junion Group and Madhouse.

Simply Theatre

8B Chemin des Couleuvres, 1295 Tannay, Switzerland
tel +41 22 860 0518
email info@simplytheatre.com
website www.simplytheatre.com
Artistic Director Thomas Grafton

Production details

Founded in 2005. A Professional English Theatre for Switzerland and Continental Europe; and an English-speaking Drama Academy. Stages 3 productions a year in the Main House (plus 3 Academy productions). Recent productions include: *Private Lives, Educating Rita,* and *Sleuth.*

Casting procedures

Holds general auditions and actors may write in at any time. Casting breakdowns are available from *Spotlight* and Casting Call Pro. Welcomes letters (with CVs & photographs) from actors previously unknown to the company, sent by post or email. Accepts showreels and invitations to view individual actors' websites.

Theatre From Oxford

B.P. 10, F-42750 St Denis de Cabanne, France
tel/fax 00-334-77-66-20-42
email theatre.oxford@virgin.net
Artistic Director Robert Southam

Founded in 1984, the main aim for the past 20 years has been to introduce audiences on the continent to the best of theatre in English. The company has toured plays by Shakespeare, Shaw, Wilde, Willy Russell, Tennessee Williams and Arthur Miller, among others. Touring for 3 months from September to Christmas in 7 European countries, the company plays in anything from the best theatres to school gyms – but nearly always to full houses. Tours again in the spring to many of the same venues, providing theatre workshops. Half of the spectators are students; the other half, adult theatre-goers. The company is shortly to have its own theatre in France.

Theatre

Actors are advised that the tours are enjoyable but demanding, and that the company seldom accepts anyone straight from drama school. Casts often include actors with RSC and RNT experience. Recently has been working with African, Asian and Latin American actors and writers, which has meant less work for British and American actors. Casting breakdowns are available by postal application (with sae) and actors are welcome to write letters or emails with their CVs and photographs. Showreels, however, are not welcomed. Offers non-Equity contracts. Will consider applications from disabled actors to play characters with disabilities.

Vienna's English Theatre

UK address: VM Theatre Productions Ltd, 16 The Street, Ash, Canterbury CT3 2HJ
tel (01304) 813330 *fax* (01304) 813330
email vanessa@vmtheatre.demon.co.uk
Theatre address: Josefsgasse 12, A-1080 Vienna, Austria
tel (43) 1 4021 2600 *fax* (43) 1 4021 26042
website www.englishtheatre.at

Founded in 1963 it is the oldest English-language theatre in continental Europe. It stages 5 shows each year in the Main House and sends 4 Theatre-in-Education tours around the schools of Austria. The season runs from September to July each year.

Casting breakdowns are posted on the website and actors may write to the UK address above with their CV and photograph at anytime. Emails not

encouraged, and showreels not accepted. "All contracts are especially written for us by Equity."

White Horse Theatre

Bördenstrasse 17, 59494 Soest-Müllingsen, Germany
tel (49) 2921 339339 *fax* (49) 2921 339336
email theatre@whitehorse.de
website www.whitehorse.de
Artistic Director Peter Griffith *Casting Director* Michael Dray

Founded in 1978. Tours schools in Germany with occasional visits to neighbouring countries. Contracts are for 10-11 months. 6 companies of 4 actors each perform 3 plays. Recent productions include: *The Glass Menagerie*, *Oliver Twist*, *A Midsummer Night's Dream* and numerous plays for 10-13 year-olds and for 14-16 year-olds.

Does not use freelance casting directors. Holds general auditions; actors should write in April requesting inclusion. Casting breakdowns are available through the website, postal application (with sae), Equity Job Information Service, *PCR* and advertisements in *The Stage*. Welcomes postal and email enquiries from actors previously unknown to the company. Invitations to view individual actors' websites are also accepted. Contracts are approved by GDBA (the German equivalent of Equity). Rarely has the opportunity to cast disabled actors since "all our actors must take part in 3 different plays, and they must also cope with the rigours of touring".

A touring actor's survival guide

Maev Alexander

Touring is more tiring, harder work, more all-consuming and more relentless than playing in one house. In order to give your best to it and get the best from it, you need to be thoroughly organised and disciplined. The main differences are, of course, the travelling and the accommodation. If you arrange these well in advance, you're on your way to having a happy and rewarding experience and saving yourself angst and money.

Getting there

At the beginning of rehearsals, or even before, you'll be given a schedule of dates and venues and a sheaf of digs lists. Work out as early as you can how you will travel and where you will stay.

If you have your own transport you can plan your journeys on a week-by-week basis, pulling maps and route finders and estimated journey times off the Internet – if you have access – both to digs and to theatres. A good company manager will supply maps of town centres with the venue clearly marked. A satnav can be reassuring, but don't rely on them in big town centres – we had to hold the curtain for a leading lady in Sheffield when her instructions were impossible to follow in a new road layout, so it's a good idea to keep your map-reading skills honed. It's amazing how they improve when you *have* to find digs and theatres within a tight timeframe.

If you don't have your own transport, ask around the company and find out if anyone lives close enough to you, and is willing, to give you lifts. Make it clear that you will contribute to petrol costs, be punctual and not bring too much luggage. If you are using public transport, book as far in advance as you can: Apex (or the equivalent) on trains and low-budget airlines will save you huge amounts of money. The touring company will expect you to do this, and will calculate the amount they give you in fares as economically as possible. Be aware that fares are worked out from venue to venue, and not to your home and out again. Remember also that you may get stuck on a Saturday night if your show comes down after the last train, which is more likely than not; this may add to your accommodation expenses. It also eats into your only day off; most No. 1 tours play Monday to Saturday, running for a week in each venue.

The rule for fares and touring allowance is: outwith 15 miles of your permanent base to qualify for fares only, and 25 miles to qualify for touring allowance. This is calculated from postcode to postcode – not by the most convenient or quickest route. Equity has negotiated sharp rises in the level of touring allowance over the last few years, and it is now reasonable. It's meant to cover accommodation and living expenses – and if you're frugal and careful, it can. You have to balance the level of comfort and convenience with which you need to live happily with the budget on which you have to do it.

Finding the right digs

Digs lists cover hotels, guesthouses, self-contained flats, houses for sharing, B&Bs and rooms in private houses. They normally tell you the price (per night or per week), the type of accommodation, the facilities, the prohibitions (i.e. no smoking, no pets), the extras (TV, kettle in room) and the distance from the theatre. The headliners can probably afford to stay in hotels (and many hotels do deals for touring actors), but other ranks will have to juggle their priorities. If you can feel comfortable in a room in a private house, sharing a bathroom and having access to a kitchen, you can do so remarkably cheaply. If you can't do without an en suite or need to be self-contained, it will obviously be more expensive, and so on up the scale; but read the list carefully and you will find something that will tick most of your boxes without too much compromise. The people who do the letting are generally friends of the theatre in some way, and the standard of accommodation is usually pretty high. I have heard horror stories of rooms booked in hotels on last-minute websites – all-night disco music and overpowering 'room fragrancers'.

Start ringing the most promising-sounding digs as soon as possible, before everyone else does. Good options are places within a 15-minute walk (obviating cabs or long, lonely walks or parking problems) or a house or cottage that is further out, possibly in countryside, to share with fellow company members both in terms of rent and transport. Beware of landlady-speak for 'a 15- to 20-minute walk' – some landladies clearly have seven-league boots! The level of rates varies from place to place: locations like Bath and Malvern tend to be more expensive across the board than, say, Southampton and Coventry. In big centres like Glasgow, Manchester, Birmingham and Leeds you will probably have to travel to the outskirts unless you can afford hotels.

When you've agreed terms with a landlord/lady, write to confirm the booking and the dates, and arrange to ring a couple of days in advance of the stay to negotiate a mutually convenient time to arrive (leave half an hour's leeway so you don't panic about getting lost). It's wise at least to drop off your luggage before the show so that you know you know where the place is, have keys and don't disturb anyone at a late hour – especially on the first night when there are likely to be drinks front-of-house afterwards. Sorting out digs gets easier the more you tour and the more contacts you acquire. Do ask experienced tourers if you're new to it – most actors are very generous about sharing the secrets of top digs. For future reference, keep records of where you've stayed and what it was like. Pay up front and remember to leave keys when you leave; get a receipt and behave well enough for the landlord/lady to wish to stay on the digs list. You represent future tourers.

What to take

It's important to pack well. Travel as light as you can, and have as much of your luggage on wheels as possible. You need enough clothes for a week, or longer if you need to go straight to the next venue; keep it simple, remembering to have something warm and something cool (because this is Britain) and something smart for the first-night drinks often provided by the host management or friends of the theatre. A towelling robe doubles as a dressing gown and post-shower gear. Take comfortable, reasonably weatherproof shoes, since you'll spend a lot of time walking. Remember your phone charger (it's worth having a spare for touring), and a toothbrush charger and adapter in case there are no shaving points. It's also worth having an emergency kit containing plasters and painkillers and cold remedies. In most places towels are provided, but pack a hand towel just in case. Travel with a hottie in winter: the only miserable digs I've had were very smart but *freezing*. I complained – do complain; you're not paying to freeze. A pocket torch is useful for unfamiliar, unlit keyholes. Don't forget comforts like books or a radio or iPod.

If you have to be away from your base for extended periods, negotiate doing your laundry with the wardrobe department. If you're home on Sunday, it saves time and hassle if you've put what needs washing into a separate bag in your case so that repacking is straightforward and quick. I was told early in my career that no proper actor has less than three weeks' worth of underwear!

You can generally travel your make-up and other dressing-room necessities, comforts and amusements in a bag or box on the truck transporting the set and props, etc. This is not an automatic right, though, so check with your company manager. Some reasonably rigid receptacle is optimum to avoid breakage; label it clearly with the name of the production and your own name and do not expect anyone else to lug it to or from your dressing room week by week. Pack it as soon as you can on Saturday night and check where you can leave it so it's not in the way of the get-out.

Eating and drinking

It's easy to be lazy about eating sensibly on tour – financially and nutritionally. Even if there are cooking facilities in your digs, it's not always convenient to be there and it's tempting to eat out all the time or grab burgers. You're going to need all your energy, so make a point of eating healthily.

In most theatres you'll have access to a microwave and possibly a fridge: ring the stage door and check. They're often in the crew room, so ask if you may use them and be considerate about clearing up after yourself. Making an interesting dressing-room picnic is a worthy challenge even if everything has to be cold. Supermarkets do better and better ranges of salads and sushi. Invest in a mini kettle for your touring box and pack a plate, a mug and cutlery. Set yourself a daily budget for food and then you'll know if you can splash out on a restaurant meal.

It's also tempting to do a great deal more after-show drinking when you're away from home: it can feel as if you're living in a bubble, out of the real world. Ask yourself if you're getting jaded/broke, and limit alcohol to within sensible limits. (The same sense of not being quite in the real world can lead too to the most unlikely affairs: be discreet, whether it involves other people or yourself.)

Bonding and recreation

After-show company meals, weekly or fortnightly, are good bonding exercises providing you all get on. Remember that it's not only part of your job to get on, but also in your best interests. It's even more important in the living-in-each-others'-pockets world of touring to be a good company member; leave your troubles firmly at the stage door and don't moan or gossip. If there's someone you find tricky, keep out of their way. In my experience, touring companies bond well and form even more of a parallel family than usual.

That said, getting away by yourself for a time is restoring. Find the local Tourist Information Office and find out about places of interest and specialist shopping. There's bound to be something that appeals to you, even if you're not a galleries/museums/castles/cathedrals person (the ABC of touring is famously, "another bloody cathedral"). I am lucky – and not alone – in regarding touring as being paid to go sightseeing. Stage door, or your company manager, can tell you of gym and leisure facilities and often arrange temporary membership; they can also point you in the direction of the nearest supermarkets and best-value restaurants.

Sussing out the theatre

One of the interesting and rewarding things about touring is playing the same show in lots of different theatres – from 900-seaters to 2000-seaters, from raked stages to flat stages, from Victorian to modern, from those with acres (seemingly) of orchestra pit to those where the front row is looking up your nose. You'll be called early on in the first day of each new venue, generally at about 5 or 6pm, to walk the stage, get to know the backstage layout and take note of significant differences. The presence or lack of a rake may mean more or fewer steps on a staircase, for instance; furniture may be closer together or further apart; wing space may be tight; prop tables may be in different places; dressing rooms will be varying distances away and you may be sharing in one venue and by yourself in another. Take time to absorb these differences, test the acoustic and plan how you're going to accommodate any changes you personally will have to make. Discuss these changes too with anyone else they may affect. Bear in mind that the audiences are always different, as well: it's amazing that what makes people laugh or weep in Cardiff is not the same as what makes people laugh or weep in Hull.

Find out when stage door opens; most theatres allow you access to your dressing room from quite early in the day, which is useful for dumping shopping or 'nesting' when it's tipping with rain. A few don't open until much later on, though, which is a great bore and makes it good to have digs close by.

Money matters

On a business level, keep a work diary and note down all your expenses (and mileages if you're driving). Have an envelope or plastic wallet in which to file all your receipts and payslips: it's much easier to lose track of these when you're away from home.

Tax offices vary in what they will allow you to claim on tour. Travel and accommodation expenses above your allowances are OK, but some accept claims for all eating expenses (again over and above), some for restaurant/cafe receipts only, and some – including my own – clearly expect you not to eat at all.

Research a mobile phone tariff that will let you keep in touch with family and friends, and your agent, as cheaply as possible.

Finally ...

More and more of the available work involves touring at some level. You might just as well maximise your chances of having a good time and making a decent profit. Regard it as an adventure.

Maev Alexander trained at the Royal Scottish Academy of Music and Drama and has been working in theatre, television and radio for 40 years. She has performed in Rep all over the country, playing everything from Cleopatra to a French poodle, been a member of the RSC, and holds the record as the longest-serving Mollie in *The Mousetrap*. She has starred in two TV series and guested in many others, presented the Newsdesk on *That's Life*, and played in dozens of radio dramas. After completing her 7th No. 1 tour in as many years, and transferring the last but one – *A Man for All Seasons* – to the Theatre Royal Haymarket in 2006, she has filmed *Death Defying Acts* with Catherine Zeta Jones and Guy Pearce, and recorded the second series of *The Eliza Stories* for BBC Radio 4.

Editors' note There are a number of websites that can help you plan your journeys to and from the locations on your tour; they may also save you money. Here are some of the major ones:

• *Maps*: **www.streetmap.co.uk**, **www.multimap.com**, and **maps.google.co.uk**. If you have a mobile phone capable of web browsing, point it to **www.google.co.uk/mmp** to access Google Maps for Mobile. Rather cleverly, if you tell it where you are, it can even give you directions to all the nearest pubs. (If you're going to be using this a lot, check how much

Internet access you have on your call plan. Google does not charge you for the service, but you may find yourself with some hefty Internet usage bills if you're not careful.)

• *Driving*: **www.theaa.com** and **www.rac.co.uk** both offer route-planning and maps, as do Google Maps and Google Maps for Mobile (see above).

• *Trains*: **www.nationalrail.co.uk** for timetables and **www.thetrainline.com** for booking the cheapest tickets available. Also worth looking at **www.megatrain.com** to check for promotional fares. In addition to these, **www.jplanner.org.uk** and **www.traveline.org.uk** are good ways of exploring options (train, coach, plane, etc.) for getting to a location. And of course, the number that the 118 companies get the most requests for: National Rail Enquiries is **08457 48 49 50**; if it's not in your phone already, why not put it there now?

• *Coaches*: **www.nationalexpress.co.uk**, **www.citylink.co.uk** (Scotland), **www.megabus.com/uk** (which often has promotional fares), and **www.eurolines.com** (destinations around Europe). In addition there are some local companies offering low-cost services to major cities such as London, which a little research should uncover.

• *London Transport*: **journeyplanner.tfl.gov.uk** or, from your mobile, text 60835 (60TFL) with 'a to b' (where 'a' and 'b' are stations, stops or postcodes in London) to find out the best way – tube, train or bus – of getting to where you're going. For example: 'Clapham Junction to The Old Vic'. Common sense and some knowledge of the geography of London may need to be applied to the directions given: in this example the text service recommends a bus journey from Waterloo Station to The Old Vic – a walk of three minutes at most.

• *Flying*: **www.travelsupermarket.com** or **www.skyscanner.net** will search out all available flights to a given destination, sorted by price.

Theatre

'Vanning it': the golden rules

Andrew Piper

Maev Alexander's article covers pretty much all you need to know about large-scale touring, and many of these principles carry over into small-scale touring too. However, the major difference between the two levels of touring is … The Van.

On a large-scale (or No. 1) tour you are generally responsible for getting to the venue yourself, since these are often in large towns with good transport links. By contrast, much of the work of mid- and small-scale companies is done in venues rather more 'off the beaten track' (a.k.a. The Middle of Nowhere), and often with only one performance in each venue. Most of these companies, then, will transport their actors around the country in a mini-bus, coach or van, which may also contain the set and lighting rig. Whereas the large-scale companies employ stage crew to do the get-ins and get-outs, on such productions it's often up to the actors and the stage manager to do everything.

'Vanning it' presents an additional set of challenges for the actor. If you don't get on with a fellow actor in a large-scale show, then you may be able to limit the amount of contact you have with them, other than your interaction on stage. If you're on a small-scale tour you will spend most of your waking hours in their company, so it's important that all company members work hard to keep a harmonious atmosphere. Van etiquette is similar to dressing-room etiquette – balancing your needs with the cast's collective needs, and the individual needs of cast members. You can never legislate for a happy company, but here are some of the 'Golden Rules' that will help enormously in that direction:

• *Pull your weight.* This kind of touring is very hard work – you may be travelling, doing a get-in, a show, and a get-out every day for several weeks or months, and slacking off is the one thing guaranteed to make you as popular as herpes. Don't dawdle in the get-out, either; being the cause of not getting to the pub in time for last orders will also not endear you to your colleagues.

• *Be punctual.* The call time is when the van *leaves*, not the time you start to leave your accommodation. Be sitting in your seat, bag stowed, ready to leave at least 5 minutes before the call time. As with almost anything in this business, you're wasting several people's time by keeping them waiting, so respect your fellow actors by being on time.

• *Music.* Bring a personal stereo or MP3 player; don't expect everyone in the van to like your taste in music. One stage manager I know resorted to telling the cast that the stereo had broken rather than sit through yet another argument about whose music to listen to. You might also want to consider a portable DVD player, either for the journeys (unless you're susceptible to travel sickness) or for something to do when you get to your accommodation. Check whether these would be covered by the company's insurance in case anything happened to them, and remember that very few pieces of electronic equipment are built to withstand the rigours of touring.

• *Mobile phones.* Keep conversations short, even (perhaps especially) with loved ones. There are few more irritating things to be forced to listen to than someone cooing to their lover for hours on end. If you're someone who gets a lot of calls, consider setting your phone to silent vibrate; there are only so many times one can listen to the Nokia tune before being overwhelmed by the urge to throw the offending phone out of the window.

• *Smoking.* *Never* smoke in the van, even if the windows are rolled down – it's inconsiderate, and most companies operate a no-smoking policy anyway. (Since the van is considered your workplace, it will also be covered by recent anti-smoking legislation.) Remember, too, that if you're puffing away seconds before climbing aboard then you will carry a strong smell of smoke with you into the van. Be considerate, too, about smelly food – curry, chips, fish, etc. – unless you're all tucking in.

• *Personal hygiene.* Important at all times in this business, but especially so when you're stuck in a confined space with the rest of the cast for what may be hours at a time, perhaps after a particularly physical show and/or get-out. Your fellow actors may be upfront enough to tell you if you're pongy – but don't rely on it. If someone else in the company is niffing, don't gossip behind their back: just tell them, in as direct and as kind a way as possible. Don't let it fester (in more senses than one!).

• *Games.* It's worth bringing a few travel games for when the conversation runs out, even if it's just a pack of playing cards – although not everyone will want to play at any given moment. A good book can help while away the time, too, although not everyone can read in a van without getting travelsick.

• *Sweets.* The 'tub of love'. It does wonders for morale if someone takes it upon themself to buy a big tub of sweets for the van.

• *Alcohol.* Check the company's policy. If it's permitted, then it's probably best that you either buy your own (sharing around if you desire) or join up with one or two other members of the cast. It's generally preferable not to have a kitty for the whole cast, because not everyone will want to drink the same stuff or the same quantities. If you are getting merry in the back of a van, be considerate to the driver: don't distract them (dangerous!) or be unreasonably raucous. S/he will have had a hard evening too, and tunelessly drunken renditions of football chants will hardly make the journey more pleasant. Remember too that requests for toilet stops when everyone's tired and wants to get home may not be popular.

• *Make the most of solo time.* When you do get some time to yourself, make the most of it. Go for a walk, listen to music, read, exercise, meditate, call friends or just sit in a coffee shop and watch the world go by. Camaraderie and team spirit are important in this kind of work, but don't be afraid to take time for yourself when you need it.

• *Plan your meals.* You may be performing in some village hall miles from the nearest source of food, so be prepared. Sometimes – in village halls, especially – sandwiches are provided by the locals, but not always, so stock up before heading off for the day's performance, and keep an emergency supply of biscuits/fruit/pot noodles in your bag just in case. Make the most of the hotel or B&B breakfast.

• *Travel light.* Remember that you will be probably be checking into several different hotels or B&Bs a week, so only take with you what you can comfortably carry by yourself in one go. For ease of access when you want to find that one pair of socks or pants, wheeled suitcases or large hold-alls are preferable to rucksacks. While you may want to have more stuff back at your base, when you're on the road stick to one large bag and a day bag.

• *Finally, keep a sense of humour and a sense of perspective.* Not always the easiest thing to do on some jobs, but you're all in this together so have a good laugh at the absurdity of it all – it may just save your sanity.

Andrew Piper trained at Bristol Old Vic Theatre School. This piece was written in the van belonging to Northumberland Theatre Company (NTC) while he was playing Herbert Pocket, Uncle Pumblechook and Orlick in their production of *Great Expectations*.

Theatre

Fringe theatres

Essentially, the idea of 'fringe theatre' began at the Edinburgh Festival more than half a century ago. It really started taking off (especially in London) in the late 1960s as an arena for 'alternative' and 'experimental' theatre. The 1990s saw a huge expansion in the number of venues being used, and a downturn in the exploration of theatre forms: the 'fringe' became more commercial and much more competitive – and not just in London and Edinburgh. Today, the terms 'alternative' and 'experimental' are far less frequently used, and the Fringe is now largely seen as a way for actors, directors and writers to showcase their work.

Casting for Fringe productions is usually advertised by one or more of the casting information services, and agents and casting directors do scout for new talent in them. However, it's highly unlikely that you will make any money from participating in such a production – you might end up with a net loss after deducting your expenses. Also agents and casting directors get blitzed with so many invitations that the chances of getting one of them to see you are not high. The only reasons for being in a Fringe production are (a) you might be 'seen'; (b) you fundamentally believe in the production's potential; and (c) it could help keep your acting-juices flowing – you might find classes less time-consuming and possibly more beneficial.

The Edinburgh Fringe Festival

There is a real sense that every actor should try this 'Carnival of theatre' experience – 'the biggest theatrical lottery in the world' – at least once. You'll meet lots of new people, make contacts and it's a great few weeks, even if your own production doesn't hit the heights.

Good advice on mounting a production on the Edinburgh Fringe is available from the Festival Office (details below).

The listings that follow are restricted to the more 'established' venues, with performance spaces for hire. Some Fringe theatres only programme-in work known to them.

Note If you are thinking of mounting a Fringe production and/or starting your own theatre company, start researching and planning well in advance. It is well worth consulting the Independent Theatre Council (ITC) – **www.itc-arts.org**.

UMBRELLA ORGANISATIONS

Edinburgh Festival Fringe

The Fringe Office, 180 High Street,
Edinburgh EH1 1QS
tel 0131-226 0026 *fax* 0131-226 0016
email admin@edfringe.com
website www.edfringe.com

The Fringe Society was formed in 1959 to coordinate publicity and ticket sales, and offer a comprehensive information service both to performers and to audiences. It compiles information about venues, press and suppliers, and produces a series of publications designed to answer frequently asked questions. Its brochure contains details for 183 Fringe venues in Edinburgh. The office is open all year round and the staff are available to help by phone, email or personal appointment.

Fringe Theatre Network (FTN)

c/o Old Red Lion, 418 St John Street,
London EC1V 4QE
tel 020-7833 3053
email helenoldredlion@yahoo.co.uk
website www.fringetheatre.org.uk
Co-ordinator Helen Devine

The FTN provides services, support and a network of contacts for venues, producing companies and individuals working on the London Fringe with the aim of increasing the level of professionalism in Fringe theatre. Acting as an umbrella organisation, the FTN puts forward the interests of Fringe theatre in its dealings with statutory authorities, funding bodies, policy-makers and other arts organsations.

OffWestEnd.com

19 Eugene Cotter House, Beckway Street, London SE17 1QS
website www.offwestend.com

A London UK theatre information and bookings site that makes it easy to find plays and performances in some of London's innovative theatres outside the West End. Tickets are sold directly from these Off West End theatres, with no fees and no commission beng charged.

LONDON FRINGE VENUES

The Albany

Douglas Way, Deptford, London SE8 4AG
020-8692 4446 020-8469 2253
email boxoffice@thealbany.org.uk
website www.thealbany.org.uk
Chief Executive Gavin Barlow

Production details

A multi-use digital arts centre programming music, spoken word, dance, comedy and family shows. The Albany is an artistic and community resource with a fully equipped theatre space, studio theatre, cafe and rehearsal and meeting rooms for hire. Has a strong commitment to working collaboratively with the diverse communities of London and encouraging participation, especially by young people and disabled communities, in the arts. As well as programming performances, the centre provides seasonal participation programmes working with young people, and is a social hub and facilitator for partnership working. Seats 300 (500 standing); 2 secondary spaces seat 60 or 70. Performances also take place in the cafe – capacity 80. All spaces have fully configurable seating; there is also seating on the balcony. Shows usually run from 1 night to 2 weeks. Hire rates may be subsidised depending on community or charity status – see website for rates of different spaces. There is disabled access. Recent productions include: *Lipsticks and Lollipops* by Deafinitely Theatre; *A Warwickshire Testimony* by April de Angelis (Mountview Theatre School); and transfer from the Royal Court of *Gone Too Far!* by Oliver Award Winner Bola Agbaje.

Casting procedures

Does not produce in-house shows.

Arcola Theatre

27 Arcola Street, London E8 2DJ
tel 020-7503 1645
email info@arcolatheatre.com
website www.arcolatheatre.com
Artistic Director Mehmet Ergen

Founded in 2000 by Artistic Director Mehmet Ergen and Executive Producer Leyla Nazli, Arcola Theatre is now one of the most respected arts venues in the UK, "blazing a trail in artistic excellence and innovative management from the outset". Housed in a converted factory in Hackney, Arcola is a favourite of established theatre literati as well as young, upwardly mobile innovators. London's largest theatre studio, it has become well known for the variety of its programming, from new writing to classic drama, music and comedy.

Arcola has staged work by some of the best living actors, writers and directors, including productions by William Gaskill, Timberlake Wertenbaker, Ariel Dorfman, Sean Holmes, Dominic Domgoole, Max Stafford-Clark and Frank McGuinness, among others. 2 Studio theatres and 4 other spaces suitable for rehearsals and other events.

artsdepot

5 Nether Street, North Finchley, London N12 0GA
tel 020-8369 5455
email info@artsdepot.co.uk
website www.artsdepot.co.uk

The only professional arts venue in the London Borough of Barnet. Committed to providing a diverse range of high-quality visual and performance arts for everyone. artsdepot has brand new, state-of-the-art facilities in the form of the large Pentland Theatre, smaller Studio Theatre and Education Spaces, for the provision of drama, dance and visual arts, and a gallery, as well as an excellent cafe and bars.

BAC (Battersea Arts Centre)

Lavender Hill, London SW11 5TN
tel 020-7326 8219
email lydias@bac.org.uk
website www.bac.org.uk
Programme Administrator Lydia Spry

BAC aims to help create and promote exciting, high-quality, collaborative arts activity. The emphasis is on devised rather than script-based work, and especially on the collaboration between different artforms. On the first Sunday of every month, *Scratch Nights* are held at which artists present no more than 10 minutes of material at a very early stage in its development – sometimes stopping in the middle for advice. The audience pays what it can to watch 3-4 of these projects and has a chance to offer feedback to the artists in the bar afterwards. Often presented as part of BAC's Opera Festival or OctoberFest are 2- or 3-night runs of *Scratch Performances*; these are rough show drafts and usually last between 40 minutes and 1 hour. Again, the audience is invited to the bar to give feedback after the show.

The next stage of development comprises 2- or 3-night runs of *Showcase Performances*, at which work is marketed to wider audiences, and is usually presented in the context of one of BAC's annual festivals.

Theatre

Following this, artists may be offered 3- to 6-week runs of *Showcase Performances* for which national reviews will be actively sought.

Artists can get on the BAC ladder of development at different stages and can progress at different rates as appropriate. Work is rarely programmed on the strength of a proposal alone, and the theatre's staff do not have time to read unsolicited scripts. Instead they prefer to build up a relationship with artists over time, viewing their work outside of BAC initially.

At certain times of year the theatre-spaces are hired out to drama schools for showcase events, but all theatre companies must go through the programming process. The BAC has 3 flexible black-box theatre spaces: Studio 1 and Studio 2 (average capacity 43/56) and the Main House (average capacity 150). For all programming enquiries, contact Lydia Spry.

Barons Court Theatre

The Curtain's Up, 28A Comeragh Rd, West Kensington, London W14 9HR
tel/fax 020-7602 0235
email londontheatre@gmail.com
Artistic Director Ron Phillips

A central London 55-seat theatre in the basement of the Curtain's Up public house and restaurant. Offers 1- to 5-week runs and can be booked up to 7 months in advance at a moderate rental. Also available for 1-day actors' showcases.

Blue Elephant Theatre

59A Bethwin Road, Camberwell, London SE5 0XT
tel 020-7701 0100
email info@blueelephanttheatre.co.uk
website www.blueelephanttheatre.co.uk
Theatre & Programme Manager Jasmine Cullingford

The only theatre in Camberwell. A vibrant arts venue aiming to nurture new and emerging artists across the performing arts. Promotes cross-art-form work and all forms of theatre, from physical and dance theatre to new writing and classics.

Co-produces all shows and is particularly interested in supporting new and emerging London-based artists across the performing arts with work that complements the black box performance space. Those interested in bringing a project to the Blue Elephant should submit a written proposal with suggested dates and a full background to Jasmine Cullingford.

The Bridewell Theatre

Bride Lane, Fleet Street, London EC4Y 8EQ
tel 020-7353 3331
website www.stbrideinstitute.org/theatre.html

The Bridewell Theatre is a versatile space, which provides both an atmospheric entertainment venue and an unique conference facility in the heart of the City. In addition to a 12x8m performance space, there is a modular tiered seating system that in standard configuration can accommodate a raked audience of 134 people. The theatre also offers dressing rooms with en suite amenities, as well as a box-office/reception area and a fully equipped bar. All areas of the theatre are accessible to disabled users via lift.

The Broadway Studio Theatre

Catford, London SE6 4RU
tel 020-8314 9472
email martin@broadwaytheatre.org.uk
website www.broadwaytheatre.org.uk
Artistic Director Martin Costello

Originally opened in 1932, the venue is Grade II listed by English Heritage as a beautiful example of 1930s art deco architecture. There are 2 venues: the Main Theatre seats 800, and the Studio Theatre seats 100. "The Broadway Studio Theatre has extremely limited availability; please contact Martin Costello to check availability and prices."

Camden People's Theatre

58-60 Hampstead Road, London NW1 2PY
tel 020-7419 4841 or (08700) 600 100 (Box Office)
fax 020-7813 3889
email admin@cptheatre.co.uk
website www.cptheatre.co.uk

A 60-seat flexible performance space, available for single nights as well as full runs. Also has rehearsal studio.

Canal Café Theatre

The Bridge House, Delamere Terrace, Little Venice, London W2 6ND
tel 020-7289 6056 *fax* 020-7266 1717
email newsrevue@mail.com
website www.newsrevue.com

A 60-seat café theatre situated above the Bridge House pub next to the canal in Little Venice. Welcomes comedy.

Chelsea Centre Theatre

World's End Place, King's Road, London SWI0 0DR
tel 020-7352 1967 *fax* 020-7352 2024

A 110-seat theatre which can be booked-up 6 months in advance. Particularly welcomes new writing.

Cockpit Theatre

Gateforth Street, London NW8 8EH
tel 020-7258 2920 *fax* 020-7258 2921
email dave.wybrow@awc.ac.uk

Theatre seats 180 (60 seats on 3 sides) and should be booked 6 months in advance. Welcomes classics, foreign-language theatre and other niche market work.

The Courtyard Theatre

Bowling Green Walk, 40 Pitfield Street, London N1 6EU

tel/fax 020-7251 6018
email info@thecourtyard.org.uk
website www.thecourtyard.org.uk

Flexible seating arrangements, 2 theatres, rehearsal rooms.

Drill Hall

16 Chenies Street, London WC1E 7EX
tel 020-7307 5060 *fax* 020-7307 5062
email admin@drillhall.co.uk
website www.drillhall.co.uk
Chief Executive & Artistic Director Julie Parker

Since opening in 1977, the Drill Hall has supported the development of unusual, unexpected and daring theatre and performance. The creation of new work, the development of new audiences and the provision of new opportunities to participate in the arts are all central to the Drill Hall's mission. Both of the fully accessible theatres and bars may be hired, as may 4 studios and 4 smaller meeting rooms.

Etcetera Theatre

Oxford Arms, 265 Camden High Street,
London NW1 7BU
tel 020-7482 4857 *fax* 020-7482 0378
email etc@etceteratheatre.com
website www.etceteratheatre.com

A black-box studio space with 42 raked seats, the theatre particularly welcomes new writing and comedy. Presents an early and a late show Tuesday to Sunday (usually running for 3 weeks or more), with one-off performances on Monday nights.

Finborough Theatre

The Finborough, 118 Finborough Road,
London SW10 9ED
tel 020-7244 7439 *fax* 020-7835 1853
email admin@finboroughtheatre.co.uk
website www.finboroughtheatre.co.uk
Artistic Director Neil McPherson

Founded in 1980, the Finborough is "one of London's leading new writing venues" (*Time Out*). It also presents rediscoveries of neglected work from 1800 onwards, music theatre and UK premières of foreign work, particularly from the US and Canada. The 50-seat theatre is available for hire for 4-week runs and 1-night performances: more information is available on the website.

See entry for Concordance, its resident company, under *Middle and smaller-scale companies* on page 194.

Greenwich Playhouse

Greenwich Station Forecourt,
189 Greenwich High Road, London SE10 8JA
tel 020-8858 9256 *fax* 020-8310 7276
email alice@galleontheatre.co.uk
Artistic Director Alice de Sousa

Theatre seats 84 and boasts state-of-the art facilities. Available for hire for short seasons at very affordable weekly rates. Visiting productions benefit free of charge from the advice and support of the resident Artistic Director – see entry for Galleon Theatre Company Ltd, under *Middle and smaller-scale companies* on page 186.

Hackney Empire Studio Theatre

291 Mare Street, London E8 1EJ
020-8510 4500 020-8510 4530
email info@hackneyempire.co.uk
website www.hackneyempire.co.uk
CEO Simon Thomsett *Head of Programming* Frank Sweeney

80-seat studio attached to the historic, Grade II* listed, Matcham-designed Hackney Empire. Contact Frank Sweeney for booking details.

Hen & Chickens Theatre

Above Hen & Chickens Theatre Bar,
109 St Paul's Road, Islington, London N1 2NA
tel 020-7704 2001

A 60-seat theatre welcoming new writing. Directly opposite station. Offers 3- to 4-week runs with Monday nights available separately.

Jacksons Lane Theatre

269A Archway Road, London N6 5AA
tel 020-8340 5226
email mail@jacksonslane.org.uk
website www.jacksonslane.org.uk

Rooms are available for hire on a daily or hourly basis for private parties, rehearsals and performances. The Lavender Room seats up to 40; the Primrose Room seats up to 40; a multipurpose space seats up to 80; the Youth Space seats up to 25; and the Main Theatre seats 125-163.

Jermyn Street Theatre

16B Jermyn Street, London SW1Y 6ST
tel 020-7434 1443 *fax* 020-7287 3232
email info@jermynstreettheatre.co.uk
website www.jermynstreettheatre.co.uk

Theatre seats 70, 5 rows facing, 2 rows on side. Stage space is 8 metres long x 4 metres deep x 3.5 metres high (to grid), 2 dressing rooms with fridges, sofas, microwaves, kettles, iron + ironing board. The theatre is air conditioned.

Hire rates

• Main Shows – Weekly rental is £2350 (this includes get-in, fit-up time, technician operating/rigging, also operates sound as well as lights). A 25% non refundable deposit is required when the contract is signed.
• Showcases / Rehearsed Readings / Seminars – £75 per hour. Theatre is available on Tuesdays / Wednesdays / Thursdays between 10am and 3pm (includes technician)
• Sunday Nights (Cabaret Evenings) – £375 for the evening, available from 6.30pm on the night for 8pm

Theatre

show, includes rehearsal Friday before (includes technician)

King's Head Theatre

115 Upper Street, Islington, London N1 1QN
tel 020-7226 8561
website www.kingsheadtheatre.org

Famous for helping to launch the careers of many new writers, directors and actors including Stephen Berkoff, Anthony Sher and Victoria Wood. The theatre is situated above a public house with flexible seating for up to 140.

The Landor Theatre

70 Landor Road, London SW9 9PH
tel 020-7737 7276
email info@landortheatre.co.uk
website www.landortheatre.co.uk

A 60-seat theatre situated above a public house.

Lion & Unicorn Theatre

42-44 Gaisford Street, Kentish Town,
London NW5 2ED
email info@giantolive.com
website www.giantolive.com

The Lion & Unicorn is the home of Giant Olive theatre company. Founded in 2008, the company has quickly developed a reputation for high-quality and imaginative theatre and dance. Giant Olive produces classical productions as well as supporting and developing new work and talent. "The Lion & Unicorn Theatre Space is available to hire at the 'Best Fringe Theatre Rates in London'. We don't just offer a black box, we can provide full production support, with everything from rehearsal space to flyer and poster design. For prices and details, and to view the venue, please contact us."

Menier Chocolate Factory

51/53 Southwark Street, London SE1 1RU
tel 020-7907 7060
email info@menierchocolatefactory.com

2900sq ft of highly versatile and atmospheric theatre space, with lighting rig, sound, and video projection. Capacity 200. Recently transferred its production of Sondheim's musical *Sunday in the Park with George* (starring Daniel Evans and Jenna Russell) to the Wyndhams Theatre in the West End.

New End Theatre

27 New End, Hampstead, London NW3 1JD
tel 020-7472 5800 fax 020-7472 5808
email mail@newendtheatre.co.uk
website www.newendtheatre.co.uk

Theatre seats 84 and has a strong tradition of presenting new plays and musicals, as well as reviving works from the classical canon. Recent productions include: Sondheim's *Assassins*; *A Dangerous Woman* (starring Fenella Fielding); and *Weill & Lenya* (directed by Ken Russell).

New Players Theatre

The Arches, Villiers Street, London WC2N 6NG
tel 020-7930 6601 fax (08456) 382102
website www.newplayerstheatre.com

The recently renovated New Players Theatre is a valuable addition to the London theatre scene and business community in the heart of the West End. Already a popular and well-known venue within the theatre, music and entertainment industries, the New Players now offers producers the opportunity to present a diverse and eclectic range of productions in an Off-Broadway-style, well-equipped, high-specification theatre, complete with on-site bars and a restaurant. It is also a distinctive setting for screenings, conference and corporate hires.

Old Red Lion

418 St John Street, Islington, London EC1V 4NJ
tel 020-7833 3053 fax 020-7833 3053
website www.oldredliontheatre.co.uk
Theatre Manager Helen Devine

Founded in 1979, the Old Red Lion Theatre is a 60-seater Fringe theatre primarily dedicated to new writing. Companies wishing to hire the venue should post a script, some company information and a production proposal to the Artistic Director. Normally programmes 3 months ahead.

Oval House Theatre

52-54 Kennington Oval, London SE11 5SW
tel 020-7582 0080
email Karena.Johnson@OvalHouse.com
website www.ovalhouse.com
Programmer Karena Johnson

Comprises 2 spaces; the upstairs theatre seats 50 and the downstairs theatre seats 100. Presents a diverse programme of work.

Pentameters

28 Heath Street, Hampstead NW3 6TE
tel 020-7435 3648
website www.pentameters.co.uk NW3 6TE

Located in the heart of Hampstead village, among an abundance of cafes, restaurants, bars, pubs and shops and just a minute's walk from Hampstead tube. Aside from the choice of venues to have pre- or post-theatre drinks or dinner, Hampstead is also well-known for its artistic character, offering a supportive, interactive and thriving local community, making it an ideal spot to promote live theatre and creative arts events. To discuss requirements, please telephone Leonie Scott-Matthews directly on the above number: "Please leave a message, and we will respond."

Pleasance Theatre London

Carpenters Mews, North Road, London N7 9EF
tel 020-7619 6868 fax 020-7700 7366
email info@pleasance.co.uk
website www.pleasance.co.uk/LONDON

The Pleasance now has 2 spaces: the Main Theatre, seating just under 300; and the Pleasance Stage Space, a new venue created to nurture the best in new theatre writing and emerging comedy talent, seating 54.

Rich Mix

35-47 Bethnal Green Road, London E1 6LA
tel 020-7613 7490 *fax* 020-7613 7499
email info@richmix.org.uk
website www.richmix.org.uk
Chief Executive Pawlet Brookes

A 132,000 square foot flagship arts and cultural centre, boasting "the best in art, performance, fashion, design, music, dance, film, theatre and comedy – 5 floors of vibrant creativity and excellence".

Riverside Studios

Crisp Road, London W6 9RL
tel 020-8237 1111 (Box Office) 020-8237 1000 (Admin) 020-8237 1015 (Hire Enquiries)
website www.riversidestudios.co.uk

Riverside Studios is an arts centre with a varied programme of both domestic and international performance, theatre, dance, music, comedy and other events. Considers work – either hires or co-productions – within the context of its artistic policy.

Studio 2 is a medium-sized black box space suited to all types of production. Comprehensive motorised grid. Flexible seating configuration, up to 400. Studio 3 is a smaller-sized black box space suited to all types of production. Comprehensive motorised grid. Retractable raked seating, up to 156. Other spaces available for hire: cinema, television studio.

Recent companies include: Forced Entertainment, LOVE&MADNESS Ensemble, Rosemary Butcher, Batsheva Dance Company, Bill Bailey, Ed Byrne, Damien Dempscy, Duran Duran, Albert & Friends – Youth Circus Festival, Tete a Tete – Opera Festival.

Rosemary Branch Theatre

2 Shepperton Road, London N1 3DT
tel 020-7704 6665
email cecilia@rosemarybranch.co.uk

Under the same management since 1996, the theatre has recently been expanded to hold a maximum of 65 seats. Presents a diverse programme including opera, classics, new writing, musicals and cabaret. A rehearsal space is also available. Normally books 3-week runs but this is negotiable. The theatre offers all visiting companies lots of support and goodwill.

Soho Theatre

21 Dean Street, London W1V 6NE
tel 020-7478 0117 *fax* 020-7287 5061
email hires@sohotheatre.com
website www.sohotheatre.com

Soho Theatre + Writers' Centre aims to discover and develop new playwrights, produce a year-round programme of new plays, and attract new audiences. Founded in 1972, the company premiered the early work of such playwrights as Caryl Churchill, David Edgar, Hanif Kureishi, Tanika Gupta, and Timberlake Wertenbaker; more recently it has presented new plays by Laura Wade, Will Eno, Adriano Shaplin, Debbie Tucker Green, Matt Charman, Rebecca Lenkiewicz and Toby Whithouse.

Soho Theatre + Writers' Centre is now a key producing venue of new plays and comedy. Offering the nation's most extensive unsolicited script-reading service, the Writers' Centre provides a range of developmental schemes including: the Writers' Attachment Programme; Launch Pad Workshops; The Verity Bargate Award; The Westminster Prize; a thriving Young Writers' Programme; commissions and seed bursaries; Writers' Rooms; and an extensive Research & Development programme of readings, workshops, script surgeries, seminars and initiatives, all of which "enable us to attract and nurture the most outstanding writers from our local community and throughout the country".

Three writers' rooms are available free of charge, complete with computer, printer and access to a growing script library. They are available to writers free of charge from 10am – 6pm, Monday to Friday and can be booked for as little as an hour or up to a month; priority will be given to writers whose work is being developed by STC.

Soho Theatre + Writers' Centre includes a flexible 144-seat theatre, a large self-contained Studio space with 85-seat capacity, theatre bar, restaurant, offices, rehearsal, writing and meeting rooms. All spaces are accessible and available for hire. For bookings and general information, please visit **www.sohotheatre.com**.

There are 4 spaces to hire at Soho Theatre. Each is air-conditioned, has full disabled access and can be set up to specific requirements. The theatre seats 144 and has a maximum stage area of 11m wide x 6m deep. The studio measures 9m x 11m and is a self-contained and sound-proofed space with an acoustic wall dividing the room into 2. The studio is equipped with a PA system and mini disc; seating is flexible with a capacity of 85. The writers' seminar room measures 7m x 3.5m; it is a light, airy room with a balcony looking over Dean Street. The terrace measures 4m x 3m and has a glass-fronted balcony. It includes a separate waiting area and is suitable for castings and small meetings. For more information, please visit the website, or telephone.

See also entry under *Producing theatres* on page 149.

Southwark Playhouse

Shipwright Yard (Corner of Tooley St & Bermondsey St), London SE1 2TF
tel 020-7407 0234 *fax* 020-7407 8350
email admin@southwarkplayhouse.co.uk
website www.southwarkplayhouse.co.uk

Theatre

Southwark Playhouse's central vision is that of a vibrant theatre in the heart of the London Borough of Southwark, serving the widest possible constituency within the Borough and beyond, providing a platform for emerging theatre practitioners and a programme of performance, education work and community drama.

Tabard Theatre

2 Bath Road, Turnham Green, London W4 1LW
tel 020-8994 5985
Artistic Director Fred Perry

Situated above the Tabard pub, close to Turnham Green tube. Offers 3- to 4-week runs which are programmed 4-5 months ahead.

The Space

269 Westferry Road, London E14 3RS
tel 020-7515 7799
website www.space.org.uk
Centre Director Adam Hemming

A multi-arts centre on the Isle of Dogs, programming a mixture of theatre, music, comedy and dance. Converted from a 19th-century church, with stained glass windows, a Steinway grand piano and flexible seating, the venue provides a uniquely atmospheric environment. The Space is also available for rehearsals and private hire.

Theatre 503

The Latchmere, 503 Battersea Park Road, London SW11 3BW
tel 020-7229 8530 *fax* 020-7229 8140
email mail@theatre503.com
website www.theatre503.com

Situated above a public house, Theatre 503 aims to provide a venue for new playwrights, comedians and directors to develop their shows. It has a working relationship with television commissioners and producers, literary managers of established theatres and literary agents, and tries to offer a stepping-stone from Fringe to 'big' theatres.

Theatro Technis

26 Crowndale Road, London NW1 1TT
tel 020-7387 6617 *fax* 020-7383 2545
email info@theatrotechnis.com
website www.theatrotechnis.co.uk

Theatro Technis' ideas and policies are realised for anyone who is interested in the development of individuals and communities. The theatre maintains a balance between classic and contemporary work, and serves to embrace a variety of diverse artforms ranging from theatre and dance to art, photography, music and film.

Toynbee Studios

28 Commercial Street, London E1 6AB
tel 020-7247 5102

email admin@artsadmin.co.uk
website www.artsadmin.co.uk/toynbeestudios

Toynbee Studios is Artsadmin's unique centre for the development and presentation of new work. The Studios comprise a 280-seat theatre, rehearsal spaces, technical facilities, and the Arts Bar & Cafe, all of which host performances and events throughout the year. Office facilities are also provided for a range of small arts organisations.

Toynbee Studios has 6 spaces catering for professional work, ranging from intimate spaces where artists can experiment to high-spec dance and theatre studios for larger productions/rehearsals, as well as ideal and unusual spaces for meetings and events. Any requests for hires for public events will be considered by Artsadmin, but must be approved by the programming team as fitting with Artsadmin's artistic objectives.

About Artsadmin: Founded in 1979, it is a unique producing organisation for contemporary artists working in theatre, dance, live art, visual arts and mixed media. Based at Toynbee Studios since 1995, the organisation offers a free advisory service for artists, mentoring and development programmes, and a number of bursary schemes.

Tristan Bates

1A Tower Street, London WC2H 9NP
tel 020-7632 8010
email itbt@actorscentre.co.uk
website www.tristanbatestheatre.co.uk
Artistic Director Matthew Lloyd

The Tristan Bates Theatre (TBT) is a venue for new work and groundbreaking experiments. The artistic policy reflects the mission of the Actors Centre, where the training of performers co-exists with the making of new work. "TBT is a launchpad for the talent we discover, and we make relationships with other organisations, producers and theatres to give further life to the work we present. We provide actors, writers and directors with a space in which they can test new ideas and be daring, at a time when the industry demands quick results on tight budgets – i.e. safe choices and tame product."

Union Theatre

204 Union Street, Southwark, London SE1 0LX
tel 020-7261 9876 *fax* 020-7261 9876
email sasha@uniontheatre.freeserve.co.uk
website www.uniontheatre.freeserve.co.uk

Primarily a new writing venue, the theatre aims to present a diverse programme featuring the best new talent. Guest performances are supplemented by regular in-house productions. Normally offers 3-week runs.

Upstairs at the Gatehouse

The Gatehouse Pub, North Road, London N6 4BD
tel 020-8340 3477

Theatre

email events@ovationproductions.com
website www.upstairsatthegatehouse.com

Seats 132 (140 in cabaret style). A rehearsal room is also available. See entry for Ovation Productions under Middle and smaller-scale companies.

White Bear Theatre
138 Kennington Park Road, London SE11 4DJ
tel 020-7793 9193

An L-shaped studio space with seating for up to 50. Generally prefers new writing but occasionally accepts revivals.

Wimbledon Studio Theatre
In Wimbledon Theatre, 103 The Broadway, London SW19 1QG
tel 0870 060 6646 (Box Office)
tel 020-8545 7900 (Admin) *fax* 020 8543 6637
email sambain@theambassadors.com
website www.ambassadortickets.com/wimbledon

A black box Studio theatre with flexible seating for up to 80. Normally offers 1-2 week runs which are programmed 6 months ahead. The auditorium is wheelchair accessible.

EDINBURGH FRINGE VENUES

Many of these venues are only available for hire during the Edinburgh Festival Fringe in August. For a full list of venues, contact the Fringe Society (see above).

Assembly Rooms
Assembly Theatre, 250 George Street, Edinburgh EH2 2LE
tel 0131-624 2442 *fax* 0131-624 7131
email info@assemblyrooms.com
website www.assemblyrooms.com

The Assembly Rooms have presented more than 1000 productions featuring most of the major names in British comedy – as well as a huge array of theatre, dance and music events which have been seen by more than 1.5 million people over the last 20 years of the Edinburgh Festival Fringe. The daily programme runs from 11.00am to 3.30am with exhibitions, a café, 2 public bars and a club bar. Aims to programme a balance of theatre, comedy and new work.

Augustine's
Augustine United Church, 41 George IV Bridge, Edinburgh EH1 1EL
tel 0131-220 1677

During the rest of the year this venue is known as Augustine United Church. It is adapted during the Festival to house 2 performance spaces (the upper venue seats 110; the lower venue seats approximately

105). Programmes theatre, musicals, dance and children's theatre from the UK and elsewhere.

Bedlam Theatre
11B Bristo Place, Edinburgh EH1 1EZ
tel 0131-225 9873
email info@bedlamtheatre.co.uk
website www.bedlamtheatre.co.uk

A 90-seat black-box theatre in central Edinburgh housed in a neo-gothic church. The theatre is available for hire when not in use by the Edinburgh University Theatre Company.

C venues
Administration Office: C Venues Limited, 5 Alexandra Mansions, Chichele Road, London NW2 3AS
email info@cvenues.com
website www.cvenues.com

Comprises 4 theatre venues in Edinburgh: C; C too; C central; C cubed. Presents drama, physical theatre, comedy, music, musicals, dance, opera, children's shows and visual arts with an emphasis on new and dynamic work. C's 4 locations include a 203-seat thrust space, 2 end-on black-box studios seating 95 and 144, and a permanent 160-seat proscenium-arch auditorium in the basement. There is also a platform stage in the bar and extensive exhibition space on each foyer level. In total there are 10 spaces including a new basement cabaret bar and 3 intimate black-box theatres at C central.

Gilded Balloon
25 Greenside Place, Edinburgh EH1 3AA
tel 0131-226 6550 or 0131-622 6555

Has a very strong comedy programme; also presents live music.

Greyfriars (Studios 1 and 2)
Greyfriars Kirk House, 86 Candlemaker Row, Edinburgh EH1 2QA

Studio 1 (upstairs, seats 60) and Studio 2 (seats around 40) are intimate spaces suited to 1- to 3-handers, storytelling or poetry. Applications should be made by February for hire during the Festival Fringe.

Hill Street Theatre
Hill Street Theatre, Universal Arts, Gateway Theatre, Elm Row, Edinburgh EH7 4AH
tel 0131-478 0195 *fax* 0131-478 0185
email hillstreet@universal-arts.com

Presents a programme of well-known works alongside new writing, musicals, dance, mime and physical theatre. Theatrical production includes comic writing but not stand-up comedy. The main theatre seats 120 while the studio theatre is a more intimate space, seating a maximum of 73. Suited to 1-

Theatre

handers, the studio can accommodate up to 8 performers comfortably.

The Netherbow Scottish Storytelling Centre

43-45 High Street, Edinburgh EH1 1SR
tel 0131-556 9579
website www.scottishstorytellingcentre.co.uk

Intimate 100-seat theatre presenting drama, poetry, storytelling and puppetry events. Offers a strong programme of family shows. The whole building, being new-build from 2005, is very wheelchair-friendly both for the public and for actors.

The Pleasance

The Pleasance Courtyard: 60 The Pleasance, Edinburgh EH8 9TJ
tel 020-7619 6868
The Pleasance Dome: 1 Bristo Square, Edinburgh EH8 9AL
The Pleasance Administration Office: Carpenters Mews, North Road, London N7 9EF
website www.pleasance.co.uk

The Pleasance presents more than 160 shows across its 16 venues during the 4 weeks of the Festival Fringe. With more than 190,000 visitors, it remains one of the most popular venues of the Fringe, offering a mix of comedy, theatre, dance and music.

The Underbelly

Off Cowgate,
Edinburgh Permanent Office: 25 Greenside Place, Edinburgh EH1 3AA
tel 0131-622 6566 *fax* 0131-622 6576
email ed@smirnoffunderbelly.co.uk
website www.theunderbelly.co.uk
Venue Manager Ed Bartlam

Comprises 6 spaces over 4 floors with 3 bars. Venues cater for audiences of 60-200 with different seating configurations available. Programmes new writing, theatre, dance and comedy.

Traverse Theatre

10 Cambridge Street, Edinburgh EH1 2ED
email mike.griffiths@traverse.co.uk
website www.traverse.co.uk
Administrative Director Mike Griffiths

Centre for new plays in Scotland. All-year-round venue in underground purpose-built theatre with 2 auditoria and off-site Rehearsal facilities. Has staged many premieres including work by David Greig, David Harrower, Rona Munro, Zinnie Harris and Gregory Burke.

OTHER FRINGE LOCATIONS

Komedia

44-47 Gardner Street, Brighton BN1 1UN
tel (01273) 647101 *fax* (01273) 647102
email info@komedia.co.uk
website www.komedia.co.uk

An upstairs and downstairs cabaret bar serving hot food and drinks, each with a capacity of 230 seated around tables, and a 160-seat theatre. Komedia presents a programme of theatre, world music, cabaret, comedy and children's shows. Has been host to names such as Graham Norton, Mel & Sue, League of Gentlemen and The Right Size.

Sevenoaks Stag Theatre

London Road, Sevenoaks, Kent TN13 1ZZ
tel (01732) 451548
email julian.woolford@stagtheatre.co.uk

The theatre can seat up to 453 and has provision for wheelchair-users. Companies should book the space up to 6 months in advance. Programmes a wide range of theatre and dance events.

Watermans Arts Centre

40 High Street, Brentford, Middlesex TW8 0DS
tel 020-8847 5651 *fax* 020-8569 8592
email enquiries@watermans.org.uk
website www.watermans.org.uk

An arts venue comprising 239-seat theatre, 125-seat cinema, studio 1 (large), studio 2 (small), gallery, restaurant and bar, and river views of the Thames. Programmes across a range of different artforms including Asian arts, new media, children's theatre, cinema and participative arts. The studios have a nominal capacity of 80 and 30 seats respectively, but these spaces are mostly used for workshops, meetings and rehearsals.

To fringe, or not to fringe

Simon Dunmore

Although it is generally regarded as 'professional' work, there is a tendency in Fringe productions for professional standards (and facilities) to be somewhat lacking – and that is sometimes an understatement. Poor technical back-up, indifferent front-of-house arrangements and general unreliability are too often the case, almost inevitably damaging the quality of the final product.

Some potential problems to watch out for

• *The ego trip.* A number of productions are set up by individuals wanting a starring vehicle for themselves – much like the old actor-managers. It is generally better to avoid such enterprises unless you can be fairly sure that the central 'ego' will not be damaging to your contribution. Ask around for objective advice before accepting a part in such a production.

• *What else will you have to do?* Will you have to do other things – like paint the set, distribute posters, help with the get-in, and so on? You may think that you can make time to do things like this, but are you sure you want to be thus distracted in the last few days before opening night?

• *Is the script good enough?* There really is no point in doing a production that's flawed before it leaves the page.

• *Can you work well with the director?* This is a highly subjective judgement, but since you are not being properly paid, it is important that you feel as sure as you can be that it'll be a worthwhile experience.

• *Can you actually afford to do it?* There is no point in taking time out from paid work in order to rehearse and perform a Fringe production unless you really think that you'll get something out of the experience. (It can be worth asking if your rehearsal-calls can be arranged around your work commitments.) Also, check whether your participation will affect your benefits in any way.

• *Your agent.* If you have one, will s/he be happy for you to do the production?

• *Contracts.* In 2005, Equity published a set of guidelines (working hours, etc.) and a suggested contract for Fringe producers. This is not intended as an alternative to Equity's other agreements; rather, it is designed to help Fringe companies develop good employment practices. Some companies issue their own contracts; it is important to read these carefully and check with Equity if you have any doubts.

• *Will the production get reviews?* A good review equals good publicity – important for any production. Some productions in the most prestigious venues get reviewed in national newspapers. However, because there are so many productions at any one time, the press has strict rules (length of run, for instance) about what they will send reviewers to. It is important to note that the perceptiveness of some of the latter is somewhat shallow (that's not sour grapes; it's a fact).

• *Will the publicity and marketing be sufficient?* After the cost of hiring the venue, publicity and marketing represent the next major cost of a Fringe production. Too many productions try to skimp on these. In such a competitive environment, they are very, very important.

• *Does the venue have a good reputation?* It is much, much harder to get people into less prestigious ones.

Theatre

• *Promises*. While enthusiasm for a project is wonderful, beware of promises when they seem over-the-top. Too much optimism can blind people to important practical realities.
• *Is it going to be properly organised?* There is far more to putting on a production than most actors realise (see below). Ask questions based on the above and, if you don't feel sufficiently satisfied, politely back away. There is no point in being miserable, as well as unpaid, for several weeks.
• *If I'm not being paid, can I not just pull out if something better comes along?* Legally, you can; morally and professionally it's an extremely dubious thing to do without the full understanding of your fellow participants – and you never know who, among them, might gain 'casting clout' in the future.

Setting up your own production

Too many people think that mounting a production is just a matter of getting a few friends together, borrowing some props and costumes, and getting on with it. What about the costs of hiring a venue, a rehearsal space, the publicity and marketing, the author's royalties (if still in copyright), and so on?

You may be lucky enough to get some, or even all, of these for free, or you might find a rich auntie. But however you fund the above essentials, you have got to do a lot of careful planning before rehearsals start. Will the playwright (and/or translator) allow you to do a production of the play in the first place? Just because a play is in print, it doesn't mean that anyone can perform it. Is the rehearsal room available enough of the time? What is the deadline for getting the poster design to the printers, so that they can get the result back to you in time for the distributors to get them displayed in good time before opening night? And so on, and so on, and so on ... Oh, and it is essential to plan and budget with contingency in both time and money – there are always several things that take more time than you'd thought, and several things that cost more than you'd thought (or forgotten to budget for in the first place).

Doing it yourself is far more complex than most people realise, but can be incredibly satisfying if you succeed. For a technically simple production you probably need to find at least £5000 – and that's without paying any of the participants. The chances of recouping this through the box office are very low; the average audience on the Fringe is about 30 per cent. A recent report stated that: "Theatres are among the most over-regulated businesses in the UK." Legal requirements like Health & Safety, VAT and performance rights cannot be neglected.

Simon Dunmore has been directing productions for over 30 years – nearly 20 years as a resident director in regional theatres and, more recently, working freelance. In that time there have been over 200 productions (of all styles, colours, shapes and sizes) – recently: several Drama School Showcases, Maugham's *Home and Beauty* and new plays about sex, WB Yeats' up-and-down relationship with Maud Gonne, one set inside a pyramid and another about Bismarck. Past favourites include: *The Promise* (Alexei Arbuzov), *Antigone* (Jean Anouilh), a seven-handed version of *Antony & Cleopatra* and too many others to mention. He also teaches acting and has worked in many drama schools and other training establishments around the country. He has written several books: *An Actor's Guide to Getting Work* (now in its fourth edition), the *Alternative Shakespeare Auditions* series and is the Consultant Editor for *Actors' Yearbook*. **www.simon.dunmore.btinternet.co.uk**

Children's, young people's and Theatre in Education companies

Paul Harman

Work in this very large sector of employment for actors in the UK varies greatly – both in the style of theatre created and presented, and in the wages and conditions offered by employers. Anyone taking work in the field should always be clear about the aims and status of their prospective employer.

Most producing theatres offer plays for young audiences as part of a season, and Christmas shows and pantomimes are mounted by a large number of receiving theatres and commercial touring companies. Some 200 independent touring companies regularly present original theatre productions, usually in schools, reaching a total audience of at least five million annually. Smaller touring companies may operate for profit, or as profit-share partnerships. Companies which are members of ITC (Independent Theatre Council) offer pay and conditions agreed with the performers' trade union, Equity.

Reality check

There is no official agency that collects reliable statistics or regulates the quality of what is offered. Your work may never be publicly reviewed – and it can be hard and demanding. Casts are often small, and living conditions on the road are sometimes difficult. The work may involve a lot of driving (if you are over 25 and insurable) as well as humping sets in and out of vans. However, the rewards for good-quality work conscientiously presented lie in the warmth of welcome from audiences and bookers alike, and a directness and openness of audience response which is often less evident at more formal, adult-orientated theatre events. In schools, you will perform in daylight, very close to children – so it helps if you like them. They can see every blemish on you, and you can see every reaction on a hundred faces.

You will need physical stamina; the ability to play many parts convincingly; and the facility to hit a peak of performance two or more times in a day, six days a week. You may need skill in playing a musical instrument. In addition, other aptitudes may be called upon. A play may be preceded or followed by workshop activity with young people – from 'hot-seating' in character to involving children in a performance. An understanding of drama education techniques is therefore an advantage, and experience of Youth Theatre useful.

What shows?

For good economic and marketing reasons, most theatre for children presented in larger houses is based on well-known stories by established authors, or on characters from TV shows. Companies may receive financial support from official agencies to present plays on health and social issues. Plays related to the National Curriculum, such as science topics, are in great demand from schools.

Theatre in Education (TIE) is a term commonly used to mean many kinds of theatre in schools. In the strict sense, TIE implies an extended theatre event, combining performance and participatory elements and designed to engage pupils in exploring their own

Theatre

knowledge, feelings and attitudes. This is quite a different process from explaining how magnets work or presenting an account of an historical event. Very few companies nowadays can afford the time and staffing needed to support real TIE, but there are many opportunities to create and present challenging educational plays on a wide variety of subjects.

Independent touring companies receiving public subsidy from Arts Councils in England, Wales, Scotland and Northern Ireland generally aim to present original, commissioned drama. A small group of writers specialises in this field, addressing personal and social topics, from fear of the dark or the break-up of families to genetics and migration. This group of companies – whose aims are primarily artistic, rather than just to entertain or deliver educational messages – find like-minded companies in 70 countries through ASSITEJ (International Association of Theatre for Children and Young People). Overseas tours and international collaborations are increasing.

Above all, don't look upon this field as an easy step towards something else. Your first experiences may well be tough, but an apprenticeship served with a supportive company will open an area of work you can return to with growing enjoyment and professional satisfaction.

Paul Harman has worked as an actor and director in professional theatre since 1963. He joined Belgrade Theatre in Education team in 1966, headed Education work at Liverpool Everyman from 1970, and founded Merseyside Young People's Theatre Company in 1978. Since 1994 he has been Artistic Director of CTC Theatre, Darlington. He is the current Chair of ASSITEJ UK.

Note Some of the companies listed are members of the Independent Theatre Council (ITC) – **www.itc-arts.org.uk**.

Action Transport Theatre

Whitby Hall, Stanney Lane, Ellesmere Port,
Cheshire CH65 9AE
tel 0151-357 2120 *fax* 0151-356 4057
email info@actiontransporttheatre.org
website www.actiontransporttheatre.org
Director Sarah Clover *Producer* Jennifer Egan *General Manager* Karen Parry *Associate Writer* Kevin Dyer *Associate Director* Nina Hajiyianni *Production Manager* Mike Francis

Production details

"A new writing company creating brave, collaborative theatre for, by and with young people." Stages 3 projects annually, with around 60 performances in 10 venues including schools, arts centres, theatres and community venues across the UK. In general 4-5 actors go on tour, playing to family (5+) and adult audiences. Incoming actors should have singing, musical instrument and physical theatre skills, and may be expected to lead workshops. Recent productions include: *Generations; The Bomb; Scratches in the Earth;* and *Night Train.*

Casting procedures

Holds general auditions and actors may write at any time to request inclusion. Casting breakdowns are available from the website, by postal application (with sae), through Equity Job Information Service and Casting Call Pro, and in *PCR* and *The Stage.* Welcomes letters (with CVs and photographs) from individual actors previously unknown to the company, sent by post or email. Will consider invitations to view individual actors' websites. Offers Equity-approved contracts as negotiated through ITC. Actively encourages applications from disabled actors, and promotes the use of inclusive casting.

Actionwork TIE

PO Box 433, Weston-Super-Mare,
Somerset BS24 0WY
tel (01934) 815163
email info@actionwork.com
website www.actionwork.com
Artistic Director Andy Hickson *Production Manager* Cath Davis

Production details

Founded in 1990. Between 2008 and 2009 toured 5 shows in the UK and abroad. Stages on average more than a hundred performances annually, touring to schools, arts centres, theatres, outdoor and community venues. In general 2-8 actors go on tour, playing to audiences aged 10 to 18. Actors may be expected to lead workshops, and it is an advantage to possess additional singing, musical instrument, dance and physical theatre skills; they should hold a current driving licence. Recent productions include: *Clash!*, 33 *Skins*, *WWW*, and *Silent Scream*.

Casting procedures

Holds general auditions; actors may write in at any time to request inclusion. Welcomes letters (with CVs and photographs) from individual actors previously unknown to the company, sent by post or email, as well as showreels and invitations to view individual actors' websites. Actively encourages applications from disabled actors, and promotes the use of inclusive casting.

Aesop's Touring Theatre Company

The Arches, 38 The Riding, Woking,
Surrey GU21 5TA
tel (01483) 724633 *mobile* (07836) 731872
fax (01483) 724633
email brooksa4@sky.com
website www.aesopstheatre.co.uk
Director Karen Brooks L.L.A.M. (Hons.) Dipl. *Other key personnel* Albert Brooks A.C.I.I. (General Manager)

Production details

Established in 1999, a professional Theatre in Education company specialising in National Curriculum based plays for the nursery and primary age range. Tours extensively on a daily basis and at the time of writing is performing 7 2-hander interactive plays and associated drama workshops. Plays are mostly performed in schools but also embrace theatres, community centres, village halls, arts centres and party venues. On average stages 300 performances each year, in 225 venues across London, in the Home Counties and further afield. 2 actors usually go on tour, plus occasionally a driver or stage manager. Applicants should be fit, versatile all-round actors with a good grasp of comedy, and should have their own transport to easily reach base for early morning starts in the company vehicle.

Casting procedures

Sometimes holds general auditions and actors may write in at any time: "We reply to all enquries." Rarely (or never) has the opportunity to cast disabled actors. "Schedules are physically demanding, and often require early morning starts."

Ape Theatre Company

32 Brook Road, Epping, Essex CM16 7BT
tel (01992) 574843
email mail@apetheatrecompany.co.uk
website www.apetheatrecompany.co.uk
Artistic Director Mr Matt Allen *Assistant Artistic Director* Mr Andrew Mulquin *Company Director / Manager* Mrs Yvonne Allen

Production details

Established in 1980. Stages 4 projects annually, with 800 performances at the same number of schools and community venues nationwide. In general 4 actors go on tour with each project, playing to audiences aged 10-plus. Actors are sometimes expected to lead workshops and should hold a clean driving licence. Dance and physical theatre skills may be an advantage. Recent productions include: *Too Much Punch for Judy*; *Legal Weapon II*; *Pills, Thrills and Automobiles*; and *Viscous Circle*.

Casting procedures

Holds general auditions, and actors are advised to write in July and November to request inclusion. Casting breakdowns are available by postal application (with sae), and via Equity Job Information Service and *PCR*. Welcomes letters (with CVs and photographs) from individual actors previously unknown to the company, sent by post and email, but does not accept unsolicited showreels or invitations to view actors' websites. Offers Equity-approved contracts as negotiated through ITC. Rarely or never has the opportunity to cast disabled actors.

Arty-Fact Theatre Co

18 Weston Lane, Crewe CW2 5AN
tel 070-2096 2096 *fax* 070-2098 2098
email artyfact@talktalk.net
Artistic Director Yvonne Peacock *Co-director* Brian Twiddy

Production details

Has been performing in schools since 1993, running history workshops, original plays and classics. Performs 6-7 projects annually, with an average annual total of 500-600 performances in 200-300 schools across England. In general 2-4 actors go on tour and perform to audiences aged 7-18. Physical theatre skills and a driving licence are required. Actors may be expected to lead workshops. Recent productions include: *Of Mice and Men*; *Much Ado About Nothing*; *Eureka!*; and *The Inventive Miss Violet*.

Casting procedures

Sometimes holds general auditions; actors are advised to write in April and July to request inclusion. Casting breakdowns are available via the website, Equity Job Information Service, *PCR* and the Actors' Centre. Welcomes letters (with CVs and photographs) from individual actors previously unknown to the company sent by post or email. Does not accept showreels or invitations to view individual actors' websites. Rarely or never has the opportunity to cast disabled actors. "Include a letter stating why you would like to work for us in particular."

Big Wheel Theatre in Education

The Institute, PO Box 18221, London EC1R 4WJ
tel 020-7689 8670 *fax* 020-7689 8670
email info@bigwheel.org.uk
website www.bigwheel.org.uk
Artistic Directors Roland Allen, Jeni Williams

Theatre

Production details

Since 1984 has developed interactive theatre for use in education and training in the UK and abroad. Normally tours 10 projects each year, with an average annual total of 400 performances and 200 different venues. Venues include schools and conference centres across the UK, Europe, Japan, Kenya and South Africa. In general 2 actors go on tour and play to audiences aged 7 upwards. Actors are required to hold a driving licence and to lead workshops. Experience in teaching or training is also useful. Recent productions include: *Introduction to Shakespeare*, a game-show-based interactive workshop; *Breakfast with Big Wheel*, a show to teach English in European schools; and a variety of workshops for the NHS about communication, partnerships and peripatetic working.

Casting procedures

Sometimes holds general auditions; actors may write at any time requesting inclusion. "It's quite specialist work. Best to have a good look at the website and only send us your stuff if you think it really is your cup of tea."

Big Wooden Horse Theatre Company Ltd

30 Northfield Road, London W13 9SY
tel 020-8567 8431
email info@bigwoodenhorse.com
website www.bigwoodenhorse.com
Artistic Director Adam Bampton-Smith *Technical Director* Will Evans

Production details

Aims to present high-quality theatre to younger audiences across the UK and to represent the best of British theatre craft abroad. Strives both to entertain and to inform young people, drawing from different cultures and traditions. On average 3 actors tour 3 projects annually, with 400 performances at around 80 venues including arts centres and theatres in the UK, US and Canada. Audiences range from 3 to 11 years. Recent productions include: *Don't Let the Pigeon Drive the Bus!* and *The Night Before Christmas*.

Casting procedures

Casting breakdowns are available from Equity Job Information Service, *PCR* and *SBS*. Welcomes approaches from actors previously unknown to the company, sent by post or email.

Bitesize Theatre Company

8 Green Meadows, New Broughton, Wrexham LL11 6SG
tel (01978) 358320 *fax* (01978) 358315
email admin@bitesizetheatre.co.uk
website www.bitesizetheatre.co.uk

Artistic Director Linda Griffiths *Administrator* Bill Robertson

Production details

Founded in 1992, the company strives to provide high-quality, entertaining theatrical productions for young people – from children's classics to Shakespeare and pantomime to new works. Also runs Theatre in Education projects and bespoke workshops. In general the company stages 11 productions each year, totalling approximately 910 performances in schools and community venues across the UK. Rehearsals take place in North Wales. Between 3-6 actors work on each show and play to audiences aged 3-19 years. Actors are required to be able to sing, dance and drive and may also be expected to participate in workshops. Recent productions include: *Much Ado About Nothing, Red Riding Hood, Where There's a Will There's a Play*, Shakespeare for year 9 SATS (*Much Ado, Tempest* & *Richard III*). Forthcoming productions include: *Romeo and Juliet, Babes in the Wood, Beauty and the Beast*, and *Aladdin*.

Casting procedures

The company holds general auditions; actors requesting inclusion in these should write in May. Casting breakdowns are available in *PCR, The Stage*, Castcall and *SBS*. Although actors are welcome to write with their CVs and photographs, the company prefers not to receive emails or showreels. Mainly takes actors from recognised drama schools; actors aged over 25 years are preferred for jobs requiring driving. All employees must pass a CRB (Criminal Records Bureau) check for work with children. Offers non-Equity contracts. Actively encourages applications from disabled actors and promotes the use of inclusive casting.

Blue Moon Theatre Company

20 Sandpiper Road, Blakespool Park, Bridgewater, Somerset TA6 5QU
tel (01278) 458253
email info@bluemoontheatre.co.uk
website www.bluemoontheatre.co.uk
Artistic Director Steve Apelt *Writer* Mark Scott-Ison *Administrator* Sue Squire

Production details

A producing "fun-packed" children's theatre with lots of participation and involvement – mainly incorporating workshops and after show discussions. Stages on average 2-3 projects annually. In general 4 actors go on tour, staging around 50 performances for young audiences at 40 UK venues including schools, arts centres, theatres, outdoor and community venues. Singing and physical theatre skills are required, as well as a clean driving licence.

Casting procedures

Sometimes holds general auditions, with casting breakdowns publicly available. Welcomes letters (with CVs and photographs) from individual actors previously unknown to the company, sent by post or email. Also welcomes showreels, and invitations to view individual actors' websites. Offers Equity-approved contracts. Actively encourages applications from disabled actors and promotes the use of inclusive casting.

Blue Star Productions

7-8 Shaldon Mansions, 132 Charing Cross Road, London WC2H 0LA
tel 020-7836 6220/4128 *fax* 020-7836 2949
email Hopkinstacey@aol.com

Production details

Blue Star Productions specialises in first-class children's musicals and Songbook Concerts. These shows tour theatres nationally. They include 8-10 performers, beautiful costumes and scenery, and always feature 'live' music. Recent productions include: *The Wonderful Wizard of Oz*; *The Adventures of Pinocchio*; *Tales from the Jungle Book*; *Alice in Wonderland*; *Snow White and the Seven Dwarfs*; and many others. Songbook Concerts include at least 4 singers, depending on venue and finance. One-man shows include: *Life Upon the Very Wicked Stage*, an audience with Barry Stacey.

Casting procedures

All casting is done in-house through Blue Star Associates, also at the above address. Holds general auditions annually, or for specific productions. Welcomes letters with CVs and photographs, and also email submissions.

Bournemouth Theatre in Education

BCCA, 93 Haviland Road, Bournemouth BH7 6HJ
tel (01202) 395759 *fax* (01202) 399597
email tie@bournemouth.gov.uk
Artistic Directors Tony Horitz, Sharon Muiruri
Administrator Shaz Watkins

Production details

Founded in 1967. "Theatre in Education service within a lifelong learning framework." Works in schools, presenting theatrical performances and facilitating drama; is also actively involved in the field of social inclusion. Normally tours 10-15 projects each year to schools, arts centres, outdoor venues, community venues, prisons and hospitals in the South of England. In general 3-4 actors go on tour and play to audiences of all ages. Actors are required to have good workshop skills and the ability to relate well to people. Recent productions include: *My Name Is Savitri*, an anti-racism play for Year 4 children; *Angel*, with a disabled actors theatre company; and *Sleeping Beauty*, with Tops (actors with learning difficulties).

Casting procedures

Sometimes holds general auditions; actors may write at any time requesting inclusion. Accepts submissions

(with CVs and photographs) from actors previously unknown to the company sent by post or email. Will also accept showreels and invitations to view individual actors' websites. "We do use professional actors on a fairly regular basis, but prefer to use those living in or around the Bournemouth area."

Box Clever Theatre Company

12 G1 The Leathermarket, Weston Street, London SE1 3ER
tel 020-7357 0550 *fax* 020-7357 8188
email admin@boxclevertheatre.co.uk
website www.boxclevertheatre.com
Artistic Director Michael Wicherek
Administrator Zareen Graves

Production details

Founded in 1996, the company produces contemporary theatre for young people: new plays, contemporary adaptations of classic texts, and issue-based and educational work. 6 major national tours are staged each year with an average annual total of approximately 600 performances in 500 different venues. The company performs to more than 60,000 young people every year. Venues include arts centres, theatres, and educational and community venues nationwide. Approximately 3 actors are involved in each production. Recent productions include: *Time for the Good Looking Boy* (for theatres); *The Buzz*, *Driving Ms Daisy*, *The Hate Plays* and *Boxed Macbeth* (for secondary schools); and *Car Story* for primary schools.

Casting procedures

Does not use freelance casting directors. Casting breakdowns are available via Equity Job Information Service, the website (normally June/July and October/November), and *PCR*. Welcomes submissions (with CVs and photographs) from actors previously unknown to the company if sent by post and if in response to casting breakdowns only. Advises actors that the company receives a huge response to advertisements placed in *PCR*, and is therefore unable to return photographs or respond in writing to applicants not invited to audition. Non-Equity contracts "in line with ITC". Considers applications from disabled actors to play characters with disabilities.

Brief Candle Theatre

Peel House, Brimington Road, Chesterfield, Derbyshire S41 7UG
tel (01246) 556161
email office@briefcandle.co.uk
website www.briefcandle.co.uk
Artistic Director David Shimwell *Writer/Director* Paul Whitfield

Production details

Established in 2002. Produces high-quality Theatre in Education and theatre for young people and family

Theatre

audiences. On average performs 5 projects each year, with 450 performances in 100 venues including schools, colleges, theatres, community venues and occasionally outdoor performances and festivals. Areas covered: Derbyshire, South Yorkshire, Lincolnshire and Wigan. On average 4 actors go on tour, playing to audiences aged 11 to adult. "We seek to work with actors who are committed to working with young people, and who have the skills required to build fast, effective working relationships with company and audience." Actors may be required to lead workshops. Recent productions include: *The Tower* – a play looking at domestic abuse and power in relationships; *Tight* – a play for 14 year olds looking at use and misuse of alcohol; *An Evening with Mallet and Ming* – a dark comedy for adults and older children, set in a Victorian Music Hall; and *No Place for Dreams* – a family show for the Edinburgh Festival.

Casting procedures

Holds general auditions and actors may write in at any time; the company keeps all submissions for consideration. Casting details are available via Spotlight Link and from the website. Prefers email applications. An approved Manager member of the ITC; all contracts are ITC Equity approved. Encourages applications from all actors, regardless of ability or disability, and promotes the use of inclusive casting.

C&T

University College Worcester, Henwick Grove, Worcester WR2 6AJ
tel (01905) 855436
email info@candt.org
website www.candt.org
Artistic Director Paul Sutton

Production details

Founded in 1988. A theatre company incorporating performance, learning and digital media. Works in schools, colleges and universities in the UK and across Europe. Normally tours 2-3 projects each year with an average annual total of 50-100 performances at 50-100 different venues. In general 2-3 actors go on tour and play to audiences aged 5-65. Dance/physical theatre skills, proficiency with computers and digital media, and a driving licence are required. Actors are also expected to lead workshops. Recent productions include: *Living Newspaper.com*, a docudrama project online for schools.

Casting procedures

Sometimes holds general auditions; actors should write in September requesting inclusion. Accepts submissions (with CVs and photographs) from actors previously unknown to the company sent by post or email. Will also accept showreels and invitations to view individual actors' websites.

Cahoots NI

109-113 Royal Avenue, Belfast BT1 1FF
tel 028-9043 4349
email info@cahootsni.com
website www.cahootsni.com
Artistic Director Paul McEneaney

Production details

Creates world-class, inspirational theatre for children aged 4 to 11 years. Aims to "expand the imagination of children, and to stimulate their artistic creativity through the visual potential of theatre and the age-old popularity of music, magic and illusion". On average tours 3 productions to schools, special schools, respite centres, councils, arts centres and theatres both nationally and internationally. 4-8 actors go on tour, performing to audiences aged 6-11. Actors should have singing, musical instrument, physical theatre, circus and magic skills, and are sometimes required to lead workshops. Recent projects include: *The Flea Pit Circus*; *The Family Hoffmann's Mystery Palace*; *The Snail and the Whale*; and *The Musician*.

Casting procedures

Sometimes holds general auditions; actors may write at any time to request inclusion. Welcomes letters (with CVs and photographs) from actors previously unknown to the company sent by post or email, and is happy to receive showreels. Does not welcome invitations to view individual actors' websites. Actively encourages applications from disabled actors, and promotes the use of inclusive casting.

Cambridge Touring Theatre

29 Worts Causeway, Cambridge CB1 8RJ
email info@cambridgetouringtheatre.co.uk
Artistic Director Rosie Humphreys

Production details

Founded in 2002. A family fun touring theatre. Stages 1 production each year, with 25 performances in 25 theatres and outdoor venues in the South, South East and East of England. In general 6 actors go on tour, playing to audiences aged 2-11. Incoming actors may be required to lead workshops; some singing, dance and driving ability is an advantage. Recent productions include: *Alice in Wonderland*, *Robin Hood*, *Wind in the Willows*, and *Sword in the Stone*.

Casting procedures

Casting breakdowns are available via the website, postal application with sae, *PCR* and CastingCallPro. Welcomes letters (with CVs and photographs) from individual actors previously unknown to the company, sent by post only. Rarely has the opportunity to cast disabled actors.

Changing Faces Theatre Company

Suite C, 226 Venner Road, Sydenham, London SE26 5HT

020-8776 8706 020-8776 7239
email info@changingfacestheatrecompany.co.uk
website www.changingfacestheatrecompany.co.uk
Artistic Director Nicholas Kessler *Company Manager* Heather Code

Production details

A not-for-profit theatre company that is "young, vibrant and ready to bring the highest quality of interactive, literacy-based theatre and workshops to primary-aged children". On average stages 3-6 projects per year, with around 200 performances and 250 workshops in 100 schools, community venues and libraries in London. In general, 2 actors perform a show or lead a workshop, working with audiences aged 4-11. Musical instrument and physical theatre skills are required, as is a clean driving licence. Puppetry, workshop skillls and classroom experience are an advantage. Recent productions include: *The Tailor of Christmas*, *The Elephant's Child*, and *The Gorgon Medusa*.

Casting procedures

Sometimes holds general auditions, and actors are advised to write in the summer (June/July/August) to request inclusion. Casting breakdowns are available via the website, Equity Job Information Service and Sportlight, or on postal application with sae. Welcomes letters (with CVs and photographs) from individual actors previously unknown to the company, but no email submissions, showreels or invitations to view individual actors' websites. Rarely or never has the opportunity to cast disabled actors.

Channel Theatre

See entry under Chalkfoot Theatre Arts (formerly Channel Theatre Company) under *Middle and smaller-scale companies* on page 192.

Creaking Door Productions

Rhys Jones House, St Peter's School, Harefield, Lympstone, Devon EX8 5AU
mobile (07711) 931768
email office@creakingdoor.co.uk
website www.creakingdoor.co.uk
Artistic Director Tom Sherman *Producer* Alix Sherman

Production details

Established in 2005. Specialises in small-scale children's theatre productions in schools and venues throughout the South West; in 2010 the company will implement its new Education Programme. Stages 2-4 productions annually with around 40 performances. In general 2-4 actors go on tour, playing to audiences aged 4 to 13, plus family audiences. Incoming actors should have singing and good basic movement skills, as well as a current driving licence. Actors may be expected to lead

workshops. Recent productions include: *Cinderella*; *The Life and Times of Isambard Kingdom Brunel*; KS2 History workshops – *From Time to Time*; *Just So Stories*; *Frogs, Kings and Golden Wings*; *Tales of Bread and Golden Thread*; and *Beauty and the Beast*.

Casting procedures

Sometimes holds general auditions; actors may write in July and October to request inclusion. Casting breakdowns are available from the website, via Equity, and from Theatre Bristol and Theatre Devon. Welcomes letters (with CVs and photographs) from individual actors previously unknown to the company, sent by post only. Rarely or never has the opportunity to cast disabled actors.

CTC Theatre

Darlington Arts Centre, Vane Terrace, Darlington DL3 7AX
tel (01325) 352004
email ctc@ctctheatre.org.uk
website www.ctctheatre.org.uk
Creative Producer Miranda Thain

Production details

Founded in 1979. A specialist producer of theatre for young audiences. Tours on average 8 projects annually, with around 240 performances in 10 schools, arts centres, theatre and outdoor venues across all regions, but mostly in the North East. In general 2-5 actors go on tour, playing to audiences aged 0-18 years. Depending on the show may require singing, musical instrument, dance and physical skills from incoming actors, and a driving licence is often required. Actors are sometimes expected to lead workshops. Recent productions include: *Five* – a contemporary dance installation for 5 year olds; *Aesop's Fables*; and *Taken* – a site-specific show about river spirits.

Casting procedures

Sometimes holds general auditions; actors are advised to write in the Autumn to request inclusion. Welcomes letters (with CVs & photographs) from individual actors previously unknown to the company, sent by post or email. Also accepts showreels and invitations to view individual actors' websites. Offers Equity approved contracts as negotiated through ITC. Will consider applications from disabled actors to play characters with disabilities.

Cwmni Theatr Arad Goch

Stryd Y Baddon, Aberystwyth, Ceredigion SY23 2NN
tel (01970) 617998 *fax* (01970) 611223
email post@aradgoch.org
Artistic Director Jeremy Turner *Administrative Manager* Nia Wyn Evans

Production details

Founded in 1989. Main focus of work is Theatre in Education. Normally tours 6 projects each year with

Theatre

an average annual total of 150 performances and more than 100 different venues. Venues include schools, theatres and community venues across Wales and occasionally abroad. In general 3-6 actors go on tour and play to audiences aged 4 upwards. Singing ability, proficiency with a musical instrument, fluency in Welsh and a driving licence are required. Actors may also be expected to lead workshops. Recent productions include: *The Impossible Parents Go Green*, for 7-11 year olds, *Winter Pictures*, for young children (4-8 year olds) and *Crash*, a community theatre piece for young people. Offers ITC/Equity approved contracts and does not subscribe to the Equity Pension Scheme.

Casting procedures

Sometimes holds general auditions; actors requesting inclusion should write before the start of the academic year. Accepts submissions (with CVs and photographs) from actors previously unknown to the company sent by post or email. Will also accept showreels and invitations to view individual actors' websites. Will consider applications from disabled actors to play disabled characters.

Daylight Theatre

66 Middle Street, Stroud, Gloucestershire GL5 1EA
tel (01453) 763808
Artistic Director Hugh Young *Key personnel* Roger Burfield

Production details

Founded in 1977. Tours educational theatre into schools. Topics have included drugs, HIV/AIDS, Shakespeare, history and mythology, and have been linked to the National Curriculum. Normally tours 7 projects each year with an average annual total of 200 performances and 150 different venues. Venues include schools (mainly primary but some secondary), arts centres and theatres across the UK, Germany and Luxembourg. In general 2-3 actors go on tour and play to audiences aged 4-18. Actors are required to hold a driving licence and may also be expected to lead workshops. Recent productions include: *Can You Take It?* – drugs, alcohol and tobacco education for 9-11 year-olds; *A Midsummer Night's Dream* and *Macbeth* for Key Stage 2 level; and *Ghostcliff Grange*, a World War II drama, also for Key Stage 2.

Casting procedures

Advises that the company rarely needs new female actors.

Fevered Sleep

c/o Young Vic, 66 The Cut, London SE1 8LZ
tel 020-7922 2988
email admin@feveredsleep.co.uk
website www.feveredsleep.com

Artistic Director David Harradine *General Manager* Sophie Pridell

Production details

Established in 1996. Creates original performance, visual art and publications, for children and for adults. "Whether in theatres, galleries or other places, our work provides exciting and intimate experiences for our audiences, and encourages people to see the world in new and unexpected ways." Tours 3 projects annually, in around 14 venues (theatres, arts centres, galleries, and site-specific) in the UK, 3 internationally, and 4 in London. In general 2-3 actors go on tour, playing to audiences aged 3-8 and 17+. Incoming actors may be expected to lead workshops, and may require dance, physical theatre and /or musical instrument skills, depending on the project. Recent productions include: *Brilliant, An Infinite Line: Brighton*, and *Stilled*.

Casting procedures

Sometimes holds general auditions, and actors may write at any time. Welcomes letters (with CVs and photographs) from individual actors previously unknown to the company, sent by post or email, as well as invitations to view individual actors' websites – but prefers not to receive showreels. Offers Equity-approved contracts as negotiated through ITC. Will consider applications from disabled actors "in line with our equal opportunities policy".

Freshwater Theatre Company

Channelsea House, Canning Road, Abbey Lane, London E15 3ND
tel 0844-800 2870
email info@freshwatertheatre.co.uk
website www.freshwatertheatre.co.uk
Directors Helen Wood, Carol Tagg *Key personnel* Brooke Gallagher (Operations Manager)

Production details

Established in 1996 with the aim of offering high-quality, affordable, innovative drama opportunites to primary school children and teachers. Runs workshops and storytelling sessions addressing a range of curriculum areas including history, geography, Shakespeare, citizenship, multicultural studies and the needs of early years pupils. Also runs drama in-service training courses for teachers. Does not tour, but provides around 40 sessions all year round at nurseries, schools and community venues in Greater London, Cambridgeshire, Suffolk, Essex, the West Midlands conurbation, and Greater Manchester. Around 40 freelance facilitators work with audiences aged 3 to 11. Relevant experience is required, and actors are expected to lead workshops. Recent workshops include: *Florence Nightingale, Leap into Language, Early Years Story Hunt*, and *An Indian Village*.

Casting procedures

Holds general auditions; actors may write in at any time. Welcomes letters (with CVs & photographs) sent by post or email, but only from experienced workshop facilitators. Does not accept showreels or invitations to view individual actors' websites. "We only engage dedicated, experienced workshop leaders to undertake our drama sessions, and will only consider those who can provide regular and ongoing availability within the areas we cover."

Fuse: New Theatre for Young People

13 Hope Street, Liverpool L1 9BH
tel 0151-708 0877 *fax* 0151-707 9950
email info@fusetheatre.com
website www.fusetheatre.co.uk
Artistic Producer Andrew Raffle *General Manager* Michael Quirke

Production details

Established in 1978. Performs 3-4 projects annually, with approximately 50 performances in schools, arts centres, theatres and community venues in the North West. In general 2-5 actors go on tour, playing to audiences aged 3 to 18 years. May require singing, musical instrument, dance and physical theatre skills; actors should hold a current driving licence, and may be expected to lead workshops. Recent productions include: *A World Away*, *Treasure*, *Portrait of a Nation*, and *Shadow Companion*.

Casting procedures

Sometimes holds general auditions: actors may write at any time to request inclusion. Casting breakdowns are available through the website and via the Arts Council's 'Artsjobs' service. Welcomes letters (with CVs and photographs) from individual actors previously unknown to the company, sent by post or email, and invitations to view individual actors' websites. Offers Equity-approved contracts as negotiated through ITC. Will consider applications from disabled actors to play characters with disabilities.

Gazebo Theatre in Education Company

Bilston Town Hall, Church Street, Bilston, West Midlands WV14 0AP
tel (01902) 313009 *fax* (01902) 313229
email gazebotie@tiscali.co.uk
website www.gazebotie.org
Artistic Director Michael O'Hara *Strategic Director* Pamela Cole-Hudson

Production details

Founded in 1979. Normally tours 3-5 projects each year plus workshops, with an average annual total of 300 performances and 250 different venues, these are mainly schools and community venues in the West Midlands and South Shropshire. In general between 1

and 3 actors go on tour and play to audiences aged 4-25. Musical ability and movement skills are sometimes required, as is a driving licence. Actors may also be expected to lead workshops. Recent productions include: *Billy No Mates!* (Special Needs); *If you see a crocodile* (Nursery & Reception); *Presents from the Past*; (KS2) *Doing our Bit* (KS3).

Casting procedures

Casting breakdowns are sometimes available by postal application (with sae) or through Equity Job Information Service. The company website will also show details of auditions and artists opportunities. Accepts submissions (with CVs and photographs) from actors previously unknown to the company if sent by post. Open auditions take place over the summer months. Will accept invitations to view individual actors' websites. Does not welcome unsolicited emails. Offers non-Equity contracts. Actively encourages applications from disabled actors and promotes the use of inclusive casting.

Gibber Theatre Ltd

Unit 9, 66 Hudson Street, North Shields, Tyne & Wear NE30 1DL
tel 0191-257 8126 *fax* 0191-257 8970
email info@gibbertraining.com
website www.gibbertheatre.com
Artistic Directors Victoria Blackburn, Tim Watt

Production details

Founded in 1999. An educational theatre company specialising in drama-based experiential learning programmes for young people of all ages. The company has built a reputation for making a difference in education, by delivering high-quality presentation, performance, workshop, road show and special events. On average performs 10 projects each year, with approximately 300 performances in 250-300 schools across the UK. Also tours to outdoor and community venues, hospitals and theatres. In general 3-4 actors go on tour, playing to audiences aged 5 to 18-plus. Actors may be required to lead workshops, and should have singing and physical theatre skills as well as a driving licence. Recent productions include: bespoke performances and workshops for London Learning Skills Council (Year 10 careers tour exploring post-16 learning and voluntary opportunities), and Newcastle Healthy Schools (KS4 tobacco education tour with a focus on tobacco-industry tactics).

Casting procedures

Sometimes holds general auditions; actors may write at any time. Casting breakdowns are available from *The Stage*, *PCR*, and Castingcallpro.com. Welcomes letters (with CVs & photographs) from actors previously unknown to the company, sent by post or email. Accepts showreels and invitations to view

Theatre

individual actors' websites. Will consider applications from disabled actors to play characters with disabilities.

The Derek Grant Organisation Ltd

Beechwood House, 13 Beechwood Road,
West Moors, Dorset BH22 0BN
tel (01202) 887439
email admin@derekgrant.co.uk
website www.derekgrant.co.uk
Artistic Director Derek Grant *Administrative Director* Michael Jones

Production details

"We present traditional children's/family shows and pantomimes. A strong storyline features in every show, along with colourful costumes and scenery, bright musical numbers and lots of joining in!" Normally tours 4 productions each year, with an average annual total of 80 performances in numerous different venues. Venues include arts centres and theatres across the UK, including Northern Ireland. In general 5-6 actors go on tour and play to audiences aged 3-93. Singing ability, dance/physical theatre skills are required. Recent productions include: *Goldilocks and the Three Bears*, *Pinocchio* and Hans Andersen's *The Snow Queen*.

Casting procedures

Sometimes holds general auditions; actors can write at any time requesting inclusion. Accepts submissions (with CVs and photographs) from actors previously unknown to the company sent by post or email. Will also accept showreels and invitations to view individual actors' websites.

Greenwich & Lewisham Young People's Theatre (GLYPT)

Royal Laboratory Office, No. 1 Street, Royal Arsenal,
London SE18 6ST
tel 020-8854 1316
email info@glypt.co.uk
website www.glypt.co.uk
Artistic Director Jeremy James *Education Officer* Caroline Edwards

Production details

GLYPT creates theatre for, with and by young people. It runs Youth Theatre workshops for 8-21 year-olds, and specialist programmes for young people with learning difficulties. The company also runs a comprehensive programme of workshops for young refugees and new arrivals. Tours 2 productions a year to young audiences across South East London and beyond; these visit schools as Theatre in Education programmes, and also play at community and arts centres and at theatres. The work explores current and provoking issues that affect the lives of young audiences, and offers a platform for aesthetic and educational debate. Recent productions have included: *Red, White, Black & Blue, Who R U Talkin' 2?* and *Master Juba*.

Casting procedures

Operates the ITC/Equity contract and works with actors committed to the young people's theatre sector. "We actively encourage applications from disabled actors and promote the use of inclusive casting." Welcomes letters and emails (with CVs) from actors and skilled workshop facilitators.

Gwent Theatre

The Drama Centre, Pen-y-Pound,
Abergavenny NP7 5UD
tel (01873) 853167 *fax* (01873) 853910
email gwenttie@aol.com
website www.gwenttie.co.uk
Artistic Director Gary Meredith *Administrator* Julia Davies

Production details

Founded in 1976. Tours at least 4 projects each year with an average annual total of 180 performances. Venues include schools, theatres, outdoor venues and community venues in Gwent and across Wales. In general 3-5 actors go on tour and play to audiences aged 6 upwards. Singing ability, proficiency with a musical instrument and dance/physical theatre skills are required. Actors may also be expected to lead workshops. Recent productions include: *Pa Mor Uchel Yw Fyny?, Home Front, The Watching* and *Shadow Seeker* (all for schools).

Casting procedures

Sometimes holds general auditions and actors can write at any time requesting inclusion. Accepts submissions (with CVs and photographs) from actors previously unknown to the company if sent by post. Does not welcome unsolicited emails. Will also accept invitations to view individual actors' websites.

Half Moon Young People's Theatre

43 Whitehorse Road, London E1 0ND
tel 020-7265 8138 *fax* 020-7709 8914
email admin@halfmoon.org.uk
website www.halfmoon.org.uk
Artistic Director Chris Elwell *Administrative Director* Jackie Eley

Production details

Founded in 1989. "Young people's theatre touring in London and nationally with a reputation for high-quality work. Also a receiving venue for young people's work." Normally tours 2 projects with an average annual total of 170 performances and 45 different venues. Venues include schools, arts centres, theatres and community venues. In general 2-3 actors go on tour and play to audiences aged under 17.

Offers ITC/Equity approved contracts and does not subscribe to the Equity Pension Scheme.

Casting procedures

Casting breakdowns are available through the website and Equity Job Information Service. Sometimes holds general auditions; actors can write at any time requesting inclusion. Accepts submissions (with CVs and photographs) from actors previously unknown to the company sent by post or email. Will also accept invitations to view individual actors' websites. Actively encourages applications from disabled actors and promotes the use of inclusive casting.

Hopscotch Theatre Company

2nd Floor, 7 Water Row, Glasgow G51 3UW
tel 0141-440 2025 *fax* 0141-440 2025
email info@hopscotchtheatre.com
website www.hopscotchtheatre.com
Artistic Director Grant Smeaton *General Manager* Susan McGregor

Production details

Founded in 1988. A Theatre in Education company touring 4 productions each year to primary schools with an average annual total of 520 performances. Venues include schools, arts centres, theatres and community venues across Scotland. In general 4 actors go on tour and play to audiences aged 5-12 years. Singing ability and some proficiency with a musical instrument are required. Recent productions include: *The Romans in Scotland, Mary Queen of Scots* and *Tam O' Shanter.*

Casting procedures

Holds general auditions; actors requesting inclusion should write in May or June. Accepts submissions (with CVs and photographs) from actors previously unknown to the company sent by post or email. Will also accept showreels. Offers non-Equity contracts. Rarely (or never) has the opportunity to cast disabled actors.

Impact Universal

Hope Bank House, Woodhead Road, Honley, Holmfirth, West Yorkshire HD9 6PF
tel (01484) 660077 *fax* (01484) 660088
email jill.beckwith@impactuniversal.com
website www.impactuniversal.com
Creative Director Brett Marshall *Creative Manager* Rosie Perkin

Production details

Established in 1994. A communications and training provider using theatrical techniques. The company's work is delivered live, fully interactive and topical, making its impact highly memorable and effective. Presentations, workshops and training events are delivered by experienced, professional actors and facilitators. In an average year tours 33 projects, staging more than 900 performances in the same number of schools, sports halls and conference centres nationwide. In general 3 actors go on tour, playing to audiences aged 11-19. Incoming actors may be expected to lead workshops; dance, physical theatre and impersonation skills are an advantage, as is a clean driving licence. Recent productions include: *Opt Into Learning* (Year 9); *HE 4 All* (Year 10); *Stay In Learning* (Year 11); and *Stay On Course* (Year 12).

Casting procedures

Holds general auditions and actors may write at any time to request inclusion. Casting breakdowns are available from Equity Job Information Service, Spotlight and Casting Call Pro. Welcomes letters (with CVs and photographs) from individual actors previously unknown to the company, sent by post or email, as well as invitations to view individual actors' websites. Rarely, or never, has the opportunity to cast disabled actors.

In Toto Theatre Company

The Colombo Centre, 34-68 Colombo Street, London SE1 8DP
tel 020-7261 1515
email sarah@in-tototheatre.co.uk
website www.in-tototheatre.co.uk
Artistic Director Sarah Carter *Associate Director* Lennie Charles

Production details

Founded in 1989 and became a charity in 2000. Provides inclusive theatre for all ages using a combination of puppetry, live music, storytelling and dance. Specialises in creating 'total theatre' by, with and for young audiences – "a highly visual musical style of theatre approach which is inclusive and accessible to a wide range of ages and abilities". Also runs participatory arts activities for families, children and young adults to make their own performance. Has completed 7 projects to date with an average of 50 performances in up to 30 venues (schools, community venues and outdoor festivals, including site-specific). On average 2-3 performers/actors tour in the company's small-scale productions devised for age groups from 18 months upwards. An additional skill is usually required of actors; playing a musical instrument and puppetry are especially valued.

Casting procedures

Does not hold general auditions. Will accept email enquiries, but unsolicited letters by post are not welcomed. Sometimes advertises casting breakdowns via Arts Jobs or Equity information line. Rather than showreels, prefers to receive links to actors' websites by email. Offers Equity approved contracts through ITC. Actively encourages applications from disabled actors and promotes the use of inclusive casting.

Theatre

"We usually recruit artists with an interest and proven experience in making theatre collaboratively, with an interdisciplinary approach. Being able to facilitate workshops is a very important requirement, and those with a background in arts therapy, social work, education or working with special needs, in addition to professional performance or visual arts training, are far more likely to be considered."

Jack Drum Arts

43/44 Gladstone Terrace, Sunniside,
Bishop Auckland, Co Durham DL13 4LS
email info@jackdrum.co.uk
Artistic Director Julie Ward *Administrator* Stacey Taylor

Production details

Founded in 1986. "Delivers a strong programme of participatory arts for all sectors of the community." Normally tours 2 projects each year with an average annual total of 40 performances at up to 40 different venues. Venues include schools, arts centres, theatres, outdoor venues and community venues across the UK and abroad, with a focus on rural touring. In general 3-4 actors go on tour and play to audiences of pre-school age and upwards. Singing ability, proficiency with a musical instrument and a driving licence are required for some shows. Actors may also be expected to lead workshops. Recent productions include: *Red Riding Hood and Her Amazing Grandmother.*

Casting procedures

Accepts submissions (with CVs and photographs) from actors in the North East area only. "We like to know who is around in the North East, especially if based in County Durham. Can help access local networks and professional development." Offers Equity & non-Equity contracts. Rarely (or never) has the opportunity to cast disabled actors, but would be interested in developing projects which can make this possible. Particularly interested in actors who have BSL skills.

Kazzum

91 Brick Lane, London E1 6QL
tel 020-7539 3500
email info@kazzum.org
website www.kazzum.org
Artistic Director Daryl Beeton

Production details

Established in 1989. "We create playful theatre and participative arts activities for young people, using art forms that reflect diverse cultural influences." Stages 1-2 productions each year, with around 40-70 performances in 30 arts centres, theatres, and outdoor and community venues across the UK. In general 3 actors go on tour, playing to audiences aged

4-8 and 10+. Incoming actors should have singing, musical instrument, dance and physical theatre skills and may be expected to lead workshops. Recent productions include: *The Boy Who Grew Flowers*; *Hunt*; *The Sorcerer's Apprentice*; and *Beginning with Blobs.*

Casting procedures

Actors may write in January through to April to request inclusion. Casting breakdowns are available from the website, through Equity Job Information Service and Arts Jobs, and in *PCR*. Welcomes letters (with CVs and photographs) from individual actors previously unknown to the company, sent by post or email. Also accepts showreels and invitations to view individual actors' websites. Offers Equity-approved contracts as negotiated through ITC. Actively encourages applications from disabled actors, and promotes the use of inclusive casting.

Kinetic Theatre Company

Suite H, The Jubilee Centre, 10-12 Lombard Road, London SW19 3TZ
tel 020-8286 2613
email paul@kinetictheatre.co.uk
website www.kinetictheatre.co.uk
Artistic Director Graham Scott *Key personnel* Paul Dunn (Production Office Manager & Casting Director)

Production details

Established in 1988. One of the country's most prominent Theatre in Education companies. Performs plays geared to the National Curriculum for Science, to schools and theatres througout the UK. Has 9 shows, 4 of which are on the road at any one time. All shows are self-contained musical comedies, all being very different in style. On average performs 12 tours every year with around 900 performances to 600 venues in England, Scotland, Wales and Northern Ireland. All shows are 2-handers, and actors play to audiences aged 5 to 12. Actors require reasonable singing and dancing skills and a driving licence is *essential*. Recent productions include: *The Hospital Force, Down to Earth, The Bunsen Towers Mystery*, and *Lamps in the Circuit.*

Casting procedures

Does not hold general auditions; lets actors know when to write in, via the usual casting breakdown sites. Casting breakdowns are widely available: consult the website for full details. Contracts are based on Equity/TMA guidelines for small-scale touring. Will consider applications from actors with disabilities to play characters with disabilities. "We cast for our productions 3 times a year, usually around February, June and October, and we *always* put out castings for our workshop-style auditions. We cannot consider applications outside these times and due to limited space do not hold details on file. Please do not send unsolicited CVs/photos as it will just waste your money. We recommend that actors check the 'auditions' page on our website for general information on when auditions are coming up, and also for more detailed information to prepare for our auditions."

Krazy Kat Theatre Company

173 Hartington Road, Brighton BN2 3PA
tel (01273) 692552 *fax* (01273) 692552
email krazykattheatre@ntlworld.com
website www.krazykattheatre.co.uk
Artistic Director Kinny Gardner

Production details

A children's theatre company founded in 1972, specialising in highly visual forms of theatre that are accessible to deaf children. Normally tours 4-6 projects each year with an average annual total of 150 performances and 75 venues. Venues include schools, arts centres, theatres, outdoor venues and community centres in Essex, Sussex, Kent and London. In general 2 actors go on tour and play to audiences aged 3-7. Singing ability, physical theatre skills, sign language and a driving licence are required. Actors may also be expected to lead workshops. Recent productions include: *Three Pigs*, *Jack & The Beanstalk*, and *The Very Magic Flute*.

Casting procedures

Sometimes holds general auditions; actors can write at any time requesting inclusion. Accepts submissions (with CVs and photographs) from actors previously unknown to the company if sent by post. Does not welcome unsolicited emails. Will also accept invitations to view individual actors' websites. Offers non-Equity contracts Actively encourages applications from disabled actors and promotes the use of inclusive casting.

The London Bus Theatre Company

37 Chestnut Close, Hockley, Essex SS5 5EQ
tel (01208) 814514 *fax* (01208) 814514
email kathy@londonbustheatre.co.uk
website www.londonbustheatre.co.uk
Principal Chris Turner *Chair* Katherine Austen

Production details

One of the most respected theatre-in-education companies in the UK, supported by the National Theatre, Arts Council, National Lottery, police and private companies as well as the Home Office. Provides innovative workshops on the subjects of drugs, bullying, anti-social behaviour, alcohol, domestic abuse, job interview techniques and knife crime. Also provides schools and colleges with the celebrated 'Kick It – Bullying', 'Kick It – Smoking' and 'Kick It – Binge Drinking' DVD series. In 2008 the company produced the award-winning 'Nutter' anti-bullying DVD. Stages an average of 20 projects each year, with approximately 200 performances in 200 venues including leisure centres, colleges and youth detention centres all over England. In general 6 actors go on tour and play to audiences aged 8-18. Actors may be expected to lead workshops and should possess singing, dance, and physical theatre skills as well as holding a driving licence. Recent productions incude: *2 Smart* (Essex police/Essex FM tour of Essex theatres in 2008): and *Nutter* (tour of schools 2008, Arts Council project 2008).

Casting procedures

Holds general auditions and actors may write in at any time. Welcomes letters (with CVs and photographs) from individual actors previously unknown to the company, sent by post or email. Accepts showreels and will consider invitations to view individual actors' websites. Considers applications from disabled actors to play characters with disabilities.

Loudmouth Education & Training

The Friends' Institute, 220 Moseley Road, Highgate, Birmingham B12 0DG
tel 0121-446 4880 *fax* 0121-440 3940
email info@loudmouth.co.uk
website www.loudmouth.co.uk
Company Directors Chris Cowan, Eleanor Bryson
Operations Manager Caroline Bridges

Production details

Founded in 1994. Supplies interactive education and training programmes for young people on personal, social and health education issues, and accessible training for adults to aid personal and professional development. On average 4 teams of 2 actors tour 14 projects around 236 UK venues each year; venues include schools, community venues and youth centres. Actors are expected to lead workshops and must have a full driving licence. Recent productions include: *Trust Me* – an interactive theatre programme focusing on STIs, contraception and unplanned pregnancy.

Casting procedures

Holds general auditions. Welcomes letters with CVs and photographs from individual actors previously unknown to the company. Will accept unsolicited CVs and photographs sent by email. Does not welcome showreels or invitations to view individual actors' websites. Rarely or never has the opportunity to cast disabled actors.

M6 Theatre Company

Studio Theatre, Hamer County Primary School, Albert Royds Street, Rochdale OL16 2SU
tel (01706) 355898 *fax* (01706) 712601

Theatre

email info@m6theatre.co.uk
website www.m6theatre.co.uk
Artistic Producer Dorothy Wood *General Manager*
Deborah Palmer

Production details

M6 Theatre Company specalises in producing and
touring high-quality, accessible and emotionally
engaging theatre for young audiences. Founded in
1977, the company tours 3-5 productions each year,
through approximately 300 performances /
workshops. Touring venues include theatres, schools,
festivals, prisons and early years settings across the
North West and nationally. Cast sizes are generally 2-
4; actors may be expected to participate in workshops
accompanying productions. Recent productions have
included: *Best Friends* for audiences aged 4+ (an
imaginative fusion of dance, theatre and original
music in collaboration with Ludus Dance Company);
Family Business for audiences aged 13+ (exploring
parent / child relationships and intergenerational
offending); and *One Little Word* (a sensitive and
moving production for children aged 3+ exploring
friendship and conflict resolution, underscored with
original music and with only one spoken word). Also
delivers a wide-ranging participatory programme
with local young people.

Casting procedures

Accepts submissions (with CVs and photographs)
from actors previously unknown to the company.
Unfortunately the company is unable to return
photos. Actor contracts are ITC / Equity approved.

Magic Carpet Theatre

18 Church Street, Sutton on Hull,
East Yorkshire HU7 4TS
tel (01682) 709539 *fax* (01682) 787362
email jon@magiccarpettheatre.com
website www.magiccarpettheatre.com
Artistic Director Jon Marshall *Company Manager*
Steve Collison

Production details

Professional young children's theatre company
presenting shows and workshops in the UK and
abroad. Tours 3-4 productions annually, with around
250 performances in 250 venues including schools,
arts and community venues, and festivals. In general
3 actors go on tour, playing to audiences aged 5-11.
Actors may be expected to lead workshops. Recent
productions include: *The Wizard of Castle Magic*;
Magic Circus.

Casting procedures

Does not hold general auditions; actors may write in
the autumn to request inclusion. Advises actors to
"ring us rather than sending CVs, etc., to see when
we are casting".

MakeBelieve Arts

The Deptford Mission, 1 Creek Road,
London SE8 3BT
tel 020-8691 3803 *fax* 020-8691 3880
email info@makebelievearts.co.uk
website www.makebelievearts.co.uk
Artistic Director Trisha Lee *Creative Projects Co-
ordinator* Alice Edwards *Company Adminsitrator*
Pippa Taylor

Production details

Established in 2002 and gained charitable status in
2006. A leading provider of high-quality arts and
education programmes, for Foundation Stage,
Primary and Secondary School pupils and their
parents and teachers. Based in South London but
works in other boroughs. In general 4-6 actors stage 1
project a year, with around 50 performances at 40
schools. Skills required depend on the production,
and actors may be asked to lead workshops. Recent
productions include: *The Woman Who Cooked
Everything*, and *Gulliver's Travels*.

Casting procedures

Holds general auditions. Casting breakdowns are
available from the website and in *PCR* and *The Stage*.
Welcomes letters (with CVs and photographs) from
individual actors previously unknown to the
company, sent by post or email. Does not however
accept showreels or invitations to view individual
actors' websites. Offers Equity-approved contracts
negotiated through ITC. Rarely has the opportunity
to cast disabled actors.

Moby Duck

12 Reservoir Retreat, Birmingham B16 9EH
tel/fax 0121-242 0400
email info@moby-duck.org
website www.moby-duck.org
Artistic Director Guy Hutchins

Production details

Founded in 1999. Performs 2 projects annually, with
more than 50 performances at the same number of
schools, arts centres, theatres and community venues
across all regions. In general 3-4 actors go on tour,
playing to audiences aged 4 to 80. Requires actors to
have "an understanding of the other cultures we
work in". Actors may be expected to lead workshops.
Singing, musical instrument, dance and physical
theatre skills are an advantage, and actors should hold
a clean driving licence. For details of recent
productions, see the website.

Casting procedures

Sometimes holds general auditions, and actors may
write at any time to request inclusion. Welcomes
letters (with CVs and photographs) from individual
actors previously unknown to the company, sent by

post or email. Also welcomes showreels and invitations to view individual actors' websites. Offers Equity-approved contracts as negotiated through ITC. Rarely or never has the opportunity to cast disabled actors.

Monster Theatre Productions Ltd

17 Prince Road, Wallsend, Tyne & Wear NE28 8DN
tel 0191-240 4011 *fax* 0191-240 4016
email info@monsterproductions.co.uk
website www.monsterproductions.co.uk
Artistic Directors Chris Speyer, Ieuan Einion
Operations Manager Doreen Ford

Production details

Set up in 2000 to continue the work for children under 7 begun by the directors at Northern Stage. Creates new music theatre for young children and runs a youth theatre programme for North Tyneside. Normally tours 2 projects each year with an average annual total of 150 performances and 30 different venues. Venues include schools, arts centres, theatres and community venues across the UK, Wales and Ireland. In general 3-5 actors go on tour and play mainly to audiences under 7 years old. Actors may also be expected to lead workshops. Recent productions include: *The Terrible Grump* and *Trouble Under Foot* (both for under-7s); and *Street of Strangers* for young people and adults.

Casting procedures

Sometimes holds general auditions; actors should write requesting inclusion when advertised in *PCR*. Accepts submissions (with CVs and photographs) from actors previously unknown to the company if sent by post. Does not welcome unsolicited emails. Will also accept invitations to view individual actors' websites. "Due to our scale of work we only employ a small number of actors each year. We favour multiracial casts to reflect our audiences. Musical and movement skills are a great advantage."

Nimble Fish

30 Wilton Square, London N1 3DW
mobile (07939) 522518
email getnimble@nimble-fish.co.uk
website www.nimble-fish.co.uk
Directors Samatha Holdsworth, Greg Klerkx

Production details

"An evolving collective of creative individuals who actively pursue collaborations with disadvantaged communities to foster positive social change." Performs 1 project annually with around 13 peformances in 14 venues, including schools, outdoor and community venues, and other site-specific venues in London, the South East and Edinburgh. Around 3-6 actors go on tour performing to adult audiences. Actors may be expected to lead

workshops. Recent productions include: *The Container* (winner of a 2007 Edinburgh Fringe First and a 2007 Amnesty International Freedom of Expression Award), and *Einstein's Dreams*. Current productions in development include: *The Trial of Wernher von Braun.*

Casting procedures

Sometimes holds general auditions. Does not welcome unsolicited approaches from individuals not previously known to the company. Offers Equity-approved contracts via ITC. Actively encourages applicatinos from disabled actors and promotes the use of inclusive casting.

Nottingham Playhouse Roundabout TIE

Nottingham Playhouse, Wellington Circus, Nottingham NG1 5AF
tel 0115-947 4361 *fax* 0115-947 5759
email andrewb@nottinghamplayhouse.co.uk
website www.nottinghamplayhouse.co.uk
Director Roundabout & Education Andrew Breakwell
Administrator Roundabout & Education Kitty Parker

Production details

Established in 1973. Has toured plays for schools and young people locally, nationally and internationally for the last 36 years. In that time hundreds of thousands of children, young people, parents and teachers have seen the company's work. Its policy is to encourage new writing, and Roundabout has "an enviable record" of adding to its repertoire of work. The company is now part of a much larger Theatre Education department of the Playhouse, and last year it offered 18 different programme strands to more than 14,000 people in over 600 different sessions.

Usually stages 4 new pieces of work each year, with 180-200 performances in over 100 schools, arts centres and small theatres in the East Midlands, East Anglia, and London. In general 3-4 actors go on tour, playing to audiences aged 4-18. It would be useful for incoming actors to have singing and musical instrument skills and a driving licence; BSL and/or Makaton desirable. Actors may be required to lead workshops. Recent productions include: *The Whale's Tooth* (for young people with profound and multiple learning difficulties); *Can You Whistle, Johanna?* (for 8-11 year olds; a new play about 2 boys who 'adopt' a grandfather); and *The Little Mermaid* (for 4-8 year olds).

Casting procedures

Holds general auditions, and actors may write in spring/summer to request inclusion. Casting is conducted by Playhouse Casting Director Sooki McShane when specific skills/types are required. Welcomes letters (with CVs and photographs) from individual actors previously unknown to the company, sent by post only. Will see shows when in

Theatre

the area. Offers Equity-approved contracts as negotiated through TMA. Encourages enquiries from actors with disabilities, and promotes the use of inclusive casting. "We welcome mature (in every sense of the word) actors for our work with young people, and candidates should be ready for a 'life on the road' with very early mornings and the 'dinner ladies'! A genuine liking of children and young people helps. In auditions I ask actors to prepare a text, chosen by myself, which we then work on together. I would expect to spend around 40 minutes with each person."

Oily Cart Company

Smallwood School Annexe, Smallwood Road, London SW17 OTW
tel 020-8672 6329 *fax* 020-8672 0792
email oilies@oilycart.org.uk
website www.oilycart.org.uk
Artistic Director Tim Webb *General Manager* Kathy Everett *Administrator* Sarah Crompton

Production details

One of the leading theatre companies in the UK, creating highly interactive multi-sensory performances for the very young (6 months to 6 years) and for young people (aged 3-19) with Profound or Multiple Learning Disabilities (PMLD) or an Autistic Spectrum Disorder (ASD). Tours national and international venues like theatres and arts centres with early years shows, and takes its special needs work to special schools around the UK. Recent productions include: *Baby Balloon* for audiences aged 6 months to 2 years; *If All The World Were Paper*; *Blue*; and *Pool Piece* – an interactive hydrotherapy pool show for young people with PMLD or ASD.

Casting procedures

Casting breakdowns are available on the website **www.oilycart.org.uk** and the Artsjobs website **www.artscouncil.org.uk/pressnews/ mailinglists.php**. Offers ITC/Equity approved contracts. Actively encourages applications from disabled actors and promotes the use of inclusive casting.

Onatti Productions Ltd

9 Field Close, Warwick, Warwickshire CV34 4QD
tel (01926) 495220 *fax* 0870-164 3629
email info@onatti.co.uk
website www.onatti.co.uk
Artistic Director Andrew Bardwell *Company Manager* Seanna Hardaker-Jones

Presents foreign-language productions for schools throughout the UK and Ireland. Plays are produced in French, German and Spanish. All plays are written by the company. Produces 4 plays each year, which tour from between 6 to 9 months. Contact Alan

Hamlet, Educational Adviser (**tie@onatti.co.uk**) for details of Theatre in Education programmes. Recent productions include: *The Way of the World*, *Premier Amour*, *Greensleeves* and *The Child King*.

Passe-Partout

13 Stanford Avenue, Brighton BN1 6AD
tel (01273) 557595
email p@sse-partout.com
Artistic Director Michele Young *Manager* Richard Crane

Production details

Founded in 1986. "Theatre for social change – assisting people to have a voice about an issue which concerns them." Normally tours 3 projects each year, with an average annual total of 20 performances and 20 different venues including schools, outdoor centres, community venues and office spaces in the UK and abroad. In general 4 actors go on tour and play to audiences of all ages. Any additional skills that actors may have will be put to use. Actors may also be expected to lead workshops. Recent projects include: *anti-bullying strategy development* (prisons, UK); *Social Capital* (various schools, Europe); *Street Children* (Nairobi, Kenya); *Bio-diversity* (Toulouse, France); and *Silkworm Journey* (France). Has an alliance with Inedit Films to produce 3-minute dramas (fact-based) for educational purposes.

Casting procedures

"We cast from the group of people who have proposed an issue they want to take forward. We sometimes build-in 1 or 2 people from outside that group who have interest and energy."

Pied Piper Theatre Company in association with the Yvonne Arnaud Theatre

1 Lilian Place, Coxcombe Lane, Chiddingfold GU8 4QA
tel (01428) 684022 *fax* (01428) 684022
email twpiedpiper@aol.com
website www.piedpipertheatre.co.uk
Artistic Director Tina Williams *Associate Director* Nicola Sangster

Production details

Founded in 1984, Pied Piper has toured nationally and internationally. Currently project-funded by Arts Council South East and Sure Start, the company is now concentrating on new writing for the age range 3-7. Combination of school and theatre touring.

Casting procedures

Holds general auditions; actors requesting inclusion should write during the summer. Casting breakdowns are available through Equity Job

Information Service. "Actors must be happy to tour. Most music is live. Must have a passion for children/ young people's theatre." Offers ITC/Equity approved contracts.

Pilot Theatre

York Theatre Royal, St Leonard's Place,
York YO1 7HD
tel (01904) 635755
email info@pilot-theatre.com
website www.pilot-theatre.com
Artistic Director Marcus Romer

Production details

A national midscale touring company producing a programme of education resources for young people. Stages on average 3-6 projects annually, with 150 performances in 20 arts centres and theatres across the UK. In general 6-10 actors go on tour, playing to audiences aged 11-25. Actors are sometimes expected to lead workshops.

Casting procedures

Actors may write in May and August to request inclusion. Casting breakdowns are available on the website or via Spotlight. Welcomes unsolicited CVs and photographs if submitted by email. Also accepts showreels and will consider invitations to view individual actors' websites. Offers Equity-approved contracts as negotiated through TMA/ITC. Actively encourages applications by disabled actors and promotes the use of inclusive casting.

The Play House

Longmore Street, Birmingham B12 9ED
tel 0121-464 5712 *fax* 0121-464 5713
email info@theplayhouse.org.uk
website www.theplayhouse.org.uk
Artistic Director Deborah Hull *Chief Executive* Gary Roskell

Production details

Established in 1986. An educational theatre charity that creates opportunites for young people to explore and make sense of the world they live in. Best known for its *Language Alive!* theatre-in-education tours, which bring the curriculum to life, and *Catalyst*, which uses theatre and drama to explore real-life issues and dilemmas. Tours an average of 15-20 projects annually, with around 1000 performances in 60-70 schools, outdoor and other venues in the West Midlands. In general 2-3 actors go on tour, performing to young audiences aged 0-18. Skills required vary according to the project and a clean driving licence is required. Actors may be expected to lead workshops.

Casting procedures

Sometimes holds general auditions; actors should write in when these are advertised. Rarely or never has the opportunity to cast disabled actors.

Playtime Theatre Company

18 Bennell's Avenue, Whitstable, Kent CT5 2HP
tel (01227) 266272 *fax* (01227) 266648
email Playtime@dircon.co.uk
website www.playtime.dircon.co.uk
Artistic Director Nicholas Champion *Administrator* Sara Kettlewell

Production details

Established in 1983 with the aim of bringing imaginative and innovative professional theatre to children and young people. Has grown to become "one of the leading children's theatre companies in the South East", and tours both nationally and internationally. Normally tours 2-4 projects each year with an average annual total of 200 performances and 190 venues. Venues include schools, arts centres, theatres, community venues and festivals. Tours have covered the South East, Yorkshire and Humberside and various countries in Europe. In general 2-4 actors go on tour and play to targeted audiences of 5-7, 4-11, 7-11 and 9-13. Actors are expected to offer 1-2 additional skills. Singing ability, proficiency with a musical instrument, physical theatre, puppetry and mime skills and a driving licence are all useful. Actors may also be expected to lead workshops. Recent productions include: *A Tale O' Two*, an adaptation of *The Canterbury Tales*; *Secrets*, a fairy-tale; and *The Happy Prince*, a co-production with a Hungarian theatre company.

Casting procedures

Holds general auditions; actors should write in August requesting inclusion. Casting breakdowns are available through the website, postal application (with sae), Equity Job Information Service, *PCR*, *The Stage* and Castcall (see entry under *The Spotlight, casting directories and information services* on page 398). Welcomes submissions (with CVs and photographs) from actors previously unknown to the company sent by post or email. Also accepts showreels and invitations to view individual actors' websites (if actor is shown performing). Advises actors to: "Be truthful. Tell us about the things that make you stand out. Tell us briefly why you want to work in children's theatre and why you like touring. Seriously consider the implications of living away from your base for months on end!" Offers non-Equity contracts. Will consider applications from disabled actors to play characters with disabilities.

Polka Theatre

240 The Broadway, Wimbledon, London SW19 1SB
tel 020-8545 8320 *fax* 020-8545 8365
email info@polkatheatre.com, casting@polkatheatre.com
website www.polkatheatre.com
Artistic Director Jonathan Lloyd *Associate Director* Roman Stefanski

Production details

Established in 1979. A theatre for children aged 0 to 13. 6 productions staged annually with 700-800 performances per year. The following skills are required from actors: singing, musical instruments, dance, puppetry and physical theatre. Offers TMA/Equity contracts.

Casting procedures

Casting breakdowns sometimes available via *SBS*. Actors are invited for specific shows. Accepts submissions (with CVs and photographs) from actors previously unknown to the company if sent by post, but not by email. Showreels and invitations to view individual actors' websites are also accepted. Actively encourages applications from disabled actors and promotes the use of inclusive casting. "Find out in advance what we're doing, come and visit Polka and see the work."

Pop-Up Theatre

27A Brewery Road, London N7 9PU
tel 020-7609 3339 *fax* 020-7609 2284
email admin@pop-up.net
website www.pop-up.net
Artistic Director Michael Dalton *Theatre & Administration Manager* Clare Knights

Production details

Founded in 1982. Produces and tours theatre for young people to an annual audience of more than 25,000 across theatres, arts centres, schools and nurseries both in the UK and overseas. Normally tours 3 projects each year, with an average annual total of 150 performances at 75 different venues. In general 2-4 actors go on tour and play to audiences aged under 11.

Casting procedures

Accepts submissions (with CVs and photographs) from actors previously unknown to the company sent by post or email. Also accepts invitations to view individual actors' websites. Offers ITC\Equity-approved contracts. Actively encourages applications from disabled actors and promotes the use of inclusive casting.

Q20 Theatre

19 Wellington Crescent, Shipley,
West Yorks BD18 3PH
Artistic Director John Lambert *Administrators* David Smith, Gillie Kerrod

Production details

Normally tours 10 projects each year with an average annual total of 350 performances. Venues include outdoor venues, corporate workspaces and shopping centres in the North East, Yorkshire and Cambridge.

In general 2 actors go on tour and play to audiences of all ages. Singing ability and dance/physical theatre skills are required. Recent productions include: *Pirate Pranks* at Wakefield Shopping Centre; *Metro Gnomes* at Metrocentre.

Casting procedures

Sometimes holds general auditions; actors should write in May or October to request inclusion. Accepts submissions (with CVs and photographs) from actors previously unknown to the company only if sent by post. Does not welcome unsolicited emails. Will also accept invitations to view individual actors' websites.

Quantum Theatre

The Old Button Factory, 1-11 Bannockburn Road, Plumstead SE18 1ET
tel/fax 020-8317 9000
email office@quantumtheatre.co.uk
website www.quantumtheatre.co.uk
Artistic Directors Michael Whitmore, Jessica Selous
Administrator Gideon Escott *Production Manager* Rachel Hogden

Established in 1993. 15 productions performed annually. National touring productions visit schools, arts centres, theatres and outdoor venues. Casting breakdowns available. Holds general auditions. Accepts submissions (with CVs and photographs) from actors previously unknown to the company if sent by post, but not by email. Showreels, voice tapes and invitations to view individual actors' websites are also accepted. Offers TMA/Equity approved contracts.

Quicksilver Theatre

The Glasshouse, 4 Enfield Road,
London N1 5AZ (registered address 2 Mayfield Road, London E8 4BB)
tel 020-7241 2942 *fax* 020-7254 3119
email talktous@quicksilvertheatre.org
website www.quicksilvertheatre.org
Artistic Directors Guy Holland, Carey English

Production details

Founded in 1977, Quicksilver, since 2008, produces 1 new production every 2 years, which is presented at a London venue as well as at partner venues around the UK, mostly small and middle-scale. Cast numbers change from production to production and vary between 1 and 5. Most of the work is aimed at young audiences, and skills required from actors varies depending on need; can include the playing of musical instruments, singing, puppeteering and dance. Actors may also be expected to lead workshops, as Quicksilver has in recent years expanded its artistic and education projects involving participation by children. Recent productons include: *Winter's Tale* (2007, adapted by None Shepphard); *Water Colours* (2007); *Primary Voices* (2007 and 2009, a playwriting project with children and professional actors; and *Ladidada* (2008 and 2010, a co-production between Quicksilver and Indefinite Articles).

Casting procedures

Casting breakdowns are available though the website, postal application (with sae), *PCR* and advertisements in *The Stage*. Accepts submissions (with CVs and photographs) from actors previously unknown to the company sent by post or email. Will also accept showreels and invitations to view individual actors' websites.

Replay Productions

Old Museum Arts Centre, 7 College Square North, Belfast BT1 6AR
tel 028-9032 2773 *fax* 028-9032 2724
email info@replayproductions.org
website www.replayproductions.org
Artistic Director David Fenton *Administrator* Ali Fitzgibbon *Development Manager* Eimear Henry *Operations Manager* Fiona Bell

Production details

"Founded in 1988, Replay aims to produce high-quality theatre and related activities that entertain, educate and stimulate children and young people." Normally tours 3 projects each year with an average annual total of 100 performances. Venues include schools, arts centres, theatres and community venues in Northern Ireland and occasionally the Republic of Ireland. In general 4 actors go on tour and play to audiences aged 3-18. Recent productions include: *Macbeth*, a site-specific production at the Crumlin Road Gaol; and *New Kid* by Dennis Foon for 8-11 year olds.

Casting procedures

Sometimes holds general auditions; casting breakdowns are available through the news section of the website. Accepts submissions (with CVs and photographs) from actors previously unknown to the company sent by post or email. Will also accept invitations to view individual actors' websites.

Scene Productions

14 Curl Way, Wokingham, Berks RG41 2TJ
tel/fax (01483) 821005
email info@sceneproductions.co.uk
website www.sceneproductions.co.uk
Artistic Directors Katharine Hurst, Kelly Taylor-Smith

Production details

Founded in 2004. Specialises in exploring new and imaginative ways of examining political contexts and social relationships, using storytelling, audience interaction, mime, puppetry and multimedia. Stages 2 projects annually, with around 80 performances in the same number of schools, arts centres and theatres ("mainly in the South East, up North twice a year, and in Jersey once a year"). In general 3-4 actors go on tour, playing to audiences aged 17+. Requires singing and physical theatre skills from incoming actors, who should hold a driving licence and may be asked to lead workshops. "You should be a good all-rounder who can cope with the pressures of small-scale touring." Recent productions include: *Fear & Misery of the Third Reich*, *The Threepenny Opera*, *The Good Person of Szechwan* (all by Brecht); *The Other Side*, a devised production which premiered at the 2009 Edinburgh Festival.

Casting procedures

Sometimes holds general auditions and actors may write in May to request inclusion. Welcomes letters (with CVs & photographs) from actors previously unknown to the company, sent by post or email. Does not accept showreels, but will consider invitations to view individual actors' websites. Rarely (or never) has the opportunity to cast disabled actors.

Shakespeare 4 Kidz

Drewshearne Barn, Crowhurst Lane End, Oxted, Surrey RH8 9NT
tel (01342) 894548 *fax* (01342) 893754
email office@shakespeare4kidz.com
website www.shakespeare4kidz.com
Producer & Director Julian Chenery *Producer* Carolyn Chenery

Production details

Founded in 1997. "Recognised as the national Shakespeare company for children and young people, it has pioneered its Music Theatre & Shakespeare and Creative Shakespeare Education Programme both in the UK and abroad." Normally tours 2 projects each year with an average annual total of 230 performances across 60 different theatres; now tours internationally from March to June. In general 13 actors go on tour and play to audiences aged 8 upwards. Singing ability and dance/physical theatre skills are required; marketing skills are also advantageous. Recent productions include: *S4K's Romeo and Juliet*; *S4K's Hamlet*; *S4K's A Midsummer Night's Dream*; and *S4K's Macbeth*.

Casting procedures

Holds general auditions; actors should write in March requesting inclusion. Casting breakdowns are available through the website, *PCR* and *The Stage*. Accepts submissions (with CVs and photographs) from actors previously unknown to the company sent by post or email. Will also accept showreels and invitations to view individual actors' websites.

Sixth Sense Theatre for Young People

c/o The Wyvern Theatre, Theatre Square, Swindon SN1 1QN

tel (01793) 614864 *fax* (01793) 616715
email sstc@dircon.co.uk
website www.sixthsensetyp.co.uk
Artistic Director Benedict Eccles *General Manager*
Mervyn Heard

Production details

Founded in 1986. Tours to schools and small-scale
venues in the South and South West. Receives
funding from Swindon Borough Council and Arts
Council England, South West and has an "excellent
reputation in the region". Normally tours 3 projects
each year with an average annual total of 150
performances across 90 venues. Venues include
schools, arts centres and community venues. In
general 3-5 actors go on tour and play to audiences
aged 5-18. Singing ability, proficiency with a musical
instrument, dance skills and a driving licence may be
required. Actors are usually expected to lead
workshops. Recent productions include: *The Rime of
the Ancient Mariner* (for 7-11 year olds), and *Sk8
Angel* (co-pro with Greenwich and Lewisham Young
People's Theatre (for 12-16 year olds).

Casting procedures

Accepts submissions (with CVs and photographs)
from actors previously unknown to the company sent
by post or email. Will also accept invitations to view
individual actors' websites. Issues ITC/Equity
contracts for 5- to 10-week tours. "Happy to receive
actors' details but can't always respond. Please don't
chase us; if we're interested we'll contact you."

Solomon Theatre Company

Penny Black, High Street, Damerham,
Fordingbridge, Hants SP6 3EU
tel (01725) 518670
email office@solomontheatre.co.uk
website www.solomontheatre.co.uk
Artistic Director Mark Hyde *Managing Director* Forest
Paget *Marketing Manager* Jo Coleman *Administrator*
Gail Newell

Production details

Founded in 2003. Specialises in communicating
messages that result in crime reduction, improved
community safety and the promotion of healthy
schools and healthy lifestyles. Has performed award-
winning plays to tens of thousands of people in
schools and community locations across the country,
as well as producing films and support material for
national programmes. Performs around 7 projects
annually in more than 300 venues, including schools,
theatres and community venues in the South West,
South East, Midlands, Wales and Northern Ireland.
On average 12 actors go on tour, performing to
audiences aged 12-16 to over 60. Actors must have a
driving licence and may be required to lead
workshops. Recent projects include: *Last Orders*

(alcohol education); *Trickster* (burglary education);
Gemma's Wardrobe (drugs education); and *Power of
Love* (domestic violence education).

Casting procedures

Holds general auditions; actors may write in July,
November and April to request inclusion. Welcomes
letters (with CVs and photographs) from actors
previously unknown to the company sent by post or
email. Also welcomes showreels and invitations to
view individual actors' websites. Does not offer
Equity-approved contracts but does offer Equity
rates. Will consider applications from disabled actors
to play characters with disabilities.

Spare Tyre Theatre Company

Hampstead Town Hall, 213 Haverstock Hill,
London NW3 4QP
tel/fax 020-7419 7007
email sttc@sparetyretheatrecompany.co.uk
website www.sparetyretheatrecompany.co.uk
Artistic Director Arti Prashar *General Manager* Bonnie
Mitchell *Administrator* Paul Margrave

Production details

The company has 3 principal strands of work:
• Work with elders: the 'HotPots' are a group of
people over 60 who perform work, often from
personal experience and using humour, about the
treatment of elders. They are committed to educating
audiences about the potential of older people.
• Work with people with learning disabilities: the
'inc.Theatre' course is a full-time, OCN (Open
College Network) approved partnership with
Redbridge College for people of all ages with learning
disabilities.
• Work with schools: professional TIE productions
for school pupils tackling homophobia in schools.
Also: 'Dealing with Difference', a workshop for
school staff looking at approaches to tackling
homophobia within schools.

Each strand of work has 1 major production a year,
touring to roughly 100 venues – from schools,
theatres and community venues to hospitals, GP
surgeries, residential homes, special needs schools
and public sector venues. Primarily covers the
London area, but also Yorkshire, Manchester, Kent
and Wales. Skills required from actors include
(ideally) a driving licence, but also workshop-leading
and facilitation skills, experience working with
community groups, and a sensitivity to and
understanding of relevant issues.

Casting procedures

Casting breakdowns are published in *The Stage* and
on the website. Unsolicited approaches – including
CVs, showreels and invitations to view individuals'
websites – at other times are discouraged. Offers ITC/
Equity approved contracts. Actively encourages

applications from disabled actors and promotes the use of inclusive casting.

Splendid Productions

I Lownes Courtyard, Boone Street, London SE13 5TB
tel 020-8318 6469 *fax* 0871-750 2166
email info@splendidproductions.co.uk
website www.splendidproductions.co.uk
Artistic Director Kerry Frampton

Production details

Founded in 2003. A theatre company and an education company creating "challenging, vibrant theatre for young people". Also provides expert training in all areas of drama, from Practitioner theory to Presentation skills. In the last 6 years the company has gained an excellent reputation for the inventiveness of its performances and the clarity of its teaching. Tours 1 main project per year (September through to March), staging on average 100 performances in 100 venues across England and Wales, including schools, arts centres and theatres (always attached to schools or colleges). 3 actors go on tour, playing to audiences aged 13 years and beyond. Actors require singing skills, strong physicality and a driving licence; they need to be able to lead workshops – or to want to learn. Recent productions include: *Dr Faustus*; *Woyzeck*; *Good Woman of Szechuan*; *Antigone*; *Animal Farm*; and *The Resistible Rise of Arturo Ui*.

Casting procedures

Does not hold general auditions. Actors may write in to request inclusion during April-June. Welcomes letters (with CVs & photographs) from actors previously unknown to the company, sent by post or email. Does not accept showreels but is happy to receive links to individual actors' websites. Will consider applications from disabled actors to play characters with disabilities. "We work hard and are very passionate about working with young people. You need to be flexible, approachable and keen to create good theatre in education. Look at our website to see what we do before getting in touch."

Stopwatch Theatre Company

Unit 318 Solent Business Centre,
Millbrook Road West, Southampton SO15 0HW
tel 023-8078 3800
email info@stopwatchtheatre.com
website www.stopwatchtheatre.com
Artistic Director Adrian New

Production details

Established in 1990. A theatre-in-education company specialising in safety and health programmes. Stages 6 productions annually, with around 800 performances in 700 schools UK-wide. In general 4 actors go on tour, playing to audiences aged 5-16. Actors are be expected to lead workshops, and driving is an advantage but not essential. Recent productions include: *Chicken!*, *Arson About*, *Footsteps the Movie*, and *The Road Race*.

Casting procedures

Holds general auditions; actors may write in June and October to request inclusion. Casting breakdowns are available from Equity Job Information Service and Casting Call Pro, and in *PCR*. Welcomes letters (with CVs and photographs) from individual actors previously unknown to the company, sent by post or email, and will consider invitations to view individual actors' websites. Rarely, or never, has the opportunity to cast actors with disabilities. "We always look favourably on those who have done some research and are evidently committed to working in quality theatre-in-education."

The Take Away Theatre Company

10 Millbank Street, Dalrymple, Ayrshire KA6 6FE
tel 0800-158 3840
email admin@takeawaytheatre.co.uk
website www.takeawaytheatre.co.uk
Artistic Director Lee O'Driscoll

Production details

Founded in 2007. A theatre-in-education company delivering "high-impact and dynamic drama projects in schools and other venues throughout the UK". Tours 9 projects annually with 270 performances at schools, arts centres, theatres and community venues. In general 4 actors go on tour, playing to audiences aged 1 to 101. Actors may be expected to lead workshops and should hold a current driving licence; singing, musical instrument, dance and physical theatre skills are an advantage. Recent productions include: *Tam O' Shanter*, *The Wind in the Willows*, *The Velveteen Rabbit*, and *Hansel & Gretel*.

Casting procedures

Sometimes holds general auditions; actors may write at any time to request inclusion. Casting breakdowns are available via the website, by postal application (with sae), and from Casting Call Pro and CastNet Ltd. Welcomes letters (with CVs and photographs) from individual actors previously unknown to the company, sent by post or email. Also accepts showreels and invitations to view individual actors' websites. Will consider applications from disabled actors to play characters with disabilities.

Ten Ten Theatre

PO Box 49063, New Southgate, London N11 1YU
tel 0845-388 3162 *fax* 0845-388 3167
email office@tententheatre.co.uk and casting@tententheatre.co.uk
website www.tententheatre.co.uk
Artistic Director Martin O'Brien

Production details

Established in 2006. Specialises in young people's theatre in primary schools, secondary schools, young offender institutions and the local community. Stages 4-6 productions annually with around 400 performances in 200 schools, arts centres, theatres and community venues across England, Scotland and Wales. In general 2-4 actors go on tour, playing to audiences aged 5 to 21. Actors may be expected to lead workshops. Recent productions include: a six-month tour of secondary schools with 3 separate plays; and a one-week residency at Feltham Young Offender Institution.

Casting procedures

Does not hold general auditions; actors may write at any time to request inclusion. Casting breakdowns are available from the website or via Equity Job Information Service, *PCR* and Spotlight. Welcomes letters (with CVs and photographs) from individual actors previously unknown to the company, sent by post or email, and will accept showreels and invitations to view individual actors' websites. Offers Equity-approved contracts as negotiated through ITC. Will consider applications from disabled actors to play characters with disabilities. "Please view our website to look at our projects and ethos before sending details."

Theatr Iolo

The Old School Building, Cefn Road, Cardiff CF14 3HS
tel 029-2061 3782 *fax* 029-2052 2225
email admin@theatriolo.com
website www.theatriolo.com
Artistic Director Kevin Lewis *Administrative Director* Wendy York

Production details

"Formed in 1987, Theatr Iolo aims to produce and programme the best of live theatre, making it widely accessible to children and young people in Cardiff and the Vale of Glamorgan to stir the imagination, inspire the heart and challenge the mind. Theatr Iolo works alongside teachers and advisers to enhance teaching and learning across the curriculum." Normally tours 5 projects each year with an average annual total of 150 performances across 120 venues. Venues include schools, arts centres and theatres in Wales and occasionally England, and international festivals. Cast sizes vary, playing to audiences aged 3-18. Singing ability, proficiency with a musical instrument, dance/physical theatre skills and a driving licence are frequently required. Actors may also be expected to lead workshops. Recent productions include: *Grimm Tales* by Carol Ann Dufy, *Lenny* by Francis Monty (trans. Paul Harman), and *Under the Carpet* by Sarah Argent.

Casting procedures

Sometimes holds general auditions; actors should write in June requesting inclusion. Casting breakdowns are available through Equity Job Information Service. Accepts submissions (with CVs and photographs) from actors previously unknown to the company if sent by post. Emails are also welcome, as long as the file is not too big. Offers ITC/Equity approved contracts. Actively encourages applications from disabled actors and promotes the use of inclusive casting.

Theatr Na N'Og

Unit 3, Millands Road Industrial Estate, Neath SA11 1NJ
tel (01639) 641771 *fax* (01639) 647941
email drama@theatr-nanog.co.uk
website www.theatr-nanog.co.uk
Artistic Director Geinor Styles *Administrator* Janet Huxtable *Education Officer* Rachel Lloyd *Outreach Officer* Samantha Timmins *Production & Touring Manager* Ceri James

Production details

"The company has been producing high-quality original theatre for young people for more than 25 years. We provide a first-class Theatre in Education service to schools in 3 county boroughs, and tour to general audiences in venues across the UK." Normally tours 3 projects each year with an average annual total of 200 performances. In general 3 actors go on tour. Singing ability is required and actors may also be expected to lead workshops.

Casting procedures

Holds general auditions; actors may write at any time requesting inclusion. Accepts submissions (with CVs and photographs) from actors previously unknown to the company sent by post or email. Will also accept invitations to view individual actors' websites. "Please learn to spell the names of the company's personnel properly!"

Theatr Powys

The Drama Centre, Tremont Road, Llandrinod Wells, Powys LD1 5EB
tel (01597) 824444 *fax* (01597) 824381
email theatr.powys@powys.gov.uk
website www.theatrpowys.co.uk
Artistic Director Ian Yeoman *General Manager* Nikki Leopold

Production details

Founded in 1976. Has an average annual total of 250 performances across 150 different venues. Venues include schools, arts centres, theatres and community venues across Wales. Recent productions include: *The Giant's Embrace*, *Gafael y Cawr* and *Angel*.

Casting procedures

Holds general auditions; actors may write at any time requesting inclusion. Casting breakdowns are available through postal application (with sae), Equity Job Information Service, *PCR* and advertisements in *The Stage*. Accepts submissions (with CVs and photographs) from actors previously unknown to the company sent by post or email. Will also accept invitations to view individual actors' websites. Offers TMA/Equity contracts and does not subscribe to the Equity Pension Scheme. Actively encourages applications from disabled actors and promotes the use of inclusive casting.

Theatre-Rites

Unit 202, The Blackfriars Foundry,
156 Blackfriars Road, London SE1 8EN
tel 020-7953 7102 *fax* 020-7953 7041
email info@theatre-rites.co.uk
website www.theatre-rites.co.uk
Artistic Director Sue Buckmaster *Executive Producer* Claire Templeton *Project Manager* John Johnston *Administrator* Roisin Caffrey

Production details

Committed to creating challenging productions which push the boundaries of theatrical form by experimenting to combine different artistic disciplines. Highly imaginative visual experiences for families to share together. Stages 2 productions annually, with around 45 performances in 12 arts centres and theatres across all English regions, in Scotland, and internationally. In general 5-8 actors go on tour, playing to audiences of various ages, often 5+. Actors are sometimes expected to lead workshops; singing, musical instrument, dance, physical theatre and puppetry skills may all be advantageous, depending on the project. Recent productions include: *Mischief* – Dance Theatre; *Hang On* – Circus Collaboration; and *Salt* – Site Specific.

Casting procedures

Sometimes holds general auditions; actors may write at any time to request inclusion. Casting breakdowns are available via the website and Equity Job Information Service. Welcomes letters (with CVs and photographs) from individual actors previously unknown to the company, sent by post or email. Also welcomes showreels and invitations to view individual actors' websites. Offers Equity-approved contracts as negotiated through ITC. Actively encourages applications from disabled actors, and promotes the use of inclusive casting. "The work is devised and often physical, so we frequently look for performers with previous experience of this kind of work."

Theatre Centre

Shoreditch Town Hall, 380 Old Street,
London EC1V 9LT
tel 020-7729 3066 *fax* 020-7739 9741
email admin@theatre-centre.co.uk
website www.theatre-centre.co.uk

Artistic Director TBA *General Manager* Charles Bishop
Associate Artist (Education) Michael Judge

Production details

Founded in 1953. A new writing company commissioning, developing and producing new plays which are toured nationally and internationally to schools, arts centres and theatres. Normally tours 3 projects each year with an average annual total of 180 performances across 100 different venues. In general 3-4 actors go on tour and play to targeted groups aged 4-18. Singing ability, proficiency with a musical instrument and dance/physical theatre skills may be required. An affinity with new writing and touring audiences is an advantage. Offers TMA/Equity approved contracts and subscribes to the Equity Pension Scheme.

Casting procedures

Casting breakdowns are available through the website, postal application (with sae), Equity Job Information Service, *PCR* and advertisements in *The Stage*. Accepts submissions (with CVs and photographs) from actors previously unknown to the company sent by post or email; actors should write around New Year or Easter. "We keep all unsolicited CVs on file and do consult them when casting – therefore do send refreshed CVs! Get to know us and our work; there are regular free open day/showcase performances to which people on the mailing list are always invited." Actively encourages applications from disabled actors and promotes the use of inclusive casting.

Theatre Company Blah Blah Blah!

West Park Centre, Spen Lane, Leeds LS16 5BE
tel 0113-274 0030
email admin@blahs.co.uk
website www.blahs.co.uk
Artistic Director Anthony Haddon *Company Manager* Stephan Aal *Youth Programme Director* Ruth Cooper

Production details

A Leeds-based Theatre in Education company founded in 1985; also produces theatre for young people with integrated workshops. Normally tours 2-3 projects each year with an average annual total of 100 performances across 60 different venues. Venues include schools, arts centres, community venues and youth centres in Yorkshire. In general 3-4 actors go on tour and play to audiences aged 5 upwards. Singing ability, proficiency with a musical instrument, dance/physical theatre skills and a driving licence are all potentially useful. Experience of TIE work is also helpful, as actors are generally expected to lead workshops. Recent productions include: *Barkin'*, a play for teenagers based on the novel *Lady – My Life as a Bitch* by Melvin Burgess, which toured youth centres; *Hansel and Gretel*, a

Theatre

series of workshops for Primary schools; *Silas Marner*, touring to rural community venues and schools with related workshops. Offers ITC/Equity approved contracts and does not subscribe to the Equity Pension Scheme.

Casting procedures

Sometimes holds general auditions; actors may write at any time requesting inclusion, as CVs are kept on file for 1 year. Accepts submissions (with CVs and photographs) from actors previously unknown to the company only if sent by post. Does not welcome unsolicited emails. Will also accept invitations to view individual actors' websites. "We are particularly interested in hearing from people with both acting and facilitation skills." will consider applications from disabled actors to play characters with disabilities.

Theatre Exchange Ltd

The Old NAAFI, Weston Drive, Caterham, Surrey CR3 5XY
tel (01883) 331545
email info@theatre-exchange.org.uk
website www.theatre-exchange.org.uk
Artistic Director Katy Potter *Education Director* Stephen Cordwent

Production details

An educational theatre company focusing on the creative exchange between young people, artists and those who work with young people. Works on up to 21 projects each year, with an average annual total of 650 performances across 400 different venues. Venues include schools, arts centres, theatres and community venues across the South East of England. In general 6 actors go on tour and play to audiences aged 4-13. Interest in and some experience of working with young people is necessary; a driving licence is also useful. Actors are also expected to lead workshops. Recent productions include: *Monsters, Myths & Legends*, *Luverly Jubilee* and *The Greeks*.

Casting procedures

Holds general auditions; actors requesting inclusion should write between May and July. Casting breakdowns are available by postal application (with sae), on Equity Job Information Service and through advertisements in *The Stage*. Accepts submissions (with CVs and photographs) from actors previously unknown to the company sent by post or email. Will also accept invitations to view individual actors' websites. "Please send a letter detailing why you are interested in working with young people, along with your CV."

Ticklish Allsorts

57 Victoria Road, Wilton, Salisbury SP2 0DZ
tel (01722) 744949
email garynunn@ntlworld.com
website www.ticklishallsorts.co.uk
Artistic Director Gary Nunn

Production details

Children's entertainers since 1981, using puppets, songs, live action, pantomime and comedy. Tours 5-6 projects annually, with 300-350 performances in 80-100 schools, arts centres, theatres, outdoor and community venues, and festivals throughout the UK. In general 1-2 actors go on tour, playing to audiences aged 4-11. Actors should possess singing and musical instrument skills, and must like comedy and working with children. They may be required to lead workshops. For details of recent productions, see the website.

Casting procedures

Actors may write to request inclusion at any time; "summer is always busy, and Christmas". Casting breakdowns are available through local drama schools. Welcomes letters (with CVs and photographs) from individual actors previously unknown to the company, sent by post or email. Rarely, or never, has the opportunity to cast disabled actors.

Tiebreak Theatre Company

42-58 St George's Street, Norwich NR3 1AB
tel (01603) 665899 *fax* (01603) 666096
website www.tiebreak-theatre.com
Artistic Director David Farmer *Administrator* Kaja Holloway

Tiebreak Theatre Company has ceased trading.

Travelling Light Theatre Company

Barton Hill Settlement, 43 Ducie Road, Barton Hill, Bristol BS5 0AX
tel 0117-377 3166 *fax* 0117-377 3167
minicom 0117-377 3168
email info@travellinglighttheatre.org.uk
website www.travlight.co.uk
Producer Jude Merrill *General Manager* Cath Greig

Production details

"Since 1984 the company has produced innovative and inspiring work for young audiences. Uses live music, visual and physical performance in its work." Normally tours 2 projects each year with an average annual total of 200 performances across 25 different venues. Venues include schools, arts centres, theatres, community venues and festivals across England, Northern Ireland, Scotland, Wales, North America and the Republic of Ireland. In general 2-3 actors go on tour and play to audiences aged 3-18. Singing ability, proficiency with a musical instrument and physical theatre skills are required. Actors may also be involved in education workshops. Recent touring productions include: *The Ugly Duckling* (for 3+ years) and *Lenny* (for 12 years upwards).

Casting procedures

Casting breakdowns are available through Equity Job Information Service, *PCR* and Castweb (see entry under *The Spotlight, casting directories and information services* on page 398). Accepts submissions (with CVs and photographs) from actors previously unknown to the company only if sent by post. Does not welcome unsolicited emails. Will also accept invitations to view individual actors' websites.

Unicorn Theatre for Children

147 Tooley Street, More London, London SE1 2HZ
tel 020-7645 0500 *fax* 020-7645 0550
email stagedoor@unicorntheatre.com
website www.unicorntheatre.com
Artistic Director Tony Graham *Associate Director* Rosamunde Hutt *Associate Director & Literary Manager* Carl Miller *Education & Youth Director* Catherine Greenwood

Production details

Founded in 1947. "The UK's professional children's theatre company has recently opened, near London Bridge, the first purpose-designed theatre for children in the UK." Performed 9 projects in 2005/06 with a total of 460 performances. Has produced site-specific works across England and in Cardiff, Glasgow and Edinburgh. In general up to 8 actors are involved in each production and play to audiences aged 4-11. Singing ability, proficiency with a musical instrument and dance/physical theatre skills are desirable. Past productions include: *Clockwork*, an opera of Philip Pullman's novel of the same name, for the Linbury Studio, Royal Opera House and touring; *Journey to the River Sea*, a co-production with Theatre Centre, adapted for the stage from the Eva Ibbotson novel. Offers TMA and ITC/Equity approved contracts and subscribes to the Equity Pension Scheme.

Casting procedures

Accepts CVs and photographs from actors previously unknown to the company only if sent by email. Advises actors to send an interesting covering note detailing why they are interested in working with Unicorn in particular. Actively encourages applications from disabled actors and promotes the use of inclusive casting.

Whirligig Theatre

14 Belvedere Drive, Wimbledon, London SW19 7BY
tel 020-8947 1732 *fax* 020-8879 7648
email davidwoodplays@virgin.net
Artistic Director David Wood

Production details

Founded in 1979, for many years Whirligig toured a musical play for children to major UK theatres, including a London season at Sadler's Wells Theatre. The company ceased regular activity in 2004, but still considers one-off projects at home and abroad. Tours, when they happen, are usually to around 15 theatre venues across the UK, playing mostly to

primary-school-age children and their families. 8-10 actors, with skills such as singing, musical instruments, dance and physical theatre, would make up the company, and they would sometimes be asked to lead workshops. Recent productions include: *The Gingerbread Man*, *Save the Human*, and *Babe, the Sheep Pig*.

Casting procedures

Holds general auditions, although advises actors to check whether or not a production is imminent. Casting breakdowns are issued through *SBS*. Welcomes letters (but not emails), with CVs and photographs, from actors previously unknown to the company. Does not welcome showreels or invitations to view actors' websites. Offers TMA/Equity approved contracts.

Whirlwind Theatre Productions with Whirlwind Children's Theatre Company

54 High Road, Halton, Lancaster LA2 6PS
tel (01524) 812851
email enquiries@whirlwindtheatre.org.uk
website www.whirlwindtheatre.org.uk
Artistic Directors Myette Godwyn, Mike Whalley
Associate Artistic Director Alistair Ganley *Patron* David Wood OBE

Production details

Formed in 2000 to produce a community play for the Museum of Cannock Chase in association with Illyria Theatre Company, and a South of England tour of a music-based show for 5-10 year-olds – *Goldie Locks and the Three Bears*. The company has close ties with the Palm Court Theatre Orchestra, and productions are period-music-based with physical and visual performance aimed at the 4-10 year age-group. Whirlwind runs a performance summer school; also has a Saturday youth theatre club and a programme of workshops.

Normally undertakes 2-3 projects each year with a total of around 150 performances. Venues include churches, arts centres, fields, schools, theatres, outdoor and community venues across England. In general 3 actors go on tour and play to audiences aged 4 upwards. Actors must be proficient in workshop-leading for this age-group; will also need singing, dance/physical theatre skills and preferably the ability to play an instrument to a high standard. A driving licence is also required and actors must be prepared to help with get-ins and get-outs. Whirlwind Theatre has a strong Christian ethos, and most rehearsals and community work are carried out at King's Community Church in Lancaster. Although the company welcomes applications from actors of all different beliefs and backgrounds, they should feel at ease with this when applying. Recent productions include: *King's New Clothes* (TIE); *Hamish Bear and*

Storytelling Magpie (TIE); *Toad of Toad Hall* (summer-school production in Ryelands Park, Lancaster).

Casting procedures

Sometimes holds general auditions; these are always held in Lancaster. Casting breakdowns are advertised in *PCR*. Welcomes letters and emails (with CVs and photographs) from actors previously unknown to the company. All actors are required to be CRB (Criminal Records Bureau) checked.

Wizard Theatre

175 Royal Crescent, Ruislip, Middlesex HA4 0PN
tel 0800-583 2373
email leon@wizardtheatre.co.uk
website www.wizardtheatre.co.uk
Artistic Director Leon Hamilton *Company Manager* Emmy Bradbury *Associate Producer* Oliver Gray

Production details

Established in 2002. Produces plays, message-based shows and workshops, conferences and training films. On average stages 10 projects annually, with more than 300 performances in 100 community and conference venues across London and the Home Counties. In general 3 actors go on tour, performing to audiences aged 2 to 80.

Actors may be required to lead workshops. Good facilitating, impro and devising skills are useful. Recent productions include: *Robin Hood*; *Tipping the Scales* (obesity conference); *Staying Safe* (Community Safety Workshop); *Pinocchio*; *OUCH!* (one-man show); and *Wind in the Willows*.

Sometimes holds general auditions; actors are welcome to write in at any time. Casting breakdowns are available via Casting Call Pro. Welcomes unsolicited approaches by actors by post or email. Also accepts showreels and will consider invitations to view individual actors' websites. Does not offer Equity-approved contracts: "Usually we pay well above Equity rates. Excellent facilitators and workshop leaders always desirable!"

Young Shakespeare Company

31 Bellevue Road, Friern Barnet, London N11 3ET
tel 020-8368 4828 *fax* 020-8368 6713
email youngshakespeare@mac.com
website www.youngshakespeare.org.uk
Artistic Directors Christopher Geelan, Sarah Gordon

Production details

One of the most well-established and respected educational theatre companies in the UK. Currently performs Shakespeare to more than 100,000 young people each year, working in schools, theatres and professional development centres to provide a year-round programme of performances, workshops and INSET courses. On average stages 10 productions each year, with around 1000 performances in 25 theatres/arts centres and 1000 schools in most regions throughout England. In general, 5 actors per show perform to audiences aged 6 to 16. Actors may be expected to lead workshops and must have a clean driving licence. Recent productions include: *Romeo and Juliet*, *Macbeth*, *The Tempest*, *Hamlet*, and *A Midsummer Night's Dream*.

Casting procedures

Holds general auditions and actors may write at any time to request inclusion. Cassting breakdowns are available via Spotlight Link. Welcomes letters (with CVs and photographs) from individual actors previously unknown to the company, sent by post or by email, but does not accept showreels or consider invitations to view individual actors' websites. Rarely has the opportunity to cast disabled actors: "All applications are considered, but please note that our touring schedule is physically demanding."

Zip Theatre

Newhampton Arts Centre, Dunkley Street, Wolverhampton WV1 4AN
tel (01902) 572250 *fax* (01902) 572251
email admin@ziptheatre.co.uk
website www.ziptheatre.co.uk
Artistic Director Jon Lingard-Lane *Administrator* Sunita Dass

Production details

Founded in 1980. Normally tours 6 projects each year with an average annual total of 300 performances. Venues include schools, arts centres, theatres, outdoor venues and community venues in the West Midlands and nationally. In general 5-6 actors go on tour and play to audiences aged 5 upwards. Singing ability and dance skills are required. Actors are also expected to lead workshops. Recent productions include: *Packers* – arts centre tour of new play by Alex Jones; *Behind a Smile* – TIE piece for junior schools based on sexual exploitation; and *The Promise* – TIE for secondary schools on post-16 options.

Casting procedures

Sometimes holds general auditions; actors may write at any time requesting inclusion any time. Accepts submissions (with CVs and photographs) from actors previously unknown to the company sent by post or email. Does not welcome unsolicited emails.

Casting calendar

Many companies are happy to receive CVs and photographs from actors at any time of the year, but some – such as those listed below – have a regular, annual schedule of casting and as such are most receptive to approaches in certain months. The table below shows the best time to approach companies, and gives information about whether their casting breakdowns are published on their website; whether they will send out breakdowns on receipt of an sae; where they publish their breakdowns (other than via the Spotlight Link); and in what section of this book their details may be found. ('JIS' is the Equity Job Information Service. Details for most of the casting breakdown services can be found under *The Spotlight, casting directories and information services* on page 398.)

Read the company's entry carefully before contacting them, to ensure that you are not wasting either their time or yours by making an inappropriate submission. The letters in brackets after the company name indicate the section in which their details may be found.
Euro = *English-language European theatre companies* (page 252)
IHP = *In-house pantomimes* (page 238)
IM = *Independent managements/theatre producers* (page 171)
MSS = *Middle and smaller-scale companies* (page 186)
PP = *Pantomime producers* (page 234)
PT = *Producing theatres* (page 136)
YP = *Children's, young people's and Theatre in Education companies* (page 273)
Companies are invited to notify us of corrections or omissions at **actorsyb@acblack.com**.

Month	Company	Breakdowns published
December/ January	Chichester Festival Theatre (PT)	
December/ January	Shakespeare's Globe (PT)	
January	Bruce James Productions (IM)	SBS, Castcall, Castweb
January	Coliseum, Oldham (PT)	Post
January	Midland Actors Theatre (MSS)	JIS, PCR
January	Nick Brooke (IM)	Web, Post
January	Nitro (MSS)	
January	Theatre Centre (YP)	JIS, PCR, The Stage
January	Traverse Theatre, Edinburgh (PT)	
January/ February	Open Air Theatre, Regent's Park (PT)	
January– March	Sheringham Little Theatre (PT)	
February	Everyman Theatre, Cheltenham (IHP)	
February	Jasperian Theatre Co (MSS)	SBS, CastNet
February	Kinetic Theatre Co (YP)	PCR, Castweb, CastNet, Castcall, CCP, JIS

Theatre

Month	Company	Breakdowns published
February	Manor Pavilion Theatre, Sidmouth (PT)	Post
February	Theatre Set-up (MSS)	
February/ March	Light Nights, Iceland (Euro)	
February/ March	Proper Pantomime Co (PP)	SBS
February/ March	Theatre Royal, Norwich (IHP)	SBS
February- July	Hammond Productions (PP)	The Stage, SBS, Castweb, Entsweb
March	Creation Theatre Co (MSS)	Post, PCR, Castfax
March	Duggie Chapman Associates (PP)	PCR, The Stage
March	Hijinx Theatre (MSS)	JIS, Web, The Stage
March	Qdos Entertainment (PP)	
March	Shakespeare 4 Kidz (YP)	PCR, The Stage
March/ April	Cambridge Arts Theatre (IHP)	
March/ April	Evolution Productions (PP)	Castweb, Web
March/ April	Library Theatre, Manchester (PT)	
March/ April	Oxford Shakespeare Co (MSS)	PCR
March/ April	Spillers Pantomimes (PP)	PCR, The Stage
March/ April	Theatre Centre (YP)	JIS, PCR, The Stage
March- May	Wish Theatre (PP)	
Spring	Dundee Repertory Theatre (PT)	
April	Citizens' Theatre, Glasgow (PT)	
April	English Theatre Frankfurt (Euro)	
April	Soloman Theatre Co (YP)	
April	White Horse Theatre, Germany (Euro)	Post, JIS, PCR, The Stage, Web
April/May	Queen's Theatre, Hornchurch (PT)	
April/May	Theatre Royal, Nottingham (IHP)	
May	Bitesize (YP)	PCR, The Stage, Castcall, SBS
May	Bruce James Productions (IM)	SBS, Castcall, Castweb
May	Frantic Theatre Co (MSS)	JIS, PCR
May	Millfield Theatre, Edmonton (IHP)	
May	Nick Brooke (IM)	Web, Post

Month	Company	Breakdowns published
May	Q20 Theatre (YP)	
May	Salisbury Playhouse (PT)	
May	20 Stories High Theatre Company (MSS)	JIS Web, PCR
May	TOSG Gaelic Theatre (MSS)	
May/June	ACT Co, France (Euro)	
May/June	Gazebo Theatre in Education Co (YP)	JIS
May-July	Greenwich Theatre (PT)	Web
May/June	Hopscotch Theatre Co (YP)	
May-July	Theatre Exchange Ltd (YP)	Post, JIS, The Stage
June	Crucible Theatre, Sheffield (PT)	Post
June	The Customs House Trust Ltd (IHP)	PCR
June	Kinetic Theatre Co (YP)	PCR, Castweb, CastNet, Castcall, CCP, JIS
June	Midland Actors Theatre (MSS)	JIS, PCR
June	NTC Touring Co (MSS)	SBS, Post
June	Orange Tree Theatre, Richmond (PT)	Post
June	Theatr Iolo (YP)	JIS
June	Theatre Royal, Winchester (IHP)	PCR
June	Torch Theatre, Milford Haven (PT)	
June-July	Box Clever Theatre Co (YP)	JIS, PCR, Web
June/July	Pied Piper Co (YP)	JIS
June/July	Replay Productions (YP)	Web
June/July	The Theatre, Chipping Norton (IHP)	Post, JIS, Web
June/July	Theatre Royal, Bury St Edmunds (PT)	
July	Kabosh (MSS)	
July	Solomon Theatre Company (YP)	
July	The Wrestling School (MSS)	Phone
July-September	Scat Theatre Co (YP)	
August	Actors of Dionysus (MSS)	PCR, Web
August	Playtime Theatre Co (YP)	Post, JIS, PCR, The Stage, Castcall
August	Theatre Royal, Bury St Edmunds (IHP)	
August/September	Cwmni Theatr Arad Goch (YP)	
August/September	English Theatre, Stockholm (Euro)	
August/September	Hackney Empire (IHP)	

Month	Company	Breakdowns published
August/ September	Kenneth More Theatre, Ilford (IHP)	
August/ October	Chaplins Ltd (PP)	Web, The Stage, Castcall
September	Bruce James Productions (IM)	SBS, Castcall, Castweb
September	C&T (YP)	
September	Jasperian Theatre Co (MSS)	SBS, CastNet
September	NTC Touring Co (MSS)	SBS, Post
September	Sixth Sense (YP)	
September	Jasperian Theatre Co (MSS)	SBS, CastNet
Sept/Oct	Magic Carpet Theatre (YP)	
Sept/Oct	Pitlochry Festival Theatre (PT)	Post
October	Crucible Theatre, Sheffield (PT)	Post
October	Kinetic Theatre Co (YP)	PCR, Castweb, CastNet, Castcall, CCP, JIS
October	Q20 Theatre (YP)	
October	Salisbury Playhouse (PT)	
October	20 Stories High Theatre Company (MSS)	JIS, Web, PCR
October/ November	Benchtours Productions Ltd (MSS)	
October/ November	Box Clever Theatre Co (YP)	JIS, PCR, Web
October/ November	Clean Break (MSS)	JIS, PCR, The Stage
October/ November	Shakespeare at The Tobacco Factory (MSS)	Web
November	Frantic Theatre Co (MSS)	JIS, PCR
November	Hijinx Theatre (MSS)	JIS, Web, The Stage
November	Kabosh (MSS)	
November	Solomon Theatre Company (YP)	
November	Southwold & Aldburgh (PT)	Phone
December	Actors of Dionysus (MSS)	PCR, Web

Festivals

These are populated by all kinds of companies listed in previous sections. Some are hired-in by a festival's organisers; others 'hire' space in order to participate – the latter predominate at the most famous festival of all, in Edinburgh. Participation in a festival can be enormous fun, and a great opportunity to meet other actors and see other productions. However, the chances of such a production transferring, let alone making money, are limited.

UMBRELLA ORGANISATIONS

British Arts Festivals Association (BAFA)
3rd Floor, The Library, 77 Whitechapel High Street, London E1 7QX
tel 020-7247 4667 *fax* 020-7247 5010
email info@artsfestivals.co.uk
website www.artsfestivals.co.uk

Provides information and a professional network for the festivals movement in the UK, working to promote the profile and status of arts festivals. As well as the arts festivals website, which catalogues festivals in the UK and provides links to festivals in Europe, BAFA also publishes a free Calendar and Directory of the 105 festival members in print, and produces an advance festivals press pack each January. Members have the opportunity to attend BAFA conferences, training courses and focus meetings. Membership is open to all arts festivals in the UK and associate membership to other arts organisations. Does not promote individual artists, companies or tours.

British Federation of Festivals for Music, Drama and Speech
Festivals House, 198 Park Lane, Macclesfield, Cheshire SK11 6UD
tel 0870-774 4290 *fax* 0870-774 4292
email julia@festivals.demon.co.uk
website www.festivals.demon.co.uk

Provides information and a network for amateur and competitive festivals in the UK. The Federation includes more than 300 festivals.

The European Festivals Association
General Secretariat, Kleine Gentstraat 46, B-9051 Gent, Belgium
email info@efa-aef.org
website www.efa-aef.org

Represents more than 90 high-quality festivals and 11 national festivals in 35 European countries. The website offers a general overview of these festivals, together with a detailed list of thousands of events and performances in its annual calendar.

UK ARTS FESTIVALS

24:7 Theatre Festival
PO Box 247, Manchester M60 2ZT
tel 0845-408 4101 *fax* 0161-286 6342
email info@247theatrefestival.co.uk
website www.247theatrefestival.co.uk

An annual festival based in Manchester which seeks to encourage and celebrate new and original work by writers, performers, directors and technical specialists. They seek to create opportunities for creative talent in all these roles. They seek to provide and promote accessible theatre for all.

24:7 uses innovative non-theatre venues, which ties in with repertory theatre pioneer Annie Horniman's connections in the area and Manchester City Council's "original-modern" marketing concept. Taking into account feedback from previous festivals, they favour venues which provide the best possible infrastructure in terms of technical and audience services, including the ability to shield the performing areas, as far as possible, from invasive noise and matching each play with the most appropriate venue.

Arundel Festival
tel (01903) 883474
email arundelfestival@btopenworld.com
website www.arundelfestival.co.uk

For 10 days each August, the market town of Arundel is host to a multi-arts festival which began in 1977. Street theatre and a festival Fringe are regular features, as are concerts, exhibitions, fireworks and jazz. The festival culminates in an open-air production of a Shakespeare play in the grounds of Arundel Castle. Each production is led by a cast of experienced professional actors, and extended with members of the local community who work with the professionals throughout the 6-week rehearsal period.

Barbican International Theatre Event (BITE)
Barbican Centre, Silk Street, London EC2Y 8DS
tel 020-7638 4141

Theatre

email theatre@barbican.org.uk
website www.barbican.org.uk/bite

Since its first programme in 1998, BITE has sought to create a venue in London dedicated to presenting some of the most significant and innovative artists around the world. The Spring 2005 season featured music, theatre and dance pieces from many different countries. Events included: Theatre O's *Astronaut*; Peter Brook's *Ta Main dans la Mienne*; and Fabulous Beast Dance Theatre's production of *Giselle*.

Bath Shakespeare Festival

Theatre Royal, Sawclose, Bath BA1 1ET
tel (01225) 448844
website www.bathshakespeare.org.uk

Presenting premières, international productions and new commissions, the Bath Shakespeare Festival takes place over 2 weeks in March. In addition to full-scale Shakespeare productions there are workshops, film screenings and education events.

Belfast Festival at Queens

25 College Gardens, Belfast BT9 6BS
tel 028-9027 2600
email a.mcGrath@qub.ac.uk
website www.belfastfestival.com

Founded in 1963, the Belfast Festival is an annual 3-week international arts festival held in October and November each year. The largest festival of its kind in Ireland, it covers all artforms including theatre, dance, classical music, literature, jazz, comedy, visual arts, folk music and popular music, attracting more than 50,000 visitors. Theatre performances in 2004 included: the Belfast Theatre Company's production of *A Most Notorious Woman*; Theatre Royal Bath's production of *Blithe Spirit* with Penelope Keith. Artists wishing to participate in the festival should submit a written proposal to the address listed above.

Birmingham ArtsFest

tel 0121-685 2605
email mail@artsfest.org.uk
website www.artsfest.org.uk

ArtsFest is one of the UK's largest free arts festivals and is held in venues across Birmingham for 2 days in September. It programmes a range of free performances including theatre, jazz, opera and dance events. Street theatre also features heavily, with musicians, jugglers, visual artists and stand-up comedians all presenting their work outside. There are also a variety of workshops on offer, ranging from screenwriting to Bollywood dancing.

Bradford International Festival Ltd

Business Innovation Centre, Angel Way, Listerhills, Bradford BD7 1BX
tel (01274) 722272 *fax* (01274) 736600
email info@bethere2003.com

The Bradford Festival has been established for 14 years and continues to grow each summer. For 2 weeks in July the festival celebrates a creative fusion of cultures from across the District and West Yorkshire. The main events are the Mela, which is the largest event of its kind in Europe; the Lord Mayor's Carnival Procession; and the Street Theatre Festival.

Brighton Festival

email info@brighton-festival.org.uk
website www.brighton-festival.org.uk

Founded in 1967. For 3 weeks in May, there are more than 300,000 attendances at 800 separate arts events taking place in venues across Brighton and Hove. Artists from a number of different countries are represented in theatre, dance, music, opera, books, events and outdoor spectaculars.

Running alongside Brighton Festival, Brighton Festival Fringe (previously called 'the Open') has been in existence for 37 years and is the biggest in England, showcasing a variety of artforms and activities. Applicants for the Fringe should first read the 'How to be in Brighton Festival Fringe' document available on the website, and then register online.

Cambridge Hotbed Festival

Junction CDC, Clifton Road, Cambridge CB1 7GX
tel (01223) 578000
email cat@junction.co.uk
website www.hotbedfest.co.uk

Following the success of the original Hotbed 2002, Menagerie Theatre Company (**www.menagerie.uk.com**) and Junction CDC (**www.junction.co.uk**) joined forces to present Hotbed 2004 and 2006, Cambridge's New Writing Theatre Festival. Over 3 weeks in July, venues around Cambridge – including CB2, Cambridge Drama Centre and Cambridge Arts Theatre's Playroom – hosted a variety of new plays by a selection of regional and national writers. Productions ranged from 15-minute lunchtime shorts to full evening performances, with a selection of workshops, talks, masterclasses and seminars also included in the programme.

The festival presents opportunities both for writers and for actors to get involved. Any writer may submit a complete play for 2 actors lasting 15-20 minutes. Successful writers will see their production professionally developed and performed at various central Cambridge venues throughout the 3-week festival. A repertory company based around the members of Menagerie Theatre Company supports the festival, and actors are welcome to audition for the company a few months in advance. For further information about the next Hotbed and how to get involved, contact Cat Moore by phone, email or post.

Canterbury Festival

Christ Church Gate, The Precincts, Canterbury, Kent CT1 2EE

tel (01227) 452853
email info@canterburyfestival.co.uk
website www.canterburyfestival.co.uk

Founded in 1929, the Canterbury Festival takes place over 2 weeks in October. The festival features music, dance, drama, opera, film, community events, talks, walks and visual arts.

The Marlowe and Gulbenkian Theatres in Canterbury and the Theatre Royal in Margate are host to major dance, drama and opera companies. Many small professional and amateur companies perform in the smaller venues and present a wide variety of drama and dance during the 2 weeks of the festival. These have included local companies as well as small foreign companies such as the Brazilian company Teatro Sao Paulo Fabrica, and Hungarian children's theatre Kolibri Theatre.

Other drama companies that have appeared at the festival include the Royal Shakespeare Company, the National Theatre Company, Actors Touring Company, Trestle Theatre, Compass Theatre, Shared Experience and Yellow Earth Theatre.

Chichester Festivities

Box Office, 45 East Street, Chichester,
West Sussex PO19 1HX
tel (01243) 780192
email info@chifest.org.uk
website www.chifest.org.uk

The Box Office is open for making reservations a month in advance of the festival. At other times consult the website or make contact by email.

Chichester Festivities are programmed over 2 weeks in July and have included performances of classical, jazz and world music, talks, contemporary sculpture in the Cathedral Cloisters, fireworks at Glorious Goodwood Racecourse and outdoor theatre productions. Founded in 1975, the festival celebrated its 30th anniversary in 2005.

The event has attracted performers such as Dame Judi Dench, Jools Holland, Fay Weldon and Nigel Kennedy.

Dumfries and Galloway Arts Festival

Gracefield Arts Centre, 28 Edinburgh Road,
Dumfries DG1 1JQ
tel (01387) 260447 *fax* (01387) 260447
email info@dgartsfestival.org.uk
website www.dgartsfestival.org.uk

An annual 9-day festival at the end of May, established in 1979. Founded with the aim of bringing high-quality international events to community audiences that would not otherwise have the opportunity to experience such talent, the festival now also presents local talent of international standing.

The festival programmes a wide range of events covering music – including classical, jazz and folk –

dance, theatre, literary, children's and the visual arts. Events take place in a range of venues throughout the region.

The Ealing Comedy Festival

Festivals and Events, Room 3.03, Ealing Town Hall, New Broadway, Ealing, London W5 2BY
tel 020-8825 6064 *fax* 020-8825 6069
email events@ealing.gov.uk
website www.ealing.gov.uk/services/ealing+summer/comedy+festival

The Ealing Comedy Festival takes place in Walpole Park over 1 week in July and reaches audiences of over 1000 each night. The festival has played host to some of the leading names in modern British comedy – including Ricky Gervais, Harry Hill, Al Murray, Rob Brydon and Jimmy Carr– and generally features around 25 comedians each year.

Edinburgh Festival Fringe

The Fringe Office, 180 High Street,
Edinburgh EH1 1QS
tel 0131-226 0026 *fax* 0131-226 0016
email admin@edfringe.com
website www.edfringe.com

The Fringe was started in 1947 to complement the first Edinburgh International Festival. It now breaks its own record every year as the largest arts festival on the planet, bringing thousands of performances of hundreds of shows in more than 200 venues across Edinburgh each August.

The Fringe Society was formed in 1959 to coordinate publicity and ticket sales and offer a comprehensive information service both to performers and to audiences. It compiles information about venues, press and suppliers and produces a series of publications designed to answer frequently asked questions. The office is open all year round and the staff are available to help by phone, email or personal appointment.

Edinburgh International Festival

The Hub, Castlehill, Edinburgh EH1 2NE
tel 0131-473 2001 *fax* 0131-473 2003
email eif@eif.co.uk
website www.eif.co.uk

Founded in 1947, the Edinburgh International Festival is an annual event held over 3 weeks in August, using all the major concert and theatre venues in the city. With music, opera, theatre, film, dance, and the Military Tattoo at the Castle, the festival is now recognised as one of the world's most important celebrations of the arts.

Also offers a programme of year-round activities, with courses and workshops on diverse subjects from playwriting to the use of digital video, and one-off projects for school children, students and adults collaborating with actors, directors, choreographers and musicians involved in the festival. Performance at the Edinburgh International Festival is by invitation only, issued by the Festival Director.

Exeter Summer Festival

Exeter City Council, Civic Centre, Paris Street, Exeter EX1 1JJ
tel (01392) 265205 *fax* (01392) 265366
email general.festivals@exeter.gov.uk
website www.exeter.gov.uk/residents/arts/exeter_festival

The city's celebration of contemporary and classical music, theatre, dance, comedy and visual arts.

Over 2 weeks in June/July, Exeter Summer Festival programmes diverse arts events, exhibitions and firework displays. Artists interested in performing should contact **artist.enquiries@exeter.gov.uk**.

Fierce!

608B The Big Reg, 120 Vyse Street, Birmingham B18 6NF
tel 0121-244 8080 *fax* 0121-244 8081
email fierce@fierceearth.com
website www.fierce.info

Annual festival of performances and events in theatres, bars, clubs, galleries and public spaces across the West Midlands. The festival takes place over 1 month in May/June.

Grassington Festival

The Festival Office, Grassington Festival, Grassington, North Yorkshire BD23 5AU
tel (01756) 752691
email arts@grassington-festival.org.uk
website www.grassington-festival.org.uk

A multi-disciplinary festival featuring contemporary and classical music, theatre, poetry and film, and taking place over 2 weeks in June/July.

Greenwich and Docklands Festivals (GDF)

6 College Approach, London SE10 9HY
tel 020-8305 1818 *fax* 020-8305 1188
email info@festival.org
website www.festival.org

Taking place over the 4 weekends of July, the Greenwich and Docklands Festival programmes multi-disciplinary arts events around East London each summer. As well as programming large-scale, visually impressive work, the festival places emphasis on educational projects and participatory arts.

The International Festival of Musical Theatre in Cardiff

Market Chambers, 5/7 St Mary Street, Cardiff CF10 1AT
tel 029-2034 6999 *fax* 029-2037 2011
email enquiries@CardiffMusicals.com
website www.CardiffMusicals.com

The 2nd International Festival of Musical Theatre was held in March 2005. The festival aims to present the best of musical theatre, old and new, large and small. Its new-writing programme, 'The Global Search for New Musicals', showcases new musicals selected from a year-long search; many of the musicals showcased in 2002 Global Search have gone on to enjoy success around the world. In addition there are masterclasses enhancing the work being shown in the festival programme; in 2005 these included a Cole Porter Day, a Stephen Sondheim Symposium and a performance masterclass from Broadway musical director, Don Pippin. Also presented as part of the festival is the BBC Radio 2 Voice of Musical Theatre, where young professional singers from around the world compete for a substantial cash prize and BBC broadcast engagements.

International Playwriting Festival

Warehouse Theatre, Dingwall Road, Croydon CR0 2NF
website www.warehousetheatre.co.uk
Festival Administrator Rose Marie Vernon *Casting* Sally Vaughan

The International Playwriting Festival has been in operation since 1986 and has consolidated the Warehouse Theatre Company's role in discovering and developing new writing talent. Launching the career of many successful playwrights, the festival has seen many of its plays transferred to the West End, the Royal Court, Hampstead Theatre and Stratford-upon-Avon.

Taking place over a few days in November, the festival is held in 2 parts. The first is a competition (for which entries must be received by June) which is judged by a panel of distinguished theatre practitioners; the second is a showcase of the selected plays in November.

The festival has received applications from writers in the USA, Hong Kong, Croatia, Holland, Australia, Estonia, Sierra Leone, Italy and New Zealand, as well as from the UK.

Lichfield Festival

7 The Close, Lichfield, Staffordshire WS13 7LD
tel (01543) 306270
email info@lichfieldfestival.org
website www.lichfieldfestival.org.uk
Administrator Peter Bacon

Annual 10-day multi-arts festival in early July, Literature Weekend in September/October, plus occasional seasonal events.

London Comedy Festival

20 Chancellors Street, Hammersmith, London W6 9RN
tel 0870-119 611
email info@londoncomedyfestival.com
website www.londoncomedyfestival.com

Theatre

The London Comedy Festival is a celebration of London's established comedy scene, with many of the capital's top clubs hosting stand-up events, a programme of humour literature events across London's libraries and bookshops including workshops, readings, competitions and debates, and major events at some of London's landmarks, along with other comedy activities. It takes place over 10 days in May.

Highlights in previous years have included the first ever open-air cinema event in Trafalgar Square; the creation of the world's largest cartoon strip; 'Wit Lit' – London's largest ever humour literature event; and the GOSH Gala, a star-studded fundraiser hosted by Graham Norton and Suggs.

Anyone can put on a show as part of the London Comedy Festival. Over the past 3 years the event has encompassed not just comedy clubs but pubs, theatres, galleries and libraries. Registration begins in January with a deadline for inclusion in the Festival Guide of mid-March.

London International Festival of Theatre (LIFT)
19/20 Great Sutton Street, London EC1V 0DR
email info@liftfest.org
website www.liftfest.org
Directors Rose Fenton, Lucy Neal

Started in 1981, LIFT is a biennial summer festival introducing some of the world's most exciting artists and theatre-makers to London. LIFT events have been staged in more than 30 London venues as well as in a number of site-specific venues such as streets, disused buildings, the river, parks and open spaces.

Also runs developmental and educational programmes exploring the nature of exchange and creativity for a range of audiences including schoolchildren and industry leaders.

London International Mime Festival
35 Little Russell Street, London WC1A 2HH
tel 020-7637 5661 *fax* 020-7323 1151
email mimefest@easynet.co.uk
website www.mimefest.co.uk
Directors Joseph Seelig, Helen Lannaghan

Founded in 1977 by Joseph Seelig and Nola Rae, the London International Mime Festival presents contemporary visual theatre. Events are non text-based and can include animation theatre, circus skills, mask, mime, clown and visual theatre. Most work will be either a UK or a London premiere.

The festival takes place over 16 days each January with the deadline for submissions in mid-July. Participation is by invitation only. To be considered, send a DVD to Helen Lannaghan and Joseph Seelig at the address above with an sae enclosed for the return of material.

Ludlow Festival
email info@ludlowfestival.co.uk
website www.ludlowfestival.co.uk

Running for more than 45 years, the Ludlow Festival takes places over 2-3 weeks in June/July with a range of music, theatre and exhibitions on offer. Each year it features open-air Shakespeare productions which are staged in the grounds of Ludlow Castle. The 2005 production was *Richard II* directed by Steven Berkoff.

The Mayor's Thames Festival
website www.thamesfestival.org

The Mayor's Thames Festival is a free annual event that takes place on and around the River Thames between Westminster and Southwark Bridges, using the river as a powerful unifying symbol for the whole of London. One of the festival's main aims is to enable more collaborations between artists and community groups. Over 1 weekend in September it programmes events such as night carnivals, fireworks spectaculars, mass choirs, music stages, a range of participatory activities, and both artist-led and river-orientated events.

Merseyside International Street Festival
tel 0151-709 3334 *fax* 0151-709 4994
email info@brouhaha.uk.com
website www.brouhaha.uk.com

Established in 1990, the Merseyside International Street Festival brings a mix of dance, drama, acrobatics, music, comedy, puppetry and street theatre to around 30,000 spectators in Liverpool each July/August.

Minack Theatre Summer Festival
Porthcurno, Penzance, Cornwall TR19 6JU
tel (01736) 810694 *fax* (01736) 810779
email minack@dial.pipex.com
website www.minack.com

Founded in 1932. An annual, 17-week summer season of plays, musicals and opera held at Minack's unique open-air theatre carved into the Cornish cliffside. Created in 1929 by Rowena Cade and her gardener Billy Rawlings, the Minack lends itself to large-cast plays. Most companies involved are amateur, although approximately 3 each year are professional.

National Student Drama Festival (NSDF)
Aberdeen Centre, 22-24 Highbury Grove, London N5 2DQ
tel 020-7354 8070
email info@nsdf.org.uk
website www.nsdf.org.uk
Director (CEO) Holly Kendrick

The National Student Drama Festival is a week-long event bringing together students and leading theatre and media professionals. Taking place in the Easter holidays, it celebrated its 50th year in 2005. The

Theatre

festival showcases and nurtures innovative theatre by young people and offers masterclasses, workshops and forums for debate and discussion. A panel of 3 eminent judges awards the prestigious NSDF Prizes, Awards and Bursaries at the end of the festival.

NSDF is open to colleges, youth theatres, community organisations and universities, and takes place each spring in Scarborough. Professionals who have attended include Mike Leigh, Willy Russell, Mark Ravenhill, Sir Alan Ayckbourn and Michael Billington.

The NSDF Ensemble is a company of talented young theatre practitioners from all over the UK. Supported by professional artists, Ensemble members take part in a one-off training/residency. On the recommendation of the NSDF selection team, members are invited to audition each year from the wide range of shows entered for the festival.

National Theatre's Watch This Space Festival

Royal National Theatre, South Bank,
London SE1 9PX
tel 020-7452 3333
email wts@nationaltheatre.org.uk
website www.nationaltheatre.org.uk/wts
Watch This Space Producer Angus MacKechnie

Takes place outside the National Theatre over the summer. The festival features theatre, music, dance, variety, film and circus from Britain and abroad. All events are free and run for about 8 weeks from late June to early September.

Pride of Place Theatre Festival

c/o Eastern Angles, Sir John Mills Theatre,
Gatacre Road, Ipswich IP1 2LQ
website www.prideofplace.org.uk

International festival held every 2 years to celebrate the work of theatre companies involved in rural touring and to debate the role of theatre in rural communities. Features seminars, discussions and performances from many of the major rural touring companies, including Eastern Angles, Farnham Maltings, Forest Forge, New Perspectives, Northumberland Theatre Company (NTC), Oxfordshire Touring, Pentabus and Proteus. In 2008 the festival was hosted in Alnwick, Northumberland by NTC Touring Theatre. See NTC's entry under *Middle and smaller-scale companies* on page 211.

Royal Court Young Writers Festival

Royal Court Theatre, Sloane Square,
London SW1W 8AS
website www.royalcourttheatre.com

A biennial festival, the Royal Court Young Writers Festival presents full professional productions and script-in-hand readings of the best new plays by British writers under 25. The festival has launched the careers of playwrights such as Leo Butler, Simon Stephens, Lucy Prebble and Laura Wade. For information about the festival, please see the Royal Court website. For casting procedures, please see the entry for the Royal Court under Producing Theatres.

Salisbury Festival

87 Crane Street, Salisbury, SP1 2PU
tel (01722) 332977 *fax* (01722) 410552
email info@salisburyfestival.co.uk
website www.salisburyfestival.co.uk

Established in 1973, for 20 years the festival consisted mostly of classical music events. It is now multi-disciplinary and combines prestigious Cathedral concerts with family street entertainment, circus, theatre and other arts events. There are normally between 30-50 different programmes and projects and a total of some 100 different events which take place at the end of May and beginning of June.

Shrewsbury Summer Season

tel (07709) 685156
website www.shrewsburysummer.co.uk

The first Shrewsbury Summer Season took place in June, July and August 2004 with a programme of visual arts, music, drama, dance, spoken word and comedy events.

Stafford Festival Shakespeare

c/o Gatehouse Theatre, Eastgate Street,
Stafford ST16 2LT
tel (01785) 253595
website www.staffordfestivalshakespeare.co.uk
Artistic Programme Manager Derrick Gask

As well as an annual pantomime, The Gatehouse Theatre, generally a receiving house, produces the Stafford Festival Shakespeare, an open air production at Stafford Castle every summer. Casting breakdowns for The Festival Shakespeare are sent out in January and casting is done by freelance casting directors. Rehearsals for The Shakespeare Festival start in June. Photos and CVs sent to the theatre by actors wishing to be considered for audition will be forwarded to the casting director. Invitations to see actors in other productions are welcomed and should be addressed to Derrick Gask. Will consider applications from disabled actors to play disabled characters.

See entry under *In-house pantomimes* on page 240 for details of the annual pantomime.

The Stratford-upon-Avon Poetry Festival

Shakespeare Birthplace Trust, Shakespeare Centre,
Henley Street, Stratford-upon-Avon,
Warwickshire CV37 6QW
tel (01789) 204016 *fax* (01789) 296083
email reception@shakespeare.org.uk (general enquiries only)
website www.shakespeare.org.uk

Established in 1954 by the Shakespeare Birthplace Trust, the festival presents recitals of poetry usually held over 9 successive Sundays in the summer. Nearly every major British poet from *Beowulf* onwards has featured somewhere in the festival, along with other poetry written or translated into English.

Over the last 50 years, many leading actors have been involved in the readings, including Judi Dench, Ralph Fiennes, John Gielgud, Ian Holm, Anthony Hopkins, Jeremy Irons, Derek Jacobi, Ben Kingsley, Ian McKellen, Helen Mirren, Vanessa Redgrave, Ian Richardson, Diana Rigg and Robert Stephens. In addition to the 9 traditional recitals, the festival now also includes a Local Poets evening, activities for children and a Poetry Mass. Most venues are wheelchair-friendly – contact the festival organisers for specific details.

Theatre

Professional role-playing

Robbie Swales

In 1992 an actor rang me and asked if I would do a job with him, which he had been offered through another actor. The job was to do a role-play with some accountants. I said, "What's role-play?" My friend explained that I had to role-play a demotivated worker, and that the purpose of the role-play was to help the accountants learn how to motivate members of their team. I did the job and enjoyed it. Since then – my first experience of role-play – this area of work for actors has expanded enormously. Although there are still networks of individual actors gaining role-play assignments, the bulk of the work for actors is provided by drama-based training companies, which provide organisations with role-players and actor/facilitators.

So why has this sector grown, and why is there a need for drama-based training companies, rather than individual actors applying directly to the end-user to offer their acting skills?

Trainers and developers within organisations have discovered that when they deliver behavioural skills training, an experiential interactive session provides better learning opportunities for the participants than the traditional talk-and-chalk approach. Because actors can put different behaviours on and take them off like a coat, they have become a valuable resource to the trainers; they make the sessions lively, interesting, interactive and memorable. Participants remember the learning and then go and use the skills in the workplace. Training and development in the workplace is only carried out if a company or organisation believes that it will improve efficiency, and therefore productivity. The use of actors for training is no exception: they help to make the behaviour of people in organisations more effective.

Drama-based training companies are what one might call one-stop shops. If an organisation, such as a high street bank, wants to employ actors to role-play on a series of development centres, the training department in the bank will find it easier to approach a role-play company. The trainer from the bank can explain their needs, check how that role-play company guarantees the quality of their actors, and then negotiate a fee. The role-play company can book the actors, brief them appropriately and arrange for them to be in the right place at the right time.

The field of drama-based training is growing more and more sophisticated, and some of these companies are becoming more like consultancies, with entire interactive theatre programmes being researched, designed, written, rehearsed and delivered by the drama-based company. For such companies to be effective at this type of work, they need a core team of full-time staff, while maintaining a freelance team of actors trained in the appropriate skills whom they can employ on a project-by-project basis.

There are, very broadly, two types of role-play work: role-playing one-to-one with a participant; and role-playing with another actor in front of an audience, with whom the actors then interact. Most role-play work is improvised; however, there are some types of interactive theatre which kick off the session with a scripted scene, before the actors then start improvising the suggestions of the audience.

One-to-one role-play

The range of work performing one-to-one role-play with a participant requires different levels of skill from the actor. An example of the simplest type of role-play is improvising a patient for an assessment centre, where no feedback is required from the actor to the participant. The Royal College of Anaesthetists requires candidates for their anaesthetist qualifying exams to role-play with a simulated patient (an actor), so that the communications and empathetic skills of the candidate can be assessed. The role-play lasts about five minutes and is not complex.

An example of a one-to-one role-play at the more challenging end of the scale would be role-playing a Senior Tax Manager being interviewed for a job. It is important to remember that an actor is used, primarily, to display different types of behaviour (e.g. being nervous, arrogant, aggressive, etc.). However, for the actor to be a convincing Senior Tax Manager for a behavioural role-play, they need to have an overall grasp of what the job entails, and they may need to throw in a few technical phrases to add reality to the situation. This kind of role-play requires a day of training for the actor so that they can learn about the role of the Tax Manager, memorise a few key technical words and phrases and rehearse the role-play encounter.

Actors are also required to give each participant with whom they role-play some high-quality feedback about their performance. At this highly sophisticated level of role-play, being able to deliver such feedback is an essential skill. Remember to frame the feedback with affirmative and supportive language.

The skills required to be a good one-to-one role-player are: the ability to go into character instantly; the ability to improvise well; the ability to understand and interpret the brief; the ability to memorise some technical terms; the ability to adjust your performance in relation to the quality of the input from the participant; and the ability to give feedback that is communicated sensitively and is useful to the participant.

Delivering an interactive theatre session

This technique has been used in schools by Theatre in Education companies for many years, and is now being used increasingly in the workplace. There are many different variations in the way that interactive theatre, or forum theatre, is delivered, but the principle is quite simple. Actors playing a scene will break out from that scene and talk to the audience, in character, asking for advice. This advice is then taken back into the scene by the actor and played out to see if it is effective.

Many aspects of development and learning can be addressed via interactive theatre: managing difficult conversations; feedback skills; diversity awareness; assertiveness skills; customer service; influencing skills; leadership; performance management; coaching; recruitment; employment law awareness.

The skills necessary for performing high-quality forum theatre are: good improvisational skills; the ability to gain a thorough understanding of the objectives of the programme; being an able facilitator in order to confidently handle the responses from the audience; and the ability to hang onto a character while improvising and facilitating.

Applying for work

There are many different types of role-play/drama-based training companies. When we created Steps in 1992, we were one of only a handful of role-play companies; I have now lost count of the number of similar organisations! They all have different cultures and different ways of approaching the work, and each individual company's style probably reflects the personalities of their creators. Some companies may only provide actors to do one-to-one role-play, while others may concentrate on providing interactive theatre. Companies may have a large database of actors; others may have a small pool of actors who work on a fairly regular basis.

My advice would be to browse through the websites of the companies listed and get a feel of what they all claim to be offering. Find out from other actors who have worked in this area about their experiences. Ask them what they think of the company who employed them. At Steps we look at all actor CVs that we receive and run audition workshops as, and when, we need to select new actors onto our team.

Role-playing for learning is no less a professional activity than professional acting. Punctuality, wearing the appropriate business/work clothes, maintaining confidentiality, interacting in an exemplary way with clients and participants, and working effectively as a member of a high-performance team with fellow role-players, are all behaviours that are required during a role-play assignment.

Being a role-player is a fascinating way for an actor to use their skills in between acting assignments while maintaining an income. Also, from the feedback I have received from role-players, the benefits are not only one-way: actors can learn a great deal from the organisations in which they role-play. The work they do can build their confidence and help them to discover new ways of managing their own careers.

Robbie Swales attended the Bristol Old Vic Theatre School from 1968 to 1970. During the 1970s he acted in Rep, toured and appeared in the West End; during the 1980s he made the most of his income from TV commercials. In 1994 Robbie joined Steps – Drama Learning Development and is now one of six directors who manage the company. In 2002 and 2003 Steps was one of the hundred fastest-growing inner-city companies in the UK, appearing on the HM Treasury-sponsored Inner City 100 Index.

Role-play companies

Actors have long used their craft in promotional areas like selling products and services over the phone and in department stores; work opportunities in these fields are advertised in *The Stage*. More recently, the idea of using theatre skills deeper inside the world of business (and the service professions, like medicine) has grown considerably. Essentially, the high level of co-operation ('interactivity') and the excitement, creativity and inspirational power of good theatre is being grasped by hierarchies 'outside the proscenium arch'. Role-play practitioners today are using techniques evolved by the Theatre in Education movement in the 1960s and 70s – but with far better-paying 'customers'.

The established companies – mostly created by actors – have built up a great deal of expertise in this new world and do not take on new 'role-players' lightly. It is therefore especially important to research each individual company's *modus operandi* before spending time and money in contacting them. However, this is a world well worth exploring as an exciting and lucrative alternative area of work.

A Corporate Act

172D Woodside Green, London SE25 5EW
tel 020-8405 5674 *mobile* (07798) 718321
email info@acorporateact.com
website www.acorporateact.com

Has several years' experience working in the corporate events industry. From initial concept to effective fulfilment of a brief, the company has built its reputation by listening to iindividual needs and client requirements, so that "whatever the occasion, a fresh, creative and dedicated approach is guaranteed .... We have assembled a reliable, knowledgeable and experienced team that will make impact at all corporate events".

Acting Out Ltd

Regal Chambers, Cavendish Street,
Chesterfield S40 1UY
tel (01246) 520014 *mobile* (07852) 320788
fax (01246) 558396
email claire.ashcroft@tesco.net
website www.acting-out.co.uk
Artistic Director Claire Hooper-Greenhill

Company's work

Supplies professional role-play actors for training for all kinds of staff, from medical and legal to bar staff and corporate training. All actors must have professional role-play experience. Clients include: NHS Trust and the National Trust.

Recruitment procedures

Periodically extends its actor-base, monthly to annually, via agents, websites, *PCR* and Equity. Welcomes letters (with CVs and photographs) from actors previously unknown to the company sent by post or email; is happy to receive showreels and invitations to view individual actors' websites. Will consider applications from disabled actors to play characters with disabilities.

Action in Management

1st Floor, Reform Place, North Road,
Durham CH1 4RZ
tel 0191-384 9900 *fax* 0191-384 9922
email aim@actioninmanagement.co.uk
website www.actioninmanagement.co.uk
Directors Chas Thomason, Diggy Wilson, Shaun Curry, Christine Pearce, Paula Smith

Company's work

Established in 1994. Interpersonal and management skills development, using forum theatre. Provides incoming actors with in-house and on-the-job training; work experience and life skills required. Clients include: BP, Conoco, Rolls Royce and the NHS.

Recruitment procedures

Periodically extends its actor-base as needed, through personal recommendation and via the website. Welcomes letters (with CVs and photographs) from actors previously unknown to the company, sent by post or email. Welcomes showreels and invitations to view individual actors' websites. Will consider applications from disabled actors for specific projects.

Activation

Riverside House, Feltham Avenue, Hampton Court, Surrey KT8 9BJ
tel 020-8783 9494 *fax* 020-8783 9345
email info@activation.co.uk
website www.activation.co.uk
Director Paul Gilmore

A leading provider of bespoke interactive training. Services include forum theatre, role-play, scriptwriting and performance, and the design and delivery of training programmes. Incoming actors are trained by the company, according to the requirements of the project. Strong acting and listening skills are required of all the actors. Recent clients include: Diageo, Barclays, and Lloyds TSB.

Periodically extends its actor-base, often by word-of-mouth but also using the Internet. Welcomes letters (with CVs and photographs) from actors previously unknown to the company if sent by post, but not by email. Does not welcome showreels, but is happy to receive invitations to view individuals' websites. Will consider applications from disabled actors to play characters with disabilities.

Actors in Industry Ltd

Talbert House, 52A Borough High Street, London SE1 1XN
tel 020-7234 9600 *fax* 020-7357 0915
email enquiries@actorsinindustry.com
website www.actorsinindustry.com
Directors Bill Cashmore, Carry Clubb, Roger Ayres, Lorraine Brunning *Head of Operations* Jeni Giffen

Established in 1992. "We are the foremost interactive training company in the UK, using role play, facilitation and interactive training and coaching to create meaningful skills improvement and behavioural change for individuals and organisations." Requires incoming actors to possess a good knowledge of business, feedback skills, and the ability to use their "third eye – the ability to put yourself in another person's position". Provides training in the form of an induction, group workshops and one-to-one sessions. Recent clients include: PWC, Linklaters, Lovelli, Barclays, Lilly, Kraft, Johnson & Johnson, IBM, and Rolls-Royce.

Extends its actor-base twice yearly, and recruits via emailed / posted CVs (business and acting) and covering letter. Rarely has the opportunity to cast disabled actors. Advises actors to "be honest about your experience; over-elaboration will be discovered very quickly".

AKT Productions

18 Grosvenor Street, London W1K 4QQ
tel 020-7495 4043 *fax* 020-7495 0692
email info@aktproductions.co.uk
website www.aktproductions.co.uk
Directors Tim Bannerman and Andy Powrie

Established in 1996. Provider of theatre-based learning resources, developing quality learning and development programmes. Incoming actors are expected to have experience of corporate role-play. Clients include: KPMG, Transport for London, Linklaters, HMPS, Shell, BP, Royal Mail. Actor-base is extended every 8-12 months via recommendations and applications.

Accepts submissions (with CVs and photographs) from actors previously unknown to them. Will also accept CVs and photographs sent via e-mail. Invitations to view individual actors' website, are also accepted. Applications from disabled actors for specific projects are considered

Apropos Productions Ltd

2nd Floor, 91a Rivington Street, London EC2A 3AY
tel 020-7739 2857 *fax* 020-7739 3852
email info@aproposltd.com
website www.aproposltd.com
Directors Paul Dubois

Established in 1999. Provides training for local, national and international clients. Key focus is on Organisational Behaviour. Training is provided for incoming actors through an induction process: client briefings. Training is given to become facilitators. Corporate experience is useful but not essential for incoming actors. Actor-base is extended annually through agents, website, Equity Job Information Service and *PCR*. Clients include: Local Government Association, Thompson Scientific, Colchester Borough Council.

Accepts submissions (with CVs and photographs) from actors previously unknown to them. Disabled actors regularly form part of their teams and are actively encouraged to apply.

Barking Productions Ltd

Regus, 1 Friary, Temple Quay, Bristol BS1 6EA
tel 0117-939 3171 *fax* 0117-939 3625
email info@barkingproductions.co.uk
website www.barkingproductions.co.uk
Key personnel Christopher Grimes, Neil Bett, Stephanie Weston

Company's work

Creative development and corporate entertainment company run by professional actors and specialising in drama-based training. The company's comedy show, *Instant Wit*, is regularly performed at corporate events. Provides incoming actors with some training in the form of familiarisation with company style and approach. Clients include: Marks & Spencer, Microsoft, Aardman Animations and Orange.

Recruitment procedures

Periodically extends its actor-base. Welcomes letters (with CVs and photographs) and always consults them when recruiting actors. Requires actors to be highly experienced with a businesslike manner (particularly for corporate work), and living in Bristol or London. Advises actors to visit the website and get a good idea of "who we are and what we do" before approaching the company.

Blue Beetle

First Floor, Aspect Court, 4 Temple Row, Birmingham B2 5HG

tel 0870-325 7000
email enquiries@bluebeetle.co.uk
website www.bluebeetle.com
Contact Graham David

A core group of 15 people, with others brought in when required. "We have a really simple statement, that tells you exactly what our training is like: Work hard. Play harder. Learn more."

Michael Browne Associates Ltd

The Cloisters, 168C Station Road, Lower Standon, Beds SG16 6JQ
tel/fax (01462) 812483
email angie@mba-roleplay.co.uk
website www.mba-roleplay.co.uk
Directors Michael Browne, Angie Smith

Established in 1997. Holds an extensive database of more than 500 professional, corporate actors. Works closely with clients to cast, devise, manage and interpret events and assessments to inform, challenge, develop, assess and train. Will provide training for incoming actors on particular clients' material as and when required. Actors should have Professional Drama training and experience in the corporate world using roleplay for assessment, training and development. Clients include: MoD, HMRC, Nationwide, Coors Brewers, Costain, VW, RBS, DVLA and Open University.

Periodically extends its actor-base when required "via interview after personal application and recommendation". Welcomes letters (with CVs & photographs) from actors previously unknown to the company sent by post or email. Accepts showreels and invitations to view individual actors' websites. Will consider applications from disabled actors for specific projects.

CentreStage Roleplay

The Stables, White Cottage, Cheapside, Ascot SL5 7QE
tel (01344) 876800
email info@centrestage-roleplay.com
Contact Pippa Shepherd

Company's work

A leading development consultancy specialising in the use of drama to enhance learning. Combines extensive business experience with a background in professional theatre and communication skills development. Uses roleplay, forum theatre, issues-based plays and other theatrical techniques "to bring learning to life without sacrificing professionalism or diluting messages".

Recruitment procedures

In the first instance, actors should send a CV outlining their acting and business experience, along with a recent photograph and covering letter, to Pippa Shepherd. Details will be kept on file until an

audition slot becomes available. "We receive many CVs: if we don't contact you, this doesn't mean we've forgotten about you."

Characters

12 Stillness Road, Honor Oak Park, London SE23 1NG
tel 020-8856 4005 mobile (07710) 493483
website www.characters.uk.com
Contact Catherine Hamilton

A well-established roleplay company with 14 years' experience. Owned by Catherine Hamilton, whose background combines a professional acting career with community health experience. Initially, the company focused on working with police forces and social services departments. It has now begun to expand into the NHS and private sector, more than doubling the client base.

Cragrats

The Cragrats Mill, Dunford Road, Huddersfield HD9 2AR
tel (01484) 686451 fax (01484) 686212
email jill@cragrats.com
website www.cragrats.com
Creative Director Mark Greenop Business Director David Bradley

Company's work

A theatrical communications company founded in 1989; specialises in corporate training, TIE and issue-based theatre nationwide. Employs 500 actors per year. Project managers and facilitators are trained in-house. Clients include: ASDA, NHS, Learning & Skills Councils, and the Royal Bank of Scotland.

Recruitment procedures

Extends its actor-base each month. Recruits actors through the website and through agents, Equity Job Information Service and advertisements in The Stage. Welcomes submissions (with CVs and photographs) by post or email from actors with at least 3 years of training at an approved drama school. "We regularly recruit actors aged 21-60. Please contact us. All rehearsals are Yorkshire-based, though work can be anywhere in the UK."

Note: Cragrats went into receivership in June 2009. However, as this book was going to press, a bidder was lined up to purchase parts of the company. See the website for the latest situation.

DramAnon

Langtons House, Templewood Lane, Farnham Common, Bucks SL2 3HD
tel (01753) 647795 mobile (01753) 647783
email info@dramanon.co.uk
website www.dramanon.co.uk
Directors Steven Brough, Melanie Nicholson

A leading provider of drama-based training in the UK. In operation for more than 11 years, the

Theatre

company has built up a client base including many police and fire services, councils and NHS Trusts within the public sector, together with professional companies, law firms, retailers, construction and pharmaceutical companies within the private sector. DramAnon expanded its activities in 2007 and now offers a wide range of services including roleplay, forum theatre, assessment, evaluation, consultation and full DVD production alongside conventional training models.

Interact

Bowden House, 14 Bowden Street, London SE11 4DS
tel 020-7793 7744 *fax* 020-7793 7755
email info@interact.eu.com
website www.interact.eu.com
Directors Derek Hollis, Ian Jessup *Company Administrator* Jamie Wright

Company's work

Founded in 1996, the company aims to bring theatre skills to business using the abilities of professional actors, writers, directors and facilitators. Role-play constitutes just 30% of output. Provides incoming actors with some training in the form of a briefing for basic role-play, rehearsal and guidance for complex work. Offers facilitators specific training in project management. Clients include: ACAS, the Foreign & Commonwealth Office, the BBC, and Royal and Sun Alliance.

Recruitment procedures

Periodically extends its actor-base. Recruits actors through the website and through agents, Equity Job Information Service, *PCR* and direct contact. Fluency, confidence and strong acting and improvisation skills are required. Business and forum theatre experience can also be an advantage. Welcomes letters (with CVs and photographs) but not email submissions. Invitations to view individual actors' websites are also accepted. Advises actors that: "Those with previous experience are most likely to be interviewed. We are unable to reply to submissions. If you are of interest to us, you will be contacted."

Maynard Leigh Associates (MLA)

Victoria House, 64 Paul Street, London EC2A 4NA
tel 020-7033 2370
email michaelm@maynardleigh.co.uk
website www.maynardleigh.co.uk

Company's work

MLA is essentially a community of about 25 people who share common values, are committed to their own and other people's personal growth, and are passionate about their work affecting an increasing number of individuals and organisations. They are required to be expert workshop leaders with an interest in the psychological aspects of human

potential development. Clients include: Hewlett Packard, Halifax plc, Ernst & Young, BBC TV, Vodafone, Barclay, Virgin and FT.com.

Recruitment procedures

All new consultants and leaders go through a rigorous and lengthy training process regardless of their professional experience. It can take up to 18 months of participation in MLA activities before an actor is allowed to represent the consultancy with clients. There are regular personal development sessions in which people explore how they are doing in MLA and how they need to develop and grow further. As MLA invests heavily in its existing Associates, its pace of growth is limited and it is unable to extend its actor-base regularly. Professional actors with a good working knowledge of business and corporate life should submit their details by email.

Pearlcatchers Ltd

Claremont House, 70-72 Alma Road,
Windsor SL4 3EZ
tel (01753) 624985 *fax* (01753) 830855
email enquiries@pearlcatchers.co.uk
website www.pearlcatchers.co.uk
Director Sharon M Young *Key personnel* Melanie Wright (Business Operations Manager), Karen Hanley (Business Development Manager)

Company's work

An event and training consultancy offering a fresh approach to learning, teambuilding and conferences. Provides actors with opportunities to shadow at events, and offers regular training afternoons and briefing sessions. Requires business skills/knowledge and prior experience in role playing and forum theatre. Clients include: AWE, BT, Ernst & Young, London Underground, Cisco, Bupa, DVLA and the RAF.

Recruitment procedures

Extends its actor base every 2 years, recruiting via *The Stage*. Welcomes letters (with CVs & photographs) from individual actors previously unknown to the company, sent by post or email. Does not accept showreels or invitations to view individual actors' websites. Considers applications from disabled actors for specific projects.

The Performance Business

78 Oatlands Drive, Weybridge, Surrey KT13 9HT
tel (01932) 888885
email info@theperformance.biz
website www.theperformance.biz
Directors Michael McNulty, Lucy Windsor

Provides incoming actors with personal assessments and one-to-one coaching. Requires excellent feedback skills and experience of working in business. Clients include: organisations in the financial, pharma, engineering, and manufacturing & public sectors.

Periodically extends its actor-base, recruiting via the website and CastNet Ltd. Welcomes letters (with CVs and photographs) from individual actors previously unknown to the company, sent by post or email. Will consider invitations to view individual actors' websites. Actively encourages applications from disabled actors and promotes the use of inclusive casting.

Power Train (UK) Ltd

15 Colston Street, Bristol BS1 5AP
tel 0117-922 1500 *fax* 0117-922 1550
email recruitment@powertrain.co.uk
website www.powertrain.co.uk
Managing Director Ian Smith *Business Support Manager* Rebecca Green

Established in 1996. Leads the way in delivering dramatic customer service performance programmes for frontline staff and their managers. The training is high impact and challenging, relevant and insightful, and deliver results that stick. Following a selection day, incoming actors will be expected to attend 2 days of training/development/workout prior to being accepted onto Power Train's approved register. No fees are paid for these days. Requires actors to have an acting qualification, and to possess experience in forum theatre and corporate role play. Clients include: Mercedes-Benz, Aviva, British Gas, Virgin Media, Virgin Trains, and Visa.

Extends its actor-base around 4 times a year. Recruits via the website, *The Stage*, and personal recommendations. Welcomes letters (with CVs and photographs) from individual actors previously unknown to the company, sent by post or email. Does not accept showreels but will consider invitations to view individual actors' websites. Rarely has the opportunity to cast disabled actors. "Being an approved Power Train associate does not guarantee work. We select teams to suit the assignment. We also expect a high degree of professionalism."

Roleplay UK

2 St Mary's Hill, Stamford, Lincs PE9 2DW
tel (01780) 761960 *fax* (01780) 764436
email actors@roleplayuk.com
website www.roleplayuk.com
Director James Larter *Commercial Manager* Ferlin Barnard *Creative Director* Andy Blair

Established in 1994. Drama-led communications and training. Provides training for incoming actors in the form of workshops. Periodically extends its actor-base every six months or every year, depending on demand. Recruits via Equity Job Information Service. Does not welcome unsolicited approaches by individuals unknown to the company, but actively encourages applications from disabled actors and promotes the use of inclusive training.

Simpatico Roleplay Agency

8 Manor Park, Histon, Cambridge CB24 9JT
tel (01223) 575259
email steve.attmore@ntlworld.com
website www.simpaticoagency.org
Director Steve Attmore

Company's work

Founded in 2002. Focuses on medical roleplay, and will provide 1-day initial training for incoming actors. Requires self-awareness in particular. Clients include: Royal College of Surgeons; East of England Deanery; and University of East Anglia Medical School.

Recruitment procedures

Extends its actor-base 6-monthly, and generally recruits via word-of-mouth. Welcomes letters (with CVs & photographs) from actors previously unknown to the agency, sent by post or email. Also welcomes invitations to view individual actors' websites, but does not accept showreels. Considers applications from disabled actors for specific projects.

Steps Drama Learning Development

Unit 4.1.1 The Leathermarket, Weston Street, London SE1 3ER
tel 020-7403 9000 *fax* 020-7403 0909
email mail@stepsdrama.com
website www.stepsdrama.com
Account Directors Robbie Swales, Richard Wilkes, Simon Thomson, Mark Shillabeer, Angela McHale

Company's work

Founded in 1990, the company supplies training to a wide variety of corporate companies through the use of drama. The work includes role-play, forum workshops and drama facilitation. Incoming actors receive training in the areas of feedback skills, forum workshops, coordinator workshops, facilitation skills and 'train the trainer'. Clients include: JP Morgan, NHS, AXA PPP, and The Audit Commission.

Recruitment procedures

Extends its actor-base once or twice a year, selecting 2-3 people in each round. Actors should submit their CV via the website. Actors should have excellent improvisation skills and be able to present themselves realistically as part of the business world in both their dress and language. Requires actors to behave in a professional manner both in their dealings with Steps and with their clients. Must be organised, reliable and good team players.

Theatre&

Church Hall, St James Road, Huddersfield HD1 4QA
tel (01484) 532967 *fax* (01484) 532962
email cmitchell@theatreand.com
website www.theatreand.com
Directors Kath Hirst, Dan Alexander, Carol Sibbald,

Theatre

Russell Watters *Casting & Events Manager* Clare Mitchell

Production details

Founded in 2005. An innovative training, development and creative presentation company working all over the UK. Designs and develops a variety of learning and communications interventions, which incorporate drama-based training techniques in order to deliver the client's desired outcomes. Theatre Development focuses on public and private sector organisations; Theatre Learning works within the education sector, delivering careers-based information to schools; and Theatre Events provides larger-scale events, such as conferences and company product launches. Offers some training to incoming actors, who should possess some touring or corporate training experience, strong improvisation skills, and the ability to use a variety of accents. Clients include: NHS, Careers Scotland, AimHigher, Scottish Enterprise, and ECITB.

Casting procedures

Regularly holds auditions to increase its database of actors, and employs up to 100 actors per year. Contract lengths range from a few weeks to 6 months. "Please send your CV and a photo, along with a covering letter detailing why you think you are a suitable candidate. We are unable to respond to everyone, but will be in touch to invite you to audition if you are successful." Accepts showreels and invitations to view individual actors' websites, and will consider applications from disabled actors for specific projects.

Theatre without Walls

Forwood House, Forwood, Gloucesterhire GL6 9AB
mobile (07962) 040441
email hello@theatrewithoutwalls.org.uk
website www.theatrewithoutwalls.org.uk
Directors Genevieve Swift, Jason Maher

Established in 2002. Award winning producing theatre company with an active training/corporate wing, working in the public and private sector. Also produces television and corporate films. Training is provided for incoming actors in the form of workshops and rehearsals in forum, roleplay and interactive drama. Incoming actors require good improvisational skills. Actors are recruited through agents and Equity Job Information Service. Clients include: National Trust, Gloucestershire Local Authority, Apollo, BBC, The Prince's Trust.

Disabled actors regularly form part of their teams and are actively encouraged to apply. See also the company's entry under *Middle and smaller-scale companies* on page 225.

Turning Point Theatre Company

20 Couper Meadows, Exeter EX2 7TF
tel (01392) 446818 *fax* (01392) 446279
email turningpoint@eclipse.co.uk
website www.turningpointtheatre.co.uk
Director Lyn Ferrand *Administrator* Anne Williams

Company's work

Founded in 1990, the company aims to raise awareness of specific health and social issues using theatre and theatre-related techniques. Gained Pavilion Award for innovations in training (2000). Works in partnership with the corporate, voluntary and statutory sectors. Creates training courses and videos for health and social service professionals; other activities include national and regional tours, residencies, workshops and conferences. Provides incoming actors with some training in forum theatre techniques if required. Clients include: Devon County Council, the Princess Royal Trust for Carers, and Rethink (NSF).

Recruitment procedures

Periodically extends its actor-base in accordance with the demands of specific projects. Actors are recruited via agents and *PCR*. Welcomes submissions (with CVs and photographs) sent by post or email. Showreels and invitations to view individual actors' websites are also accepted.

Media
Introduction

The last decade has seen incredibly rapid advancements in recording technology, computers, digital media and the Internet. There has also been an enormous growth in the principal broadcasting companies contracting-out much of their output; this in turn has led to an increase in the number of independent companies employing actors. (There are also companies whose output does not include drama – these have not been included in the listings.)

Most film and television companies use casting directors, and it's usually a waste of time and money writing to anyone else unless you have a personal contact. It is worth remembering that many companies do work for businesses – training and promotional films, for instance.

Student films may be a somewhat poor relation to Hollywood blockbusters, in terms of pay (if any) and exposure, but they can provide useful experiences, be a good addition to your CV, and have the potential to lead onto something that is properly paid and much more prestigious. Extracts from such a film could also be useful for your showreel.

Casting for radio is much more akin to that for theatre, although often without the use of a casting director.

Recorded Media

Countdown to 'Action!'

Edward Hicks

The shooting process will vary slightly from production to production, and will present different challenges. But the one element that is certain – be it multi-camera studio or single-camera location – is the waiting. It's hardly surprising that actors have a reputation for story-swapping; it helps to pass the time! However, as actors spend the day unable to fully relax, in a permanent state of standby ready for 'Action', the waiting can be strangely tiring.

The average shooting day is long, and even though a finished shot lasts seconds on-screen, setting up a shot and lighting takes hours. If the sequence involves stunts, special-effects, animals or supporting artistes, it can take several days. For the actor, this means intense moments of concentrated activity (lasting minutes) followed by long periods of waiting (lasting hours). This balance between being relaxed, yet at the same time remaining focused and energised, can be difficult to achieve. Then, when things fall behind schedule (which inevitably they do), the pressure to get it right intensifies – making it even harder to relax.

A small role in an episode of a long-running television programme can frequently be far more nerve-racking than a larger part. I've often seen actors sitting around all day waiting to do a few lines, only to discover that their little scene is to be covered in one shot ... which is to be the last shot of the day. The director knows that the crew (who have worked flat-out all day) must finish on time, as there's no money in the budget for overtime; a good 1st AD won't be shy about reminding the director of this. So with only ten minutes to get the scene in the can, you're frantically called to the set (not a good moment to leave a jacket or prop in your dressing room!); you're introduced to the 1st AD (the person responsible for keeping the director on schedule); you do a rough block with the director, followed by final make-up and wardrobe checks; then someone screams "turn over", the board is read out and the director yells "Action!" Suddenly, with all eyes on you (not to mention a camera), the pressure to get it right first time is enormous. This kind of scenario may sound extreme, but every actor will experience it.

Every production will be slightly different, but the countdown to a standard shoot (if such a thing exists) will probably be as follows.

Firstly, the audition. Remember that getting one is an achievement in itself – so make the most of it. It's hard to get seen for TV and films, and even if you don't land this job, the audition may lead to others. Nearly all castings are handled by a casting director who liaises with the agents and assembles various actors to meet the director. These castings are more like an interview than an audition, involving a brief chat followed by a reading. Arrive early, as you may find a couple of pages waiting for you at reception. Don't be surprised if you only get to read the scene a couple of times; that's quite normal and the casting director usually reads the other roles. It will probably be filmed and may only last ten minutes or so.

Having been cast, you'll be sent a script (possibly a revised draft) and a schedule. Read them both carefully. The schedule is an important document and should help to answer a lot of your questions. At the very least, it will contain a call sheet with details of where you need to be and when; most are far more detailed than that, and include cast lists, crew lists, phone numbers, maps, directions to locations, travel arrangements, health and safety regulations, etc. Check that your contact details are correct and that the dates on the schedule are the dates you were booked for. It's rare for them to be wrong, but it's always best to check as you may start work before your contract arrives. Your agent would have the original booking dates from when the company first checked your availability.

Next you'll receive several phone calls. Firstly, one from the 2nd AD or a production assistant confirming your call. If you have any questions that the schedule can't answer, this is the time to ask. For instance, if by this stage you've not received a script, mention it. They listed me as the wrong character on a schedule once and when I mentioned it to the 2nd AD, it turned out that some of the lines and my character's name had been changed. Nobody had told me and I had learnt the wrong role. Luckily, I still had time to learn the right one! Then, you'll probably get calls from someone in the Costume and Make-up departments. Depending on the scale of the production they may arrange fittings and make-up tests. Either way, make sure you know all your measurements for Costume, including hat and glove sizes. (Incidentally, it's not uncommon in TV for you not to try on your costume until you arrive for the shoot – so give them your real sizes, not the sizes you wish to be!) Also, if your hair is different from your Spotlight photo, tell them, as they might be making decisions based on it.

While waiting for your shooting day to come around, work on your script; familiarise yourself with the lines and characters. Any work you do at home that better prepares you before the shoot could prove useful, especially as less and less time is allocated for rehearsing on set. Don't forget to work on the standby scenes too; these are scenes that are held in reserve in case the schedule is changed at the last minute. They'll be on the call sheet listed as standby scenes or wet weather scenes. You'll probably then hear nothing until a day or two before you start, when they'll ring to confirm your call.

When you arrive at the unit base, the first person you'll meet will most likely be the 2nd AD who, among other things, is responsible for your whereabouts during the shoot. Make sure that they or someone else knows where you are at all times: 2nd ADs are full of stories about wandering actors bringing shoots to a grinding halt because they decided to look around a location. Remember, you'll end up looking foolish – but the 2nd AD gets the blame.

Having arrived at the unit base or the studios, and provided the shoot is running to schedule, you'll be shown to a dressing room or green room. If the schedule has been changed (it often is), you'll be taken straight to Costume and Make-up. If on location, the unit base will either be a building or various trailers and trucks. You'll probably be left on your own as most people will be shooting somewhere else, but there may be other actors around (and if on location, catering people and various drivers). However, at some point you'll be collected and taken to Costume and Make-up. First thing in the morning these places are a hive of activity, so look out for the other actors in your first scene that day. The chances are that some of them will be in make-up at the same time as you.

Depending on the size of the production, you may have your own make-up artist and your own dresser who will be responsible for your costumes. As you will end up spending a lot of time with these people, they'll be a large factor towards your enjoyment of the shoot. I know one director who judges the mood of his cast and crew by the atmosphere in the Wardrobe, Make-up and Catering trailers.

Once you are in costume and have been to Make-up, you'll probably get sent back to your dressing room or trailer. How long you spend waiting to be called will depend on how well they are sticking to the schedule ... and how you pass the time is up to you. Every actor I've met has their own way (I know of one actor who used to spend his time trying to write sitcom scripts, and ended up becoming a very successful writer). Some actors (but not all!) like to get together and run lines, which is great if you are inexperienced as it can help calm the nerves. However, the important thing to remember is that you have to be ready, so that whenever you are called to the set, you are able to do the best you can when the director yells, "Action!"

Every actor knows that work generates work. So no matter how small your role is, never forget that you've been given an opportunity many other actors would relish. I can't think of a more exciting place than a film set full of talented technicians and actors, who are all pulling together to create something. So make the most of it and enjoy it, because if you're lucky, you can work in some amazing places with some incredibly talented people.

Edward Hicks is currently Head of Film, TV and Radio at RADA – a post sponsored by Warner Bros. He has directed numerous Shorts, commercials and promos, is a graduate and former governor of LFS, has various film projects in development, and has written articles on screen acting in addition to being a regular contributor to *Actors' Yearbook*. Ed has taught at various Drama Schools including East 15, where in 2001 he created the first media-based acting course to gain NCDT accreditation. Under the name Edward Rawle-Hicks he started his professional career as a child actor (from the age of ten), appearing at the RSC, in the West End and in numerous commercials, films and television projects.

Television companies

These almost always use casting directors who, in turn, will circulate casting breakdowns to agents they trust. However, a carefully timed (and crafted) submission from an individual can occasionally excite interest.

Recorded Media

BBC network television

For more information, visit the BBC website – **www.bbc.co.uk**.

The new structure

Major restructuring, introduced by the former Director-General, Greg Dyke, resulted in the creation of five programming divisions:

- Radio and Music
- Drama, Entertainment and CBBC (Children)
- Factual and Learning
- Sport
- News

BBC Broadcast and BBC Production have been abolished. In the areas of sport, children's and education, commissioning and programme-making are now integrated. A New Media division is developing the BBC's interactive television online activities.

Television genre commissioners in drama, entertainment and features now work with the television channel controllers to strengthen the BBC's output in these areas.

The disbanding of the Independent Commissioning Group has not diminished the value the BBC now places on the contribution of independents. However, in future they will take the same commissioning routes as in-house producers.

The restructuring also gives output guarantees for in-house departments, including Nations and English Regions, and longer-term commissions to enable better planning and a greater focus on creativity.

Casting information

The BBC no longer has a central casting department. Casting advisers are appointed to each specific programme as required. Output includes: *Casualty*, *Holby City*, *Doctors*, *EastEnders*, *Born and Bred*, *The Inspector Lynley Mysteries*, *Waking the Dead*, *Judge John Deed*, *Dalziel and Pascoe*, *Silent Witness* and *Spooks*. The various programmes' casting departments will accept letters from actors previously unknown to them (with CVs, photographs and performance notices); however, actors are advised that while casting personnel are on the lookout for new talent and do attend shows, they are extremely busy and tend to use agents when casting.

The recently launched BBC Talent initiative is designed to offer 'raw talent' (actors without formal qualifications or experience) the opportunity to act their way onto a major drama. In 2003, several of the actors cast for the BBC1 drama, *The Canterbury Tales*, were winners of BBC Talent auditions. For the latest information on BBC Talent's projects, see the website – **www.bbc.co.uk/talent**.

Drama

Drama has departments in London, Birmingham and Manchester and produces a broad range of plays, serials, series and readings for TV, film, BBC Radio 3, BBC Radio 4 and BBC World service.

London
BBC Television, Wood Lane, London W12 7RJ
tel 020-8743 8000
BBC Elstree, Neptune House, Clarendon Road, Borehamwood WD6 1JF
website www.bbc.co.uk/drama
Director of Vision Jana Bennett *Director, Drama Production* Nicolas Brown *Head of Drama, BBC*

Wales Julie Gardner *Head of Series and Serials* Kate Harwood *Head of Drama Serials* Laura Mackie *Head of Drama, BBC Scotland* Anne Mensah *Head of Independent Drama* Lucy Richer *Executive Producer, EastEnders* Diederick Santer *Head of Drama, BBC Northern Ireland* Patrick Spence *Controller, BBC Fiction, BBC Vision* Jane Tranter *Creative Director, Drama* Sally Woodward Gentle *Controller, Drama Production Studios* John Yorke

Note that while most of these senior programme makers are based at Wood Lane, many BBC casting directors are based at the Elstree site. See the Casting Directors section on page 115 for more information.

Birmingham
BBC Birmingham TV Drama Village, Archibald House, 1059 Bristol Road, Selly Oak, Birmingham B29 6LT
tel 0121-432 8888
website www.bbc.co.uk/birmingham
Executive Producer Birmingham Drama Will Trotter

Manchester
New Broadcasting House, Oxford Road, Manchester M60 1SJ
tel 0161-200 2020
website www.bbc.co.uk/manchester
Executive Producer Manchester Drama Anne Mensah
Executive Producer, Radio Drama, Manchester Sue Roberts

The New Writing Initiative
BBC Writersroom, 1 Mortimer Street, London W1T 3JA
tel 020-7765 2703
email writersroom@bbc.co.uk
website www.bbc.co.uk/writersroom
Creative Director Kate Rowland *Development Manager* Paul Ashton

Entertainment
BBC Television Centre, Wood Lane, London W12 7RJ
tel 020-8743 8000
website www.bbc.co.uk/entertainment
Head of Comedy Sophie Clark-Jervoise *Head of Comedy Entertainment* Jon Plowman

Entertainment welcomes new half-hour TV situation comedy scripts, and material is reviewed by its Comedy Script Unit. Radio is also a good entry-point for new comedy writers, performers and ground-breaking innovative series such as sketch shows and panel games.

CBBC (Children)
BBC Television Centre, Wood Lane, London W12 7RJ
tel 020-8743 8000
Head of Drama Jan East *Head of Entertainment* Joe Godwin

There are opportunities for new writers in this highly competitive area. Unsolicited material is read by the department, preferably in the form of synopses of ideas. The preferred genres are contemporary comedy and drama.

Entertainment and Features, Manchester
BBC New Broadcasting House, PO Box 27, Oxford Road, Manchester M60 1SJ
tel 0161-200 2020

A bi-media department which makes programmes for both radio and TV. It is responsible for a wide range of factual, entertainment and music programming, and specialises in spotting new comedy talent; aims to see all new stand-up performers/writers in the North West. Write with details of events to Comedy Entertainment, Room 4033.

Network Production, Birmingham
BBC Birmingham, Pebble Mill Road, Birmingham B5 7QQ
tel 0121-432 8888
Editor, Radio Drama, The Archers Vanessa Whitburn

A vast range of radio and TV programming which encompasses Asian, consumer affairs, leisure, lifestyle, motoring, music and rural affairs.

BBC Northern Ireland
BBC Broadcasting House, Ormeau Avenue, Belfast BT2 8HQ
tel 028-9033 8000
website www.bbc.co.uk/ni
Entertainment and Events Mike Edgar *Head of Drama* Patrick Spence

BBC Northern Ireland produces a broad spectrum of radio and TV programmes, both for the BBC's networks and for its home audience. Output includes news and current affairs, documentaries, education, entertainment, sport, music, Irish language and religious programmes. It also has a thriving drama department which reads unsolicited scripts across all genres, i.e. single, serials, series, feature films and the short-film scheme Northern Lights, which is aimed at new talent from within Northern Ireland.

In addition to making network radio programmes, broadcasting on BBC Radio 1, 2, 3, 4, and 5 Live and BBC World Service, BBC Northern Ireland also makes programmes for its local radiolisteners.

BBC Scotland
40 Pacific Quay, Glasgow G51 1DA
tel 0141-339 8844
website www.bbc.co.uk/scotland
Head of Drama Anne Mensah

BBC Scotland is the BBC's most varied production centre outside London, providing BBC TV and radio networks and BBC World Service with pivotal drama, comedy, entertainment, children's, leisure, documentaries, religion, education, arts, music, special events news, current affairs and political coverage. Internet development is also a key element of production activity.

In addition to making network output, more than 850 hours of TV programming per year is transmitted on BBC1 Scotland and BBC2 Scotland. BBC Radio Scotland is the country's only national radio station, and is on air 18 hours a day, 7 days a week. Local programmes are also broadcast on Radio Scotland's FM frequency in the Northern Isles, and there are daily local bulletins for listeners in the Highlands, Grampian, Borders, and the southwest. BBC Radio Nan Gaidheal provides a Gaelic service on a separate FM frequency for around 40 hours a week.

The BBC offices are wheelchair accessible.

BBC Wales

BBC Broadcasting House, Llandaff, Cardiff CF5 2YQ
tel 029-203 22000
website www.bbc.co.uk/wales
Head of Drama Piers Wenger

BBC Wales provides a range of services in both English and Welsh, on radio, television and online.

The Drama department produces programmes for local and network BBC television channels and local and network radio stations. Notable recent successes of the department include *Doctor Who*, *Torchwood*, *The Sarah Jane Adventures*, *Life on Mars* and *Ashes to Ashes* for television, and the serialised and single dramas for radio, *The Wooden Overcoat*, *Investigating Mr Thomas*, and *Solo Behind the Iron Curtain*.

Casting for television

Janie Frazer

There are now many casting directors working in television, and each will have their own way of working. This is my own viewpoint and may not be shared by others, but I hope it may be helpful.

I came into casting by way of the theatre. When I was a schoolgirl I fell in love with the theatre and, being good at English, thought perhaps I could become a drama critic. However, some wise person suggested that before writing about the theatre I should work within it, and so I managed to get a job – at first unpaid, sweeping the stage and as a dresser, and subsequently as an ASM and then handling publicity for the Citizens Theatre Glasgow. I had also been involved in the big auditions held at the start of each season for the Citizens, and had come to realise that the actors were the thing that interested me most about the theatre. Subsequently I moved to London and incessantly badgered LWT for a job as a casting assistant, which finally transpired. I have worked there, through several mergers which have resulted in the company currently known as ITV, for many years. I have cast for all types of television productions; mainly drama, comedy drama and situation comedy, but also sketch comedy, factual drama, hidden camera, animation (voice-over), and various others programmes which defy definition.

Each production has its own specificity, but there are basic requirements that apply to all.

The script

This is the first principle and the foundation for everything else, even though the script may change beyond recognition during the process of getting the production to the screen. The script contains the characters, their descriptions, and the dialogue; from this, in consultation with the director and producer, I will put together a list of suggested actors for the roles.

Casting for television carries with it certain commercial considerations. The casting of the main characters is often crucial to a programme getting commissioned in the first place, since in commercial television the advertisers need to be assured of getting a specific audience for the programmes around and within which they buy advertising space. This is the reason for the often-heard grumble that the same well-known faces crop up again and again, and the reason for it is that they have good form – i.e., the programmes they appear in produce good viewing figures, which is what both ITV and the BBC are striving to maintain.

Beyond the 'name' casting, the casting for other roles involves interpreting the director's vision, style, ideas and the tone of the piece to come up with suggestions that will best express the way in which the director wants to portray the material. Therefore, the same script may elicit different suggestions from me, according to the individual director.

Suggestions for actors

How do I arrive at these? I have many lists, and many files, sorted in an idiosyncratic fashion over the years and added to constantly after seeing actors' work on stage and screen. Also there is *Spotlight*, which is the casting director's invaluable and indispensable tool. If there was only one piece of advice I could offer to an actor, it would be to appear in *Spotlight*, and to keep one's entry accurate and up to date. I now use *Spotlight* almost exclusively via the Internet, as the information contained on the website is wonderfully comprehensive and well organised, and allows me to do cross-reference searching (e.g. for a 30-year-old Punjabi speaker with a Manchester accent) which is extremely swift and useful. The information contained on the site does however rely entirely on the input of the actors who subscribe to *Spotlight*, and it is therefore very important that actors keep their credits and personal details current.

Also and most importantly, their photographs. To state the crashingly obvious, television is a visual medium. It's vital that an actor's photograph is up to date and actually looks like them. Vanity should not be the issue, as television requires all types and ages to be portrayed; moreover, an inaccurate photograph can be misleading and time-wasting. The Spotlight's website has now progressed to offer audio and video clips of each actor, and I have found that these can be really useful to play to a director when discussing casting. Therefore, I would strongly recommend that actors make full use of all the opportunities offered by *Spotlight* to show their wares.

Via the Spotlight Link I am also able to send out a breakdown of characters to the agents, who then relay back their suggestions, which I can order, prioritise and follow up. I will discuss with the director and producer the various suggestions we have made between us, and those that have come from agents; I will then arrange casting sessions for the various roles.

Getting in touch

I would love to be able to say that receiving letters with photos and CVs, or emails with all those attachments, is always a boon – but I'm afraid it's not usually the case. More useful is to be notified of actors' forthcoming performances: even if it's not always possible to cover these, it's good to know what work you are doing, and one may ask other casting directors if they have seen you in the piece.

Showreels on VHS/CD can be useful to view as examples of an actor's work, but tend not to be so significant if they arrive unsolicited – there are simply not enough hours in the day to watch everything that is sent in. I find I am most likely to watch them if they are directly relevant to a current project (for instance, if I am looking for young Northern actors, or working on a sketch comedy show, I will select to watch those that might fall into the relevant categories).

When you are called for audition

Almost invariably now, casting sessions for television dramas and comedy are video-taped. This allows for greater scrutiny of the actor, and assessment of their presence on screen away from the social context of the audition. It does not mean that the actor has had to produce a flawless reading, but many things emerge from watching an actor on screen which may have been missed during the live reading. The camera is sensitive to minute changes in thought-processes and expression as the actor is being filmed in close-up; this is something the actor needs to bear in mind during a television casting audition – that the performance will be watched at close hand, and therefore a loud voice and large expressions will convey considerable impact which may need to be scaled down.

Whatever an actor's looks, the most important feature on screen is the eyes. The people casting the programme need to see yours. Therefore, it will help enormously if you are able to absorb, familiarise yourself with, or best of all learn the scene so that you are able to raise your eyes from the script. Almost all 'sides' or scenes for reading will have been emailed to your agent or yourself prior to audition. Make sure you have an email address. Acquaint yourself with script formats such as Final Draft (at the time of writing, a free download for viewing scripts in Final Draft format is available from the website **www.finaldraft.com**). If you wear glasses, print the scene in a large font so that you can still read it if at the casting they would prefer to see you without glasses.

Other basic things to bear in mind are to arrive on time; make sure you know the specific whereabouts of the casting venue, and how long it is likely to take you to get there. You may be unavoidably kept waiting, in which case make sure you let the casting director know if you have another appointment you need to get to. If you can, do some prior research, both about the project, and also about the producer and director of the programme. You can find out about their previous work via the IMDb website, **www.imdb.com** – and since they will after all be looking at your CV, they may be impressed and flattered if you also know something about theirs.

Spend some time thinking about the material you've seen, so you have something to say about it. Many actors would be surprised at how much their observations have contributed to the final version of the script. In television as in film, time is money. Pre-production periods have been reduced to the minimum, which means that there is often very little time for rehearsal once shooting begins. Directors often therefore use the casting process to try out ways in which they would like to scenes to play – this can be rewarding for the actor, and useful even if they do not finally land the part; often directors keep their interview lists and bear actors in mind whom they've liked but who haven't been quite right for the part in question.

If you look good, I look good

Sometimes actors view casting interviews as an exam, or as some sort of test they have to pass. However, there is at least one person in the room who is completely on your side – the casting director. The casting director's reputation relies on the calibre of the actors invited for interview, and if the actors aren't up to it then the casting director is the one who's on the line. Therefore, by getting you in for audition, the casting director is demonstrating faith in your ability and rightness for the part.

Know your value

Everyone has their own USP – their unique selling point. Even if you are Mr/s Ordinary, then that's it. It's valuable. Get to know what it is that is most intriguing about you, and play to your strengths. Ask your colleagues for constructive criticism and listen to it. Emphasise your strengths and don't pretend to be what you are not. Whereas the theatre can thrive on disguise and artifice, the camera takes no hostages and is ruthless in its exposure.

Did you get it?

If you got the part, then congratulations! But an actor is often confused as well as disappointed about not getting a part. They will ask: should I have done it like this, dressed like that, what did I do wrong? It's hard to explain to an actor that the choice is not dependent on something they did or didn't do, but often is the result of someone else being more right for the part than they are. This is a nebulous assessment which I can appreciate is very unsatisfactory to hear, but it is nevertheless the truth. Those actors who have ever been on the other side of the casting process often remark how they now understand what this means, but it doesn't help much with the feeling of frustration. One can only suggest that by the law of averages, eventually the part will come up for which you are the most right; that you've done pretty well to get the interview in the first place; that the director may well have clocked you for the future – and that the whole experience stands you in good stead.

Janie Frazer worked for the Citizens Theatre Glasgow and the Bristol Old Vic before joining LWT's Casting Department, where she worked as a casting assistant before becoming a casting director in her own right in 1994. She has cast single dramas, drama series, continuing drama, factual drama, comedy drama, situation comedy, single comedy, sketch comedy and animation series. She is also currently the London-based casting director for *Coronation Street*.

Independent television

ITV (**www.itv.com**) is the biggest commercial television network in the UK. It is made up of a network of 15 different regional licences, each with its own set of obligations and conditions designed to reflect the particular character of their region and the interests of their viewers. ITV plc (**www.itvplc.com**) owns 12 of the ITV licences; the remainder are owned by SMG, Ulster, and Channel.

ITV1 is the most popular commercial television channel in Britain. Watched on average by 45 million people every week, it has the largest programme budget of any commercial channel in Europe. Network programmes are commissioned by the ITV network controllers purely on merit. At least 25 per cent of programmes shown on ITV1 each year come from independent producers. Regional programmes are commissioned by each regional company.

Note Neither Channel 4 nor Channel 5 make any of their own programmes, so do not have casting departments.

Channel Television

The Television Centre, St Helier, Jersey JE1 3ZD
tel (01534) 816816 *fax* (01534) 816777
website www.channelonline.tv

Provides programmes for the Channel Islands during the whole week, relating mainly to Channel Islands news, events and current affairs. Does not produce any in-house drama.

Grampian Television

Television Centre, Craigshaw Business Park,
West Tullos, Aberdeen AB12 3QH
tel (01224) 848848
Harbour Chambers, Dock Street, Dundee DD1 3HW
tel (01382) 591000 *fax* (01382) 591010
23-25 Huntly Street, Inverness IV3 5PR
tel (01463) 242624
website www.grampiantv.co.uk

Provides programmes for North Scotland during the whole week.

ITV Anglia

Anglia House, Norwich NR1 3JG
tel (01603) 615151 *fax* (01603) 631032
website www.itvregions.com/Anglia

Provides programmes for the East of England, daytime discussion programmes, documentaries and factual programmes for UK and international broadcasters. Does not produce any in-house drama.

ITV Border

The Television Centre, Carlisle CA1 3NT
website www.itvregions.com/Border

Provides programmes for Cumbria, the Borders and the Isle of Man during the whole week.

ITV Central

Gas Street, Birmingham B1 2JT
tel 0121-643 9898 *fax* 0121-643 4897
website www.itvregions.com/Central

Provides ITV programmes for the East, West and South Midlands every day.

ITV Granada

Granada Television Centre, Manchester M60 9EA
tel 0161-832 7211
email casting@itv.com
website www.itvregions.com/Granada
Casting Director, Coronation Street Gennie Radcliffe
Casting Director June West

The ITV franchise holder for the North West of England. Produces programmes across a broad range for both its region and the ITV network.

Welcomes submissions (with CVs and photographs) from actors previously unknown to the company sent by post or email. As the Casting Department is extremely busy, it cannot guarantee to respond to all submissions. Advises actors to call to find out what projects are being cast, and to send in their details as and when appropriate.

ITV London

South Bank, London SE1 9LT
tel 020-7261 3338
email david.wheal@itv.com
Casting Director Janie Frazer *Asst Casting Director* Stephanie Dawes *Casting Assistant* David Wheal

ITV Productions/Granada produces programmes primarily for the ITV network, but also for other channels such as BBC1, BBC2, BBC3, C4, C5 and Sky.

Unsolicited photos and CVs from actors are not especially encouraged, but advance notification of stage or screen performances is welcomed.

ITV Meridian

Forum One, Solent Business Park, Whiteley, Hants PO15 7PA
tel (08448) 812000
website www.itvlocal.com

The ITV franchise-holder for the South and South East coast of England. Does not produce any in-house drama.

ITV Tyne Tees

Television House, The Watermark, Gateshead, Tyne and Wear NE11 9SZ
tel 0191-404 8700
website www.itvregions.com/Tyne_Tees

Broadcasts to the North of England 7 days a week, 24 hours a day.

ITV Wales

ITV Wales, The Television Centre, Culverhouse Cross, Cardiff CF5 6XJ
tel 029-2059 0590
website www.itvregions.com/Wales

Provides programmes for Wales during the whole week. Produces programmes for home and international sales.

ITV West

Television Centre, Bath Road, Bristol BS4 3HG
tel 0117-972 2722 *fax* 0117-971 7685
website www.itvregions.com/west

Produces programmes for the West of England and for use across the ITV network. Also runs the ITV West Television Workshop, aimed at young people (up to 26) to offer experience in the performance and production skills required for TV, film, theatre and radio. See **www.itvworkshop.co.uk** for more information.

ITV Westcountry

Langage Science Park, Plymouth PL7 5BQ
tel (01752) 333333 *fax* (01752) 333444
website www.itvregions.com/Westcountry

Provides programmes for South West England throughout the week. In-house production is mainly news, sport, and regional current affairs; other regional features are commissioned from independent producers.

ITV Yorkshire (YTV)

The Television Centre, Leeds LS3 1JS
tel 0113-243 8283 *fax* 0113-244 5107
website www.itvregions.com/Yorkshire
Casting Director Sue Jackson *Assistant Casting Director* Faye Styring

Established in 1968, YTV is one of the biggest ITV companies. Following the new Communications Act and the merger of Granada and Carlton, it is part of the new single ITV plc which began life on 2nd February 2004.

YTV continues to produce a range of drama and light entertainment programmes, including: *A Touch of Frost*; *Emmerdale* (shown on the network every weekday night); and *Heartbeat* – ITV1's most popular long-running drama series. In 2003 a new sister programme, *The Royal*, attracted 11.3 million viewers and a 41.3% share of the television audience. In addition to its drama series, YTV has made a number of one-off dramas for the ITV network, including: *Booze Cruise* and *Brides in the Bath*. With an audience of 9.7 million viewers and a 44% audience share, *Booze Cruise* ranked as the best performing Single Drama from any channel for the whole of 2003.

The Casting Department generally works through agents, but will accept submissions (with CVs and photographs) from actors previously unknown to the company if sent by post. As the Department is very busy it cannot guarantee to acknowledge all submissions, but advises actors to enclose an sae for a quicker response. Prefers not to be contacted by telephone or email.

London Weekend Television (LWT)

See entry for ITV London on page 331.

SMG TV Productions Ltd (formerly Scottish Television)

Pacific Quay, Glasgow G51 1PQ
tel 0141-300 3000
website www.smgproductions.tv
Head of Drama Eric Coulter

Network television production arm of SMG plc, incorporating London-based Ginger Productions. It's client list includes all terrestrial networks and major satellite and cable channels. Output includes drama, factual/factual entertainment, entertainment and children's programming.

The Drama Department has more than 20 years' experience of producing network drama for ITV1. Credits include: *Taggart*; *Dr Finlay*; *Rebus* and *Goodbye Mr Chips*. The Drama team is based at the SMG Productions offices in Glasgow. Casting procedures differ from project to project; generally uses independent casting directors, but also accepts letters from actors 'on spec' (with CVs and photographs). Where appropriate these will be passed on to a relevant programme or project.

UTV

Havelock House, Ormeau Road, Belfast, Northern Ireland BT7 1EB
tel 028-9032 8122 *fax* 028-9024 6695
email info@u.tv
website www.u.tv/television

Provides programmes for Northern Ireland. All drama is produced by the ITV network.

Working in a soap

Susan Penhaligon

I had never been in a soap. When I started back in the seventies, doing a soap was seen to be a bit down market and selling out. If you wanted to be considered a 'serious actor' you avoided them like the plague – a bit grand maybe, but that was the perceived wisdom then. Now, all that has changed. With the nature of TV – reality shows, multi channel choices, repeats - most actors today would be very happy to get a few episodes or even a long term engagement on a prime time terrestrial channel performing in front of an audience of ten million. For an established actor like me, it's a chance to let everyone know I'm not dead! And for a young actor it can be a fantastic way of upping your profile and introducing yourself (let alone earning some money to put in the bank) so when the call came for me to get on the train to Leeds to audition for *Emmerdale* I was both delighted and very nervous. I was lucky and got the part and a six month contract which was then extended for another six months. The work process was completely new to me and after thirty years in the business it was a challenge. My observations are obviously personal and about *Emmerdale*. Another actor might have a different view, but hopefully they will be useful to you.

Auditioning often means you have to travel to either Leeds or Manchester, or if it's *Eastenders*, to Elstree. Make sure you arrive on time. This is very important as it tells the casting director you are punctual and reliable (very important for soap schedules). I went by train to Leeds which allowed me to look at the script on the way up.

Do try to learn the scenes they send you and to go in with confidence, different actors have different methods, I convince myself I don't want the job, apparently producers and directors feel uneasy if someone is needy and desperate! Sometimes you are handed the script when you arrive so try and get there early to pick up the pages, take them away and learn as much as you can. This shows you can learn lines quickly, a useful tool for soap acting. Often, if it's going to be a long-term contract, they will give you an emotional scene and a funny scene and it can be hard to do without preparation. I focus on the lines and the emotion, trying to make the lines come off the page, but don't be surprised if you come away thinking you've done badly. Its part of the process. If you get the part, the ability to learn quickly and focus emotion without much discussion will be very handy.

Don't worry about accommodation. Most TV companies have lists of hotels and B&Bs for your initial weeks. If you are going to be a long term character you might want to rent a flat or, after you get settled, share with another actor. At the *Emmerdale* studios there is a notice board outside the actors' Green Room where people advertise rooms and flat sharing.

I found most of the regulars on *Emmerdale* had moved within commuting distance and had families. This can make you feel a bit lonely. After a day's work they go back to their cosy homes while you sit in a hotel room. But the young actors on the show had a great social life and I found most people to be extremely friendly and welcoming. Given time, you find a life for yourself. It's a help if you know friends in the area you can visit who are not in the show, so you can debrief. It's not a good idea to let off steam with people you are working with. Tread carefully to begin with. Keep your own counsel.

A word of warning: when I was in *Emmerdale*, the way expenses were paid was changed after much consultation between Equity and management. The result was that individual expenses are now paid on top of your fee. The flat-rate expenses for everyone became redundant. Your agent needs to sort this out for you. Also I found that the expenses were sent a few weeks after I had to pay my rent, so be prepared to have those funds available or have your agent arrange an advance.

You will probably be asked to go on a costume trip with the costume supervisor before you start. I would advise that you have a good idea of how you would like the character to look, particularly if you are on a long contract, as the bulk of your wardrobe will be bought at the beginning (obviously if you are involved in a wedding scene or special occasion, another shopping trip will be done). In fact I would go as far as having a chat with the producer about how you see the character and what they have planned for you.

A good producer will suggest that you go to them if you have any problems. Be bold about doing this, it's important. I foolishly didn't clarify some issues I had, and for me there was always a grey area about where my character came from, what social band she belonged to and how she fitted in with the three main regulars – the family she joined. *And* I never discussed with the producer what kind of clothes she wore.

This also goes for later on, when you might feel strongly about a speech change or story line you're not sure about. The names and extension numbers of the script editors are in the Green Room and they don't mind if you ring to discuss any lines you feel don't work.

The layout of the *Emmerdale* studios is a bit like a factory! The management are on top, the workers are on the shop floor, so it's easy to get to see someone. I'm sure it's true for the other soaps.

I have to say that my first day passed in a flurry of nerves, meeting people, attempting to remember names, constantly changing costume and trying to figure out which camera was on me. Most of the soaps do what they call a multi camera set up, i.e. you have four cameras recording the scene at the same time. If this is a new experience for you, it can be a bit nerve-wracking – but don't worry. Actually you don't have to know which camera is on you, and if the director needs you to be aware for whatever reason, he will make a point of telling you on the appropriate line. Eventually it becomes like second nature; you kind of see the red light going on in the corner of your eye and it won't throw you. On location you will only have at most, two cameras – it's easier.

In the studio, which is more like a warehouse, the different sets are lined up side by side. This is very confusing for a beginner, and it's easy to get lost. Even after a year, I could still be found wandering aimlessly around muttering, "Where's the Woolpack?" Try not to feel a fool just because the long-termers know exactly where they are going. I used to follow the herd, but sometimes ended up in the wrong set! The runners (or third assistant directors), who give you the morning calls, will tell you the number of the next scene and come and get you when you are needed on set. They are wonderful. They're young and keen; anything you need to know – ask them.

Emmerdale does three blocks of four scripts every fortnight. You may be involved in four or five episodes, but no more than eight, over two blocks. Each block has its own crew, A/Ds and director. There are three units working at all times, but you will only be involved with two units. One unit is usually out at the *Emmerdale* village, the other in the studio and during the day you will be taxied between the two. Most soaps do between 20 and 30 scenes a day (*Emmerdale* tries to do 38). You won't be involved in all those scenes, but you could do up to 20.

Your scenes will be out of sequence and in different blocks, so you might be changing your costume from scene to scene (when you start, it's best to ask the costume department after each scene if you need to change). This sounds simple, but I found that when I had a lot to do, the speed at which you finish a scene, rush back to your dressing room, change and then rush back to the studio can be very confusing at first. The costume department will choose your clothes for the scenes and are on the ball with continuity. They are usually willing to bring you something else out of your wardrobe if you are unhappy, but generally it's best to wear what they have chosen for you; otherwise you can spend the whole day discussing or even arguing, and it's not worth it.

I did find the make up, costume department, production team and crew amazing. They worked the longest hours of anybody, with professionalism and good humour. And the latter is one of the essential ingredients to creating a happy work atmosphere. Particularly in the hot house environment of a soap!

This brings me on to another important problem: how to divide your script up. I found that every actor had their own method. Some of them had large folders with each filming day, date and episode cross-referenced with the director's name and a short break-down of the story order. (People called the blocks by the director's name.)

I found my own way, which was to put the scenes together in a daily shooting order with the day and date at the top. I made sure I read the episode thoroughly before I split it up, hoping I would remember the story order on the set. I did come a cropper once, forgetting that in a scene I had shot the week before I was tearful and vengeful, only to be too sunny and smiley in the following scene. A pitfall of shooting out of sequence. Some of the directors are very good at reminding you of the story order. The regulars seem to have an uncanny ability to make every scene work as well as it can with the minimal amount of effort and worry about story order.

The changing nature of soap story lines has no logic. To begin with it's frustrating, particularly if you've been lucky enough to work in an environment where all the right questions are asked about your character's motivations and behaviour. I advise you to give all that up; there just isn't time. A soap is about narrative, so your lines are taking the story forward (not necessarily revealing anything about your character). This is why people are always seen in the same sort of costume or hat – it identifies them (if you start off carrying a dog you'll probably carry the dog in every scene!).

Unlike a play, or an episode of *Casualty*, there is no beginning, middle and end. You step onto the roller-coaster and you go with it until you leave. I found if you play the emotion in the scene for what it is, as real and as truthfully as possible, without thinking about what has happened to the character in the past or what's coming up in the future, it saves you a lot of angst and time trying to talk to the director about your motivation while the first assistant is looking at her watch, making, 'got to GET ON' noises. The shooting schedules are such that directors rarely have time to discuss the scenes in depth (although there are exceptions) and a lot of the time the scenes can't take too much analysing.

Obviously if the only line you have all week is, "Pull us another pint, Val," then there's not much you can do except arrive on time, be friendly, have a laugh and know your words.

If you have a short stint in the soap then you might only work with one director, but if it's a year or so you can work with a lot more. I found this to be the single most confusing part of being in a soap. After years of working on productions where you build a relationship with a director, acknowledging that they are team leader, taking notes from them, trying to collectively put their vision on the stage or screen, I discovered that in a soap this is all topsy turvy. Directors come and go. They do a block at a time, which will involve three or four story lines, then go away to edit while the story machine rolls on with another director. There are often first-time directors and you will know more about your character than they do. If a director has been away for six months on other jobs, they can't possibly catch up on all the story lines – so you end up explaining that no, you can't get in the car and drive out of the village because two episodes ago you lost your licence. Having said that, I worked with some very good directors who did a lot of other TV work, so it's best you understand that they can be as frustrated as you. For both of you it's the nature of the format that describes your working methods.

A typical day would be getting up at 6am, either driving yourself to the studio or paying for a taxi (if you are on location, a studio car will pick you up). You arrive in your dressing room to put on costume, then into make up to be ready on set for 8am. You might work through the day until 7pm (not necessarily in every scene). So you wait either in your dressing room or in the Green Room to be called. The A/Ds don't like you to leave the building or location. Such is the nature of schedules that you can have one scene first thing in the morning and five more starting at 6pm – be prepared for this. I used to take a book; some actors spend the time learning their lines. I always preferred to learn my lines the night before, even if I got in late. And a word on learning: don't over learn, it's not like a play. And learn to learn quickly. It's quite possible that you could be given a new piece of script just before going into the studio ... this happens, and there are always rewrites. Don't feel bad about drying on set either. Everyone does it. Obviously if you dry all the time people will get fed up with you. But I discovered that fluffing and drying is very much part of a day's work.

More than likely you will have blocks out when you can get home. I had a month out when I came back from Leeds to London. On top of that you are entitled to two weeks' holiday a year. At Emmerdale the blocks are posted up on a notice board with the episode numbers running along the top and the characters names involved down the side, so you can have some idea of your work pattern. But, not only did I need a degree to understand this schedule, I also found that it changed, so don't take it as gospel. There is always a friendly soul nearby to explain everything to you but don't expect to be told. Ask, ask, ask would be my motto. *Nobody sits you down and says this is how it all works.* Including when the canteen opens and shuts. Find out to avoid disappointment! (The canteen is subsidised, by the way, so really OK food is very cheap.)

Although most people know how to behave, just a little word. Too much ego is frowned on. Without losing your own identity, it's common sense that you should acknowledge there are actors who have been doing the show much longer than you. A modicum of humility is appreciated, along with a bit of respect. They will respect you in return. Being able to laugh or make people laugh is at a premium. I had a day when I had 18 scenes and by mid-afternoon I couldn't remember my own name. So a bit of banter relieves the pressure.

Believe me, it's hard work doing a soap. It's not a doddle, like a friend of mine suggested. The days can be long with a lot of scenes to remember, or very tedious, when you have little or no story line and you are needed for a non-speaking background appearance. You can be playing high emotions one minute and a lighter moment the next, and there is very little feedback apart from 'that's fine, next scene'. There's no audience to clap you and producers are busy people, so they can't be on the studio floor the whole time telling actors how good they are. don't expect it. If it happens, and it can, be happy. I found that it was the other actors who encouraged me. They were kind and supportive, a lovely crowd.

Now, there is that thing called FAME. After about six months, depending on your story lines and the success of your character, you will be noticing people looking oddly at you on the train, or someone comes up and says, "Didn't I meet you on holiday in The Himalayas last year?" Six months on and the general public think they know you. They'll call you by your soap name, ask for your autograph and generally be pleased to see you.

Along with all this good feeling comes publicity. If you are young and good looking, the soap publicity machine will want to use you. It's part of the job – but if you feel adamant that you don't want the readers of *Heat* magazine to know what underpants you wear, then don't do it. I personally think there is a way of doing the publicity while keeping your private life intact, but be careful. If you become a successful soap actor you have to watch your back. There will always be a photographer when you least expect it, or a member of the public will snap you staggering legless out of a club. There is nothing wrong with getting your name known; the problem with a soap is that you become known as your character. That's ok if you are happy to stay in the show for as long as they'll have you, but if you have ambitions to play other parts, it can take time to erase the memory of the character you played. Of course there are some actors who come out of soaps and do very well. But there are more young actors who seem to fall by the wayside. And some, sadly, hardly work at all. If you do go down the celebrity route, I would say go for it big time. Make sure your *own name* is printed large in the paper and in people's minds.

And please, please don't believe your own publicity. It's a fickle game. If it's decided that your character has run its course, they will write you out and the publicity stops. So keep your feet on the ground, however famous the attention makes you feel.

And there's something else. If you are good in your part and show you are serious about the process of acting, people take notice; the word goes around. You can be in a soap and still be rated as a good actor. Sometimes you'll get the chance to play a well-written scene with substance so you can show what you're made of. I found that the actors in *Emmerdale* worked hard to keep the standard of acting high, sometimes against all odds. They cared about it and wanted it to do well in the ratings.

I had a wonderful year and I learnt a lot. That's very satisfying when you've been working for as long as I have.

Susan Penhaligon's first appearance in theatre was playing Juliet in *Romeo ond Juliet* at the Connaught Theatre, Worthing. Since then stage appearances include two seasons with the Royal Exchange Theatre (Manchester) and parts in productions at the Nuffield Theatre (Southampton), Birmingham Rep and the Palace Theatre (Watford). In the West End her appearances include Natasha in *The Three Sisters*, a leading role in Richard Harris' *The Maintenance Men,* and Annie in *The Real Thing*. She has appeared many times on television; early work included *The Taming of the Shrew, Doctor Who, Upstairs Downstairs, Tales of the Unexpected* and *Dracula* with Louis Jordan. She is best known to viewers as Pru in *Bouquet of Barbed Wire* and as Judi Dench's sister in *A Fine Romance*. Among other film parts Susan played Mae Rose Cottage in the movie of *Under Milk Wood* and appeared in Paul Verhoven's film *Survival Run*. She has published her first collection of poems in collaboration with Sara Kestelman, called *Two Hander* (Do-Not Press).

The world of children's television

Iain Lauchlan

What are the special skills you need for this murky world of children's TV? Well, to answer that I would have to divide my reply into three sections: children's drama, children's presenting, and animation voice-over work.

Children's drama has to be tackled like an adult drama. You have to commit to the part, find and play the truth of the part and be sure to play the relationships with the other characters in a believable and truthful way. Children are not a separate race; they are just like little adults with less experience. They tend to like the same things – good quality storytelling and characters that entertain.

Children's drama is like any other kind of drama. You need to be able to act, audition well and be handy with a pen and paper to write to the producers and commissioning editors. There is so little drama done for children that you need to be sending letters to these people constantly, as they need to be reminded of your existence. The truth of the matter is that there is no money around for big children's drama productions anymore: as a result the producers never get to know many actors, so you need to keep writing to them.

There is a move to increase the drama output by the BBC and by Channel 5 for children, so hopefully the possibility of doing a drama may increase.

Children's presenting is another story altogether. Not every actor can present ... it's a different skill. Some actors master it easily, and some have great difficulty. If you are an actor that likes pantomime and enjoys breaking the fourth wall to contact the audience directly, then the chances are you will enjoy presenting.

Finally the voice-over artiste. There are many opportunities in this field, as voices are always required for animation characters, puppet characters and costume characters.

As an actor it can be a very enjoyable experience exploring what your voice can do. I often get voice CDs sent to me that only explore the different accents that an actor can do, but it is important to explore the different qualities of voice you can achieve, because these are the artistes that get the work.

You must explore how high a voice you can sustain, how low you can go, how odd you can make it. Where in your mouth, throat or nose you can place the voice so that you can switch voices when asked to in a session.

I find that if you study pictures of characters from children's books and give them the voice you think suits them, then you can begin to expand the limits you have set on your voice. It will amaze you the different qualities of voice you can achieve without falling back on accents.

There are many animations made every year in this country and they all need voices. Once you have settled on some crazy voices as well as a selection of normal ones, then get them down on a clear CD. Not a tape done in your living room, as these are painful to listen to when you are searching regularly. And get them out there. Send them to everyone. Tell people you exist and that you have a very useful collection of voices.

Here are three 'C's which are important to remember when acting presenting and performing voices for children– whether it is in the theatre, recording studio or in a TV studio… **Commitment, Contact and Communication.**

Firstly you must **commit** to whatever age range you are presenting to or acting for. This means getting to know your audience, whether it be pre-school, 7-10 year olds, 10-12 year olds, or teenagers. Each age range needs to be spoken to in a way that is not condescending, that is truthful and that seems to treat them as older than they are. All children are aspirational and will only engage with a presenter, actor or programme if they feel that it caters for older children as well.

Contact is the most important aspect of presenting and acting. Particularly presenting. You have to commit to the audience and let your performance either cross the footlights or drive its way down the lens of the camera to contact and connect with your young audience. Many actors are more comfortable with their performance staying within the fourth wall and allowing the audience to have a passive experience enjoying the relationships, together with the twists and turns in the plot.

Presenters must contact the audience directly and have a dialogue with them. The experience must be an active one from the audience's point of view, and is a commitment by the presenter to the audience with a similar commitment back to the presenter. If I can mention the actor in the pantomime again, this is a half-way house for a character like Idle Jack. Although he is playing a character and telling a story, his performance will not be complete until he has an audience and builds a rapport with them. The audience is the final member of the cast. This is also true for a presenter.

If you are performing with others on stage then the process of communication must be an imaginary triangle that begins with you and travels to the other presenter via the audience. This is just as important if you are having a dialogue on stage between two presenters. It is essential that you have contact with your audience at all times. This contact is most important when presenting to a pre-school audience. There must be a trust, a respect and an entertaining rapport built up that should never falter.

Communication is therefore a key factor in performing to children. If you are not communicating – be it dialogue, a song or a comedy routine – then the audience will not be engaged and will get bored. They will either chat if they are in a theatre, or walk away from the screen if they are in a cinema. Children will give a very honest response.

If you feel that you are one of those actors that could be a successful presenter, then how do you break into the world of children's television?

There are many types of children's programming, like animations, live action with costume characters, live action with presenters, documentaries, game shows and magazine programmes. Some of them do not require presenters, but others do – and ask presenters to offer information, facts, link songs and comedy routines. Experience as an actor will come in very useful when required to do these things and should be played up when writing for work. Time spent as a Holiday Camp host is also invaluable; you experience at first hand the reaction children have to you and to your material. When I audition for presenters or costume characters, I often see Red Coats.

How do they know I exist?

It is the old story here yet again. You must write to the producers who make children's programmes and tell them you exist. This will be all of the major children's broadcasters like BBC, ITV, Channel 5 and Nickelodeon, plus many of the Independent Production Companies that now produce a large percentage of children's programming for the above broadcasters.

You must tell them you are around and what you are capable of and keep telling them. Every time they are casting for their latest production your letter must be on their desk, otherwise they will not think about you. A good clear CV with relevant information including your height, age, weight, experience and skills, together with a professional looking letter showing clearly your contact details and a good, truthful photograph, is all that is required. I am not a great lover of showreels as they often show the limitations of the artist rather than their true capabilities. They are also way too expensive to produce.

Yes, there is a children's TV world out there, and it is possible to break into it. The advice you must keep in mind at all times is this: make sure that people know about you and what you can do. Don't just tell them – *keep* telling them.

Start collecting a list of production companies and who runs them. They keep changing, so keep up to date with them. *Contacts* should be able to provide you with the broadcasters information, and PACT should have a list of Independent Producers. Good luck!

Iain Lauchlan has been involved with children's television since 1980, when he fell into being a presenter on *Playschool* which he did regularly for eight years. During this time he also presented *Fingermouse* and a selection of children's radio programmes. Iain then ran his own company, which created children's programmes such as *The Tweenies, Boo, BB3B* and latterly *Jim Jam and Sunny*. During most of this time he has tried to keep his 'acting' career going, which is a challenge if you make it as a presenter. The most important thing he has learned is to make sure people know you exist.

Independent film, video and TV production companies

Companies in this field start up and close down all the time, and it is very important to have a proper contract if offered work with an independent. If in doubt, check with Equity.

Absolutely Productions

Alhambra House, 27-31 Charing Cross Road,
London WC2H 0AU
tel 020-7930 3113 *fax* 020-7930 4114
email info@absolutely-uk.com
website www.absolutely-uk.com
Managing Director Miles Bullough

Founded in 1988. Produces drama and comedy for cinema and TV, and TV entertainment programmes. Recent credits include: *Dead Air* (C4), and *Skin and Blister* (short film).

Actaeon Films Ltd

50 Gracefield Gardens, London, SW16 2ST
tel 020-8769 3339 *fax* 0870-134 7980
email info@actaeonfilms.com
website www.actaeonfilms.com
Company Director/Producer Daniel Cormack *Producer* Matt Gunner *Head of Development* Becky Connell

Production details

A London-based production company established in 2004 to develop and produce theatrical motion pictures, both drama and comedy. Recent productions include: the Tiscali Award-winning *Amelia and Michael* (35mm, 2007) starring Anthony Head; the UK Film Council completion-funded *A Fitting Tribute* (HD/Super 8mm, 2007); and the micro-short comedy *Nightwalking* (HD, 2008) starring Raquel Cassidy.

Casting procedures

Uses freelance casting directors and publishes casting breakdowns in *PCR*. Offers PACT/Equity approved contracts and does not subscribe to the Equity Pension Scheme. Actively encourages applications from disabled actors and promotes the use of inclusive casting. "We welcome invitations to showcases, screenings and theatrical productions and will view showreels, but we don't advise sending CVs/headshots unless in relevant response to a current casting call."

Anglo-Fortunato Films Ltd

170 Popes Lane, London W5 4NJ
tel 020-8932 7676 *fax* 020-8932 7491
email anglofortunato@aol.com
Contact Luciano Celentino (Managing Director)

Produces action drama, comedy and psychological thrillers. Offers Equity approved contracts and does not subscribe the the Equity Pension Scheme. Actively encourages applications from disabled actors.

APT Films

APT Films, Ealing Studios, Ealing Green,
London W5 5EP
tel 020-8280 9125 *fax* 020-8280 9111
email admin@aptfilms.com
website www.aptfilms.com
Managing Director Jonny Persey, *Director* Paul Morrison, *Producers* Stewart le Marechal, Al Morrow

Enterprise dedicated to the development and production of feature films for national and international audiences. Also produces short films. The company has a number of feature films in development.

Recent credits include: *Deep Water, Wondrous Oblivion* and *Soloman & Gaenor*. Upcoming work includes: *Heavy Load* and *The Pied Piper of Hutzovina*.

The Ashford Entertainment Corporation Ltd

20 The Chase, Coulsdon, Surrey CR5 2EG
tel 020 8660 9609 *fax* 0870 166 4142
email info@ashford-entertainment.co.uk
website www.ashford-entertainment.co.uk
Managing Director Frazer Ashford

The Ashford Entertainment Corporation Ltd was established in 1996 by producer Frazer Ashford with the aim of developing film and television programming for the international marketplace. The company is also the major shareholder in The Reel Thing Ltd, a UK-based corporate television and events company.

Avalon Television Ltd

4A Exmoor Street, London W10 6BD
tel 020-7598 7280 *fax* 020-7598 7300
website www.avalonuk.com
Directors Jon Thoday, Richard Allen-Turner, Sally Debonnaire

Production details

TV, film and radio company producing drama, comedy and documentaries. Recent credits include:

The Frank Skinner Show, Shane, Harry Hill's TV Burp, and The Sketch Show.

Casting procedures

Always casts through freelance casting directors and does not issue public casting breakdowns. Does not welcome unsolicited contact of any kind from actors previously unknown to the company. Offers Equity approved contracts.

Bentley Productions

Pinewood Studios, Pinewood Road, Iver,
Bucks SL0 ONH
tel (01753) 656594 fax (01753) 652638
website www.all3media.com/companies/bentley.html
Managing Director Brian True-May

Specialises in high-quality drama, and has completed productions for both ITV1 and BBC1, including Midsomer Murders. Bentley followed the success of Midsomer Murders with an action thriller for ITV1, Ultimate Force.

Big Bear Films

36 Courtnell Street, London W2 5BX
tel 020-7229 5982 fax 020-7221 0767
email office@bigbearfilms.co.uk
website www.bigbearfilms.co.uk
Producer/Directors Marcus Mortimer and John Stroud Head of Development Suzi McIntosh

Established in 1998. Makes comedy, drama, and factual entertainment programmes for all networks. Recent productions include: My Hero (BBC1), Get A Grip (ITV with Ben Elton), Strange (BBC1), The Hairy Bikers Cookbook (BBC2). Casting done by freelance casting directors Tracey Gillham and Sara Crowe. Actors are employed under Equity approved contracts. Actively encourage applications from disabled actors. "Please come to auditions with some knowledge of the part and the production."

Big Red Button Ltd

91 Brick Lane, London E1 6QL
email hello@bigredbutton.tv
website www.bigredbutton.tv
Key personnel John Burns, Pier Van Tijn, Sagar Shah

Production details

Established in 2002. Specialises in short films and music videos. Works in live action, puppetry and animation. Also employs actors in drama, comedy and commercials.

Casting procedures

Holds general auditions and actors can write to request inclusion at anytime. Casting breakdowns are available on the website and in PCR. Welcomes letters (with CVs and photographs) from actors previously unknown to the company if sent by post, but not by email. Invitations to view individual

actors' websites are not accepted, but showreels are welcome. Does not offer Equity approved contracts. Rarely has the opportunity to cast disabled actors.

Blakeway Productions

6 Anglers Lane, London NW5 3DG
tel 020-7428 3100 fax 020-7284 0626
email admin@blakeway.co.uk
website www.blakeway.co.uk

Established in 1994. In 2004 the company was bought by Ten Alps PLC and in 2007 it merged with 3BM Television and Ten Alps TV, bringing together strong track records of successful production across the genres of documentaries, docu-dramas, current affairs and factual entertainment formats.

Has produced more than 200 hours of prestigious programming for the BBC, Channel 4, More 4, ITV1 and Five in the UK, and leading US broadcasters including PBS, National Geographic, HBO, The History Channal and Discovery. Recent hits include: the Emmy nominated docu-drama 9/11: The Twin Towers, a co-production with Dangerous Films for BBC1 and Discovery; The Clinton Years for Radio 4; and the Bafta winning docu-drama Nuremberg: Goering's Last Stand for Channel 4 and The History Channel.

Blue Wand Productions Ltd

2nd Floor, 12 Weltje Road, London W6 9TG
tel 020-8741 2038 mobile (07885) 528743
fax 020-8741 2038
email lino@bluewand.co.uk
Managing Director Lino Omoboni Executive Producer Paola Omobomi

Established in 1990, the production company works exclusively in feature film production. Recent credits include: Camelot.

Box TV

151 Wardour Street, London W1F 8WE
tel 020-7297 8040 fax 020-7297 8041
email info@box-tv.co.uk
website www.box-tv.co.uk
Executive Producer Gub Neal

Founded in 2000 by award-winning producer Gub Neal, formerly Head of Drama at Channel 4 and Controller of Drama at Granada Television. Produces film and television of the highest quality and vision for markets throughout the world. The company was joined in 2006 by Adrian Bate, formerly Head of Film & Drama at Zenith Entertainment.

Bryant Whittle Ltd

49 Federation Road, Abbey Wood, London SE2 0JT
tel 020-8311 8752
email romy@bryantwhittle.com
website www.bryantwhittle.com
Directors John Bryant, Amanda Whittle Assistant Romy Tennant

Production details

An independent production company working in feature film production, with a slate of live action and CGI animated movies. Also offers a script editing service. Employs actors in drama and voice-over.

Casting procedures

Uses freelance casting directors and actors may write at any time to request inclusion; details will be kept on file. Offers Equity-approved contracts.

Cactus TV

Cactus TV Studios, 373 Kennington Road, London SE11 4PA
tel 020-7091 4900 *fax* 020-7091 4901
email touch.us@cactustv.co.uk
website www.cactustv.co.uk
Joint Managing Directors Amanda Ross, Simon Ross

Specalises in broad-based entertainment, features and chat shows. Since its inception in 1994 Cactus has produced 41 distinct titles in the UK, for 10 different channels.

Carlton Television Productions

35-38 Portman Square, London W1H 0NU
tel 020-7486 6688 *fax* 020-7486 1132
Director of Programmes Steve Hewlett

Comprises Carlton Television Productions, Planet 24 and Action Time. Makes drama programmes for all UK major broadcasters (ITV, BBC, Channel 4, Channel 5 and Sky) and regional programmes for Carlton Central, Carlton London and Carlton Westcountry.

Carnival Film & Television Ltd

47 Marylebone Lane, London W1U 2NT
tel 020-7317 1370
email info@carnivalfilms.co.uk
website www.carnivalfilms.co.uk
Managing Director Gareth Neame *Creative Director* Sally Woodward-Gentle

Production details

Founded in 1978. Works mainly in TV production, creating drama with a popular and international feel. Employs actors for drama. Commissioned by major UK broadcasters including BBC, Channel 4 and ITV. Has received various prestigious awards/nominations, including Oscars and BAFTAs. Recent credits include: *Poirot*, *BUGS*, *Traffik*, *The Grid*, *Hotel Babylon* and *Rosemary and Thyme*.

Casting procedures

Uses freelance casting directors, does not deal directly with actors. Offers PACT/Equity contracts. Will consider casting disabled actors to play disabled characters.

Celador Films Ltd

39 Long Acre, London WC2E 9LG
tel 020-7845 6800 *fax* 020-7845 1147
website www.celador.co.uk
Chairman Paul Smith *Managing Director* Christian Colson

Works also in television and radio. TV output is mostly non-fiction and light entertainment – e.g. *Who Wants to be a Millionaire?* and *You Are What You Eat* – although the company produced the sitcom, *All About Me*, starring Jasper Carrott and Meera Syal.

"The company is developing a number of other projects, including a further Neil Marshall project for production; BAFTA-winner Adrian Hodges' adaptation of Claire Tomalin's Whitbread Award-winning biography of Samuel Pepys, *The Unequalled Self*; *Farang*, a low-budget road movie set in Thailand – a collaboration with writer Richard Cottan and director Peter Webber; an original screenplay from Paul Webb, based on events following the accession of Lyndon Baines Johnson to the United States presidency in the aftermath of Kennedy's assassination; and *Big Deal*, a comedy about a hapless English journalist attempting to navigate the shark-infested waters of the international poker circuit."

Celtic Films

Lodge House, 69 Beaufort Street, London SW3 5AH
tel 020-7351 0909 *fax* 020-7351 4139
email info@celticfilms.co.uk
website www.celticfilms.co.uk

Production details

Established in 1986, Celtic Films has acted as a co-producer for 15 feature-length episodes of *Sharpe* for ITV, and for the award-winning *The Girl from Rio*.

Casting procedures

Accepts submissions (with CVs and photographs) from actors previously unknown to the company if sent by email. Showreels, voice tapes and invitations to view individual actors' websites are also accepted. Offers Equity approved contracts. Will consider applications from disabled actors to play characters with disabilities.

Chatsworth Television Ltd

97-99 Dean Street, London W1D 3TE
tel 020-7734 4302 *fax* 020-7437 3301
email television@chatsworth-tv.co.uk
website www.chatsworth-tv.co.uk
Managing Director Malcolm Heyworth

Founded in 1980, the company produces entertainment, factual programmes and drama. Has sister companies in TV distribution and licensing.

Children's Film and Television Foundation Ltd

Elstree Film and Television Studios, Borehamwood, Herts WD6 1JG

tel 020-8953 0844 *fax* 020-8207 0860

Involved in the development and co-production of films for children and the family, both for the theatrical market and for television.

Coastal Productions

25B Broad Chare, Quayside,
Newcastle upon Tyne NE1 3DQ
tel 0191-222 3160
email coastalproductions@msn.com
website www.coastalproductions.co.uk

Created in 1997 by Sandra Jobling and Robson Green with the aim of making feature films and TV dramas in the North East of England – and supporting local young people wanting to get into the industry. The company's many production and co-production credits include: *Take Me, Blind Ambition, The Last Musketeer, Touching Evil, Close and True, Grafters 1 & 2, Rhinoceros, Hereafter, Unconditional Love, Rocketman,* and *Wire in the Blood.*

Collingwood O'Hare Productions Ltd

10-14 Crown Street, London W3 8SB
tel 020-8993 3666 *fax* 020-8993 9595
email info@crownstreet.co.uk
website www.collingwoodohare.com
Head of Development Helen Stroud

Founded in 1988. Animation series and specials for children. Does not deal directly with actors: prefers to deal with agents.

The Comedy Unit

Glasgow: 6th Floor, 53 Bothwell Street,
Glasgow G2 6TS
tel 0141-220 6400 *fax* 0141-220 6444
London: 3-6 Kenrick Place, London W1U 6HD
tel 020-7317 2230 *fax* 020-7317 2231
email info@comedyunit.co.uk
website www.comedyunit.co.uk
Managing Director April Chamberlain *Creative Director* Colin Gilbert

Produces some of Scotland's best-loved television and radio shows, as well as a range of programmes for transmission across network and satellite channels. Formed in 1996, became part of the RDF Media Group in 2006.

Company Pictures

Suffolk House, Whitfield Place, London W1T 5JU
tel 020-7380 3900 *fax* 020-7380 1166
email enquiries@companypictures.co.uk
website www.companypictures.co.uk
Managing Directors George Faber, Charlie Pattinson
Head of Film Robyn Slovo *Executive Producer (TV)* Suzan Harrison

Does not accept unsolicited submissions; proposals should be submitted through agents.

Cowboy Films

34-35 Berwick Street, London W1F 8RP
tel 020-7758 4102 *fax* 020-7758 4108

email info@cowboyfilms.co.uk,
charles@cowboyfilms.co.uk
website www.cowboyfilms.co.uk
Managing Director Charles Steel

Until recently, Cowboy Films represented a range of top-quality commercials and music video directors, and also worked on feature films such as *The Hole* and *Goodbye Charlie Bright.* Sister company Crossroads Films in the US has taken over the roster of music video and commercial projects, while Cowboy continues to work on features. Kevin Macdonald's *The Last King of Scotland* is the company's most recent project.

Create Media Ventures (formerly Create TV & Film)

52 New Concordia Wharf, Mill Street,
London SE12 2BB
tel 020-7154 6960
email assistant@cmventures.co.uk
website www.cmventures.co.uk
Key personnel Vanessa Chapman, David Kerney

Production details

Originally established in 2000 (as Create TV & Film) and relaunched in 2005 as Create Media Ventures. Specialises in TV and film in the areas of drama, children and animation. Recent credits include: *Little Robots* and *Bionicle* (employing voice cast).

Casting procedures

Casting breakdowns can be obtained via the casting director. General auditions are held, and actors are advised to apply in January and September for inclusion.

Welcomes letters (with CVs and photographs) from actors previously unknown to the company if sent by post, but not by email. Invitations to view individual actors' websites are also accepted. Actively encourages applications from disabled actors and promotes the use of inclusive casting.

Dalton Films Ltd

127 Hamilton Terrace, London NW8 9QR
tel 020-7328 6169 *fax* 020-7624 4420

Production details

Established in 1987. Working mainly in film drama. Recent credits include: *Oscar and Lucinda, Country Life, Madame Sousatzka.*

Casting procedures

Casting is carried out by freelance casting directors. Actors should only make contact in response to announcements in the trade press – does not welcome any form of unsolicited communication from actors. "Do not waste time or postage until a film is actively being cast or being developed." Rarely or never has the opportunity to cast disabled actors.

Don Productions Ltd

2 Soskett Mews, Shackwell Lane, London E8 2BZ
tel 020-7254 0044 *fax* 020-9227 3283
email london@donproductions.com
website www.donproductions.com
Director Donald Harding

Japanese/English bilingual TV and media production
company based in London. Produces TV drama,
documentaries, news and sports programmes. Clients
include: Japan Broadcasting Corporation, Nippon
Television and Channel 4. Recent work includes: *The
Life of Charles Darwin.*

The Drama House

The Clockhouse, St Mary Street,
Nether Stowey TA5 1LJ
tel (01278) 733336
email jack@dramahouse.co.uk
website www.dramahouse.co.uk
Chairman/Chief Executive Jack Emery

Produces drama and drama-documentaries for film
and TV. Recent credits include: *Inquisition* for
Channel 5, one of the first HD drama shoots –
starring Derek Jacobi; also *Breaking the Code, Witness
Against Hitler, Little White Lies* and *Suffer the Little
Children.* Commissioned by major UK broadcasters:
BBCTV, Channel 4 and C5. Also international PBS
and HBO. Winner of many international and
national awards. Hopes that high-profile work will
encourage writers and other professionals to come to
the Drama House.

Ecosse Films Ltd

Brigade House, 8 Parsons Green, London SW6 4TN
tel 020-7371 0290 *fax* 020-7736 3436
email info@ecossefilms.com
website www.ecossefilms.com
Director Douglas Rae *Head of Drama* Robert
Bernstein

Founded in 1988. Works mainly in TV and feature
film production and employs actors in dramas and
comedies. Recent credits include: *Mrs Brown,
Charlotte Gray, Monarch of the Glen* and *Amnesia.*
Uses freelance casting directors and does not deal
directly with actors.

Elstree Film and Television Studios

Borehamwood, Hertfordshire WD6 1JG
tel 020-8953 0844 *fax* 020-8207 0860
email annahome@cftf.onyxnet.co.uk

Elstree is involved in the development and co-
production of films for children and the family, both
for the theatrical market and for television.

Eye Film and Television

Chamberlain House, 2 Dove Street, Norwich,
Norfolk NR2 1DE
tel (01603) 762551 *fax* (01603) 762420
email production@eyefilmandtv.co.uk
website www.eyefilmandtv.co.uk
Managing Director Charlie Gauvain

Independent producers of film and TV drama and
documentaries. Also produces corporate,
commercial, education and training material. Clients
include: BBC, ITV1/Anglia, Channel 4, Five, and First
Take Films. Recent credits include: *The Secret of Eel
Island* and *POV.*

The Farnham Film Company

34 Burnt Hill Road, Lower Bourne,
Farnham GU10 3LZ
tel (01252) 710313 *fax* (01252) 725855
email info@farnfilm.com
website www.farnfilm.com
Key personnel Ian Lewis, Melloney Roffe

Production details

Areas of work include film, TV, video, documentaries
and corporate. Recent productions include: *Children
of the Lake, The Chef's Apprentice,* and *Mona the
Vampire.*

Casting procedures

Casting breakdowns are available via the website and
in *PCR.* Offers Equity contracts. Does not welcome
unsolicited CVs. Actively encourages applications
from disabled actors and promotes the use of
inclusive casting.

Feelgood Fiction Ltd

49 Goldhawk Road, London W12 8QP
tel 020-8746 2535 *fax* 020-8740 6177
email feelgood@feelgoodfiction.co.uk
Managing Director Philip Clarke *Drama
Producer* Laurence Bowen

Producers of film and TV drama.

Film & General Productions Ltd

4 Bradbrook House, Studio Place, London SW1X 8EL
tel 020-7235 4495
email cparsons@filmgen.co.uk
Directors Clive Parsons, Davina Belling

Founded in 1971, the company produces a wide
range of feature films, television drama and children's
drama. Work includes: *Gregory's Girl, Scum, I Am
David, Tea with Mussolini, The Queen's Nose* and
Green-Eyed Monster. Does not accept unsolicited
submissions. Producers may send short synopsis by
email to Clive Parsons, but the company only accepts
showreels from agents.

Flashback Television Ltd

58 Farringdon Road, London EC1R 3PB
tel 020-7490 8996 *fax* 020-7490 5610
email mailbox@flashbacktv.co.uk
website www.flashbacktelevision.com
Managing Director & Executive Producer Taylor
Downing *Creative Director & Executive
Producer* David Edgar *Director of Production* Tim Ball

Flashback Television has been in continuous
production since 1982 and is one of the top rated

production companies in the UK. The company has a reputation for the quality of its work, for high visual standards and powerful story-telling. Flashback produces factual, factual entertainment and drama programming for broadcasters in the UK and around the world. In the UK Flashback has worked for all the other major British broadcasters including the BBC, Channel Four, ITV, Five and BSkyB. Recent credits include *Nigella's Christmas Kitchen* (BBC), *Married to the Prime Minister* (C4), *Secrets of the Classroom* (C4) and *Beau Brummell: This Charming Man* (BBC). Flashback also produces many hours of programming each year for the UK Government-backed channel Teachers' TV.

Flashback has a long track record of production in the international market. For over a decade the company has been producing series direct for North American broadcasters Arts & Entertainment Television Networks and Discovery. They have also co-produced several major projects with FR2 in France. Recent credits include *The Lost Evidence* (The History Channel), *Superhomes* (Discovery), *Top Tens* (Discovery), and *Weaponology* (Discovery).

Flashback also produces interactive material including the website *History Quest* for Channel 4 Learning, and educational podcasts for the British Council.

Flashback Television is based in London and Bristol. More information can be found at **www.flashbacktelevision.com**.

Focus Films Ltd

The Rotunda Studios, rear of 116-118 Finchley Road, London NW3 5HT
tel 020-7435 9004 *fax* 020-7431 3562
email focus@focusfilms.co.uk
website www.focusfilms.co.uk
Director David Pupkewitz *Head of Production* Lucinda Van Rie

An independent feature film development and production company founded in 1982 by David Pupkewitz and Marsha Levin. Early successes with TV documentaries and dramas preceded a transition to feature films in the 1990s. Recent productions include: *51st State* with Robert Carlyle and Samuel L Jackson; *Book of Eve* with Claire Bloom and Julian Glover; and *Crimetime* with Stephen Baldwin and Pete Postlethwaite. Upcoming projects include: *Heaven and Earth* and *Chemical Wedding*.

Focus Productions Ltd

58 Shelley Road, Stratford-upon-Avon, Warwickshire CV37 7JS
tel (01789) 298948 *fax* (01789) 294845
email maddern@focuspublishers.co.uk
website www.focusproductions.co.uk
Directors Ralph Maddern, Martin Weitz

Production details

Established 1993. Specialising in TV features and documentaries. Employs actors in TV, radio and film.

Also for presentation and voice-overs. Recent credits include: *The Real Rain Man* (C5), *Painting the Mind* (C4), *The Piano Player* (C5) and *Vivaldi's Fantasia* (film).

Casting procedures

Holds general auditions. Actors are advised to apply requesting inclusion at any time. Casting breakdowns are available by telephone. Welcomes letters (with CVs and photograph) from actors previously unknown to the company if sent by post, but not by email. Also accepts invitations to view individual actors' websites. Offers Equity approved contracts. Rarely has the opportunity to cast disabled actors.

Mark Forstater Productions Ltd

11 Keslake Road, London NW6 6DJ
tel 020-8933 5475

Works in film and TV production.

Fremantle Media

1 Stephen Street, London W1T 1AL
tel 020-7691 6000 *fax* 020-7691 6100
website www.fremantlemedia.com

Leading producers of prime-time drama, serial drama, entertainment and factual entertainment, programming in around 43 territories. Runs production operations in more than 25 countries worldwide. Brands include: Pop Idol, Grand Designs and Never Mind the Buzzcocks.

Funny Face Films Ltd

8A Warwick Road, Hampton Wick, Surrey KT1 4DW
Director Steven Drew

Production details

Works mainly in Film/Video.

Casting procedures

Uses in-house Casting Director. Sometimes holds general auditions. Welcomes letters (with CVs & photographs) from actors previously unknown to the company, sent by post or email. Accepts showreels and will consider invitations to view individual actors' websites. Will consider applications from disabled actors to play characters with disabilities.

Galleon Films Ltd

Greenwich Playhouse, 189 Greenwich High Road, London SE10 8JA
tel 020-8310 7276
email alice@galleontheatre.co.uk
website www.galleonfilms.co.uk
Chief Executive Alice De Sousa

Production details

An independent film and drama production company.

Casting procedures

Uses freelance casting directors and sometimes holds general auditions. Casting breakdowns are publicly available via all actor-accessible publications and the website. Does not welcome unsolicited letters and CVs or showreels, but will consider invitations to view individual actors' websites. Actors are employed under Equity approved contracts.

Green Umbrella

2 Home Farm Court, Shillinglee, Surrey GU8 4SY
tel (01428) 707933 *fax* (01793) 778212
email jules@gumedia.co.uk
website www.gupublishing.co.uk
Producers Steve Gammond, Bruce Vigar *Managing Director* Jules Gammond

Founded in 1990. Works in DVD and book publishing and distribution. Recent credits include: *Destination South Africa*, *Easyfit*, and *Betjeman's Britain*.

Greenwich Village Productions

Greenwich Village Productions,
14 Greenwich Church Street, London SE10 9BJ
tel 020-8853 5100 *fax* 020-8293 3001
email info@greenwichvillage.tv
website www.fictionfactory.co.uk/gvtv
Producer/Director John Taylor

An established producer of documentaries for the BBC World Service and BBC Radio 4, Greenwich Village Productions specialises in "intelligent entertainment". Recent credits include: *Adlestrop* and *Love & The Art of War*.

Hat Trick Productions Ltd

10 Livonia Street, London W1F 8AF
tel 020-7434 2451 *fax* 020-7287 9791
email info@hattrick.com
website www.hattrick.com
Joint Managing Directors Denise O'Donoghue, Jimmy Mulville

Founded in 1986, Hat Trick Productions is one of the UK's most successful independent production companies working in situation and drama comedy series and light entertainment shows. Recent credits include: *The Kumars at No. 42*, *Worst Week of my Life*, *Have I Got News for You* and *Room 101*.

Heavy Entertainment Ltd

111 Wardour Street, London W1F 0UH
tel 020-7494 1000 *fax* 020-7494 1100
email info@heavy-entertainment.com
website www.heavy-entertainment.com
Director David Roper

Established in 1992. Audio and video producers. Areas of work include drama, corporate, commercials and audiobooks. Offers Equity approved contracts. Welcomes showreels, voice tapes and invitations to view individual actors' websites.

Hurricane Films Ltd

17 Hope Street, Liverpool L1 9BQ
tel 0151-707 9700 *fax* 0151-707 9149
email sol@hurricanefilms.co.uk
website www.hurricanefilms.net
Managing Director Solon Papadopoulos

Founded in 2000, produces single films and documentary series from original ideas. Recent credits include: *Warship* (in association with Granada TV); *Comm-Raid on the Potemkin* (FilmFour); and *Wrecked* (BBC2).

J I Productions

10 Linden Grove, Great Linford, Milton Keynes, Bucks MK14 5HF
mobile (07732) 476409
email jason.impey@freeuk.com
website www.jasonimpey.co.uk
Director Jason Impey

Production details

Works mainly in film, making feature horror films. Also employs actors in the fields of drama, comedy and documentary. Recent credits include: *Tortured*, *Troubled*, *Home Made* (1 & 2), *Revenge of the Dead*, *Demon Scroll*, *Lust*, *The Bridge*, and *Woods of Terror*.

Casting procedures

Uses freelance casting directors and holds general auditions; actors may write in at any time requesting inclusion. Casting breakdowns available via postal application with sae. Welcomes letters (with CVs and photographs) from individual actors previously unknown to the company, sent by post or email. Also accepts showreels and invitations to view individual actors' websites. Actively encourages applications from disabled actors and promotes the use of inclusive casting. "Always on the lookout for new talent."

Kelpie Films

227 St Andrews Road, Glasgow G41 1PD
tel 0871-874 0328 *fax* 0871-874 0329
email yearbook@kelpiefilms.com
website www.kelpiefilms.com

Independent production company that produces a range of broadcast and corporate/commercial work, from computer-animated children's programmes to documentaries in the Middle East and low-budget feature films. Credits include: BAFTA-nominated animation, *Cannonman*; Grierson Award-winning documentary, *And So Goodbye*; and large-scale corporate work for global clients such as Shell and the UK Government.

Lexitricity Ltd

15-25 Vereker Road, West Kensington, London W14 9JU
tel 0870-840 4466

Recorded Media

email alexandra@lexitricity.com,
production@lexitricity.com

Founded in 2006. An independent production company making short films, music promos, documentaries and actors' showreels. Comprises a writer, director, producer and storyboard artist, teamed up with an experienced professional crew employed on a freelance basis. Work includes experience on feature films, BBC dramas and documentaries as well as award-winning short films. Will take clients through the entire production process, from concept and storyboard to a creative shoot and edit. Works closely with photographers, illustrators and graphic artists to produce original marketing material including flyers, posters and DVD cover designs.

LWT and United Productions

London TV Centre, Upper Ground, London SE1 9LT
tel 020-7620 1620
Controller of Drama Michele Buck

Founded in 1996. Producers of TV and film.

Maverick Television

Units 1-4 Progress Works, Heath Mill Lane,
Birmingham B9 4AL
tel 0121-771 1812 *fax* 0121-771 1550
website www.mavericktv.co.uk
Casting Director Alexandra Fraser *Executive Producer* Jim Sayer

Production details

Established in 1994. Television production company producing broadcast and non-broadcast content to all terrestrial and specialist channels. Recent productions include: *10 Years Younger, The Property Chain, VEETV, Born Too Soon* and *The Comedy Lab*.

Casting procedures

Accepts submissions (with CVs and photographs) from actors previously unknown to the company, sent by post only – no emails please. Welcomes invitations to view individual actors' websites; does not accept showreels. Offers Equity approved contracts. Actively encourages applications from disabled actors.

Maya Vision International Ltd

6 Kinghorn Street, London EC1A 7HW
tel 020-7796 4842 *fax* 020-7796 4580
email info@mayavisionint.com
website www.mayavisionint.com
Producer/Director Rebecca Dobbs *Producer* Sally Thomas *Writer* Michael Wood

Maya Vision International is an independent film and television production company, founded in 1983. Since then it has won many awards, and become renowned for making work of the highest quality.

Specialising in producing "original, landmark documentaries, features and drama for film and television", Maya Vision has developed a unique style, making some of history's great stories accessible to a wider public.

Working alongside many broadcasters and funders, including the BBC, ITV, Channel 4, five, PBS, UK Film Council and Arts Council England, Maya Vision's acclaimed catalogue has been screened in more than 140 territories worldwide. Since 2002 the company has been managing the UK Film Festval's successful Short Film Completion Fund, and has helped support nearly 60 titles that have gone on to win more than 150 awards and appeared in at least as many festivals worldwide. See the website for how to apply for funds.

NFD Productions Ltd

PO Box 76, Leeds LS25 9AG
tel/fax (01977) 681949
email alyson@nfdproductions.com
website www.nfdproductions.com
website www.film-tv-casting.com
website www.film-tv-agency.com
Director Alyson Connew

Production details

Production company producing Adverts, Exhibition Video, Corporate Video, Educational content, Training Videos, Wedding videos, Streaming Video and Multi-Media.

Casting procedures

Casting is done via an online agency and actors are encouraged to register their details at **www.film-tv-agency.com**. Note that commission will be charged on work obtained through the agency.

On Screen Productions Ltd

Ashborne House, 33 Bridge Street,
Chepstow NP16 5GA
tel (01291) 636300 *fax* (01291) 636301
email action@OnScreenProductions.com
website www.OnScreenProductions.com
Director and Producer Richard Cobourne *Producer and Director* Alison King *Assistant Producer and Production Manager* Esther Prosser

Production details

Established in 1992. Creative, business-led, integrated visual communications company producing the full range of broadcast and non-broadcast TV, video, TV commercials, interactive media, training, live events, conferences, exhibitions etc. Frequently uses actors across many of its productions – the majority of which are non-broadcast (60% for Health and Pharmaceutical companies).

Casting procedures

Casting is done by freelance casting directors as needed, or in-house by Joe Allansen. Accepts submissions (with CVs and photographs) from individual actors previously unknown to the company if sent by post or email (postal submissions are preferred). Invitations to view showreels and individual actors' websites are also accepted. Deals in 'buy out' contracts (except broadcast and theatrical). "We do not discriminate either positively or negatively against disabled actors."

OVC Media Ltd

88 Berkeley Court, Baker Street, London NW1 5ND
tel 020-7402 9111 *fax* 020-7723 3044
email eliot@ovcmedia.com
website www.ovcmedia.com
Director Joanne Cohen

Production details

Established in 1982. Areas of work include TV, film, video and documentary production. Recent credits include: *History of the World Cup, African Odyssey* and *My Matisse*.

Casting procedures

Accepts submissions (with CVs and photographs) from actors previously unknown to the company if sent by post, but not by email. Showreels, voice tapes and invitations to view individual actors' websites are also accepted. Offers Equity approved contracts and does not subscribe to the Equity Pension Scheme. Will consider submissions from disabled actors to play disabled characters.

Park Village Ltd

1 Park Village East, Regents Park, London NW1 7PX
tel 020-7387 8077 *fax* 020-7388 3051
email reception@parkvillage.co.uk
website www.parkvillage.co.uk
Managing Director Tom Webb *Directors* Thor, Sven Harding, Simon Burill, Mark Brozel, Mark Emberton, Andy Welch, Marek Losey, Nuno Dias, Max Rocket, Rowena True

Established in 1972. Commercials production company working mainly in commercials and content/interactive. Casting is done by freelance casting directors. Recent credits include Marks & Spencer Food. Actors are employed under Equity approved contracts. Will consider applications from disabled actors to play disabled characters.

Penumbra Productions Ltd

80 Brondesbury Road, London NW6 6RX
tel 020-7328 4550 *fax* 020-7328 3844
email nazpenumbra@aol.com
Contact HO Nazareth

Founded in 1981. Independent film and TV producer making contemporary social-issue drama and documentaries. Also produces non-broadcast videos when commissioned.

Picture Palace Films Ltd

13 Egbert Street, London NW1 8LJ
tel 020-7586 8763 *fax* 020-7586 9048

email info@picturepalace.com
website www.picturepalace.com
Producer & Chief Executive Malcom Craddock

Founded in 1972. Works mainly in feature films and TV drama production. Recent credits include: *Sharpe's Peril, Sharpe's Challenge, Frances Tuesday* and *Extremely Dangerous* (all ITV); *Rebel Heart* (BBC); *A Life for a Life (The True Story of Stefan Kizko)*; and the *Sharpe* series.

Red Rose Chain

1 Fore Hamlet, Ipswich IP3 8AA
tel (01473) 288886
email info@Redrosechain.com
website www.redrosechain.co.uk
Director Joanna Carrick *Key personnel* David Newborn (Producer), Jimmy Grimes (Designer)

Production details

Established in 1997, a theatre and film company that focuses on tackling challenging subjects such as domestic violence, teenage pregnancy and child abuse. As well as being screened at international festivals and winning a number of awards, the company's films – which are used in 50% of UK schools – aim to raise awareness and train health and social care professionals and young people. Recent productions include: *Valentine's Day, Friday Night Shirt*, and *Walking Away*.

Casting procedures

Sometimes holds general auditions: actors may write in Jan/Feb to request inclusion, but are asked to "please check the website regularly for information regarding upcoming film or theatre work". Welcomes letters (with CVs & photographs) from actors previously unknown to the company sent by post, but not by email. Accepts showreels but prefers not to receive invitations to view individual actors' websites. Actively encourages applications from disabled actors and promotes the use of inclusive casting.

The Reel Thing Ltd

20 The Chase, Coulsdon, Surrey CR5 2EG
tel 0845-357 6393
email info@reelthing.tv
website www.reelthing.tv
Key personnel Frazer Ashford, Chris Day

Established in 2001. Specialising in corporate and business TV production. Working the UK and worldwide for small, local clients and large multinationals. Recent credits include: *Fire Safety* (Homebase Ltd) and *Lake Avalon* (US). Does not welcome unsolicited CVs. Offers non-Equity contracts and does not subscribe to the Equity Pension Scheme. Actively encourages applications from disabled actors and promotes the use of inclusive casting.

Recorded Media

Replay Film & New Media

25 Museum Street, London WC1 1ST
tel 020-7637 0473
email solutions@replayfilms.co.uk
website www.replayfilms.co.uk
Directors Dave Young, Stuart Slade *Production Manager* Danny Scollard *Creative Director* Tim Copsey

Established in 1990. Activities include: drama, documentary, corporate, E-learning, training, consultancy. Involved in all aspects of film and new media, web design, working mainly in TV, video and computer media production. Casting breakdowns are available publicly on the website and Castweb. Invitations to view individual actors' websites are accepted.

September Films

22 Glenthorne Road, London W6 ONG
tel 020-8563 9393 *fax* 020-8741 7214
email september@septemberfilms.com
website www.septemberfilms.com
Chairman David Green *Director of Production* Elaine Day

September Films is a leading UK independent television and film production company with offices in London and Los Angeles. It was founded in 1992 by feature film director, David Green, who devised the groundbreaking *Hollywood Women* series that launched the company. Having produced over 1000 hours of primetime television during the last 13 years, September is an established specialist in factual entertainment, features, reality programming and entertainment formats.

Seven Stones Media Ltd

The Old Butcher's Shop, High Street, St Briavels, Gloucester GL15 6TA
tel (01594) 530708 *fax* (01594) 530094
email info@sevenstonesmedia.com
website www.sevenstonesmedia.com
Managing Director Adam Alexander *Creative Director* Jeremy Gibson

Established in 2005. Recent productions include: *Return to Tuscany* and *Urban Chef*. Does not welcome unsolicited CVs.

Sightline

Dylan House, Town End Street, Godalming, Surrey GU7 IBQ
tel (01483) 861555 *fax* (01483) 861516
email alex@sightline.co.uk
website www.sightline.co.uk
Director Keith Thomas *PA to Director* Alex Hayes

Production details

Established in 1985. Complete in-house multimedia production company specialising in corporate videos, CD Roms, DVDs and websites. Employs actors in corporate work and commercials. Recent credits include: Edexcel, BAA and London and Quadrant HT.

Casting procedures

Welcomes letters (with CVs and photographs) from actors previously unknown to the company – please send by email, not by post. Invitations to view individual actors' websites are welcome. Does not offer Equity approved contracts or subscribe to the Equity Pension Scheme. Rarely has the opportunity to cast disabled actors.

Sixteen Films

2nd Floor, 187 Wardour Street, London W2 5SH
tel 020-7734 0168 *fax* 020-7439 4196
email info@sixteenfilms.co.uk
website www.sixteenfilms.co.uk
Director Ken Loach *Producer* Rebecca O'Brien

Sixteen Films was set up by Ken Loach and Rebecca O'Brien following the dissolution of Parallax Pictures in Spring 2002. They are joined by Paul Laverty as Associate Director.

Speakeasy Productions Ltd

2 Sheraton Street, London W1F 8BH
tel 020-7851 4676 *fax* 020-7117 1132
email info@speak.co.uk
website www.speak.co.uk
Director Jim Adamson *Head of Production* Jeremy Hewitt *Head of Post-production* Magnus Wake *Production Manager* Simone Bett

Production details

Corporate media production company and event management company based in London and Perth. Works mainly in video production, employing actors in documentary, corporate, and commercials. Occasionally holds general auditions. Recent credits include: Royal Bank of Scotland *Raid Video* with Fiona Bruce; *Recipe for Success* events for Food Standards Agency with Phil Vickery.

Casting procedures

Accepts submissions (with CVs and photographs) from actors previously unknown to the company. Will also accept CVs and photographs sent via email. Invitations to view showreels and individual actors' websites are also accepted. Promotes inclusive casting and applications from disabled actors are considered.

Spellbound Productions Ltd

90 Cowdenbeath Path, Islington, London N1 0LG
tel 020-7713 8066 *fax* 020-7713 8066
email phspellbound@hotmail.com
Producer Paul Harris

Small independent production company specialising in feature films and drama for television. Current projects include: *Twist of Fate*, a romantic comedy in development with Columbia Pictures (LA); plus other 'genre' projects in development.

Stagescreen Productions

12 Upper St Martin's Lane, London WC2H 9JY
tel 020-7497 2510 *fax* 020-7497 2208
Director Jeffrey Taylor *Development Executive* John Segal

Founded in 1986, Stagescreen is a film and TV production company with offices in London and Los Angeles. Recent credits include: *What's Cooking*, directed by Gurinder Chadha (Lionsgate); *Alexander The Great* directed by Jalal Merhi (ProSeiben); and *Jekyll*, directed by Douglas Mackinnon and Matt Lipsey (BBC). Forthcoming work includes: *Young Cleopatra*.

Offers PACT/Equity approved contracts and does not subscribe to the Equity Pension Scheme. Will consider applications from disabled actors to play disabled characters.

Table Top Productions

1 The Orchard, Chiswick, London W4 1JZ
tel 020-8994 1269 *fax* 020-8742 0507
email berry@tabletopproductions.com
website www.tabletopproductions.com
Director Alvin Rakoff *Production Manager* Ben Berry

Production details

Established in 1967. Credits include: *A Voyage Round My Father*, *Romeo and Juliet*, *Liberty Tree*, *Don Quixote*, *Dance to the Music of Time* (C4) and *Separate Tables* (Mill at Sonning Theatre).

Casting procedures

Casting breakdowns are available via the website; apply only when in production. Offers Equity approved contracts. Does not welcome unsolicited CVs. Rarely has the opportunity to cast disabled actors.

TalkBack Productions

20-21 Newman Street, London W1T 1PG
tel 020-7861 8000 *fax* 020-7861 8001
website www.talkback.co.uk

Founded in 1981. Produces TV situation comedies and comedy dramas, features, and straight drama. Credits include: *Property Ladder*, *Jamie's Kitchen*, *Smack the Pony*, *The 11 O' Clock Show* and *Da Ali G Show*. TalkBack is part of the Fremantle Media Group (see page 346).

The Ashford Entertainment Corporation Ltd

20 The Chase, Coulsdon, Surrey CR5 2EG
tel 0844-351 0042
email info@ashford-entertainment.co.uk
website www.ashford-entertainment.co.uk
Key personnel Frazer Ashford

Established in 1996 to supply drama and documentary programming to the UK and overseas markets. Does not welcome unsolicited CVs.

Tiger Aspect Productions

Drama address: 5 Soho Square, London W1V 5DE
tel 020-7434 0672 *fax* 020-7544 1665
email general@tigeraspect.co.uk
Comedy address: 7 Soho Street, London W1D 3DQ
tel 020-7434 0700 *fax* 020-7434 1798
website www.tigeraspect.co.uk
Head of Drama Greg Brenman

Founded in 1993. Produces TV drama, comedy and sitcoms with the aim of "investing in and working with the leading writers, performers and programme-makers to produce original, creative and successful programming". Credits include: *Teachers* (C4), *My Fragile Heart* (ITV), and *Playing the Field* (BBC1).

Trafalgar 1 Limited

153 Burnham Towers, Adelaide Road, London NW3 3JN
tel 020-7722 7789 *fax* 020-7483 0662
email t1ltd@blueyonder.co.uk

Production details

Established 1985. Produces feature films, music videos, documentaries and short films. Recent productions include: *Rough Cut and Ready Dubbed*, *Art of the Critic* and *11th Dimension*.

Casting procedures

Welcomes letters (with CVs and photographs) from actors previously unknown to the company sent by post or email. Showreels, voice tapes and invitations to view individual actors' websites are also accepted. Offers Equity approved contracts. "We rarely have the opportunity to cast disabled actors."

Twenty Twenty Television

20 Kentish Town Road, London NW1 9NX
tel 020-7284 2020 *fax* 020-7284 1810
email mail@twentytwentytv.co.uk
website www.twentytwenty.tv
Managing Director Peter Casely-Hayford *Executive Producer* Claudia Milne *Head of Development* George Kay

Twenty Twenty Television is one of the UK's leading independent television production companies, making award-winning documentaries, hard-hitting current affairs, popular drama and attention-grabbing living history series. Its recent primetime children's shows are also bringing success in an exciting and challenging genre. *The Choir* won a 2007 BAFTA Award; the series *That'll Teach 'Em* won an Indie Award and was nominated for a British Academy Award. The *Lads Army* series gained the Royal Television Society primetime features award as well as a BAFTA nomination, and the international

Recorded Media

factual hit *Brat Camp* brought home an International Emmy from New York in November 2004.

Formed in 1982 by 'hands on' programme-makers, Twenty Twenty Television has always grown organically. Its industry-wide reputation for quality, intelligence and rigour was built in factual programmes. Twenty Twenty remains truly independent and is still run by creative and enthusiastic programme-makers. Its work has been broadcast by networks around the world including the BBC, CBBC, ITV, Channels 4 and Five in the UK, and ABC, The Discovery Channel, Turner Original Productions, Sundance Channel, CNN, The Arts and Entertainment Channel and WGBH in the USA.

TwoFour Productions Ltd

TwoFour Studios, Estover, Plymouth PL6 7RG
tel (01752) 727400 *fax* (01752) 727450
email eng@twofour.co.uk
website www.twofour.co.uk
Director of Broadcast Melanie Leach *Press & Publicity* Amanda Wood

Production details

Established in 1987. Independent television production company specialising in factual, lifestyle and documentary programming. Recent credits include: *Accidents Can Happen* (BBC1); *Cruise with Stelios* (Sky); *The Hotel Inspector* (C5); *Why Men Wear Frocks* (Channel 4) and *Life Begins Again* (C4).

Casting procedures

Welcomes actors' showreels. Offers Equity approved contracts. Will consider applications from disabled actors to play characters with disabilities.

Video Enterprises

12 Barbers Wood Road, High Wycombe, Bucks HP12 4EP
tel (01494) 534144 *mobile* (07831) 875216
email videoenterprises@ntlworld.com
website www.videoenterprises.co.uk
Director Maurice R Fleisher

Video Enterprises is a UK-based video production and crewing company specialising in Broadcast, Corporate, Industrial, Theatrical and Social Events programme-making.

Videotel Productions

84 Newman Street, London W1T 3EU
tel 020-7299 1800 *fax* 020-7299 1818
email mail@videotelmail,com
website www.videotel.co.uk
Casting Directors Stephen Bond, Peter Wilde, Kathrein Guenther

Production details

Established in 1975, Award-winning Videotel is "the world leader for the production of DVD/video,

multimedia and web-deliverable training material for the maritime industry".

Casting procedures

Hold general auditions, casting information available via the website, Spotlight, Talent Circle, Casting Call Pro and CastNet UK. Offers Equity approved contracts. Accepts submissions (with CVs and photographs) from actors previously unknown to the company sent by post or email. Showreels, voice tapes and invitations to view individual actors' websites are also accepted. Rarely has the opportunity to cast disabled actors due to the fact that most of the company's work is filmed aboard ships.

Walsh Bros Ltd

29 Trafalgar Grove, London SE10 9TB
tel 020-8858 6870 *mobile* (07879) 816426
email info@walshbros.co.uk
website www.walshbros.co.uk

BAFTA-nominated productions range from television series and dramas for BBC 'Sofa Surfers', Channel 4's *Don't Make Me Angry*, and feature film production *Monarch*. The BBC documentary series *Headhunting the Homeless* was shortlisted for the Grierson Awards 2004.

Wilder Films

21 Little Portland Street, London W1W 8BT
tel 020-7631 3417 *fax* 020-7636 4439
email molliehalford@wilderfilms.co.uk
website www.wilderfilms.co.uk
Director Paul Gowers *Managing Director* Richard Batty

Production details

Established in 2003. Works mainly in film and video production, especially corporate, brand and short films, and commercials. Recent credits include: *Ripple* – a comedy short film; British Gas recruitment; Aston Martin corporate; and Olympic bid films.

Casting procedures

Uses in-house and freelance casting directors and holds general auditions – but "will look for people if needed". Does not welcome unsolicited approaches but may accept invitations to view individual actors' websites.

Michael Winner Ltd/Scimitar Films

219 Kensington High Street, London W8 6BD
tel 020-7603 7272 *fax* 020-7602 9217
email winner@ftech.co.uk
Directors Michael Winner, John Fraser

Production details

Established in 1956. Specialises in film and television commercial production. Employs actors in drama, comedy and commercials.

Casting procedures

Welcomes letters (with CVs and photographs) from actors previously unknown to the company if sent by post, but not by email. Offers Equity approved contracts.

Working Title Films

76 Oxford Street, London W1N 9FD
tel 020-7307 3000 *fax* 020-7307 3003
email dan.shepherd@unistudios.com
website www.workingtitlefilms.com
Chairmen Tim Bevan, Eric Fellner *President* Liza Chasin *President UK Production* Debra Hayward

Recent films include *Atonement* (with James McAvoy, Keira Knightly, Romola Garai, Saoirse Ronan and Vanessa Redgrave) and *The Golden Age* (with Cate Blanchett and Geoffrey Rush, who reprise the roles they orginated in the award-winning *Elizabeth*, joined this time by Clive Owen).

World Productions Ltd

12-14 St Christophers Place, 2nd Floor,
London W1U 1NH
tel 0203-179 1800 0203-179 1801
email firstname@world-productions.com
website www.world-productions.com
Executive Producer Tony Garnett *Executive Producer/Head of Development* Simon Heath *PA & Office Manager* Helen Saunders

Produces TV drama features, series and serials. Recent credits include: *Between the Lines, Ballykissangel* and *Love Again* – a film about Philip Larkin (BBC).

Zenith Productions Ltd

43-45 Dorset Street, London W1U 7NA
tel 020-7224 2440 *fax* 020-7224 3194
email general@zenith-entertainment.co.uk
website www.zenith.tv.co.uk
Managing Director Ivan Rendall *Casting Director* Matt Western *Head of Drama* Adrian Bate

Founded in 1984. Part of the Zenith group, which comprises Zenith North and Zenith Productions. Works mainly in producing a wide range of programmes for terrestrial, satellite and cable television and feature films for worldwide theatrical distribution.

Recorded Media

Film schools

Although the work is minimally paid (if at all), it is well worth contacting film schools for casting consideration. Despite the fact that you'll often find yourself in the hands of a director with no idea about actors and acting, the potential of gaining something from the experience is possibly greater than that of participating in a Fringe theatre production – and the end result could contain material worthy of use in a showreel. Some schools keep files of actors' CVs and photographs for students to refer to when casting.

Castings for many low- or non-paid films are advertised on Shooting People (**www.shootingpeople.org**) – see entry on page 461.

The Arts Institute at Bournemouth
Wallisdown, Poole, Dorset BG12 5HH
tel (01292) 533011
Key contact/Lecturer Mike Fisher

Students do not only consider local actors for their short films. Actors are generally offered their expenses and a VHS copy. Welcomes enquiries (containing CV, photograph and covering letter) from new actors; actors' details are kept on file.

ARTTS International (Advanced Residential Theatre and Television Skillcentre)
Highfield Grange, Bubwith,
North Yorkshire YO8 7DP
tel (01757) 288088 *fax* (01757) 288253
email admin@artts.co.uk
website www.artts.co.uk
Key contact Geoffrey Bicker

The basis of ARTTS' training is multi-skilling, offering fast-track, intensive training in a single year. Every aspect of the training gears students practically towards a career in the entertainment industry. All our trainers are people who have already worked at high levels within the fields of film, television, theatre and radio, and who understand the demands and realities of the marketplace.

100% practical 'on-the-job' training results in students working at the very highest standards, both technically and personally – making them far better equipped to walk into a paid job in the media industry anywhere in the world. ARTTS has an impressive 94% graduate employment record. Using broadcast-standard, state-of-the-art technology, students have the opportunity to work on external corporate videos under the guidance of professional directors and producers. ARTTS Skillcentre houses a dedicated production company with a satellite office based in London, developing material for the corporate and broadcast market.

Actors interested in working on student short films should submit their details to Geoffrey Bicker at the address above.

Brighton Film School
Administration, 13 Tudor Close, Dean Court Road,
Rottingdean BN2 7DF
tel (01273) 302166 *fax* (01273) 302163
email info@brightonfilmschool.org.uk
website www.brightonfilmschool.org.uk
Key contact Franz von Habsburg

Film-industry-recognised. Provides training in all aspects of motion pictures production: screenwriting, directing, cinematography, editing and production management. More than 30 student short films are made each year; students generally recruit actors through Shooting People (**www.shootingpeople.org**). There is no formal agreement with Equity. Students do not only consider local actors. Actors are generally offered their expenses and a VHS copy. Welcomes enquiries (containing photograph and 1-page CV) from new actors if sent by post.

International Film School Wales
University of Wales College, Caerleon Campus,
PO Box 179, Newport NP18 3YG
tel (01633) 432677 *fax* (01633) 432680
email post.ifsw@newport.ac.uk
website www.ifsw.newport.ac.uk
Head of School Humphry Trevelyan

A recognised Welsh national institution for the production and development of the audiovisual culture of Wales, through training, education and postgraduate research. On average 60-80 student short films are made each year. Students generally recruit actors through agents, casting directors, Equity Job Information Service and public notices at the Royal Welsh College of Music & Drama. There is no formal agreement with Equity. Actors' details are held on file. Welcomes enquiries (with CV, photograph and covering letter) from new actors. Students at BA and MA level increasingly work in production groupings and cast professionally. "As the main centre for film education and training in Wales, we seek, encourage and support the casting of professional actors wherever possible. We also require actors to teach part-time on our BA Hons in Performance course."

London College of Communication
Elephant & Castle, London SE1 6SB
tel 020-7514 7935 *fax* 020-7514 6843
email s.jeans@lcc.arts.ac.uk
website www.arts.ac.uk
Course Director Sarah Jeans

A long-established film and television course with both BA and FdA programmes. Students work on 16mm, video and HD, and cast for projects throughout the year. Letters and CVs are welcome. Expenses only are offered, but a copy of finished work is supplied for showreels.

London Film Academy
52a Walham Grove, Fulham, London SW6 1QR
020-7386 7711 020-7381 6116
email info@londonfilmacademy.com
website www.londonfilmacademy.com
Key contact Laura Tovey

Specialise in professional full-time film training. Students make a series of short graduation films and commercials using both professional and non professional actors. Students train in all areas of filmmaking.

"Students use agents, casting directors, and the various Internet websites and paper casting publications to recruit actors." Accept submissions (with CVs and photographs) from actors previously unknown to them. Actors' details are kept on file for the student's reference and the actor is contacted directly. Payment to actors depends on the individual project budgets. Expenses will usually be paid and the actor will receive a copy of the showreel.

The London Film School
24 Shelton Street, London WC2H 9UB
tel 020-7240 0161 *fax* 020-7240 0167
email c.bright@lfs.org.uk
website www.lfs.org.uk
Librarian/Casting Chrissy Bright

London Film School offers a 2-year MA Course in the art and technique of filmmaking, with approximately 120-130 student short films being made each year. Students generally recruit actors through Spotlight, *PCR*, Star Now, Talent Circle, Acting Faces. Expenses and a DVD/VHS copy of the film are normally offered to actors cast in student films. The School welcomes enquiries from actors (with CVs and photographs) and will be happy to keep their details on file for future productions. We also have a 1-year MA Screenwriting Course.

National Film and Television School
Beaconsfield Studios, Station Road,
Beaconsfield HP9 1LG

tel (01494) 671234 *fax* (01494) 674042
email admin@nftsfilm-tv.ac.uk
website www.nftsfilm.ac.uk
Key personnel Shakil Mohammed

Offers 2-year MA courses including fiction direction, cinematography, production design, editing, sound, animation, and documentary. Students generally recruit actors through casting directors, *Spotlight*, Shooting People (**www.shootingpeople.org**) and from actors' files kept by Shakil Mohammed. Has a formal agreement with Equity. Students do not only consider local actors. Actors are generally offered their expenses. Welcomes enquiries (with CVs and photographs) from new actors which should be marked for the attention of Shakil Mohammed. Actors' details are held on file. Actors are also required throughout the year for workshops, and files are kept for this purpose. Graduation projects are cast by external casting directors.

UCCA Farnham (Surrey Institute of Art and Design)
Falkner Road, Farnham GU9 7DS
tel (01252) 722441 *fax* (01252) 892787
email sjeans@ucreative.co.uk
website www.ucreative.ac.uk
Director of Studies (Media) Sarah Jeans

The course, accredited by the British Kinematograph, Sound & Television Society, offers a broad grounding in film and video practice. Students work on both 16mm productions and video. The course emphasises film as social practice, and the study of issue-based work is a dominant theme. An average of 40-50 student short films are made each year. Actors are recruited through *Spotlight*, *PCR* and Shooting People. Only local actors are considered. Travel expenses and a copy of the film are offered, although it is not always possible to provide transfers of 16mm projects. Welcomes CVs and photographs (sent by post, not email) from actors.

University of Westminster
University of Westminster, Watford Road, Northwick Park, Harrow, Middlesex HA1 3TP
email hortp@westminster.co.uk
website www.westminster.ac.uk/filmschool
Key personnel Peter Hort, Malcolm Mowbray, Simon Passmore, Zoe Allsop

Makes around 40 short films per year from 3 minutes to 20 minutes in length, on 16mm film and video. Expenses and DVD copy of the film to actors. Welcomes letters (including CV and photograph) from actors previously unknown to the school.

Recorded Media

The essentials of screen acting

Mel Churcher

The first question I always ask when I run a film acting workshop is, "What are the differences between screen acting and theatre acting?" The first and most fundamental difference is always the last one that actors tell me, and yet it is the most crucial.

In theatre, there is an audience. In film, there is no audience.

It sounds so simple and obvious but this awareness has a deep and subtle effect on your work. When you perform for the stage, you are always sharing with the people out there in the darkness, even if it is a tiny space with an audience of one. Even in the most intimate production, there is live interplay between you and the audience – the watchers and the watched.

In film, you do your work surrounded by technicians but they are not your audience. They are there to do their own important tasks and, apart from making sure that their aspect of the work is as good as they can get it, most have little interest in, or knowledge about, what you are doing. In fact only a few key people like the director, the producer, script supervisor, sound crew and dialogue coach are wearing headphones to hear what you are saying!

Certainly, the camera isn't your audience. It is an inanimate object that is there to record your secret life. You need to open yourself up to being minutely scrutinised by it, but you share with it at your peril: once you start to 'show' to it, you will be perceived as false.

In other words, you have to believe that this weird world full of cameras, microphones and people is a form of real life. You have to believe that there is no one there but the other characters who also inhabit this strange reality. You have to think extremely hard at every moment and trust that the camera sees that. And it will. Martin Scorsese calls it 'the physic strength of the lens'. Thinking is enough and you have to trust it. You must never 'show' us what you are thinking. If you do that, we won't believe you are living this real life that we are privileged to observe from our safe position in the darkened cinema or from the corner of our sofa. That explains why it would be possible to move a close-up of a good actor from one film situation to another. The camera can see you thinking – but it doesn't know what you are thinking. You can test this out. Look around you in the tube and watch someone closely who is just sitting and thinking. Now, in your imagination, try putting them into different situations. Perhaps they are looking at a loved one, worrying about a bill or thinking about a hidden secret. You will see how, in life, they could be in any of those scenarios and yet look the same. Of course, I don't mean you should be consciously deadpan. We can see emotion when you feel and think. Your eyes literally shine with all the thoughts that light them up. Too often, this light dims when an actor is speaking learned text. You need all the thoughts, memories and pictures in your head to be as specific and extra-ordinary as they are in life, but not 'acted'.

One day you hope that an audience will see the assembled jigsaw of your film flickering on a screen, but that audience has nothing to do with your work at the time of shooting.

The next most important difference between screen and live work is that a film is shot out of order. You may bury your lover before you've met them or murder your boss before you've interviewed for the job. Each scene is done from many different angles (or set-ups).

The bigger the production, the more of these set-ups there will be. Then each set-up can involve many takes and each take needs to be fresh and spontaneous. So film takes tremendous imagination and focus, not to mention stamina.

You also need to know where you are in the story. You, as the role, can only live in the moment, but you, as the actor, need to know exactly where you are in the story. How long ago did you hurt your knee? Do you know about that affair yet? Exactly how drunk are you?

I have a quick tip for this. Take a pack of filing cards. Now write a card for each scene you are in, including the ones where you don't have any dialogue. Write the scene number at the top of the card. Then put down where you've come from and, at the bottom of the card, put where you're going to. Write who is in the scene with you and what you know or feel about them at this time. For example, is this before or after you're pregnant? Do you know about the robbery yet? Then put down anything else that's important – I'm feeling hungry, I've just run a mile, it's a heat wave, etc. Now tie all your cards together and you have a flickbook of your journey through the film.

Now when they pick you up at 5am and tell you you're not doing scene 32 but scene 64 because the set blew down in the night, you won't spend the next hour in a panic, thumbing through the script trying to find out where you are in the story and how bad your limp is!

You don't need to write down your dialogue – that's in your script. Why can't you write these notes there too? Because, in a big film, that script will change a dozen times and you'll end up with a rainbow-coloured script of re-writes. You'll never have the energy to keep transferring your notes. Also, it is bulkier than your little carry-around flickbook. And doing this work really makes sure you read the script thoroughly!

Of course the technology makes filming so different to live theatre. It comes hard to realise that no matter how well you act, if the camera doesn't see it, it doesn't exist. There's only one reality and that's what ends up on that screen. That means hitting your mark or you'll be out of focus, watching your continuity or the shot can't be used, having to be closer than you want to be to your partner because the camera, with its two-dimensional nature, changes spatial relationships and enduring long hours of waiting for that technology to work properly.

You need tremendous, specific imagination. You may have to imagine strange alien creatures whilst staring at a blue or green screen, Your partner may not be able to be in your eye-line for your close-ups. And you need to be thinking the whole time and visualising what you talk about.

Which brings me to rehearsal. There's not much rehearsal for film – well, not as we know it in theatre, If you're very lucky, there may be a few weeks of pre-production but it is unusual for all the cast to attend at the same time. You'll have a script reading of sorts (where everyone will want to change the text), and meetings with the director. You'll have costume fittings, make-up tests, horse-riding, sword-fighting and dialect coaching where applicable. But, until you arrive on that set for shooting, you may never have rehearsed with, or even met, the person you are going to play the scene with.

And yet you do need to do a tremendous amount of preparation before you get to that stage. But it must be the right kind. Beware of imposing a 'character', as the camera will read it as overdone and false. You really do need to 'inhabit' the role. It needs to be you 'as if' you were in that situation or living in that time. And that 'as if' could mean a complete change of physicality, depending on the life you've led in the role. You might be a medieval peasant who digs the ground or an astronaut who has trained for a weightless environment. So 'Who am I?' and 'Where am I?' will take the life you've led and the period into account. But you have to reach it organically through research, work and specific imagination.

Now you need to ask. 'What do I want? Your needs must be powerful and strong. You may not show those needs to the other people in the story (that's sub-text), but strong needs must drive you.

Beware of deciding how you get what you want. If you plot a course or decide how to play the scene, you will not be open to react in the moment. And you don't know what the other people will bring to the scene yet. Until you have that short but valuable rehearsal on set before shooting, you need to stay open to all possibilities.

What you can also do on your own or with a willing partner is to improvise scenes that fill in the gaps. You can't break up with someone till you've met and loved them. So if your only scene is a divorce, improvise your first meeting at home. Or imagine waking up and thinking of them the morning after the first date. Act out stories you're going to tell in the dialogue so that you've already lived through the events and have powerful specific pictures in your head when you come to tell them on the screen.

You are a unique exciting human being – don't let your character be less engaging than you are!

So keep open, really listen, think hard and react in the moment. And also sit back. This sounds silly but nerves and a desire to please will often make you crane forward. Good actors are comfortable in their own skins and we are drawn to people who show a little 'attitude'. We shy away from people who are needy, insecure or sorry for themselves.

Find out the size of the shot from the camera crew so that you can work out technical problems and know how much you can move to stay in shot.

Remember to warm up. Your breathing should be relaxed and centred. Make sure you're releasing your abdominal area as you breathe in and not holding it tight and breathing high up in your upper chest. When you are relaxed, you will feel your stomach gently moving away from you as you breathe in and flattening back as you breathe out. You need to make sure that you continue to breathe like this when, with the excitement of shooting, adrenalin is pumping round your body. This will keep you relaxed and your face clear. It will put you in touch with your feelings, so that you don't 'push' emotions. If your face keeps screwing up or overworking, it is a sure sign that you are not centred and you're manufacturing emotion. The breathing work will also help to keep your voice warm and resonant. You only need to use the level of voice you'd need in life but don't choose a half-whispered sound that doesn't carry any emotional life and will mean you'll need to record it again in post-production because no-one could hear you! This is an expensive business and it is much harder to re-find your performance months later, standing in a recording studio trying to match your lip-movements to your image on screen.

Finally, forget anything you've ever heard about theatre work being big and screen work being small. Films and TV plays are about extreme situations, emotions or characters. How can that be small? If you are truly rooted in truth, you can be as big as you'll need to be (allowing for the technical aspect of where you can move in a close-up). If the director says it's too big, then sure thing, you're sharing or manufacturing or signalling what you want us to feel and it's not too big – it's just not truthful.

Mel Churcher was an actor for many years but now works as a director and international acting and voice coach. Her theatre voice work includes The Royal Shakespeare Company, Shakespeare's Globe and The Open Air Theatre, Regent's Park, where she was resident voice and text coach from 1996 to 2007. Mel has coached on dozens of major movies including *Control* (BAFTA nominated), *The Count of Monte Cristo*, *King Arthur*, *The Fifth Element*, *The Hole*, *Lara Croft: Tomb Raider*, *Tristan & Isolde*, *Danny the Dog*, *Eragon* and *Incendiary*. She runs regular film acting workshops at the Actors Centres and leading drama schools. She has an MA in Performing Arts (Mddx), and Voice Studies (CSSD) Her book *Acting for Film: Truth 24 Times a Second* is published by Virgin Books. **www.melchurcher.com**

Recorded Media

Fringe film: low-budget shorts, student films and web-based work

Edward Hicks

A challenging and changing environment

Fringe theatre is familiar to most actors as an area for potential work which may be low-paid, but which can give you the chance to experiment and/or stretch yourself more than you might in commercial theatre. The equivalent is happening in screen work, with a growing area of possible opportunities that splits into two categories: Short films (including Student films), and web-based work. It's this new and expanding area of potential screen work that I am referring to under the umbrella title of 'fringe film'. Is it time to take this work more seriously, or is it just another example of how actors are poorly paid and sadly exploited?

With filmmaking equipment being more accessible than ever before (even phones now have cameras), more and more people are 'Shooting'. The days of needing to hire expensive equipment and a huge crew to make a film are now behind us, thanks to digital technology. A reasonable digital camera from your local high street and a computer with an editing program (some even come with free editing software) is all you need to shoot and edit a film that could be of sufficiently high technical quality to be broadcast (provided the filmmakers know what they are doing!). But remember, just because a person can use a computer does not mean they can write a novel. The technology may have opened the doors to more filmmakers, but the abilities and artistic choices of everyone involved in the project, and how the equipment is used, are – and always will be – the most important factor.

So this changing environment of 'fringe film' presents a dilemma for the professional actor. On the one hand, there is more potential screen work out there; on the other, the quality of this work varies hugely. In the past some of this work was seen as being a little amateur, not taken too seriously and perhaps considered not really appropriate work for the professional actor. However, it could also be argued that just as fringe theatre may not be as well paid as the more traditional commercial theatre, it can still prove a worthwhile commitment for an actor to take on – after all, a few West End shows started on the fringe. There is also a popular misconception that this area of work is always expenses-only and unpaid, whereas in reality that is not always the case.

Short films

Film schools and websites such as Shooting People (**www.shootingpeople.org**) are a good place to start finding work in Shorts. Although the majority are Student films listed under the Lo/No Budget category (usually meaning expenses-only), don't presume that the film will be rubbish. The script is all-important, and I'm often amazed by the creative ideas of young filmmakers who are desperate to make their films despite the lack of funds.

It's also worth noting that despite the new HD technology, some of the best-regarded film schools shoot some films on 35mm (celluloid), which is far more expensive; they see it as fundamental to the film training. These films can provide a fantastic opportunity for an actor to experience being surrounded by expensive equipment and a large crew – an opportunity that might not present itself with projects that are shot digitally. And there's always the additional chance that the student director you work with today will be a successful feature-film director tomorrow.

However, be under no illusion. The vast majority of Shorts (and indeed web-based work) will be expenses-only, and therefore as a professional actor you need to consider carefully if working for free is something that you wish to do and/or promote. Some actors argue that working for free should not be allowed, and that actors are being unfairly treated – taken advantage of, in fact. I can understand this point or view, since nobody wishes to see anyone being exploited. That said, it is a reality of the world we live in that there are budding, often very talented, filmmakers out there who are also struggling and failing to secure funding. Funding for film is extremely competitive, and can be a simple matter of a particular film or filmmaker not fitting one single criterion. They are then left with no choice but to fund the film themselves – which goes some way to explaining the lack of money available with which to pay crew and actors. Simply put, for some projects, paying both actors and crew can mean that the Short does not get made. For more advice on this, and with any specific queries or concerns, contact Equity (**www.equity.org.uk**).

So don't rule out an expenses-only Short if the project provides you with an exciting challenge: an opportunity to stretch yourself and experiment, gain more experience on camera, make material for a showreel, and forge new contacts. One advantage of Shorts is that the shooting process is quick (not just for budgetary reasons) – often only taking a few days. Therefore your time commitment is minimal, and you can squeeze it around any castings that may come up. Most people working in this area will try and accommodate you (especially if they are not paying you), because they understand that, just like them, you are trying to earn a living and can't turn down a casting or a paid job. I've known several actors who have even managed to work on a Short during the day while performing in the theatre at night, as the shooting schedule was designed around the performance times.

There is a huge international film festival circuit for Short films, which caters to every level – from the more established and respected events that include a Short film section, to festivals that are aimed purely at Shorts. It's not unusual for some of the better Shorts that win prizes at the biggest festivals to end up being broadcast on television. However, if the filmmakers claim they are submitting the Short to Cannes as an incentive to get you on board, remember that *submitting* a film to a festival does not mean that it will automatically be accepted.

Make sure you fully understand what it is you are getting involved in, and if the filmmakers are new and you don't know them, do some research (consult IMDB, the International Movie Database; browse via various search engines; talk to fellow actors and so on). You could ask to see examples of the director's work, find out if any of his or her films have ever been selected for a festival, and then research the festivals (there are some that take anything and everything!).

I would also recommend you always ask to see the script before a meeting, especially if they are not paying you. The best advice I ever heard given to actors about Shorts was, *"If the script and project do not excite you, walk away."* Remember, if you commit to a project like this, you have a responsibility to take it as seriously as you would anything else you do, regardless of salary. If your professionalism is not reciprocated by the people you are working with, word will soon spread – and you cannot afford to be tarnished by the wrong kind of association.

Bear in mind too that not all Shorts will be Student films, expenses-only or made by the DIY filmmaker. Some will have competed for funding, and the criteria for gaining funds may include paying a fee to the actors and crew. It's not uncommon for Shorts to win funding, provided this is matched by the production company – and some film schools have been known to pay a token fee to the actors. Peter *'Lord of the Rings'* Jackson made a Short in order to test a new type of camera; directors often make a Short in order to help gain funding for a feature film project. Shorts at this level are more likely to be funded, and to have an established production company on board to produce them, as well as a casting director to cast them.

Web-based work

You only have to look at the number of Shorts, commercials, virals (web content that is aimed at triggering an online following which builds its own momentum as it spreads – a commercial of sorts) that are posted on sites like YouTube to see how the web has become a huge growth area for screen work. However, it also highlights how quality standards can vary massively. At one end of the scale are huge multinational companies with budgets to match, employing production companies to make virals, commercials and Short films; and at the other is the DIY filmmaker filming his dog on a skateboard. Just as with the Short film market, do your research, make sure you know what you are getting involved in, and check with Equity.

Advertising agencies continue to look for less traditional outlets for their work, and the web is becoming an important area for them – which in turn means more potential screen roles for actors. I know one actor who has been able to establish himself as a cabaret act, based on a character that he originally helped to create for a web-based advertising campaign. More recently, too, web-based TV shows have started to spring up: projects that are made exclusively for the web and not broadcast on traditional TV. The first web-based soap was sold not long ago to a TV network, having established a large initial following on the Internet. With more and more of the population now watching TV over the web rather than on traditional TV sets, this phenomenon looks set to grow and grow over the next few years; actors will need to be especially careful as to what they sign in terms of agreements over future sales.

So, if you're a new actor who has just left drama school and wants more screen experience, or a more experienced actor keen to stretch yourself, this growth area I refer to as 'Fringe Film' might be worth considering. However, like all new growth areas, approach with caution. Despite people's best efforts and intentions, quality is never guaranteed. You must be realistic about what it is you are doing – and be honest with yourself about why.

Edward Hicks is currently Head of Film, TV and Radio at RADA – a post sponsored by Warner Bros. He has directed numerous Shorts, commercials and promos, is a graduate and former governor of LFS, has various film projects in development, and has written articles on screen acting in addition to being a regular contributor to *Actors' Yearbook*. Ed has taught at various Drama Schools including East 15, where in 2001 he created the first media-based acting course to gain NCDT accreditation. Under the name Edward Rawle-Hicks he started his professional career as a child actor (from the age of ten), appearing at the RSC, the West End and in numerous commercials, film and television projects.

Acting for radio

Gordon House

I remember once, in a burst of evangelical enthusiasm at having decided never to touch a cigarette again, upbraiding a distinguished member of the Radio Drama Company for her constant disappearances to the Green Room to light up. (Nowadays, of course, all BBC Green rooms are smoke-free, and your poor cigarette-smoking actor has to shiver in the car park.) "My dear man," she wheezed grandly. "The only reason you employ me on the wireless is because of my nicotine-nourished, port-soaked larynx. Living badly has made me the radio actress I am today!"

Well – it's a point of view. Just as the camera relishes certain skin textures, so the microphone may embellish the actor or actress who has lived a little – resulting in, shall we say, an idiosyncratic oesophagus. But as a way of getting a radio part, it's not a course of action I'd recommend. Radio simply doesn't pay enough to sustain a life of alcoholic debauchery.

So how do you get into radio? "It's a closed shop," moaned one actor to me the other day. "You hear the same names, time and again – and there's no way of breaking into this magic circle." I personally have worked with well over 800 actors, so it can't be that much of a closed shop ... though it's true that given the ruthless time constraints of the medium (a 60-minute play will be rehearsed and recorded in two days), there's a natural tendency for producers to work with those actors whom they know can 'deliver' quickly. There's no joy to be had in the seventh take of a difficult scene when your nervous newcomer is finally coming to grips with the ambiguities of his or her character, as well as the technical demands of this strange new medium, while everyone else's performances have long-since peaked and are now beginning to sound tired and lacklustre.

But that said, new writers and new actors are the lifeblood of the medium. And what do you need to be a good actor on radio? It's simple. You need to be a good actor. If you're successful in the theatre, in film, on TV – then of course you can be successful on radio. A good actor is a good actor. It obviously helps if your voice doesn't sound like a creaking door (given that creaking doors are a staple diet of many a radio play), and the medium has no place for prima donnas. With every producer sparingly counting his or her loose change, there's no such happy luxury as a radio 'extra'; so if you're cast as Hamlet, you can also expect to do your fair share of off-mic mumbling in Claudius' court. And if that doesn't appeal, don't do radio.

You also have to be prepared to work fast and make almost instant decisions. Over the years I've worked with a few actors whom I admire hugely; whom I've seen – in other media – give performances of rare charm and intelligence; but who in radio have simply been unable to 'come off the page' – make the character they're playing sound truthful and real. Of course this may simply be attributed to the crass inadequacy of the director. But for some actors the sheer speed at which they have to make decisions about character, motivation, sub-text and so forth is incredibly daunting. And then there's the physical absurdity of much of what they have to do: "How the xxx do you expect me to be 'truthful' when I'm carrying a xxxing great script in my left hand, a glass of water, masquerading as gin, in my right, and you want me to walk through a carpet of scrunched-up audio tape and pretend it's a meadow," shrieked one despairing actor to me a couple of years ago.

And yet that's exactly what we expect – truth. There's no medium as unforgiving for exposing over-acting or over-emoting (or worse – simple 'reading'). A radio play – and particularly a contemporary, naturalistic play – should make listeners feel that they are eavesdropping on real conversation. It's a medium that may owe much to theatre for providing it with great writing and acting talent (though the reverse is equally true), but the technique of radio acting is far closer to that of film than of theatre. "Less is more! Less is more!" as my erstwhile colleague, Martin Jenkins, one of Radio Drama's finest practitioners, used to impress on his casts. (It was Martin, incidentally, who uttered the memorable phrase: "Good Luck – Please!" before the umpteenth take of one particularly stressful scene.)

How do you bring yourself to the attention of radio producers? Well – there's no denying the fact that a lovingly crafted CD arriving on your desk just as you're in the process of casting your next play, and can't for the life of you think who you can get to play the embittered Glaswegian ex-shipbuilder who's contemplating a sex change, can make all the difference. But choose the pieces you record with care – and keep them short. There's no point in doing all sorts of varied accents, if varied accents are not a speciality. Obviously, it's a great asset to be master – or mistress – of many different voices, this being a medium where 'doubling' and 'trebling' is done with impunity. But a CD where the truthfulness of most of your extracts is undone by your game but doomed attempt to do a passable Geordie, won't help anyone. Many years ago I remember auditioning Jeremy Sinden for a part. "What accents do you do?" I asked him. "I do two actually," he said. "I do posh. And I do very posh." Well a mere two accents didn't stop Jeremy getting a load of work in every medium – including radio – in his all-too-brief, but exhilarating, career.

Having recorded your tape or (preferably) CD, you can, of course, circulate it to every producer who's ever made a radio play. But my advice would be to be a little more discerning. Listen to some radio plays (a great way of determining for yourself what works and what doesn't) and note the names of the producers whose productions particularly appeal to you. You can then write a personal note to them – you know the kind: "I must say, Mr House, I really enjoyed your fascinating and unusual interpretation of *Hedda Gabler* on Radio 3 last night, and incidentally Hedda is a part I've always yearned to play myself,"(etc.). I'm not saying it will get you a part, but producers are as vain as the next person (I should know) and it may well make them more inclined to slip your CD into the CD player, on the basis that anyone with such discerning judgement as yours must be worth hearing.

Radio is a fantastic, and hugely under-rated medium, and actors, by and large, love working for it. It can also be the stepping-stone to fame and fortune. For many years we've been running our own radio bursary scheme for accredited drama schools – the Carleton Hobbs Competition (named after one of the great 20th century radio actors) – and the role-call of actors who have been winners, from Richard Griffiths to Stephen Tompkinson, from Nerys Hughes to Emma Fielding, is hugely impressive. Our new bursary scheme, the Norman Beaton Fellowship, for actors who didn't go to an accredited drama school, is also providing us with some excellent new talent. Details of both these schemes can be found on the BBC website.

And of course we producers don't simply wait to receive your CDs, but are constantly on the lookout for new and exciting talent from wherever we can find it. You may not need to approach us – we may approach you! As World Service Drama producers, Hilary Norrish and myself gave a young actor called Ewan MacGregor his first two professional jobs, having seen him in a drama school showcase. And Ewan – if you ever get to read this – where are the invitations to those glamorous film previews you promised you'd send us when you were famous? Remember – it was radio that gave you your first break!

Gordon House is the former Head of the BBC Radio Drama Department. He joined the BBC as a studio manager in 1972, working in Children's Television and Radio Sport before becoming a drama director. For 14 years he headed the small BBC World Service Drama team, during which time the Unit won more than 30 national and international awards. In 1998 Gordon won the Writers' Guild Special Prize for services for his work with new writers, and has twice won the Sony Drama Award. He is a founder member of The Worldplay Group, a radio association of drama directors from broadcasting stations around the world, which initiates a yearly season of international radios dramas broadcast on BBC World Service, ABC, CBC, RTE, Radio New Zealand and Radio Television Hong Kong.

Radio companies and other 'voice-work' opportunities

Unlike in the visual media, many radio directors have their roots in theatre and will go to stage productions to inform their future casting. And, unlike their visual media counterparts, they have a far greater understanding of actors and acting, and are far more open to casting against obvious physical type.

The BBC has by far and away the biggest radio drama output, and it also uses actors to read poetry, narrations and stories. Some of this 'output' is made in-house; a good proportion is contracted-out to independent companies. This is one area of work that doesn't very often use casting directors. It is a good idea to listen to radio drama to become aware of its ways – you won't hear much swearing, for instance. Also see 'Voice-over agents' (page 106) and 'Showreel and voice-demo companies' (page 423); some of the latter have excellent advice on making a voice demo on their websites.

BBC Radio Drama

Bush House, The Strand, London WC2B 4PH
tel 020-7557 1013
website www.bbc.co.uk/drama/radio
website www.bbc.co.uk/soundstart
Head of Radio Drama Alison Hindell *Coordinator, Drama Company* Cynthia Fagan *Production Executive, Radio Drama* Rebecca Wilmshurst

BBC Radio Drama Department is the biggest producer of drama on radio in the world. It provides more than 700 hours of drama a year for Radio 3, Radio 4, BBC World Service, BBC7 and the BBC Asian Network. Plays are broadcast every day of the week and can be heard at any time, either on air or on the website. An audience of about half a million people is listening every time a play is aired. Output includes: *Westway* (drama set in a London health centre); *The Archers* (countryside soap opera); the Friday and Saturday plays (thrillers, mysteries and love stories); afternoon plays, classic serials, Woman's Hour Drama (weekday drama serial); play of the week (from around the world); book of the week (non-fiction); book at bedtime (fiction, including modern classics).

The Radio Drama Company was founded in 1940 as the BBC Repertory Company, and is still frequently referred to as The Rep. The company's focus allows new acting talent to work alongside established actors in a variety of radio productions. Actors joining the RDC have already worked with many eminent artists such as Julia Mackenzie, Derek Jacobi, Richard Griffiths, Cheryl Campbell, Anna Massey and Daniel Day-Lewis.

Past members of the company have included Stephen Tompkinson, Alex Jennings, Adjoa Andoh, Norman Bird, Emma Fielding, Anthony Daniels, Ben Onwukwe, Joanna Monro, Ann Beach, Janet Maw, Suzanna Hamilton and Carolyn Pickles.

The RDC does not use freelance casting directors and casting breakdowns are not publicly available. Sometimes holds general auditions and actors can write at any time requesting inclusion. Welcomes postal submissions from individual actors previously unknown to the company, but does not accept email enquiries. Voice demos and invitations to view individual actors' websites are also accepted. More information can be found under 'FAQs' at **www.bbc.co.uk/soundstart**

The Norman Beaton Fellowship is part of BBC Radio Drama's commitment to place integrated casting at the heart of its output. The NBF aims to provide access to BBC Radio Drama for talented actors from non-traditional training backgrounds, and particularly those from minority ethnic backgrounds who are currently under-represented in radio drama.

The Radio Drama Company will also be forging links with theatre companies all over Britain to help develop and nurture new talent for both radio and the stage and to find new NBF bursary winners. Consult the website for information about the next Norman Beaton Fellowship and for details of eligibility requirements.

The Carleton Hobbs Bursary is aimed at students graduating from accredited drama courses across the country. Looks for distinctive, versatile radio voices to form the next season's Radio Drama Company. It aims to recruit 4-6 winners annually. Students will be seen through an audition process, from which an equal mix of men and women will be selected. Winners receive a 6-month binding contract as members of the Radio Drama Company. Up to 4 runners-up will be engaged as freelance actors in one-off productions.

BBC Radio Drama (Belfast)
Room 3.07 Blackstaff House, Great Victoria Street, Belfast BT2 7BB
tel 028-9033 8476 *fax* 028-9033 8462
email heather.larmour@bbc.co.uk
website www.bbc.co.uk/ni/drama
Producers Gemma McMullan, Eoin O'Callaghan, Lawrence Jackson *Executive Producer* Anne Simpson
Key contact Heather Larmour

Production details
Produces drama (29 plays last year) and readings for Radio Ulster, Radio 3, Radio 4 and BBC 7; particularly welcomes enquiries from actors with regional dialects and singing ability.

Casting procedures
Casts in-house; does not issue casting breakdowns. Happy to receive approaches from actors unknown to the company, either by post (with a CD voice reel, preferably with no commercials) or by email to Heather Larmour. Offers Equity approved contracts. Rarely has the opportunity to cast disabled actors.

Shell Like
81 Whitfield Street, London W1T 4HG
tel 020-7255 5224
email enquiries@shelllike.com
website www.shelllike.com
Casting Directors Mike Blunt, Richard Donaghue

Production details
Specialises in audio production and radio commercials. Works mainly in radio. Employs actors for corporate and commercials. Recent credits include: T-mobile and NSPCC (both radio).

Casting procedures
Sometimes uses freelance casting directors and may hold general auditions. Does not encourage unsolicited approaches but will accept invitations to view individual actors' websites. Actively encourages applications from disabled actors and promotes the use of inclusive casting. "We are happy to advise actors on how to get into voice-over work, and how to get a showreel made."

World Service
Bush House, Strand, London WC2B 4PH
tel 020-7557 2941
website www.bbc.co.uk/worldservice

BBC World Service provides radio services in English and 42 other languages, via short wave and, in an increasing number of cities around the world, on MW and FM. The English service is also available 24

hours a day in real audio on the Internet. Classic contemporary drama, novels, short stories, soap operas and poetry are all a feature of its English service, plus a wide range of arts, documentaries, education, features, music, religious affairs, science, sports and youth programmes. In addition, BBC World Service provides on-the-spot coverage of world news, giving a global perspective of international events.

INDEPENDENT RADIO COMPANIES

Above the Title Productions
Level 2, 10-11 St George's Mews, London NW1 8XE
tel 020-7916 1984 *fax* 020-7722 5706
email mail@abovethetitle.com
website www.abovethetitle.com
Managing Director Helen Chattwell

Founded in 1998, Above the Title Productions has made over 500 hours of radio programming covering a range of genres, from comedy to factual programmes, drama, discussion programmes, and music and the arts. See the website for detailed programme credits.

All casting is done through agents; direct contact with actors is not welcomed. Is no longer able to accept voice demos and CVs, as the company has received such a large number of applications in the past.

Art and Adventure Ltd
L'Ocean Ltd, 5 Darling Road, London SE4 1YQ
tel/fax 020-8692 0145
email roger@artandadventure.org
website www.artandadventure.org
Producers/Directors Roger Elsgood, Willi Richards

A production company specialising in making high-production-value, location-recorded long-form drama for BBC Radio 3 and 4 with international casts and directors. Recent work includes: *The Two Gentlemen of Valasna* and *The Mrichhakatikaa* for Radio 3, both recorded entirely on location in India; *To the Wedding* for Radio 3 – a collaboration with Complicite; *Shooting Stars*, for Radio 3 (directed by Mike Hodges and starring Michael Gambon, Michael Sheen and Clive Owen); *King Trash*, the second play in Mike Hodges' radio trilogy; and *Inferno* with Corin Redgrave, Alex Jennings and Laurie Anderson.

The company is always happy to receive submissions and voice demos from actors (preferably as hard copy), and auditions as necessary. It sometimes offers Equity contracts. Actively encourages applications from disabled actors and promotes the use of inclusive casting.

The Comedy Unit Ltd
Glasgow TV and Film Studio, Craigmont Street, Glasgow G20 9BT
tel 0141-305 6666 *fax* 0141-305 6600

email general@comedy unit.co.uk
website www.comedyunit.co.uk
Producers/Directors Colin Gilbert, Niall Clark, Rab Christie

Founded in 1996. Works in TV and radio productions – has produced approximately 30 hours of TV and 25 hours of radio. Areas of work include drama, sitcoms, comedy and other light entertainment. Recent drama credits include: *Ronan the Amphibian* and *Coming Home*.

Sometimes holds general auditions. Actors can write at any time requesting inclusion. Submissions from actors previously unknown to the company are accepted, sent by post or email. Voice demos and invitations to view individual actors' websites are also accepted.

CSA Word

6a Archway Mews, 241a Putney Bridge Road, London SW15 2PE
tel 020-8871 0220 *fax* 020-8877 0712
email info@csaword.co.uk
website www.csaword.co.uk
Key personnel Victoria Williams, Clive Stanhope

Founded in 1991. Producer of audiobooks, drama, readings, feature programmes and documentaries for BBC Radios 4, 2 and BBC World Service.

Does not hold general auditions, as the company tends to use agents for casting. Invitations to view individual actors' websites are accepted. Equity contracts are not used, "but we usually pay above Equity minimum." Happy to consider disabled actors: "We work mainly in speech, audio and radio work, so rarely an issue with regard to physical disability."

Culture Wise

1 Chiswick Staithe, London W4 3TP
Key personnel Mukti Jain Campion, Chris Eldon Lee

Founded in 1988. Areas of work include TV and radio documentaries. Does not hold general auditions. Invitations to view individual actors' websites are accepted. The company rarely employs actors, as the primary focus is on factual output: actors are generally used for short readings only within a feature programme.

Curtains for Radio

58 St Helen's Gardens, London W10 6LH
tel 020-8964 0111
email aparesi@aol.com
website www.curtainsforradio.co.uk
Producers/Directors Andrew McGibbon, Jonathan Ruffle, Nick Romero

Established in 2001. Specialises in comedy, comedy drama, comedy archive and music. The ability to perform in foreign languages, regional dialects and singing are among the skills required by actors.

Records one play annually. Recent titles include: *Wheeler's Fortune* (2003), *Wheeler's Wonder* (2004), I *Was Morrissey's Drummer* (2005), *Reality Is An Illusion Caused By Lack Of N.F.Simpson* (2007). Casting is carried out by freelance casting director Rachel Freck.

Accepts submissions from actors previously unknown to them. Voice demos and invitations to view individual actors' website are also accepted. "Voice demos should only be sent on a CD that can be played in any CD player." Voiceover artists are employed under Equity approved contracts. Actively encourage applications from disabled actors.

Devlin Morris Productions Ltd

97b West Bow, Edinburgh EH1 2JP
Key personnel Morris Paton

Producers of theatre, radio and cultural tourism projects. Areas of work include drama and light entertainment. Recent drama credits include: features for BBC Scotland, Radios 4 and 3, and the World Service. Does not hold general auditions. Actors can write at any time requesting inclusion. Submissions from actors previously unknown to the company are accepted if sent by post. Voice demos and invitations to view individual actors' websites are also accepted. Does not accept email enquiries.

Falling Tree Productions (formerly Alan Hall Associates)

13 Cliffview Road, London SE13 7DD
tel 020-8305 6936
email alan.hall@easynet.co.uk
website www.fallingtree.co.uk
Executive Director Alan Hall

Founded in 1998, Falling Tree Productions is an independent supplier to BBC Network Radio (3 and 4 principally) and foreign broadcasters, crafting documentaries and music feature productions. Winner of the Sony Gold in 2004 feature category, and previously, in the music feature category too. Has also been awarded the Prix Italia (twice) and the Prix Bohemia. The company has employed actors in documentaries, music features, anthology programmes and museum guides. Recent credits include: *Song on the Death of Children, Brahms' Beard* and *Something Understood*.

Will accept submissions (written or emailed) and voice tapes from actors previously unknown to the company. Welcomes invitations to view an actor's website. Advises that actors are used mainly for readings in radio productions, but also in the production of numerous voice-overs for museum and art gallery audioguides.

The Fiction Factory

14 Greenwich Church Street, London SE10 9BJ
tel 020-8853 5100 *fax* 020-8293 3001
email info@fictionfactory.co.uk
website www.fictionfactory.co.uk

Key personnel John Taylor, Celia de Wolff, Joanna Green, Roland Jaquarello, Marina Calderone

Founded in 1993. Makes radio drama and features for the BBC and has recently expanded into video production. Areas of work include drama, documentaries, light entertainment and voice-overs. Recent drama credits include: *In Search of Lost Time*; *Markheim*; *Abrogate*; *London, This is Washington* (Radio 4).

Does not hold general auditions. Submissions from actors previously unknown to the company are accepted if sent by post. Voice demos are also accepted. Does not welcome email submissions or invitations to view individual actors' websites. "It is helpful if showreels contain material appropriate to the kind of work sought; for example, corporate voice-overs or radio advertisements don't necessarily show off acting skills."

First Writes

Lime Kiln Cottage, High Starlings, Banham, Norwich NR16 2BS
tel (01953) 888525 *fax* (01953) 888974
email ellen@firstwrites.fsnet.c.uk
website www.firstwrites.co.uk
Key personnel Ellen Dryden, Richard Blake, Jonathan Dryden Taylor

Established in 1992. Areas of work include BBC Radio Drama for Radios 3 and 4, and World Service. Recent credits include: *The Franchise Affair, I Was Born There* and *The Eliza Stories*. Offers Equity approved contracts and does not subscribe to the Equity Pension Scheme. Accepts submissions from actors previously unknown to the company if sent by post, but not by email. Welcomes voice demos and invitations to view actors' websites. Aims for inclusive casting where possible.

Heavy Entertainment Ltd

111 Wardour Street, London W1F 0UH
tel 020-7494 1000 *fax* 020-7494 1100
email info@heavy-entertainment.com
website www.heavy-entertainment.com
Director David Roper

Established in 1992. Audio and video producers. Areas of work include drama, corporate, commercials and audiobooks. Offers Equity approved contracts. Welcomes showreels, voice tapes and invitations to view individual actors' websites.

Ladbroke Productions

Essex House, 29 Foley Street, London W1W 7JW
tel 020-7323 2770 *fax* 020-7079 2080
email info@electricairwaves.com
website www.electricairwaves.com
Producers/Directors Neil Gardner, Richard Bannerman, Paul Kent, Andy Jordan *Assistant Producer* Anna Van Dieken

Founded in 1975, Ladbroke Productions produces for all BBC networks in many genres, including drama,

documentaries, music, light entertainment and features. Its studio and production facilities are also used by BBC Drama, BBC Readings and BBC Factual Learning. Actors are mainly employed by the company in its drama and documentary production. Recent credits include: *Sitting in Limbo* (BBC World Service) and *In the Company of Men* (BBC Radio 3).

Will accept unsolicited submissions (written or emailed), voice demos and invitations to view actors' websites. April and September are generally better months to write.

Loftus Audio Ltd

2A Aldine Street, London W12 8AN
tel 020-8740 4666 and 01620-893 876
website www.loftusproductions.co.uk
Directors Joanne Coombs, David Smith, Matt Thompson

Small award winning audio and radio production company based in West London and North Berwick, East Lothian specialising in features, documentaries and readings, mostly for BBC Radio 3 and 4. Require plain narration from actors. Record three plays and two audiobooks a year. Recent titles include: *Blindness* for BBC Radio 3, *Leni* (Riefenstahl) for Radio 4's Book of the Week.

Accept submissions from individual actors previously unknown to them. Will also accept submissions sent via e-mail. Straight narration is preferred on voice demos and should be sent either as an MP3 or CD with name on the spine of CD box (unable to return demo CDs). Actors are employed under Equity approved contracts. Applications from disabled actors are welcomed.

Pennine Productions

17 Crimicar Lane, Sheffield S10 4FA
tel 0161-427 1460
website www.pennine.biz
Contact Janet Graves

Founded in 2000. Has made documentaries and features for BBC Radio 4 since 2001, and programmes for BBC Radio 3 since 2004. Has produced book readings for Radio 4 since 2005. Broadcasts northern, national and international stories. Main areas of work include documentaries and readings. Recent credits include: *Israel in East Africa, When Jesus Rode into Bristol* and *Land of the Oval Ball* (all Radio 4, 2003). Offers Equity approved contracts and does not subscribe to the Equity Pension Scheme.

"We only welcome unsolicited approaches from actors with significant broadcast experience, particularly of book readings – or other audiobook productions. We are too small to be useful to actors trying to break into the network radio or TV." Happy to consider applications from disabled actors: "radio experience is the over-riding concern."

Pier Productions

8 St Georges Place, Brighton BN1 4GB
tel (01273) 691401 *fax* (01273) 693658

Managing Director Peter Hoare

Founded in 1993, Pier is an award-winning Brighton-based company and is a significant supplier of factual and drama productions to BBC Radio 4. The company employs actors for drama productions and is keen to work with talent located in Brighton and the surrounding area. Recent productions include: aa production of JM Barrie's *Little White Bird* and dramatisations of *Scenes from Married Life* and *The Nutcracker*.

The company does not hold general auditions. Submissions from actors are accepted by post and email, but we do not welcome invitations to view individual actors' websites. It must be emphasised that opportunities in radio drama are limited and that the company does not use the services of voice-over artists.

So Radio Ltd

18 Hatfields, London SE1 8GN
tel 020-7960 2000 *fax* 020-7960 2095
email info@sotelevision.co.uk
website www.sotelevision.co.uk
Producer/Director Graham Stuart

Founded in 2003 as the radio arm of So Television Ltd. Recent credits include: *The Storyman with Andrew Clover* and *It's that Jo Caulfield Again* for BBC Radio 4. The company has employed actors mainly for light entertainment productions.

Does not accept unsolicited written submissions. As the company is small it cannot promise to reply to all enquiries. Offers Equity approved contracts (where applicable). Actively encourages applications from disabled actors and promotes the use of inclusive casting.

Lou Stein Associates Ltd

14a Tavistock Place, London WC1H 9RD
email info@loustein.co.uk
Producer/Director Lou Stein **Co-Director** Deirdre Gribbin

Lou Stein founded the Gate Theatre, Notting Hill, and was Artistic Director of the Palace Theatre, Watford. Lou Stein Associates was formed to continue Lou's interest in new work, adaptations, music theatre and media. Employs actors for drama programmes. Recent drama credits include: *Fear and Loathing in Las Vegas* (adapted and directed by Lou Stein, starring Harry Dean Stanton); *My Month with Carmen* (starring Miriam Colon and Julian Glover); *Grace Notes* by Lou Stein (based on the Bernard MacLaverty novel, starring Amanda Burton); *Embers* (adapted by Lou Stein from the novel by Sandor Marai and starring Patrick Stewart); *The Possessed* (written and directed by Lou Stein from the Dostoevsky novel, starring Paul McGann); *Performances* by Brian Friel (Wilton's Music Hall, starring Henry Goodman and Rosamund Pike).

Voice demos and invitations to view individual actors' websites are accepted, but actors are requested to email in the first instance. Please note that no reply will be given unless the actor is suitable for immediate casting. Names will be retained on file. Offers Equity approved contracts. Actively encourages applications from disabled actors and promotes the use of inclusive casting.

TalkingPEN books

Global House, 303 Ballards Lane, London N12 8NP
tel 020-8445 5123 *fax* 020-8446 7745
email info@talkingpen.co.uk
website www.talkingpen.co.uk
Producers/Directors R. Dutta, D.M. Chatterji, Henriette Barkow

Established in 2002. Produces Audiobooks, E-books, Talkingpen books and posters. The ability to perform in foreign languages, singing and storytelling are often required of actors. Voice demos should include short story telling in English or other language. Records 20 audiobooks annually. Recent titles include: *Hansel and Gretel, Jill and the Beanstalk, English Terms Explained.*

Accepts submissions from actors previously unknown to them. Voice demos and invitations to view individual actors' website are also accepted. Actively encourages applications from disabled actors.

Tintinna Productions

Summerfield, Bristol Road, Bristol BS40 8UB
tel (01275) 333128 *fax* (01275) 332316
email tintinna@aol.com
Producer Ian Bell **Research & Production** Sandy Bell

Founded in 1998. Specialises in factual documentaries including history, lifestyle and human interest. Main area of work is documentaries. Does not hold general auditions. Submissions from actors previously unknown to the company are accepted if sent by post. Voice demos are also accepted. Does not welcome email submissions or invitations to view individual actors' websites.

Unique

50 Lisson Street, London NW1 5DF
Executive Producer: Drama & Entertainment Frank Stirling

Produces drama, documentaries, comedy and light entertainment for radio. Recent drama credits include: *Zazie* (World Service), *A Confidential Agent, Fragile!* (Radio 4), *Professor Bernhardi, Bajazet* (Radio 3), and *Something Understood* (poetry and prose readings for Radio 4).

Submissions from actors previously unknown to the company are accepted sent by post or email. Voice demos are also accepted. Does not welcome invitations to view individual actors' websites. Advises actors to "include radio work on demo". "We regret that we cannot reply to all submissions, but your details will be kept on file."

Whistledown Productions

8A Ayres Street, London SE1 0AS
tel 020-7407 8001

email davidprest@whistledown.net
website www.whistledown.net
Producers/Directors David Prest, Sarah Cuddon

Founded in 1993. One of the largest independent suppliers to BBC Radio, with a background in features and landmark documentaries, as well as programme strands such as *The Reunion*, *Traveller's Tree*, and *Questions Questions*. Also produces voice demos in custom-build studio.

AUDIO BOOKS

Barefoot Audio Books Ltd
123 Walcot Street, Bath BA1 5BG
Director Tessa Strickland *Group Project Manager* Emma Parkin

Recent titles include: *Mrs Moon*, *Animal Boogie* and *Tales of Wisdom and Wonder*. Does not use freelance casting directors. Accepts submissions from actors previously unknown to the company if sent by post, but does not welcome email enquiries. Voice demos and invitations to view individual actors' websites are also accepted. Singing ability is required from actors, and Caribbean and African voices are needed in particular.

HarperCollins Audio
77-85 Fulham Palace Road, London W6 8JB
tel 020-8307 4630 *fax* 020-8307 4517
email rosalie.george@harpercollins.co.uk
website www.harpercollins.co.uk
Director Rosalie George *Editorial/Production Manager* Nicola Townsend

Has produced more than 1000 titles for both children and adults over the last 15 years. Work spans all genres including crime, comedy, literary fiction, mass market fiction, non-fiction, poetry and classics. Recent titles include: *Brick Lane* by Monica Ali; *Sharpe's Havoc* by Bernard Cornwell; and *Lovers and Liars* by Josephine Cox.

Foreign languages and regional dialect skills are required from actors. Does not use freelance casting directors. Advises actors to make contact by email or telephone, or preferably through an agent. Also accepts invitations to view individual actors' websites.

Isis Audio Books
7 Centremead, Osney Mead, Oxford OX2 0ES
tel (01865) 250333 *fax* (01865) 790358
email sales@isis-publishing.co.uk
website www.isis-publishing.co.uk
Audio Production Manager Catherine Thompson

Founded in 1975. Publishes unabridged audiobooks. Recent titles include: *Twelve Sharp* by Janet Evanovich; *The Vanishing Act of Esme Lennox* by Maggie O'Farrell; *Tenderness of Wolves* by Stet Penney; and *The Good Husband of Zebra Drive* by Alexander McCall Smith.

Does not use freelance casting directors. Accepts submissions from actors with proven audiobook experience if sent by post or email, but does not welcome telephone enquiries. Actors should have a range of voices and good sight-reading ability. Offers non-Equity contracts and does not subscribe to the Equity Pension Scheme. Actively encourages applications from disabled actors and promotes the use of inclusive casting.

Macmillan Audio Books
20 New Wharf Road, London N1 9RR
Audio Publisher Alison Muirden *Audio Editorial Coordinator* Rebecca Folkard-Ward

Casts in-house. Accepts submissions from actors previously unknown to the company if sent by post, but does not welcome email enquiries. Voice demos are also accepted. Does not offer Equity contracts or subscribe to the Equity Pension Scheme. Will consider applications from disabled actors to play disabled characters.

Naxos Audio Books
40A High Street, Welwyn, Herts AL6 9EQ
tel (01438) 717808 *fax* (01438) 717809
email nicolas.soames@naxosaudiobooks.com
Producer/Director Nicolas Soames

Founded in 1984. Produces classic fiction, modern fiction, drama, poetry and children's classics for CD and download. Recent titles include: *The Canterbury Tales*, *Heidi* and *King Lear*. Regional dialect skills are required from actors. Accepts voice demos.

Orion Audio Books
5 Upper St Martin's Lane, London WC2H 9EA
tel 020-7240 3444 *fax* 020-7379 6158
email audio@orionbooks.co.uk
website www.orionbooks.co.uk
Audio Manager Pandora White *Audio Assistant* Victoria Nicholl *Audio Publicity Manager* Jonathan Weir

Started in 1996, Orion audio draws mainly on the Orion Group lists, but also acquires elsewhere. With notable authors such as Ian Rankin, Maeve Binchy, Michael Palin, Francesca Simon, Antonia Fraser, Michelle Paver, Terry Wogan, Raymond Khoury, Kate Mosse, Michael Connelly, Miss Read, and Dan Brown. Orion Audiobooks prides itself on its diversity with continued success at creating and using new packaging. Orion's strong marketing skills allow its titles to reach a very wide range of non-traditional outlets, and now firmly established in the digital download market. Produces 50-60 audiobooks a year. Recent titles include: *Horrid Henry's Christmas Cracker*, *Grizzly Tales: Nasty Little Beasts 1.1*, *The Naming of the Dead*, *Whitethorn Woods*, *Salmon Fishing in the Yemen*, *Love and Louis XIV* and *Young Stalin*.

Casts in-house. Useful skills include regional dialects and occasionally singing ability. Welcomes submissions and voice-demos from actors previously unknown to the company. Offers Equity approved contracts. Happy to receive submissions from disabled and non-disabled actors with the right skills for the job.

Random House Audio Books

20 Vauxhall Bridge Road, London SW1V 2SA
tel 020-7840 8400 *fax* 020-7834 2509
email jlewis@randomhouse.co.uk
Editorial Director Zoe Howes *Editorial Assistant* Jenni Lewis

Created in 1991, the Audiobooks division of Random House publishes writers such as James Patterson, John Grisham, Andy McNab, Ruth Rendell and Kathy Reichs.

Uses freelance casting directors. Accepts submissions from actors previously unknown to the company, sent by post. Voice demos and invitations to view individual actors' websites are also accepted.

Soundings Audiobooks Ltd

Isis House, Kings Drive, Whitley Bay,
Tyne & Wear NE26 2JT
tel 0191-253 4155 *fax* 0191-251 0662
website www.isispublishing.co.uk
General Manager Gillian Bell

Founded in 1984, the company records around 190 audiobooks a year. Recent productions include: Robert Ludlum's *The Ambler Warning*; Anna Jacobs' *Seasons of Love*; and Alexandra Connor's *The Tailor's Wife*.

Casts in-house and does not issue casting breakdowns. Welcomes letters (not emails) with voice demos or invitations to view individuals' websites. Prefers voice demos without commercials. Uses non-Equity contracts. "We rarely (or never) have the opportunity to cast disabled actors."

Media festivals

These are geared towards showcasing directors, rather than actors. However, they can be useful places to network, learn and (if your film is short-listed) gain extra exposure.

Belfast Film Festival

The Exchange Place, 23 Donegal Street,
Belfast BT1 2FF
tel 028-9032 5913 *fax* 028-9032 5911
email info@belfastfilmfestival.org
website www.belfastfilmfestival.org

Normally held in March/April each year, the Belfast Film Festival brings the best of independent, world, local and classic cinema to screens across Belfast. In addition there are panel discussions, workshops, music events and a series of related club events in venues across the city.

Candidates may submit features, shorts, animation and documentaries for inclusion in the festival. The deadline for submissions is normally early December. While all categories will be considered for screening, the only competitive category is the Irish short film. To be eligible for the £1000 Kodak Short Film Prize, films must have been shot in Ireland during the previous year and last no longer than 20 minutes.

BFM International Film Festival

tel 020-8527 9582 *fax* 0870-132 2249
email festival@bfmmedia.com
website www.blackfilmmakermag.com/festival

Presenting the UK's premier black film event each September across venues in London, the BFM promotes the range and diversity of black cinema and television around the world. Showcasing an array of award-winning features, documentaries, animation and short films by established international talent alongside black British film-makers, the BFM also screens a substantial amount of high-quality work from up-and-coming filmmakers. In addition there are exclusive preview screenings, seminars, workshops and masterclasses on offer. Awards are presented to winners in the following categories: best actor, best actress, best film, best cinematography, and best screenplay.

Birmingham Screen Festival

9 Margaret Street, Birmingham B3 3BS
tel 0121-643 0631
email info@birminghamscreenfestival.com
website www.birminghamscreenfestival.com
Director Barbara Chapman

A 6-day event in March celebrating the best of film, television and interactive software at venues across Birmingham. The programme features UK premières, previews, retrospective work, experimental work, shorts, documentaries, animation, international cinema, masterclasses and community events. Awards include: the Norman Beaton Award for Film and TV Drama; the Samuelson Award for Achievement in Drama; Birmingham Screen Festival Best Newcomer Award; Birmingham Screen Festival Special Award for Lifetime Achievement.

Applications are by invitation only; contact the festival for further details.

Bite the Mango

National Museum of Photography,
Film & Television, Bradford BD1 1NQ
tel (01274) 203326 *fax* (01274) 203387
email adeni.rutter@nmsi.ac.uk
website www.bitethemango.org.uk

Founded in 1994, Bite the Mango aims to promote the best in world cinema with an eclectic mix of features, shorts and documentaries from many countries around the world. The festival runs for 1 week in September and features premières, previews, retrospectives, masterclasses and seminars by leading figures in world cinema.

Bradford Film Festival

National Museum of Photography,
Film & Television, Bradford BD1 1NQ
tel (01274) 203308 *fax* (01274) 770217
email ben.eagle@nmsi.ac.uk
website www.bradfordfilmfestival.org.uk
Director Tony Earnshaw *Contact* Ben Eagle

Held each year in March, the Bradford Film Festival presents a number of special guests, tributes, screentalk interviews, masterclasses, spotlights, the Crash symposium and the Widescreen weekend over a 15-day period.

Features, shorts, documentaries and experimental work submitted for competition must have been completed during the previous 2 years.

Brief Encounters Festival

Watershed Media Centre, 1 Canon's Road,
Harbourside, Bristol BS1 5TX
tel 0117-915 0186 *fax* 0117-930 9967
email info@brief-encounters.org.uk
website www.brief-encounters.org.uk

Brief Encounters is an international short film festival which runs for 1 week in November and promotes new talent in the film industry. With more than 20 screenings of diverse new shorts from around the world, special guests and events, parties, awards, seminars, masterclasses, surgeries and focus sessions, the festival offers insights and advice from industry professionals about every aspect of film. For advice about funding and submitting your work, visit the website.

Cambridge Film Festival

Arts Picture House, 38-39 St Andrew's Street, Cambridge CB2 3AR
tel (01223) 500082 *fax* (01223) 462555
email cff@picturehouses.co.uk
website www.cambridgefilmfestival.org.uk

Established in 1977, the festival was relaunched in 2001 after a 5-year hiatus and now runs for 10 days in July. Aiming to screen the best of current international cinema and to rediscover neglected films of the past, it also runs a programme for children supported by events and workshops, and organises free outdoor screenings and touring events across the Eastern region. The festival is attended by many actors and directors and is complemented by parties, receptions, drive-in movies and educational events. Recent visitors include Cate Blanchett, Richard Harris, Timothy Spall and Joel Schumacher.

Directors such as Peter Greenaway, Patrice Chereau, Philip Kaufman and Francesco Rosi have also presented work at the festival, and many acclaimed films – including *Reservoir Dogs*, *Intimacy*, *Bowling for Columbine*, *Goodbye Lenin!* and *La Haine* – received their UK première in Cambridge.

Cardiff Screen Festival

10 Mount Stuart Square, Cardiff CF10 5EE
tel 029-2033 3324 *fax* 029-2033 3320
email enq@iffw.co.uk
website www.iffw.co.uk
Festival Manager Sarah Howells

Celebrating film, TV and new media from Wales and further afield, the festival offers a wide selection of screenings, special guest appearances, debates and programmed industry events for 10 days each November.

The DM Davies award is open to any short-film director who is of Welsh origin or has been a native of Wales for 2 or more years. It is one of the largest short-film prizes in Europe; previous winners have included Justin Kerrigan (*Human Traffic*) and Sara Sugarman (*Very Annie Mary*). Entries are screened towards the end of the festival, with many of the directors in attendance. The winner receives a comprehensive package of funding, facilities and assistance to shoot a 10-minute film in Wales.

Celtic Film & Television Festival

249 West George Street, Glasgow G2 4QE
tel 0141-302 1737
email mail@celticfilm.co.uk
website www.celticfilm.co.uk

The Celtic Film Festival celebrates the cultures and languages of Cornwall, Brittany, Ireland, Scotland and Wales in film and in television broadcasting. Awards include: Short Drama Award, Drama Feature Award and Drama Series Award. The festival is attended by producers, directors, commissioning editors, film executives, media students, distributors and schedulers.

The Seaward Chichester Film Festival

Chichester Cinema at New Park, New Park Road, Chichester PO19 1XN
tel (01243) 786650 *fax* (01243) 790235
email info@chichestercinema.org
website www.chichestercinema.org
Director Roger Gibson

An 18-day festival in August/September presenting more than 70 feature films, Q&As with visiting directors, and related talks. More than half the films shown are previews and premières; the remainder form retrospectives on important contributors to the film world.

The Commonwealth Film Festival

Unit 9, Greenheys Business Centre, Manchester Science Park, 10 Pencroft Way, Manchester M15 6JJ
tel 0161-342 0044 *fax* 0161-342 0055
email info@commonwealthfilm.com
website www.commonwealthfilm.com
Director Mathieu Ravier

The festival promotes filmmaking talent in the Commonwealth and seeks to develop new audiences for their work. Committed to inclusivity and excellence, it also aims to promote respect for human rights, equality, freedom and sustainable economic development. Founded in 2001, the festival presents documentaries, short films, seminars, workshops, industry networking events and parties during its 10-day run across April/May, and is the largest festival showcase for Indian, Canadian and South African cinema in Europe. Submissions must be made in or co-produced with one of the 72 nations of the Commonwealth.

Disability Film Festival

London Disability Arts Forum, 20-22 Waterson Street, London E2 8HE
tel 020-7749 4352 *fax* 020-7749 4363
email caglar@disabilityfilm.org
website www.disabilityfilm.co.uk
Festival Coordinator Caglar Kimyoncu

Showcasing the talent of disabled filmmakers, the Disability Film Festival takes place over 4 days in December, and is hosted by the BFI Southbank (formerly the National Film Theatre). The festival offers filmmakers, film-goers and industry professionals the opportunity to meet, exchange feedback, network and socialise. It has also become a forum for debate, challenging the exclusion of disabled people either on screen or as filmmakers. Submission forms and guidelines are available to download from the website.

Edinburgh International Film Festival

Filmhouse, 88 Lothian Road, Edinburgh EH3 9BZ
tel 0131-228 4051 *fax* 0131-229 5501
email info@edfilmfest.org.uk
website www.edfilmfest.org.uk
Artistic Director Hannah McGill *Managing Director* Ginnie Atkinson

Celebrating cinema for over 60 years, the festival aims to entertain, challenge and inspire audiences for 10 days each August. The programme covers a range of different areas such as British Cinema, red carpet gala events, live interviews with cinema greats, retrospectives, debuts and second films from new filmmaking talent, short films and special events. Previous events have included the National 48 Hour Film Challenge, Script Factory masterclasses and performed readings, a BAFTA-sponsored interview with Sir Sean Connery, and a Skillset event on Careers in Film.

Submissions should be received by April; all the forms, rules and regulations can be downloaded from the website. Films submitted from outside the UK must have been produced during the 2 years previous to the festival, and British films during the year beforehand. All films must be UK premieres.

Foyle Film Festival

The Nerve Centre, 7-8 Magazine Street, Derry, BT48 6HU Northern Ireland
tel 028-7126 7432 *fax* 028-7137 1738
email competition@nerve-centre.org.uk
website www.foylefilmfestival.com
Director Shauna Kelpie *Programmer* Brónagh Corr

Established in 1987, the Foyle Film Festival runs for 10 days each November, screening more than 200 films and featuring a number of special guests, events, presentations, workshops and seminars.

Awards are available for the Best Irish Short, Best International Short, Best Animation, Best Feature and Best Documentary. The application forms and rules and regulations for the competition can be downloaded from the Foyle Film Festival website. Send an email or call the office to request a hard copy.

Hull International Short Film Festival

Hull Film, Danish Buildings, 44-46 High Street, Hull HU1 1PS
tel (01482) 381512 *fax* (01482) 381517
email office@hullfilm.co.uk
website www.hullfilm.co.uk
Director Esther Johnson

Held over 5 days in late September, the festival shows short narrative, documentary, animated and experimental films. The aim is to show international and local short films as an innovative and exciting artform, as well as to provide training opportunities in the region. The festival also includes outdoor screenings, music and film events, international speakers and archive events.

Leeds International Film Festival

PO Box 596, Leeds LS2 8YQ
tel 0113-247 7952 *fax* 0113-247 8397
email filmfestival@leeds.gov.uk
website www.leedsfilm.com
Director Chris Fell

Leeds International Film Festival has been presenting extensive programmes of new and unseen cinema from around the world since 1987, supported by a number of events and workshops for those wanting to get into film and TV. The Yorkshire Short Film Competition highlights emerging new filmmaking talents in the Yorkshire region, while the Louis Le Prince International Short Film Competition promotes some of the best fiction completed in the last year around the world. The key features of the festival include UK Film Week, an annual showcase of emerging talent; Film Festival Fringe, where the bars and clubs of Leeds host human rights films, music documentaries and special events; the Main Programme; Unique Retrospectives.

The festival is complemented by the Leeds Children's and Young People's Film Festival held in April each year, with an award for National Young Filmmaker of the Year.

London Film Festival

BFI South Bank, London SE1 8XT
tel 020-7815 1322 or 020-7815 1323
fax 020-7633 0786
website www.lff.org.uk

The BFI London Film Festival is Europe's largest public film event, screening an average of 280 films from 60 countries in October/November each year. Leading figures in the film industry present their work at the festival, and the programme is supported by a number of interviews, industry and public forums, lectures, education events, Gala films and special screenings promoting the best in cinema across the world.

London Lesbian & Gay Film Festival

c/o BFI Southbank, Belvedere Road, South Bank, Waterloo, London SE1 8XT
tel 020-7928 3535 or 020-7928 3232 (Box Office)
website www.bfi.org.uk/llgff
Senior Programmer Brian Robinson *Head of Festivals (bfi)* Sandra Hebron *Festival Producer* Helen de Witt

The London Lesbian and Gay Film Festival presents the best of British and international Queer Cinema in all its forms – mainstream and avant garde. Features and shorts are complemented by discussions and interviews with writers and filmmakers. The London run of the festival is based at the BFI Southbank (formerly known as the National Film Theatre), with other screenings taking place in Leicester Square. Following this run in March and April, it continues on tour around the UK until the autumn. See the website for programme details, including the tour schedule, or contact the BFI box office for a brochure of the London run.

Manchester International Short Film Festival

Kinofilm, 42 Edge Street, Manchester M4 1HN
tel 0161-288 2494 *fax* 0161-281 1374
email john.kino@good.co.uk
website www.kinofilm.org.uk
Director John Wojowski

British New Wave and an International Panorama of film provide the main focus to the festival, with a regional showcase, 'Made up North', aimed at promoting films from local and regional filmmakers. Education and Professional Development events are also hosted by the festival and are presented by external curators and organisations.

The festival is open for film submissions each year from January to June, with shortlisted entries being screened at the festival itself in October. Short films on any theme, subject or category and made on any format are eligible, as long as they run no longer than 20 minutes and have been made within the 18 months prior to the festival. The Kinofilm Awards acknowledge outstanding achievements in short film, with awards in many categories. Rules, regulations and application forms are available on the website.

Raindance Film Festival Ltd

81 Berwick Street, London W1F 8TW
tel 020-7287 3833 *fax* 020-7439 2243
email info@raindance.co.uk
website www.raindance.co.uk/festival
Producer Jesse Vile

Running for 2 weeks in October, Raindance is the UK's largest independent film festival and is

committed to screening the boldest, most innovative and challenging films from the UK and around the world. Weighted heavily towards new talent, the festival offers more than 100 features (many of which are directorial debuts), 20 shorts programmes and a wide range of events, workshops and parties.

Rushes Soho Shorts Festival

PO Box 2868, London W1A 5QL
tel 020-7851 6207 *fax* 020-7851 6369
email info@sohoshorts.com
website www.sohoshorts.com

Taking place for 1 week in July/August, shortlisted films are screened free of charge throughout Soho's cafes, bars and cinemas, as well as other special events and screenings being held. In addition, Vue cinemas around the country will also be holding screenings throughout that week. The festival culminates in an awards cremony with winners being announced in the following categories: Short Film, Newcomer, Animation, Music Video, and Title Sequence & Idents. Patrons of the festival include BAFTA and the Directors' Guild of Great Britain.

Films for submission should be no longer than 12 minutes, and should have been produced in the 12 months prior to the deadline.

UK Jewish Film Festival

PO Box 3217, Brighton BN1 6QA
tel (01273) 735522 *fax* (01753) 327766
website www.ukjewishfilmfestival.org.uk

Established in 1997, the festival is committed to showing a wide variety of films which celebrate the diversity of Jewish cultures and identity, and which reach both Jewish and wider audiences. In addition to film screenings there are education projects and talks with directors. The UK Jewish Film Festival Short Film Fund offers a grant of up to £15,000 for the production of a short film or video (drama, animation or factual) of a Jewish theme and with a significance to Jewish and general public audiences. For application details, consult the website.

Disabled actors
Introduction

This section brings together companies and organisations of specific interest to disabled actors. It should also be noted that (a) some agents and companies now welcome enquiries from disabled actors (see listings), and (b) the Conference of Drama Schools (CDS) states that, "All members of the Conference of Drama Schools are committed to a policy of widening access, to reflect the social and cultural diversity of society." Some drama schools have more detail on their disability admissions policies on their websites.

A number of television companies want to increase the representation of disabled performers, contributors and production crew in their programme-making. To this end they have set up databases of disabled people with interests and/or skills in acting, reporting, and other aspects of film, television and radio production. The contact details are as follows:
• *BBC Diversity Database*. Contact David Pain, Room DG20, BBC Centre House, Wood Lane, London W12 8SB (send CV and photograph); alternatively, please email **diversity.database@bbc.co.uk**.
• *Channel 4*. Contact Alison Walsh (**awalsh@channel4.com**) or 020-7306 8125; **www.channel4.com/4disabledtalent**.
• *ITV*. Contact Janie Frazer (performers only) on 020-7261 3848. More contact details are in the casting directors' section, and Janie's details are on page 121.
In addition, disabled Equity members can add their details to the *Disability Register*, which is published by The Spotlight. Casting directors looking for disabled actors can search this register via the Spotlight website.

Note The UK Government recognised BSL as an official language in March 2003, and the editors acknowledge that many deaf people consider themselves to be members of a linguistic and cultural minority – Deaf with a capital 'D' – rather than disabled people. For the sake of simplicity, however, this book uses a broad definition of disability to encompass Deaf people (although an individual entry will retain the distinction if present in the material provided to us by that company).

The editors would like to thank Silvie Fisch (of The National Disability Arts Forum) and the staff of Graeae Theatre Company for their help in compiling this section.

TRAINING

Apart from the training offered by drama schools, a number of theatre companies and organisations operate training schemes or courses for disabled actors. Many of these schemes are relatively short – a few days or weeks – but Lawnmower's Liberdade, Chicken Shed's BTEC National Diploma, Mind the Gap's Staging Change, and Shysters' ShysterShadows operate over a longer term. Shorter courses are run by (among others) Birds of Paradise, Blue Eyed Soul, CandoCo, and Oily Cart. These are often advertised through the NDAF's email newsletter, EtCetera – **www.ndaf.org** has more information about how to subscribe – or contact the company concerned for more information. (Details for all the theatre companies listed here can be found in the *Sources of work* section below.)

SOURCES OF WORK

Amici Dance Theatre Company

Turtle Key Arts, Ladbroke Hall, 79 Barbly Road,
London W10 6AZ
tel 020-8964 5060 *fax* 020-8964 4080
email info@amicidance.org
website www.amicidance.org
Artistic Director Wolfgang Stange

Dance theatre company integrating disabled and
non-disabled artists and performers.

Anjali Dance Company

The Mill Arts Centre, Spiceball Park, Banbury,
Oxfordshire OX16 8QE
tel/fax (01295) 251909
email info@anjali.co.uk or education@anjali.co.uk
website www.anjali.co.uk
Artistic Director Nicole Thomson *Admin Officer*
Adrienne Szabo

Production details

A professional contemporary dance company. All
Anjali's dancers have a learning disability. The
company produces and tours performances, and
undertakes Educational and Outreach work; it is one
of the first of its kind in the world. Aims to show that
disability is no barrier to creativity. Stages 1-2
productions a year with up to 10 performances over
6-8 venues around the country, such as the Mill Arts
Centre (Banbury), Stratford Circus (London), and
the Pegasus Theatre (Oxford).

Casting procedures

Casts in-house, does not issue casting breakdowns,
and welcomes letters (but not emails) from
individuals previously unknown to the company.
Welcomes invitations to view individuals' websites,
but no showreels.

Apropos Productions Ltd

2nd Floor, 91a Rivington Street, London EC2A 3AY
tel 020-7739 2857 *fax* 020-7739 3852
email info@aproposltd.com
website www.aproposltd.com
Directors Paul Dubois

Established in 1999. Provides training for local,
national and international clients. Key focus is on
Organisational Behaviour. Training is provided for
incoming actors through an induction process: client
briefings. Training is given to become facilitators.
Corporate experience is useful but not essential for
incoming actors. Actor-base is extended annually
through agents, website, Equity Job Information
Service and *PCR*. Clients include: Local Government
Association, Thompson Scientific, Colchester
Borough Council.

Accepts submissions (with CVs and photographs)
from actors previously unknown to them. Disabled

actors regularly form part of their teams and are
actively encouraged to apply.

art+power

Spike Island, 133 Cumberland Road, Bristol BS1 6UX
tel 0117-946 8630 *fax* 0117-946 8631
minicom 0117-946 8632
email info@artandpower.com
website www.artandpower.com
Key contact Joanne Goldsworthy

Bristol-based organisation that uses the arts to
empower disabled people and build a more equal,
inclusive and creative society. art+power runs a
Personal Arts Support scheme (PASS) in
Performance and produces theatre, dance and live art
projects.

Birds of Paradise Theatre Company

333 Woodlands Road, Glasgow G3 6NG
tel 0141-339 1155 *fax* 0141-339 1177
email all@birdsofparadisetheatre.co.uk
website www.birdsofparadise.co.uk
Artistic Director Morven Gregor *Projects Manager*
Shona Rattray *'Agent for Change'* Robert Softley

A professional touring theatre company which
produces adventurous and challenging work that
places disability issues in the public arena. The
company has toured throughout Scotland for 12
years with inventive programmes of performances
and workshops, both for traditional theatre-going
audiences and people who have difficulty
experiencing theatre due to disability or geographical
isolation.

Birds of Paradise shares its knowledge of good
practice across the arts and disability sector with a
clear objective: to increase the number of disabled
professional theatre practitioners working in
Scotland. The company recognises that in order to
reverse hundreds of years of discrimination against
disabled people, it needs to present high-quality work
and positive role models for contemporary Scottish
Theatre, its audiences and practitioners. These role
models are also engaged to support the company's
work with physically disabled young people, who
continue to be excluded from participating and
engaging in the arts.

Since 1995, the company has intensively trained 150
people over 22 acting courses and technical skills. 400
general Outreach and Taster Workshops have been
run, involving approximately 4800 people, and there
have been 7 inclusive touring productions with
disabled and non-disabled performers and stage
workers. 23 disabled actors have been employed; 12
non-disabled actors have also been employed. 4
disabled people were employed in technical jobs.

Previous productions include: *The Farce of
Circumstance* by Tom Lannon (1995); *The Resistible
Rise of Arturo Ui* by Bertolt Brecht (1996); *Tongues* by
Sam Shephard and Joseph Chaikin (1997); *Working
Legs* by Alistair Gray (1998 commission); *Playing for*

Keeps by Archie Hind (1998 commission); *Merman* by Susan McClymont and Dave Buchanan (2000 commission); *Twelve Black Candles* by Des Dillon (2001); *The Irish Giant* by Garry Robson (2003); *Brazil 12 Scotland 0* by Ian Stephen (2005 commission); *Mouth of Silence* by Gerry Loose (2006 commission); and *Beneath You – Spider Girls are Everywhere!* by Kathy McKean (2007 commission). Birds of Paradise Theatre Company in association with The Citizens' Theatre produced *Offshore* by Alan Wilkins, directed by Morven Gregor, in September 2008.

Blue Eyed Soul Dance Company

The Lantern, Meadow Farm Drive, Sundorne, Shrewsbury SY1 4NG
tel (01743) 210830 *fax* (01743) 466854
email admin@blueeyedsouldance.com
website www.blueeyedsouldance.com
Artistic Director Rachel Freeman

Production details

Founded in 1994, Blue Eyed Soul is a successful inclusive dance company, which offers a dance repertoire, and education and training programmes. It embraces difference, and actively seeks out creative partnerships between disabled and non-disabled people. It stages 1 production a year, with an average of 20 performances in a wide range of locations including arts centres, theatres, outdoor venues, educational and community venues. Areas covered have included the West Midlands, London, North West and the South East.

Casting procedures

Uses freelance casting directors, and holds general auditions. Casting breakdowns are available by postal application (with sae). Does not welcome unsolicited CVs, showreels or invitations to view individuals' websites from dancers unknown to the company. Offers non-Equity contracts.

CandoCo Dance Company

2T Leroy House, 436 Essex Road, London N1 3QP
tel 020-7704 6845 *fax* 020-7704 1645
email info@candoco.co.uk
website www.candoco.co.uk
Joint Artistic Directors Stine Nilsen, Pedro Machado
Executive Director Lauren Scholey *Administrator* Joanne Lyons *Marketing Manager* Nadja Dias
Education Manager Luke Pell *Finance Manager* Elizabeth Charman *Technical Manager* Ed Trotter

CandoCo Dance Company is the contemporary dance company of disabled and non-disabled dancers. By producing creatively ambitious dance performances, the company aims to push the boundaries of contemporary dance and to broaden people's perception of what dance is and who can dance.

CandoCo was founded in 1991 and through its performances and education work has developed into the world's leading exponent of inclusive dance practice. The company regularly commissions artists and choreographers to create new dance work that tours nationally and internationally. It also runs a variety of training courses, residencies, workshops and 3 Youth Dance Companies.

Chicken Shed

Chase Side, Southgate, London N14 4PE
tel 020-8351 6161 *minicom* 020-8350 0676
website www.chickenshed.org.uk
Key contact Susan Jamson

Children and young people's theatre company producing shows that are inclusive and accessible to all. Performs a wide range of works, spanning experimental pieces to full-scale productions; original works to Shakespeare. In addition the company runs:

• An inclusive theatre education workshop programme for nearly 700 members from the ages of 5 to 24 (550 up to the age of 18)
• The only inclusive BTEC National Diploma in Performing Arts in the country
• Special interactive performances to pre-school children and their parents and carers
• Training and work experience in performance and all aspects of theatre production to young people
• Training in inclusive practice through workshops and seminars to a range of professionals from the fields of education, social services and health
• A community facility that is completely accessible physically and has a warm and welcoming ambience
• A national training and development programme with mainstream and special educational needs schools; this has already established 15 new inclusive children's and youth theatre companies across the country, with more on the way

Common Ground Sign Dance Theatre

32-36 Hanover Street, Gostin's Building (4th Floor), Hanover Street, Liverpool L1 4LN
tel/fax 0151-707 8033
textphone 0151-707 8380
email info@signdance.com
website www.signdance.com
Artistic Director & Choreographer Denise Armstrong
Administrative Director Simeon Hart

Founded in 1986, Common Ground is a dance theatre company creating unique performances (through the fusion of sign language, dance and physical theatre) which are accessible to all audiences.

Deafinitely Theatre

Office 7, The Beethoven Centre, Third Avenue, London W10 4JL
minicom 020-8968 1589
textphone 020-8968 1589
email paula@deafinitelytheatre.co.uk
website www.deafinitelytheatre.co.uk

Artistic Director Paula Garfield *General Manager* Mark Sands

Actors with Disabilities

Founded in 2002 to produce performance ideas by Deaf people. All the company's work is Deaf-led but is accessible to hearing people as well. The company runs projects and workshops for Deaf people and colleges in writing, acting and technical theatre. Recent productions include: *Dysfunction* (Soho Theatre); *Children of a Greater God* (Jackson's Lane); *Motherland* (Jackson's Lane); *Two Chairs* (Oval House).

Full Body & The Voice

Lawrence Batley Theatre, Queen's Street, Huddersfield HD1 2SP
tel (01484) 484441 *fax* (01484) 484443
email fullbody@lbt-uk.org
website www.fullbody.org.uk
Key contact Jon Palmer

Production details

Established in 2000. Production company exploring a range of projects that include actors with learning disabilities and promote inclusive working practices. Approximately 1 production per year touring to 10-15 venues, including arts centres and theatres in Yorkshire, the North West and internationally. Roughly 5-8 actors are used in each production.

Casting procedures

Occasionally uses freelance casting directors. Does not welcome unsolicited CVs. Actively encourages applications from disabled actors and promotes the use of inclusive casting. Offers Equity approved contracts.

Graeae Theatre Company

Bradbury Studios, 138 Kingsland Road, London E2 8DY
tel 020-7613 6900 *fax* 020-7613 6919
email info@graeae.org
website www.graeae.org
Artistic Director Jenny Sealey

Production details

Founded in 1980. Produces theatre made by disabled people (actors, directors and other theatre practitioners) with physical and sensory impairments. Stages 3 productions annually and gives 70 performances at 50 venues each year. Venues include arts centres and theatres in England, Scotland, Wales and Ireland. 3-6 actors are involved in each production. Recent productions include: national tour of *Blasted* by Sarah Kane, and *Whiter Than Snow* by Mike Kenny, which was a co-production with Birmingham Rep. Graeae/New Wolsey Theatre co-produced *Flower Girls* by Richard Cameron in Autumn 2007, and Graeae/Suspect Culture co-produced a new play in Spring 2008.

Casting procedures

Sometimes holds general auditions. Welcomes postal or email submissions (with CVs and photographs)

from actors with physical and sensory impairments. Also accepts showreels and invitations to view individual actors' websites. Offers ITC/Equity approved contracts.

Into The Scene is a new Arts Council England initiative led by Graeae. Works with leading drama schools on inclusive practice to encourage drama schools to recruit more disabled actors onto their training courses.

Scene Change is a Graeae initiative working with venues, drama schools and colleges offering taster workshops to encourage more young people to apply to drama schools.

The company offers Continued Professional Development workshops for actors. Past workshops have included Comedy Acting with director Gordon Anderson (ATC/Catherine Tate), and Singing with Barb Jungr.

Hijinx Theatre

Wales Millennium Centre, Bute Place, Cardiff CF10 5AL
tel 029-2030 0331 *fax* 029 2063 5621
email info@hijinx.org.uk
website www.hijinx.org.uk
Artistic Director Gaynor Lougher *Associate Director* Louise Osborn *Administrative Director* Val Hill

Production details

Founded in 1981, the company stages at least 2 professional productions a year on a one-night-stand basis across Wales and England, for community and theatre venues. In general the Spring show is aimed at a learning disabled audience and their communities, while the Autumn and Winter tours target the general public.

The company has developed a strong commitment to new writing over the years, commissioning plays from many of Wales' leading playwrights. On average 4 actors work on each production, which includes a strong musical element. Recent productions include: *Chasing Rainbows* (touring day centres, gateway clubs, community centres and colleges); and *The Other Woman* (Wales Millennium Centre, Torch Theatre and community venues). Offers ITC/Equity approved contracts and does not subscribe to the Equity Pension Scheme.

Casting procedures

Shows are cast by the artistic and associate director. Welcomes letters, CVs and photographs from actors previously unknown to the company. Does not accept emails or showreels. Welcomes applications from disabled and non-disabled actors.

IMPACT Theatre Company

The Stirling Road Centre, Stirling Road, Acton, London W3 8DJ
tel 020-8575 9911
email impact-theatre@btconnect.com
website www.impactondisabilityarts.com
Artistic Directors Kim Mughan, Amanda Braggins

IMPACT (IMagine, Perform And Create Together) Theatre Company was founded in 1999. It was set up by and for adults with learning disabilities facilitated by two Artistic Directors. While not a professional company, IMPACT helps to develop skills of performance and self-expression for its actors.

Krazy Kat Theatre Company

173 Hartington Road, Brighton BN2 3PA
tel (01273) 692552 *fax* (01273) 692552
email krazykattheatre@ntlworld.com
website www.krazykattheatre.co.uk
Artistic Director Kinny Gardner

Production details

A children's theatre company founded in 1972, specialising in highly visual forms of theatre that are accessible to deaf children. Normally tours 4-6 projects each year with an average annual total of 150 performances and 75 venues. Venues include schools, arts centres, theatres, outdoor venues and community centres in Essex, Sussex, Kent and London. In general 2 actors go on tour and play to audiences aged 3-7. Singing ability, physical theatre skills, sign language and a driving licence are required. Actors may also be expected to lead workshops. Recent productions include: *Three Pigs*, *Jack & The Beanstalk*, and *The Very Magic Flute*.

Casting procedures

Sometimes holds general auditions; actors can write at any time requesting inclusion. Accepts submissions (with CVs and photographs) from actors previously unknown to the company if sent by post. Does not welcome unsolicited emails. Will also accept invitations to view individual actors' websites. Offers non-Equity contracts. Actively encourages applications from disabled actors and promotes the use of inclusive casting.

Lawnmowers Independent Theatre Company & Liberdade

Swinburn House, Swinburn Street,
Gateshead NE8 1AX
tel/fax 0191-478 9200
email thelawnmowers@onetel.net.uk
website www.thelawnmowers.co.uk
Arts Director Geraldine Ling *Apprenticeship Coordinator* Rob Huggins

Theatre company addressing issues of concern for people with learning difficulties, often with an international dimension. Uses theatre and drama as a means for people with learning difficulties to explore and develop ideas, and help plan and take control of their futures.

Also runs the Liberdade Apprenticeship Scheme, a 3-year physical theatre apprenticeship scheme for young adults with learning difficulties who aim to form their own theatre company.

Magpie Dance

The Churchill Theatre, High Street,
Bromley BR1 1HA
tel 020-8290 6633
email info@magpiedance.org.uk
website www.magpiedance.org.uk
Artistic Director Avril Hitman *General Manager* Laura Riches

Magpie Dance is a company for people with learning disabilities; based in Bromley, Magpie can also deliver workshops to any region in the UK. With an emphasis on ability rather than disability, the company has a national reputation for its exciting approach to inclusive dance.

Mind the Gap

Mind the Gap Studios Bradford, Silk Warehouse, Patent Street, Bradford BD9 4SA
tel (01274) 544683 *fax* (01274) 544501
email arts@mind-the-gap.org.uk
website www.mind-the-gap.org.uk
Artistic Director Tim Wheeler *Administrative Director* Julia Skelton *Outreach Director* Emma Gee *Project Manager* Rachel Porter

Production details

Founded in 1988, Mind the Gap is a theatre company with a belief in quality, equality and inclusion, and a mission to dismantle barriers to artistic excellence so that learning disabled and non-disabled actors can appear as equals. The company has 5 main areas of activity:

• National Touring: in 2000, Mind the Gap progressed from devised work to adaptations of well-known texts. In recent years the company has produced: *Of Mice and Men* (2000 and 2005); *Dr Jekyll and Mr Hyde* (2001); *Pygmalion* (2002); *Don Quixote* (2003 – collaboration with Northern Stage); and *Cyrano* (2004). Total audiences for the 2005 tour were approximately 6700.
• Learning & Skills: each year Mind the Gap runs a full-time accredited training course for people with learning disabilities. In addition, as part of the DaDA awards scheme, the company runs Staging Change – a residential, nationally recruited training course for people with learning disabilities, working in partnership with 5 of the country's leading mainstream drama schools.
• Acting Company: comprising 7 learning-disabled graduates of Mind the Gap's training courses who work on National Touring productions and their own programme of local and regional performance work and workshops.
• Outreach: each year, Mind the Gap's Outreach programme works with 300 young learning-disabled people from West Yorkshire on short-term drama training and performance projects.
• Advocacy: Mind the Gap advocates for people who are traditionally excluded or marginalised from mainstream practices. Mind the Gap is also commissioned to do a variety of performance projects: e.g. *Finding their Feet* – a production commissioned by Bradford School of Health Studies; and *Inside Knowledge* – commissioned by Tonic as

Actors with Disabilities

part of a consultation to provide guidance for the design of a new cancer care centre in Leeds.

Stages 1 or 2 national tours annually (25-30 performances each), 1 large-scale regional performance project (3-6 performances), and 1 or 2 regional schools tours (12 performances). The national tour visits 15-20 venues: in 2005 these included West Yorkshire Playhouse; The Theatre, Chipping Norton; Ustinov Studio, Bath; Norwich Playhouse; Rose Theatre, Ormskirk; New Vic, Newcastle-under-Lyme; and Jackson's Lane Theatre, London. 3-5 actors are involved in the national tour, up to 7 actors in the schools tour, and over 20 performers in the regional performance project.

Casting procedures

Casts in-house. When the company is seeking to recruit an actor outside of the core company, it contacts agents, and advertises in *The Stage* and on its website. Casting breakdowns are available on request. Welcomes letters (with CVs and photographs) as well as showreels and invitations to view individuals' websites, "although we do not often employ actors who are not known to us. For national touring work we rarely cast outside our core Acting Company, but we do keep on record details which have been sent to us. We are particularly interested in hearing from disabled artists". Offers TMA/Equity approved contracts.

Nasty Girls

email info@nasty-girls.co.uk
website www.nasty-girls.co.uk

Disabled/Deaf women who devise, write and perform their own material specialising in cardboard characters, overblown egos, cheap laughs and slapstick.

Oily Cart Company

Smallwood School Annexe, Smallwood Road, London SW17 OTW
tel 020-8672 6329 *fax* 020-8672 0792
email oilies@oilycart.org.uk
website www.oilycart.org.uk
Artistic Director Tim Webb *General Manager* Kathy Everett *Administrator* Sarah Crompton

Production details

One of the leading theatre companies in the UK, creating highly interactive multi-sensory performances for the very young (6 months to 6 years) and for young people (aged 3-19) with Profound or Multiple Learning Disabilities (PMLD) or an Autistic Spectrum Disorder (ASD). Tours national and international venues like theatres and arts centres with early years shows, and takes its special needs work to special schools around the UK. Recent productions include: *Baby Balloon* for audiences aged 6 months to 2 years; *If All The World Were Paper*; *Blue*; and *Pool Piece* – an interactive hydrotherapy pool show for young people with PMLD or ASD.

Casting procedures

Casting breakdowns are available on the website www.oilycart.org.uk and the Artsjobs website www.artscouncil.org.uk/pressnews/ mailinglists.php. Offers ITC/Equity approved contracts. Actively encourages applications from disabled actors and promotes the use of inclusive casting.

Pride of Place Theatre Festival

The Pride of Place group of Rural Touring theatre companies hold a general audition each summer specifically to see disabled actors that they have not met before. As general auditions they do not necessarily result in immediate work, but are about establishing a relationship with the companies for future opportunities.

See the entry on page 308 for more details of the Pride of Place Festival and the companies involved.

Contact Brendan Murray of Oxfordshire Theatre Company or visit the OTTC website for more information about the auditions. Contact details for Brendan Murray and OTTC can be found on page 213.

Salamanda Tandem

14-16 Bridgford Road, Nottingham NG2 6AB
tel/fax 0845-293 2989
email info@salamanda-tandem.org
website www.salamanda-tandem.org
Artistic Director Isabel Jones

Producer of contemporary art works, creative environments and sensory performances, where people can choose to observe or become part of the artwork itself. Works with a wide spectrum of people, and in particular people with disabilities. Strong advocate for ethical practice in arts and health. Publishes articles and conducts training and professional education.

Shed MK (part of Inter-action MK)

The Old Rectory, Waterside, Peartree Bridge, Milton Keynes MK6 3EJ
tel (01908) 678514
email mandy@interaction.clara.co.uk
website www.interactionmk.org.uk/shedmk.html
Project Manager Hannah Kitchen

Inspired by the work of Chicken Shed Theatre Company (see page 379), Shed MK runs various inclusive performance projects – among them, youth theatre projects for 7-11 and 12-16 year-olds.

Shoot Your Mouth Off

Unit B, Cromwell Business Park, Cromwell Street, Hartlepool TS24 7LP
tel (01429) 42349 *mobile* (07960) 532554
email karensheader@aol.com
Director Karen Sheader

Shoot Your Mouth Off is a film company run by a disabled producer/actor, Karen Sheader. SYMO began making films with a local professional video production company, Carpet Films, in 2001; Carpet Films has since become part of SYMO. The company has made 12 films to date, many of which have been screened at both disability and mainstream festivals in the UK and internationally, including San Francisco and Moscow. An award-winning production company based in the North-East of England, it works with actors who consider themselves to be disabled – "all our films explore some aspect of the experience of being a person with impairments in a disabling society". Makes comedies, dramas, documentaries and interactive digital media.

the shysters (part of open theatre company)

AUEW Building, 57-61 Corporation Street, Coventry CV1 1GX
tel/fax (024) 7623 9186
email shysters@opentheatre.co.uk
website www.theshysters.co.uk
Artistic Director Richard Hayhow *Associate Director* Kathy Joyce *Company Manager* Sue Walker

The shysters theatre company was set up by open theatre company (otc) in partnership with the Belgrade Theatre, Coventry in 1997, but is now incorporated fully into the work of otc. "The company uses an ensemble way of working that reflects our unique characteristics (which we call 'shysterness') and which has its roots in learning disability". The shysters are keen to collaborate with others and are always looking for new ways to develop and make theatre.

In 2002 the shysters set up the shystershadows to offer training in performing arts skills and 'shysterness' to young people with learning disabilities.

Spare Tyre Theatre Company

Hampstead Town Hall, 213 Haverstock Hill, London NW3 4QP
tel/fax 020-7419 7007
email sttc@sparetyretheatrecompany.co.uk
website www.sparetyretheatrecompany.co.uk
Artistic Director Arti Prashar *General Manager* Bonnie Mitchell *Administrator* Paul Margrave

Production details

The company has 3 principal strands of work:

• Work with elders: the 'HotPots' are a group of people over 60 who perform work, often from personal experience and using humour, about the treatment of elders. They are committed to educating audiences about the potential of older people.
• Work with people with learning disabilities: the 'inc.Theatre' course is a full-time, OCN (Open College Network) approved partnership with Redbridge College for people of all ages with learning disabilities.

• Work with schools: professional TIE productions for school pupils tackling homophobia in schools. Also: 'Dealing with Difference', a workshop for school staff looking at approaches to tackling homophobia within schools.

Each strand of work has 1 major production a year, touring to roughly 100 venues – from schools, theatres and community venues to hospitals, GP surgeries, residential homes, special needs schools and public sector venues. Primarily covers the London area, but also Yorkshire, Manchester, Kent and Wales. Skills required from actors include (ideally) a driving licence, but also workshop-leading and facilitation skills, experience working with community groups, and a sensitivity to and understanding of relevant issues.

Casting procedures

Casting breakdowns are published in *The Stage* and on the website. Unsolicited approaches – including CVs, showreels and invitations to view individuals' websites – at other times are discouraged. Offers ITC/Equity approved contracts. Actively encourages applications from disabled actors and promotes the use of inclusive casting.

Spiral

See entry for First Movement on page 385.

Starfish Theatre Company (formerly Jumpstart)

See entry for Prism Arts on page 386.

StopGAP Dance Company

Farnham Maltings, Bridge Square, Farnham, Surrey GU9 7QR
tel (01252) 718664
email vicki@stopgap.uk.com
website www.stopgap.uk.com
Artistic Director Vicki Balaam

A vibrant integrated dance company that includes disabled and non-disabled dancers. It challenges traditional notions about dance by using each dancer's physical and intellectual potential as a starting point for creating new work. "We work from a philosophy of physical, psychological and social integration. In so doing, we recognise and celebrate individuality and the differences between people, while continually seeking artistic and technical excellence in all that we do."

Theatre without Walls

Forwood House, Forwood, Gloucesterhire GL6 9AB
mobile (07962) 040441
email hello@theatrewithoutwalls.org.uk
website www.theatrewithoutwalls.org.uk
Directors Genevieve Swift, Jason Maher

Established in 2002. Award winning producing theatre company with an active training/corporate wing, working in the public and private sector. Also produces television and corporate films. Training is provided for incoming actors in the form of workshops and rehearsals in forum, roleplay and interactive drama. Incoming actors require good improvisational skills. Actors are recruited through agents and Equity Job Information Service. Clients include: National Trust, Gloucestershire Local Authority, Apollo, BBC, The Prince's Trust.

Disabled actors regularly form part of their teams and are actively encouraged to apply. See also the company's entry under *Middle and smaller-scale companies* on page 225.

Theatre Workshop

34 Hamilton Place, Edinburgh EH3 5AX
tel 0131-225 7942 *fax* 0131-220 0112
email afleming@twe.org.uk
website www.theatre-workshop.com
Artistic Director Robert Rae *Company Manager* Anne Fleming

Production details

Founded in 1965; stages 4 productions a year with around 60 performances across 2 theatre venues. Occasionally tours internationally. Employs an average of 5 actors on each production, using ITC/Equity approved contracts. Recent productions include: *The Jasmine Road* (No Limits International Theatre Festival, Berlin); and *The Threepenny Opera* (Edinburgh Festival Theatre & Tramway, Glasgow).

Casting procedures

Casting breakdowns are available from the website and Equity Job Information Service. Welcomes letters and emails (with CVs and photographs) from individuals previously unknown to the company. Also happy to receive showreels and invitations to view individuals' websites. Encourages applications from disabled actors and promotes the use of inclusive casting. "Theatre Workshop casts both disabled and non-disabled actors in all our productions."

Touchdown Dance

Waterside Arts Centre, Sale M33 7ZF
tel 0161-912 5760 *fax* 0161-912 5783
email info@touchdowndance.co.uk
website www.touchdowndance.co.uk
Director Katy Dymoke

Touchdown Dance provides dance workshops for visually impaired and sighted people of all ages and ability, ranging from 'jam' weekends to more intensive courses.

VisABLE People

PO Box 80, Droitwich WR9 0ZE
tel (01905) 776631
email louise@visablepeople.com
website www.visablepeople.com
Agent Louise Dyson

Founded in 1996, VisABLE is the UK's first agency representing only disabled people for professional engagements. It represents artistes with a wide range of impairments and in every age group, including children. 1 agent represents around 50 artistes in all areas of acting, including presenting.

Does not welcome performance notices: "Sorry, no time to get out and see them usually; existing clients only." Happy to receive other enquiries (with CVs and photographs) from disabled actors via email only. Showreels should always be accompanied by an sae for return. Also happy to receive invitations to view individual actors' websites. Recommends the photographer Derek Lee. *Commission*: 10-17%

Wolf + Water

The Plough, 9-11 Fore Street, Torrington,
Devon EX38 8HQ
tel (01805) 625533
email w+w@eclipse.co.uk
website www.wolfandwater.org
Co-founders Steve Newton, Philip Robinson
Administrator Peter Smith

Since establishing itself independently in 1991 after 3 years as the Beaford Centre's 'Common Sense Project', Wolf + Water Arts Company has brought its creative and therapeutic approaches to a wide variety of groups locally, nationally and internationally. These groups have included people with learning difficulties, people with mental health issues, people in conflict situations, offenders, communities, young people at risk, children with life-threatening illnesses and their families, and staff groups working with all the above. The company produces original topical performances for conferences and for tour, and provides a wide range of training courses for those wishing to use drama and arts techniques in special needs situations. Work has taken the company throughout the UK, Eire, Scandinavia, the Middle East and the Balkans.

FESTIVALS

Disability Film Festival

London Disability Arts Forum,
20-22 Waterson Street, London E2 8HE
tel 020-7749 4352 *fax* 020-7749 4363
email caglar@disabilityfilm.org
website www.disabilityfilm.co.uk
Festival Coordinator Caglar Kimyoncu

Showcasing the talent of disabled filmmakers, the Disability Film Festival takes place over 4 days in December, and is hosted by the BFI Southbank (formerly the National Film Theatre). The festival offers filmmakers, film-goers and industry professionals the opportunity to meet, exchange feedback, network and socialise. It has also become a forum for debate, challenging the exclusion of disabled people either on screen or as filmmakers. Submission forms and guidelines are available to download from the website.

ARTS ORGANISATIONS

Acadea (formerly Northern Disability Arts Forum)

MEA House, Ellison Place,
Newcastle upon Tyne NE1 8XS
tel/fax 0191-222 0708
minicom 0191-261 2238
email info@arcadea.org
website www.arcadea.org

Arcadea aims to promote the artistic and cultural equality of disabled people in the North East region, serving Co. Durham, Northumberland, Tees Valley and Tyne & Wear.

Articulate

Cleveland Arts, 3rd Floor, Melrose House,
Melrose Street, Middlesbrough TS1 2HZ
tel (01642) 264651 *fax* (01642) 264955
email feedback@articulate.org.uk
website www.articulate.org.uk

Articulate is a programme run by Cleveland Arts which aims to develop cutting-edge arts projects inspired by, involving and relating to disabled people.

Artlink Central

Cowane Centre, Cowane Street , Stirling FK8 1JP
tel (01786) 450971 *fax* (01786) 465958
email info@artlinkcentral.org
website www.artlinkcentral.org

Established in February 1988, Artlink Central is a registered charity founded in the belief that involvement in the arts is life-enhancing and should be available to all. It enables a wide range of disabled and/or marginalised people to work with experienced professional artists on high-quality arts projects in the Stirling, Falkirk and Clackmannanshire areas of Central Scotland.

Artlink Edinburgh

13a Spittal Street, Edinburgh
tel 0131-229 3555 *fax* 0131-228 5257
website www.artlinkedinburgh.co.uk

As Artlink Central, but based in Edinburgh and the Lothians.

Artsline

c/o 21 Pine Court, Wood Lodge Gardens,
Bromley BR1 2WA
tel 020-7388 2227 *fax* 020-7383 2653
minicom 020-7388 2227
email access@artsline.org.uk
website www.artsline.org.uk

Founded in 1981 with the aim of increasing disabled people's participation in the arts, and to provide them with accurate information about access to arts and cultural events in London. In collaboration with the London Disability Arts Forum, it began producing *Disability Arts in London* (*DAIL*) magazine in 1986, and now provides a newly launched access database with details for arts and entertainment venues across London, including: theatres, cinemas, museums, art centres, tourist attractions, comedy, music venues and selected restaurants. For details of other publications, projects and services available, consult the website.

Carousel

Community Base, 113 Queens Road,
Brighton BN1 3XG
tel (01273) 234734 *fax* (01273) 234735
Artistic Director Mark Richardson *Executive Director* Liz Hall *Administrator* Mark Tidmarsh

Carousel was founded in 1982, and operates primarily in the South East of England. It is a Brighton-based arts organisation that works with people who have learning disabilities. Among its projects are the High Spin Dance Company and the Oskabright Film Festival.

DaDa-Disability & Deaf Arts

The Bluecoat, School Lane, Liverpool L1 3BX
tel 0151-707 1733 *minicom* 0151-706 0365
fax 0151-708 9355
email info@dadahello.com
website www.dadahello.com
CEO Ruth Gould

DaDa-Disability & Deaf Arts is a disabled and Deaf led organisation. It aims to facilitate the active participation of disabled and Deaf people in all aspects of the arts and creative industries, and to promote and celebrate disability and Deaf arts and culture. Based in Liverpool City Centre, the company's work covers the whole of the northwest and the UK, as well as operating on an international scale.

Disability Arts Cymru

Sbectrwm, Bwlch Road, Fairwater, Cardiff CF5 3EF
tel 029-2055 1040 *textphone* 029-2055 1040
fax 029-2055 1036
email post@dacymru.com
website www.dacymru.com
Director Maggie Hampton

Disability Arts Cymru is the only organisation in Wales providing Disability Equality Training (DET) specifically for arts providers; it lists among its clients the Arts Council of Wales and the Royal Welsh College of Music and Drama. A number of documents are available from its excellent website, which offer advice on a range of subjects including access issues for touring companies. In June 2006 the company ran 'The Unusual Stage School', a free 11-day course aimed at disabled would-be actors living in Wales.

First Movement

Level Centre, Old Station Close, Rowsley,
Derbyshire DE4 2EL
tel (01629) 57687

email fmt@first-movement.org.uk
website www.first-movement.org.uk

First Movement is an experimental arts organisation developing projects which uniquely reflect the experiences, choices and abilities of groups of people with severe and profound learning disabilities. Runs a performance company called Spiral.

National Disability Arts Forum (NDAF)

59 Lime Street, Newcastle upon Tyne NE1 2PQ
tel 0191-261 1628 *minicom* 0191-261 2237
fax 0191-222 0573
email ndaf@ndaf.org
website www.ndaf.org

The National Disability Arts Forum aims to create equality of opportunity for disabled people in all aspects of the arts. It does this by:

• Supporting the development of Disability Arts Agencies, both regional and local, throughout the UK
• Maintaining and developing a network through which these Agencies can support and assist each others' development
• Establishing favourable conditions within which disabled people can explore and express the condition of disability through the arts
• Promoting the value of art by disabled people

It also:
• Promotes and supports examples of good and/or innovative practice that encourages the participation of disabled people in the arts
• Assists organisations in developing good and/or innovative practice that encourages the participation of disabled people in the arts

The members of the Forum believe that it should be disabled people themselves who determine where and with whom responsibility for decision-making and advocacy on their behalf should lie. Hence, the organisation is accountable to, and controlled and managed by, disabled people.

Like other 'self-led' disability organisations in the UK, NDAF is committed to promoting equal opportunities and prioritises the employment of disabled people, as well as operating an ethical fundraising programme to finance its projects. It works to promote similar practices throughout the arts community, and supports other arts organisations with corresponding policies.

The Forum's main strategy for delivering its mission is to support and work with others whose work involves making their products or services more accessible or attractive to disabled people, those who are engaged in producing and promoting Disability Arts, and those who provide specialist arts services to disabled people, such as workshops or exhibitions.

NDAF aims to undertake at least 1 major arts project a year that is targeted directly at disabled people. Usually these are 'model' projects, or projects that are designed to break new ground.

Note Visit the website to sign up to *EtCetera*, NDAF's email newsletter, which contains (among other things) job opportunities, training and workshops, and a Pick-of-the-Week for television and radio. Also on the website you can listen and subscribe to its Disability Arts podcast.

Northern Ireland Arts & Disability Forum

Cathedral Quarter Managed Workspace,
109-113 Royal Avenue, Belfast BT1 1FF
tel 028-90 239 450
email info@adf.ie
website www.adf.ie
Chief Executive Officer Chris Ledger

A non-profit-making voluntary organisation that aims to provide:

• Information to disabled people and organisations – both inside and outside the arts sector
• A body that advocates on behalf of disabled people in the arts sector
• A networking, developmental and coordinating body
• A body that identifies and fills gaps in training provisions for disabled people working in the arts
• A focus for campaigning

Also runs a gallery to exhibit the work of disabled artists.

Prism Arts

Unit 003, Warwick Mill Business Village,
Warwick Mill, Carlisle, Cumbria CA4 8RR
tel (01697) 745011 *fax* (01697) 745006
email office@prismarts.fsnet.co.uk
website www.prismarts.co.uk
Director Catherine Coulthard

Promotes disabled people's access to creative arts activities in Cumbria. Runs Starfish Theatre Company, a group of learning-disabled performers.

Shape

Deane House Studios, 27 Greenwood Place,
London NW5 1LB
tel 020-7619 6160 *minicom* 020-7619 6161
fax 020-7619 6162
email info@shapearts.org.uk
website www.shapearts.org.uk

Shape is based in North London with offices in Hammersmith and Fulham, Wandsworth and Islington. It is a charity that opens up access to the arts, enabling greater participation by disabled and older people.

RIGHTS, ADVICE AND SUPPORT

Broadcasting & Creative Industries Disability Network (BCIDN) – see Employers' Forum on Disability.

Directgov

website www.direct.gov.uk/disability

The government's Public Services portal, with links to information and advice on employment, home and housing options, financial support, health, education and training, rights and obligations, transport, travel and holidays, leisure and recreation, and caring for someone.

Disability Rights Commission

DRC Helpline, FREEPOST MID02164, Stratford upon Avon CV37 9BR
tel (08457) 622633 *textphone* 08457) 622644
(You can speak to an operator at any time between 8am and 8pm, Monday to Friday) *fax* (08457) 778878

The Disability Rights Commission (DRC) is an independent body established in April 2000 by Act of Parliament to stop discrimination, and to promote equality of opportunity for disabled people.

The DRC:

• Gives advice and information to disabled people, employers and service providers – its Helpline has taken more than half a million calls
• Supports disabled people in getting their rights under the DDA
• Helps solve problems, often without going to a court or employment tribunal
• Supports legal cases to test the limits of the law: it funded 84 legal cases in 2002/3
• Provides an independent Disability Conciliation Service for disabled people and service providers through Mediation UK
• Campaigns to strengthen the law
• Organises campaigns, such as the Open 4 All campaign, to change policy, practice and awareness
• Produces policy statements and research on disability issues, and publications on rights and good practice for disabled people, employers and service providers.

Employers' Forum on Disability

Nutmeg House, 60 Gainsford Street, London SE1 2NY
tel 020-7403 3020 *fax* 020-7403 0404
minicom 020-7403 0040
email clare.morrow@efd.org.uk
website www.efd.org.uk
BCIDN Network Manager Clare Morrow

The leading employers' organisation focused on disability as it affects business. Funded and managed by more than 400 members, the Forum works to make it easier for companies to recruit and retain disabled employees and to serve disabled customers. Umbrella organisation for the Broadcasting & Creative Industries Disability Network (BCIDN), a forum for the UK's major broadcasters to explore and address disability as it relates to the media industry. It is advised by a panel of associates – 14 disabled people with considerable media experience who work in different areas of broadcasting and the media in general.

FASED

website fased.org

Freelance and self-employed disabled people in the arts. East Midlands-based organisation, primarily aimed at visual artists, but with some good general advice for freelancers on their Documents page.

Ouch!

website www.bbc.co.uk/ouch

The BBC's online disability magazine, including weblogs, message board, and a monthly podcast.

Skill: National Bureau for Students with Disabilities

Unit 3, Floor 3, Radisson Court, 219 Long Lane, London SE1 4PR
tel 020-7450 0620 *fax* 020-7450 0650
minicom 020-7450 0620
email info@skill.org.uk
website www.skill.org.uk
Chief Executive Barbara Waters

An independent UK charity that, since 1974 has promoted opportunities in learning and employment for disabled adults (over 16) from all impairment groups. Skill believes that for many disabled people, education is the key to leading a fulfilling and independent life. Information Service: open Tuesdays: 11.30am – 1.30pm; Thursdays: 1.30 – 3.30pm; *tel* 0800-328 5050 (freephone)and 020-7657 2337. "Ringing us on the second phone number saves us money – thanks!"

Provides a free information and advice service for individual disabled people and the professionals who work with them, via a freephone helpline, email and the website. This information and advice helps disabled people to overcome financial and physical barriers, ignorance and discrimination so that they can study, train or find work.

Informs and influences key policy-makers to improve legal rights and support for disabled people in post-16 education and training. Skill works together with individual disabled people, professionals working in education, training and careers, employers and disability organisations to influence government. "We listen to the people who contact our Information Service so that we know what the real issues are."

Promotes best practice through:

• Skill membership: keeping professionals up to date and informed about policy changes, providing the opportunity for exchanging information and ideas and to be more closely involved with Skill's work
• Running topical conferences and seminars
• Producing informative and practical publications
• Providing consultancy and staff training for colleges, universities and other organisations

Conducts research and develops projects on education and disability issues to address gaps in provision and to take forward new ideas.

Actors with Disabilities

Opportunities for disabled actors

Jamie Beddard

The plethora of journeys and experiences of disabled performers over the past 30 years has ranged from the lonely, demoralising, and depressing to the downright bizarre. The barriers encountered far outreach the regular obstacles preventing non-disabled actors from learning, and plying their trade. Performance attributes of technique, voice, improvisation and movement seem distant concepts when you cannot get through the doors of drama school, producers baulk at the idea of employing disabled performers, and most training and employment opportunities are based around strict notions of 'the classical actor'. This is altogether surprising in the creative industries, which should surely celebrate uniqueness, individuality and diversity. However, where once black actors were denied access to stage and screen, so those with different bodies have fought similar battles for opportunity, acknowledgement and representation. This, against a backdrop in which esteemed, non-disabled actors regularly pick up Oscars for their touching portrayal of characters with disability; Daniel Day Lewis in *My Left Foot*; Jamie Foxx in *Ray*; John Voight in *Coming Home*; Tom Hanks in *Forrest Gump* – the list is endless. One-dimensional replication of impediments, far outweighing any considerations around full and meaningful characterisations. Authenticity has been a label seldom attached to the portrayal of disability in the mainstream.

Personal anecdotes are perhaps best served in exploring the issues faced by disabled performers, as until recently, there have been no formal routes of progression into the industry. Those few who have made the periphery have tended to have random and short-lived paths based around such indeterminates as maverick directors, word of mouth or, as in my particular case, luck. The groundbreaking film *Skalligrigg* – a road movie in which a rag tag of disabled characters take to the road on a mythical quest – threw my staid career path into chaos, and levered a window (previously boarded up!) into performance. In the absence of disabled actors, many first-timers with no experience were suddenly thrust onto a film set; I thought the sound-boom was a cheap prop! 'Rough diamonds' probably most accurately described those of us fortunate enough to get such a break, and for me, the film opened up a completely new, and exciting, world. A mixture of bluff, wide-eyed enthusiasm and no little begging had to suffice in the absence of any formal training.

This 'new and exciting world' was also populated by baffling and disheartening prejudices, and initial enthusiasm soon became tinged with disappointment and anger. A casting director for *Eastenders* once informed me that a disabled character – played by a disabled actor, heaven forbid! – would place the programme in the realm of freak show. So much for diverse communities and gritty realism! This attitude is unfortunately still painfully prevalent and theatre directors are worried that their audiences will be put off by seeing a disabled person on stage.

I contacted Graeae Theatre Company – a company that had been going since the early 1980s, and was run by, and for, actors with sensory and physical disabilities. Graeae had become accustomed to (and was hardened by) irksome battles against prevalent prejudices and barriers. I found a group of like-minded individuals who were challenging these ridiculous, outdated and offensive attitudes, and determined to pursue careers considered impractical and unrealistic. They were developing, writing and performing theatre as does any small-scale company; sometimes very good, and sometimes not so good. However, the normal critical faculties brought to bear on other companies seemed strangely absent from assessment of Graeae's work, with emphasis on the 'oh so strange impairments' rather than art. The *Independent*, when reviewing Graeae's 2002 production – *Peeling* – came up with such helpful insights as, "Beaty is four feet tall; Coral has tiny limbs and a torso about the same size as her head." Apart from gross inaccuracies, the obvious offence to the individual actors involved and the banality of such revelations, what relevance has this to the art? Hopefully, the paying public didn't recoil in shock at this assembled collection of bizarre physical specimens!

I always yearned for a bad – rather than ignorant, ill informed and avoiding – review, because this would suggest a considered judgement based on the same criteria as any other performer. Undoubtedly, I have been involved in a few 'turkeys', and they should be recognised as such! However, fascination with individual impediment always seems the central tenet of any assessment of performance. Perhaps it would be interesting to apply such criteria to the wider acting fraternity – solely judging Woody Allen on his glasses, Tom Hanks on his stature, or Kenneth Williams on his nasal inflection.

Over the years the profile of Graeae, and of disabled performers in general, has grown, and there has been a gradual acceptance that it is no longer acceptable to marginalise their talents, aspirations and contributions. In many ways the Arts have lagged behind society in taking the first steps towards embracing and committing to diversity. Although, there has, in many quarters, been a genuine will to broaden participation, the stick of the Disability Discrimination Act has been instrumental in initiating fundamental appraisal and change. The possibility of legal challenges has shaken many organisations, venues and makers from their comfy inertia. Even tokenism is preferable to apartheid!

Drama schools, in particular, have found the concept of students with disability difficult to grasp, but the introduction of the Dance & Drama Awards has started the process of drama schools thinking not only about the physical access to their buildings, but also the attitudinal access and ways to promote inclusive teaching. This is very exciting and will no doubt pave the way for young disabled people to go through mainstream training rather than be reliant on Graeae.

While the process of change will take time (especially the attitudinal aspect), Graeae has had to respond to the obvious demand by setting up the training course in conjunction with London Metropolitan University. The course offers all the elements found in drama schools, and provides the skills, disciplines and training that were denied people of my age. Lack of sufficiently trained and experienced disabled actors has long been an excuse for the 'cripping up' of non-disabled actors, while training providers continually stress the unlikelihood of disabled graduates sustaining careers in the industry. A classic chicken-and-egg situation, in which aspirant disabled performers are denied entrance at all levels. However, the percentage of those who have graduated through Missing Piece, and gone into the industry, compares favourably with other drama schools, and Graeae is frequently approached by casting directors looking for disabled talent. So, young people with disabilities do share the same aspirations as any others; there is an increasing demand for such actors; and the institutions are failing to shoulder responsibility.

Missing Piece is fulfilling this vacuum, and has now been running since 2000. The nine-month (September to May) intensive training allows disabled students to work with a wide range of theatre practitioners – both specialist and mainstream. The course can act as a foundation course to further education or drama school – access- and will-permitting! – or, as is often the case, a direct gateway into the industry. Academic and practical elements of performance are covered, and opportunities for showcasing and touring afforded. Recent years have culminated in professional touring productions of *Mother Courage* and *George Dandin*, and many relationships have been brokered between our performers and directors, producers and casting directors. There is a crossover with the Performing Arts degree at London Metropolitan, with our disabled performers working alongside and in collaboration with tutors and students at the University. As well as the main Missing Piece course, Graeae run a series of taster workshops throughout the year for prospective actors.

So strides are being made by Graeae, and by other companies; the excuses and barriers preventing inclusion are slowly being dismantled. There are viable careers for those with the talent, determination and thick skin when necessary.

BBC has set up a talent fund for disabled actors to try and address dated attitudes, and to encourage writers to write storylines which are not always hospital-based or about the whole 'disability thing'!

However the failure of mainstream films such as *Inside I'm Dancing*, which continue to propagate stereotypes and exclusion – with all the main disabled characters played by non-disabled actors – will hopefully mark a sea-change in attitudes and imaginations among creators. The existing, and perspective, body of talent out there no longer allows for petty excuses or wilful misrepresentation. Disabled people, like any others, can make good, bad or indifferent performers, and should be judged as such. However, we have a right to expect the same opportunities, treatments and prospects as all. Banging the door down has become boring – just let us in. It's not rocket science!

Jamie Beddard is an actor, writer and director. Involved with Graeae since 1991, he was Associate Director of the company for some years. He is currently working as a freelance director and co-editor of *DAIL* magazine. Graeae productions 2006/7 include *Blasted* by Sarah Kane, touring March to May; *Once Beyond These Walls, A Girl* by Richard Cameron, touring October to November; and *Whiter Than Snow* by Mike Kenny – a co-production with Birmingham Rep, touring February to April 2007. For full details, visit the website **www.graeae.org**. For information on Missing Piece, contact: **ellie@graeae.org**.

Resources
Introduction

This section covers those practical items (and sources of more detailed help and advice) that are, to the actor, what tools and a first-aid kit are to a carpenter. Some may be irrelevant to you – for instance, you may feel as though you could never have the organisational skills to set up your own company. Others are essential to all actors: good photographs, for example. Whatever your needs, time taken to formulate clearly your requirements before approaching any of the contacts listed below will be time well spent.

Equity

Louise Grainger

Equity is the only Trade Union to represent performers and people working creatively across the entire spectrum of arts and entertainment, both live and recorded. The main function of Equity is to negotiate minimum terms and conditions of employment throughout the entire world of entertainment, and to endeavour to ensure that these take account of social and economic changes. We look to the future as well, negotiating agreements to embrace the new and emerging technologies which affect performers – so satellite, digital television, new media and so on are all covered, as are the more traditional areas. We also work at national level by lobbying government and other bodies on issues of paramount importance to the membership. In addition we operate at an international level through the Federation of International Artists which Equity helped to establish, the International Committee for Artistic Freedom, and through agreements with sister unions overseas.

As well as these core activities, Equity strives to provide a wide range of services for members so that they are eligible for a whole host of benefits which are continually being revised and developed. These include helplines, job information, insurance cover, members' pension scheme, charities and others. (For more information, visit the Equity website **www.equity.org.uk**. For details of Equity's Job Information Service, see entry under The Spotlight, casting directories and information services.)

Louise Grainger is a Marketing & Membership Services Officer for Equity.

Equity
Head Office, Guild House, Upper St Martins Lane, London WC2H 9EG
tel 020-7379 6000 *fax* 020-7379 7001
email info@equity.org.uk
website www.equity.org.uk
- Job Information Service: 0870-901 0900
- Theatre, Variety, Opera & Dance Helpline: 020-7670 0237
- Film, Television, Radio & Audiovisual Helpline: 020-7670 0247
- Tax & Benefits Helpline (Tuesdays & Thursdays only): 020-7670 0223
- Bullying Reporting Line: 020-7670 0268
- Subscription Enquiries: 020-7670 0219

Regional offices:

Midlands
Office 1, Steeple House, Percy Street, Coventry CV1 3BY
tel (02476) 553612
email info@midlands-equity.org.uk

North East
The Workstation, 15 Paternoster Row, Sheffield, S1 2BX
tel 0114-275 9746
email njones@sheffield.equity.org.uk

North West and Isle of Man
Express Networks, 1 George Leigh Street, Manchester M4 5DL
tel 0161-244 5995 *fax* 0161-244 5971
email info@manchester-equity.org.uk

Scotland and Northern Ireland
114 Union Street, Glasgow G1 3QQ
tel 0141-248 2472 *fax* 0141-248 2473
email igilcrist@glasgow.equity.org.uk

South East
Guild House, Upper St Martins Lane, London WC2H 9EG
tel 020-7670 0229 *fax* 020-7379 7001
email jainslie@equity.org.uk

Wales and South West
Transport House, 1 Cathedral Road, Cardiff CF1 9SD
tel 029-2039 7971 *fax* 029-2023 0754
email info@cardiff-equity.org.uk

Equity Pension Scheme

Did you know that you could get your theatre employer to contribute to your Equity Pension Scheme?

Successful negotiations by Equity in 1997 saw the launch of the EPS. Initially it catered for members working mainly in television, but further negotiations meant that by January 2001 the EPS had been expanded to include actors, actresses and stage management working in theatre.

• Firstly the EPS was launched in the West End with SOLT Managers participating. These were quickly followed by the RNT, the Globe on the Southbank and Walt Disney Theatrical (UK). The RSC joined in January 2002.

• 1st April 2004 saw further expansion of the EPS with the inclusion of Subsidised Repertory Theatre (TMA, Grade 1) and Commercial Theatre Managers.

• From 1st April 2005 this extended to Grade 2 and 3 theatres.

• Most recently, for the 2005/06 season onwards QDOS Entertainment is also party to the EPS.

This means that the majority of theatre engagements will benefit from contributions to the EPS.

What is the EPS?

• The EPS is a Stakeholder compliant product, which is administered by First Act, the appointed insurance intermediaries to Equity and its members.

• The funds are managed by Norwich Union; the UK's largest insurer with over £230 billion of funds under management. The EPS has access to over 60 investment funds, catering for all attitudes to investment risk including ethical funds. Details of these funds can be supplied upon request.

• You have total flexibility. You can contribute when you are working, and when you are not; you can take a break.

• The EPS is penalty free and has a maximum charge of 0.75% per annum of the funds under management i.e. £0.75 for every £100 in your fund.

How the EPS works

As an EPS member you benefit from a contribution paid by your employers, equal to a percentage of your weekly rehearsal of performance fee. Details of these and the participating employers are shown below.

To qualify, you agree to make a contribution from your weekly fee. Again details are shown below.

The employer contribution is added to your salary and then deducted together with your personal contributions.

There is no need for a direct debit or chance of spending the contributions by mistake as both yours and the employer contributions are sent directly by the employer to First Act, for investment on your behalf.

Once with Norwich Union, basic rate tax relief is added.

An example (SOLT)

If your weekly performance fee was £400:

• Your contribution £10 per week

• Employer contribution £20 per week
• Total Net contribution £130 per month
• Total Gross contribution £166.67 per month

As you can see, you would have paid £40, but a monthly investment of £166.67 is achieved.

The EPS can work in a number of ways.

1. You can make contributions related to your engagement only, this way you can pay in when you are working but freeze payments when you are not, **and**
2. you can make additional personal payments by direct debit on a monthly basis, **and**
3. you can make additional personal contributions by cheque on an add hoc basis.

As you would expect, this document is only a brief introduction to the EPS and not a full explanation.

If you are already a member of the EPS, you must make sure that you have inserted your EPS membership number onto your contract/addendum **or** advised your Company Manager of your EPS membership number.

More information – including an application form – can be found on the Equity website. If you have any questions please contact Andrew Barker of First Act, *tel* 020-8686 5050, *fax* 020-8686 5559, *email* **eps@firstact.co.uk**.

The role of an Equity deputy

Steve Fortune

The Equity deputy of a show is generally the first point of contact between the performers and the union in the event of any problems arising, and can offer advice on the many issues that Equity is involved in.

In an ideal world, at some time during the first week of a rehearsal process for a new production of either a play or a musical, a meeting would be called of the acting company and stage management team, and at this meeting they would elect someone to act as the Equity deputy for the duration of the show. In reality, this meeting is often a snatched 5 minutes halfway through rehearsals and the person elected is the unfortunate soul who happened to be in the toilet at the time!

Once elected, the deputy then contacts Equity who puts him or her in touch with the correct official – the organiser who deals with the specific area that the show might be in (e.g. West End Theatre, Commercial tour or Subsidised Repertory). The organiser will then send out a 'dep's pack'. This contains information about Equity; leaflets about current activities; and a cast list detailing those who are already members and those who aren't, as well as the current status of members, such as whether they are 'in benefit' or 'out of benefit'. To be in benefit, a member has to be 'paid up' – that is, they have paid their subscription for the year. If the subscription is more than 13 weeks overdue then the member is 'out of benefit', which means that they would not be eligible for legal assistance, public liability insurance and all of the other services which Equity provide to its members.

Until the employment act of 1990 made it illegal to refuse to employ someone who was not a member of a trade union, Equity was what is known as a 'closed shop': you had to be a member of the union in order to work in theatre, television and film. In order to become a member you had to get work that offered an Equity contract and allowed you to apply for a provisional membership card. This enabled you to work in certain areas of the profession, but not in all. To work in the West End and other areas you had to be a 'full member', which meant that you had to prove that you had completed 40 weeks' professional work on recognised Equity contracts. Nowadays, thought, there is no requirement for you to be a member of Equity in order to work in the profession, so another function of the deputy is to recruit new members by showing them the advantages and benefits of membership. The deputy will also collect subscriptions from existing members where necessary, in order to retain their membership. Currently the Equity subscription rate is £100 per year for those earning £20,000 or less a year and can be paid by direct debit monthly, quarterly or annually. A number of managements will also arrange for them to be taken from the salaries on a weekly basis.

As a deputy one of the most common questions I am asked is: "Why should I join the union?" For me the answer is simple and straightforward. It is only because we have a union that we are able to negotiate from a position of strength for pay and working conditions. Over the years Equity has secured agreements governing minimum pay and conditions across the entertainment industry. It also produces guidelines for work in areas where there are no representative bodies with whom to negotiate. These benefits are enjoyed by members and non-members alike, but without some tough negotiations they would not exist, and one doesn't have to look far today to find examples of employees on buy-out contracts working long hours for low set payments. The old adage of strength in numbers is why it is important to join the union, and the more members it has within the industry, the stronger its position when it comes to negotiating.

A deputy is often required to act as the company spokesperson, voicing any concerns or problems which members of the company may have with the management – even when these concerns have little or nothing to do with the Equity agreement! For this reason it is very useful to have a good working relationship with the company manager of the show; it enables you to speak freely and comfortably with them in order to resolve any issues before they escalate and involve the union officials. One contentious area that has arisen a number of times when I have been a deputy is an issue called 'push and pull'. This involves a payment for an artist when they are asked to change the set or move scenery, furniture or props other than in character or as part of the action of a scene. Quite often a director will decide that it is much better stylistically for a production if the cast themselves are involved in scene changes, rather than having crew members trooping on stage and moving everything. However, in an attempt to avoid extra wage costs, producers will sometimes try and maintain that these scene changes are wholly part of the action and in character, and therefore should not attract a payment. I once had to take up such a case on behalf of a company of actors. Initially the employing company refused to pay, but the union took up the case and eventually the performers involved got the relevant remuneration. This was backdated to the first night of the production, and represented a bonus all in all of about £250 each! As you can imagine, it wasn't too hard to convince those people to pay their union dues!

Original cast recordings are great fun to be involved in, but for a deputy it can also be a test of his or her diplomatic and negotiating skills. When a cast album of a show is going to be recorded, the record producer must pay the artists a recording fee plus a royalty on sales of the album. The royalty payment is based on 90% of the dealer price of each CD, and is 6.5% for the first 75,000 sales – so if the dealer price were, say, £9 then the royalty would be 52 pence per CD. This royalty is then divided into points, which are split between the artists and stage management involved in the recording. This is where it can get tricky, because if someone is playing a lead role in a show and singing a lot of solos, they may feel that they are entitled to a greater share than the person who only has one song, or less still, maybe just one line in a song. So the points have to be divided up in such a way as to keep everyone happy (although of course the more points that the royalty is divided into, the less each point is actually worth!). Usually, though, as long as the status quo appears to have been retained, everyone is happy. The issue is generally academic anyway, because – with a few notable exceptions, such as *Les Miserables* and *Phantom of the Opera* – most cast albums never sell anything like 75,000 copies and royalties are either fairly small or virtually non-existent.

An Equity deputy is also involved in areas of health and safety, making sure that any accidents are reported promptly and noted in the accident book in as much detail as possible. They may also be asked to communicate with the management about things such as a slippery stage, which can be dangerous, particularly if dancers are being asked to perform on it. Other things, such as a lack of heating in changing areas backstage and in dressing rooms, may also be brought to the deputy to convey to the management.

One of Equity's greatest success stories in recent years has been the establishment of a pension scheme for people working in theatre and television and the BBC, into which both employer and employee contribute. Although the scheme is administered by a professional financial services company, it is often the deputy who brings it to the attention of new and existing members.

Deputies working in West End theatre are eligible to attend monthly deputies' meetings, which are held at the Equity head office in Upper St Martin's Lane. As well as being an enjoyable way of meeting people from all the other shows and plays in London, these meetings are a good opportunity to learn about any negotiations or developments within the industry that Equity are involved with, as well as providing a useful forum to discuss any areas of concern which you may have.

Equity plays a vital role in the working life of anyone involved in the entertainment industry, and the benefits of membership far exceed the cost of subscription. The union:
• Provides medical support through the British Performing Arts Medicine Trust.
• Automatically covers its members for public liability of up to £10 million, as well as for backstage and accident insurance.
• Distributes hundreds of thousands of pounds each year in payments for use of members' work in television and film re-runs, video sales and audio recordings.
• Offers members free legal advice and support in disputes over professional engagements, including personal injury claims.
• Provides members with free advice on National Insurance, taxation, benefits, pensions and welfare issues, taking cases to tribunal level if needed.
• Protects members' names, so that no two subscribers can use the same professional name.
And all this comes at a cost of less than £2 per week, for most people.

Being an Equity deputy is an unpaid job, but you can if you wish claim commission on the subscriptions you collect. The work can be stressful at times when there are a lot of problems, but it is also rewarding and interesting. It's always a pleasure to see the faces of member who has just been told that as a result of your negotiation they will be receiving extra money for filming or overtime. The job generally takes up very little time, and it serves a vital role in providing a line of communication between the union members, the management and the union. Support the union, join Equity and the next time you are in a show, agree to be the Equity deputy ... you just might find you enjoy it so much that you want to do it again and again!

Steve Fortune has appeared in a number of West End shows. Most recently he played the Constable in *Fiddler on the Roof* at the Savoy Theatre; he has also appeared in *Noises Off* at the Piccadilly Theatre, *Jesus Christ Superstar* at the Lyceum, *Hard Times* at the Theatre Royal Haymarket, *Chess* at the Prince Edward, *Annie Get Your Gun* at the Aldwych and *Underneath the Arches* at the Prince of Wales Theatre. On television he has appeared in *Casualty*, *The Bill*, *Eastenders*, *Only Fools and Horses*, *Birds of a Feather* and *The Jump*, and in numerous commercials advertising everything from woodstain to bananas. He once played a salsa-dancing laxative user...

Resources

The Spotlight, casting directories and information services

Spotlight is a fundamental part of the fabric of the acting profession, and it is essential to have an entry. (It is a false economy not to have one.) The growth of the Internet has seen a rise in companies offering similar services – usually, for a lower subscription. Once again it is important to research thoroughly the value to you of investing in one of these. As well as trying to assess whether such an investment will really enhance your visibility to employers, an essential part of that research is to read the 'small print' properly.

With some exceptions (major musicals, for instance), many employers do not openly advertise the properly paid acting work they have to offer. It's simpler to contact agents whom they know and trust for casting suggestions. This limits the number of submissions, largely prevents (time-wasting) unsuitable applicants, and goes some way towards ensuring that those suggested for consideration are really suitable for the parts available. Consequently, the time required to consider all the CVs and photographs submitted is contained within reasonable limits. It can take a day's work to go through a thousand submissions to select whom to interview; it can take another day's work to interview just 30 of these.

Casting information services – often allied to Internet casting directories – glean their information from all kinds of sources. The important thing to remember is that some of the information about 'properly paid acting work' is of a second-hand nature – that is, it was not sent directly to them in the first instance. Consequently, it is important to research reputations for accuracy (and 'up-to-dateness') before committing your funds to such companies. However, many Fringe production and student film opportunities are directly advertised in such publications, and such opportunities might lead on to 'properly paid acting work'.

The Spotlight

Head Office, 7 Leicester Place, London WC2H 7RJ
tel 020-7437 7631 *fax* 020-7437 5881
email info@spotlight.com
website www.spotlight.com

The Spotlight was founded in 1927 and has since become world-famous for its casting directories. Today more than 30,000 performers appear in the book and Internet versions of *Spotlight*, including actors and actresses, child artists, presenters, dancers and stunt artists. As the industry's leading casting resource, *Spotlight* is used by TV, film, radio and theatrical companies throughout the UK, and many worldwide. Its Internet casting services have become an essential communication tool, uniting actors, agents and production professionals more quickly and easily than ever before.

Membership of The Spotlight means that a performer is promoted to casting opportunities in a number of ways. Firstly, each artist has a photo and contact details in the *Spotlight Directories*, which are printed once per year. Their details are also held on an Artists' Records telephone database, so that casting/production professionals know immediately where to call when they want to get in touch.

Additionally, every performer is promoted on Spotlight Interactive (**www.spotlight.com**) – the online version of *Spotlight*. Here, casting professionals can search performers' details according to very specific criteria. For example: "Show me all actors with black hair, aged 35-40, who can speak French and play the guitar." In 2006, The Spotlight website received over one million artist searches, and actor CVs were viewed a total of 5,753,312 times.

Performers can upload showreels, voice-clips and additional photos to enhance their online CVs, which is a far quicker and more cost-effective way of promoting themselves than sending out endless copies to casting directors and agents in the post. Artists are also issued with a pair of unique PIN numbers which allow them respectively to access their CV whenever they wish – keeping credits and skills up-to-date – or to email to others, a link to their *Spotlight* CV.

Spotlight is also used on a daily basis by production professionals sending out casting briefs to agents. In 2006, a weekly average of 160 casting breakdowns was sent out via The Spotlight Link, with more than 33,370 artists submitted weekly for an average of 541 individual roles, spanning a wide variety of TV, film, theatre, radio and commercial work. This makes The Spotlight by far the busiest casting service in the UK. The Spotlight is also due to launch a job information service which goes directly to artists themselves: see the website for the latest details.

The Spotlight also publishes *Contacts* every November. This is a directory of companies and individuals working across TV, film, stage and radio, and costs £11.99.

To join The Spotlight, visit the website **www.spotlight.com**, call 020 7437 7631, or email **info@spotlight.com** for application forms. Entry is strictly limited to professionally trained and/or professionally experienced performers, and applications are always vetted.

AT2 UK (Actors-Inc)

FREEPOST RLZY-TBYA-UATX,
Sandhurst GU47 0FR
email info@actors-inc.co.uk
website www.AT2Global.co.uk

Details of casting information services

Casting breakdowns are delivered instantly via email, in addition to a weekly newsletter which is sent every Friday afternoon. Members can search the website for information, advice and details of workshops and events, as well as a full listing of virtually all theatrical agencies in the UK. Job advertisements for casual temporary work geared towards resting actors are also posted on a daily basis.

Actors' details are included in a fully searchable database which is accessible to casting professionals, and a personal profile and web address which may be used for easy self-promotion, networking etc. Audio samples and video showreels can also be incorporated. AT2 is an expanding global company, with offices in the UK, USA, South Africa, Australia, New Zealand, and with more territories due to be joining forces in 2007/08. As part of your membership, you may easily transfer your profile to different host countries if you are travelling abroad.

The monthly membership fee is £6 for the standard package, or £7.50 if you'd like to incorporate video and audio samples – plus a month's free trial to evaluate the service. Recent productions cast include Skins (E4 – Sally Broome Casting), Crimewatch (BBC – Vital Productions), Grease (West End – Debbie O'Brien Casting), Sony (Commercial - Casting Unlimited), Nike (Commercial – Ali Fearnley

Casting) along with student films, profit share, TIE etc.

Castcall

106 Wilsden Avenue, Luton LU1 5HR
tel (01582) 456213 *fax* (01582) 480736
email info@castcall.co.uk
website www.castcall.co.uk

Details of casting information services

Established in 1986. Information service is available by email or fax, with regular updates throughout the week. Actors should be professionally trained or experienced to be included. Charges £34 for 12 weeks. Allows actors to put subscriptions on hold if required and to resume when appropriate. Also offers general advice and free image scanning.

Sources of casting breakdowns have included: Crocodile Casting, Casting Unlimited, Panto People, Layton & Norcliffe, Pippa Ailion, Jayne Collins, Vital Productions, the BBC, Greenwich Films, Nina Gold and many repertory theatres.

Casting Call Pro

138 Upper Street, London, N1 1QP
tel 020-7288 2233
email info@castingcallpro.com
website uk.castingcallpro.com

Details of casting information services

Established in 2004, Casting Call Pro is an online service now used by over 14,000 professional actors. The site is updated daily with a wide range of casting breakdowns which include films, theatre tours, corporate work and commercials. Details of appropriate opportunities are sent directly to users as they become available. Users can select which types of opportunities (e.g. film, theatre) they wish to receive information about. Members can then apply for opportunities through their CCP profile. CCP profiles feature actors' headshots and basic details along with their work history and skills and can include a show-reel or voice-reel if required. Casting Call Pro also fosters a lively community of actors. Whether you need advice on how to handle problem situations, want feedback on your new head shots or need the right audition piece CCP's 'Green Room' and other features help users keep control of their career. Casting Call Pro's unique interface even allows users to keep track of old contacts, and forge new ones by giving you access to the company, agency and service provider directories. More information and a full breakdown of features are available online.

The standard service from Casting Call Pro is entirely free. They also offer a Premium Service offering a wider range of features. To discover more about the benefits of using Casting Call Pro as well as current subscription rates and latest updates to the service, please visit the website at **uk.castingcallpro.com**. All members are also included in their online directory which is viewed over 30,000 times each week.

To join Casting Call Pro you must have graduated from an NCDT accredited course, be a current Equity member or have at least 3 professional acting credits (no extra, or non-speaking roles).

CastNet Ltd

20 Sparrows Herne, Bushey,
Hertfordshire WD23 1FU
tel 020-8420 4209 *fax* 020-8421 9666
email admin@castingnetwork.co.uk
website www.castingnetwork.co.uk
Key contact Alyson Sharron

Details of casting information services

Established in 1997. The information service is only available online, with information circulated to members by email every day. Casting information is tailored to the exact requirements of the actor; if an actor is not interested in working in certain areas, such as student films or TIE, they will not be sent details of those projects. Information is also filtered according to the skills and physical characteristics of actors. When suitable casting opportunities do arise, CastNet will send actors free text messages and emails. Actors may make a submission for any project via the website or by telephone; CastNet will then send their CV, headshot and a covering letter to the casting director.

All reproductions of photos and postage costs are included in the subscription charge. Sends a weekly summary report by email, detailing every production for which actors have been submitted. CastNet receives casting breakdowns from a range of clients including Fringe theatre, mainstream films and TV.

Details of actors' Internet directories

All actors must meet the following criteria to be included: have graduated from an NCDT-accredited course; have a minimum of 3 professional theatre, film or acting credits (does not include extra or drama school work); be able to use 1 UK-based accent to a 'native' standard; have full membership of Equity (or be eligible); have a professionally taken b&w publicity photograph; and be at least 18 years old at the time of application.

Admits new members every week. The CastNet Directory is distributed to more than 1500 casting directors and production companies. Actors' CVs are included on the website, with instant messaging facility for casting directors to contact them by email or text message. Will also include up to 4 photos, showreel and voice demo at no extra charge. Registers personal domain name for each actor and points it directly to their online CV. Anyone can access online directory, but printed directory is only available to industry professionals. Members' online details are updated daily and the book is updated on a quarterly basis. For details of current clients (both actors and casting professionals), consult the website.

The weekly subscription rate is £6.50 and includes all the services listed above.

Castweb

7 St Luke's Avenue, London SW4 7LG
tel 020-7720 9002
email info@castweb.co.uk
website www.castweb.co.uk
Key contact Patrick Warrington

Details of casting information services

Established in 1999. A daily information service is available online, with casting breakdowns circulated to subscribers throughout the day. Subscription starts at £17.95 per month. Castweb has circulated casting opportunities for over 1200 production companies and casting directors, and subscription is strictly for the use of professional actors and established agents only. It is now received by more than 1000 agents across Europe, as well as over 400 in the UK. At just 39p per day, it remains the essential source of casting opportunities for professional performers in the UK.

Equity Job Information Service (JIS)

Guild House, Upper St Martin's Lane,
London WC2H 9EG
website www.equity.org.uk

Details of casting information services

Launched in 1999, this service is now available (to members only) 24 hours a day via the Equity website; the phone line was discontinued in August 2007. It is available free of charge to all members. The service provides details of job opportunities in the wide range of fields in which Equity members work. Users of the service can search for jobs in acting, singing, dance, variety, light entertainment and circus, and in non-performance work such as stage management. All the work listed is at least reasonably paid (although not necessarily at full Equity-agreed rates), thoroughly checked for accuracy, and the job-providers checked for their record of fair treatment of employees.

The effectiveness of this service relies on members only submitting themselves for suitable roles. Too many unwanted applications will make employers reluctant to advertise on JIS in the future, and reduce the number of opportunities for actors.

Mandy.com

website www.mandy.com

Posts casting calls for actors for film. See entry under *Publications, libraries, references and booksellers* on page 458.

Performers Directory

PO Box 29942, London SW6 1FL
tel 020-7610 6699 *fax* 020-7736 6088

email admin@performersdirectory.co.uk
website www.performersdirectory.co.uk
Directors Antonia Stratton, Clive Stevens

Details of casting information services

Established in 1995. Information is available online only, with emails being circulated to subscribers every day.

Details of actors' Internet directories

Includes actors' CVs, photos and voice samples in the online directory, which is accessible only to casting professionals. Members' details are updated as and when requested. Clients have included: Disney, the BBC, Bollywood producers, Universal, the National Theatre and the Royal Shakespeare Company. Has also suggested actors for *The Bill*, *Jonathan Creek*, *Jerry Springer the Opera* (West End), Walkers Crisps commercials, Selfridges' Fashion Show and various club events.

Annual subscription rate is £37 and includes all services listed above.

Production & Casting Report (PCR)

PO Box 11, London N1 7JZ
tel (01843) 860885
email info@pcrsubscriptions.com
website www.pcrnewsletter.com

Details of casting information services

Established in 1968. Available in print and online, *PCR* is a weekly newsletter which carries details of casting and crew opportunities in film, television and theatre. Information is checked carefully by staff and always comes directly from the production company or casting director – *PCR* never prints second-hand information. A free telephone information line is also available to help subscribers track down casting leads. Every week, dozens of opportunities are featured from such sources as Hubbard Casting, David Grindrod, Lucinda Syson, Birmingham Stage, Red Shift and Jeremy Zimmermann, among others. Low-budget film, voice-over, pop promo, commercial, corporate video and Fringe casting calls are also featured.

The subscription rate is £31.04 for 5 weeks but other rates are available, including £22.46 per month by direct debit.

Other publications include:

• *Filmlog*: lists feature films in pre-production and development, with details of studios, locations, key people and addresses (£40 for 12 months)

SBS (Script Breakdown Services)

Suite 204, 254 Belsize Road, London NW6 4BT
tel 020-8451 2852

SBS is a publication giving casting breakdown information. It is circulated to agents *only*. It is not available to individuals.

Shooting People

email contact@shootingpeople.org
website www.shootingpeople.org
Co-founders Cath LeCouteur, Jess Search *Casting Editor* Andrew Robertson

Shooting People allows thousands of people working in independent film to exchange information via a range of daily email bulletins, including a daily UK Casting Bulletin. This allows actors to discuss their craft and receive casting calls from directors, producers and casting directors. Shooting People's overall membership is currently more than 34,000. Actors can create a public casting profile as well as getting significant discounts off key film products and services.

Part-membership allows subscribers to receive email bulletins only, and is free. Full membership costs £20 per year and entitles users to a range of other services. See entry under *Publications, libraries, references and booksellers* on page 461 for further details.

The Stage

47 Bermondsey Street, London SE1 3XT
tel 020-7403 1818 *subscriptions* (01858) 438895
email newsdesk@thestage.co.uk
website www.thestage.co.uk
Managing Director Catherine Comerford *Editor* Brian Attwood

Online and weekly print publication for the entertainment industry. News, reviews, features and recruitment for theatre, light entertainment, opera, dance, TV, radio, backstage and technical, management, education and training. Established 1880

Talent Circle

website www.talentcircle.co.uk

Details of casting information services

Established in 2003. Provides a free online casting information service and resource where emails are circulated to members on a daily basis.

Details of actors' Internet directories

Directory is open to all actors free of charge and is publicly accessible. Casting directors can select level of experience required at sign-up, as no minimum criteria are demanded of members. Members can update their own entry (to include photograph, voice sample and CV) at any time.

Talent Spot UK

1 Colindale Avenue, Edgware Road, London NW9 5DS
tel 0845-045 4111
email info@talentspotuk.com
website www.talentspotuk.com
Key contact (for new members) Dean Ezekiel

Resources

Details of casting information services

Established in 2002. Casting bulletins are posted online each week and can be accessed for £6.99 per month at the time of writing. Produces a montly newsletter and circulates related special offers to members.

Details of actors' Internet directories

Admits new members on a daily basis at a charge of £6.99 per month, or £59.99 per year at the time of writing. Actors' CVs, photos and voice samples are posted on the website. "Specialises in providing networking and lifestyle services for the talent and entertainment industry."

UK Theatre Network

PO Box 3009, Glasgow G60 5ET
tel 0870-760 6033 *fax* 0870-760 6033

email editor@uktheatre.net
website www.uktheatre.net

Details of casting information services

Established 2001. Casting information is circulated to members daily, by email. In addition the company offers webmail, website hosting, reviews, contacts and listings of what's on. All services are provided free of charge. New members should contact **uktheatre-daily@getresponse.com**.

Details of actors' Internet directories

This service is available free of charge to all active performers aged 16 upwards. Members' details are available publicly and can be updated by the actor at any time. Actors can include their CV, photograph and voice sample on the directory.

Getting the most from your photographs

Angus Deuchar

When searching for actors, most casting directors or directors start with a pile of photographs. Their time is limited, so they really only want to see the people who stand a chance of being right for a part – and the picture will be a vital part of their decision-making process. It's important therefore, to ensure that the photographs you use are as good as they can possibly be.

Have a flick through *Spotlight*. As well as being compulsive entertainment for any actor, it can be a great way to decide what works and what doesn't. If *you* were the casting director, who would (and wouldn't) you see? Try it for different types of production: a musical, a Shakespeare play, a TV drama. You may be surprised at the assumptions you make based on the photographs.

I'm going to look at what makes a good actor's photograph; help you think through how to choose a photographer; and discuss how you can get the best results from a photo session. Here is a list of, in my opinion, some important qualities to look for in a good headshot. It should be:

• **Honest.** This to me is the key to a good actor's photograph. Decisions at interviews are often largely made in the first few seconds, so it's important that the person who walks through the door is the person they saw in the photograph. If an actor looks different in some way, the interviewer's first reaction may well be disappointment. Which can't be a good start!

• **Well lit.** The face and hair should be well lit. If there are excessively bright areas or shadows on the face, the photo is probably not doing the actor any favours.

• **In focus.**

• **A good connection with the eyes.** These are possibly the most important feature, as these are what we generally look at first. We make a connection with the eyes. They should be well lit, in focus, looking *at* the camera and not squinting. They should also be 'alive' and not glazed over.

• **Well framed.** Ideally just head and shoulders. Not too close up, as it can look a bit overbearing. Likewise, not too far away as the face becomes too small.

• **Nothing 'tricksy'.** No fake hand-gestures, and certainly no props!

Can't I just get my friend to take some pictures in the back garden? Well, you could (in fact, some do). But what kind of image of yourself would that portray? You can always see such pictures in *Spotlight* – the actor looking awkward, squinting into the sunlight or the picture out of focus. Again, if you were the casting director, would you consider that actor to be serious? There's no point in cutting costs here. Decent photographs can more than pay for themselves.

Finding a photographer

Assuming you've decided to employ a photographer, how do you find the right one? Professional photographers are not all alike. Some who may be fantastic at, say, press or fashion, may not be good at actors' portraits. It's important that the photographer knows the business of Acting. There are countless listings of specialist actors' photographers – in publications like this one; as adverts in *Contacts*; or on posters in Actors Centres; but the style of photographs, and the ability of the photographers, are as varied as the prices and packages. It is therefore essential to check out their work for yourself. Have a look at their website if they have one, or at least try to see several different examples of their work.

Don't make a choice based solely on price. The amount a photographer charges is not necessarily an indication of how good (or bad) they are. Wherever possible, make your decision about a photographer based mostly on the *work* they produce, rather than how much they charge. It's important ultimately that you get the best possible photographs.

Find out the following:

• **Studio or natural light?** Studio light is easier to standardise and can be used at any time of the day or night and during any weather. It can be made to flatter someone, but won't necessarily show what they will look like in 'real life'. I prefer natural light, as I believe it to be generally more honest. Good natural light can still show someone at their best, but it won't deceive. It can also be more relaxing for the subject to be outside for the session. Casting directors often prefer natural light as it gives a better indication of who is actually going to walk through the door.

• **Film or digital?** Digital technology has moved on to such an extent that the quality of either format is comparable. Digital tends to produce a cleaner, less grainy image *and* you can check the results as you go along. It is essential however, that whoever is preparing the final photograph knows how to convert the image into a good-quality black and white print, with decent contrast and without loss of detail. This takes a reasonable amount of skill and know-how.

• **How much do they charge?** Does that include VAT? If relevant, you may want to ask about concessions for students.

• **How many photos do I get?** Find out how many photos will actually be taken at the session and how many different, finished 8x10 prints you can choose.

• **How will I view my proofs?** Some photographers will put your proofs onto a website enabling you to view them blown up on the screen. You may prefer a paper contact sheet, which, although much smaller to view, is more portable. If you want both, you may need to pay extra – so ask.

• **How long until I see my proofs?** Websites can often be published the same day as the session, while a paper contact will usually need to be produced and posted, so will take a few days. Some photographers will show you pictures on a computer straight away. This can be useful as a guide, but you probably shouldn't try to make final decisions without a bit of time to think.

• **How long will it take until I get my finished prints?** Try to get an indication of how long you should expect to wait after placing your final order. Hopefully, no more than a few days.

• **Do I get a CD?** As well as the prints, a few electronic versions of the final photos are extremely useful. They can be used on a website, to send a submission via email, to send to The Spotlight, to print out yourself, or to act as the master-copy for your 'repros'. Find out if the photographer will provide you with a few different versions on a CD, and if it's included in the price.

The session itself

Here are some important things to prepare before – or think about during – your photo session.

• **Your 'look'.** Do you want to appear neutral or as a particular 'type'? For instance, earrings (on men especially) or other piercings, may limit you to modern or even 'alternative' characters. A formal jacket might suggest a business person or MP. Any of these looks may be fine, as they can make you 'ideal' for a particular type of role – but it's likely that that's all you'll ever be seen for while using that photograph! You decide – it really depends upon how you are marketing yourself.

• **Make-up and hair.** Preferably little or no make-up, but certainly no more than you would wear normally, day to day. Some photographers provide a 'hair and make-up' service but I would strongly discourage actors from using this. Don't confuse actors' portraits with having a glamorous photo to stick on top of the piano! If someone else prepares you, you're unlikely to look like the 'normal' you and it may be difficult to recreate that look in the future. Likewise, if you're planning to get a new hairstyle before your session, do so several days in advance to give you a chance to get used to it.

• **What to wear.** Concentrate on the neckline. Wear something you feel comfortable in, but avoid distracting patterns or logos. Most colours are fine, and black often works well. Bright white can affect the exposure so is less helpful. A jacket of some sort for some of the photos can often work well. Jewellery can be distracting so is usually best avoided.

• **Facial expression.** A big smile is often great for musicals or front-of-house pictures, but for other casting purposes it can seem a little over the top. Any kind of 'emoting' can seem over-earnest or, worse, corny. I tend to favour a good neutral expression with 'spark' behind the eyes. A kind of a relaxed, open look with the smallest hint of a smile.

Ultimately, photographs play an important part in helping you get a foot in the door. But once you've been called for the interview, it's over to you ...

Angus Deuchar trained as an actor, during which time he subsidised his grant by taking photographs of his fellow students. When he left drama school in 1987 he soon realised that this was an ideal way to make a living between jobs! He pursued both careers for the first seven years, but has continued with just the photography since then. A website showing examples of his work can be seen at **www.actorsphotos.co.uk**.

Photographers and repro companies

Good photographs (and quality reproductions of same) are an essential part of an actor's professional armoury and there is absolutely no point in trying to scrimp on them. ('A picture is worth a thousand words.')

Your photograph is a silent, static, two-dimensional representation of vocal, mobile, three-dimensional you. It should be of your head down to your shoulders, reasonably stylish and well produced without necessarily being too glamorous. It should look natural and have life, energy and personality – especially in the eyes, the most important part of your face. Your photo should say, 'Here I am; I know who I am; I'm OK with Rowwho I am.' Also, it is very important that your photograph really looks like you when you arrive for interview.

Crucial to the final result is finding a good photographer (a) who understands the world that the end result is intended for and (b) with whom you can work well. In the listings that follow, you'll find a wide range of prices and deals. It is important to research as many of these as possible, without making cost your prime consideration. Ask friends, teachers and your agent (if you have one) for recommendations, and check through *Spotlight* and websites to see samples of work. Read the details under each listing to get a 'feel' for who might produce the 'goods' for you. Once you have a shortlist of possibilities, phone each with appropriate questions (what to wear, studio or natural light, and so forth) in order to get a sense of how well you might be able to work with him/her. Only *after* you've done all this research should cost be a consideration. Even then, a cheap deal could mean that the photographer will spend much less time, and take fewer photographs, than a more expensive one. You might be lucky with the former, but you'll enhance your chances of getting really good results with the latter.

Note Allow plenty of time for this research. Also, bear in mind that as the deadline for *Spotlight* gets nearer, photographers become increasingly busy and it becomes more difficult to book a session.

Copyright

Under the Copyright, Designs & Patents Act 1988, the photographer owns the copyright on any new photograph, even though you've already paid for the original. That means that you have to obtain his/her permission to have new photographs reproduced in *Spotlight* or anywhere else. Your photographer may be happy to approve such reproduction, but may not be so happy about any cropping or other alterations: you must get permission if you intend to do this. The other important new legal requirement is that your photographer must be credited on any reproduction of the original. Some of the repro companies are now doing this as a matter of course.

Repros

You could get subsequent, high-quality reproductions done by your photographer or by someone else nominated by him/her. However, these will be expensive. The specialist repro companies can do this significantly more cheaply with minimal loss of quality. Once again, check with others about the quality (and service and reliability) of individual companies before taking costs into consideration. It is also useful to overestimate the number of copies you might need over the lifetime (generally, about two years) of your chosen photograph – because (a) you'll almost always find that you underestimate that number in the first place, and (b) you can take advantage of cheaper unit costs.

Note It is often preferable to send a 10x8in (25x20cm) photograph for submissions; however, good-quality 'jpegs' (around 400 pixels wide) inserted into your CV are becoming increasingly acceptable. If you're planning to email a CV containing your photograph, make sure that the total document size is not more than about 200kb, or you'll end up clogging up the casting director's mailbox. (Most image editing software will have a menu option to allow you to reduce the image size if required.)

10 out of 10 Photography
Forest Hill Business Centre, Clyde Vale, London SE23 3JF
tel 0845-123 5664
email pauljneed@hotmail.com
website www.pauljneed.co.uk
Photographer Paul J Need

Services & rates

Charges £80 for a photo shoot. Photographer has a background in theatre, film, concert and television lighting, as well as teaching lighting design at RADA. Offers digital photography.

Abacus Photography
156 Kingshill Road, Swindon SN1 4LN
tel (01793) 537257 *mobile* (07966) 551909
fax (01793) 344208
email nickabacus@fsdial.co.uk
website www.abacus-photography.co.uk

Services & rates

Charges £50 for a photo shoot which includes photographer's fee and studio and equipment costs. This does not include the cost of any 10x8in (25x20cm) prints which are priced at £5 each. A variety of packages is also available. Offers discounts for group bookings. Digital photography is also available at a charge of £50 for 24 images. Always advises clients to bring a change of clothing and discuss their requirements before the shoot.

Work portfolio

Established in 1992. Photographs can be viewed on the website. Has taken publicity shots for around 20-30 actors.

The Actor's One-Stop Shop
54 Belsize Avenue, Palmers Green, London N13 4TJ
tel 020-8888 7006 *fax* 020-8888 9666
email info@actorsone-stopshop.com
website www.actorsone-stopshop.com

Services & rates

Charges £195 for a photo shoot which includes photographer's fee, studio and equipment costs,

processing of 1 b&w 36exps, contact sheet and 4 10x8in (25x20cm) prints. Offers 10% discount for group (2 or more) bookings. Offers both pre-shoot and post-shoot consultancy, advising clients on clothing, image projection and selection of photos, as well as general advice on how best to promote themselves within the acting industry.

Work portfolio

Established in 1997. Photographs can be viewed on the website or in person by visiting the studio. Has taken publicity shots for around 250 actors. Recent clients include: Tagforce (an actor register), Omar Khan, Samuel L Jackson, Anna Friel and Rachel Watkins.

Stuart Allen
mobile (07776) 258829
email info@stuartallenphotos.com
website www.stuartallenphotos.com

Services & rates

Charges £150 for a digital photo shoot which includes 360-500+ images, your own website for proof viewing the whole shoot with email links to you and your agent, contact sheets emailed to you as Adobe PDF files, updated contact sheets emailed to you as you narrow down your selection, cost of retouching four images, photos prepared for *Spotlight*, Casting Call Pro and Castnet, images emailed to *Spotlight*, Casting Call Pro and Castnet (if applicable). Shoot taken in natural light and typically last 2-3+ hours. All the images can be in black & white and/or colour. "The photos are captured in uncompressed high resolution 'RAW' format so as to give you the best possible quality and maximum control over the final image. This is the digital equivalent of a negative. It is superior to the other smaller and lower quality digital formats."

Film shoots also available at £130 for two 36 exp films and contact sheets. Competitive print service available. Offers full advice on clothing, makeup and hair.

Areas that are covered in the UK for headshots are London, Bath, Bristol, Brighton, Cardiff, Cheltenham, Guilford, Oxford, Warwick and

Resources

Winchester. If you do not live near one of these cities please check on availability.

Work portfolio

Stuart studied photography at Salisbury College of Art and Design. Since then he has worked in numerous spheres of the entertainment industry taking photographs. Shooting headshots of actors for almost a decade his work can be seen on his website, Casting Call Pro website and *Contacts*. Please check website for latest prices.

AM-London Photography

3A Godolphin Road, London W12 8JE
tel 020-7193 1868 *mobile* (07974) 188105
email studio@am-london.com
website www.am-london.com

Offers 2 types of headshot session; please see details below (student discount price is given in brackets):

• 1.5 hr Headshot Session (Studio and Natural Light) at £280 (£230). The package includes: 1.5 hour shoot in studio and natural light (outdoor). Variety of portraits and character shots. 250+ images supplied colour and black & white high res on disc. 4 retouched 10x8in prints
• 50 min Headshot Session (Studio only) at £210 (£180). The package includes: 50 min shoot – studio shots & variety of portraits. 150+ images supplied colour and black & white high res on disc. 2 retouched 10x8in prints

"With both sessions we make sure we get lots of variety. This means using different lighting setups, different backdrops and a number of outfit changes."

Ric Bacon

30 Fortis Green Road, Muswell Hill,
London N10 3HN
mobile (07970) 970799
website www.ricbacon.co.uk

Services & rates

Charges £280 for a photo shoot which includes photographer's fee, processing of 2 b&w 36exps, 6x4in print of every shot (rather than a contact sheet) and all negatives. Offers reduced rates to students. Shoots in a very relaxed manner, in natural light or studio, and offers advice on all aspects including clothing and make-up. Prints are ready to view in 1 hour and will be reviewed with the client, offering advice on selection of images for self-promotion if needed. Happy to look at old photographs of the client that they particularly like or dislike. Works with film or digital.

Work portfolio

Established in 1999. Photographs can be viewed on the website and has a comprehensive portfolio at The Spotlight offices. Has taken publicity shots for around 500 actors.

Chris Baker

tel 020-8441 3851
email chrisbaker@photos2000.demon.co.uk
website www.chrisbakerphotographer.com

Service & rates

A photographer since 1974, charges £245 for a photo shoot including 2 b&w 36exps, contact sheets and 5 10x8in prints. Student rate is £210 for the same service. Also offers a digital service at the same rates for around 60 digital images and 5 retouched photos on disk. Shoot takes place in a studio or outdoor location – only the outdoor location is wheelchair-accessible.

Work portfolio

Examples of work can be seen on the website or at The Spotlight offices. Has taken photographs for several thousand actors, among them Sally Anne Triplett, Julia Sawalha, Kim Medcalf, Todd Carty, and David Griffin. "Informality and relaxation are the secret to a successful photo session. Clients get 2 hours, giving us time to have a cup of tea and discuss their requirements.

I recommend that clients look as natural as possible, and discourage the use of make-up artists as it's far more important that my subjects look 'like themselves'! Tops should be unfussy and typical of the wearer. If in doubt, a simple black shirt is hard to beat.

I shoot digital or film, depending on the preference of my client, and am happy to advise on which will work best for you. I retouch the final selected images whether they're prints or on disc, eliminating stray hairs, spots or anything else that distracts from the real you.

I've been doing this for 30 years and am a full-time professional – not someone just dabbling as a sideline! My work is of the highest technical quality, but more importantly reflects the personality and potential of my clients; that's why so many of them come back."

Sophie Baker

tel 020-8340 3850
email sophiebaker@totalise.co.uk

Services & rates

A photographer since 1972 initially working in theatre front of house – National Theatre, Royal Shakespeare Theatre and many West End shows – no relation to Chris. Rate is £190 plus £10 for digital for two rolls of film and five 10x8in photographs. Student rates are £150 solo sitting (including digital and four 10x8in photographs) and £200 for a shared sitting providing three 10x8in photographs each. Photographs taken mostly in natural light in third floor studio overlooking Hampstead Heath and outside in the park.

Work portfolio

Work portfolio can be seen at the Spotlight offices. A website is planned!

"As a former student at the Central School of Speech and Drama (after the first year I realised that 'acting' wasn't for me – I would be happier behind the camera) I am aware of the discomfort and tensions the sitter can feel so I attempt to empathise and look to make the subject feel as comfortable as possible. The sessions are therefore relaxed and tailored to create a calm atmosphere. I have seen many directors and casting agents looking through books of photographs and therefore aim for a 'bright eyed and bushy tailed look' but not to overglamorize. It is important that a portrait photo attracts the eye of the director but it must be an honest reflection of the sitter. I suggest the client has a good night's sleep before hand and comes with a mixture of tops and necklines. It is not easy to dictate what will work over the phone."

Taken photographs for as many as 14,000 actors, among them Judi Dench, Ian Holm, Nigel Hawthorne, Ben Whitrow, Hugh Bonneville, Jane Horrocks, Rachel Weisz and John Lynch. "As I have been working for over 35 years the list is long. Over a period of 25 years I was also a film stills photographer working with Ken Loach, Stephen Frears, Louis Malle, Denys Arcand, Atom Egoyan to name a few but now prefer working on my own and not at the dictate of crazy film scheduling hours."

Paul Barrass

Unit 6, Ellingfort Road, London E8 3PA
mobile (07973) 265931
email paul@paulbarrass.co.uk
website www.paulbarrass.co.uk

Services & rates

Session price is £120. Includes four 10x8in prints. Special student rate of £100. All photography is digital. Photos can be taken either in the studio or outdoors. All locations have wheelchair access. Images are viewed during the photo session on a monitor. Has photographed in excess of 1000 actors.

Helen Bartlett Photography

Based in London and Cambridge
tel 0845-603 1373
email info@helenbartlett.co.uk
website www.helenbartlett.co.uk

Services & rates

Established in 2003. All photography is digital. Cost of headshot photo shoot is £150; £185 for headshots and full length. Photos are proofed online by way of a private gallery for the client. Usually around 30 images to choose from. The cost includes three photographs which are provided digitally on a CD so the client can make their own prints. Additional images are available at £35 each and a set of printed contact sheets are available for £40. Photos taken in outdoor locations or client's home. Photo sessions can be arranged at a mutually convenient location in either London or Cambridge so locations that are wheelchair accessible can be organised.

Work portfolio

Has photographed approximately 45 actors. Has photographed many of the clients of Rhino Management. Sessions take approximately 2 hours and can include a variety of locations.

"I recommend bringing a selection of tops with simple necklines, avoiding white."

A Beautiful Image Photography & Design (Debal Bagachi)

31 Church Walk, Brentford, Middlesex TW8 8DB
tel 020-8568 2122 *mobile* (07956) 861698
email debal@abeautifulimage.com
website www.abeautifulimage.com

Services & rates

Charges £150 for a photo shoot which includes photographer's fee, studio and equipment costs, processing of 2 b&w 36exps, contact sheets and 2 10x8in (25x20cm) prints (either hand- or digitally printed). Occasionally offers 10% discount for clients sharing a shoot. Digital photography is also available at the same rate; images can be supplied on CD Rom. Also able to provide website and print publicity. Advises actors to keep make-up simple for b&w photography and wear unfussy, unpatterned tops with simple necklines.

Work portfolio

Established in 1994. Photographs can be viewed on the website and at The Spotlight offices. Has taken publicity shots for around 50 actors. Recent clients include: Elizabeth Alexander, Patrick Regis, Fiona Marchant and Diane Cracknell.

Sheila Burnett

email sheilab33@ntlworld.net
website www.sheilaburnett-photography.com

Services & rates

Charges £200 + VAT (£180 + VAT for students) for a photo shoot. Includes 4 10x8in prints. Offers digital photography. Photos taken in studio. Works with 170 actors per year, including Imelda Staunton, Catherine Tate, David Soul, Paul Freeman, Simon Pegg, Anita Harris and Jackie Clune.

"Appointments can be made either online or by phone. I always advise on what is good to bring to the session. I'm open to any questions and happy to have a chat about what it is you want to achieve. My sessions always start with a 10-minute warm-up, this is mainly for me to adjust the lights and find the best position. It is also a good time for you to acclimatise to my studio and the tungsten lights. Because we are indoors, this makes it possible for you to freshen up upon arrival and to change outfits, apply make-up etc., and, for the boys, to shave if you want. I also rather like to have a cup of tea and a chat before we start. "

Will C

Studio 55d Dartmouth Road, London NW2 4EP
tel 020-8438 0303 *mobile* (07712) 669953
email billy_snapper@hotmail.com
website www.theukphotographerexhibition.co.uk
website www.billysnapper.com
website www.london-photographer.com

Services & rates

Established in 1968. £160 includes 80 colour, 80 b/w and 2 high-res CDs with all photos at 14 million pixels, delivered to the client in the studio. All photos are seen at the moment of taking on a large screen. Make up and hair can be provided in full attendance for the whole photo session for £80. Prints are obtained from an independent printer for £5.00 (b/w) and £7.00 (colour). Majority of photos taken in studio (home studio), other location prices are available on request. No wheelchair access to studio.

Work portfolio

Has photographed approximately 6500 performers including: Dame Judi Dench, Will Young, Charles Dance. Advice: "Neutral colours for clothes, no patterns, simplicity".

Jon Campling Headshots

206 Ellison Road, London SW16 5DJ
tel 020-8679 8671 *mobile* (07941) 421101
email photo@joncampling.com
website www.joncamplingheadshots.com

Services & rates

Established in 2004. All photography is digital. £100 includes online contact sheet, CD of all images in full resolution, and full digital correction of 4 images, only payable if client uses the images. Uses instant full size preview at session. Happy to give free advice via email or telephone. Prints of images are available at £1.99 each or 99p if order 20 or more of each. Photos are taken in home studio. No wheelchair access. Has photographed over 150 actors which include: Shenna Ellis, Dominic Cazenove, Charlotte Graham. "I am an actor myself ... I advise a simple approach to make up and clothing."

Robert Carpenter Turner Photography

The Studio, 62 Hemstal Road, London NW6 2AD
tel 020-7624 2225

email robert@carpenterturner.co.uk
website www.carpenterturner.co.uk

Services & rates

Charges £225 for a photo shoot which includes all costs and at which at least 70 high-quality digital photographs are taken. These are then displayed on the web with a private code for only the customer and agent to view. From these are ordered 6 pictures, which are corrected and improved as required, or changed to high-quality b&w images before being written to CD Rom. 2 10x8in prints are included. Time allowed for photoshoot is 2 hours.

Work portfolio

Established in 1960. Portfolio of photographs, latest rates and other information can be viewed on the website. He has taken publicity pictures for many hundreds of actors and performers over the past 40 years. Studio contains a grand piano for use by musicians.

Charlie Carter

tel/fax 020-8222 8742
email charlie@charliecarter.com

Services & rates

Established in 1998. Charges £375 for photo shoot including 3 x 36exps films and 4 x 10x8in prints. Starting to work with digital, but still mostly film. Sessions are in a home studio on the second floor, so not wheelchair-accessible. Examples of work can be viewed at The Spotlight offices. Clients include: Kenneth Branagh, Tom Hollander, Roger Allam, Emily Blunt, Isla Blair, Eve Best, Harry Enfield, Eleanor Bron, Martin Shaw, Kerry Condon, Paul McEwan, Serena Evans and Charlie Condou – as well as agents Ken McReddie Ltd, Rebecca Blond Associates, Conway van Gelder, ICM, PFD, Hamilton Andrews, Elinor Hilton, and Billboard.

Advises clients to start preparing several days beforehand – timing haircuts so that there's time for it to grow out a little, cutting out alcohol, drinking lots of water, taking exercise – so that skin and eyes will look their best. "Ladies, please check your diaries to avoid your session clashing with the worst part of PMT – mad to have pictures done when you are not at your loveliest ... By the time you add together the cost of photographs, repros and *Spotlight*, it's a lot of money – so protect your investment by doing everything you can to feel as good about yourself as possible. The session will take as long as it takes."

Andrew Chapman

198 Western Road, Sheffield S10 1LF
tel 0114-266 3579 *mobile* (07779) 861921
email andrew@chapmanphotographer.eclipse.co.uk
website www.andrewsphotos.co.uk

Services & rates

Charges from £125 for a photo shoot, which includes all photography and computer labour charges, studio and equipment costs. The session includes 40-70 photos, b&w and/or colour) which are transferred to the computer; you may select any or all images and these are written to a CD for you to take away for immediate use. Prints and contacts are available (e.g. a 10x8in is £15) if required, but in most cases images are emailed directly to *Spotlight* and for repros. Also gives clients a 'release note' so that photos can be used for PR, repros, agents, *Spotlight*, etc.

Black and bright colours work well in b&w, and higher necklines are usually better than low: "I always advise people on an individual basis. Ideally, allow about 2 hours for the session."

Work portfolio

Has more than 3500 actors on database as well as singers, dancers, models, martial artists and others. Clients are from agents across the country; they include: Philippa Howell, Sharron Ashcroft, Jane Hollowood, Liberty Management, David Daly, Direct Line, and Act One. "Qualified member of BIPP, SWPP, BPPA with over 20 years' experience."

John Clark Photo Digital

tel 020-8854 4069
email info@johnclarkphotography.com
website www.johnclarkphotography.com

Services & rates

Charges £145 per hour for digital photography.

Work portfolio

Established in 1982. Photographs and advice can be found on the website. Has taken publicity shots for around 500-600 actors. Recent clients include: actors represented by Roger Carey Associates, Collis Management, Crawfords, Rossmore and Langford Associates.

CW Photos

Southampton
tel (02380) 732550
email cwp@cwphotos.co.uk
website www.cwphotos.co.uk

Services & rates

Charges from £75 for a photo shoot, which includes fees, studio, processing and contact shots (5 selected from 40 taken). Offers an option of either 10x8in prints or files on CD. Special packages for actors (including students) include a 10-image portfolio disc from £145 (head shots, 3/4 length, full length, different backgrounds and lighting, and 10 selected finished images from 100 taken). Other packages are available to suit all budgets. Digital photography also offered, and all locations are possible: the main studio is wheelchair-accessible.

Work portfolio

Established in 1990. Has taken photographs for more than 100 productions and of more than 50 actors.

Clients include: Ros Liddiard, Steven Fawell, Susannah Steadman, James Norton and Joanna Russel. "We recommend bringing a selection of 2 or 3 different necklines, as then we can advise the optimum for each individual. The same applies to make-up, etc. Each client gets a personal assessment and recommendation."

Grant David Photography

34a Manor Park Road, London N2 OSJ
tel 020-8815 9789
email grantdavidphotos@tiscali.co.uk
website www.grantdavid.co.uk

Services & rates

Charges £100 for a photo shoot: this includes all fees and studio costs, processing of 2 b&w 36 exps, contact sheets and 2 10x8in prints. Offers the same package to students at the reduced rate of £60. Digital photography is also available at the same rates and will enable the client to leave the session with all the shots on CD. Advises clients to use very little make-up and to bring 3 tops, keeping patterns and jewellery to a minimum. Post-production includes air-brushing on blemishes/spots for free.

Work portfolio

Established in 1992. Photographs can be viewed on the website and at The Spotlight offices. Has photographed around 600 actors, with recent clients including: Janine Smith, Amanda Fulton and Luke Long.

Angus Deuchar

PO Box 25799, London SW19 1WQ
tel 020-8286 3303 *mobile* (07973) 600728
email angus@actorsphotos.co.uk
website www.actorsphotos.co.uk

Services & rates

Charges £230 for a photo shoot taken in natural light. Price includes approximately 120 proofs viewed on a website, 4 finished b&w 10x8in (real!) photographic prints and a CD with various electronic versions. Student deals available. Telephone or email for further information.

Work portfolio

Photographs and "advice to actors seeking photographs" can be viewed on the website. Has around 20 years' experience of taking actors' portraits, and used to be an actor himself. Clients include: Neil and Adrian Rayment (*The Matrix Reloaded*), Anne Reid, James Bolam, John Alderton and Richard Lumsden.

DF: Photographer

Studio 29-31, Stafford Road, Brighton BN1 5PE
tel (01273) 549967 *mobile* (07958) 272333

Resources

email info@image2film.com
website www.image2film.com
Photographer David Fernandes

Has worked as a photographer since 1995, and has taken photographs for roughly 500 actors. Charges £85 for a photo shoot including 2 10x8in prints, using either film or digital. Special 'shared sitting' rates are available to students. Works in a studio, outdoors or in the client's home. Shoots and edits actors' showreels; please phone for prices. The studio is not wheelchair-accessible. Advises clients to "bring a selection of tops with different necklines. Not too 'fussy'. A black top always works well".

Mike Eddowes

tel (01903) 882525 *mobile* (07970) 141005
email mike@photo-publicity.co.uk
website www.theatre-photography.co.uk

Services & rates

Established in 1975. Services offered include: headshots, editorial publicity shoots, editorial portraits, poster images and theatre production photography. Cost of portrait photo-shoots is £225. This includes 6 10x8in prints plus CD with 50 images. Special discount of £30 is offered to clients who mention *Actors' Yearbook*. Studio in Kennington, London SE11, or natural daylight outdoor shoots in West Sussex. London studio is not wheelchair accessible. More details are available from the website.

Work portfolio

Examples of photography can be seen on the website. Has photographed several hundred actors. Testimonials are available on their website along with examples of photography.

"Don't wear too much makeup; bring clothes which are you as yourself (not dressing up!); and have an early night before the photography session. Try and build a relationship with a photographer and stick with him or her. Don't get a keen amateur friend to try and take your photos – acting is a very tough career and you need all the help you can get!"

Elliott Franks Photography Services

PO Box 29801, London SW19 1WW
tel 020-8544 0156 *mobile* (07802) 537220
email frankse@aol.com
website www.elliottfranks.com

Services & rates

Charges £85 (reduced from £160 for *Actors' Yearbook* readers) for a 2-hour photo shoot in Wimbledon studio with 5 changes of tops, 3 rolls of medium-format film (high quality) with 12 shots per roll, and 3 contact sheets. Usually shoots a fourth roll for fun which is supplied on CD Rom. One-off 10x8in (25x20cm) prints are priced at £11.31 each; repros of 12 10x8in prints are priced at £1.85 each.

Work portfolio

Established in 1997. Photographs can be viewed on the website and at The Spotlight offices. Has taken publicity shots for more than 300 actors. Recent clients include: actors represented by ICM and Wendy Lee Management Ltd.

James Gill

6 Hanover Gardens, London SE11 5TL
tel 020-7735 5632

Services & rates

Charges £85 for a photo shoot which includes photographer's fee, studio and equipment costs, processing of 1 b&w 36exps, contact sheet and 2 10x8in (25x20cm) prints. Increases to £130 for 2 rolls and 4 10x8in prints. Extra 10x8in prints are priced at £12.50 each. Advises actors to keep it simple. Will take photos of actors as they wish to be presented, and will take all the time necessary.

Work portfolio

Established in 1992. Photographs can be viewed at The Spotlight offices. Has taken publicity shots for around 500 actors and in addition has more than 40 years' experience of working in theatres, both in casting and as company manager.

Nick Gregan Photography

Unit 3, 10A Ellingfort Road, London Fields, London E8 3PA
tel 020-8533 3003 *mobile* (07774) 421878
email info@nickgregan.com
website www.nickgregan.com

Services & rates

Charges £145 for a photo shoot, which includes fees, studio, processing and contact sheets (around 300 shots are taken). The first two 10x8in prints are free; £10 per print thereafter. Students are offered an extra discount of £35 on production of a valid student card. Also offers digital photography, for which the same rates apply. Photos are taken in a studio or outdoor location and both are wheelchair-accessible.

Work portfolio

Established in 1992. Has taken publicity photos for more than 3000 clients, including Paul Danan, Lucinda Rhodes and Henry Luxemburg. "My website offers '7 secrets to a great head shot' – check it out for loads of useful information."

Charles Griffin Photography

PO Box 36, Deeside, Chester CH5 3WP
tel (01244) 535252
email studio@charlesgriffinphotography.co.uk
website www.charlesgriffinphotography.co.uk

Services & rates

Photographer since 1993. Charges £149 for photo shoot, which includes processing of 2 x 12exps medium-format (high-quality) rolls, contact sheets and 2 10x8in prints. (Offers this service at £92.83 if client mentions *Actors' Yearbook* when booking a 2-hour session. Student rates are also available – telephone or email for information.) Digital service also available at the same rates, although an extra charge is made to provide the images on CD. Uses studio and outdoor location (both wheelchair-accessible).

Work portfolio

Examples of work can be seen on the website. Has taken photographs for around 250 actors, among them Raquel Lee, Gemma Gray, Sam Gratton, Paul Draw. "Sessions are conducted in a relaxed atmosphere: I will shoot images of actors as they wish. Clients should bring a variety of plain tops: those with high neckline or v-neck in red, grey or black are most useful."

Claire Grogan

12 Calverley Grove, London N19 3LG
tel 020-7272 1845
email claire@clairegrogan.co.uk
website www.clairegrogan.co.uk

Services & rates

Charges £225+vat for photo shoot including photographer's fee, studio and equipment costs, 2 roll B&W 36 exps contact sheets and 4 10x8s. This shoot can be either outdoors, studio or combination of both. Also offers 1 roll 36 exps and 2 10x8s studio only for £150+vat. Special rates for full time drama students are £170+vat for 2 roll session or £110 for 1 roll session. Offers full advice on clothing and make-up when a booking is made. Sessions last approx 2 and a quarter hours in a relaxed atmosphere. "I make a point of capturing shots that really reflect the actor's personality and casting potential."

Work portfolio

Established in 1991. Photographs can be viewed on the website and at Spotlight offices. Takes around 400 publicity shots for actors each year and is recommended by a number of agents. Clients have included Steve McFadden, Lindsey Coulson, Stephen Tompkinson, Heather Peace, Nicola Blackman, Ben Richards, Debbie Arnold, Chris Walker, Caroline O'Neill, Phil Whitchurch, Tiffany Chapman, Philip Brown.

"Sorry no wheelchair access at present."

Jamie Hughes Photography

mobile (07850) 122977
website www.jamiehughesphotography.com/headshots

Services & rates

Charges £250 for a digital photo shoot (including fee, approx. 100 images supplied on CD Rom, and

retouching and processing of 3 10x8in prints). Additional prints (including retouching) are available for £10 each. Uses a studio and outdoor location, both of which are wheelchair-accessible. Examples of his work – featuring some very famous faces – can be seen on the website.

Remy Hunter

Flat 2, 9 Belsize Park, London NW3 4ES
tel 020-7431 8055 *mobile* (07766) 760724
email remy_hunter@hotmail.com
website www.remyhunter.co.uk

Services & rates

Established in 2003. Charges £190 and £140 for a 4 hour and 2 hour Actors session respectively. Includes 80 digital shots taken for 4 hour session and 40 shots for 2 hour session. Also includes CD of all shots given to client at end of session and a further CD of 6 high resolution images for 4 hour session and 4 images for 2 hour session. Student discount available as follows: £150 for a 4 hour session and £120 for a 2 hour session. Shared sessions available for half of the above prices per person. Also includes two CDs. Studio and outdoor shots available during same session. Free retouching of images where necessary. Uses a studio that is not accessible to wheelchair users.

Work portfolio

Has taken photographs for roughly 500 actors, including (with Spotlight PIN in brackets): Freya Dominic (2211-8979-4470), Gemma Harvey (0615-5643-5877), Julie Pollin (0459-1206-3661), Jonathan Grace (aka James Dillinger – 2517-8940-4373). Advises clients to "bring a range of tops with varying necklines. Black tends to come out best, so a couple of black tops are a good idea. For make-up bring what you'd wear from day-to-day".

David James Photography

mobile (07808) 597362
email info@davidjamesphotos.com
website www.davidjamesphotos.com

Established 2001. Charges £230 for photo shoot including processing of 2 x 36bw films, and four 10x8in prints. Also offers digital shoot at the same price. Uses studio, outdoor locations and client's own home for the shoot; the studio is not accessible for wheelchair users. Has taken photographs for around 200 actors including clients of ICM, PFD and Markham & Froggatt.

Matt Jamie

London N19
mobile (07976) 890643
email photos@mattjamie.co.uk
website www.mattjamie.co.uk/portraits

Services & rates

Established in 2000. Digital photography. Cost of photo shoot is £125. This includes shooting indoor and outdoor session with over 100 images taken (viewable on camera during the shoot and then afterwards in an online portfolio), and 3 images with any retouching necessary on CD Rom. The disk also includes a digital 'contact sheet' of all the images from the shoot. Further images may be selected at a later date. Offers 100% satisfaction promise – a free re-shoot or refund if not satisfied with shots taken. No prints are included, these are charged at £2.50 for small numbers of prints (10x8in) or £30 for sets of 25. Further details are available on the website. Special packages include: £95 for individual student rate or £85 per person for bookings of 3 or more students from the same drama school. Photos taken in studio or outdoor locations. Will travel to outdoor locations selected by client for small extra fee to cover expenses. Local outdoor locations used are wheelchair accessible. Studio sessions at drama schools can also be arranged.

Work portfolio

Examples of photography can be seen in portfolio at Spotlight offices. Has photographed more than 100 actors, including commissions from Ambassador Theatre Group, Whats On Stage.com, TheatreMAD and *Theatregoer Magazine* to photograph stars including Kevin Spacey, Kristin Scott Thomas, Patrick Swayze and John Barrowman.

"I offer a relaxed, informal shoot which can take as long as you need. You can bring a variety of different clothes (I suggest at least 2 different necklines, and generally plain colours – bring something you feel confident in), wigs, friends, or anything else you might want with you to make you feel relaxed."

JK Photography

17 Delamere Road, West Wimbledon, London SW20 8PS
mobile (07816) 825578
email jkph0t0@yahoo.com
website www.jk-photography.net

Services & rates

Established in 1997. Charges £145 for a photo shoot in studio or outdoor location (includes 100 shots plus fee, studio, processing and contact sheets). £10 per print. Offers a 10% discount for students.

Work portfolio

Has taken photographs for around 300 actors. "Stick to plain colours with no patterns or logos, and bring a range of different necklines. Professional hair and make up will be provided on the day."

Steve Johnston

mobile (07775) 991834
email steve@smj-cp.com
website www.smjcp.com

Services & rates

Established in 1994. Based in London, offering bespoke casting photography service to actors,

musicians and dancers. Shoot lasts 1-2 hours either on location, in the studio or the client's home. Only outdoor locations are wheelchair accessible. Only shoots digitally. This enables critique as images are taken. A 1-2 hour session would normally result in around 40-60 final images. Contacts are either presented on secure online website or printed off. Images can be colour or black and white. Price per session is £165 incl. VAT. This includes online contact sheet and light retouching of 4 selected images. Prints of any selected/retouched images cost £8.00 each. Any further retouching is charged at £10 per image. Also offers free online upload of images to Spotlight and Castingcallpro. Special student rate £130.

Work portfolio

Examples of photography available on website. Has photographed approximately 20 actors. Recent clients include: Janet Jefferies, Davina Silver, Carrie Jones and Julie Ford. "Bring along a change of tops, black or white would be best, with no patterns or stripes and simple uncomplicated necklines (shirts work well). Keep makeup as natural looking as possible. Keep hair as you would normally wear it. Feel free to bring along any images showing styles you particularly like and any previous spotlight/casting images."

Neil Kendall Photography

19 Oakfield Court, Haslemere Road, London N8 9RA
tel 020-8340 4214 *mobile* (07776) 198332
email mondo.nez@virgin.net
website www.neilkendallphotography.com

Services & rates

Charges £135 for a photo shoot which includes photographer's fee, studio and equipment costs, processing of 3 b&w 36exps, contact sheets and 2 10x8in (25x20cm) prints. Uses both studio and natural light.

Work portfolio

Photographs can be viewed on the website. Has taken publicity shots for around 30-35 actors. Recent clients include: Vanessa Earl, Peter Ackyroyd, Graham Norton and Liberty X.

Jack Ladenburg Photography

mobile (07932) 053743
email info@jackladenburg.co.uk
website www.jackladenburg.co.uk

Services & rates

Established in 2006. Only digital photography. Cost of photo shoot is £195. This includes three 10x8in prints. Student discount of £30; further discounts for group bookings. Will retouch and resize according to clients' wishes and send them previews of their selected shots before printing. Photos taken in studio or outdoor locations. Only outdoor locations are wheelchair accessible.

Work portfolio

Portfolio is available to view at the Spotlight offices. Has photographed approximately 200 actors. Recent clients include Julian Rhind-Tutt, Nicholas Day, Tara Summers and Katherine Tozer. "I place a big emphasis on making sure that my clients are happy and relaxed before we start the shoot, and that they enjoy themselves on the day. I never rush through a session and always devote either a morning or an afternoon to one shoot. I don't set a limit on how many photos I'll take in a session, and make sure we concentrate on the casting needs of each actor."

Carole Latimer

113 Ledbury Road, Notting Hill, London W11 2AQ
tel 020-7727 9371
email carole.latimer@freenet.co.uk
website www.carolelatimer.com

Services & rates

Professional photographer for over 25 years. Charge for actors' headshots is £300 inc. VAT (student rate is £250). This includes three 10x8in prints. Extra prints are charged at £16 each. Digital photography is also offered. Photographs are taken in a studio and occasionally outdoor locations. The studio does not have wheelchair access.

Work portfolio

Provided publicity photos for approximately 2000 actors including: Kate O'Mara, Alistair McGowan, Maureen Lipman, Zoe Lucker and clients from the following agencies ICM, Conway Van Gelder, Narrow Road. "No large patterns, if black and white shoot, at least one black top always bring a selection of tops so I have a choice. I have an exceptional daylight studio with full lighting equipment. Good facilities for make-up."

Steve Lawton

134 Randolph Avenue, Maida Vale, London W9 1PG
mobile (07973) 307487
email stevelawton2@msn.com
website www.stevelawton.com

Services & rates

Charges £265 for a photo shoot, which includes 4 b&w 10x8in prints. The same package is offered to students at the reduced price of £240. 10x8in prints are priced at £6.50 each and digital photography is also available. Advises clients not to bring patterned tops; fitted t-shirts and v-necks in blue, grey or black are most effective.

Work portfolio

Established in 2001. Has taken photographs for more than 1500 actors and is recommended by Curtis

Brown, Independent Talent Group, United Agents, Jorg Betts, Shane Collins, International Artists and Bronia Buchanan, amongst others. A full portfolio and price information is available on the website.

LB Photography

36 Nutley Lane, Reigate, Surrey RH2 9HS
tel (01737) 224578 *mobile* (07885) 966192
email labowerman@hotmail.com

Services & rates

Charges £160 for a photo shoot (£150 student rate), which includes photographer's fee, studio and equipment costs, processing of b&w 36 exposures and poster-sized contact sheet, and 2 10x8 prints. Price increases to £185 for 2 sheets; additional 10x8 prints are £10 each. There is no VAT charged at any stage. CD transfer also available. 6-7 Hi Res shots for £25. Photographs may be viewed at The Spotlight offices, in *Contacts* and on the Castingcallpro website.

Work portfolio

Photographs may be viewed at The Spotlight offices, in *Contacts*, and on the Castingcallpro website. Has taken publicity shots for over 3000 actors. More than 50 agencies send clients on a regular basis, including Narrow Road, Evans & Reiss, Brown and Simcocks, Hatton & McEwan and CAM.

Peter Le May

mobile (07703) 649246
email photo@petelemay.co.uk
website www.petelemay.co.uk

Services & rates

Typically charges £175 for a photo shoot including at least 75 printed proofs and licenced images on CD. A full price-list is available on request, with special rates for students. Photos are taken at a location of your choice, either outdoor or indoor using natural light. It is important for you to be relaxed and confident throughout so I am keen to listen to your requirements and ideas. I always recommend keeping hair, make-up and clothes very simple so that they don't distract from your face. All photography is digitial, allowing you to review and discuss photos during the shoot, and minor retouching is available on the selected images.

Work portfolio

Established 2002 and has photographed approximately 50 actors. Recent clients include: Blake Ritson (Conway Van Gelder), Kevin Trainor (Ken McReddie Associates), Cicely Giddings (RDF Management).

Murray Lenton

2 Toll Bar Barn, High Hesket, Near Carlisle, Cumbria CA4 OHR

tel (01697) 475442 *mobile* (07941) 427458
email murray.lenton@btinternet.com

Services & rates

Digital or film as required. Rates to be discussed at time of booking. Theatre photography and portraits since 1997. General photography since 1983.

Work portfolio

Established as a general photographer in 1983, and as a theatre photographer in 1997. Recent clients include: Tamsin Greig, Simon Dormandy, Luke Sorba and Wild Girls.

MAD Photography

200 Gladbeck Way, Enfield EN2 7HS
tel 020-8363 4182 *mobile* (07949) 581909
email mad.photo@onetel.net
website www.mad-photography.co.uk

Services & rates

Charges £185 for actors' photo shoot which includes photographer's fee, studio and location shoot, 75 proofs contact sheets emailed same day and 4 10x8in prints. Offers discounted rate of £125 to students (includes as above, but with 2 10x8in prints); also offers student shared shoots at £85 each (includes as above, but with 50 proofs contact sheets and 2 prints). Extra 10x8in prints are priced at £15.95 each and images on disc are £20. "Hair and make-up should be natural. Bring 4 tops in any colours: one v-neck, one collar, one t-shirt and one jacket. No white!"

Work portfolio

Established in 1997. Photographs can be viewed on the website and in *Contacts* and CastingCallPro. Has taken publicity shots for over 6000 actors and student actors. Clients include: Shane Richie, Michelle Ryan, Susan Penhaligon, Michael Knowles, Jessica Wallace, John Partridge, Tom Law, Belinda Owusu, Janie Dee and Phoebe Thomas.

Gemma Mount Photography

3rd Floor, 5 Torrens Street, London EC1V 1NQ
mobile (07976) 824923
email gemma@gemmamountphotography.com
website www.gemmamountphotography.com

Services and rates

Charges £190 for a photo shoot, which includes 60-100 shots on CD. Rates are reduced to £125 for students, and to £150 if you book with a friend. Prints are charged at £5 each. All photos are taken in a converted factory with natural light, and outdoors.

Advises clients as follows: "Simple clothes are best; nothing should distract from the face or limit the casting. Bring a variety of tops – it is always better to have too many. V-necks are generally most flattering for women, because round necks tend to make a face look broader. A dark shirt is often good for guys and a selection of plain t-shirts. White can be great outside and often makes an actor look younger. If you have long hair, avoid colours that are a similar tone, or your hair won't stand out. Matte make-up is good; avoid anything shiny, as you want to look as natural as possible."

Work portfolio

Established in 1998. Has taken photos of around 400 actors, including Frazer Douglas, Paddy Crawley, Geraldine Barry Murphy, Kirsty Jeffery, Stephanie Mottershead, Susan Barrett, Felicity Houlbrooke and Emily Altneu.

Adam Parker

1 Hoxton House, 34 Hoxton Street, London N1 6LR
tel 020-7684 2005 *mobile* (07710) 787708
email actors@adamparker.co.uk
website www.adamparker.co.uk

Established in 1996. Rates: £200-250 for a photo shoot; includes retouching and four 10x8in prints. Lower rates for students and groups. Photos taken in studio or at an alternative location by arrangement. Offers digital photography.

"I shoot fashion and beauty and will use this experience to make you look good but still look like you! I use the highest quality equipment and take great care to deliver a top service. Make-up / hair and fashion stylists can be arrangement if desired."

Michael Pollard Photographer

Manchester-based
tel 0161-456 7470
email info@michaelpollard.co.uk
website www.michaelpollard.co.uk

Services & rates

Charges £75 for a 40 shot contact sheet including the first image chosen either to CD or print. £110 for a 70-80 shot contact sheet including the first 2 images chosen either to CD or print. "I shoot as many shots as I think we need to edit down so the actors have a good set of images to choose from." Student rates are available. Shoots can be indoors or outdoors or a mixture of both.

Encourages actors to bring 2-3 tops ranging from lighter to darker tones. "Tops should be simple and comfortable with either a round or V-neck. Hair needs to be tidy but avoid going to the hairdresser the day before you have it cut. For women make-up should be simple and sparing, avoiding lip liner or lipstick that is too dark or too red. The key is to keep things simple and natural and to be positive and be prepared. Think how you want to look and how you don't want to look. Enjoy it and be yourself!"

Work portfolio

Established in 1982 (1993 for actors). Photographs can be viewed on the website and at the Northern

Actors Centre, Manchester. Has taken publicity shots for around 2500 actors. Recent clients include: Sarah Jayne Dunn (*Hollyoaks*), Rebecca Atkinson (*Shameless*), Samantha Siddall (*Shameless*), Sophia Di Martino.

David Price Photography

69 Pevensy Road, London SW17 0HT
mobile (07950) 542494
email info@davidpricephotography.co.uk
website www.davidpricephotography.co.uk

Services & rates

Prices start from £150. Informal sessions shooting in daylight and studio light. Session includes: 2-3hr shoot, CD with 6 final edited images and two 10x8in prints. Uploading of final images to an actor's agent is also included. Online ordering from **www.photoboxgallery.com/davidpricephotography** (prints are no longer available through Visualeyes). Film sessions available; please refer to website for prices.

"Portable studio equipment allows me to visit clients' homes at special request." Hair and make-up available if booked in advance at £40. 10% student discount available.

Studio is not accessible for wheelchair users.

Work portfolio

Clients include, Narrow Road, Hobson's International, Stephanie Evans Associates, Jackie Palmer Stage School, Bristol Old Vic Theatre School, Lamda, RAM and Central School of Speech and Drama, and commissions from theatres across the country.

David has connections with The Actor's Workshop Youth Theatre and also does Headshot Introduction workshops for acting students.

"Your headshots should be a fair and flattering portrait of the professional that you are. I aim to achieve a strong, confident image that represents the person that will walk through that door at the audition or casting. I am more than happy to give advice on the nature of the industry and the best way in which to market yourself."

Prices are subject to change. Please check the website for the latest prices.

Howard Sayer Photography

Kingston-on-Thames
mobile (07860) 559891
email howard@howardsayer.com
website www.howardsayer.co.uk

Services & rates

Charges £125 for a photo shoot which includes photographer's fee, studio and equipment costs, processing of 2 b&w 36exps and contact sheets.

10x8in (25x20cm) prints are priced at £6 each. Also offers digital photography at the same rates. Actors can preview images during the photo shoot. Includes a CD containing 10 best images as part of a student package. Images can be reproduced in either colour or b&w.

Work portfolio

Established in 1987. Photographs can be viewed on the website. Has taken publicity shots for around 1000 actors. Recent clients include: actors working for the BBC, Teddington Studios and Benedict Productions.

Karen Scott Photography

London
mobile (07958) 975950
email info@karenscottphotography.com
website www.karenscottphotography.com

Services & rates

Charges £175 for a digital shoot, which includes b/w portfolio and a selection of colour shots – approximately 80 images selected, cropped and finished, slight re-touching applied if necessary and provided on CD. All photographs provided as high-resolution. Includes contact sheets for reference and two 10x8 prints. Session is very relaxed and unlimited in time, allowing several clothing changes and shot using flattering natural light, be that outdoors or indoors. £125 discounted rate is offered to all students. Live performance shoots undertaken for individuals and theatre companies for an arranged fee. Your individual needs within any discipline in the arts discussed before each shoot and advice on clothing and make up offered. "An honest yet striking image, portraying the qualities behind the photograph."

Work portfolio

Photographs can be viewed on the website and in The Spotlight offices, and also in *Contacts*.

Catherine Shakespeare Lane

The Monsell Stores, 43 Monsell Road,
London N4 2EF
tel 020-7226 7694
email cat@csl-art.co.uk
website www.csl-art.co.uk

Services & rates

Charges £390 for a photo shoot which includes photographer's fee, studio and equipment costs, processing of 2 b&w 36exps, contact sheets and 4 10x8in prints. Offers a student package for £270 (1 roll of 36 and 2 10x8in prints). In special circumstances this package is also available to non-students for £280. Uses natural light inside and favours a natural look. "My aim is to show my clients at their most interesting."

Work portfolio

Established in 1975. Photographs can be viewed at The Spotlight offices and in *Contacts*. Has taken publicity shots for more than 2000 actors.

Peter Simpkin

17 Grove Avenue, London N10 2AS
tel 020-8883 2727
email petersimpkin@aol.com
website www.petersimpkin.co.uk

Services & rates

Charges £411.25 (inclusive of VAT) for a photo shoot which includes photographer's fee, studio and equipment costs, processing of 3 b&w 36exps, contact sheets and 6 10x8in (25x20cm) prints (also supplied with a CD). Student price is £352.50 inclusive of VAT.

Work portfolio

Established in 1973. Photographs can be viewed on the website. Has taken publicity shots for thousands of actors. Recent clients include: actors represented by ARG, Curtis Brown, Christina Shepherd Associates; students from Webber Douglas (now Central School of Speech & Drama), LAMDA, Mountview and Bristol Old Vic.

Rosie Still

391 Sidcup Road, London SE9 4EU
tel 020-8857 6920
email rosie391@talktalk.net
website www.rosiestillphotography.com

Services & rates

A professional photographer for 35 years. Charges a special price for actors of £120 for a portrait session (normally £150). This includes session fee, proof sheet and two 10x8in b&w prints of the client's choice. The price accommodates up to 4 changes of top. Also offers a special reduction for students to £80, which includes all of the above but accommodates 2 changes of top.

Takes as many shots as are necessary, depending on the client's needs. Offers an airbrushing service at no extra cost; for an additional £10 can also provide the whole shoot on CD for the client to take home (normal price, £20). Additional prints are £5 each, but the price is reduced if a number of the same prints are required. Also does repros, z-cards, photo business cards and photo CVs. All sessions are carried out in own South London studio, approx. 5 minutes' train journey from London Bridge station and with parking spaces directly outside. The studio is wheelchair accessible.

Work portfolio

Portfolio includes many pop stars and TV celebrities, but specialises now in publicity shots for actors and drama students. Clients include: Debra Stephenson, Charlie Clements, Liz Frazer, Bella Emberg, Christopher Parker, Chris Jarvis, Zoe Heyes, Maureen Sweeney, John Leyton, Gabrielle Bradshaw and Mia McKenna-Bruce. Examples of work can be seen on the website **www.rosiestillphotography.com** and on Castingcallpro.

"Ladies should keep make-up to the minimum – as if going out for the evening, nothing heavier. Men should wear none at all. My priority is to finish a shoot with the client 100% satisfied with their results."

TM Photography & Design

Suite 228, Business Design Centre, 52 Upper Street, Islington, London N1 0QH
tel 020-7288 6846
email info@tmphotography.co.uk
website www.tmphotography.co.uk

Services & rates

Established in 1995. All photography is digital. Cost of photo shoot is £70. The cost includes one 10x8in print which can be taken away on the day of the shoot. Images can be viewed by the client as they are taken. Images are loaded on to a private webpage to be viewed. Orders can be placed online. Student photoshoot is discounted at £40. Photos taken in studio or outdoor locations or client's home. Studio is wheelchair accessible.

Work portfolio

Has photographed approximately 3000 actors, walkons and background artists. Has photographed many of the clients of Allsorts Agency, Ray Knight, G2, Guys & Dolls. Actors photographed include: Fraser Hines, Antonia Okonma. Photoshoots can be booked at short notice. Also offers repro service and promotional products such as websites, model cards and CV creation.

ToShoot.Com (formerly 7LA Studios)

42b Medina Road, London N7 7LA
tel/fax 020-7686 2324
mobile (07960) 726957
email hi@toshoot.com
website www.toshoot.com
Photographer Carlos Cicchelli

Services & rates

Established in 2003. "Actors' and models' headshots and portfolios done on digital of film. Prices vary depending on the job. Email for quotation."

Steve Ullathorne

London
tel (07961) 380969
email steve@ullapix.com
website www.ullapix.com

Services & rates

Charges £185 for a digital photo shoot; this covers all fees and studio costs, contact sheets and 5 10x8in prints. Will offer a discount to students, negotiable at the time of booking. All clients receive an online contact sheet with a web address that they can pass on to their agent. Prior to the shoot, clothing and locations will be discussed with the client on the telephone. All photos are retouched in Photoshop to remove any blemishes plus any other light retouching required by the actor. Email proofs are sent of each chosen image. Rather than specifying a number of images, prices are dictated by duration of the shoot, which is 1.5 hours. Actors usually end up with more than 100 shots to choose from.

Work portfolio

Please see website for samples. Agency recommendations include: Brown and Simcocks, Mike Leigh Associates, and Conway van Gelder.

Martin Usborne Photography

mobile (07747) 607930
email mail@martinusborne.com
website www.martinusborne.com

Services & rates

Established in 2000. Shoots exclusively on high end digital cameras so all shots can be seen directly after the session on a computer. Clients select prints which are then processed immediately and printed off on professional lab printer. Images can be colour or black and white. Charge for photo session is £200. This includes two 10x8in prints and CD of all shots at full resolution. Touch up service is offered at an extra cost of £50. Photo session lasts 2 hours. Student discount £175. Photos taken in studio or outdoor locations. Only outdoor locations are wheelchair accessible.

Luke Varley

mobile (07711) 183631
email luke@lukevarley.com
website www.lukevarley.com

Established in 2004. Charges £210 for a photo shoot, which includes approximately 130 shots and 4 10x8in prints. Shoots take place in a studio (inc. home studio) or at an outdoor location that is wheelchair-accessible. Has taken publicity photos for several hundred actors, including clients from the following agencies: Ken McKreddie, Troika, McFarlane Chard and Bronia Buchanan.

Robin Watson

tel 020-7833 1982
email robin@robinwatson.biz
website www.robinwatson.biz

Services & rates

Charges £180 for a photo shoot. This includes all fees and studio costs, processing of 2 b&w 36exps, contact sheets and 2 10x8in prints. Digital photography is also available and costs an additional £10 for transferring images to CD. Advises clients to keep clothing simple with unfussy necklines and mid-tone single colours, not black and white. Make-up should also be simple, perhaps a little eye-liner and some foundation powder if the complexion is shiny.

Work portfolio

Established in 1994. Photographs can be viewed on the website or in *Spotlight*. Has taken photographs of hundreds of actors, with recent clients including: Rula Lenska, Christopher Timothy and Finty Williams.

Robert Workman

32 West Kensington Mansions, Beaumont Crescent, London W14 9PF
tel 020-7385 5442
email bob@robertworkman.demon.co.uk
Studio address: Studio 103B, The Business Village, Broomhill Road, London SW18 4JQ
website www.robertworkman.demon.co.uk

Services & rates

Charges £250 plus VAT for a photo shoot which includes photographer's fee, studio and equipment costs, processing of 2 b&w 36exps, contact sheets, 5 10x8in (25x20cm) prints and a CD for digital submissions to casting directors and *Spotlight* online. Special student portrait session costs £150 plus VAT.

Work portfolio

Photographs can be viewed on the website. Has been taking around 200 publicity shots for actors every year for 20 years. Recent clients include: Caroline Quentin, Jude Law and Philip Middlemiss.

REPRO COMPANIES

Denbry Repros Ltd

57 High Street, Hemel Hempstead, Herts HP1 3AF
tel (01442) 242411
email info@denbryrepros.com
website www.denbryrepros.com

Charges £7.20 plus VAT for the initial copy of a b&w negative. Can also reproduce from a digital image.

Repros of a b&w 10x8in (25x20cm) are priced as follows:
£26 for 25, £47.05 for 50, £89.05 for 100, £178.10 for 200, £200.40 for 250 and £393.75 for 500.

Repros of a b&w postcard print are priced as follows:
£19.50 for 25, £36.30 for 50, £66.05 for 100, £132.10 for 200, £133.75 for 250 and £234.95 for 500.

All prices exclude VAT. Colour repros are also available at an increased price.

Other services include a studio for casting photography, downloading images from the Internet and supplying images on CD in colour or b&w.

Resources

Denman Repros

Burgess House, Main Street, Farnsfield,
Nottinghamshire NG22 8EFF
tel (01623) 882272 *fax* (01623) 882272

Initial scan of a 10x8in (25x20cm) print is free. Can
also work with CDs, negatives and transparencies.

Repros of a b&w 10x8in are priced as follows:
£48 for 100, £64 for 250 and £88 for 500.

Repros of a b&w postcard print are priced as follows:
£34 for 100, £39 for 250 and £64 for 500.

Note Please ring for latest prices for colour repros.

Faces Prints

10 Avondale Road, Carlton, Nottingham NG4 1AF
tel 0115-847 5640 *fax* 0115-847 5640
email facesprints@ntlworld.com

Initial scan is free.

Repros of b&w 10x8in are priced as follows:
£28 for 25, £43 for 50, £56 for 100, £73 for 200, £85
for 250 and £99 for 500.

Repros of a b&w postcard print are priced as follows:
£22 for 25, £32 for 50, £37 for 100, £49 for 200, £59
for 250 and £85 for 500.

Will also provide a free gloss on quantity of 25, free
photo retouch, free design on 'z-cards', and email
proofing and free name/caption insertion.

Moorfields Photographic

Old Hall Street, Liverpool L3 9RQ
tel 0151-236 1611
email info@moorfieldsphoto.com

Established in 1981. Please refer to the website, and to
the separate advertisement in this Yearbook, for full
details.

Profile Prints

Courtwood Photographic Ltd, FREEPOST TO55,
Penzance, Cornwall TR18 2BF
tel (01736) 741222 *fax* (01736) 741255
email sales@courtwood.co.uk (images to
jlewis.courtwood@virgin.net)
website www.courtwood.co.uk

One-off charge of £2.75 for negative from email, CD
or original. All media accepted.

Repros of 10x8in b&w or colour are priced as follows:
£29.75 for 24, £52.25 for 50, and £94.25 for 100.

Credit card-sized self-adhesive 'minis' (great for
CVs):
£13 for 50, and £18.25 for 100.

Produces all sizes, postcards and z-cards. Prices
include p&p and VAT.

Visualeyes Imaging Services

95 Mortimer Street, London W1W 7ST
tel 020-7323 7430 *fax* 020-7323 7438
website www.visphoto.co.uk

Reproducing actors' headshots for more than 30
years. True photographic printing from 6x4in to
16x12in. Other services include digital printing,
scanning, retouching and image archiving. Visit the
website for full information on services, prices,
ordering and despatch options. Offers a discount to
students, free clean-up of images, and free
transmission of image to *Spotlight*.

Voice-overs

Bernard Shaw

'Voice-overs' are very buoyant, with more available work than ever before and more opportunities for 'newcomers' to find their place in this exciting world. The voice business is strictly that – business! Learn how it works and learn how to earn your place within it. Focused and targeted effort will be rewarded; a business-like approach might well open lucrative doors for you.

You are unlikely to make any professional progress without a 'demo' CD showing the quality and range of your natural voice. Newcomers are more likely to be booked for their 'own' voice than for their ability to perform a multitude of doubtful regional accents and unrecognisable impressions. Given that very few employers actively seek a 'versatile voice', there is little point in marketing yourself under this rather old-fashioned banner. Identify your natural strengths and market them in places where they might be in demand. Demonstrate, briefly, what you can do well.

Historically, actors had interminable voice-demo cassettes designed to be all things to all listeners, with many of them containing up to 20 tracks ranging from Shakespeare to coffee ads. These are no longer acceptable: anyone sending out such a thing will be regarded as out of touch with current reality and will not be taken seriously. The medium of choice is now CD and the preferred running length is three minutes! The BBC and other companies producing Radio Drama will tolerate eight or nine minutes. Voice Actors (the cool way to describe yourself) should have a master CD containing a range of material which can be 'picked and mixed' to suit a variety of recipients. Home computers make it very easy to create a different content and running order for each CD produced.

This master CD ought to be produced and recorded by one of the few reputable studios specialising in this work and should contain only genuine material. Do not write your own scripts or rely on 'spoofs'. Your recordings need to sound as professional as the real thing and should be complete with music and sound effects. For work voicing ads you should have three or four 30-second commercial scripts such as hard sell, soft sell, real person, and 'character' voice. For documentary work, you could have a two-minute 'wildlife' read together with a contrasting piece 'explaining' a concept or process. This material is easily found as there are thousands of scripts available on the Internet.

If you have specialised knowledge (perhaps from a former profession or hobby), you should include a recording demonstrating this. Computer games are now bigger business than Hollywood films so it would be wise to record some material for this market. You might be possessed of the deep tones of a Super Hero or discover the ability to voice cutesy cuddly toys – or both! The voices required for these games are similar in range and extremes to those heard in cartoon films and children's stories. Games companies do not normally cast on the strength of a 'demo' CD, but professionally produced recordings might well get you a place on their audition list.

Radio Drama producers expect to receive a CD containing four pieces no longer than two minutes each. The material should be one 'classical', one 'contemporary', one 'comic' and a poem. The ideal is to produce a balanced listen which gives an overall glimpse of your range and abilities, but without straying into the trap of attempting to demonstrate your skill (or lack thereof) in producing large numbers of accents and characters. Be yourself!

Your CDs should be well and imaginatively labelled and packaged. Ideally they should be as impressive, interesting and memorable as anything bought in a high street shop. Full-time Voice Actors spend much time, effort and money on designing their packaging. It should be memorable enough for the CD to be found from within a pile of 100 others long after the name of the artist has faded from memory. Use a memorable 'catch phrase' with a coordinated picture or design. You cannot rely solely on the quality of your voice, nor on the open-mindedness of employers and agents, to get you a hearing. High-quality, imaginative packaging is essential. The software which helps you produce it is to be found in most modern computers; if it is not resident on your desktop, it can be bought for only £10.

There are two ways to find work. You can either ask an agent to put you on their books, or you can contact the employers yourself. Before a voice-over agent agrees to represent you, it will be necessary for you to demonstrate that you can provide them with a new income stream. The primary function of any agent is to make money for themselves; it is a waste of time and effort to approach agents who already represent someone who sounds the same as you. Agents have Internet sites where their clients' voices can be heard; visit these sites, and if you hear someone sounding like you, don't waste your time and energy on a pointless phone call. When you find someone who does not already represent what you have to offer you will be able to call them from a position of strength and confidence.

Many successful Voice Actors choose to represent themselves. They enjoy the challenge of running what is essentially a 'Small Business' from home. Their core reference book is Mr Osborne's *Voice-Over Contacts*, which is a most useful and reasonably priced publication containing details of a large number of employers and other important contacts within the voice business. Full details can be found at **www.voiceovercontacts.co.uk**. Newcomers may be surprised to find their phone calls meeting with a much warmer response from the advertising agents than from the voice agents.

Treat the voice world in a professional and business-like manner, and it will, at the very least, listen to what you have to offer. Always present yourself as a 'solution' rather than a 'problem' and, above all, try to match your strengths to their needs. Good luck!

Bernard Shaw is the author of *Voice-Overs: A Practical Guide* – a popular training manual on both sides of the Atlantic. He runs regular Voice-Over and Radio Acting workshops at the Actors Centres in London, Birmingham, Manchester and Newcastle. He works full time in the voice business and is one of the most experienced producers of voice demos in the world. His website, **www.bernardshaw.co.uk**, contains further advice and interesting links.

Showreel and voice demo companies

The rapid growth in recording technology has seen an explosion of such companies over the last decade. There has also been a significant increase in the amount of (sometimes contradictory) advice offered on content, length, and so on. Much of this 'advice' is available on individual companies' websites, where you can sometimes also find samples of their work.

Voice demos (also known as 'voice reels' and 'showreels') have been around for several decades, and a good one could attract the attention of a voice agent. However, the world of voice-overs is hard to break into and so a quality-produced demo is very important. Showreels are a more recent innovation and are not yet the 'norm' – some agents and casting directors won't watch them. However, a good one might just tip the balance in your favour.

If you intend to travel down these routes, check the details (including pricing) of each possible company and the quality of their work. You should also assess whether the financial investment(s) involved could produce sufficient return. These additional 'calling cards' need to be of broadcast quality and professionally packaged to have any impact. As with photographers, it is very important to research as thoroughly as possible before committing your meagre funds. Is there a real possibility that one (or both) will enhance your chances of acting work?

Note It is very important that you have permission from the copyright-holders of any material that you intend to use. Some companies will help with this.

Accent Bank

420 Falcon Wharf, 34 Lombard Road, London SW11 3RF
tel 020-7223 5160
email enquiries@accentbank.co.uk
website www.accentbank.co.uk
Director Lisa Paterson

A voice-over portal distributed to an international market. Acts as a shop window for experienced voice-over talent specialising in authentic regional and international voices. "Accent Bank provides bespoke one-on-one coaching and workshops for those new to the business. We pride ourselves on a very personal service, using the best coaches and directors, original material and excellent production facilities to bring out the best in your voice. For more information, or to have a chat, contact us by phone or email."

Actor Showreels

97B Central Hill, London SE19 1BY
tel (07853) 637965
email post@actorshowreels.co.uk
website www.actorshowreels.co.uk
Key contact Hugh Lee
established 2007

Showreel services

Each actor works in collaboration with an editor to select material from pre-existing clips. The editor uploads the material online so that the actor's agent can also view the edit. Once the client is fully satisfied, the DVD goes to print.

Charges £200 for producing a showreel as above; the cost includes 10 additional copies. The average duration of a showreel is 5 minutes.

Recent clients have included: Jennifer Hennessy (Curtis Brown); Nathalie Armin (Lou Coulson Associates).

The Actor's One-Stop Shop

First Floor, Above the Gate Pub, Station Road, London N22 7SS
tel 020-8888 7006 *fax* 020-8888 9666
email info@actorsonestopshop.com
website www.actorsonestopshop.com
established 1997

Showreel services

Offers broadcast-quality, professionally packaged reels. Scenes are crafted like film/TV excerpts rather than being 'audition pieces'. Actors can choose either monologue or dialogue scenes, in any combination they wish. A single scene (monologue) reel costs £310 (including final copy in box DVD presentation).

Also edits reels from past work at a cost of £60 per hour; clients sit-in on the edit and receive the

Resources

finished product the same day. Price includes full archiving of material so that the reel can be easily and affordably updated in the future. Actors can order DVD, CD Rom or VHS copies. The company also supplies 'streamed' copies for agency and The Spotlight websites.

Recommended by several agents, The Spotlight and CastingCall Pro. See website for reel samples.

Ben Crowe
23 John Aird Court, Little Venice, London W2 1UY
mobile (07952) 784911
email bencrowe@hotmail.co.uk
Key contact Ben Crowe

Charges £65 for producing a voice demo from scratch (or £55 with Spotlight card, and for students). Includes 2 additional CD copies. Average duration of the demo is 60-90 minutes. "Select 4 30-second speeches for Spotlight voice clips."

Crying Out Loud Productions
Soho, London
tel 020-3262 3076 *fax* (07809) 549887
email simon@cryingoutloud.co.uk
website www.cryingoutloud.co.uk
Key contacts Simon Cryer, Marina Caldarone

Voice demo services

Established in 1999. Charges from £280 to produce a bespoke voice demo from scratch; this includes a face-to-face consultation with Marina Caldarone to select material, studio time with both producer and director, full editing and production, a 2-minute MEGAMIX, a 2-year archive, a Master Audio CD and a data CD containing MP3 files and Contacts Brochure.

There are no hidden costs. Clients will record a selection of material consisting of around 5 Commercials, 2 Narratives, 1 Documentary and 3 Dramas. Each client meets with the director, Marina Calderone, for a 90-minute consultation to select the most suitable material for their voice. Clients should aim to leave at least 7 days between consultation and recording session so they have sufficient time to prepare.

Recent clients have included: Charles (Lord) Brocket, Andrew Castle, Sky, Elizabeth Norman (the voice of BT 1571), the Disasters Emergency Committee (DEC), Ubisoft, and Sally Gunnell OBE. Both Simon Cryer and Marina Caldarone are practitioners in the industry working in Radio Commercials and Radio Drama.

Cut Glass Productions
Studio 185, 181-187 Queens Crescent, Camden, London NW5 4DS
tel 020-7267 2339
email info@cutglassproductions.com
website www.cutglassproductions.com
Producer Phil Corran

Voice-demo services

Three package options:
- £210 'Revive' – created for artists who wish to update or make changes to an existing showreel.
- £250 'Create' – for actors/artists who need a completely new reel. A lot of support and advice is given to beginners. Includes script consultation and 4 hours' studio time.
- £350 'Raw Talent' – this package is for complete newcomers to the voice industry who feel they are going to need the freedom of unlimited time in the studio.

Once each actor's showreel expectations are established, there is a detailed pre-consultation by phone – this enables Cut Glass to get to know you and select material suitable for your playing age/ range. Cut Glass doesn't recycle scripts – each piece (4-5 commercials, 2 narrations or documentaries, maybe an animation/story piece) will be unique to you. There is also a detailed consultation on the day to discuss selected material. The recording session itself is a creative experience in terms of ideas and performance, with Phil Corran directing and producing the session. You will be guided throughout the production, and go home with your mastered reel and 1 extra copy. Showreels are around 4 mins long, with an option to produce a 90-second punchy 'montage' which sits at the beginning of your reel and can be emailed to casting directors as an MP3 or used on Spotlight.

As well as specialising in creating high-quality voice-over showreels, Cut Glass is a digital voice-over production studio and creative voice agency. As such, the company has a diverse range of clients – both professional voice-over jobs and showreel customers – and works with animation/computer games companies, corporates, the BBC and independent production companies. It regularly produces audio guides and comedy podcasts, and produces showreels for other agencies as well as its own. See the website for examples of 'montages' of the agency's showreels.

Advice to beginners: As voice-over agents (see entry on page 106), Cut Glass recommends that your showreel be no longer than around 4 mins; any longer and you will have lost the casting director/agent's attention. Talk to people who work in the voice industry, and listen to recommendations. It's so important to get your showreel production spot-on, because it's your one chance to showcase your vocal talent.

MyClips
Flat 1, 2 Blackdown Close, London N2 8JF
tel 020-8371 9526
email info@myclipsdvd.co.uk
website www.myclipsdvd.com
Key personnel Ruth Hutchinson, Alex Perkins

Showreel services

Edits showreel credits into individual clips. Because a myclips DVD is non-linear, the casting director or agent can choose the order of the clips they wish to view. Footage can be supplied in DVD, VHS or 8mm video format. The company can also improve the quality of the clips, for example by altering the colour balance or removing some of the hiss from VHS credits. Charges £199 to provide a showreel including 5 DVD copies, each presented in a clear slimline myclips DVD case. Also designs and prints print full-colour, photographic quality, double-sided DVD case inserts with more information about the client. The standard insert includes photo, CV, biography and contact details. On request, the company can include further details to suit individual needs, including a promotional flyer for an upcoming performance. Prints a full-colour, photographic quality design directly onto the DVD face: "No more sticky labels." Each DVD also has animated menus so that the viewer can see a preview before choosing which clips they wish to watch. "A myclips DVD is incredibly user-friendly." An upgrade package is also available at £99.

Opus Productions Ltd

9a Coverdale Road, London W12 8JJ
tel 020-8743 3910 *fax* 020-8749 4537
email into@opusproductions.com
website www.opusproductions.co.uk
Key personnel Claire Bidwell, Neil Wilkes

Established in 1999. Works mainly in computer media production. Specialises in video and audio encoding, DVD authoring, video editing, graphic design and website design. Will edit, produce and encode video and DVD showreels for actors.

The Reel Deal Showreel Co

6 Charlotte Road, Wallington, Surrey SM6 9AX
tel 020-8647 1235
email info@thereel-deal.co.uk
website www.thereel-deal.co.uk
established 2003

Showreel services

Has 2 rates for editing a showreel: £199 for a full day's editing, which includes 2 free hours in the first year to update the reel, and 2 free DVDs; or the hourly rate of £35 for actors who don't have a lot of material. A discount of 15% is offered if you mention this publication when booking your edit. Clients include: James McAvoy, Rory Kinnear, Rula Lenska, Shane Richie and Shobna Gulati, amongst others.

Replay Film & New Media

25 Museum Street, London WC1 1ST
tel 020-7637 0473
email showreels@replayfilms.co.uk
website www.replayfilms.com
established 1991

Showreel services

Although Replay can record presentations and performances from scratch, for most clients the task is to produce a carefully constructed compilation of highlights from existing TV and film performances. Advises that the correct selection and juxtaposition of these clips is essential, and it is therefore vital that clients sit-in on the editing process to ensure that they are happy with the final result. Most showreels last 4-7 minutes. Will supply scripts if requested, but does not organise for copyright clearance.

As most showreels take around 4 hours to edit, Replay has put together the following package for a fixed fee: up to 4 hours in the edit studio with the editor (digitising existing clips from VHS, capturing digitised clips onto an Avid editing suite, editing the captured clips and inserting titles where required); and 3 VHS copies. The digital master tape will be archived at 2 sites. Exact prices are available on application only. Discounted rates are available to actors, presenters, students and non-commercial theatre companies. Overtime (anything over 4 hours) is charged at approximately 50% of the commercial editing rate.

Recent clients include: Donald Standen, Julian Hanshaw, Justine Waddel, Michael Mears, Patsy Kensit, Shared Experience Theatre Company and Vicky Johnson.

Bernard Shaw

Horton Manor, Canterbury CT4 7LG
tel (01227) 730843
email bernard@bernardshaw.co.uk
website www.bernardshaw.co.uk
established 1980

Voice-demo services

Supplies scripts for actors to use if desired. Charges £350 to produce a voice demo from scratch. This includes the company fee, studio and equipment costs, recording and editing of new material and 1 CD copy. Normally produces voice demos lasting 6-15 minutes but this varies according to the wishes and ability of the client. Charges £60 per hour to produce a voice demo from existing material only. Advises actors to reproduce CDs with a specialist duplicator for a cheaper price.

Material is selected in consultation with the client, either from their resources or from an extensive in-house library. Does not organise for the copyright clearance of material chosen. Recent clients include: actors from major agencies and broadcasting organisations such as BBC Radio Drama. Has also provided services for actors at the Royal Shakespeare Company, the Royal National Theatre and various drama schools. Work can be heard on nearly all voice agents' websites, The Spotlight online casting directory, Castingcallpro.com, or on Bernard's own website **www.bernardshaw.co.uk**.

Bernard Shaw is a voice-over tutor at the Actors Centres in London, Birmingham, Manchester and Newcastle (see entries under *Short-term and part-time courses* on page 38) and is the author of *Voice-Overs, a Practical Guide* published by A & C Black Publishers Ltd. He specialises in directing and producing tapes for BBC Radio acting.

Advises actors to attend classes at the Actors Centres, research voice-over websites, talk to people working in the field and study *Voice-Overs*. Also see **www.voiceovercontacts.co.uk** for a recommended publication.

The Showreel Ltd

Knightsbridge House, 229 Acton Lane, Chiswick, London, W4 5DD
tel 020-7043 8660 *fax* 020-8995 2144
email info@theshowreel.com
website www.theshowreel.com

Showreelz

Chiswick, London W4
mobile (07885) 253477
email brad@showreelz.com
website www.showreelz.com
established 1998

Showreel services

Showreelz.com has been filming and editing showreels for performers for more than 10 years. The company now has a base in Chiswick, London W4. Rates are £50 per hour for filming and £30 per hour for editing.

• Shooting reels from scratch: total cost approx. £200-250. This includes company fee, studio and equipment costs, recording and editing of new material and 2 DVDs with full colour print on the DVD. Offers free consultation to actors shooting from scratch, ascertaining the roles they are most likely to be cast in and selecting pieces accordingly.
• Editing: produces reels lasting on average 2-5 minutes. Charges £30 for editing from existing material and can accept most formats. £40 DVD mastering charge to include menu design if required, full colour print on the DVD, clamshell cases and 2 copies. Further copies from £3 each. Can also put reels online or prepare reels for uploading to casting services.

Also films showcases, productions and auditions. Recent clients include: Ricci Harnett, Tamer Hassan, Rosemary Ashe, Justine Glenton, Isabel Losada, JC Mac, Eugene Washington, Abbin Galeya, Satnam Bhogul, Amy Darcy. Online payment now accepted. Offers a 15% discount on editing to actors mentioning this publication.

Voice-demo services

Supplies scripts for actors to use if desired. Total cost approx. £120 to produce a voice demo from scratch. This includes the company fee, studio and equipment costs, recording and editing of material and 2 CD copies. Rates are set at £30/hour. Normally produces voice demos lasting 2-3 minutes. Will offer a 10% discount to actors quoting this publication. Recent

clients include: Kelsey Cameron, Kal Mansoor, David Lee, Brian Scoltock and Eugene Washington.

Silver-Tongued Productions

178 Ramillies Road, Sidcup DA15 9JH
tel 020-8309 0659
email contactus@silver-tongued.co.uk
website www.silver-tongued.co.uk
established 1996

Voice-demo services

Prices start at £120, depending on length of time required in studio. Silver-Tongued Productions is a small independent company. They will guide you through the whole process of recording your voice reel, from choosing scripts to directing you during the recording session, making it as simple and as easy as possible. They supply the commercials which are selected in consultation with the actor, taking into consideration the style of the voice, age etc., showing as much variety as possible. The readings are the actor's choice and can be from plays, books, poetry or prose. Again, try to show a variety. For a free brochure and a sample CD, visit their website and fill in the brochure request form on their "Contact Us" page, or give them a call.

Recent clients include: Philip Glenister, Aiden McArdle, Robert Duncan, Pip Torrens, Guy Masterton, and Jeremy Edwards. Agency recommendations include: Ken McReddie Ltd, Hobson's Voices, Foreign Voices, Break-A-Leg.

Small Screen Showreels

17 Knole Road, Crayford, London DA1 3JN
tel 020-8816 8896
email info@smallscreenshowreels.co.uk
website www.smallscreenshowreels.co.uk
Key contact Anthony Holmes

Established in 1999. Supplies scripts, premises are wheelchair-accesssible. Does not organise copyright clearance. Recent clients include: Frank Scantori, Ralph Gassmann (both Narrow Road Company), Vidal Sancho (Andrew Manson). Charges £60 per hour for filming (client selects material) plus £40 per hour (or £500 package price with assistance selecting material). If working from existing material, charges £40 per hour with client present, or £200 plus p&p (package price) for editing-by-mail. Charges up to 10 copies £3 each, up to 30 copies £2.50 each, up to 100 copies, £2 each, over 100 copies price on request. Average duration of a showreel is 3.5 minutes. Spotlight members, or those who quote *Actors' Yearbook* when booking, will receive a 10% discount. Also offers assistance with selection of material for existing footage if required (assistance with selecting material for filming service only applies with package price). Does not record voice demos, but is able to edit existing ones if required.

SonicPond Studio

70 Mildmay Grove South, Islington, London N1 4PJ
tel 020-7690 8561

email martin@sonicpond.co.uk
website www.sonicpond.co.uk
Key contact Martin Fisher

Showreel services

Supplies scripts for actors to use if desired. Charges £200 (£175 for students) to film a showreel from existing material only, with 3 copies included in the price and extra copies charged at £2.50 each. The average duration of a showreel is 4 minutes. Clients include: Edmund Kente and Annie Cooper (Felix de Wolfe); Deborah Baxter (Crawfords); Rhian Green (Emptage Hallett); and Katharine Bennett-Fox (Global Artists). Advises actors: "Don't worry that you may not have enough material; you most likely do. Less is truly more with showreels. Also, don't wait for that copy of the student film you have been waiting to be sent, think of the reel as an organic growing thing which you will add to and change for the whole of your career. Just get it started."

Voice-demo services

Supplies scripts for actors to use if desired. Charges £290 to produce a voice demo from scratch; working from existing material the hourly rate is £35 plus vat. 3 CDs are included in the package, with extra copies charged at £2 each. Average total duration of the demo is 7-8 minutes. Students receive a discounted package of £250 for a full voicereel; for actors, Spotlight clips (4 x 30-second pieces) are charged at £85. Voice clients include: Bob Golding (Hobsons); Nicholas Keith (Yakety Yak); Christina Pickard (Lip Service); Pete Gallagher (Another Tongue); Zoe Lister (Bronia Buchanan Associates); and James Alexandrou (Earache). Advises actors: "Don't worry about the pieces – everyone does! We will work together to find you the best material; it's much more about finding the tone for each piece on the day, which is our job in directing you. In the meantime, listen to as much voiceover as possible, and think about what works and why."

Take Five

37 Beak Street, London W1F
tel 020-7287 2120 *fax* 020-7287 3035
email info@takefivestudio.co.uk
website www.takefivestudio.co.uk
Key contact Charlie Lort-Phillips
established 1995

Showreel services

Charges £70 per hour for filming and £45 per hour for editing (this includes all studio and equipment costs). VHS copies are priced at £6 each, DVDs at £13 each and CDs at £6 each. Discounts are offered for bigger quantities.

A script consultation is held with each actor, preferably 7 days prior to filming. Scenes can be shot in the studio or on location and benefit from professional direction, lighting and cameramen. Most

showreels last around 5 minutes. The company advises actors who are sending in existing material only to cue scenes on the tape or to have the timecodes written down to speed up the capturing process.

Recent clients include: Siobhan Hewlett (Hamilton Hodell), Harry Eden (ICM), Lee Ingleby (Conway van Gelder) and Tim Barlow (Paul Becker).

The Reel McCoy

4 Kirkdale, Sydenham, London SE26 4NE
mobile (07708) 626477
email reelmccoyservice@aol.com
website www.reelmccoy.notlong.com
Key contact James Hyland

Established in 2005. Offers a highly specialised service in which existing material is re-edited so that the actor becomes the primary focus of each of his or her chosen segments, while still maintaining the narrative of the scene. Also specialises in creating non-verbal montages with music. Clients include: Nick Bartlett (Narrow Road), Hassani Shapi (Nancy Hudson Associates Ltd), and Nicola Preece (City Actors Management). Charges £20 for producing a showreel with an average duration of 5 minutes. This includes 1 DVD, with further copies charged at £3 each. Offers a free consultation session and portfolio photo-reel included on the completed DVD. Recommends actors to "make sure they have noted the time in which their chosen footage appears on their VHS tapes or DVDs. This will save time in the editing room".

Twitch Films

22 Grove End Gardens, 18 Abbey Road, London NW8 9LL
tel 020-7266 0946
email post@twitchfilms.co.uk
website www.twitchfilms.co.uk

Established in 2006; offices are fully wheelchair-accessible. Working with existing material, charges a flat fee of £200, which includes editing, design of DVD interface and discprint, 10 professionally printed and packaged DVDs, digital files for use on the Internet, websites and for emailing, and full archiving. For shorter edits and updates the hourly rate is £40; additional discs can be ordered from £2.50 each, depending on quantity. The average duration of a showreel is 3-5 minutes.

"We advise recording material from scratch only in exceptional circumstances, primarily when an aspect of the actor's range, which would be key to their castability, is under-represented in their existing footage. We do not provide scripts, but will give detailed advice on what scripts may be appropriate, and assist in making the selection." Recent clients include: Darren Boyd and Eleanor Matsuura (Amanda Howard Associates); Colin Salmon (GMM); Jane Perry (Andrew Manson Personal Management); Kevork Malikyan (United Agents); and Trevor White (Price Gardner Management).

Skillset and Equity Careers Advice Service

Give your career the attention it deserves, with this invaluable advice from **Beverley Hills**, one of Skillset's three Equity-accredited performance careers advisers.

As an actress I am lucky to have carved for myself what has been termed a 'freelance portfolio career'. This means that I do several freelance jobs in between performing.

My own journey in the Arts began working backstage at the Birmingham Rep, moving on to dressing at the RSC, then designing Opera in Italy, before becoming a jazz singer and finally an actress. I am also a writer with a Masters degree that gave me knowledge of Higher and Further Education, plus the funding issues that face freelancers. Experiencing all these different backgrounds at first hand gives me a distinct advantage when it comes to my work as a Skillset performance careers adviser.

Who are Skillset?

Skillset is the sector skills council for Creative and Media. The organisation is industry- and Government-funded, and the Careers department provides information, advice and guidance to anyone wishing to work, or currently working, in all aspects of the film and television industry, from training to funding to networking.

Traditionally Skillset was set up to provide industry with a way of training people to have the right skills at the right time on the technical side of things, i.e. behind the camera. There are 34 freelance Skillset advisers in total: whatever your discipline – director, sound, camera – your adviser will be a freelance practitioner working in your chosen field of discipline.

Thanks to external funding from the Union Learning Fund, Equity and Skillset have been able to train Careers and Learning Advisers, and Skillset's brief has expanded to include one-to-one careers advice and careers workshops for performers. Across the UK there are only three performance advisers fully accredited by Equity who are specifically trained to deliver this unique and confidential service, and I am one of them.

What are the benefits?

We performance advisers (two in London and one in the North West) are all working practitioners with a wealth of experience between us that covers stage, TV, radio and theatre, plus our own specialisms. We're not stuck behind a dusty computer terminal looking at stats telling you how it should be; we're out there in the field gathering vital practical information about this wonderful ever-changing business of ours. We are also experienced in the age-old problem of how to survive when you're not working.

The wonderful thing about being an accredited adviser is the privileged access to the profession I now have, with professional links to casting agents, agents, directors, produc- ers, etc. that are usually denied the working actor. I can ask direct questions and pass this information straight on to you, the client – telling it like it actually is, rather than reverting to mere speculation or outdated hearsay.

Who is the service for?

Our careers advice service is available to all performers. When we use the term 'performer', this could refer to anything from, say, a circus performer to a dancer, actor, singer, variety performer, DJ, VJ, (Video Jockey), burlesque stripper – you name it! Anything you can do in front of an audience is termed 'performance' (steady now!).

As well as new entrants, returners or those who feel stuck in a rut, I've advised people at the very top of their game. One big TV/film celebrity (who of course shall remain nameless) needed help not to find work, but to rediscover their passion for performing.

How does it work?

To apply, you need first to fill out an application form online at the Skillset or Equity websites, stating where you are in your career and what you would like to achieve. Perhaps you are a returner, having been out of the business for a while for whatever reason; or you haven't worked for a spell, or need to know how to find an agent. Whatever your position, is up to me to help facilitate movement or change.

One-to-one sessions take place in central London and last for 60-90 minutes, depending on a performer's experience. There are two 'stages': Stage One (60 minutes), for those with less than two industry years' experience; and Stage Two (90 minutes), aimed at more experienced practitioners. During the meeting we work together to devise a tailor-made action plan, which is specifically designed to encourage progression.

Subsequent to this initial meeting we offer a follow-up service, where you have the opportunity to see the same adviser for the sake of continuity, or to talk to another in order to get a fresh perspective. You can also take advantage of the free email service for any questions that may spring up as a result of the meeting(s). There's no need to feel isolated any longer, which is a common trait in our business; you are fully supported for as long as you want to be.

To set your mind at rest, if you see me I am also a trained councillor and so can, and often do, deal with other personal issues that might culminate in an actor feeling 'stuck'.

What if I change my mind?

After a performer has filled out their application form, I will do some research into how best to help them achieve their goals. Occasionally, they change their mind between filling out the form and meeting me – and that's fine. The important thing is to be honest with yourself, to make the most out of our work together. Writing down your list of goals can help clarify the muddy waters.

It can be hard for performers to talk rationally about their careers: spouses and agents have heard it all before, and fellow professionals are probably in the same boat. It can all end up with a collective moan down the pub, which may be therapeutic but is not necessarily productive! Our service is objective, confidential and based in extensive experience as we look honestly at your career and give you up-to-date advice about CVs, photos, agents, marketing and all the other business of being a performer.

Does the service work?

That depends on how much effort you think your career is worth. Last year, when acting work was once again thin on the ground, I took a long, hard and *objective* look at myself as a performer. I noted where I could make some changes – some of the same changes I encourage my clients to make. It took me a year to make all the adjustments, which included some classes, a revamp of my marketing strategy and, most of all, significant weight loss.

And did it work? Put it this way: I got my first theatre job in a long time. I played Shirley Valentine at The Garrick, which was sold-out every night and broke all box-office records.

What will it cost me?

The current prices in **England and Northern Ireland** are:

Stage One (60-minute session):	£45
Stage Two (90-minute session):	£70
Follow-up (90-minute session):	£45

If you live in **Scotland**, all sessions are charged at a flat rate of £30, thanks to funding from Scottish Screen.

The current prices in **Wales** are:

Stage One (60-minute session):	£30
Stage Two (90-minute session):	£60
Follow-up (90-minute session):	£30

You can receive a 50 per cent discount if you are a member of any of the following unions affiliated to the Federation of Entertainment Unions:

• Broadcasting, Entertainment Cinematograph and Theatre Union (BECTU)
• Equity
• The Writers' Guild of Great Britain (WGGB)
• National Union of Journalists (NUJ)
• Musicians' Union (MU)

You'll have to provide a valid membership number in order to qualify.

Other discretionary discounts may be available for applicants who are unemployed and in receipt of benefits, on a low income or from under-represented groups.

To apply, or for further details, please visit **www.skillset.org/careers** or **www.equity.org.uk**.

Beverley Hills (**www.beverleyhills.co.uk**) has extensive experience as an actress, voice-over artiste, TV writer and presenter, Equity/Skillset adviser and Skillset course accreditor, NCDT performance reviewer and ITC trainer – and much more. She loves her job as a Skillset performance adviser: "Every performer is different and every need is distinctive, but we all have one essential similarity at heart – a passion for our work."

Between engagements

or 'How to survive until the next job'
Andrew Piper

All the articles in this publication are one person's perspective, and as such need to be tested against your own judgement and experience. None more so than this article, because like you I'm an actor. Unless you are extremely lucky (or have only just graduated from drama school), you will have experienced periods of unemployment, and will have come up with your own strategies for coping with this. What follows is a collection of thoughts on what seems *to me* to be good advice for any actor finding themself temporarily out of work. I don't always follow this advice, but it does seem to help when I do. Not everything here will be right for you, but I hope that some of it will make it easier for you get to your next acting job with body and soul intact.

I've grouped the suggestions in this article under four headings: stay solvent, stay employable, stay visible, and stay sane. Do all these things, and acting work should never be too far away.

Stay solvent

It might surprise you that I start with this, but money problems can make all the other suggestions in this article so much more difficult to do. Your first priority as an actor, therefore, is to make sure that you can keep a roof over your head, food in your fridge, and your creditors (if any) off your back. Without these things it becomes next to impossible to present a confident face to the world, to maintain the self-esteem and self-belief that one needs to survive as an actor, and to plan any strategies for finding acting work. So with this in mind – and recognising that this is the least interesting bit – here are my tips for staying solvent:

• Save money when you are working. That's not easy if you're on the sort of wages that are common in theatre, but the more money you can save now, the more you'll have in reserve for the lean times ahead. Even if you have another job to go onto after this one, the chances are that there will be a few weeks between finishing one and starting the next, and that's time that potentially no one will be paying you for. Remember too that your wages will rarely have tax deducted from them, which means you will need something in reserve for when the tax bill is due. If you're doing a long theatre job, then consider setting up a standing order to a savings account – even if you only manage to save a few pounds a week, you may be glad of it further down the line.

• Live as cheaply as you can. The lower your overheads, the more you can save and the longer you can ride out a period of reduced income.

• Make your extravagances count. If you've been frugal during the week, then you can treat yourself at the weekend. Something as simple as making your own sandwiches may save you enough to pay for a meal out in as little as a few days. Skipping two or three nights of drinking and clubbing could even save you enough for a weekend in Paris or Prague.

• Probably the largest single expense you'll have is your rent or mortgage. This is generally unavoidable – unless of course you're still living with your parents – but if you're someone who does a lot of touring then it can be frustrating to be paying some exorbitant London rent for a room that you're hardly using. (Mortgages are different, of course, because at least you'll own something at the end of it.) However, for most people, having a place you can call home and look forward to returning to is immensely important. Whether or not you feel there are savings that can be made – by subletting while away, say, or moving to a cheaper area – don't leave it out of the equation when looking at keeping your costs down.

• Get a second phone. That might seem perverse, but if you don't have access to a landline (for example, if you're away from home) and you have an 'anytime minutes' contract with one of the operators, get yourself an old mobile phone (eBay is quite good for this) and put a pay-as-you-go SIM card in it for making all your off-peak calls. That way, all your long off-peak chats to your mum/partner/best mate won't eat up your valuable 'anytime' minutes. Shop around, and see what will work out best for you.

• Have a look at **www.moneysavingexpert.com**. Run by the journalist Martin Lewis, this website has all sorts of tips and tricks for making your money go further.

• Get a 'day job'. Even Kenneth Tynan's actor mistress once observed that "the worse thing about not working is having to work". And ain't that the truth! Sooner or later most of us – especially those who work mostly in theatre – have to knuckle down to something unrelated to acting in order to pay the bills. What form this takes will depend on your particular skills – it doesn't hurt to get some IT and typing skills under your belt when you get the chance – but consider office temping, waiting and bar work, call centres (one company, RSVP – **www.rsvp.co.uk** – is even run by actors), and shop work, for starters. If you have a teaching qualification, then you could make some slightly better money by doing 'supply teaching', covering for full-time teachers in case of illness. Many of the photographers listed in this book are (or were) also working actors – although this shouldn't be regarded as a way to a quick buck: those guys have worked long and hard at perfecting their skills. One of the most popular ways of earning cash between jobs is promotions work. Have a look at these sites for more information: **www.stuckforstaff.com**, **www.turns.net**, **www.ays.co.uk** and **www.promojobspro.com** (this last one is run by the same people as CastingCall Pro). I've even turned my hand (if that's the right expression) to artists' life-modelling, although I've never managed to earn more than beer money for it. One friend of mine took a course in massage in order to have another string to his bow – although I'm generally cautious about diverting money, time and energy into training that won't actually improve your employment prospects as an actor. One job I wouldn't recommend is 'extras' work, unless what you aspire to be is a background artiste. Never did a job so eloquently encapsulate the meaning of the phrase, 'so near, and yet so far'. (*Note* This point doesn't really belong in the 'stay solvent' section, but while we're on the subject of day jobs: Never take a job that you couldn't in good conscience drop at short notice to go to an audition or accept acting work, unless you want to be stuck doing that job for the rest of your life. Alas, almost any job that one could describe as 'interesting' or 'stimulating' also requires a degree of commitment. For this reason, most 'day jobs' that are suitable for actors are tedium incarnate. I wish it were otherwise. I really *really* wish it were otherwise.)

• Don't sit around waiting for the money to run out. If you have managed to bring in a good chunk of money, paid off your debts, set aside enough for your tax bill, had a holiday, and still have enough left not to need to work for a while … get a part-time job. Your savings will last you longer, and instead of turning into a couch potato (which can happen frighteningly quickly) you will retain a sense of yourself as a working, earning person. By all means do the other things you never had time to do before – take classes, see films, visit galleries, meet friends – but do these on your days off.

• Know what State Benefits you're entitled to, and claim them (and if you're not entitled, then don't). I loathe and detest signing on – Jobcentres are rarely beacons of hope and optimism – and will do almost any kind of work rather than do so, but if you do find yourself without work then it is worth taking the time to fill in the forms. Talk to Equity if the Jobcentre is sniffy about you signing on as an actor.

• Act quickly if you do get into financial trouble. If you find yourself borrowing money for your day-to-day living expenses (including using credit cards) or to make payments on existing debts, then you have a problem, and one that must be dealt with as soon as possible. This is too big an issue for me to tackle here, but you can get advice on dealing with unmanageable debts from your local Citizens' Advice Bureau, **www.citizensadvice.org.uk** (in Scotland this is **www.cas.org.uk**); from National Debtline, **www.nationaldebtline.co.uk** or *tel* 0808-808 4000; and from Consumer Credit Counselling Service, **www.cccs.co.uk** or *tel* 0800-138 1111. Whatever you do, don't be tempted to take out another credit card (even a zero interest one) or another loan unless this will allow you to cancel your existing credit cards, because you'll spiral even further into debt. Never *ever* touch those 'debt consolidation', 'one-easy-payment' companies that advertise on daytime TV – they just want to make money out of you and will make matters worse. It doesn't have to be scary – you have more power than you might think. The banks want their money back, of course, but would much prefer to accept a repayment plan which fits your budget, than go through the expense of legal proceedings when they know you can't pay.

Stay employable

This is perhaps the easiest section for me to write, because, well, we all know it all already. But do we do it? No, neither do I. Time and money are big factors, of course, but so are simple inertia and laziness. "Chance," said Louis Pasteur, "favours the prepared mind," so here's my list of best practices, given in the knowledge that I rarely get around to more than a handful of them when I'm between jobs.

• Brush up your skills – voice, dance, singing, stage combat, Shakespeare, Alexander Technique, etc. – and learn new ones. There are various places in London and around the country that offer professional-grade courses in these, such as the London and Manchester Actors Centres, The City Lit, and the drama schools and universities listed in the Short Courses section of this book. Get a driving licence if you don't already have one.

• Keep fit, whatever your preferred means is. Sport, gym, dance, swimming, walking, martial arts – even regular bouts of acrobatic sex would do it, I suppose, as long as afterwards you didn't light up or order pizza. Aerobic fitness is most important as this provides both the stamina to get through an evening's performance (I'm talking theatre now, not sex) and the twinkle in the eye that says 'energy and vitality' to an auditioning director. (A twinkle that says 'regular, acrobatic sex' is probably quite effective too, in certain circumstances.)

• Brush up on your audition speeches and songs. How would you feel if, at short notice, you got an audition for a great job, and you fluffed it because your speeches or songs were rusty or tired? It's happened to me; don't let it happen to you.

• Read plays. Not because you *should* (because if that's your reason then you won't) but because they're *fun*. A lot of us came into this business because we loved plays – it's odd that once we got here we read so few of them. (Keep an eye open for good audition speeches while you're reading.)

• Keep in touch with what's going on in the business. Read *The Stage*, talk to your agent and your actor friends, keep your finger on the pulse. Know which theatres have new artistic directors, which casting directors are working on which projects, and so on. Remind yourself that you're an actor – not always easy after the umpteenth week of photocopying and filing in some awful temp job.

• Watch TV. And no, I don't mean *Trisha* or *Cash in the Attic* – watch drama on TV, and go to the theatre and cinema. Remind yourself of how it's done, and make a note of the performers, directors, casting directors and production companies whose work you most admire.

• Visit your dentist. That smile of yours is important, so look after it. You don't have to go getting expensive cosmetic work done (unless your gnashers are particularly hideous, or unless you're up for a lot of romantic leads in film and television), but get a check-up with your regular dentist and make sure any problems are spotted early. I had an abscess while on tour once, and was in agony for several days. This pain was as nothing, though, compared to the shock of the bill I had for a (private) emergency dentist to perform root canal surgery. Don't let it happen to you: get them sorted before you go away.

• Lastly, but perhaps most importantly: keep yourself **available**. Remember what your real job is. As I mentioned in the previous section, it's a sad fact that almost any job that's interesting will require a degree of commitment, but if you are so committed to your 'day job' that you can't drop everything for an audition or acting work then you are putting yourself and your acting career at a real disadvantage. Talk to your agent (if you have one) when you're planning a holiday – he or she must know your every movement, even if it's only a long weekend, because both you and your agent will look stupid if an audition is arranged for a time when you're actually going to be sunning yourself on some Mediterranean beach, or giving the Best Man's speech at your brother's wedding. Talk to your agent, too, if you're considering applying for Fringe work. In some circumstances this can be a good showcase for your talents, but this must be offset against the fact that it will put you out of the running for any paid work – talk it through with your agent and discuss what you hope to get out of it. Keep your mobile phone switched on whenever possible, and return calls from your agent immediately.

Stay visible

All the preparation in the world won't count for much if nobody knows you're there. There are thousands of us out there, all chasing too few jobs, and it can be hard enough to get noticed even when you're doing everything right. That means that being a wallflower just isn't an option, however much you might hate the idea of marketing yourself. So here are a few (relatively painless) suggestions for keeping your name and face in employers' minds.

• Keep your *Spotlight* CV up to date. An entry in *Spotlight* is essential for film, television and increasingly also theatre jobs. Unless your CV is up to date then (a) the casting director's picture of you is incomplete and (b) it will look like you haven't worked for the last x years.

• Keep your photo up to date. Angus Deuchar's excellent article on page 403 will tell you why, and what to do if it's not. It's significant that all the casting directors who have written for this book have stressed how important it is that your photograph actually looks like you.

• Keep in touch with past employers. Unless you've disgraced yourself while working for them, these people represent your best chance for further work. Send a friendly email or postcard to let them know what you've been doing, with perhaps a mention that you'd love to work with them again and would appreciate a call next time they're casting.

• The best time to write to other potential employers and casting directors is when you're working and can invite them to see you. Of course there's a pretty slim chance that any London-based employers will travel up to Pitlochry to see your Stanley Kowalski or Blanche Dubois, but that's not the point: they will see that you are working – not 'just finished' working (the meaning of which can be curiously flexible) – but actually working, right now.

• Keep covering letters brief, but as individual as possible. Most companies get stacks of CVs from actors with nothing but the baldest of covering notes, so a sentence along the lines of "I'm hoping to see your *Macbeth* when it comes to Leeds" or "My friend John Smith is having a great time working for you at the moment" may make yours stand out from the rest.

• Think about your marketing materials: photo, CV, covering letter. Are they well presented? They represent you: do they do a good job? Are the CV and letter on good-quality paper or the nasty, cheap stuff you get in photocopiers? Get someone who knows what they're talking about to give constructive criticism about them. There are differing opinions about this, but I think it's always worth printing your photo onto the CV itself. If it's well printed then many theatre companies are quite happy with this instead of a full 10x8. If you're sending out a lot of letters and CVs, then it might be worth asking your local printer to quote for some headed notepaper with your photo at the top. Don't get him to print the whole CV – it will go out of date long before you get round to mailing them all. (I should say that my agent completely disagrees with this idea – he reckons you should always send 10x8s, and leave printing your photo on your CV for when you've run out of photos. As I said, opinion is divided.)

• Additional marketing tools. Websites can be quite a good way of getting someone to spend time finding out about you, and of putting across a particular image. The cost of commissioning one from scratch can vary wildly, but someone with only a modicum of computer know-how should be able to knock together something quite presentable using a site like **www.moonfruit.com** or **www.easily.co.uk** (this latter also allows you to register quite cheaply your own domain name – e.g. andrew-piper.com). Don't fret if you haven't got one – your *Spotlight* web page already carries all the important information. Personal websites are currently a 'nice-to-have' not a 'need-to-have'.

• Postcards and business cards. Not a substitute for the CV and photo, but quite a useful additional tool – something to give or send someone who has met you, as a reminder of who you are. Postcards can also make quite good performance notices – something a casting director can read easily while eating breakfast. Have a look at **www.vistaprint.co.uk** (and there are many others) for business cards, including ones with your photo on. There are a number of companies which can produce postcards quite cheaply: **www.justpostcards.co.uk** and **www.goodprint.co.uk** are two but there are others if you hunt around.

Resources

• Apply for jobs. Sounds obvious, but plenty of actors wait for their agent to submit them for everything. Even if the agent is doing their job, in practice this will mean that your CV arrives with a pile of others, with little or nothing to indicate why you are (a) particularly good for this job or (b) interested in working for this company. Find out what's casting – the listings in this book will tell you how best to do that for each company, and your agent may also be happy to tell you – and make your own applications. Tell your agent who you're writing to, and make sure that the CV your agent sends out on your behalf is accurate and up to date.

• On the subject of agents, stay visible to yours. Quite a number of agents have far too large a client list (30 to 35 per agent is about right, I reckon) so it's easy for them to forget about those they haven't heard from in a while. Some form of contact – phone or email, say – every week or two isn't unreasonable when you're not working. Make it a constructive call – not just "have you got me any auditions?" – and talk about what you can be doing to generate work: what's casting, who to write to, ideas for people to approach for general auditions (especially if you're travelling), and so on. Remember that they work for you, so make the most of their skills.

• Write to directors, producers and casting directors whose work you have seen, and tell them how much you enjoyed or admired it.

• Network. Go to see friends in plays, especially first nights, and get yourself invited to the party or pub afterwards. No need to be pushy – just be sociable. When you meet the director don't be tempted to 'do an audition' – casting is almost certainly the last thing on his or her mind right now, and you'll just alienate them. Conversely, don't *not* talk to them just because they're the director – that can be just as irritating. Remember that they're human beings. You won't be able to forget that they're the director, but try to see them as just someone you're meeting at a party. Then follow it up with a CV or showreel in the post. (Have one to hand in case they ask for one.)

• Showcase your talents. The Actors Centres run showcase evenings to which casting professionals are invited, and there are various others around – although be careful, before you stump up too much cash, that they are reputable. One recent addition to the collection is London Bites, which is monthly at Turnmills in Clerkenwell (**www.standupdrama.com**). Also worth considering is Fringe theatre. It is a huge commitment in terms of time and money (in lost earnings alone) to embark on a Fringe production, so make sure you'll get something out of it. If you want to work on *Holby City*, ask yourself if a Fringe production of *Godspell* is really the best showcase for you. Also, if you want casting directors to travel to see you, is it going to be worth your while doing something dark and disturbing in some tiny, God-forsaken flea-pit in the middle of nowhere? More problematic is the question, 'Is it likely to be any good?' – and for that you'll have to do your homework. Find out what the director (and writer if it's a new play) has done before, because you may not want to give up several weeks' earnings to work with a first-time director straight out of college. Everyone has to start somewhere, but you've a right to be able to make an informed judgement if you're working for next to nothing. Google, Whatsonstage.com and Theatre Record may be helpful here. (See the introduction to the Fringe theatre section for more pitfalls to watch out for.)

• Do a short film. These can be useful camera experience, and occasionally provide material for a showreel. Some of these are paid (often badly); a great many are not. These days every kid with a media studies degree wants to be the next Guy Ritchie, so again if you're working for nothing, make sure you have confidence in your director and producer before committing yourself. You're not a charity, and you're not an amateur who just does it for fun.

Stay sane

Being an actor should carry a mental health warning – working away from home, unemployment, rejection, failure, insecurity, poverty: all of these can take their toll on your psychological health and on your relationships. And the worse thing about that is that it makes it even harder to find and get acting jobs – few things kill your chances in an audition quicker than the smell of desperation. After all, if *you* don't have confidence in yourself, why should they? So look after yourself, and take responsibility for your own wellbeing. Here are my suggestions for psychological pick-me-ups …

• Be sociable, even if you don't feel like it. It can be a lonely business when you're out of work – and often even when you're working – so make the most of the time to see as much of friends and family as possible. This is particularly important with partners, especially if the kind of work you tend to get means being away from home. Throw parties or invite your friends to dinner when you're feeling up, and call your actor friends for an understanding shoulder to cry on when you're not.

• Make time for things you enjoy, that make you feel good about yourself. Perhaps this may mean setting yourself challenges – do the garden, DIY around the home, learn French, run a marathon – or may just mean setting aside 'me' time. Yoga and meditation are particularly good for this, and some people draw great strength from religious observance.

• If (like me) you are a naturally anxious person, and meditation or yoga don't appeal, then consider getting some relaxation tapes and spend some time every day listening to them. If anxiety and self-image are your problem, don't go buying some motivational 'You too can be rich and famous' hypnosis tape or you could make things worse: deal with the problem in hand. Have a look at **www.relax-uk.com** or **www.relaxaudio.com** for some examples.

• Get out in the fresh air. Remember when you were younger, when adults urged you to switch off the telly and get outdoors? Well, they were right – exercise and sunlight are vitally important for both your physical and mental health, particularly in the winter months when daylight is in short supply. Even when we're working, often much of our time is spent in windowless boxes, so make the most of a nice day and go for a walk.

• Take a holiday. That's really not easy to do, especially at the start of one's career. A week away from the 'day job' is a week not earning money, which can be expensive if you've already used up your holiday pay subsidising those days or weeks of involuntary unemployment that often occur just before or just after an acting job. But everyone needs to recharge their batteries from time to time, even if it's just a long weekend visiting old friends.

• Detox. Most actors drink – I think it was Gene Hackman who once observed that all actors eventually become either directors or drunks – but if your last job involved a lot of boozing (or if you're currently waking up with one or more hangovers a week), then try a few weeks off the sauce. Drink two litres of water a day, get plenty of early nights, and try to make fruit and fresh veg a good fifty per cent of everything you eat. Some people also find it beneficial to give up bread or go veggie or vegan for a while. Go back to beer-

and-burgers after that if you want, but notice the difference in your mood and concentration when you do.

• Keep a positive attitude. Remember, you're in this for the long term, so although six months or more can feel like a long time, compared with the 30- or 40-year career you have ahead of you, it's really not so long. Almost all actors are out of work for periods in their career – even very good ones – so don't panic.

• Don't give yourself a hard time about past failures: learn the lesson and move on. Make here and now your starting point, and plan for the future based on what *is* rather than what *might have been.*

• Silence your inner critic. Brendan Behan wrote that "Critics are like eunuchs in a harem: they know how it's done, they've seen it done every day, but they're unable to do it themselves." We all have a critic within us, but the less room we give it, the less we'll feel like eunuchs ourselves. Be generous to your fellow professionals, understanding of what they go through, and don't be threatened by their success. A friend of a friend of mine is doing very well for himself – very good-looking, great agent, lovely telly and film roles coming his way – and I so wanted to dislike him. But meeting him again at a party recently he was warm, relaxed, interested in what I was doing, remembered things I'd told him last time we met – in short, utterly charming. And I realised that that's actually what made him the star. Not just the looks or the talent – both of which he does have in spades – but also the generosity of spirit, the belief that 'I'm ok, you're ok'. It might be the acidic queen with the barbed tongue who gets the laughs at the party, but it's people like that actor who will in the end do well. So resist pressure to join in bashing reputations or impugning characters, and learn compassion for yourself and for others.

• Don't just wait for your agent to call. Be proactive. Take charge of your career. Keep doing the things listed above that will improve your chances of finding work.

• Finally – and you may be surprised that I give this advice in an actors' yearbook – if it really is getting too much for you, then it may be time to call it quits. Acting can be a very cruel business, and not everyone is built to withstand the emotional battering that visits most actors from time to time. If there is anything at all that you could be happy doing instead of acting, then do it: there is no shame at all in looking after your sanity. A very talented friend of mine who left the business after years of frustration described her new situation to me thus: "I'm doing a job that I hate and I'm happier than I've been in years." Many people who leave acting find related work – teaching, for example, or work in some aspect of production – but I know some who have found that proximity to what they've left behind to be too painful, and have opted for entirely unrelated occupations. In the end, it comes down to what makes you happy, where you feel at home, and what ultimately brings you peace. Enjoying acting is not the same as enjoying being an actor.

There's a 'prayer' that runs, 'Grant me the serenity to accept the things I cannot change, courage to change the things I can, and wisdom to know the difference.' This seems to me to be a good motto for any actor. A great many decisions affecting our lives as actors are out of our hands, but a great many more we *do* have control over. The trick to staying sane in this business seems to be knowing (and accepting) which are which.

Andrew Piper trained at the Bristol Old Vic Theatre School. More information can be found at **www.andrew-piper.com**. He edited the 2007 and 2008 editions of *Actors' Yearbook.*

Physical and mental fitness for actors

Alex Caan

The instrument or tool of the actor is the body. Like a musical instrument, if it is left idle it will become out of tune and lose its ability to function effectively.

Actors need to constantly develop their instrument to get the best out of it. Unlike a musical instrument, we carry our tool with us every day. With good habits and practice we can alleviate many of the problems that need to be fixed before they start. The work required to have a positive ongoing effect is not as great or as demanding as one would expect. Before we look at what we can do to make our bodies outstanding, let's look at what our bodies really are.

In a person of average weight and build, 70 per cent of the mass of the body is muscle and bone. Therefore we can have a large effect on our bodies, by focusing on our muscles and bones. Before we can affect change in our muscles and bones we need to understand how they work and what relationships they have with each other.

The structure of the body is extremely complicated but can be viewed in quite a simplistic manner. Originally we would have walked on all fours, which is why our upper limbs have very similar corresponding joints to our lower limbs. Each hand has five digits, with a dominant thumb; our corresponding lower body part is the opposite foot, with the big toe as the dominant digit. The wrist and ankle are similar multi-directional joints, whereas the elbow and knee are both hinged joints. The shoulder and hip are ball and socket joints.

The upper and lower limbs are also connected by corresponding groups of muscles. The quads, which are in the front of the thigh, are related to the upper body through the triceps, which are in the back of the upper arm. The hamstrings, at the back of the upper leg, are related to the biceps. The gluteus or buttocks are related to the pectorals or chest muscles. So rather than looking at muscular activity in isolation, we must see muscles as groups working together.

When the body moves forward, the opposite arm and leg swing. The combination of muscles working together propels our bodies. Muscles move limbs by shortening.

Muscles work together synergistically and in a healthy, well-maintained body are balanced. If bad habits occur, this simplicity of movement can lead to long-term health problems by over-use of some muscles, and under-use of others. This constant over-use/under-use will lead to a tired or sore body part in a specific area, often one side of the neck or lower back.

As we move forward, the chain of movements pass through the centre of the body. This passing through the centre is a clue to the focus of long-term fitness and wellbeing for the actor.

The centre of the body is the place where all life stems from. It is here that a baby is connected to its mother through the placenta, that later becomes the belly button. In the centre of the body is the diaphragm, from which, through correct training, all breath should originate.

The movement of our bodies creates heat and energy. Contrary to what some directors believe, we are not beings that live in our head or brain space. We live in our bodies and movement produces powerful emotional responses. This is encapsulated in the phrase 'Motion creates Emotion'. This is why actors talk about getting the walk of the character, because this allows them to get into the body of the character, which in turn allows them to get into the personality of the character. Some actors do this instinctively, but it is and can be a learned skill.

Actors communicate thoughts in the vast majority by speaking. There are, of course, actors who use mime and dance to communicate, but mainly thoughts are communicated verbally, using speech or song. Words are merely a manipulation of breath using the tongue, mouth and vocal cords. Without breath we have nothing to carry our thoughts over large theatrical space.

Coincidentally, breath or oxygen is the most important nourishment our bodies need. Without food one can live for 40 days or more; without water one can live for 7-10 days; but if you don't breathe for five minutes you will die.

Using this as our guide, the focus of the actors' fitness should be built around the development of a robust powerful tool that can create large amounts of powerful breath. Not just large volumes of breath, but outstanding control of the mechanism that delivers that breath.

The mechanism that delivers the breath is the lungs and diaphragm and their supporting muscles. These muscles need to be strong, but also need to be mobile and have excellent endurance.

Lastly, the value of water cannot be underestimated. A 5 per cent drop in hydration can lead to mild dehydration, which can lead to a large drop in bodily function, both mental and physical. Even a 2 per cent drop in hydration can have a very damaging and negative effect on our voice. In temperate climates we lose 2.5 litres of water throughout an average day. If we are performing, rehearsing or undertaking strenuous physical activity we will use much greater amounts of water than this. Therefore we must monitor our bodies and increase water intake when needed. Passing clear urine is a good indicator of hydration – if not first thing in the morning, then definitely throughout the day.

So where does one start in the nitty-gritty of training the actor's body? Actors come in all shapes and sizes. I am not advocating that all actors try to become slim and pert: who would play all the non-slim, non-pert roles? Equally, I am not advocating that all actors develop muscular physiques. We need to be limber in the joints and muscles, but there is no point in the serious actor developing big muscles at the expense of range of movement. I believe that you can be tall, short, slim, rotund, lanky or squat and at the same time be very fit. Olympic shot putters are very large but all can run great distances and move like ballet dancers.

Fitness for actors doesn't require a massive overloading of the body. To reach Olympic-standard fitness we would need to break the body down systematically over a period of time, in order to allow the body to regenerate stronger than before. This regeneration occurs during periods of rest. But this overloading is not really needed for general fitness for actors.

In all of our fitness development we need to place breath control and posture at the forefront. The ideas and concepts of the Alexander Technique are pivotal to this. Its values are based on excellent posture and good use of muscles, rather than overuse and bad postural habits. So when performing any movement, be aware of the alignment of the head, neck and back. Often actors strain their voices because they are tight in another part of their body, which pulls the head and neck out of alignment, resulting in a sore throat or strained voice. For those of you who are not familiar with the Alexander Technique, I would recommend that an awareness of posture and balance is vital to long-term fitness.

A simple starting point for general fitness for actors is walking. Walking is the most underused and undervalued exercise we can do. It involves a good pair of training shoes and a place to go! Between 20 and 60 minutes' continuous walking a day will increase lung capacity and make our heart a great deal stronger. I know many actors say that they walk at least that in a day – going shopping, walking to the bus or train, and so on. I am not discounting that, but I am advocating a steady brisk walk with arms swinging back and forth in time with the opposing leg. By doing this, the whole body is being exercised and the core muscles through the centre of the body are activated. It is akin to the phase of human development, that we know as crawling. The same benefits cannot be achieved through passive day-to-day walking.

Walking has a very effective return for the amount of effort expended, because there is little detrimental impact on the joints of the lower limbs. The swinging of opposing arms and legs also helps reinforce correct neurological pathways. This helps us to move our bodies more effectively and efficiently as a kinetic chain, rather than as disjointed isolated movements.

A walking regime three days a week is a good place to start. You will not only build your lungs and heart, but also the tissues around your joints in the legs, arms and back. These need time to adapt and grow to the new stresses being placed on them. Taking a day off in between will allow the tissues throughout your body to regenerate during the periods of rest.

If you are a fitness novice, then building up to an hour-long walk is an achievable goal. Start with a ten-minute walk that builds systematically over a period of between four and six weeks, rather than blazing into a brisk hour-long walk initially. Increasing your walks by three minutes each walk will let you achieve an hour-long walk from a ten-minute starting point in just six weeks. Three minutes may sound a lot, but since it requires adding just one and a half minutes to your outward journey, it is not an unrealistic amount.

Swimming is also an excellent way to work the heart and lungs without placing any stress on the joints, as it is a non-weight bearing form of exercise. However, it is important to swim using the front crawl and backstroke rather than predominantly using the breast stroke, so that we continue to move opposing upper and lower limbs to work our core muscles. A mixture of all swimming strokes would be best to work the greatest range of muscle groups and minimise the likelihood of housemaid's knee (a common breast stroke-related injury)! Learning to swim with your head partially submerged in the water is vital, in order to maintain correct alignment of the spine.

The same incremental approach to developing fitness through walking, as recommended above, should be applied when undertaking a swimming regime. Rather than using the increment of time, the number of lengths swum is a very simple starting point. Do bear in mind the length of each pool that you may swim in may vary! It is likely that the more often you swim, the quicker you will become. So increasing the number of lengths that you swim each session may require little or no extra time in the pool.

We have exercised the heart and lungs with walking and swimming. We need now to develop our range of movement and strength. Basic Yoga movements are also a simple and effective way to increase inner strength and develop range of movement and good posture. I am not looking at the more physical jumping around or sauna types of Yoga. I am advocating basic Yoga moves.

Yoga has many positive effects, which include large ranges of movement and mobility. By getting into certain Yoga positions we are not only stretching the muscles, but also massaging the internal organs. Yoga also has the benefit of establishing excellent breath control. The breath floods into the centre of the body and has to be released with control and in a sustained manner. This has a very relaxing and meditative effect. This helps us switch off our overactive minds, the value of which cannot be underestimated.

Buying a book or DVD on Yoga or joining a Yoga class is an excellent place to start. If Yoga doesn't appeal to you, then Pilates is an excellent alternative. Both Yoga and Pilates are fantastic for developing breath control and posture control techniques.

Let us look at a sample week's exercise programme – for example, walking or swimming on Monday, Thursday and Saturday, with Yoga or Pilates on Tuesday and Friday. This gives you two days off, on Wednesday and Sunday, which follow either two or three days of activity. Rest is vital to regeneration. We only become fitter and stronger by allowing our bodies to

> **Further information**
>
> For more information about any of the suggested forms of exercise, see the websites listed below:
>
> Alexander Technique www.alexandertechnique.com
> Walking www.thewalkingsite.com
> Swimming www.britishswimming.org
> Yoga www.bwy.org.uk (British Wheel of Yoga)
> Pilates www.pilatesfoundation.com

recover and grow. These days off give the individual physical downtime, which can then be filled with mental stimulation of some kind, including meditation, vocal and singing practice, reading or other pursuits that aid the actor's development as a whole.

This is a brief overview of the most suitable and simple exercises to cover what is required for the stresses and strains of most acting jobs. All of these suggestions can be carried out from home or on tour. The time and effort required to train in this manner will not be detrimental to the actor's performance. By starting small, and increasing gradually, the actor will feel more invigorated and energised from undertaking an exercise programme.

The actor's body should be viewed as a communication tool. Bodies require stimulation to develop. Without stimulus, the body and mind will deteriorate. Permitting this to happen is an injustice to the craft of acting. We all only have one body, and we need to look after it and maintain it for our specific needs.

Alex Caan was an international athlete before training at RADA for three years. Since graduation, he has worked extensively in theatre, TV and radio. Alex works as a business consultant, teaching powerful communication through effective use of the body. He also teaches acting for animators to the world's leading computer games company. Alex has coached Premiership football and rugby players to international level, and advised several Premiership football academies on their development programmes. He is currently coaching sportsmen and women at Olympic and World level in a range of different athletic disciplines. **www.raiseyourbar.com**

Do actors need to live in the South-East?

Nigel Collins

I was appalled to be asked to write this article as I did not realise that here in Wakefield in West Yorkshire we were not in the South-East. Actually, fellow professionals who live in Northumberland would claim that we are just about a suburb of London. In fact, it is possible to be in the heart of London within a couple of hours of leaving home via GNER and tube or cab. If there is enough notice of auditions it is also possible to buy fairly cheap train tickets online (yes, we have entered the 21st century oop North!).

Having left drama school in Manchester nearly 28 years ago and only living in London when needing to do so when working there, I feel confident in being able to say that it is possible to live outside the southeast and have an acting career. However, wherever we live as actors, we all depend on the contacts we make, the hard work of our agent, good fortune and to a large extent our network of friends in the business locally. There are many such networks outside London. For instance, many actors in Newcastle or Liverpool can and do have rewarding and busy careers without ever having to consider leaving their home cities as there is plenty of work around in local theatres and regional television dramas and series. Speaking personally, as a 'regional actor', i.e. what film-school hot-shot directors refer to as 'General Northern', I have done pretty well playing the 'Yorkshire' card over the years, a card that could well be trumped if played anywhere but in the relevant area. The resultant casting opportunities are almost always in the north – Manchester or Leeds generally for ITV, but increasingly over recent years the BBC have been casting in London productions to be shot in the regions; during the 80s and 90s they seemed to cast away from headquarters, but alas not as often these days. There was probably some money-saving memo from a corporate suit who had never been further north than Hampstead. Of course, I am willing to withdraw this slur immediately for the sake of a casting opportunity. No use upsetting people unnecessarily.

Earlier I mentioned the need for a good agent. Vital anywhere, but perhaps more so in the regions; in the south-east and London it is possible to keep up with all the latest tittle-tattle, gossip, rumour and speculation if one is a skilled networker, being physically remote from London means that one is very reliant on the hard work of an agent to keep up with all the latest casting news and to act on it.

We can all supplement the work that our agent does by looking at theatre websites and writing suggesting our suitability for whatever is coming up in the next season. Obviously, this can be done from anywhere, but, if the casting breakdown is for certain theatre companies it is a positive advantage to be northern based. Barrie Rutter at Northern Broadsides and John Godber at Hull Truck are just two directors who discriminate positively in favour of northern-based northerners. In part, this is to do with cost savings that are available by employing an actor who does not qualify for subsistence but more usually because directors have long realised that there is a large 'pool' of good performers on their doorstep. So there is no real need to trudge down the M 1 to spend a couple of days in some overpriced church hall with no heating, a comedy reverberating echo and a steady stream of RADA and Central graduates doing their 'Ee bah gum, I'll go to t' foot of our stairs' salt-of-the-earth types when they know very well that they only have to whistle down the nearest Actor's Centre workshop in Manchester or Leeds to have half a dozen potential David Threlfalls or Judi Denches champing at the bit to give their 'Now is the winter..' in their best Brighouse dialect. None of this is intended to give the impression that we regional types regard ourselves as somehow 'special' or more, how shall I put it, gifted, than our fellow strugglers marooned in the congestion zone that is the southeast, but we know what we know. But you knew that already didn't you?

Within an hour's drive of our affordable three bedroom mid-nineteenth century cottage there are at least a dozen theatres creating new and interesting work alongside the usual rep fare needed to guarantee their continued existence. I am thinking about places with international reputations such as West Yorkshire Playhouse in Leeds, The Royal Exchange in Manchester, Crucible Theatre in Sheffield, Hull Truck and Pilot Theatre in York. A little further afield there is NTC National Touring in Northumberland (which in 2008 will be hosting the Pride of Place festival for touring theatre companies), Theatre By The Lake in Keswick and Duke's Playhouse in Lancaster amongst others.

There is not a great deal of fringe theatre around out of London; which many of us think of as rather a good thing! In-between jobs are also more difficult to come by in parts of the country with higher unemployment, with proportionately more people competing for what few opportunities there are. In the past it was always possible to 'pick up' a job for a while, leave to fulfil a theatre contract and return to the same employer. More recently, those same employers are likely to recruit permanent staff that can be relied on to be there all the time. In these days of ongoing employee development, staff appraisals and one-to-ones actors do not seem to fit into the corporate structure. Except when we are employed by that same organisation to enter the workplace to role-play during training days!

Fortunately, many corporate videos and training films are made around the country in addition to a constant stream of TV and film commercials, usually cast (in my case) in Manchester or Leeds. Of course the usual ratio of castings to jobs applies – about 50 to 1! To a certain extent the availability of such jobs depends on the economy and the willingness of companies to spend money. In times of recession it is noticeable that this aspect of the business tends to withdraw back to the southeast.

On a practical level there are plenty of photographers, voice coaches and singing teachers available. I travel 30 miles down the M1 to Sheffield for my publicity shots, but due to the joys of the internet am able to have the repros printed in London and mailed direct to my agent in Manchester. I mentioned the Actor's Centre earlier; there are many and varied workshops that take place in Manchester and Leeds, which are very popular with us northerners. There is not yet a voice class to help get rid of the RP that seeps into our natural speech from time to time but I'm sure it is on the cards.

Most actors would answer 'quality of life' if asked why they choose to live away from London. The cost of living, housing, insurance and travel are all far lower. It is possible to find a good state school without too much trouble. A car journey is measured in minutes and hours, not days and weeks. We have fantastic open spaces in our cities, most of which have undergone regeneration that puts them on a par with many of our European neighbours. The Lake District, North York Moors, Yorkshire Dales and the Peak District National Parks are all an easy drive. The rugged coastline of North Yorkshire and the pleasures of Blackpool are 90 minutes away.

The one thing that the vast majority of we 'distance-theatricals' accept is the need to be prepared to travel to London at short notice for auditions and interviews (on occasion, for theatres or TV companies not far from home!). This can be expensive if there is no time to purchase cheaper tickets, making a £150 hole in the weekly budget, but that is the price one has to be prepared to pay to stay in the mainstream of the business. There are actors, as I mentioned above, who manage to work consistently in their local areas and have no desire to travel elsewhere. For instance, in Newcastle, some actors have been in the ensemble at Northern Stage for approaching 8 years. This consistency of employment benefits local theatres and TV companies who have a reliable pool of experienced actors to choose from and the actors themselves who do not need to worry about chasing every job prospect in other 'circles' of the industry.

The reader must understand that all of the above is written from the standpoint of a Tyke and all that that entails. In no way should any of this piece be construed as an invitation to sell up and move to the regions. We're not very welcoming and we can do without any upward inflation on house prices, thank you very much.

Nigel Collins was born in the late 1950s at the correct side of the Pennines, and grew up in the Heavy Woollen District of the West Riding of Yorkshire in an area famed as the World capital of mungo and shoddy manufacture. Not having much clue as to what these (allegedly) textile processes might entail, he took the safe option and went to Manchester Poly School of Theatre. Not having much clue what that entailed either. However, learning the intricacies of collar studs, phonetics and 5&9 has been a boon ever since, especially useful for small scale touring. Realising that it WAS possible for 'Oop Northerners' to work in theatre and television despite what he had been told, Nigel has assiduously extended his playing age from 23 to 63. By the time you come to read this it may be old news as Nigel fully expects the industry to come to its senses, so you will probably have heard him telling his story on *Desert Island Discs*, *Parky* or at the very least *Friday Night with Jonathon Ross*.

Tax and National Insurance for actors
Philippe Carden

Actors enjoy a rare hybrid status. They are treated as self-employed for income tax purposes but as employees for National Insurance. This combination brings with it a number of advantages, but also certain complications. Many actors choose to instruct an accountant to benefit from those advantages, and to avoid the pitfalls created by the complications.

The income tax advantages include being able to claim a deduction for expenses against income in arriving at taxable net profit (or allowable loss), provided that those expenses are incurred "wholly and exclusively for the purposes of the trade". *The Equity Advice and Rights Guide,* available free of charge to its members, provides a very helpful list of usually allowable expenses, with suitable notes to restrain the enthusiasm of actors to stretch definitions to their limits. Self-imposed restraint in claiming for expenses is sensible in minimising the risk of being selected for an Inland Revenue enquiry. Some accountants produce their own list.

It is helpful to assess the types of expense according to the risk of being challenged by the Revenue. Here are some examples:

Low risk or No risk
• Commission paid to agent (including VAT)
• Annual subscription to Equity
• Travel and subsistence on tour
• Photographs and publicity (repros, *Spotlight* entry)
• Classes to maintain skills, e.g. voice, movement
• Business stationery and postage
• Fee paid to accountant

Medium risk
• Professional library – scripts, books, CDs
• Publications – *The Stage, Time Out*
• Travel and subsistence when not on tour
• Visits to theatre and cinema

High risk
• Wardrobe – renewal, dry cleaning and repair
• Hairdressing and make-up
• Gratuities to dressers and stage door-keepers
• Home as office

As the risk rises, so too must the care taken in deciding which to claim and which to discard. Engaging an accountant to use his or her experience, skill and judgement in carrying out a review of expenditure claims is a source of considerable reassurance to many actors. It is worth noting that entertaining, as in paying a meal for another person (even if a casting director), is never allowed.

An accountant's review may also be key in calculating the business proportions of motor car expenses, land-line and mobile telephone charges, and television and video hire and television licence. An accountant's help in computing capital allowances for expenditure on capital items (computer, motor car, musical instruments) is appreciated by all but the most self-confident.

The emphasis so far has been on the income tax advantages of being self-employed. Whilst many actors are happy to register themselves as self-employed within the three-month time limit, others enlist the help of an accountant even at that stage to provide a buffer-zone between themselves and the Inland Revenue. Once registration is done, a Unique Taxpayer Reference ('UTR') will be issued, often still referred to as a Schedule D number. Unless preventative action is taken at the time of registration, or very soon afterwards, a costly national insurance (NI) pitfall will trap the unwary actor.

If an actor is to be treated as an employee for NI, s/he certainly does not want to be seen as self-employed for NI as well. Such duplication is costly and usually brings no additional benefits. A common solution is to apply for small earnings exception (SEE) from the flat-rate weekly NI paid by 'normal' self-employed people – Class 2 – by completing and submitting form CF10.

For actors who do some work abroad and/or who write and direct as well as perform, the solution is more likely to involve paying Class 2 but applying for deferment of Class 4. That class of NI is the earnings-related charge borne by 'normal' self-employed people in addition to the flat-rate Class 2. It confers no benefits to the payer and is collected by the Inland Revenue as part of the self-assessment system.

The complexities of the NI regime, and especially the interaction of its different classes, encourage co-operation between actor and accountant at least as much as does the application of the criteria for acceptability of expenses for income tax purposes.

So, the basic bundle of services provided by an accountant includes the following:
• Annual income and expenditure account
• Capital allowances computations
• Advice on NI and the necessary form-filling
• Completion of the annual Tax Return
• Preparing a tax calculation and checking the Revenue's version
Additional services would include completing quarterly returns for actors successful enough to be registered for VAT, and advice on the tax and NI implications of performing abroad.

Most accountants charge according to time spent and the seniority and expertise of the persons doing the work. Here is an example of how this might work in practice for a young actor: he would need four hours of a book-keeper at £30 per hour (£120), plus an hour for a manager's review and tax return (£50); an hour of the manager's time to sort out the NI (£50); and finally half-an-hour of the principal's/partner's time for overall review and quality control (£50). With perhaps a few telephone calls or a shortish meeting, the annual fee would typically be £340 plus VAT, i.e. £399.50.

In my experience, as the cost of the initial meeting is rarely charged for, I make a loss in year 1 of a new client. I break even in year 2, and only make a profit in year 3 and subsequent years. It is not a surprise therefore that I see my relationship with a client as a long-term one, one which has time and effort invested in it by both actor and accountant.

To an actor in the early years of his career, the accountant's annual fee of about £400 represents a significant expense. The decision to instruct an accountant is a personal one. Some actors are much more comfortable and confident than others in dealing with money matters, taxation and National Insurance. Others shy away from such a course of action and choose to have an ally in the form of an accountant.

In general terms, for an actor with gross earnings of less than £15,000 but who still makes a profit, having an accountant is optional. For one with smaller earnings and who makes a loss, having an accountant could be worthwhile to use that loss effectively. For those with gross earnings in excess of £15,000, the choice is compelling.

Having made the decision to use an accountant, choose the firm carefully. The most desired method is word of mouth. A personal recommendation from another actor, from your drama school or indeed from the company manager works well. It is important that the accountant selected know about the taxation and NI of actors rather than being a general practitioner. It is also important that the accountant be a member of one of the professional bodies of accountants as an indication of quality – and just in case a dispute arises which cannot be resolved amicably. Most of the institutes have a system of arbitration for fee disputes, for example, which can be used as a last resort.

Another factor in the choice of accountant is the size of the firm. The range is huge: from a sole practitioner to a multinational firm employing thousands. The former will be suitable for an actor of modest means, while the latter might be a good match for a performer with very considerable earnings and royalties from several countries around the world. In between those extremes are smaller firms with one to five partners and which specialise in the tax affairs of those who work in theatre, television and film, and larger firms which have an entertainment and media department with a similar specialism. The smaller firms are likely to provide a more personal service and lower fees. The larger are likely to have access to a greater breadth of related expertise (such as film finance, production accounting) but fees will be correspondingly higher.

Each accountant will have his or her favoured way for actors to keep records. The most important point is that an actor must co-operate with his or her accountant to save time and maximise the return on effort. Here are some guidelines and handy hints:

• Keep all agent's remittance advices, payslips and invoices.
• Only claim expenses incurred "wholly and exclusively for the purposes of the trade".
• Use the Equity list of usually allowable expenses for guidance.
• Keep receipts for all expenses and write explanatory notes on them, e.g. for audition with ...
• File away carefully details of any interest or dividends received, jobseeker's allowance claimed, Gift Aid payments made and any other item which may be needed to complete your tax return.
• Deliver your accounts papers to your accountant as soon as you can after the end of the tax year – never leave it until close to the 31st January deadline!*

Philippe Carden is a chartered accountant specialising in the taxation of actors and other individuals working in theatre, film, television and dance, onstage and backstage, artistic and technical. He co-wrote *Investing in West End Theatrical Productions* (Robert Hale, 1992) and has written articles for *The Guardian*, *The Stage* and other publications.

* *Note* From 2008, all paper self-assessment returns must be received by 30th September. If you file online, you will have another two months until 30th November. Deadline for payment of any tax owing remains 31st January.

Accountants

M Barnfather & Co
15 Birley Street, Blackpool FY1 1DU
tel (01253) 622519 *fax* (01253) 294179
email mike@mikebarnfather.co.uk
Accountant Michael Barnfather

Founded in 1974. Charges between £150 and £250 for preparation of accounts and submission of tax return. Provides support by means of face-to-face meetings, phone and email (mostly phone and email). Provides Excel spreadsheets and Money Manager (cashbook accounting software, compatible with most PCs but not Mac or Linux) if necessary. 3 clients are actors, but other clients include circus artistes, magicians, singers and dancers. Offices are not wheelchair-accessible (2nd floor). "We encourage all clients to keep proper accounting records (we advise them on their specific requirements), and to forward tax correspondence (including Self-Assessment return forms) directly to us as soon as received."

Breckman & Company
49 South Molton Street, London W1K 5LH
tel 020-7499 2292 *fax* 020-7408 1151
email info@breckmanandcompany.co.uk
website www.breckmanandcompany.co.uk
Accountants Kevin Beals, Graham Berry, Robert Breckman, Richard Nelson

Established for more than 40 years. Charges £100-£150 + VAT for simple accounts; upwards of that for preparing formal accounts. Costs are dictated by complexity and time spent. Initial meeting is free during which the 'fixed fee' structure will be discussed. Client support includes face-to-face meetings, phone and email (included in the price). Advises actors "to place as much importance on finding the right accountant (and not based solely on cost) as you would your agent". Also mentions that "we have some rather unique offices, that alone are worth a visit!".

P O'N Carden
56-58 High Street, Ewell, Surrey KT17 1RW
tel 020-8394 2957 *fax* 020-8394 2722
email philippe@poncarden.com
Accountants Philippe Carden, Marine Head

Founded in 1977. Charges £400 ("in the early years") for a complete set of accounts and tax return. "Time and complexity increase this – up to £2000 to include quarterly VAT returns. Tailor-made packages for really complex cases." Provides face-to-face meetings in central London. "My actor clients make clear how much support they feel they need, and the programme of work is tailored accordingly." Provides Excel spreadsheets appropriate to the client's needs.

40% of clients are actors; 45% are other entertainment industry professionals. The offices are not wheelchair accessible, but meetings can be held in wheelchair-accessible locations. Advises actors *not* to "just give your accountant bags of receipts. Provide information about why you are claiming particular expenses. Do be obsessive about keeping payslips and remittance advices".

Mark Carr & Co
Garrick House, 26-27 Southampton Street, Covent Garden, London WC2E 7RS
tel 020-7717 8474
email info@markcarr.co.uk
63 Lansdowne Place, Hove, East Sussex BN3 1FL
tel (01273) 778802 *fax* (01273) 778822
website www.markcarr.co.uk
Accountant Mark Carr (FCCA)

Provides individual service according to the client's requirements. Annual accounts for the HM Revenue & Customs tax return as well as a whole range of services are offered. Fees can be calculated on time spent basis or a fixed fee – £250 upwards, depending on the complexity. Payment terms can be varied to suit the client. First meeting is free of charge. Free advice service on a one-to-one basis on tax and book-keeping are offered at The Actors Centre. Very popular free downloadable Excel spreadsheets available from the website to clients and non-clients. 50% of client base are actors, 50% are other entertainment professionals. The London office has wheelchair access. "We have over 370 clients, who range from those starting out to those with celebrity status."

Count & See Ltd
219 Macmillan Way, London SW17 6AW
tel 020-8767 7882 *fax* 0845-004 3454
email info@countandsee.com
website www.countandsee.com
Director Miss Shereena Nathwani

Charges an annual fee of £250 (plus VAT) upwards, depending on the amount of work involved. Provides actor clients with face-to-face, phone and email support: there may be an additional charge at £70-100 per hour (plus VAT). If requested, supplies software templates in Excel suitable for Windows 95, Win98 & ME, Win XP, and Vista. A small proportion of the company's clients are actors and other entertainment-industry professionals. The trading office is wheelchair-accessible. "Before setting up my own practice, I worked for a number of firms specialising in the entertainment industry, so I have experience in advising such clients."

Dub & Co
7 Torriano Mews, Torriano Avenue, London NW5 2RZ

Resources

tel 020-7284 8686 *fax* 020-7284 8687
email office@dub.co.uk
Accountants George Dub, Joyce Davies

Chartered, certified accountants established in 1979. Charges from £400 + VAT for preparation of accounts for a tax return. Provides face-to-face meetings, phone and email support included in this fee. Does not provide software or spreadsheet templates to clients. Handles the tax and accountancy affairs of around 50 actors and 100 other entertainment industry professionals. The company's offices are wheelchair accessible.

Dunbar & Co

70 South Lambeth Road, London SW8 1RL
tel 020-7820 0082 *fax* 020-7820 0806
email mason@equitax.co.uk
Accountants Nick Mason (Senior Partner), Bob Long

Founded in 1896. Fees are on a time-cost basis, depending on the complexity of the client's tax affairs, but a typical fee range for an actor would be £330-£420 p.a. Support is provided via various means, including face-to-face meetings, phone and email. Provides spreadsheet templates for clients, which require Microsoft Excel. 50% of clients are actors, with a further 15%, other entertainment-industry professionals. Offices are wheelchair-accessible.

"We offer a full accountancy service, including bookkeeping, VAT, tax returns, tax advice, assistance with Revenue investigations, limited company accounts, personal and corporate tax planning. Our sister company, Sandford Dunbar, is authorised by the FSA as an independent financial adviser specialising in personal financial and pension planning."

Fisher Berger & Associates

Devonshire House, 582 Honeypot Lane, Stanmore, Middlesex HA7 1JS
tel 020-8732 5500 *fax* 020-8732 5501
email nik@fisherberger.com
website www.fisherberger.com
Accountant Nik Fisher FFA FCCA

Established in 2005. Charges between £250 and £750 on average, depending on the amount of work involved. Offers actors face-to-face and email / phone support: "as much as they require; our policy is to teach actors how best to keep their books and records, to save on accountancy fees". Provides spreadsheet templates in Excel and for VAT analysis, suitable for a range of software platforms. Around 15% of clients are actors, and 25% other professionals in the entertainment industry.

Jonathan Ford & Co

The Coach House, 31 View Road, Rainhill, Merseyside L35 0LF
tel 0151-426 4512

email info@jonathanford.co.uk
website www.jonathanford.co.uk
Accountant Jonathan Ford

Charges from £275 to £450, depending on the level of bookkeeping the client has done themselves. All fees are agreed in advance. Client service is comprehensive and includes face-to-face meetings, telephone and email support, all included within the fee. "Using the Internet we can meet the needs of clients all over the country." Supplies Excel spreadsheet templates, so MS Office is required; the software is suitable for all operating systems. Has around 10 actor clients and 40 other entertainment industry professionals. Offices are not wheelchair-accessible. Advises actors to "see our 10 tax commandments!".

Goldwins

75 Maygrove Road, London NW6 2EG
tel 020-7372 6494 *fax* 020-7624 0053
email aepton@goldwins.co.uk
website www.goldwins.co.uk
Accountant Anthony Epton

Established in 1987. Specialises in the entertainment industry, handling the tax and bookkeeping affairs of around 200 actors. Charges around £400 for preparation of an actor's tax return, although this can vary from £250 up to £1000 depending on the complexity of the job. Provides face-to-face meetings, phone and email support included in this price. Does not provide software or spreadsheet templates. The company's offices are wheelchair accessible.

Goodman Jones LLP

29/30 Fitzroy Square, London W1P 6LQ
tel 020-7388 2444 *fax* 020-7388 6736
email jrf@goodmanjones.com
website www.goodmanjones.com
Partner Julian Flitter

Founded in 1934. "Each person is different and we tailor our support to the clients needs, so costs can range from £250 to £500 for more complex returns involving international aspects and multiple categories of income." This amount would include any support required in the form of face-to-face meetings, phone calls, letters and emails. "The range of services we offer includes tax compliance services from personal tax returns and VAT returns, advice on whether or not to incorporate as a limited company, when to register for VAT, how to deal with working abroad, bookkeeping services, preparation of financial accounts (limited company, sole trader, LLP or partnership) as well as full personal tax planning and company secretarial and payroll services." Can supply software templates to clients as required, but recommends "keeping it simple". Offices are wheelchair accessible.

Hard Dowdy

23-28 Great Russell Street, London WC1B 3NG
tel 020-7436 2171 *fax* 020-7436 4923

email info@harddowdy.com
website www.harddowdy.com
Accountants Tim Waters, Jacqui Lee Foster

Fees are charged on a time-spent basis and on average range between £450 and £750, depending on the complexity and quality of the records provided. Client support includes face-to-face meetings, telephone and email services. The company is based in the West End and currently acts as auditors and advisers to Equity – "a specialist firm, offering a comprehensive service". Depending on the size of a client's business, offers Sage accounting packages to tailored Excel spreadsheets. Has around 350 actor clients and 50 other entertainment industry professionals. Offices are wheelchair accessible. "Accurate records, maintained regularly, will save time, tax and accountancy fees!"

Harris Coombs & Co

5 Jaggard Way, London SW12 8SG
tel 020-8675 6880 *fax* 020-8675 7017
email mailbox@harriscoombs.co.uk
website www.harriscoombs.co.uk

Partners Graham Harris FCCA, Richard Coombs FCA

Charges to prepare actors' accounts for annual Inland Revenue tax returns range from £500-£1000. Charges vary depending on figures and VAT. Client support includes: face-to-face meetings, phone, email (all included in the price). Personal service in all financial matters: tax, NI, VAT etc. Of client base 15% are actors and 20% are other entertainment industry professionals.

Harveys LLP

The Old Winery, Lamberhurst Vineyard, Lamberhurst, Kent TN3 8ER
tel (01892) 890388 *fax* (01892) 891892
email tax@harveysllp.com
website www.harveysllp.com
Accountants Damian McGee, Lynnette Lawrence

Established in 2008. Charges £600 plus VAT per annum. Client support includes face-to-face meetings, telephone and email, as well as fee protection insurance and freepost record envelopes. Accounts support is charged at £40 per hour; tax compliance at £60 per hour; and partner at £90 to £150 per hour. Supplies clients with MS Excel spreadsheet templates suitable for Windows XP and Vista. 50% of the client base comprises actors, and 30% other entertainment industry professionals. Offices are wheelchair-accessible.

Hayles & Partners Ltd

39 Castle Street, Leicester LE1 5WN
tel 0116-233 8500 *fax* 0116-233 7288
email geoff.banks@hayles.co.uk
website www.hayles.co.uk
Accountants Geoff Banks, Amanda Jelley

Charges from £150 for preparation of a basic tax return. Provides face-to-face meetings, phone and email support. Initial consultation or advice is offered free of charge. Does not supply software or spreadsheet templates to clients. Advises actors to "open a separate business bank account and identify all receipts and payments, retaining all supporting documentation".

Horwath Clark Whitehill

St Bride's House, 10 Salisbury Square, London EC4Y 8EH
tel 020-7842 7100
website www.horwathcw.co.uk
Accountants David Ford, Tim Norkett

Established in 1982. Provides flexible solutions to clients' tax problems; initial meeting is offered free of charge. Supports clients via meetings, phone and email. Will supply software and/or spreadsheet templates that are tailor-made to individual requirements. Current client list includes 20 actors and 20 other entertainment industry professionals. Offices are wheelchair-accessible. Fees vary according to the complexity of the service(s) required: £400 + VAT is the minimum. "The better the quality of the client's recordkeeping, the lower the fees."

J Morris and Co

17 St Ann's Square, Manchester M2 7PW
tel 0161-832 4841 *fax* 0161-835 2539
email johne@alexander.co.uk
website www.alexander.co.uk
Accountant John Evans

An accountant since 1969, John Evans merged the J Morris & Co practice with Alexander & Co in 2005. Charges for completion of accounts and submission of tax return start at £250 "dependent on complexity of case". Provides support by means of face-to-face meetings, phone, email and written correspondence, and can offer introduction to further specialist advice (e.g. legal) where required. Provides PC (Windows) compatible software or spreadsheets as required. Offices are not wheelchair accessible. "We deal with a number of actors and entertainers, and we are on Equity's list."

Nyman Libson Paul

Regina House, 124 Finchley Road, London NW3 5JS
tel 020-7433 2400 *fax* 020-7433 2401
email entertainment@nlpca.co.uk
website www.nlpca.co.uk

75 years in the entertainment industry.

Shaw Walker

26 Great Queen Street, London WC2B 5BB
tel 020-7242 1134 *fax* 020-7831 7232
email alison@shawwalker.co.uk
website www.shawwalker.co.uk
Accountants Mrs A McCarthy, Mr P Skinner, Mr T K Chong

Established in 1925, charges from £400 to prepare actors' accounts for the tax return, depending on the complexity of the accounts. Provides a face-to-face initial meeting; support thereafter is as convenient to the client, and this is included in the fee. Provides a complete range of accounting services – VAT, tax, PAYE, business support, book keeping *et al.* Software and/or spreadsheets are provided to the client as required. Offices are not easily wheelchair-accessible. Advice to actors: "Seek a *qualified* accountant."

David Summers & Co

Argo House, Kilburn Park Road, London NW6 5LF
tel 020-7644 0478 *fax* 020-7644 0678
email dsummersfca@hotmail.com
website www.dsummers.co.uk
Accountants David Summers and Chet Haria

Established in 1982. Charges start from £200 + VAT for preparation of annual self-employed accounts and the self-assessment tax return. A quote is given at the initial meeting, which is free of charge. The services offered also include preparation of limited company accounts and corporate tax returns, VAT registration, payroll, tax planning advice, etc. Client support includes face-to-face meetings, phone, email, and dealing with day-to-day queries as they may arise (all included in the price). Approximately 10% of clients are actors or members of the entertainment industry. "We tailor advice to each individual's requirements."

TWD Accountants

Grosvenor House, St Thomas Place,
Stockport SK1 3TZ
tel 0845-058 2223 *fax* 0845-059 2292
email bernard@taxrebates.com
website www.twdaccounts.co.uk
Director Bernard Oster *Accountant (for actors)* Mike Parkes

Founded in 1996, formerly Tax Watchdog Direct. A fixed-fee tax and accountancy service, charging £169 + VAT (£198.58) per year. Provides phone and email support to clients, as well as free bookkeeping software. "TWD Online is a new easy to use web-based bookkeeping programme available on a 90-day free trial (1 year if you sign up for the accountancy package). The system can be accessed at **www.twdonline.co.uk** and is ideally suited to entertainment professionals." 15% of clients are actors; 5% are other entertainment-industry professionals.

Vantis

Torrington House, Holywell Hill, St Albans, Hertfordshire AL1 1HD
tel (01727) 838255 *fax* (01727) 861052
email stalbans@vantisplc.com
website www.vantisplc.com/stalbanshh
Accountant Paula Jeffs

Charges to prepare actors' accounts for annual Inland Revenue tax returns range from £470-£700. Level of accountancy work done by actor reduces the fee. Client support includes: face-to-face meetings, phone, email (all included in the price). Level of client support ranges from proactive advice, regular meetings, seminar programmes and direct phone link to dedicated professional. Excel Spreadsheets/templates are provided to clients. Of client base 10% are actors and 5% are other entertainment industry professionals. Offices have no wheelchair access. They advise clients "keep it simple; keep records of expenditure as you go; pass it over as soon as possible after tax year end; keep talking to us – we can take the strain off you."

Wyatts Accounts

18 Highbury New Park, London N5 2DB
mobile (07710) 160442
fax 020-7226 0211

Friendly and clear service. Specialists with actors, artists and performers. Reasonable and transparent scaled fees and charges. Provides software and/or templates for Sage, Excel, Quickbooks and Money Manager for Apple or PC. Client base is 100 per cent arts and entertainment industry professionals. Offices are not wheelchair-accessible.

Funding bodies

The competition for funding is so fierce that it is important to allow sufficient time for research, planning and proper presentation of your proposed project. It is well worth checking to see what information is available on the websites listed in this section. Many funding bodies are happy to advise on form-filling, what kind of projects stand a chance and what could constitute a realistic amount to ask for. It is also well worth going on one (or more) of the Independent Theatre Council's (ITC; see page 468) courses for assistance in the complex world of funding applications.

Bodies that offer individual funding should be approached with similar care and attention.

NATIONAL ARTS COUNCILS

Arts Council England
14 Great Peter Street, London SW1P 3NQ
tel 0845-300 6200 *fax* 020-7973 6590
textphone 020-7973 6564
email enquiries@artscouncil.org.uk
website www.artscouncil.org.uk

Arts Council England is the national development agency for the arts in England, promoting excellence, innovation and diversity within the arts. It awards grants to individuals, arts organisations and national touring projects using public money from government and the National Lottery.

Grants for individuals are generally between £200 and £30,000, while those for organisations range from £200 up to a maximum of £100,000. Most grants, however, will be under £30,000. National touring grants are available for individuals and organisations touring to 2 or more Arts Council England regions, and normally vary between £5000 and £200,000. Grants for individuals, organisations and national touring can cover activities lasting up to 3 years.

All applicants should apply to the region in which they are based. Application forms, guidance notes and information sheets can be downloaded from the website. A wide range of resources, publications, links and information about other funding sources is also accessible on the website.

Editor's Note: At the time this edition of *Actors' Yearbook* went to print, Arts Council England announced a major restructure to save on administration costs. The key elements of their proposal were as follows:
• a smaller head office – focused on strategy and support to frontline staff
• 9 regional offices – smaller and more focused on frontline delivery, working with the organisations it funds, artists and other key partners
• regional offices grouped under 4 area executive directors – with a strong senior management team to streamline internal processes and encourage knowledge-sharing

• a central Grants for the Arts processing team – relieving regional offices of administrative burden and making grant-giving more equitable; this team will be based in Manchester
• a streamlined advocacy and communications team – a specialist head office team and 3 area advocacy teams supporting regional offices, line-managed in the areas but forming a clear professional family
• a smaller executive board (9 members, as opposed to the current 14), with a balance of regional knowledge and a strategic overview, making quicker decisions

Implementation of the new structure began in mid-July 2009, to become fully operational from April 2010. As a consequence, some of the information given above (and that given under 'Regional Arts Council Offices') may be outdated within the lifetime of this edition. Please check **www.artscouncil.org.uk** for latest updates.

Arts Council of Northern Ireland
MacNeice House, 77 Malone Road, Belfast BT9 6AQ
tel 028-9038 5200
email publicaffairs@artscouncil-ni.org
website www.artscouncil-ni.org

The prime distributor of public support for the arts, the Arts Council of Northern Ireland is committed to increasing opportunities for artists to develop challenging and innovative work. In addition to funding schemes for organisations and community groups, the council has developed a special programme of schemes to extend support for the individual artist. This programme includes the General Arts Award, which provides funding for specific projects, specialised research and personal artistic development; and the Major Individual Award, which supports established artists in the development of ambitious work.

Arts Council of Wales
9 Museum Place, Cardiff CF10 3NX
tel 029-2037 6500
email info@artswales.org.uk
website www.artswales.org.uk

Responsible for funding and developing the arts in Wales using money from Welsh Assembly Government and the National Lottery. Provides arts organisations and individuals in Wales with the opportunity to apply for funding towards clearly defined arts-related projects. Scheme Guidelines for the funding programmes are available on the website. Anyone applying for funding should speak to an Arts Development Officer in their local office to discuss how well the project aligns with national and regional priorities. Contact information for all local offices can be found on the website.

Scottish Arts Council

12 Manor Place, Edinburgh EH3 7DD
tel 0131-226 6051
email help.desk@scottisharts.org.uk
website www.scottisharts.org.uk

The Scottish Arts Council is the principal channel of public funding for the arts in Scotland, distributing money from the Scottish Government and the National Lottery to those working at a professional level in the arts. Funding is available to individuals and organisations for arts projects, productions and presentation of work, research and development including short-term or one-off training courses, conference fees, master classes, mentoring, travel to see work, establishing contacts and partnerships and exploring opportunities for future projects.

REGIONAL ARTS COUNCIL OFFICES

Arts Council England, London

2 Pear Tree Court, London EC1R 0DS
tel 0845-300 6200 *textphone* 020-7973 6564

Area covered: Greater London.

Arts Council England, East

Eden House, 48-49 Bateman Street,
Cambridge CB2 1LR
tel 0845-300 6200 *fax* 0870-242 1271
textphone (01223) 306893

Area covered: Bedfordshire, Cambridgeshire, Essex, Hertfordshire, Norfolk, Suffolk; and unitary authorities of Luton, Peterborough, Southend-on-Sea, Thurrock.

Arts Council England, East Midlands

St Nicholas Court, 25-27 Castle Gate,
Nottingham NG1 7AR
tel 0845-300 6200 *fax* 0115-950 2467

Area covered: Derbyshire, Leicestershire, Lincolnshire (excluding North and North East Lincolnshire), Northamptonshire, Nottinghamshire; and unitary authorities of Derby, Leicester, Nottingham, Rutland.

Arts Council England, North East

Central Square, Forth Street,
Newcastle upon Tyne NE1 3PJ
tel 0845-300 6200 *fax* 0191-230 1020
textphone 0191-255 8585

Area covered: Durham, Northumberland; metropolitan authorities of Gateshead, Newcastle upon Tyne, North Tyneside, South Tyneside, Sunderland; and unitary authorities of Darlington, Hartlepool, Middlesbrough, Redcar and Cleveland, Stockton-on-Tees.

Arts Council England, North West

Manchester House, 22 Bridge Street,
Manchester M3 3AB
tel 0845-300 6200 *fax* 0161-834 6969
textphone 0161-834 9131

Area covered: Cheshire, Cumbria, Lancashire; metropolitan authorities of Bolton, Bury, Knowsley, Liverpool, Manchester, Oldham, Rochdale, St Helens, Salford, Sefton, Stockport, Tameside, Trafford, Wigan, Wirral; and unitary authorities of Blackburn with Darwen, Blackpool, Halton, Warrington.

Arts Council England, South East

Sovereign House, Church Street, Brighton BN1 1RA
tel 0845-300 6200 *fax* 0870-242 1257
textphone (01273) 710659

Area covered: Buckinghamshire, East Sussex, Hampshire, Isle of Wight, Kent, Oxfordshire, Surrey, West Sussex; and unitary authorities of Bracknell Forest, Brighton & Hove, Medway Towns, Milton Keynes, Portsmouth, Reading, Slough, Southampton, West Berkshire, Windsor and Maidenhead, Wokingham.

Arts Council England, South West

Senate Court, Southernhay Gardens, Exeter EX1 1UG
tel 0845-300 6200 *fax* (01392) 229229
textphone (01392) 433503

Area covered: Cornwall, Devon, Dorset, Gloucestershire, Somerset, Wiltshire; unitary authorities of Bath and North East Somerset, Bournemouth, Bristol, North Somerset, Plymouth, Poole, South Gloucestershire, Swindon, Torbay.

Arts Council England, West Midlands

82 Granville Street, Birmingham B1 2LH
tel 0845-300 6200 *fax* 0121-643 7239
textphone 0121-643 2815
website www.artscouncil.org.uk
Literature Officer Adrian Johnson *Literature Assistant* Maeve Haughey

Area covered: Shropshire, Staffordshire, Warwickshire, Worcestershire; metropolitan authorities of Birmingham, Coventry, Dudley, Sandwell, Solihull, Walsall, Wolverhampton; and unitary authorities of Herefordshire, Stoke-on-Trent, Telford and Wrekin. Supports Ledbury Poetry Festival, *Poetry on Loan* in public libraries, and individual writers through grant aid, which can be applied for by using the organisation's *Grants for the Arts* pack. Telephone for a full application pack.

Arts Council England, Yorkshire

21 Bond Street, Dewsbury,
West Yorkshire WF13 1AX

tel 0845-300 6200 *fax* (01924) 466522
textphone (01924) 438585

Area covered: North Yorkshire; metropolitan
authorities of Barnsley, Bradford, Calderdale,
Doncaster, Kirklees, Leeds, Rotherham, Sheffield,
Wakefield; and unitary authorities of East Riding of
Yorkshire, Kingston upon Hull, North Lincolnshire,
North East Lincolnshire, York. Premises are
wheelchair-user friendly. For information on disabled
parking, please phone in advance.

NATIONAL AND REGIONAL FILM AGENCIES

UK Film Council
10 Little Portland Street, London W1W 7JG
tel 020-7861 7861
email info@filmcouncil.org.uk
website www.filmcouncil.org.uk

Established by the Government in 2000, the UK Film
Council supports the development of the British film
industry and film culture. Offers a variety of funding
schemes to nurture new filmmaking talent and
provides money to regional film agencies for
distribution to local projects.

For general enquiries about any of the UK Film
Council's short film schemes, and to be kept
informed of future opportunities, contact
shorts@ukfilmcouncil.org.uk.

Scottish Screen
249 West George Street, Glasgow G2 4QE
tel 0141-302 1700
email info@scottishscreen.com
website www.scottishscreen.com

Wales Screen Commission (formerly Sgrin Media Agency for Wales)
6G Parc Gwyddoniaeth, Cefn Llan, Aberystwyth,
Ceredigion SY23 3AH
tel (01970) 627186/627831 *fax* (01970) 617942
email enquiry@walesscreencommission.co.uk
website www.walesscreencommission.co.uk

The Northern Ireland Screen
3rd Floor, 21 Alfred House, Belfast BT2 8ED
tel 028-9023 2444
website www.northernirelandscreen.co.uk

EM Media
35-37 St Mary's Gate, Nottingham NG1 1PU
tel 0115-934 9090
email info@em-media.org.uk
website www.em-media.org.uk

Film London (formerly London Film & Video Development Agency)
Suite 6.10, The Tea Building,
56 Shoreditch High Street, London E1 6JJ
tel 020-7613 7676 *fax* 020-7613 7677

email info@filmlondon.org.uk
website www.filmlondon.org.uk

North West Vision
233 The Tea Factory, 82 Wood Street,
Liverpool L1 4DQ
tel 0151-708 2967 *fax* 0151-708 2974
email info@northwestvision.co.uk
website www.northwestvision.co.uk

Northern Film & Media
Central Square, Forth Street,
Newcastle upon Tyne NE1 3PJ
tel 0191-269 9200
email info@northernmedia.org
website www.northernmedia.org

Screen East
2 Millennium Plain, Norwich NR1 3JG
tel (01603) 776920
email info@screeneast.co.uk
website www.screeneast.co.uk

Screen South
The Wedge, 75-81 Tontine Street, Folkestone,
Kent CT20 1JR
tel (01303) 259777 *fax* (01303) 259786
email info@screensouth.org
website www.screensouth.org

Screen West Midlands
Screen West Midlands, 9 Regent Place,
Birmingham B1 3NJ
tel 0121-265 7120 *fax* 0121-265 7180
email info@screenwm.co.uk
website www.screenwm.co.uk

Screen Yorkshire
Studio 22, 46 The Calls, Leeds LS2 7EY
tel 0113-294 4410
email info@screenyorkshire.co.uk
website www.screenyorkshire.co.uk

Screen Yorkshire has an actors' database of talent
from the Yorkshire and Humber region. Those who
wish to be included should send a full CV, together
with 2 b&w full-face shots, no smaller than A5 size.

South West Screen
St Bartholomews Court, Lewins Mead,
Bristol BS1 5BT
tel 0117-952 9977
email info@swscreen.co.uk
website www.swscreen.co.uk

OTHER SOURCES OF FUNDING

Additional information about various entertainment
charities and benevolent funds can be found on the
website of The Actors' Charitable Trust
www.tactactors.org. Unless explicitly mentioned,
most of the organisations listed below and on the
TACT website do not provide assistance with drama
school fees or maintenance.

Actors' Benevolent Fund

6 Adam Street, London WC2N 6AD
tel 020-7836 6378 *fax* 020-7836 8978
email office@abf.org.uk
website www.actorsbenevolentfund.co.uk

For more than 125 years the Actors' Benevolent Fund has provided financial assistance to actors unable to work due to poor health, an accident or old age. To be eligible for assistance, applicants need several years of professional acting experience.

The Actors' Charitable Trust (TACT)

58 Bloomsbury Street, London WC1B 3QT
tel 020-7636 7868
email robert@tactactors.org
website www.tactactors.org
General Secretary Robert Ashby

Grant, advice and support for the children of professional actors. Also administers TACT Education Fund: Maintenance grants for students on arts courses who have a parent who is or was a professional actor.

Calouste Gulbenkian Foundation

98 Portland Place, London W1B 1ET
tel 020-7636 5313 *fax* 020-7908 7580
email info@gulbenkian.org.uk
website www.gulbenkian.org.uk

Awards grants to professional organisations or professional artists, working in partnerships or groups, developing new art in any artform.

Department for Business, Innovation & Skills

Castle View House, East Lane, Runcom WA7 2GJ
tel 020-7215 5555
website www.bis.gov.uk

This new (as of June 2009) organisation now covers Further & Higher Education. Its work was formerly the responsibility of the Department for Education & Skills.

Equity Charitable Trust

Plouviez House, 19-20 Hatton Place,
London EC1N 8RU
tel 020-7831 1926 *fax* 020-7242 7995

The trust seeks to further education through support and development of the performing arts, and to provide for the welfare and health of professional performers, former performers, their relatives and dependants. Also offers free debt counselling and benefits advice.

Evelyn Norris Trust

222 Africa House, 64 Kingsway, London WC2B 6BD
tel 020-7404 6041
Secretary Keith Carter

The Evelyn Norris Trust is a charity that accepts applications for grants from members of the concert and theatrical professions. The Trust aims to help with the cost of convalesence or a recuperative holiday following illness, injury or surgery.

First Light

Studio 28, Fazeley Studios, Fazeley Street,
Birmingham B5 5SE
tel 0121-224 7511

First Light is the UK's leading initiative enabling young people to realise their potential via creative digital film and media projects. It operates a number of youth funding schemes, including:

• The Young Film Fund – the UK Film Council's Lottery-funded filmmaking initiative for 5-19 year olds. For guidelines and information on how to apply, go to **www.firstlightonline.co.uk**
• Mediabox – a Department for Children, Schools & Families fund to help young people establish a positive voice in the media. It offers disadvantaged 13-19 year olds the opportunity to develop and produce creative media projects using film, print, television, radio or online platforms. There are grants of up to £40,000 available now. For more information, visit **www.media-box.co.uk**
• Second Light – a talent development scheme which, through production-based training, will give 30 talented young people aged 18 to 23, from BME backgrounds, supported opportunities to move into the film industry. For more information go to **www.firstlightonline.co.uk**

The Foyle Foundation

Rugby Chambers, 2 Rugby Street,
London WC1N 3QU
tel 020-7430 9119 *fax* 020-7430 9830
email information@foylefoundation.org.uk
website www.foylefoundation.org.uk

The Foyle Foundation makes grants to registered charities in the UK whose core remit covers the arts, learning or health. It has supported tours, festivals and education projects, and helped to develop new work. It will also consider funding the building or updating of arts facilities. The average size of grant is between £5000 and £20,000. Application forms and guidelines are available to download from the website.

The Jerwood Charitable Foundation

171 Union Street, London SE1 0LN
tel 020-7261 0279
email info@jerwood.org
website www.jerwood.org

Awards grants to young people, mainly aged 20 to 35, who have demonstrated achievement, commitment and excellence, particularly in the performing arts. Financial support has been offered to young actors, dancers, choreographers, playwrights, filmmakers, singers and musicians and others in the performing and visual arts. The charity seeks to make grants which will produce tangible and visible results and whose beneficial effects will extend beyond the immediate recipient of the grant.

National Theatre Foundation

c/o National Theatre, South Bank, London SE1 9PX
tel 020 7452 3366 *fax* 020 7452 3364

email foundation@nationaltheatre.org.uk
website www.nationaltheatre.org.uk/foundation
Administrator Lucy Francis *Welfare Counsellor* Mary Hill

The Royal National Theatre Foundation exists to help anybody who works or has worked at the National Theatre and is in need of help – usually in circumstances where he or she cannot afford the normal things of life which most people take for granted. This may take the form of a loan or a one-off grant towards a range of things, depending on the individual's circumstances. Each case is treated on its merit and involves the applicant submitting a confidential application form which includes details of savings and a statement of regular income and expenditure. More information including an application form is available at **www.nationaltheatre.org.uk/foundation** or email foundation@nationaltheatre.org.uk. The Welfare Counsellor can be contacted directly on 020-7452 3737.

NESTA (National Endowment for Science, Technology and the Arts)

Fishmongers' Chambers, 110 Upper Thames Street, London EC4R 3TW
tel 020-7645 9500
email nesta@nesta.org.uk
website www.nesta.org.uk

Offers a variety of funding schemes to promote innovation within the fields of science, technology and the arts.

The Oxford Samuel Beckett Theatre Trust Award

PO Box 2637, Ascot, Berks SL5 8ZN
email info@osbttrust.com
website www.osbttrust.com
Director Romilly Walton Masters

The purpose of this annual award is, in particular, to help the development of emerging practitioners in the field of innovative theatre/performance and, in general, to encourage the new generation of creative artists. Artists from all disciplines are encouraged to apply.

The award is for a site-responsive, non-traditional show to take place in one of the 5 host Boroughs for the Olympic and Paralympic Games. The show will be part of the Barbican BITE season and CREATE Festival in East London.

Performance Initiative Network

School of Arts, Brunel University, Uxbridge UB8 3PH
tel (01895) 266505
email info@perform.tv
email kerry.irvine@brunel.ac.uk
website www.perform.tv

Contact Kerry Irvine

Supporting the professional small theatre company and theatre artist to make and produce their work. Runs the GroundWork Festival, eVolve, and the PiLab series of projects.

The Royal Theatrical Fund

11 Garrick Street, London WC2E 9AR
tel 020-7836 3322 *fax* 020-7379 8273
email admin@trtf.com
website www.trtf.com

Founded in 1839, the Royal Theatrical Fund makes grants which will alleviate the suffering, assist the recovery, or reduce the need, hardship or distress of theatrical artists or their families/dependants. To be eligible to receive a grant, a person must have professionally practised or contributed to the theatrical arts (on stage, radio, film or television) for a minimum of 7 years.

Sophie's Silver Lining Fund

17 Silver Street, Chacombe, Banbury, Oxon OX17 2JR
tel (01295) 711155
email TheLarges@aol.com
website www.silverlining.org.uk

Provides assistance to needy acting and singing students with the cost of their training.

TACT Educational Fund

See entry under The Actors' Charitable Trust

The Wellcome Trust

Arts Awards, 210 Euston Road, London NW1 2BE
email arts@wellcome.ac.uk
website www.wellcome.ac.uk/arts

The Wellcome Trust Arts Awards is the Trust's new funding scheme, which continues to support arts projects that engage with biomedical science.

"The Arts Awards provide funding for a range of projects that bring together any art form and any area of biomedical science. We encourage collaboration between professionals from different disciplines, between adults and young people, and between experts and the public. The scheme builds on the success of previous schemes such as Sciart, Pulse and Science on Stage and Screen, and is part of the Trust's £3.2million Engaging Science programme. 2 levels of funding are available – small to medium sized projects (up to and including £30,000) and large projects (above £30,000). Full details are available on our website, including details of pending deadlines for large and small grants, application guidelines, examples of previously funded projects, and the application form."

Publications, libraries, references and booksellers

This section lists the major sources for scripts and sheet music – and routes to finding that elusive script or score. While Internet search engines can be extremely useful in such a quest, it sometimes requires some lateral thinking to find what you want. It is possible to find out-of-print plays via libraries or book-finding services and by combing second-hand book shops. Some publishers (even a few playwrights' agencies) will organise a photocopy – for a fee. Also, the British Library (in theory) has a copy of every play ever performed in this country, but there can be complications in actually getting hold of a copy. Start with your local library if you're determined to find a specific play; if they don't have it, they may well be able to get it from another library (via the inter-library loan system), but be prepared for it to take a long time. Another route is to try to find a theatre at which the play has been performed: they may be able to help.

AbeBooks.com
website www.abebooks.com

Excellent website which will search the catalogues of hundreds of secondhand booksellers in this country and around the world.

Amazon.co.uk & Amazon.com
website www.amazon.co.uk or www.amazon.com

UK and US sites (respectively) for books, DVDs, CDs and all sorts of other things. Secondhand items are listed alongside the new, so often a good place to find cheap scripts.

Barbican Library
Barbican Centre, London EC2Y 8DS
tel 020-7638 0569
website www.cityoflondon.gov.uk/barbicanlibrary

Situated on level 2 of the Barbican Centre, this is the largest lending library in the City of London. In addition to the general library, the strong arts and music sections reflect the Barbican Centre's emphasis on the arts. The library is fully accessible by wheelchair and has a number of other access facilities including hearing induction loops and a reading magnifier machine. *Opening hours*: Monday and Wednesday: 9.30am – 5.30pm; Tuesday and Thursday: 9.30am – 7.30pm; Friday: 9.30am – 2pm; Saturday: 9.30am – 4pm.

BookBarn
White Cross, Somerset BS39 6EX
tel (01761) 451777
website www.bookbarn.co.uk

"The UK's largest used book warehouse," with many thousands of cheap secondhand scripts and a searchable catalogue online.

The British Library
96 Euston Road, London NW1 2DB
tel 0870-444 1500 (Switchboard), 020-7412 7676 (Advance Reservations, St Pancras Reading Rooms and Humanities enquiries), 020-7412 7702 (Maps), 020-7412 7513 (Manuscripts), 020-7412 7772 (Music), 020-7412 7873 (Asia, Pacific & Africa Collections)
website www.bl.uk

The British Library is the national library of the United Kingdom and contains a substantial collection of plays and manuscripts from the UK and Ireland, as well as from other parts of the world. The sound archive also includes just about everything from the sound of Amazonian tree frogs to classic recordings of Shakespeare's plays. Users need a Reader's Pass (details on how to acquire same is on the website) to access and read particular publications. The library will, for a fee, allow photocopying – subject to copyright legislation.

Chappell of Bond Street
152-160 Wardour Street, London W1F 8YA
tel 020-7432 4400 *fax* 020-7432 4410
email enquiries_bs@chappell-bond-st.co.uk
website www.chappellofbondstreet.co.uk

Stocks the largest range of printed music anywhere in Europe, covering everything from popular chart books to medieval instrumentals, exam pieces to orchestral scores. *Opening Hours*: Monday to Friday: 9.30am – 6pm; Saturday: 9.30am – 5pm.

Contacts
See separate section on The Spotlight.

Doollee.com

website www.doollee.com

An excellent free online guide to modern playwrights and theatre plays which have been written, or translated, into English since the production of *Look Back in Anger* in 1956.

The Drama Student

Top Floor, 66 Wansey Street, London SE17 1JP
tel 020-7701 4536 *fax* (07092) 846523
email editor@thedramastudent.co.uk
website www.thedramastudent.co.uk
Editor Phil Matthews

Recently launched as the only magazine dedicated to drama students across the UK. Published quarterly, the first issue appeared in January 2009. The magazine brings together an exciting community of current and prospective students actively pursuing a career in theatre, film, television or radio, either as an actor or behind the scenes. *The Drama Student* is their essential reference, a publication with both enthusiasm and substance.

Dress Circle

57-59 Monmouth Street, Upper St Martin's Lane, London WC2H 9DG
tel 020-7240 2227 *fax* 020-7379 8540
email info@dresscircle.co.uk
website www.dresscircle.co.uk

Dress Circle was founded over 25 years ago to supply the widest possible selection of Musical Theatre and Cabaret-related products from around the world – CDs, cassettes, videos, DVDs, posters, cards, mugs, collectibles and more. Opening Hours: Monday to Saturday: 10.00am – 6.30pm. "If we can't get it – no one can!"

Samuel French Theatre Bookshop

52 Fitzroy Street, London W1T 5JR
tel 020-7255 4300 *fax* 020-7387 2161
website www.samuelfrench-london.co.uk

Samuel French has been publishing, selling and leasing plays for performance since 1830. Today it has more than 2000 playscripts available, covering all elements of performing theatre – from comedies to tragedies, sketches to full-scale musicals. In addition, the bookshop stocks a comprehensive range of playscripts and technical books on all aspects of theatre. Publishes *The Guide to Selecting Plays*, which lists plays according to genre and cast size. Bookshop is wheelchair-friendly, staff are helpful and signage suitable for visually-impaired. Enlarged print catalogue & lists on demand.

Internet Movie Database

website uk.imdb.com

A comprehensive database and news round-up of film and television around the world.

The Knowledge

CMP Data & Information Services,
CMP Information Ltd, Riverbank House,
Angel Lane, Tonbridge, Kent TN9 1SE
tel (01732) 377041
email knowledge@cmpinformation.com
website www.theknowledgeonline.com

Covering all aspects of production, The Knowledge Online contains contacts and services for the UK film, television, video and commercial production industry. Its *Know-How* section contains studio and post-production charts, production guidelines, articles and maps, and in 2003 it introduced an overview of international co-production by the British Film Commission.

Limited access can be gained by registering online, but for full access to over 18,000 entries and to the *Know-How*, users must pay a £50 annual subscription.

London Arrangements

30 Maryland Square, London E15 1HE
tel 020-8221 2381 *fax* 020-8926 2724
email enquiries@londonarrangements.co.uk
website www.londonarrangements.co.uk
Director Stephen Robinson

Specialises in the production of hard-to-find backing tracks. Main genres covered are big band, theatre, film, easy listening and classical. Samples of all tracks can be listened to online, and the majority may be ordered in any key at no extra charge.

London Theatre

website www.londontheatre.co.uk

A website containing news, reviews, events, booking information and seating plans for London's theatre scene plus maps, hotels and general tourist information.

Mandy.com

website www.mandy.com

An online service providing a directory of 40,000 technicians, facilities and producers and a vacancy list for jobs in production, crew, art departments and post-production. Also posts casting calls for actors, classified ads and information about films for sale and distribution on its website.

Musicroom

www.musicroom.com
email info@musicroom.com

The world's largest online retailer of sheet music, tutor methods, instructional DVDs & videos, music software and instruments & accessories.

National Theatre Bookshop

National Theatre, South Bank, London SE1 9PX
tel 020-7452 3456 *fax* 020-7452 3457

Resources

email bookshop@nationaltheatre.org.uk
website www.nationaltheatre.org.uk/bookshop

Opening Hours: Monday to Saturday: 9.30am –
10.45pm (this varies on certain public holidays);
12pm – 6pm on Sundays when there is a
performance. David Hare once described it as "the
most varied and complete performing arts bookshop
in the English-speaking world".

Offstage Bookshop

34 Tavistock Street, Covent Garden,
London WC2E 7PB
tel 020-7240 3883 *mobile* (07970) 582529
email offstagebookshop@aol.com
website www.offstagebookshop.com
Contact Brian Schwartz

"Our aim is to help teachers, librarians and anyone
else involved with buying books for schools.
Although our speciality is theatre and cinema, we can
research / source any book you care to name. We
offer an uncomplicated method for getting in set
texts, single titles, and audio and DVD material.
Please phone, write or email."

PlayDatabase.com

website www.playdatabase.com

US site that helps theatre-lovers find monologues and
plays for production.

Playregistry.com

email info@playregistry.com
website www.playregistry.com

A database containing thousands of well- and lesser-
known plays; the list is growing all the time. "Search
through our vast database to find detailed
information about the plays and playwrights,
including synopses, biographies, character
breakdowns, production histories and much more."

Production & Casting Report (PCR)

See entry under *The Spotlight, casting directories and
information services* on page 398.

Project Gutenberg

website www.gutenberg.org

An online library of more than 18,000 books – and
many classic plays – which have gone out of
copyright in the US. Also a growing collection of
music recordings and scores. Possibly the largest of its
kind in the world.

Rogues and Vagabonds

13 Elm Road, London SW14 7JL
tel 020-8876 1175
email contact@roguesandvagabonds.co.uk
website www.roguesandvagabonds.co.uk

"*Rogues & Vagabonds* is an online publication for
everyone who loves theatre with news, reviews (plays,

books, exhibitions), interviews, comment and debate
from freelance contributors, and is as much about
our theatrical heritage as the present and future of the
performing arts. There are specific resources for
professionals, including free casting information,
links to useful websites and information on a range of
services for actors."

The most recent entries are fully accessible but
registration is required to see articles going back to
April 2001.

Royal Court Theatre Bookshop

Sloane Square, London SW1W 8AS
tel 020-7565 5024
email bookshop@royalcourttheatre.com
website www.royalcourttheatre.com

Offers a diverse selection of contemporary plays and
publications on the theory and practice of modern
drama. The staff specialise in assisting with the
selection of audition monologues and scenes. Royal
Court playtexts from past and present productions
cost £2. The Bookshop is situated in the downstairs
Royal Court Bar & Food area. *Opening Hours*:
Monday to Friday: 3pm – 10pm; Saturday: 2.30pm –
10pm.

Screen International

EMAP Media, 33-39 Bowling Green Lane,
London EC1R 0DA
tel 020-7505 8080 *fax* 020-7505 8117
email ScreenInternational@compuserve.com
website www.screendaily.com
Editor Colin Brown

International news and features on the film business.
Subscriptions cost £135 p.a. for 48 issues plus
unlimited access to **ScreenDaily.com**.

Script Websites

Although subject to rules on copyright, a number of
websites make the scripts for films and television
shows, and suggestions for audition speeches,
available online. These sites tend to come and go, but
here are some that are current at the time of going to
press:

- **www.script-o-rama.com**
- **www.sfy.ru**
- **www.imsdb.com**
- **www.playscripts.com**
- **www.simplyscripts.com**
- **www.whysanity.net/monos**
- **www.singlelane.com**
- **www.ubishops.ca/ccc/div/hum/dra/audition.htm**

The Sheetmusic Warehouse

www.sheetmusicwarehouse.co.uk
email pianoman@globalnet.co.uk

Specialists supplying old music, rare music, music
from the shows, musicals and operetta, popular

music, wartime music, jazz music, Deep South
American music. Music Hall music, classical music,
modern music ... "You name it, we've probably got it.
Music to play, music to sing to or music to frame and
hang on your wall!"

Shooting People
27 Hedingham Close, London N1 8UA
email contact@shootingpeople.org
website www.shootingpeople.org

Shooting People allows thousands of people working
in independent film to exchange information via a
range of daily email bulletins. These include:

• Daily UK Filmmakers Bulletin – for directors,
producers and crew to share information on the latest
technologies, get advice, find crew, locations,
production deals, events & screenings, training and
more. Currently more than 22,000 members
• Daily UK Screenwriters Bulletin – writers all over
the UK use this email network to discuss writing,
share ideas and hear about competitions,
opportunities and training. Currently more than
13,000 members
• Daily UK Casting Bulletin – for actors to discuss
their craft and receive casting calls from directors,
producers and casting directors. Currently more than
14,000 members
• Weekly UK Script Pitch Bulletin – a weekly
collection of script pitches offered to producers and
directors by the writers on the Screenwriters
Network. Currently more than 11,000 members

Both part and full membership are available. Part
membership allows subscribers to receive email
bulletins only, and is free. Full membership costs £20
per year and entitles users to a range of other services.
Full members can create an actors' personal profile
with a photograph and be listed in the online
directory, post to any bulletin and download guides
on various confusing aspects of film-making such as
actor contracts, health & safety and distribution. They
are also entitled to create member cards and browse
other member cards to find potential local
collaborators.

Shooting People also organises a number of parties,
screenings, workshops and other events for which full
members receive advanced notice.

Skoob Books
66 The Brunswick, Marchmont Street,
London WC1N 1AE
tel 020-7278 8760
website www.skoob.com

An excellent collection of secondhand plays,
including many translated works and as-new titles at
half RRP. Strong theatre, film, music and TV sections
in a very large basement bookshop. All academic
areas covered, and masses of paperback fiction. Lift
access and knowledgeable, friendly staff. Thousands

more books in its Oxford Warehouse, sent to the
shop on request. Experienced in set-dressing, offering
advice, samples and loan or purchase of books and
ephemera.

The Spotlight
See *The Spotlight, casting directories and information
services* on page 398.

The Stage
47 Bermondsey Street, London SE1 3XT
tel 020-7403 1818 *subscriptions* (01858) 438895
email newsdesk@thestage.co.uk
website www.thestage.co.uk
Managing Director Catherine Comerford *Editor* Brian
Attwood

Online and weekly print publication for the
entertainment industry. News, reviews, features and
recruitment for theatre, light entertainment, opera,
dance, TV, radio, backstage and technical,
management, education and training. Established
1880

Theatre Record
PO Box 445, Chichester, West Sussex PO19 3ZH
tel (01243) 539437 *fax* (01243) 539437
email (subscriptions) ruth@trsubs.co.uk
website www.theatrerecord.com

Established in 1981 as *London Theatre Record*, the
magazine was renamed in 1990 to cover work across
the UK. *Theatre Record* publishes the complete,
unabridged reviews of all new shows covered by
national press and leading listing magazines. Fringe
shows get extra attention from the critical teams of
Time Out and *Metro* (London), while special
supplements cover festivals and seasons such as
Edinburgh (official and Fringe), LIFT and the
London International Mime Festival.

As well as reviews, each show is represented by a full
listing of cast, technical credits and, where possible,
production photographs. Also lists opening nights for
forthcoming productions. Issued fortnightly.

Virtual Library of Theatre & Drama
website www.vl-theatre.com

Lists online versions of plays and resources in more
than 50 countries.

Westminster Reference Library
35 St Martin's Street, London WC2H 7HP
tel 020-7641 4638
website www.westminster.gov.uk/libraries/
findalibrary/westref

General reference library with an extensive
performing arts section. *Opening Hours*: Monday to
Friday: 10.00am – 8.00pm; Saturday: 10.00am –
5.00pm.

Resources

Wikipedia

website en.wikipedia.org

A free, online encyclopedia with over one million articles. Originally created by an army of volunteers in 2001, it can be added to or edited by anyone at all – a very democratic publication. This democracy can sometimes mean that contentious or politically sensitive issues are not always presented in the most balanced way, although some measures are in place to prevent flagrant abuse of the system. Occasionally too, the editing process makes for some slightly disjointed articles. However, as a free source of information on just about any topic, it is unsurpassed. The theatre section can be accessed via the following link: **en.wikipedia.org/wiki/Portal:Theatre**.

The World of Musicals

website www.mtishows.com

A great resource for researching songs – some of which can be partially listened to and read about on this site.

The Writers' Guild of Great Britain

40 Rosebury Avenue, London EC1X 4RX
tel 020-7833 0777 (switchboard) 020-3372 8404 (direct)
email erik@writersguild.org.uk
website www.writersguild.org.uk

A trade union for all professional writers working in TV, radio, film, theatre, books and multimedia, it is affiliated to the Trades Union Congress (TUC) and has more than 2300 members. The Guild represents writers in matters such as terms of pay and credits for their work. The Minimum Terms Agreements and advice services aim to safeguard writers against exploitation. Also offered are professional, cultural and social activities to help provide writers with a sense of community, making writing a less isolated occupation. Members receive *UK Writer*, a glossy quarterly magazine, plus a weekly email bulletin containing news and work opportunities. Further information and advice for writers working in theatre, film, radio or TV can be found in *Writers' & Artists' Yearbook* (A&C Black).

Organisations, associations and societies

This section contains details of all kinds of ways of getting involved, sourcing useful information, learning, finding interesting lectures, networking, and simply keeping in touch with what's going on. It is important for the 'jobbing' actor to keep up-to-date with developments within the industry, and getting involved in related activities can pay dividends in the future.

Actors' Benevolent Fund

See entry under *Funding bodies*.

Actors Centre (London)

See entry under *Short-term and part-time courses*.

Actors Centre North

See entry under *Short-term and part-time courses*.

Actors Centre North East

See entry under *Short-term and part-time courses* on page 39.

Actors' Church Union

St Paul's Church, Bedford Street, London WC2E 9ED
tel 020-7240 0344
email actors_church_union@yahoo.co.uk
website www.actorschurchunion.org
Administrator Lorraine Spenceley *President* The Rt Revd Frank Sargeant *Senior Chaplain* Canon Bill Hall *Rector of St Paul's* Father Simon Grigg

Provides pastoral support for all members of the entertainment world, regardless of beliefs. Runs a network of voluntary chaplains for theatres, clubs and studios, in the UK and overseas. Also runs a charitable trust for children of parents in entertainment.

The Agents' Association (GB)

54 Keyes House, Dolphin Square,
London SW1V 3NA
tel 020-7834 0515 *fax* 020-7821 0261
email association@agents-uk.com
website www.agents-uk.com

Established in 1927 to represent and enhance the interests of entertainment agents in the United Kingdom and to standardise practice. Boasts a membership of more than 430 agencies, covering all fields of the entertainment industry.

Arts & Business

Nutmeg House, 60 Gainsford Street, Butlers Wharf, London SE1 2NY

tel 020-7378 8143 *fax* 020-7407 7527
email info@aandb.org.uk
website www.aandb.org.uk

With support from the Department for Culture, Media Sport and Arts Council England, Arts & Business delivers a range of services to arts organisations of all sizes across the UK promoting the effectiveness and creativity of business and arts partnerships.

Services include sponsoring seminar workshops, training courses, a resource centre, development forums, one-to-one advice sessions and a wide range of publications. Contact details for regional offices are available on the website.

Arts Councils (National and Regional)

See entries under *Funding Bodies*.

Arts Venues

website www.arts-venues.co.uk

Commissioned by the Arts Council England, this online guide brings together detailed information from venues, promoters and festivals across England.

The guide provides extensive information on each organisation, including contact details, artistic policy, programmes of work, artforms covered, spaces and stages available, facilities for companies, facilities for patrons, and details of public services available. Also provides each organisation's email address and website, plus a detailed location map. All material for the entries is supplied directly by the venues, promoters and festivals themselves.

ASSITEJ International

Nova ves 69, HR-10 000 Zagreb, Croatia
tel +385 1 4667034 *fax* +385 1 4667225
email sec.gen@assitej-international.org
website www.assitej-international.org/english/home.aspx

ASSITEJ International (Association Internationale du Theatre pour l'Enfance et la Jeunesse) states: "Since the theatrical art is a universal expression of

Resources

mankind, and possesses the influence and power to link large groups of the world's people in the service of peace, and considering the role theatre can play in the education of younger generations, an autonomous international organisation has been formed which bears the name of the International Association of Theatre for Children and Young People." Also see Theatre for Young Audiences (TYA), below.

British Academy of Dramatic Combat

3 Castle View, Helmsley, North Yorkshire YO62 5AU
email enquiries@badc.co.uk
website www.badc.co.uk

See entry under *Short-term and part-time courses* on page 41 for further details.

British Academy of Film and Television Arts (BAFTA)

195 Piccadilly, London W1J 9LN
tel 020-7734 0022 *fax* 020-7292 5868
email membership@bafta.org
website www.bafta.org

Founded in 1947, BAFTA provides facilities for screening and discussions, runs a popular and varied events programme coverings all aspects of film, television and interactive entertainment, encourages research and experimentation, and presents the annual Orange British Academy Film Awards.

Approximately 4 events are available to members each month. These range from major industry debates to pre-release screenings of film or television productions, followed by a question-and-answer session with the producer, director, writer and/or cast. A series of Networking Evenings was launched in 2001 to facilitate informal meetings and the exchange of ideas between industry professionals. One of the key events in the programme is the annual David Lean Lecture which has been given by such luminaries as Woody Allen, Ken Loach, John Boorman, Robert Altman and Sidney Pollack.

Applicants must have a minimum of 4 years' professional experience in the film, television or video games industries (or any combination of these) and must be able to demonstrate a significant professional contribution to the industry.

The British Academy of Stage & Screen Combat

Suite 280, 14 Tottenham Court Road,
London W1T 1JY
tel (07981) 806265
email info@bassc.org
website www.bassc.org

The British Academy of Stage & Screen Combat was founded in 1993 with the aim of improving the standards of safety, quality and training of stage

combat and promoting a unified code of practice for the training, teaching and assessing of stage combat within the United Kingdom.

All BASSC teachers have undergone a rigorous training programme and the examining members of the BASSC are highly qualified, experienced professionals with a tradition of working in theatre, television and film productions such as *Alexander, Troy, Stardust, Closer, The Last Legion* and *The Golden Compass.*

Since its formation the BASSC has established a reputation as the invigorating driving force behind stage combat in the United Kingdom and is respected, both nationally and internationally, as the leading provider of professional level level stage combat training.

As a result of this British Equity, in 1997, recognised the BASSC's Advanced Certificate as a valid qualification for entry onto the Equity Fight Directors' Training scheme and in 2001 the BASSC was appointed by the Equity Council for the training and assessment of Fight Directors candidates applying to join the Equity Fight Directors' Register.

The BASSC now has training schemes in place which allow for development from actor/combatant to Certified Teacher as well as assessment and training of Fight Directors for the Equity register.

British Association for Performing Arts Medicine

4th Floor,
Totara Park House 34-36 Gray's Inn Road London WC1X 8HR
tel 020-7404 8444 (London Helpline)
tel 0845-602 0235 (Helpline elsewhere)
tel 020-7404 5888 (Admin) *fax* 020 7404 3222
website Web: www.bapam.org.uk

The British Association for Performing Arts Medicine is a specialist charity, founded in 1984. It deals with the occupational health field of performing arts medicine.

BAPAM aims are to:

• Assist performers either by seeing them in the advisory clinics run by BAPAM or directing them on to appropriate places for treatment.
• Undertake research into the particular medical and psychological problems that afflict performers, in order to build up knowledge and skills in the treatment of these problems.

BAPAM keeps a database of healthcare practitioners to whom patients can be referred after a free assessment. This includes conventional and complementary therapies, physical and psychological expertise: GPs and consultants, physiotherapists, chiropractors, osteopaths, Alexander practitioners, counsellors, voice-therapists, all of whom take a special interest in the needs of performers.

BAPAM also administers AMABO (The Association for Medical Advisers to British Orchestras). This scheme ensures that there is appropriate medical treatment available for orchestral musicians. The scheme is run on a similar basis to the provision of medical care available to football, rugby and cricket teams. Doctors provide, on an honorary basis, the kind of specialist advice and medical care specifically geared towards musicians, which might not normally be available from a patient's own GP.

All calls are treated in confidence. Information and referral to the assessment clinics is free. Most often, even if it is then necessary to refer on to a specialist consultant, the appointment is available quickly, either free or at reduced cost.

British Council

Arts Group, 10 Spring Gardens, London SW1A 2BN
tel 020-7389 3194 *fax* 020-7389 3199
email artweb@britishcouncil.org
Norwich Union House, 7 Fountain Street, Belfast BT1 5EG
tel 028-9024 8220 *fax* 028-9023 7592
email collette.norwood@britishcouncil.org
The Tun, 3rd Floor, 4 Jackson's Entry, Holyrood Road, Edinburgh EH8 8PJ
tel 0131-524 5714 *fax* 0131-524 5714
email art.scotland@britishcouncil.org
28 Park Place, Cardiff CF10 3QE
tel 029-2039 7346 *fax* 029-2023 7494
email chris.ricketts@britishcouncil.org
website www.britishcouncil.org/arts

The British Council is the UK's public diplomacy and cultural organisation and works in 100 countries, in arts, education, governance and science. The Arts Group supports around 2000 arts events every year encouraging international collaborations, performances and exchanges with some of the top UK artists. In addition they support arts-based workshops, seminars and online events.

The form of support which is offered varies according to the project. In most cases the Council acts as an advisory body and brokers partnerships with overseas contacts such as artistic programmers and producers, venues, choreographers and festival directors. Although most work is geared towards young people aged 16-35, this isn't an exclusive emphasis and classic or traditional work is supported, especially if it has a modern slant.

Resources available on the website include an annual directory of UK drama, dance, live art and street art companies that have work suitable for overseas touring; specialist information about drama/performing arts education in the UK; and *Britfilms* **www.britfilms.com** – a portal site for the UK film industry with information about international film festivals, UK film directors and films, making a film in the UK, training and careers advice.

Not open to the public except by appointment. Write, phone or email to establish contact or get in touch with an artform specialist.

British Film Commission

See UK Film Council International.

British Film Institute (BFI)

BFI National Library, 21 Stephen Street, London W1T 1LN
tel 020-7255 1444
email library@bfi.org.uk
BFI Southbank, Belvedere Road, South Bank, Waterloo, London SE1 8XT
tel 020-7928 3535
email nft@bfi.org.uk
website www.bfi.org.uk

Established in 1933, the BFI strives to increase the level of understanding, appreciation and access to film and television culture. In addition to the BFI National Library which holds the largest film archive in the world, the organisation runs BFI Southbank (formerly the National Film Theatre) and London Film Festival (see entry under *Media festivals*), and the BFI IMAX Cinema. It also publishes books, releases films in cinemas, on video and DVD, runs educational programmes and has one of the largest collections of film stills and film posters in the world.

British Music Hall Society

82 Fernlea Road, London SW12 9RW
tel 020-8673 2175
website www.music-hall-society.com
Secretary Daphne Masterton

Founded in 1963 and with offices across England, the society aims to preserve the history of music hall and variety, to recall the artistes who created it and to support entertainers working today. Members receive copies of the society's quarterly magazine *The Call-Boy* containing news, views and information about the sector; they also have the opportunity to attend evening and weekend study group meetings. Arranges live theatre shows and it is possible for members to take part in such performances on these occasions.

Casting Directors Guild

website www.thecdg.co.uk

A professional organisation which represents casting directors working in film, television, theatre and commercials. The Casting Directors Guild aims to standardise professional working practice and to enable the exchange of information and ideas between members.

Election to the Guild is at the discretion of the Committee. Full members must have worked in 1 or more areas of the industry for at least 5 years and are entitled to use the initials CDG after their name. Probationary members must have worked as an assistant to a casting director for 3 years.

Members are listed on the website with information about their areas of work and recent credits.

Co-operative Personal Management Association

The Secretary, c/o 1 Mellor Road, Leicester LE3 6HN
mobile (07894) 345310
email cpmauk@yahoo.co.uk
website www.cpma.coop

Founded in 2002, the CPMA works to further and promote the interests of its members, who are acting agencies located across the UK. Backed by Equity, it seeks to raise the profile of co-ops with both employers and actors, and to represent the interests of co-ops with external bodies. Also works with members to identify and assist in solving the unique problems of a co-operative, to enourage good practice, to develop training skills and opportunities, and to act as an advocate for co-operative working.

The John Colclough Consultancy

tel 020-8873 1763
website www.johncolclough.co.uk

Practical independent guidance for actors & actresses. When The Spotlight decided to end their advisory service in March 2005, John Colclough decided to carry on an 'advisory' service independently using the knowledge he had gained at The Spotlight and also from his shop-floor experience as an actor, director and producer.

Sessions take place over the telephone. Please refer to the website for current charges. Payments may be made either by cheque or credit/debit card after the consultation has taken place. Telephone calls are free to landlines. Calls to mobiles will be charged for, unless the caller offers to return the call. For a consultation, telephone John on 020-8873 1763.

Conference of Drama Schools (CDS)

PO Box 34252, London NW5 1XJ
email info@cds.drama.ac.uk
website www.drama.ac.uk

Founded in 1969 to strengthen the voice of member drama schools and encourage the highest standards of training, the CDS also helps students understand the range of courses on offer and how to apply for them. The CDS played a key role in the negotiations which led to the formation of the National Council for Drama Training (see entry below).

The 22 member schools offer courses in Acting, Musical Theatre, Directing and Technical Theatre training. CDS members offer courses that are professional, intensive and vocational. They are often mentally and physically demanding and, unlike most degree courses at universities and colleges, do not generally contain a high proportion of academic work.

Produces the *Guide to Professional Training in Drama and Technical Theatre* for careers officers, teachers and applicants, providing a description of each member school, its policy and the courses it offers together with information about funding. It also provides details of summer schools. The printed version is available free of charge from French's Theatre Bookshop (see entry on page 459). Alternatively it can be downloaded from the CDS website. (CDS also publishes *The Guide to Careers Backstage* which is also available from French's and from the CDS website.)

Conservatoire for Dance and Drama (CDD)

1-7 Woburn Walk, London WC1H 0JJ
tel 020-7387 5101 *fax* 020-7387 5103
email info@cdd.ac.uk
website www.cdd.ac.uk

The Conservatoire is one of the newest and most exciting higher education institutions in the country, established in 2001 to secure the future of conservatoire-level vocational training in dance and drama in England. It has a unique structure, made up of 8 affiliate schools. All are small, specialist, vocational training institutions with international reputations for high-quality training in dance, drama or circus arts. Through the Conservatoire, all the affiliates receive funding from the Higher Education Funding Council for England, which helps to ensure that the most talented students benefit from vocational training, to which access can given regardless of background or financial circumstances.

The Conservatoire welcomes applications from disabled people and judges applicants solely on their talent and potential to develop the skills required for their chosen profession. "We are committed to admitting and supporting disabled students and warmly encourage you to inform the school so that appropriate support can be put into place as soon as possible."

The eight Conservatoire affiliate schools are: Bristol Old Vic Theatre School, Central School of Ballet, Circus Space, The London Academy of Music and Dramatic Art (LAMDA), London Contemporary Dance School, Northern School of Contemporary Dance, Rambert School of Ballet and Contemporary Dance, Royal Academy of Dramatic Art (RADA)

Council for Dance Education and Training (CDET)

Old Brewer's Yard, 17-19 Neal Street, Covent Garden, London WC2H 9UY
tel 020-7240 5703 *fax* 020-7240 2547
email info@cdet.org.uk
website www.cdet.org.uk

The Council for Dance Education and Training is the national standards body of the professional dance industry. It accredits programmes of training in vocational dance schools and holds the Register of Dance Awarding Bodies – the directory of teaching societies whose syllabuses have been inspected and approved by the Council. It is the body of advocacy of the dance education and training communities, and offers a free and comprehensive information service, *Answers for Dancers*, on all aspects of vocational dance provision to students, parents, teachers, dance artists and employers.

Culture.info
website www.culture.info

The aim of Culture.Info is to be the first port-of-call for users seeking cultural information on a particular topic. Each Culture.Info sub-portal provides a carefully researched set of listings of links to information that is more focused and useful than can usually be obtained from the vast majority of existing listings or search engines.

Dance UK
Battersea Arts Centre, Lavender Hill, London SW11 5TN
tel 020-7728 4990 *fax* 020-7223 0074
email info@danceuk.org
website www.danceuk.org

Dance UK was founded in 1982 and works with and on behalf of dance, providing information, publications, networks, forums for debate and conferences and a unified voice for all its members. It has about 130 corporate members, including most of the major dance companies, venues, agencies, funders and educational institutions. Individual members include individual dance artists, choreographers, administrators, managers, technicians, teachers, students, writers and members of dance audiences.

The organisation is active in 3 main areas: Communication, Professional Development and Healthier Dance. As well as the website, Dance UK manages email groups for choreographers, dance managers and independent dance artists, and produces *Dance UK News* which is mailed quarterly to members. Has set up a number of practical initiatives to promote longer-lasting careers and professional development in dance including insurance schemes for teachers, the UK Choreographers Directory, and books and information sheets on floors, pensions, insurance and copyright.

Promoting the health and well-being of dancers, it also generates research, educational talks and events, posters, information sheets and books. The Practitioners Register is a telephone help-line providing contact information for local medical and complementary therapists with experience of working with dancers. For information about other dance organisations and performing companies, visit the links page on the website.

Denville Hall
62 Ducks Hill Road, Northwood, Middlesex HA6 2SB
tel (01923) 825843 *fax* (01923) 841855
email deborah.gray@btconnect.com

The care home for elderly actors, including residential, nursing and dementia care and short respite stays.

Department of Culture, Media and Sport (DCMS)
Information Centre, 2-4 Cockspur Street, London SW1Y 5DH
tel 020-7211 6200
email enquiries@culture.gov.uk
website www.culture.gov.uk

The DCMS is responsible for Government policy on the arts, sport, the National Lottery, tourism, libraries, museums and galleries, broadcasting, film, the music industry, press freedom and regulation, licensing, gambling and the historic environment.

Arts policies are carried out in partnership with Arts Council England and its Regional Arts Councils, other government departments such as the Department for Education and Skills, and with regional bodies such as local authorities.

Directors Guild of Great Britain & Directors Guild Trust
4 Windmill Street, London W1T 2HZ
tel 020-7580 9131 *fax* 020-7580 9132
email guild@dggb.org
website www.dggb.org

The Directors Guild of Great Britain and Directors Guild Trust work together to promote and support directing across all media: film, television, theatre, radio, opera, commercials, music videos, corporate film, multimedia and new technology. The Guild hosts events and training, produces and sponsors publications, has a respected public voice on arts and media policy, and is a Forum for members to meet and share experiences and skills. "We welcome professional directors in all media, students of directing and associated studies, educational establishments teaching directing in theatre, film and television, corporate members who would like access to our facilities, and everyone interested in the art and craft of directing."

Actors can obtain information about the Guild's members and their career profile using the online searchable database. For information on directors who are not members of the Guild, the DGGB has a number of suggestions on their website. Actors may wish to consult the following websites for information on international directors:

• www.dga.org (Directors Guild of America)
• www.dgc.ca (Directors Guild of Canada)

Resources

• www.asdafilm.org.au (Australian Screen Directors Association)

Directors UK

20-22 Bedford Row, London WC1R 4EB
tel 020-7269 0677 *fax* 020-7269 0676
email info@Directors.UK.com
website www.directors.uk.com

Directors UK (formerly the Directors' & Producers' Rights Society (DPRS)) is the collecting society which represents British film and television directors. It collects and distributes money due to directors for the exploitation of their work. The Society is also a campaigning organisation, working to establish and protect directors' rights in the UK and abroad. It works closely with the Directors Guild of Great Britain (DGGB) and the Broadcasting, Entertainment, Cinematograph and Theatre Union (BECTU) to improve the conditions and terms under which directors are employed. The current membership runs to 4000 directors and estates, working in all fields of film and television: from features to soap, from fly-on-the-wall to natural history.

Drama Association of Wales

The Old Library, Singleton Road, Splott, Cardiff CF24 2ET
tel 029-2045 2200 *fax* 029-2045 2277
email teresa@dramawales.org.uk
website www.dramawales.org.uk
Key contact Teresa Hennessy

Founded in 1934 and a registered charity since 1973, the Drama Association of Wales aims to increase opportunities for people in the community to be creatively involved in high-quality drama.

Its main activities are an extensive mail-order library service with more than 300,000 volumes of plays, biographies, critical works and technical theatre books, and training courses in all aspects of theatre, including a 7-day residential summer school.

Also runs several new writing schemes offering a script-reading service, a playwriting competition, workshops and support for first productions, and organises the Welsh National Drama Festival from March to June, culminating in the Wales One Act Festival.

UK membership costs £18 per year for individuals and £40 for groups, both professional and amateur.

Dramaturgs' Network

69 Hounslow Road, Twickenham, Middlesex TW2 7HA
tel (07939) 270556
email info@dramaturgy.co.uk
website ee.dramaturgy.co.uk

The Dramaturgs' Network is a professional organisation which promotes the role of the dramaturg in the UK. Providing members with a network of support, the organisation brings dramaturgs, literary managers and script editors together to create opportunities for debate and sharing of information and experiences. In collaboration with other professional bodies such as the Directors Guild of Great Britain and Equity, the organisation seeks to standardise the definition and working practice of dramaturgs in the UK.

The website contains details of members, activities, a newletter archive and other information.

Equity

See entry on page 392.

Euclid

website www.euclid.info

Euclid is the official UK 'Contact Point' for the EU's Culture funding programme (2007-2013).

Independent Theatre Council (ITC)

12 The Leathermarket, Weston Street, London SE1 3ER
tel 020-7403 1727 *fax* 020-7403 1745
email admin@itc-arts.org
website www.itc-arts.org

Founded in 1974, the Independent Theatre Council (ITC) is the management association and political voice of around 700 performing arts professionals and organisations. ITC provides its members with legal and management advice, training and professional development, networking, regular newsletters and a comprehensive web resource. Additionally ITC initiates and develops projects to enrich, enhance and raise the profile of the performing arts.

Working across a variety of art forms including drama, dance, opera, music theatre, puppetry, mixed media, mime, physical theatre and circus, ITC members usually operate on the middle and small scale and are dedicated to producing innovative work, often in unconventional performance spaces.

ITC has commissioned a wide range of publications which offer guidance on potentially difficult aspects of working in the performing arts, advice on good practice and further sources of information. For more than 20 years the Independent Theatre Council has been organising training for managers and staff across the performing arts. ITC now runs nearly 50 different courses each year. In addition it has broadened its service to become leader in the field providing Action Learning sets, team building events and Executive Coaching.

For details of how to join and other benefits available to members, consult the website.

International Federation of Actors (FIA)

Guild House, Upper St Martin's Lane, London WC2H 9EG

tel 020-7379 0900 *fax* 020-7379 8260
email office@fia-actors.com
website www.fia-actors.com

The FIA currently represents 105 performers' unions and guilds in 75 countries around the world. Membership is limited to unions, guilds and professional associations – individual actors may not join. FIA works internationally to represent and co-ordinate the interests of performing artists and their professional organisations.

Services: Lobbying at European and international level on behalf of performers; defence of artists' freedom; trade union development; information exchange through conferences and meetings; networking.

Objectives: To promote a better understanding of performers' concerns and challenges around the world; the ensure that all main decision-making processes take due consideration of the specific needs of performers; to contribute to improve the social and professional conditions of performers worldwide; to facilitate the sharing of knowledge and experience on all issues of common interest between member organisations.

National Association of Youth Theatres (NAYT)

Arts Centre, Vane Terrace, Darlington DL3 7AX
tel (01325) 363330 *fax* (01325) 363313
email nayt@btconnect.com
website www.nayt.org.uk

Founded in 1982, the National Association of Youth Theatres (NAYT) is the development agency for youth theatre practice in England. The organisation supports the development of youth theatre activity through training, advocacy, participation programmes and information services. Registration is open to any group or individual using theatre techniques in their work with young people, outside formal education. NAYT is an educational charity (No. 1046042) and a company limited by guarantee (No. 2989999).

NAYT responds to more than 800 enquiries a year from young people, teachers, parents, carers, youth workers and social services looking for information and advice about youth theatre provision or career and educational opportunities. This free service puts young people in direct contact with youth theatres.

National Council for Drama Training (NCDT)

249 Tooley Street, London SE1 2JX
tel 020-7407 3686
email info@ncdt.co.uk
website www.ncdt.co.uk

The National Council for Drama Training is a partnership of employers in the theatre, broadcast and media industry, employee representatives and training providers who work together to increase support for professional drama training and education.

It seeks to maintain the highest standards and provides a credible process of quality assurance through accreditation for vocational drama, reassuring students that the courses they choose are recognised and respected by the drama profession.

National Operatic and Dramatic Association (NODA)

58-60 Lincoln Road, Peterborough PE1 2RZ
tel (01733) 865790 *fax* (01733) 319506
email info@noda.org.uk
website www.noda.org.uk
Patron The Lord Lloyd Webber

Founded in 1899, NODA is the main representative body for amateur theatre in the UK. It has a membership of around 2500 amateur/community theatre groups and 3000 individual enthusiasts throughout the UK, staging musicals, operas, plays, concerts and pantomimes in a variety of performing venues, ranging from professional theatres to village halls.

Produces a quarterly national magazine, *NODA National News*, containing advice and information for the amateur theatre sector, listings of performances in the National Theatre Diary and classified ads. Also holds area and national conferences, workshops and summer schools.

National Theatre Platforms

South Bank, London SE1 9PX
tel 020-7452 3333
email angus@nationaltheatre.org.uk
website www.nationaltheatre.org.uk/platforms
Platforms Producer Angus MacKechnie

An eclectic programme of pre-performance events celebrates all aspects of the arts, offering the chance to learn about the National's work and discover more about theatre in general. Platforms usually start at 6pm, lasting for 45 minutes – there are occasional afternoon events, usually starting at 2.30pm. Tickets: £3.50 (£2.50 concessions).

New Producers Alliance (NPA)

NPA Film Centre, Suite 1.07 The Tea Building, 56 Shoreditch High Street, London E1 6JJ
tel 020-7613 0440 *fax* 020-7729 1852
email queries@npa.org.uk
website www.npa.org.uk

The NPA is the UK's national membership and training organisation for independent new producers and filmmakers. It provides access to contacts, information and advice for more than 800 members, from film students to major production companies and industry affiliates. Individual membership costs

£75 per year (£50 for students and the unemployed) and is open to producers, directors and writers.

North American Actors Association (NAAA)

tel 020-7938 4722
email americanactors@aol.com
website www.naaa.org.uk

The North American Actors Association is a network serving the entertainment industry by supporting North American actors with a base in Britain.

Membership is open to professional actors who can work on both sides of the Atlantic without restriction, are full members in good standing of at least one entertainment union, and have proof of professional contracts. To those involved in casting, we act as a resource of genuine North American actors, and are happy to provide agent and other contact details of our members.

Pact (Producers Alliance for Cinema and Television)

3rd Floor, Fitzrovia House,
153–157 Cleveland Street, London W1T 6QW
tel 020-7380 8230
email info@pact.co.uk
website www.pact.co.uk
Online Resources Manager David Alan Mills

The UK trade association that represents and promotes the commercial interests of independent feature film, television, animation and interactive media companies. Headquartered in London, it has regional representation throughout the UK, in order to support its members. An effective lobbying organisation, it has regular and constructive dialogues with government, regulators, public agencies and opinion formers on all issues affecting its members and contributes to key public policy debates on the media industry, both in the UK and in Europe. It negotiates terms of trade with all public service broadcasters in the UK and supports members in their business dealings with cable and satellite channels. It also lobbies for a properly structured and funded UK film industry and maintains close contact with the UK Film Council and other relevant film organisations and government departments.

Personal Managers' Association

Rivercroft, 1 Summer Road, East Molesey,
Surrey KT8 9LX
tel 020-8398 9796 *fax* 020-8398 9796
email info@thepma.com
website www.thepma.com

Founded in 1950, the PMA is an association of artists' and dramatists' agents which provides members with a forum to exchange ideas and information. The association maintains a code of conduct and acts as a lobby when necessary.

Royal Television Society (RTS)

Kildare House, 3 Dorset Rise, London EC4Y 8EN
tel 020-7822 2810 *fax* 020-7822 2811
email info@rts.org.uk
website www.rts.org.uk

Provides the leading forum for discussion and debate on all aspects of the television industry, with opportunities for networking and professional development for people at all levels and across every sector. The RTS has 14 national and regional centres in the UK which draw up an annual programme to suit the needs of their members.

Events organised by the RTS include dinners, lectures, conventions, conferences and awards ceremonies. In addition it produces a monthly magazine, *Television*, outlining key industry debates and developments.

The Royal Theatrical Fund

See entry under *Funding bodies*.

The Screenwriters' Workshop

Now part of the New Producers Alliance (NPA) - see entry on page 469.

Society of London Theatre (SOLT)

32 Rose Street, London WC2E 9ET
tel 020-7557 6700 *fax* 020-7557 6799
email enquiries@solttma.co.uk
website www.officiallondontheatre.co.uk

Founded in 1908 by Sir Charles Wyndham, the Society of London Theatre is the trade association which represents the producers, theatre owners and managers of the major commercial and grant-aided theatres in central London.

Today the Society combines its long-standing roles in such areas as industrial relations and legal advice for members with a campaigning role for the industry, together with a wide range of audience-development programmes to promote theatre-going.

The Society of Teachers of Speech and Drama (STSD)

73 Berry Hill Road, Mansfield,
Nottinghamshire NG18 4RU
email stsd@stsd.org.uk
website www.stsd.org.uk

Protecting the professional interests of qualified, specialist teachers of Speech & Drama, the STSD encourages good standards of teaching and promotes the study and knowledge of speech and dramatic art in every form. Has established close links with drama schools and examination boards and its publications are read worldwide.

Members receive copies of its newsletters, information sheets and the journal *Speech & Drama*.

They are entitled to free advice, to be included in a register of members and to attend its summer conference.

Students of Speech & Drama can search for suitable teachers using the online database.

The Stephen Sondheim Society
265 Wollaton Vale, Wollaton, Nottingham NG8 2PX
email sondheimsociety@sondheim.org
website www.sondheim.org
Chair Mandy Dixon *Administrator* Lynne Chapman

Society to promote the works of the composer and lyricist Stephen Sondheim. Keeps track of all productions (professional and amateur) of Sondheim's musicals, publishes a newsletter, arranges theatre visits, and from time to time also sponsors appropriate productions.

At the time of writing, membership is £15 (single), £10 (concession) or £20 (joint) but please consult the website for the latest rates.

StartaTheatreCompany.com
email admin@startatheatrecompany.com
website www.startatheatrecompany.com

An online guide to starting and developing a performing arts company. An e-learning course with 6 comprehensive modules, covering all you need to know about building a successful and sustainable enterprise. Delivered through fortnightly video and audio lessons, the guide is presented by tutor Sinead Mac Manus. Sinead has many years of experience working with and training performing arts companies, and has brought this experience to the world of e-learning.

Studio Salford
King's Arms, 11 Bloom Street, Salford M3 6AN
website www.studiosalford.com

Studio Salford is an umbrella group representing and promoting several theatre companies, raising the profile of Salford as a viable artistic location and promoting artists from all over Salford and Manchester. Their performance venue is the intimate and unique space upstairs at The King's Arms.

The Radio Independents Group (RIG)
c/o Square Dog Radio, Kilmagadwood Cottage, Scotlandwell, Kinross KY13 9HY
email chair@radioindies.org
website www.radioindependentsgroup.org
Chair Mike Hally

A non-profit-making trade body funded through membership fees and other fund-raising activities, representing the interests and needs of the UK's independent radio production industry. Formed in July 2004, RIG currently represents two-thirds of the industry, and membership continues to grow – to include globe-spanning commercial giants through to one-person companies, partnerships and solo producers. As well as representing members' and the industry's needs in negotiations with the BBC, commercial radio and other groups, and the government, RIG offers support, resources, information, access and training. Its aim is to bring together the knowledge of the thousands of dedicated and skilled people in the independent radio production sector, and to make as much of it available to all as is possible.

The Society of Teachers of the Alexander Technique (STAT)
1st Floor, Linton House, 39-51 Highgate Road, London NW5 1RS
tel 020-7482 5135 *fax* 020-7482 5435
email office@stat.org.uk
website www.stat.org.uk

The Alexander Technique has been taught for more than 100 years. In 1958, the Society of Teachers of the Alexander Technique (STAT) was founded in the UK by teachers who were trained personally by FM Alexander. STAT's first aim is to ensure the highest standards of teacher training and professional practice.

Teaching members of STAT:
• Are registered (MSTAT) to teach the Technique after completing a 3-year, full-time training course approved by the Society or one of the Affiliated Societies overseas
• Are required to adhere to the Society's published *Code of Professional Conduct and Competence*, and are covered by the professional indemnity insurance.

There are currently more than 2500 teaching members of STAT and its Affiliated Societies worldwide. Graduates of STAT training courses are assessed by a system of external moderation; the Society also runs a postgraduate programme of Continuing Professional Development. STAT's further aims are to promote public awareness and understanding of the Alexander Technique, and to encourage research. The Society publishes a regular newsletter, *STATNews*, and *The Alexander Journal*.

The Standing Conference of University Drama Departments (SCUDD)
website www.scudd.org.uk

Represents the interests of Drama, Theatre and Performing Arts in the Higher Education Sector in the UK. Acts as a mediating body with organisations such as funding councils, the AHRC and the Arts Councils, and is consulted by such organisations when matters of future policy are discussed and decided.

Theatre for Young Audiences (TYA)
16 Victoria Embankment, Darlington DL1 5JR
tel (01325) 483259

email paul.harman63@ntlworld.com
website www.tya-uk.org
Contact Paul Harman

TYA (UK Centre of ASSITEJ) is a network for makers and promoters of professional theatre for young audiences, linking the UK to theatres, organisations and individual artists around the world. Works for a fuller awareness of the value of theatre for young audiences.

The Theatre Museum – see entry under V&A Theatre Collections (formerly The Theatre Museum)

Theatre Royal Haymarket Masterclasses

Theatre Royal Haymarket, London SW1Y 4HT
tel 020-7389 9660 *fax* 020-7389 9697
email masterclass@trh.co.uk
website www.trh.co.uk/masterclass
Patrons Sir Peter Hall, Sir David Hare, Maureen Lipman CBE

Masterclass is an arts initiative which allows young people aged 17-30 to attend workshops and talks given by leading actors, directors, designers and writers working in theatre today. All events take place at the Theatre Royal Haymarket and are free of charge to young people aged 17-30. People over the age of 30 may also take part and contribute to the project by joining the Masterclass Friends scheme.

In addition to the masterclass events, the programme includes a longer-term new writing project and a series that gives career advice and support. Previous Masters have included Steven Berkoff, Simon Callow, Mike Leigh, Alan Rickman, Prunella Scales and Janet Suzman. For details of forthcoming events, consult the website.

Theatres Trust

22 Charing Cross Road, London WC2H OQL
tel 020-7836 8591 *fax* 020-7836 3302
email info@theatrestrust.org.uk
website www.theatrestrust.org.uk

The National Advisory Public Body for Theatres, protecting theatres for everyone. Operates nationally in England, Wales, Scotland and Northern Ireland, providing an authoritative and knowledgeable source of expert advice and information on theatres. The Theatres Trust provides a range of advisory services, is a statutory consultee on planning applications, and provides guidance on design, conservation, property and planning matters to theatre operators, local authorities and official bodies, and also runs an information service. Its archives include records of over 3500 theatre buildings and some 30,000 images, as well as plans and other documents.

Theatrical Management Association (TMA)

32 Rose Street, London WC2E 9ET
tel 020-7557 6700 *fax* 020-7557 6799

email enquiries@solttma.co.uk
website www.tmauk.org
Chief Executive Richard Pulford

TMA is the pre-eminent UK wide organisation dedicated to providing a professional support network for the performing arts industry. Founded in 1894 by Sir Henry Irving, it is now an association of people and throughout the UK professionally involved in the production and presentation of the performing arts. Its members include repertory and producing theatres, arts centres and touring venues, major national companies and independent producers, opera and dance companies, and associated individuals and businesses.

TMA is run by a Council elected from and by the membership. This Council represents all sectors of the business and employs the professional staff team who provide the services for members. Diverse as they are, TMA members share a common conviction that the professional and social advantages of membership increase their ability to run successful businesses. Member organisations are encouraged to follow best professional practice and are given advice to enable them to do so. Individuals can benefit from training and networking opportunities to help develop their careers.

TMA shares a common staff with the Society of London Theatre (SOLT).

UK Centre of the International Association of Theatre for Children & Young People

Arad Goch, Strydy Baddon, Aberystwyth, Dyfed SY23 2NN
tel (01970) 617998 *fax* (01970) 611223
email j.turner@apt.org.uk
website www.assitej.org
Contact Jeremy Turner

Supporting the provision of professional theatre for young people, APT encourages and enables the exchange of ideas, experience and advice between theatre companies in the UK and abroad. Information about member companies and their work is available on the website.

UK Film Council

See entry under *Funding bodies*.

V&A Theatre Collections (formerly The Theatre Museum)

tel 020-7942 2697 *fax* 020-7942 2733
email tmenquiries@vam.ac.uk
website www.vam.ac.uk/tco

The V&A's Theatre Collections hold the UK's national collection of material about live performance in the UK since Shakespeare's day, covering drama, dance, musical theatre, circus, musical hall, rock and pop, and other forms of live entertainment.

In March 2009, the new Theatre and Performance galleries at the V&A opened to the public. The galleries replace those at the Theatre Museum in Covent Garden, which closed in 2007. The new displays explore the process of performance, from the initial conception, through the design and development stages, to audiences' reactions.

Women in Film and Television (WFTV)

6 Langley Street, London WC2H 9JA
tel 020-7240 4875
email emily@wftv.org.uk
website www.wftv.org.uk
Membership & Events Manager Emily Compton

A membership association open to women with a minimum of 1 year's professional experience in the television, film or digital media industries. With more than 800 members including writers, actresses and directors, the WFTV promotes the interests and diversity of women working at all levels in these industries. Offers a network of national and international contacts with an online directory of members, and provides a number of social forums, workshops, seminars and preview screenings.

Youngblood

Top Floor, 57 Paddington Street, Marylebone, London W1U 4HZ
tel 020-7193 3207
email info@youngblood.co.uk
website www.youngblood.co.uk

A company of fight directors and stage-combat teachers. Runs ongoing classes for professional actors in various locations around London. Also provides fight directors and trainers for film, television and theatre projects, including low-budget productions.

An actor's guide to keeping sane

Tim Bentinck

This is not a flippant title. The psychological battle of being an actor/breadwinner is the war; doing the job is just the fighting.

If you're a good builder and you're not getting work, it's probably because you're being undercut by the East Europeans, but you still know you're a good builder.

If you're an actor, you have no such objective take on the matter. In order to be a professional actor, you *have* to believe you're bloody good, or you can't even get started, let alone continue. The problem is that your own estimation of your talent is inherently biased, because when a builder has finished a roof conversion that looks beautiful and doesn't leak, no one rings him to complain. When an actor has done a part on telly and no-one rings, is it because (a) they weren't watching? (b) they thought you were good but didn't bother to ring? (c) they thought you were crap? or (d) they didn't like you anyway and turned over the minute you appeared? Even when your best friends think you're crap, they almost never say.

Therefore, you have to rely on your own judgement, and as an actor it's extremely difficult to be objective, disinterested and honest about your own performance. On stage you get a good idea when your jokes fall flat and people talk about the set in the bar afterwards, but on screen and on radio, you really are not the best judge. Everyone, myself included, can believe they're being brilliant when they're not. When you start off as an actor you *have* to have at heart a naïve belief that your originality, eccentricity, new interpretation of a text, your life experience, your pain, your joy, your discovery of sex for the first time in history, your raw talent, or your chutzpah and charm will blow them all away.

This, dear actor, we all have. You can't *be* an actor without empathising with some part of the above.

The reality, *quelle malheur*, is mostly down to luck – the right place, the right time, and almost nothing more. Oh, and probably being unconventionally good-looking or sexy. Being good at it is an added bonus.

I'm 52. About 25 years ago someone I knew fairly well said to me drunkenly at a party, "Oh I saw you in that thing on telly last night, you were *awful*! Jeremy did you see it? Wasn't Tim dreadful?! Ha ha ha." At the time I was really hurt. I was shocked and rocked to the core. I had to find a way to deal with it, so I just decided she was a cow and mad and had no taste and didn't get it, and got on with life. About a year ago, when I watched the episode in question again on DVD, I realised she was painfully closer to the truth than I'd realised. I'd never done telly before and had just done nine months as a pirate in the West End and I was way OTT — lots of *acting* going on. I hadn't learned the 'do nothing' rule. In my defence I was fairly dishy and the swordfights were good. Yes she was a rude cow for saying it, but the point I'm circumlocutorily trying to reach is this: At the time, everyone said I was brilliant. No – I was *alright*. Beware the flatterers. Make people tell you the truth and then do something about it. Never be afraid of criticism; it's usually well founded, and sometimes well meant.

So in order to remain sane in this business, it is important that you have a very strong belief – backed up by some rigorous interrogation of your most trusted friends, your family, your loved ones and your fans – that you have what it takes, if given the chance, to be an astonishingly brilliant actor. Because unless you're very lucky, you are going to be hurt, rejected, abused, disrespected, talked down to, patronised, dismissed, ignored, not appreciated, paid badly, not paid at all, taken for granted and generally ground down for the rest of your life ... so if you can't face that, forget it.

From then on, one of three things is going to happen. The first is that you become a megastar. End of story, read a different book. The second is that you become a professional actor, earning some kind of living. The third is that it's a total bloody disaster. Here are some suggestions for how to remain sane with option two.

About five years ago, I spent a good six months of that year worrying about what things were going to be like five years in the future. Here I am today and everything's pretty fine. So I had effectively *wasted* all that time of my life worrying about something that didn't happen. Absurd. You have got to seize the day, or the night if that's your thing – *carpe noctem,* even!

Depression is a killer; it killed someone close to me, and I've been down that road too. But you can talk yourself out of it. You can bully yourself. Buy a bike and ride it, swim, have more sex, go to the pub and meet new people, get drunk with them and solve the problems of the world, sign up for a rally driving course, use the credit card to pamper yourself and don't worry about tomorrow (if that doesn't work, take Prozac but don't do the drinking thing – it's unhealthy, expensive and doesn't work). Do that until you've stopped being depressed, then you can worry about the debt with a more sanguine view – sanguine and proactive (dreadful word but can't think of an alternative).

You have *got* to treat it as a business. You're the product and if someone else isn't selling you (PR or agent), then it's down to you. My very first agent came from the world of PR and said to me that he knew nothing about acting, but aimed to get my name on the desks of everyone who mattered, every day of the week. He made me a lot of money. You're up against the PR might of comedians, footballers, models, weather-girls, body-builders, basketball players, TV presenters, extras, personal fitness coaches to the stars, drunks, reality-show winners, reality-show runners up, Pop Idols, and specifically Jade (insert adjective of choice, like 'talented', 'intelligent', 'thin', 'attractive') Goody.

Get a website, make a voice tape, make a video compilation, send them to Spotlight, send them to your agent, send a DVD to casting directors. Get yourself in the press, get yourself on radio, write plays, write songs, drive trucks, plant gardens, do classes, keep fit, look good, raise a family, change the nappies. Live a life, the experience of which you can bring to your acting. Be in trim and ready to grab the bits of luck that come your way with bold confidence.

Another thing: work on your memory, or carry a notebook. Remember the names of the casting directors; remember the directors you work for; be pleasant to the runner, because s/he'll be the producer/director in six year's time; remember what your agent looks like when you meet him/her at parties; remember the voice-overs you did and who directed them; also, get a copy of everything to add to your showreel. Remember to keep all your receipts and put money aside for tax; if you're VAT registered, you're being paid to be a tax collector, so do it yourself – keep the money and have a holiday.

If you're young – *do it now do it now*! Over 40? – you've learned the game, so play it; you're just a more mature version of you at 20. If you're over 50, this is the time to strike:

be bold, we've learned it all, we've got it all to give. Young filmmakers take heed: we are what you will be in 30 years' time, so we represent what you aspire to. You're pretty bright now, but don't you reckon that after 30 years you'll have learned a whole shed-load more? Well that's *us*. Welcome to Saga and the days of low insurance, paid-off mortgages and, finally, the bus pass, which I admit is still hard, at my age, to contemplate. It's eight years away though. Hmmm.

All the bloody pain and insecurity and rejection is mitigated, though, by this:

You could face a cavalry charge in the Crimea. You could star in a West End musical. You could fly an F3 Tornado simulator. You could fight duels and fire machine guns. You could sit on a rubber pad on the top of a mountain inside the Arctic circle in Norway for three days waiting for the fog to clear to shoot a commercial for beer and get frostbite. You could be protected at night from elephant and tiger by armed guards in the Masai Mara, filming an ad for ice cream – and get sunstroke. You could dice for the lead with Damon Hill in a Formula One Kart. You could re-voice Gerard Dèpardieu in a movie, be the voice of James Bond in a computer game and say "Mind The Gap" on the Piccadilly Line. You could be kissed by Kevin Kline or thrown overboard by Roger Moore. You could die in the arms of Sean Bean and snog loads of beautiful women. You could have Claudia Schiffer looking into your eyes saying, "Ich liebe dich, ich liebe dich...". You could dub the lucky guy who shags Sharon Stone in *Basic Instinct 2*. You could earn your living with an earring in your ear and a sword around your waist. You could star in sitcoms, television series and radio soaps. You could do live improvisation games on stage and be filmed on horseback, scuba diving, canyoning, parachuting and piloting a flying boat. You could time a kiss, on a beach on the Great Barrier Reef, so that the setting sun shines between your closing lips as the waves lap around your suntanned body.

Sorry, but look we're all bloody show-offs after all, and if after 30 years I couldn't give a list like the above, I'd have given it up.

It's a great, great adventure. It's a business and you have to run it. If it isn't working, give it up. I know plenty of ex-actors who are hugely successful at their new jobs. When I was training at Bristol, I remember thinking that *everybody* should do this course – not just actors, but everyone. If you've acted professionally for a while, it's a brilliant intro to everything else. Look at politicians – crap actors. Local government – the same. Most businessmen talking to their staff – abysmal. Actors can turn their hands to anything, so if you give it up, it wasn't wasted; it was part of your life-training.

Downer. What I mean is this: I've seen the highs and I've dived down deep with the lows. I know the reality but I'm still fired by the dream. That's what keeps us going.

Churchill said it most accurately, with all the power of the struggle of the war behind him: "Keep Buggering On."

See you on the green.

More about **Tim Bentinck** can be found at **www.bentinck.net**.

Bibliography

Books for aspiring, student and young actors

Margo Annett, *Actor's Guide to Auditions and Interviews* (3rd edition, A & C Black, 2004). A useful guide outlining some of the techniques needed for success.

Peter Barkworth, *The Complete About Acting* (Methuen, 1991). Another very good book about acting and getting work.

Simon Dunmore, *An Actor's Guide to Getting Work* (4th edition, A & C Black, 2004). A practical, comprehensive guide covering all aspects of marketing yourself as an actor.

Simon Dunmore, *Alternative Shakespeare Auditions for Women* (A & C Black, 1997). A collection of 50 less-well-known speeches for women.

Simon Dunmore, *MORE Alternative Shakespeare Auditions for Women* (A & C Black, 1999). Another collection of 50 less-well-known speeches for women.

Simon Dunmore, *Alternative Shakespeare Auditions for Men* (A & C Black, 1997). A collection of 50 less-well-known speeches for men.

Simon Dunmore, *MORE Alternative Shakespeare Auditions for Men* (A & C Black, 2002). Another collection of 50 less-well-known speeches for men.

Ellis Jones, *Teach Yourself Acting* (Hodder & Stoughton Ltd, 1998). A good overview of acting and the profession.

Jennifer Reischel, *So You Want to Tread the Boards: The Everything-you-need-to-know, Insider's Guide to a Career in the Performing Arts* (JR Books Ltd, 2007)

Anna Scher, *Desperate to Act* (Lions, 1988). Brilliant, basic advice for those so 'desperate', from a lady who should know.

William Shakespeare, *Hamlet, Prince of Denmark*. Especially Hamlet's advice to the players (Act 3, scene 2), which is some of the best advice on acting ever given.

Bernard Graham Shaw, *Voice-Overs, A Practical Guide* (A & C Black, 2000). A useful guide which explains and teaches the skills of voicing radio and television commercials.

Clive Swift, *The Job of Acting* (Harrap, revised 1984). Although some of it is out-of-date, this book is a wonderful read from an experienced and caring professional.

Malcolm Taylor, *The Actor and the Camera* (A & C Black, 1994). Another good 'primer' for the beginner.

Other career advice books for actors

Ed Hooks, *The Audition Book* (3rd edition, Back Stage Books, 2000). Excellent reading if you're thinking of trying your hand in the USA. It's also worth looking at Ed's website for his excellent 'Craft Notes' (**www.edhooks.com**).

Peter Messaline and Miriam Newhouse, *The Actor's Survival Kit* (3rd edition, Simon & Pierre, 1999). Well worth reading if you're thinking of trying your hand in Canada.

Books for any actor

Stephen Aaron, *Stage Fright: Its Role in Acting* (University of Chicago Press, 1986). Fascinating book, written by a psychotherapist who is also an experienced director and teacher.

Brian Bates, *The Way of the Actor* (Century Hutchinson, 1986). Very interesting insights into the inner workings of the actor's psyche.

Peter Brook, *The Empty Space* (Penguin, 1990). Written in the 1960s, but still essential reading.

Adrian Cairns, *The Making of the Professional Actor* (Peter Owen Publishers, 1996). A fascinating study of the history, and possible future, of the art of acting.

Simon Callow, *Being an Actor* (Penguin, 1995). Autobiographical books by famous actors are generally useless in terms of practical career advice. However, this one – part autobiography and part advice – has a great deal of down-to-earth common sense. His famous 'manifesto' on directors' theatre is spot on.

Mel Churcher, *Acting for Film: Truth 24 Times a Second* (Virgin Books, 2003). Invaluable insights into the specific techniques involved.

Nicholas Craig, *I, an Actor* (Pavilion Books, 1988). A very funny send-up of the starry actor's autobiography. A must.

Declan Donnellan, *The Actor and the Target* (Nick Hern Books, 2005) A fresh approach to the actor's art from the artistic director of Cheek by Jowl

John Gillett, *Acting on Impulse: reclaiming the Stanislavski approach* (A&C Black, 2007). An excellent demystification of Stanislavski.

Uta Hagen, *A Challenge for the Actor* (Macmillan, 1991). One of the best books on acting ever written.

Richard Hornby, *The End of Acting: a radical view* (Applause Books, 1992). Revelatory insights into the processes of acting.

David Mamet, *True and False* (Faber & Faber, 1998). This book cuts through much of the mythology that surrounds acting.

Fintan O'Toole, *Shakespeare Is Hard, But So Is Life: A Radical Guide to Shakespearean Tragedy* (Granta Books, 2002)

Kenneth Rea, *A Better Direction* (Calouste Gulbenkian Foundation, 1989). A very thorough inquiry into directors and the need for more training opportunities.

Patsy Rodenburg, *An Actor Speaks* (Methuen, 1997). An entirely practical guide with excellent advice and exercises to help develop the performer's voice.

Michael Sanderson, *From Irving to Olivier – A Social History of the Acting Profession* (Athlone Press, 1984). A very expensive, but nevertheless fascinating, study of the actor's world over the last century.

Edda Sharpe & Jan Haydn Rowles, *How to Do Any Accent: The Essential Handbook for Every Actor* (Oberon Books, 2007)

Michael Shurtleff, *Audition* (Walker & Company, 1984). An American book which should be read. It contains brilliant insights and thoughts to help any actor.

The Spotlight, *Contacts* (The Spotlight, annually in October). Contact details for everything you can think of (and more) that relates to the performing arts in general.

Webography

What follows is a selected collection of the most important websites for aspirants and professionals, and some others which the editors have found extremely useful, but don't quite fit elsewhere in this book.

Important websites for aspirants and professionals

www.actorscentre.co.uk – Actors Centre London

www.agents-uk.com – Agents' Association of Great Britain

www.bbc.co.uk – BBC homepage

www.bbc.co.uk/drama/radio – BBC Radio Drama

www.bis.gov.uk – Department for Business, Innovation & Skills, now covering universities; formerly the job of the Department for Education & Skills (www.dfes.gov.uk)

www.thecdg.co.uk – Casting Directors Guild

www.cpma.coop – The Co-operative Personal Management Association

www.drama.ac.uk – Conference of Drama Schools, with links to member schools' websites

www.eif.co.uk – Edinburgh International Festival

www.edfringe.com – Edinburgh Festival Fringe

www.equity.org.uk – Equity

www.fringetheatre.org.uk – Fringe theatre network, with listings of and links to London Fringe venues

www.itc-arts.org – Independent Theatre Council homepage with links to member companies' websites

www.imdb.com – Internet Movie Database; catalogues all sorts of information on more than 250,000 films and the 900,000 people who helped to make them

www.ncdt.co.uk – National Council for Drama Training

www.northernactorscentre.co.uk – Northern Actors Centre

www.thepma.com – Personal Managers' Association

www.scudd.org.uk – Standing Conference of University Drama Departments

www.spotlight.com – The Spotlight publishes the most important actors' directories

www.thestage.co.uk – *The Stage*, contains news, information and job advertisements which are updated each Thursday

www.ucas.ac.uk – UCAS, the central organisation that processes applications for full-time undergraduate courses at UK universities and colleges

Other useful websites

www.artsline.org.uk – Arts-Line, provides access information on arts venues

www.bfi.org.uk/filmtvinfo/ftvdb – the British Film Institute's film and television database

www.britfilms.com – an extensive source of information on the UK film industry

www.britishtheatreguide.info – lots of articles, reviews and links about British theatre

www.companieshouse.gov.uk – Companies House: useful for checking background details (like date of foundation) of individual companies

www.edhooks.com – contains some interesting articles on acting

www.excellentvoice.co.uk – information and advice for voice-over artists with examples of good voice demos online

www.hiddenextra.com – a useful online guide for those looking to become supporting artistes

www.its-behind-you.com – seemingly a comprehensive list of pantomimes and their producers

www.ku.edu/~idea – the International Dialects of English Archive (IDEA) is a useful collection of English-language dialects and English spoken in the accents of other languages

www.officiallondontheatre.co.uk – Society of London Theatre website with news, reviews and booking information

www.royalist.info – a database that provides biographical details of thousands of individuals who have either belonged to, or been connected with, the royal family of England and Scotland during more than 1000 years of history

www.shakespeare-online.com – electronic copies of the plays and poems, along with other related material of interest. These copies of the texts should be checked against published editions before use in audition or performance, in order to gain the benefit of modern scholarship

www.simon.dunmore.btinternet.co.uk – advice on many aspects of the profession, including auditioning, marketing and good professional practice

www.sound.co.uk – information and advice for voice-over artists with links to many other sites

www.susan.croft.btinternet.co.uk/Supplements/Blackplays.htm – lists the work of those Afro-Caribbean and Asian playwrights whose work has been published, and in most cases produced, in Britain

www.theatredigs.com – a site aimed solely at touring professionals within the UK entertainment industry

www.theatrenet.com – news, events and special offers and links to agents, producers, theatre companies, venues and more

www.uksponsorship.com – an online database of UK sponsorship opportunities

www.uktw.co.uk – UK Theatre Web, with information, events and tickets for theatre in the UK

www.usefee.tv – a site which lets performers, their representatives and employers quickly calculate the appropriate use fee for featured players in TV commercials based on the established, industry-endorsed method approved by the Personal Managers' Association, the Association of Model Agents and Equity

www.visit4info.com – a site where you can see recent television and cinema commercials and get details of the companies who created them

www.vocalist.org.uk – a site for singers, vocalists, singing teachers and students of voice of all ages, standards and styles. The site contains useful information on aspects of singing, performance, plus free online singing lessons and articles for vocalists related to singing and getting into the music industry

www.voiceovers.co.uk – a forum for voice-over artists to advertise themselves

www.whatsonstage.com – a UK theatre listing service with search facilities, a ticket-ordering service, reviews, news and debate

Index